MOON

PRAGUE & BUDAPEST

TOM DIRLIS

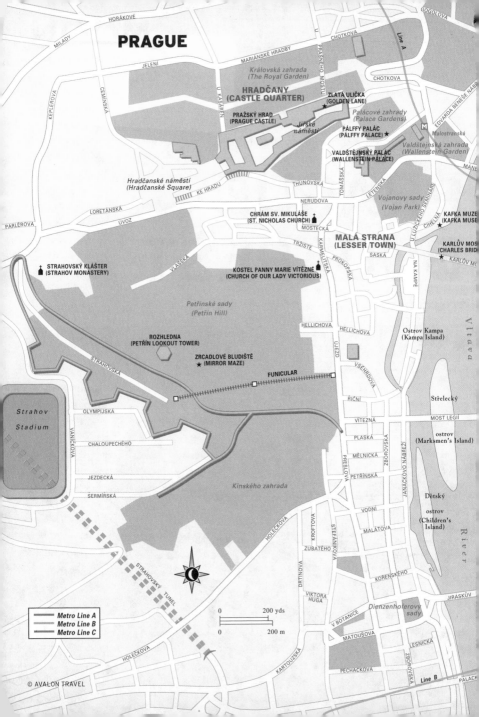

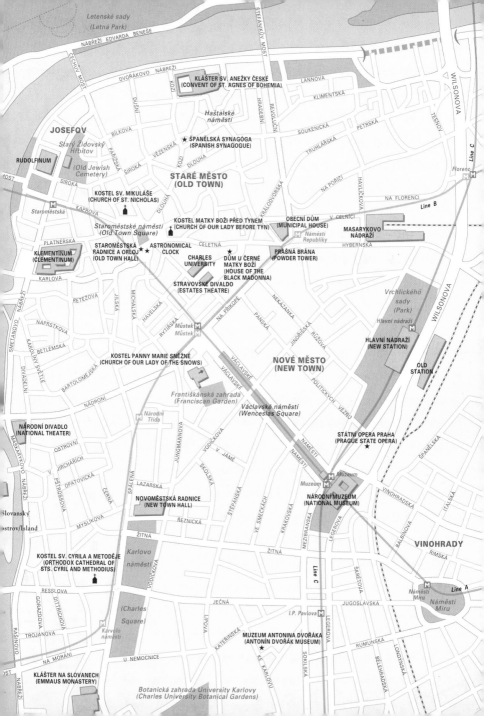

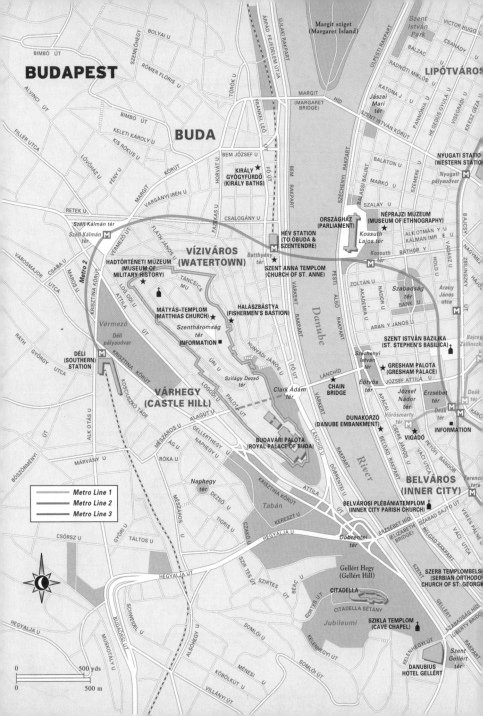

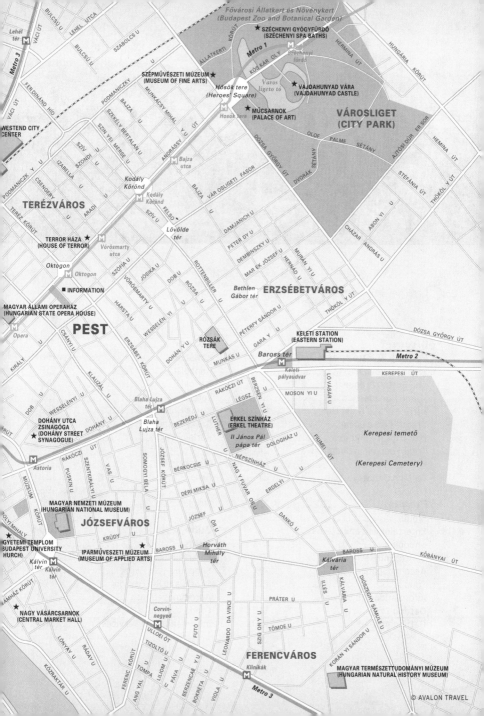

Contents

DISCOVER

Prague & Budapest

Renowned for their storied pasts, Prague and Budapest have also established themselves as steadfast beacons of a brightly burning future. A visit here will expand your mind and enrich your soul.

Prague, thanks to its breathtaking architecture, resembles a forgotten fairy tale more than a Central European capital. From the top of Wenceslas Square to the majestic Prague Castle, it is just as beautiful as Paris and Venice, though far less expensive and a lot more liberal-minded than either. This is the capital of Bohemia, after all, where beer is cheaper than bottled water and freedom of expression perseveres.

Faster, bigger, and rougher around the edges than Prague, Budapest nevertheless abounds in beauty, harmony, and incontestable charm. Whether it's the no-nonsense bustle of Pest or the Dickensian backstreets of Buda, the people's passion for music, drink, and romance expresses itself brazenly on every corner.

The myriad of changes Prague and Budapest have undergone is obvious as previously foreign concepts like cell phones, fast food, and high fashion trends are now ubiquitous. Come to Prague and Budapest and have your eyes opened and your heart stirred by a seamless blend of the Old World with the new.

Planning Your Trip

Where to Go

Prague
The Golden City is not only one of the most beautiful capitals in the world, it is one of the hottest destinations in the region as well thanks to its well-preserved historic buildings and laid-back, anything-goes attitude that continues to attract artists, foreigners, and anyone else looking for a bit of the Bohemian in their lives. Whether it's the majesty of Prague Castle, the picturesque streets of Malá Strana, or the breathtaking beauty of Charles Bridge and Old Town Square, Prague is a city that never fails to leave an indelible impression on visitors.

Bohemia
The country's largest region boasts plenty of pretty castles and sleepy towns that make for excellent day trips. Karlštejn, Konopiště, and Křivoklát are remarkable castles, unique in both architecture and beauty. Český Krumlov's castle, meanwhile, is the second largest in the country and overlooks the stunning medieval town of the same name. Fans of the morbid will be fascinated by the macabre bone church in Kutná Hora, while those looking to heal amid gorgeous natural surroundings will be impressed by Karlovy Vary's curative springs.

Moravia
Moravia represents the country's wine region. Steeped in tradition, Moravians are proud of their land as well as their capital, Brno, a fine place to visit for a couple of days. Aside from its historic old town, it's also the scene of countless cultural events that add to the overall university-town vibe. Meanwhile, UNESCO-listed Telč has one of the prettiest squares in the country, and its surrounding lakes and forests make for a peaceful getaway. And don't forget magical Mikulov, which has served as Moravia's leading wine center for centuries.

Budapest
The famed Danube River separates Buda's hilly west bank from Pest's bustling streets. In Pest, visitors can enjoy the remarkable St. Stephen's Basilica and Heroes Square, as well as lingering romantic strolls along the Danube Embankment. Meanwhile, Buda's ancient tranquility persists in tiny residential streets, the Royal Palace of Buda, and the serene and otherworldly Buda Hills.

Beyond Budapest
It'd be a shame if you didn't get beyond Budapest. The artist colony Szentendre, with its promenade, Mediterranean restaurants, and colorful shops, is a popular day trip. Esztergom, meanwhile, is a must for history fans, who'll practically faint at the sight of the awe-inspiring Basilica. Then there's legendary Lake Balaton. Central Europe's largest lake attracts countless visitors looking for parties in Siófok or wine tasting in traditional villages up north, all easily accessible from Budapest.

If You Have . . .

- **A LONG WEEKEND:** Spend two days each in Prague and Budapest.
- **ONE WEEK:** Add some time in Bohemia and Moravia.
- **TWO WEEKS:** Add a trip to Lake Balaton.

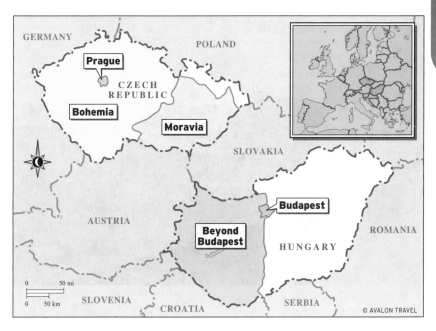

When to Go

In the spring, flowers begin to bloom, the land turns a healthy shade of green, and temperatures start to climb. Fairs and festivals begin, too, with both cities hosting popular Spring Festivals.

The summer season is easily the busiest time of year. Prague's streets are overrun with families and tour groups, while students and backpackers fill the bars and clubs. In Budapest, finding a table at an outdoor café becomes considerably harder, while Danube Bend towns come alive and Lake Balaton becomes the place to let your hair down.

Those not interested in battling the crowds should visit in the fall, when the capitals turn into cozier and cheaper destinations. Prague's parks, along with Margaret Island and the Buda Hills, turn red and gold, providing picturesque backdrops to breathtaking skylines.

While admittedly cold and unnervingly dark, the winter is still a charming time to visit. Prague affects a Kafkaesque aura whose mysterious beauty is compounded by snow-capped buildings. Budapest, in turn, sees its streets and squares settle back into the majestic beauty they're renowned for. Both cities boast Christmas markets and legendary New Year's Eve parties, while Bohemia's ski resorts ring loudly with the merriment of snowboarders, skiers, and nighttime revelers. The main drawback to visiting at this time is that Czech castles and gardens close till spring, while Hungary's most important sites keep shorter hours.

winter in Prague

Before You Go

Visas and Officialdom

Visitors from the United States and Canada need a valid passport to gain entry to both the Czech Republic and Hungary. Citizens of the European Union, the United States, and Canada do not need a visa to enter either country, provided their visits are less than 90 days in length. Visitors from other countries should check with their local Czech and Hungarian consulates, as requirements change often.

What to Take

If visiting in the winter, bring a heavy coat, wool cap, gloves, and boots with lining and treads. If you plan on traveling through the region or simply love to walk, bring a pair of long underwear, too.

Frequent rainfalls are common during spring or fall, so bring an umbrella and a waterproof jacket. Sweaters, fleeces, and warm coats are also good ideas due to the chilly evenings.

In the summer, flaunt it if you got it. Short skirts, sandals, and halter tops rule female fashion, while men stick to shorts and T-shirts. A long-sleeved shirt or two won't hurt, nor will a sweater or light jacket. If you plan on camping, hiking, or tanning, don't forget the insect repellent and sunblock.

Finally, those planning on patronizing expensive restaurants or chic clubs should bring semiformal attire. Suits and formal wear, on the other hand, are appropriate when visiting classical music concerts or the opera.

The Best of Prague and Budapest

Ten days is enough time to take in all the major sights both cities have to offer, but it does mean sticking to a tight schedule and forgoing a few museums. Be prepared to do a lot of walking, and get your camera ready—you're about to experience a few Kodak moments.

Prague

DAY 1

Fly into Prague's Václav Havel Airport and head for your hotel. Staying in Nové Město (Old Town) means being within spitting distance of a wide array of shops, restaurants, sights, and nighttime action. Conversely, if it's a more peaceful, picturesque environment you're looking for, Malá Strana (Lesser Town) is hard to beat.

DAY 2

Start your first full day at the top of Nové Město on the National Museum's steps, where you can see the length of bustling Wenceslas Square stretching out before you. If natural history isn't your thing, forgo the museum and make your way slowly down the square. There are countless shopping possibilities on either side of the boulevard as well as numerous cafés and restaurants that are perfect for people watching. When you're ready to move on again, continue down to the bottom of the square, otherwise known as Můstek. On the right is Na Příkopě Street, which is filled with even more shops, cafés, and restaurants as well as casinos and museums. Those interested in learning more about the Czech Republic's Communist past should definitely pay a visit to the highly informative Museum of Communism. Farther along Na Příkopě Street, you'll come upon the Powder Tower and art nouveau masterpiece the Municipal House. Have lunch, then head for Old Town Square, taking time to admire the gorgeous facades and wide array of beautiful buildings like the Church of Our Lady Before Týn and Church of St. Nicholas. Drink in Old Town

headstones in the Old Jewish Cemetery in Prague

St. Vitus Cathedral in Prague

Church of Our Lady Before Týn in Prague

Hall and the Astronomical Clock, and make sure to catch the wooden marionette show, *The Walk of the Apostles*, performed at the top of every hour. From there, take a stroll down chic Pařížská Street with its trendy boutiques and designer cafés. Stop for coffee then continue on to Josefov, Prague's famed Jewish quarter and home of the magnificent Spanish Synagogue and haunting Old Jewish Cemetery. Lose yourself among the winding picturesque streets, then settle in for an evening of traditional food and drink, or head back to Nové Město for a more cultured evening, taking in a classical concert or opera at the Municipal House, National Theater, or State Opera House.

DAY 3
Start your day bright and early by heading to Prague Castle, the city's most popular and recognizable landmark. Admire the view of Prague down below before wandering through the courtyards and entering jaw-dropping St. Vitus Cathedral. Bask in the glory of its massive nave, stained glass windows, and ornate frescoes, then follow the crowds to tiny Golden Lane, onetime home of the incomparable Franz Kafka.

Backtrack to the castle's front gates and ease on down Nerudova Street, peeking into its plethora of souvenir shops before arriving at legendary Malostranska Square. Enjoy a traditional Czech lunch, then burn those calories off with an enjoyable walk through Lesser Town's romantic cobblestone streets. You'll find no shortage of art galleries, cafés, and glass shops, but make sure to leave time for a visit to Kampa Island. Rest on one of its park benches, and when you've had enough of the remarkable view of Old Town and the lazy Vltava River, head for the Charles Bridge and see for yourself why it's widely considered one of Prague's most memorable structures. Take your pick from any one of the district's many fantastic restaurants, and cap it off with a live show or drinks. Don't go too wild, however. You're traveling tomorrow.

Stopover in Brno
DAY 4
Hit the road early and head for Brno, your halfway point between Prague and Budapest. Once there, get yourself settled and head for Old Town for a tasty Moravian lunch. Take a stroll through Freedom Square and check out the shops on Masarykova Street for any

friendly deals. Take in Old Town Hall and the Cabbage Market then head on up to Špilberk Castle for a taste of history and the finest views in town. Brush up on your history at the Brno City Museum, including the grislier side of the times at the castle's Casemates. Finish off your whirlwind tour with a visit to St. Peter and Paul's Cathedral and the Capuchin Crypt then consult this guide's listings for a memorable dinner and fun night out. Exercise discipline once again, however, as tomorrow's another travel day.

Budapest
DAY 5
Today is another travel day, so pack your bags and head for the airport, bus station, car rental office, or train station. Upon arriving in Budapest, settle into your hotel, freshen up, and hit the Belváros. Vörösmarty Square is the city's social hub and the site of the world-famous Café Gerbeaud. Don't miss the opportunity to grab a delicious cup of coffee and scrumptious dessert before heading on to Váci Street, the country's best-known pedestrian shopping district. At the end of the street is the cavernous Central Market Hall, which, if still open by the time you reach it, will overwhelm you with countless stalls selling everything from wine and paprika to traditional clothing and gifts. If you still have some energy left, take a romantic walk down Budapest's famed Danube Embankment, home to cozy outdoor restaurants and cafés as well as gorgeous views of Buda Castle and Gellért Hill.

DAY 6
Begin at the Royal Palace of Buda, and if time or interest allows, spend a couple of hours admiring the artwork in the massive Hungarian National Gallery. A hop, skip, and a jump will take you to Szentháromság Square and monumental Matthias Church, as well as kitschy yet playful Fishermen's Bastion. Grab some lunch, and when you're done admiring the maze of streets and royal views, head on back down the hill and over the striking Chain Bridge.

Spend the afternoon exploring grand boulevard Andrássy Avenue, whose numerous shops are bound to keep you occupied for

statue of Prince Eugene of Savoy in the Royal Palace of Buda in Budapest

some time. You'll soon come upon the grand Opera House, a tour of which is highly recommended whether you're a fan of opera or not. A little farther on is Nagymező Street, Budapest's Broadway, the site of charming outdoor cafés, popular theaters, and the city's very own Moulin Rouge club. Just down from that is Franz Liszt Square, a bustling collection of outdoor restaurants, bars, and cafés—the perfect place to enjoy an excellent meal, fine wine, and a well-deserved evening of fun.

DAY 7

Kick things off bright and early with gigantic Heroes Square. It's flanked on either side by the Palace of Art and Museum of Fine Arts, both of which are perfect for fans of culture and high art. Nearby is eclectic Vajdahunyad Castle and its collection of Gothic, Renaissance, and baroque buildings. If you have the time, soothe your aches and pains in one of Europe's largest spa complexes, the Széchenyi Spa Baths. If traveling with kids, visit family fave Vidám Park, full of Old World charm and home to a 100-year-old merry-go-round. Have some lunch on or

around Andrássy út as you head back toward the center and over to St. Stephen's Basilica, Hungary's largest church. Enjoy a cup of coffee or light snack at one of the cafés bordering the square, then continue on past peaceful Liberty Square to Kossuth Lajos Square and the remarkable Parliament building, a tour of which is highly recommended. As evening descends, treat yourself to a tasty Hungarian dinner and some excellent domestic wine.

DAY 8

Spend a peaceful and relaxing morning on beautiful Margaret Island, where lazy strolls among its gardens and ruins will reward you with an amusing Musical Fountain, the historic Dominican Convent, and open-air water complex Palatinus Strand. After lunch, head for the Buda Hills. Take a breathtaking ride up the hills via the Cog-Wheel Railroad and the Children's Railroad, stopping to enjoy the serenity of Normafa before reaching Jánoshegy—Budapest's highest point. Make your way back down slowly, savoring the natural surroundings before returning to the realities

the Chain Bridge and Parliament in Budapest

St. Stephen's Basilica in Budapest

The Perfect Night Out

While there is certainly no shortage of things to do at night in either capital, it is this same dizzying array of choices that can leave some travelers overwhelmed. But fear not: Below you'll find the perfect recipe for a successful night on the town that kicks off with a proper traditional meal before moving on to cocktails, live music, clubbing, and a nightcap or two as the sun begins to rise. Follow one or all these suggestions and prepare yourself for an evening to remember.

BEST TRADITIONAL FOOD

· **U Pinkasů** (Prague): Time-honored Czech restaurant serves up delicious traditional fare and a rare unpasteurized version of Pilsner Urquell–the country's finest brew.

· **Zeller Bistro** (Budapest): Pleasant and affordable restaurant offers mouth-watering Hungarian dishes prepared with ingredients grown on the owners' farm.

BEST COCKTAILS

· **Blue Light** (Prague): Bustling bar with a hip, cozy vibe serves some of the finest cocktails in Malá Strana.

· **400** (Budapest): Lively bar in the Jewish Quarter features local DJs and a large outdoor terrace packed with late-night revelers.

BEST LIVE MUSIC

· **Jazz Dock** (Prague): Warm and friendly jazz club offers an excellent range of live acts jamming till the wee hours along Prague's famed riverbank.

· **A38** (Budapest): Unique concert hall located in the bowels of a former Ukrainian stone-carrier ship comes complete with restaurant and thumping outdoor terrace.

BEST CLUB

· **Roxy** (Prague): Popular with locals and tourists alike, Prague's most famous club continues to attract world-class bands and DJs on a weekly basis.

· **Instant** (Budapest): This high-energy club with a house-party feel is filled to capacity on any given night with youngsters looking to groove the night away.

BEST AFTER-HOURS BAR

· **Le Clan** (Prague): Laid-back after-hours club attracts partiers of all stripes looking to stave off their inevitable comedown.

· **Corvintető** (Budapest): Old-school after-hours club throws legendary parties and offers gorgeous panoramic views of Budapest from its enormous rooftop patio.

---

of the big city. Once back, reward yourself for all the walking you've done with a delicious meal and top it off with domestic wine and a tantalizing dessert.

Day Trip to Szentendre
DAY 9

Pack a bag and power up your camera; it's time to head 13 miles north to the picturesque and historical artist colony of Szentendre. Once there, begin at the main square, Szentendre's nerve center, taking your time to enjoy the

lovely baroque and rococo architecture as well as the large number of shops, cafés, and restaurants that populate the busy Bogdányi Street strip. Have lunch at one of the popular restaurants mentioned in this guide then take a long, leisurely stroll along the beautiful and romantic embankment, Szentendre's very own Danube Embankment. If time permits, check out the historical works of local artists at the Ferenczy Museum, or the extensive collection of Hungary's most celebrated ceramics artist at the Margit Kovács Museum. Upon returning to Budapest, spoil yourself with a scrumptious meal and loads of last-minute fun. It is your last night in town, after all.

Back to Prague
DAY 10
Have a hearty breakfast and squeeze in the impressive Dohány Street Synagogue, the largest functioning synagogue on the continent. Then it's on the road again for the trip back to Prague. If you get to Prague at a reasonable hour, take a final stroll around the city's magical streets and try to visit Charles Bridge one last time. You'll be happy you did.

DAY 11
Head to Václav Havel Airport and start figuring out how soon you can conceivably come back.

Prague Like a Local

Everybody knows what the main sights, bars, and restaurants are, but what if you'd like to live like a local? Eat, drink, and stroll where they do—here are a few local tips.

Day 1
Start your day with an affordable breakfast and bottomless cup of coffee at Bohemia Bagel by Charles Bridge. Pick up an extra bagel or two if you like because you'll be doing a lot of walking. Start with the streets of Malá Strana (Lesser Town) and work your way through Kampa Island over to Petřín Hill. Take the funicular or do as the brave do and make your way slowly up the hill on foot, resting and admiring the view below as often as you like. When you get to the top, stroll through the large grounds and, if you have the energy, climb up Petřín Lookout Tower for an excellent panoramic view. Grab a delicious and healthy lunch at Malý Buddha, then continue on to the castle. When you're done there, leave the tourist hordes behind and head on over for more peaceful walking through both Wallenstein Gardens and Vojan Park, and say hello to the peacocks in the

entering the Lesser Town from Charles Bridge

view of the Lesser Town and Petřín Hill from Prague Castle

latter. Enjoy a delicious Balkan dinner at the unbeatable Gitanes, and when you're ready to rock and roll with the local contingent, start drinking at Klub Újezd, where anything goes. If something a little more upscale is to your liking, get on over to Blue Light for cocktails and impromptu conversations. Both bars stay open until very late, so dig in and get ready to party like a Bohemian.

Day 2

Enjoy breakfast at the charming Café Louvre, then make your way to Stromovka Park, one of Prague's more serene getaways, where you can breathe in the fresh air and clear your head among laughing children, playful dogs, and the fortunate locals who don't have a day job. Come out on the end where Výstaviště is located and take your pick from amusement rides, the Lapidárium, or Sea World. Have lunch at one of the local restaurants and walk it off with a romantic stroll through Letná Park before grabbing a picnic bench at its popular beer garden for informal drinks and excellent views of the city below. Have a fun dinner at local favorite Hostinec na Staré Kovárně before

moving a couple of doors down to Fraktal, where free-form conversation comes more naturally than you might think. Order a beer. Drink. Repeat.

Day 3

Take your pick from the countless restaurants along Wenceslas Square and have breakfast while watching the people go by. Next, it's shopping along Na Příkopě Street whose boutiques, malls, and specialty shops will easily keep you busy till lunch. For a real local experience, break bread at U Govindy Vegetarian Club. Spend a few hours browsing the myriad of shops lining both Celetná and Pařížská Streets, picking up gifts and mooning over outfits you can't afford. Have a cup of coffee with local artists and students at Café Montmartre, then explore the back streets of Staré Město (Old Town) while asking yourself if a downtown core can really be this beautiful. An exotic dinner at Zebra Asian Noodle Bar will provide the sturdy base you'll need for drinks at the always fun and rowdy Harley's Bar. If cocktails and the in-crowd are more your speed, then a night at M1 Secret Lounge should do the trick.

Day Trips from Prague

As great as the Golden City is, it would be a shame if you didn't expand your horizons a little bit by hitting the road and enjoying some of the more interesting and inspiring day trips the country has to offer. From castles to colonnades, museums and mom-and-pop wine cellars, you'll quickly come to realize that the Czech Republic has a lot more going for it than the its castle or the Charles Bridge.

Bohemia
KARLŠTEJN

After breakfast, jump on a train or in the car and head to Karlštejn Castle. Enjoy the trip along the Berounka River, and when you get to the castle, don't be put off by the busloads of tourists—there simply isn't a down time here. Settle on a tour of your liking and have fun roaming through the castle's various rooms and chapels. For lunch, try either Koruna or U Janů for tasty traditional Czech fare.

KUTNÁ HORA

Kutná Hora, part of UNESCO's World Cultural Heritage List, boasts the masterfully Gothic St. Barbara's Cathedral. Take your time admiring its remarkable interiors, then set off for another memorable interior—the morbid yet fascinating Sedlec Ossuary with its unbelievable collection of human bones. If you haven't lost your appetite, try Pivnice Dačický for a traditional Czech lunch or local fave U Šneka Pohodáře for yummy pizza pie. Depending on time or interest, check out the Czech Silver Museum and Medieval Mine or take a walk through town and soak up life in a slower, friendlier Bohemia.

ČESKÝ KRUMLOV

Leave Prague as early as possible because you'll want to maximize your time in the medieval paradise that is Český Krumlov. Stroll through the town's historic center and stop for lunch at either Tavern U dwau Maryí or Cikánská jizba before heading off to the castle, where tours through Masquerade Hall and Mirror Hall will simply astound. Don't forget to peer into the Bear Moat, and if shopping is

Telč's town square

Karlštejn Castle

in the cards for you, definitely stop by Egon Schiele Art Centrum for funky, creative souvenirs.

KARLOVY VARY

Up and at 'em nice and early before making your way to Karlovy Vary, the Czech Republic's largest and most famous spa. Head straight for the springs and see whether you can actually stomach the metallic-tasting water. Enjoy walking around the town's five colonnades, stopping only for lunch before wandering around the peaceful town some more. Visit historical sights like the Russian Orthodox Church of St. Peter and Paul or take a tour of the Becherovka factory, where one of the country's most popular liqueurs is made.

Moravia
TELČ

Hit the road for a trip to the peaceful, picturesque, and UNESCO-listed town of Telč. The town square, one of the prettiest in the country, deserves a slow, appreciative stroll through it, so take time to enjoy all the well-preserved examples of Renaissance and baroque architecture. Have lunch on the charming summer terrace of Šenk pod věží, then head up to remarkable Telč Castle, where a tour of its lavishly decorated halls will leave you breathless. If there's time, make sure to explore a few of the countryside's numerous lakes and forests.

MIKULOV

Pay a visit to the heart of wine country and the town of Mikulov. Start with the remarkably well-preserved Renaissance buildings that characterize the town square. Pop your head into the Church of St. Wenceslas for a look at one of the country's most valuable church organs then settle in for lunch. Afterward, up to Mikulov Castle you go, where you can learn plenty about Moravia's wine history at the Regional Museum of Mikulov as well as feast your eyes on Central Europe's second-largest wine barrel. Spend the rest of your time sampling the local wine at various wineries and wine cellars, and make sure to buy a few bottles for friends and family back home.

Treat Yourself in Budapest

Those who like to treat themselves to something extra special while on holiday will find no shortage of opportunities to do so in Budapest. Whether it's upscale shops, fine dining, or world-class baths, this city has it all. Here are a few tips on how you can make your stay here an extra cozy one.

Shopping

Begin where everyone else does—on Váci Street. Ignore the plethora of souvenir shops with their knockoff T-shirts and cheap mugs. Head instead for the boutiques and name-brand outlets, where you'll find everything from a new pair of shoes to that expensive but amazing item of clothing you wouldn't dare buy at home.

Another unique shopping experience can be found at the one and only WestEnd City Center, Central Europe's largest shopping center. With over 400 shops at your disposal, you'll not only find whatever it is you're looking for, but probably one or two things you weren't. Grand Andrássy Avenue will definitely keep you busy for at least a couple of hours thanks to large bountiful shops selling everything from high fashion to creative gift items. Make a list and check it twice; you're off to Central Market Hall. Browse the countless stalls selling fresh fruits and vegetables, every kind of conceivable deli meat, tons of domestic wine, traditional folk costumes, and a whole lot more.

Food and Drink

Stop at least once for a delicious lunch at famed Café Gerbeaud and make sure to leave room for a scrumptious and decadent dessert. When you're done with the day's sightseeing, opt for dinner and drinks on trendy Ráday Street, where you can take your pick from an amazing variety of top-notch restaurants and bars. Feel like feasting? Try Kárpátia, one of the city's better-known Hungarian restaurants, whose rich interiors, excellent service, and traditional dishes like pike perch and

Széchenyi Spa Baths in Budapest

Strange Brews

Everybody knows that a surefire way to make good with the locals is to imbibe the local brew. But what if it looks funny, smells weird, or you've heard it tastes like Grandma's homemade cough syrup? Brace yourself by reading the following descriptions to both countries' local liquors, then buck up and give them a try. If they're not to your liking, take solace in the fact that you can always wash them down with some of the world's finest wine and beer.

ABSINTHE

The mysterious mind-altering effects of absinthe have made this spirit famous around the world. The origin of absinthe can be traced back to the end of the 18th century when French doctor Pierre Ordinaire began using wormwood (*Artemisia absinthium*) together with anise, fennel, hyssop, and numerous other herbs distilled in an alcoholic base as an herbal remedy for his patients. Absinthe is still banned in most countries today, but you'll find it readily available in plenty of Prague bars, which play up the drink's magical history. If you decide to give it a whirl, it will most likely be served to you in a small glass, along with a teaspoon and packet of sugar. Pour some sugar onto the spoon, then soak the spoonful with absinthe and light it in order to caramelize the sugar. When the flame goes out, stir the sugar into your drink, and drink it all down. You'll soon realize why most bars have a two-absinthe maximum. And don't worry—the "mind-altering effects" are largely exaggerations. Try some of the "Green Fairy" at **Red Room, Harley's Bar,** and **Batalion** in Prague.

BECHEROVKA

Becherovka is an interesting 100 percent natural alcoholic drink. The sweet herbal liquid has a maturation process before it is filtered and bottled, and the recipe hasn't changed in over 200 years. Becherovka is very popular among Czechs, but it is really an acquired taste. Give it a try, but don't feel bad if it's not to your liking. You can find Becherovka pretty much anywhere, including **J.J. Murphy's, Fraktal,** and **M1 Secret Lounge.**

PÁLINKA

Almost always drunk as a shot, *pálinka* is an integral part of Hungarian drinking culture. The word's origin comes from the Slavic word *páliť* (distill). Made from plums, apples, pears, apricots, and sometimes cherries, a shot of this brandy was traditionally used as a digestion aid. Today, it can be found in most Budapest bars, including **Szoda, 400,** and **Morrison's Music Pub.**

UNICUM

"Das ist ein Unikum!" (That is special/ unique!) is the phrase most associated with this digestive liqueur that dates back to Kaiser Joseph II of Austria. Made from 40 different herbs and spices, it is one of Hungary's most requested spirits. Don't let its tar-black color and syrupy consistency scare you away; just prepare yourself for a considerably earthier version of Jägermeister with a bitter aftertaste. Try it at **Szimpla kert** and **Corvintető,** both in Budapest.

FERNET

Popular with hipsters the world over, Fernet is an herbal liquor for anyone who likes the strong stuff. In Prague and Budapest, you can find two flavors: Fernet Stock (bitter) and Fernet Citrus (lemon flavored). The recipe is heavily guarded, and with ingredients such as gentian root, quinine, orange peels, and Roman chamomile, you probably are better off not knowing it. An Italian original, this spirit is best served cold or with ice, but it also makes for a potent shooter. Try a shot of Fernet in Prague along with your beer at **Duende, Chapeau Rouge,** and **Blue Light.**

the lip-smackingly good strudel will make you feel like the king or queen you've always known you are.

All that vacation food and drink is bound to catch up with you, so why not burn a few calories the fun way by walking over to Buda and taking in the glorious surroundings? From Buda Palace to Matthias Church, Rózsadomb to the Víziváros, you'll have no shortage of sights to gawk at and more than enough to do until you've built that appetite back up again. Since you're already on the Buda side, don't miss the opportunity to enjoy an upscale dinner at Arany Kaviár, where, if you really feel like spoiling yourself, the Gourmet Menu is the only appropriate choice.

Enjoy lunch on bustling Franz Liszt Square and unwind as you watch the world go by. Take a long, leisurely stroll down Andrássy Avenue toward mighty Heroes Square, taking time to stop and appreciate the dilapidated extravagance of Kodály körönd. Upon reaching Heroes Square, check out Hungary's largest collection of contemporary art at the Palace of Art or the treasure trove of art history at the Museum of Fine Arts. If you happen to have seen enough high culture for one day, don't fret—simply take your pick from less intellectually imposing activities such as the Budapest Zoo and Botanical Garden, the Hungarian State Circus, or venerable Vidám Park. When the day's fun is over, have dinner at the always impressive Gundel, one of the country's best known and most respected restaurants.

Take your time strolling down Budapest's historic Danube Embankment, making sure to absorb the beautiful view of Buda Castle on the opposite side of the river, then choose from any number of restaurants offering excellent traditional fare.

Spas

Shopping and eating can take a lot out of a person, so make your way to the remarkable Gellért Baths and splash around in the lavish indoor pool or bask in the steam rooms and saunas. Feel like a makeover? Cruise up and down Andrássy Avenue and choose from any number of salons offering all kinds of aesthetic boosts. When it comes to pampering and relaxation, the Széchenyi Spa Baths are always a sure bet. Chill out with the natives in the gigantic outdoor swimming pool or head straight for the impressive set of steam rooms, saunas, and Turkish baths.

Enjoy life the old-fashioned way by having a picnic on Margaret Island. Afterward, spend the day strolling past colorful flower gardens, romantic ruins, and a lovely mini zoo, or take in the entire 225 acres via bicycle or electric car, both of which are available to rent. When you're ready to spoil yourself a little, make a beeline for open-air complex Palatinus Strand. With three thermal pools, a water slide, table tennis, and trampolines, you may never want to leave.

Balaton Getaway

Whether you like to party till you drop, appreciate nature, or crave cultured evenings sipping the region's finest wines, you will find that Hungary's Lake Balaton has something for everyone.

Day 1: Budapest to Siófok

Get in the car or jump on one of the trains regularly leaving Budapest's Keleti and Déli train stations and prepare yourself for Siófok—Lake Balaton's Dionysian capital. Upon arrival, find the hostel, guesthouse, or wellness center you've secured a room at, then waste no time heading for Siófok Beach. Work on that tan or stay in shape by joining a game of beach volleyball. When hunger strikes, grab a snack at any of the many kiosks or dive into a tasty traditional dish at the excellent Csárdás Restaurant. Spend some time walking down the tree-lined promenades, and if you're looking for a different place to take an afternoon dip, check out either the Aranypart (Gold Coast) or Ezüstpart (Silver Coast). Freshen up and grab some dinner before beginning what is sure to be a long night. Head back to Siófok Beach for nonstop fun at the Coke Club or hit the Palace Dance Club or Bacardi Music Café for dancing till dawn.

Day 2: Siófok

Sleep in, shake off that hangover, and head back to whatever beach you fancy for more fun in the sun. Add some culture to your visit by checking out peaceful and romantic Millennium Park—the perfect antidote to the frenzy of activity that surrounds the rest of town. Head for the railroad and have an unbelievable lunch at Hintaló Vendéglő, known to satisfy even the most finicky of diners. Drop by the unique Evangelical Lutheran Church, designed by Ybl Prize-winning architect Imre Makovecz, then make your way through the shops and stalls of Kálmán Promenade and pick up a souvenir or two. After dinner, take a nice long walk, enjoy

view of Lake Balaton from Tihany Benedictine Abbey

the sunset, and figure out whether you really want to knock off early in a town that was born ready to party.

Day 3: Balatonfüred

Head north to pretty Balatonfüred, where the old world meets the new. Check into your hotel, then make your way to the center of town, where you'll find Lajos Kossuth Spring. Drink deeply from its curative springs and feel the debauchery of Siófok pleasantly fade away. Have lunch at the outdoor Cimbora Grill Garden and gorge on the wide array of grilled meat dishes as well as the generous salad bar on offer. Walk around town admiring the tasteful villas and charming residential districts, stopping for a cup of coffee or souvenir shopping along the way. Enjoy a fantastic meal on Stefánia Vitorlás Restaurant's sunny terrace and make sure to save some room for one of the over 40 desserts available. If you feel rested enough and could do with another party, check out Café La Luna or Waikiki Cocktail Bar for tasty cocktails and remarkable views of the lake.

Day 4: Tihany

Take the boat over to Tihany and settle into a nice hotel or inn along the bay. Give yourself a couple of hours to explore the peninsula's pretty interior, which includes the Inner Lake and Outer Lake, accessible via a trail from Tihany village. Once you've built up an appetite, head for Fogas Csárda, Tihany's oldest traditional restaurant and a hit with both visitors and locals. Stroll along the cobblestone streets of charming Tihany village and have a look at all the handicrafts, wine, and embroidery for sale before moving on to impressive Tihany Benedictine Abbey. When you're done admiring the wood carvings and baroque pulpit inside, take the path to the left of the church leading up to Echo Hill. Enjoy gorgeous views of the lake

and shout a few words when you get to the top to find out how the hill got its name. Unwind with dinner at the superb Ferenc Cellar Tavern and finish the evening with a glass of wine or a pleasant walk.

Day 5: Badacsony

Take the train west to beautiful Badacsony and find yourself a nice hotel along the shore or guesthouse in the center of town. Take one of the many walking trails leading to the legendary Basalt Hills and lose yourself among the geological gems. For lunch, try the excellent pike perch at the Szent Orban Wine-House and Restaurant and drink in the wonderful panoramic view from its summer terrace. Spend the rest of the day wine tasting, moving from wine cellar to wine cellar and enjoying the beautiful vistas along the way. If visiting during the end of July, make sure to stick around for at least one day and night of the Badacsony Wine Festival.

Day 6: Keszthely

Get up at a decent hour and head to Keszthely, located at the far western tip of the lake. Check into a pension along the shore or in the center of town and waste no time getting to Festetics Palace, Hungary's fourth-largest palace. Enjoy a tasty lunch at Jóbarát Vendéglő, then spend a couple of hours at the highly informative Balaton Museum or enjoy an afternoon of walking around town checking out the shops and Keszthely's open-air market. This is your last night at Lake Balaton, so spoil yourself with a wonderful dinner and then cap off the night with drinks at John's Pub or the more alternative 512 Club.

Day 7: Back to Budapest

After finishing breakfast, jump in the car or on the train and make your way back to the capital.

PRAGUE

It has been a quarter of a century since Communism fell and the doors to Soviet Bloc countries flew open. Since then, Prague has established itself as the hottest travel destination in central Europe thanks in large part to its breathtaking surroundings that boast lush wooded parks and architectural marvels that have been left relatively untouched despite two world wars.

HIGHLIGHTS

LOOK FOR ◖ TO FIND RECOMMENDED SIGHTS, ACTIVITIES, DINING, AND LODGING.

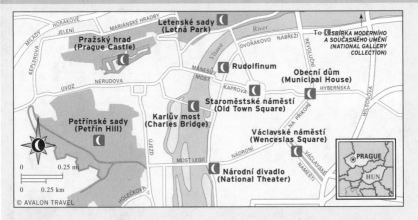

◖ **Václavské náměstí (Wenceslas Square):** Commercial center by day, neon jungle by night, the hub of the city pulses with a lively mix of human traffic no matter what time it is (page 36).

◖ **Obecní dům (Municipal House):** Sit back and enjoy the Prague Philharmonic Orchestra perform classical masterpieces in the city's finest example of art nouveau architecture (page 41).

◖ **Národní divadlo (National Theater):** This icon of Czech culture is the perfect place to take in drama, opera, or the ballet. A tour of the magnificent playhouse is also available (page 43).

◖ **Staroměstské náměstí (Old Town Square):** Abuzz with shops, hotels, restaurants, and bars, this is *the* place to meet fellow travelers, take in some of the city's most jaw-dropping sights, and enjoy intoxicating nightlife (page 46).

◖ **Karlův most (Charles Bridge):** Take a long romantic stroll past artists, musicians, and souvenir hawkers vying for your attention, along with breathtaking views of the city (page 53).

◖ **Rudolfinum:** Home of the Czech Philharmonic Orchestra, this magnificent example of neo-Renaissance architecture also houses some of the city's most interesting art retrospectives (page 60).

◖ **Petřínské sady (Petřín Hill):** Take the funicular or walk all the way up Prague's highest and greenest hill to get away from the maddening crowd (page 72).

◖ **Pražský hrad (Prague Castle):** Whether it's St. Vitus Cathedral, Golden Lane, or the Royal Garden that brings them here, this is one place *everybody* goes at some point during their stay. It's the epitome of Prague's national pride and international identity (page 73).

◖ **Sbírka moderního a současného umění (National Gallery Collection of 19th-, 20th-, and 21st-Century Art):** The 20th-century Bohemian art on display includes cubism and surrealism alongside thought-provoking and often hair-raising Stalin-era work (page 86).

◖ **Letenské sady (Letná Park):** Pull up a bench and drink in the city's mesmerizing skyline (page 86).

Who can remain unimpressed by the awe-inspiring Prague Castle and St. Vitus Cathedral, or the inherent beauty of Petřín Hill and Kampa Island? Is there anybody who has walked up and down Charles Bridge and not felt its palpable perfection deep in their heart? The simple truth is that Prague is a magical, melancholy city that mesmerizes all of its visitors without fail season after season. There are also thousands of foreigners who've made the capital their home, many of whom had initially arrived with the intention of staying for a month or two but found they couldn't resist the city's "claws" Kafka once famously warned of.

Not just a living, breathing museum of arresting architecture, Prague also boasts legendary nightlife that attracts thousands of visitors who are desperate to party with Bohemians while getting a taste of the world's best beer. Others come to shop along trendy Pařížská and pricey Na Příkopě Streets, while still others choose Prague as their honeymoon destination, strolling hand in hand down its cobblestone streets and sealing their lifelong pledge of love with a romantic Old World kiss. Whether you come here to party, soak up the history, or simply check out what everybody's been buzzing about, Prague will resonate deep within you long after you've reluctantly left.

PLANNING YOUR TIME

Most come to Prague for a quick whirlwind tour of the major sights and better-known bars and rarely stay longer than a weekend. It's true that the city center and its immediate surroundings can easily be covered in a couple of well-planned days, though a four-day visit offers you a better chance to get an authentic taste of all Prague has to offer, and five days is ideal if you'd like to investigate the outlying neighborhoods or get in a day trip to one of the many nearby castles and towns.

Prague is a breeze to get around thanks to the fact that the most important sights are situated in Prague 1, starting from the top of Wenceslas Square in Nové Město all the way down to Old Town Square in Staré Město then over Charles Bridge into picturesque

Malá Strana and Prague Castle. While most people prefer to stroll along the romantic cobblestone streets, others are more than satisfied with Prague's exceptional public transportation system, which offers subway stations near and around all sights, as well as numerous trams that lead right to the doorstep of the most significant monuments. Public transportation is also the best and easiest way to reach outlying neighborhoods like Dejvice, Holešovice, Vinohrady, and Žižkov. These particular districts will be of interest primarily to those who are looking to learn more about how the city really ticks. The deeper you delve into these areas, the more you'll shed the hordes of visitors that crowd the center and the closer you'll come to understanding what exactly it is that makes Praguers so proud of their magical city.

ORIENTATION
Nové Město
(New Town)

Located in Prague 1, Nové Město is one of the city's busiest districts and is characterized by Václavské náměstí (Wenceslas Square). Starting from its natural top at the National Museum, it stretches down toward Můstek, interrupted halfway by busy Vodičkova Street. Turning northeast at Můstek leads you down pedestrian Na Příkopě Street, which eventually ends at Náměstí republiky; heading southwest from Můstek will take you to Národní třída and the Vltava River.

The major subway stops are Muzeum, Můstek, Náměstí Republiky, Karlovo náměstí, and Národní třída. The major tram lines are 3, 4, 5, 8, 9, 10, 14, 16, 18, 22, 23, 24, and 26.

Staré Město
(Old Town)

The eastern tip of Celetná Street marks the border between Old Town and New Town. Heading west brings you to Staroměstské náměstí (Old Town Square). Walking past Old Town Hall takes you to jam-packed Karlova Street, which winds its way to the Old Town side of Charles Bridge. Behind the Jan Hus monument in Old Town Square is the start

PRAGUE

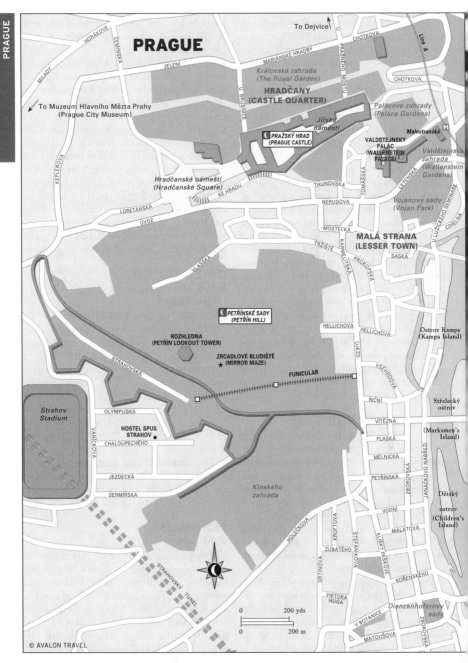

PRAGUE

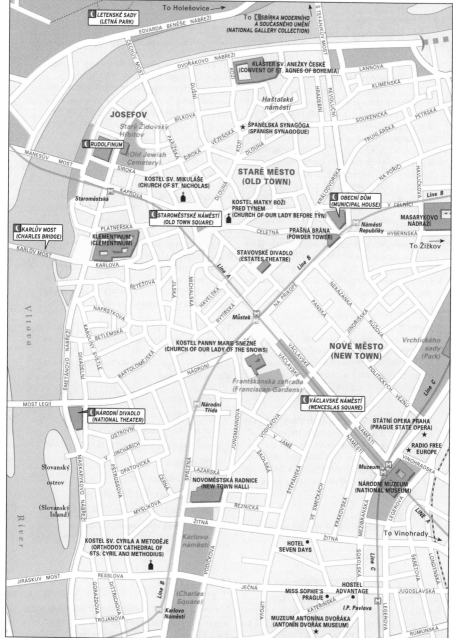

To Holešovice →

LETENSKÉ SADY
(LETNÁ PARK)

EDVARDA BENEŠE NÁBŘEŽÍ

ČECHŮV MOST

DVOŘÁKOVO NÁBŘEŽÍ

To SBÍRKA MODERNÍHO
A SOUČASNÉHO UMĚNÍ
(NATIONAL GALLERY COLLECTION)

Š. ŠTEFÁNIKŮV MOST

KLÁŠTER SV. ANEŽKY ČESKÉ
(CONVENT OF ST. AGNES OF BOHEMIA)

LANNOVA

HRADEBNÍ

REVOLUČNÍ

KLIMENSKÁ

DUŠNÍ

Haštalské
náměstí

JOSEFOV

Starý Židovský
Hřbitov

BÍLKOVA

SOUKENICKÁ

PETRSKÁ

VĚZEŇSKÁ

ŠPANĚLSKÁ SYNAGÓGA
(SPANISH SYNAGOGUE)

TRUHLÁŘSKÁ

RUDOLFINUM

PAŘÍŽSKÁ

ŠIROKÁ

KOZÍ

DLOUHÁ

NA POŘÍČÍ

MÁNESŮV   MOST

(Old Jewish
Cemetery)

ŠIROKÁ

HAVLÍČKOVA

KOSTEL SV. MIKULÁŠE
(CHURCH OF ST. NICHOLAS)

STARÉ MĚSTO
(OLD TOWN)

KRÁLODVORSKÁ

KAPROVÁ

Staroměstská

DLOUHÁ

OBECNÍ DŮM
(MUNICIPAL HOUSE)

Line B

KOSTEL MATKY BOŽÍ
PRED TÝNEM
(CHURCH OF OUR LADY BEFORE TÝN)

V CELNICI

MASARYKOVO
NÁDRAŽÍ

PLATNÉŘSKÁ

STAROMĚSTSKÉ NÁMĚSTÍ
(OLD TOWN SQUARE)

ČELETNÁ

PRAŠNÁ BRÁNA
(POWDER TOWER)

Náměstí
Republiky

HYBERNSKÁ

KARLŮV MOST
(CHARLES BRIDGE)

KLEMENTINUM
(CLEMENTINUM)

To Žižkov

KARLŮV MOST

KARLOVA

STAVOVSKÉ DIVADLO
(ESTATES THEATRE)

Line B

ŘETĚZOVÁ

JILSKÁ

Line A

NEKÁZANKA

Vltava

NAPRSTKOVA

MICHALSKÁ

HAVELSKÁ

RYTÍŘSKÁ

NA PŘÍKOPĚ

PANSKÁ

JINDŘIŠSKÁ

RŮŽOVÁ

KAROLÍNY SVĚTLÉ

BETLÉMSKÁ

Můstek

SMETANOVO NÁBŘEŽÍ

DIVADELNÍ

BARTOLOMĚJSKÁ

KOSTEL PANNY MARIE SNĚŽNÉ
(CHURCH OF OUR LADY OF THE SNOWS)

NÁDRONÍ

VÁCLAVSKÉ

VÁCLAVSKÉ

NOVÉ MĚSTO
(NEW TOWN)

Vrchlického
sady
(Park)

POLITICKÝCH   VĚZŇŮ

Line C

MOST LEGIÍ

Frantškánská zahrada
(Franciscan Gardens)

Národní
Třída

VÁCLAVSKÉ NÁMĚSTÍ
(WENCESLAS SQUARE)

NÁRODNÍ DIVADLO
(NATIONAL THEATER)

OSTROVNÍ

JUNGMANNOVA

VODIČKOVA

NÁMĚSTÍ

STÁTNÍ OPERA PRAHA
(PRAGUE STATE OPERA)

JIRCHÁŘÍCH

V JÁMĚ

NÁMĚSTÍ

RADIO FREE
EUROPE

Slovanský
ostrov

MASARYKOVO NÁBŘEŽÍ

PŘÍTROSSOVA

OPATOVICKÁ

ČERNÁ

SPÁLENÁ

ŠKOLSKÁ

VINOHRADSKÁ

Muzeum

(Slovanský
Island)

MYSLÍKOVA

LAZARSKÁ

NOVOMĚSTSKÁ RADNICE
(NEW TOWN HALL)

ŠTĚPÁNSKÁ

VE SMEČKÁCH

KRAKOVSKÁ

NÁRODNÍ MUZEUM
(NATIONAL MUSEUM)

LEGEROVA

LINE A

River

ŽITNÁ

REZNICKÁ

MĚZIBRÁNSKÁ

To Vinohrady

KOSTEL SV. CYRILA A METODĚJE
(ORTHODOX CATHEDRAL OF
STS. CYRIL AND METHODIUS)

Karlovo
náměstí

VODIČKOVA

ŽITNÁ

HOTEL
SEVEN DAYS

SOKOLSKÁ

Line C

ŠKRÉTOVA

LONDÝNSKÁ

JIRÁSKŮV MOST

RESSLOVA

JEČNÁ

MISS SOPHIE'S
PRAGUE

HOSTEL
ADVANTAGE

JUGOSLÁVSKÁ

GORAZDOVA

DITTRICHOVA

Line B

(Charles
Square)

Karlovo
Náměstí

LIPOVÁ

KATEŘINSKÁ

I.P. Pavlova

LEGEROVA

TROJANOVA

MUZEUM ANTONÍNA DVOŘÁKA
(ANTONÍN DVOŘÁK MUSEUM)

RUMUNSKÁ

Prague Addresses and Districts

Prague is separated into 10 postal districts, the numbers of which are generally included when giving an address. For example, the proper full address for the excellent Café Louvre would be written like this: Národní 20, Praha 1. Oftentimes, the address given will also state the specific neighborhood within the district: Národní 20, Praha 1, Nové Město. This, of course, makes it even easier to locate a particular address. The most common districts and their corresponding neighborhoods:

Praha 1
The city's most central and by far most popular district, Prague 1 is home to the tourist-driven neighborhoods of Hradčany, Malá Strana, Staré Město, Josefov, and northern Nové Město. All the major sights are here: Prague Castle, Charles Bridge, and Wenceslas Square, along with the city's major shops, restaurants, hotels, and businesses.

Praha 2
Prague 2 comprises the tail end of southern Nové Město, Vyšehrad, and western Vinohrady. A good deal of its charm lies in its quiet residential streets, cozy wine bars, intimate restaurants, and wooded parks.

Praha 3
Eastern Vinohrady and Žižkov make up the city's third district. Still close to the center, it's full of old decrepit buildings, though it's been going through a bit of a makeover the last few years. Žižkov, in particular, is known for its countless bars and rather Bohemian expat residents.

Praha 5
Prague 5 is situated on the Vltava River's left bank, just south of Malá Strana. Its main neighborhood, Smíchov, has undergone dramatic changes over the last five years, transforming itself from a dodgy area into a bustling commercial center full of cinemas, shopping centers, and administrative offices.

Praha 6
Prague 6's main neighborhood is Dejvice. Home to Divoká Šárka, Břevnov Monastery, and Hvězda Summer Palace, it is mainly characterized by embassies, ambassadors' villas, university campuses, and residential areas.

Praha 7
Continuous reconstruction of Holešovice, Prague's former industrial zone, has made the seventh district one of the hotter locations to invest in real estate these days. This relatively central neighborhood is home to Stromovka Park, Letná Park, and Výstaviště.

TERMS
The Czech language is a notoriously difficult one, but learning a few of the terms below ought to help you navigate the city's streets with relative ease.

- *most*–bridge
- *nábřeží*–quay
- *nádraží*–train station
- *náměstí* (also abbreviated as *nám.*)–square
- *ostrov*–island
- *sady/zahrada*–garden(s)
- *třída* (also abbreviated as *tr.*)–avenue
- *ulice* (also abbreviated as *ul.*)–street
- *zastávka*–bus, tram, subway stop

of fashionable Pařížská Street and the beginning of Josefov, Prague's Jewish quarter, which stretches all the way down to the Vltava River.

The major subway stop is Staroměstská. The major tram lines are 12, 17, and 18.

Malá Strana (Lesser Town)
Malostranské náměstí is the district's center, where all visitors eventually find themselves. This is where you'll find legendary Nerudova

PRAGUE

© LUCIE ERICKSEN

Prague Castle looms over the Lesser Town.

Street, lined with restaurants and souvenir shops as it stretches up to Prague Castle.

The major subway stop is Malostranská. The major tram lines are 12, 18, 20, 22, and 23.

Hradčany

Hradčany is defined by Prague Castle. The center of the castle complex is Jiřské náměstí, which leads off to plenty of sights, including lovely Golden Lane. Opposite the castle's gated entrance is the gorgeous Hradčanské náměstí, home to the Archbishop's Palace, Sternberg Palace, and Schwarzenberg Palace. Just west of the square is Loretánské náměstí, characterized by the magnificent Loreto.

The major subway stop is Hradčanská. The major tram lines are 1, 8, 15, 22, 23, and 25.

Dejvice

The center of the sixth district is the busy roundabout known as Vitězné náměstí. Evropská Street connects to this square and leads to both Divoká Šárka and Václav Havel Airport.

The major subway stop is Dejvická. The major tram lines are 2, 8, 20, and 26.

Holešovice

Prague's seventh district is reached via Milady Horákove, which delves into the depths of Holešovice, passing Letná Park and busy commercial square Letenské náměstí before ending at Strossmayerovo náměstí. From here, it's just a few blocks to the National Gallery Collection of 19th-, 20th-, and 21st-Century Art, Výstaviště's exhibition grounds, and beautiful Stromovka Park.

The major subway stops are Vltavská and Nádraží Holešovice. The major tram lines are 1, 5, 8, 12, 14, 15, 17, 25, and 26.

Žižkov

Žižkov is Prague's sprawling third district, and its main square is Náměstí Jiřiho z Poděbrad. On the opposite side of the district is Žižkov Hill as well as main road Seifertová, whose tram lines connect the area with the center of town.

The major subway stops are Florenc and Jiřiho z Poděbrad. The major tram lines are 5, 9, 10, 11, and 26.

Vinohrady

Vinohrady is located in the heart of Prague's second district and boasts two main squares: the heavily congested I. P. Pavlova, with its endless stream of trams, shoppers, and area workers, and the grander, more peaceful Náměstí Míru, where comfortable benches and the magnificent Church of St. Ludmilla provide the perfect antidote to I. P.'s bustle. The area's two main streets are Ječná, which leads to Karlovo náměstí, and Vinohradská, which starts right behind the National Museum.

The major subway stops are Náměstí Míru and I. P. Pavlova. The major tram lines are 4, 6, 10, 16, 22, and 23.

Sights

NOVÉ MĚSTO (NEW TOWN)

Founded by Charles IV in 1348, Nové Město is a predominantly commercial district that is home to many of the city's finer shops, most of its financial institutions, and a plethora of restaurants, bars, and hotels. Bustling both day and night with all walks of life, it stretches north and east to Národní, Na Příkopě, and Revoluční, where it borders Staré Město (Old Town).

(Václavské náměstí and Vicinity (Wenceslas Square)

More a boulevard than a square, the 2,462-foot-long, 197-foot-wide Wenceslas Square is named after St. Wenceslas, former duke and present

Wenceslas Square

© LUCIE ERICKSEN

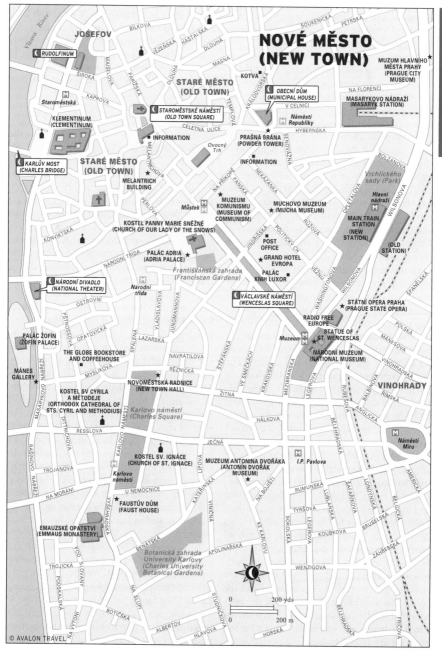

JOSEFOV

RUDOLFINUM

Vltava River

BÍLKOVA

SOUKENICKÁ

PETRSKÁ

NOVÉ MĚSTO (NEW TOWN)

MUZUM HLAVNÍHO MĚSTA PRAHY (PRAGUE CITY MUSEUM)

ŠIROKÁ

MAISELOVA

VĚZEŇSKÁ

HAŠTALSKÁ

DLOUHÁ

MASNÁ

KOTVA

OBECNÍ DŮM (MUNICIPAL HOUSE)

NA FLORENCI

MASARYKOVO NÁDRAŽÍ (MASARYK STATION)

KAPROVA

PAŘÍŽSKÁ

DLOUHÁ

STARÉ MĚSTO (OLD TOWN)

V CELNICI

Staroměstská

STAROMĚSTSKÉ NÁMĚSTÍ (OLD TOWN SQUARE)

TEMPLOVÁ

KRÁLODVORSKÁ

Náměstí Republiky

HYBERNSKÁ

BOLZANOVA

KLEMENTINUM (CLEMENTINUM)

CELETNÁ ULICE

INFORMATION

Ovocný Trh

PRAŠNÁ BRÁNA (POWDER TOWER)

SENOVÁŽNÁ

Vrchlického sady (Park)

KARLŮV MOST (CHARLES BRIDGE)

MELANTRICHOVA

STARÉ MĚSTO (OLD TOWN)

INFORMATION

NA PŘÍKOPĚ

PANSKÁ

NEKÁZANKA

OPLETALOVA

Hlavní nádraží

WILSONOVA

MELANTRICH BUILDING

PERLOVÁ

KONVIKTSKÁ

Můstek

MUZEUM KOMUNISMU (MUSEUM OF COMMUNISM)

MUCHOVO MUZEUM (MUCHA MUSEUM)

RŮŽOVÁ

MAIN TRAIN STATION (NEW STATION)

(OLD STATION)

KOSTEL PANNY MARIE SNĚŽNÉ (CHURCH OF OUR LADY OF THE SNOWS)

JINDŘIŠSKÁ

POLITICKÝCH

POST OFFICE

VĚZŇŮ

WASHINGTONOVA

WILSONOVA

ŠPANĚLSKÁ

NÁRODNÍ TŘÍDA

PALÁC ADRIA (ADRIA PALACE)

Františkánská zahrada (Franciscan Gardens)

GRAND HOTEL EVROPA

PALÁC KNIH LUXOR

NÁRODNÍ DIVADLO (NATIONAL THEATER)

Národní třída

VÁCLAVSKÉ NÁMĚSTÍ (WENCESLAS SQUARE)

STÁTNÍ OPERA PRAHA (PRAGUE STATE OPERA)

OSTROVNÍ

PŠTROSSOVA

OPATOVICKÁ

VLADISLAVOVA

JUNGMANNOVA

ŠPÁLENA

LAZARSKÁ

RADIO FREE EUROPE

STATUE OF ST. WENCESLAS

POLSKÁ

MÁNESOVA

PALÁC ŽOFÍN (ŽOFÍN PALACE)

THE GLOBE BOOKSTORE AND COFFEEHOUSE

NAVRÁTILOVA

ŠTĚPÁNSKÁ

VE SMEČKÁCH

KRAKOVSKÁ

MEZIBRANSKÁ

Muzeum

NÁRODNÍ MUZEUM (NATIONAL MUSEUM)

VINOHRADSKÁ

VINOHRADY

ŘÍMSKÁ

MÁNES GALLERY

MASARYKOVO NÁBŘEŽÍ

MYSLÍKOVA

ŘEZNICKÁ

ŽITNÁ

LEGEROVA

RUBEŠOVA

BALBÍNOVA

ANGLICKÁ

KOSTEL SV CYRILA A METODĚJE (ORTHODOX CATHEDRAL OF STS. CYRIL AND METHODIUS)

NOVOMĚSTSKÁ RADNICE (NEW TOWN HALL)

Karlovo náměstí (Charles Square)

HÁLKOVA

BĚLEHRADSKÁ

RAŠÍNOVO NÁBŘEŽÍ

DITTRICHOVA

TROJANOVA

RESSLOVA

KARLOVO NÁMĚSTÍ

JEČNÁ

LIPOVÁ

KATEŘINSKÁ

NA BOJIŠTI

RUMUNSKÁ

LUBLAŇSKÁ

ŠAFAŘÍKOVA

LONDÝNSKÁ

AMERICKÁ

Náměstí Miru

NA MORÁNI

KOSTEL SV. IGNÁCE (CHURCH OF ST. IGNACE)

Karlovo náměstí

MUZEUM ANTONÍNA DVOŘÁKA (ANTONÍN DVOŘÁK MUSEUM)

I.P. Pavlova

I.P. Pavlova

BELGICKÁ

U NEMOCNICE

VINIČNÁ

TYRŠOVA

SOKOLSKÁ

LEGEROVA

KOUBKOVA

BRUSELSKÁ

ZÁHŘEBSKÁ

FAUSTŮV DŮM (FAUST HOUSE)

EMAUZSKÉ OPATSTVÍ (EMMAUS MONASTERY)

VYŠEHRADSKÁ

BENÁTSKÁ

APOLINÁŘSKÁ

KE KARLOVU

WENZIGOVA

TROJICKÁ

POD SLOVANY

PODSKALSKÁ

NA SLUPI

Botanická zahrada University Karlovy (Charles University Botanical Gardens)

STUDNIČKOVA

FRIČOVA

BOTIČSKÁ

ALBERTOV

HLAVOVA

HORSKÁ

BĚLEHRADSKÁ

0   200 yds

0   200 m

© AVALON TRAVEL

patron saint of Bohemia who, legend has it, was murdered while on his way to church by mercenaries hired by his brother Boleslav.

The square operates as the unofficial hub of the city and was the site of nearly every major historical event that the country underwent during the 20th century. On October 28, 1918, droves of Praguers filled the square to hear Czechoslovakia proclaimed an independent republic. During the Nazi occupation, the streets were the scene of mass demonstrations. The brief hope-filled Prague Spring of 1968 came and went here, and on January 19, 1969, university student Jan Palach set himself ablaze in protest of the Soviet invasion. It was here, too, on November 17, 1989, that the world tuned in to see hundreds of thousands of Czechs celebrating their first taste of democracy in over 40 years.

In the early morning, while locals head to work and travelers sleep off their hangovers, the boulevard is relatively quiet, making it easy to drink in some of the historical buildings that line it. At number 34 for example, you'll find the **Wiehl House,** a beautiful neo-Renaissance building designed in 1895-1896 that boasts colorful murals, gables, turrets, and a belfry. The **Melantrich Building** at number 30 will stay in the hearts and minds of Czechs for a long time to come, as this is the spot where Václav Havel and Alexander Dubček stood on the second balcony and announced to a delirious crowd on November 24, 1989, that Communism was finally over. At number 25 stands the infamous art nouveau **Grand Hotel Evropa,** which, despite its magnificent facade, has fallen way behind the times in the realm of hotel service and makes for a much better photograph than a place to rest your head.

Wenceslas Square becomes a lively mix of hurried workers and souvenir-laden visitors as the day unfolds. It can get somewhat overwhelming at times, but one way to avoid the crush of human traffic is to cross over to the island that runs down the middle of the boulevard. Lined with benches and well-manicured little gardens, the meridian is a far less crowded affair and makes for a perfect place

to rest your feet, have a snack, or simply look around and admire the view without hurry. At night, Wenceslas Square sheds the day's overtly commercial slant and fills up with a barrage of thrill-seekers, giving the area a carnival-like atmosphere that extends well into the wee hours.

NÁRODNÍ MUZEUM (NATIONAL MUSEUM)

At the southern end of the square sits the **National Museum** (Václavské náměstí 68, tel. 224 497 111, www.nm.cz, closed for reconstruction until June 2015), a grand neo-Renaissance building that was built between 1885 and 1891 based on the designs of Josef Schulz. Weather-beaten and war-weary, it survived near-bankruptcy during the World War I and a German bomb during the World War II. Soviet soldiers senselessly opened fire on its facade in 1968, and underground blasting during the construction of the Museum subway station in 1978 caused further damage, as did the construction of what was then dubbed the "North-South Highway" (Wilsonova/Mezibranska St.), which runs past the front of the building.

Today, scores of visitors congregate at the top of the museum's steps to enjoy the view encompassing the length of the square. Inside, permanent exhibitions include the primeval history of Bohemia, Moravia, and Slovakia as well as various zoological and mineral collections. The truth is that most of what's on display here is rather unimpressive, but the majestic lobby and opulent staircase are well worth a look. In front of the museum, you'll notice two small mounds embedded in the cobblestone street. They are there to commemorate Jan Palach, who set himself on fire in protest against the Soviets, as well as Jan Zajíc, who followed suit a month later.

In front of the National Museum, on the other side of Wilsonova Street, is an imposing equestrian **statue of St. Wenceslas,** designed by famed Czech sculptor Josef Myslbek. Simply called "The Horse," it marks the beginning of the boulevard and is one of Prague's favorite meeting spots, not to mention the starting point of countless walking tours. St. Wenceslas

Velvet Václav: From Dissident to President

It is a very clear understanding that the only kind of politics that truly makes sense is one that is guided by conscience.

Václav Havel (1936-2011)

Playwright, poet, political prisoner, and president, Václav Havel was one of the foremost intellectual figures and moral forces in Eastern Europe, bringing the world's attention to the absurdity of regulated thought and speech under Communist rule and emphasizing the moral revival of the individual amid changes in the social order. Born into an affluent family in Prague, Havel was denied entry to university due to his "bourgeois" background. He ended up studying at a technical college from 1955 to 1957, then served in the Czechoslovak army between 1957 and 1959 before joining the progressive Theater on the Balustrade in 1960. Starting as a stagehand, Havel eventually saw his first play, *The Garden Party*, performed on stage in 1963. It satirized modern bureaucracy and was a critical success both at home and abroad. In 1965 he picked up where he left off, writing *The Memorandum*, in which he introduced an artificial language constructed with the express purpose of creating greater precision in communication. The theme was further explored a few years later in 1968 with *The Increased Difficulty of Concentration,* which attacked fashionable sociological terminology, the era's own specific brand of political correctness. During this time, Havel was also a member of the editorial board of the literary magazine *Tvár,* which quickly started to annoy the conservative Writers Association. The magazine was ground to a halt in 1969, the same year Havel's passport was confiscated on the grounds that his writings were considered subversive and therefore a danger to the state.

Communism's "normalization" period began in the 1970s, a period that saw tens of thousands of writers and artists arbitrarily threatened, expelled from the country, or simply locked away. Things began to look bleak, and Havel saw his country becoming more and more apathetic and demoralized in the face of increased repression. In 1975 he sat down and wrote a letter to Gustav Husak, Czechoslovakia's then-ruler, and lambasted him in systematic detail as to how totalitarianism was ruining the country: "So far, you and your government have chosen the easy way out for yourselves, and the most dangerous road for society: the path of inner decay for the sake of outward appearances; of deadening life for the sake of increasing uniformity; of deepening the spiritual and moral crisis of our society and ceaselessly degrading human dignity for the puny sake of protecting your own power." Broadcast over Radio Free Europe and illegally typed and distributed among numerous underground artistic and political circles, Havel's letter sent ripples of rebellion throughout the region, causing many to stop and realize that they too could stand up, ignore the potential consequences, and put their oppressors on the defensive.

Havel continued to fight the good fight, sparking the Charter 77 movement that defended civil liberties, specifically rock music and its musicians, who had recently been brought to the courts as dangers to society and the state. Imprisoned in 1979 for 4.5 years for subversion of the republic, Havel was released in 1983 due to illness and instantly became the unofficial leader of the Czechoslovak human rights movement. He continued to write powerful plays and political essays as well as deliver impassioned speeches and pleas that began gaining the attention and sympathy of neighboring Western countries. In November 1989, Havel formed a political opposition group named the Civic Forum and was elected by direct popular vote as president of the Czech and Slovak Federal Republic when Communism finally fell. The so-called Velvet Revolution of 1989, named after Havel's favorite band The Velvet Underground, may very well have been a political inevitability, but it was Havel himself who stood up time and again for the right of individuals to speak freely and, as he liked to put it, "live in truth."

keeps company with fellow Bohemian patron saints Agnes, Adelbert, Procopius, and Wenceslas's own grandmother, Ludmila. At the foot of the statue rests a **memorial to the victims of Communism,** depicting the images of Palach and Zajíc, two protesters who sacrificed their lives for their beliefs.

RADIO FREE EUROPE

East of the National Museum is the former home of the Stock Exchange (1936-1938), which later became the Federal Assembly Building in 1973 and continued as such until Czechoslovakia split into two republics in 1993. Today, the dull-looking building is the headquarters of **Radio Free Europe** (Vinohradská 1, tel. 221 122 114, www.rferl.org) and has been surrounded by concrete barriers and heavy security ever since a bomb threat was called in shortly after the tragic events of 9/11.

STÁTNÍ OPERA PRAHA
(PRAGUE STATE OPERA)

East of Radio Free Europe is the pretty **Prague State Opera** (Wilsonova 4, tel. 224 901 448, www.sop.cz, box office daily 10am-6pm), which opened on January 5, 1888, with a performance of Wagner's *The Mastersingers of Nuremberg.* Every season brings above-average artists from all over Europe who perform the classics, along with a few lesser-known works now and again to keep things interesting. Tickets are rather inexpensive compared to Western prices, and the elegant neo-rococo auditorium alone is worth the visit.

Northern Nové Město

The north side of Wenceslas Square is named Můstek, or "little bridge" in Czech. Indeed, a bridge once connected Old and New Town here, the partial remains of which can still be seen down in the depths of the Můstek subway station. Today, Můstek is surrounded by a wide variety of shops as well as food stands offering all kinds of greasy burgers, sausages, and hometown late-night favorite *smažený sýr* (deep-fried cheese). Continuing straight past the square, with the National Museum at your back, you

will eventually end up in Old Town Square. Turning southwest at Můstek will take you to southern Nové Město and the Vltava River; heading northeast sends you down Na Příkopě, an unapologetically expensive street filled with shops, restaurants, casinos, and cafés, not to mention museums, the Municipal House, and Powder Tower.

MUZEUM KOMUNISMU
(MUSEUM OF COMMUNISM)

Starting with the coup in February 1948 and spanning four full decades before Communism's collapse in 1989, the thought-provoking **Museum of Communism** (Na Příkopě 10, tel. 224 212 966, www.muzeum-komunismu.cz, daily 9am-9pm, 190 Kč) recreates a memorable account of the totalitarian regime that changed the face of the country and is still felt and remembered by many today. The theme of the museum is "Communism—the Dream, the Reality, and the Nightmare," and visitors are invited to experience what life was like behind the iron curtain. An old schoolroom and interrogation room have been recreated, while news footage of the era in the museum's Television Time Machine both chill and inspire. This is a great introduction to life under Communism and a vivid reminder of what many Czechs endured not all that long ago.

MUCHOVO MUZEUM
(MUCHA MUSEUM)

Alfons Mucha (1860-1939) is arguably the Czech Republic's best-known visual artist. More than 100 exhibits featuring various paintings, photographs, and personal memorabilia can be found at the **Mucha Museum** (Kaunický palác, Panská 7, tel. 224 216 415, www.mucha.cz, daily 10am-6pm, 180 Kč). Most often remembered for the unconventional yet beautiful posters he designed for Sarah Bernhardt, he also played a key role in influencing French art nouveau at the turn of the 20th century. A 30-minute video detailing Mucha's life and a re-creation of his Parisian studio are also part of the exhibition, and visitors can purchase

© TOM DIRLIS

the mighty and majestic Municipal House

concert hall. Taking in a classical concert here is an unforgettable experience and highly recommended to anyone who is a fan of the music.

PRAŠNÁ BRÁNA (POWDER TOWER)

Next to the Municipal House is the 213-foot-tall **Powder Tower** (tel. 724 911 461, www.prazskeveze.eu, Oct. and Mar. daily 10am-8pm, Nov.-Feb. daily 10am-6pm, Apr.-Sept. daily 10am-10pm, 75 Kč). This Gothic structure originally served as the gateway to the Royal Route that wound through Old Town, over Charles Bridge, and up to the Castle. Built in 1475, it was one of Prague's original 13 city gates and was originally named Mountain Tower. The name changed in the 17th century when the structure was used to store gunpowder. Renovated in the 1990s, visitors can now climb the 186 steps to the top for excellent views of the city, along with a permanent exhibition dealing with the history of Prague and its towers.

MUZEUM HLAVNÍHO MĚSTA PRAHY (PRAGUE CITY MUSEUM)

Tracing Prague's development from the earliest settlement of the Prague Basin all the way to the late 18th century, the **Prague City Museum** (Na Poříčí 52, tel. 221 709 674, www.muzeumprahy.cz, Tues.-Sun. 9am-6pm, 120 Kč) is an interesting and educational way to spend an hour or two. Full of historical artifacts, weapons, maps, and signs, its most prized possession is a remarkable huge cardboard model of the city designed from 1826 to 1837 by Antonin Lanweil. Masterfully crafted, this model accurately depicts the city as it was before large areas of the center were cleared during the 19th and 20th centuries.

Southern Nové Město

FRANTIŠKÁNSKÁ ZAHRADA (FRANCISCAN GARDENS)

Located just off Vodičkova Street behind Světozor Cinema are the **Franciscan Gardens,** formerly a monastic garden built by—you guessed it—the Franciscans. The

reprints of many of his colorful works from the museum's gift shop.

OBECNÍ DŮM (MUNICIPAL HOUSE)

Prague's most prominent art nouveau building also happens to be one of its most beautiful. Situated on the site of the former Royal Court Palace, the **Municipal House** (Náměstí Republiky 5, tel. 222 002 101, www.obecnidum.cz, guided tours 290 Kč, times vary) was constructed between 1905 and 1911 and decorated with intricate stained glass windows, gold trimmings, the finest in Czech crystal, and magnificent frescoes painted by the country's most talented 20th-century artists, including Alfons Mucha and Karel Spillar, who is also responsible for the mosaic, titled *Homage to Prague,* above the building's main entrance. The Municipal House contains several upper-class restaurants, bars, conference rooms, and the like, but its essence can be found in Smetana Hall, named after the famous Czech composer and which remains Prague's largest

The Royal Route: Walking with Kings

One of the most enjoyable ways to see the best of Prague's offerings is to follow the Royal Route—the historical path Bohemian monarchs took on their way to being crowned at Prague Castle's St. Vitus Cathedral. The route starts at the Powder Tower located next to the magnificent Municipal House. It continues down colorful Celetná Street, home to countless souvenir shops as well as beautiful murals, facades, and important pieces of architecture, including the House of the Black Madonna. Following Celetná will lead you to Old Town Square and all of the beauty that comes with it: the astronomical clock, Týn Church, and St. Nicholas Church, among others. Continue on down Karlova Street and its wide array of shops and restaurants until you hit Charles Bridge, one of Prague's most celebrated attractions. Here you can enjoy the wonderful view of Prague Castle, the lovely Vltava River, buskers, artisans, and 30 remarkable statues that cause everybody to stop, stare, and admire. Coming off the bridge, take adjoining Mostecká Street up to Malostranské náměstí and pause for a moment to enjoy its collection of historical buildings, including the awe-inspiring St. Nicholas Church. From there, it's on to steep Nerudova Street and its never-ending shops, restaurants, and cafés filled with visitors and locals, all enjoying the grandeur of times long gone but not forgotten. At the top of Nerudova, follow the curve to the right and you'll come upon Matthias Gate and Prague Castle, which served as the official end of the coronation procession. The path itself is very easy to navigate, but if you find yourself confused or feel that you've lost your way, look down—there are silver arrows in the ground labeled "Silver Line" outlining the entire path.

© LUCIE ERICKSEN

The Royal Route takes you across Charles Bridge.

small park is a peaceful oasis amid the rush and rumble of Nové Město and is often inhabited by office workers on their lunch break, students playing hooky, or just about anybody else looking to rest on one of the many comfortable benches. It's a perfect place to take a break from the crowds.

PALÁC ADRIA
(ADRIA PALACE)
Located southwest of Můstek is Jungmannovo náměstí, and the **Adria Palace** is at number 28. Built in 1925, it is arguably the city's finest example of rondocubist architecture. It's now home to modern offices, apartments, and shops, but it still makes for an excellent photograph.

KOSTEL PANNY MARIE SNĚŽNÉ
(CHURCH OF OUR LADY
OF THE SNOWS)
Founded in 1347 by Charles IV, the **Church of Our Lady of the Snows** (Jungmannovo náměstí 18, tel. 222 246 243, http://pms.ofm.cz, daily 7am-7:30pm) was intended to be Prague's most exalted place of worship.

© LUCIE ERICKSEN

National Theater

The Hussite Wars put an end to that dream, however, and only one-third of the church was ever completed. Visitors will nevertheless be impressed by the church's vaulted ceilings and altarpiece as well as the 95-foot-tall main altar that was designed in the mid-17th century and still stands as Prague's tallest.

◖ NÁRODNÍ DIVADLO (NATIONAL THEATER)

The neo-Renaissance **National Theater** (Ostrovní 1, tel. 224 901 448, www.narodni-divadlo.cz, box office daily 10am-6pm), lined with a balustrade of wild horses and topped with a golden dome, is one of the country's strongest symbols of a people who wanted to unify their Czech nation and culture. Funded completely with donations from people of all social strata, the ceremonial foundation stone was laid on May 16, 1868, and the theater opened officially on June 11, 1881, in honor of Crown Prince Rudolf's visit. Tragedy struck scarcely two months later, however, when a fire broke out while additional work was being done

on the building, destroying the copper dome, stage, and auditorium. Once again the Czech people got together and amassed an incredible one million florins in just 47 days. Finally, on November 18, 1883, the theater opened officially with a performance of Bedřich Smetana's opera *Libuše*. Today, the theater continues to be a beacon of culture and entertainment, offering consistently sold-out audiences the very best in ballet, opera, and theater.

Tours of the National Theater are Saturday-Sunday 8:30am-11am. The tour lasts one hour and costs 200 Kč pp. For information, email tourinfo@pis.cz.

PALÁC ŽOFÍN (ŽOFÍN PALACE)

The gorgeous **Žofín Palace** (Slovanský ostrov 226, tel. 224 934 880, www.zofin.cz), a neo-Renaissance mansion located on Slovanský Island, was built during 1885-1887 in honor of the Archduchess Sophie, mother of Emperor Franz Joseph I. Offering tremendous views of the city, including Prague Castle, it has seen some of the world's finest composers perform, including Smetana, Dvořák, Berlioz, Liszt, and Wagner. Its huge halls are ideal for concerts and balls, both of which continue to this day, along with congresses, gala receptions, and major business events.

MÁNES GALLERY
Designed by Otakar Novotný and completed in 1934, the functionalist-looking **Mánes Gallery** (Masarykovo nábřeží 250, tel. 224 932 938, www.galeriemanes.cz, Tues.-Sun. 10am-8pm, admission varies) is home to three spacious floors of regularly scheduled international art shows as well as popular exhibits of contemporary Czech artists. If you have the time, treat yourself to a cup of coffee and a wonderful panoramic view of the city on the gallery's restaurant terraces.

Karlovo náměstí and Vicinity (Charles Square)
Charles IV took it upon himself to create a square large enough to rival the one found in Old Town. He certainly accomplished what he set out to do. Originally a cattle market, Charles Square remains the largest square in the capital. Choked by busy roads and an endless stream of trams, the park in the middle of the square is nevertheless an enjoyable place to walk the dog, read a book, or soak your tired feet in the fountain. Plenty of shops, restaurants, and offices are found in the area, along with interesting historical sights, including New Town Hall, the baroque Cathedral of St. Ignatius, Emause Monastery, and the Faust House. Although it's an excellent place to take a stroll and soak up some rays, the park is known to become a rather popular place for drug users and petty criminals at night. Use caution and common sense when walking through the square after dusk.

NOVOMĚSTSKÁ RADNICE (NEW TOWN HALL)
Operating as the home of New Town authorities from 1377 to 1784, **New Town Hall** (Karlovo náměstí 1/23, tel. 224 948 229, www.

novomestskaradnice.cz, Tues.-Sun. 10am-6pm, 50 Kč) was also the site of Prague's First Defenestration. On July 30, 1419, an angry mob led by Jan Želivský demanded the release of Hussite prisoners that were being held in the building. When the Roman Catholic councilors refused, the outraged crowd stormed the building and went about throwing all the present councilors out the window. Those who somehow managed to survive the fall were beaten to death. It was here, then, that Prague's first protest and the beginning of the Hussite Revolution took place. Today, the building's three lovely halls are used for far more enjoyable purposes such as cultural events and weddings.

KOSTEL SV. IGNÁCE (CHURCH OF ST. IGNATIUS)
The full-on gilding and flamboyant stucco work found on the **Church of St. Ignatius** (Karlovo náměstí, corner of Ječná and Resslova, open only for mass Mon.-Fri. 6:15am, 7:30am, 5:30pm, Sat. 6:30am, 7:30am, 5:30pm, Sun. 7am, 9am, 11am in Latin, 5:30pm) is quite typical of the kind of baroque churches the Jesuits were apt to build in order to convince others of the power of their faith. It was built by Carlo Lurago in 1665 and finished in 1687 by Paul Ignatz Bayer, who added the church's tower. Both architects were also responsible for the adjoining Jesuit College, which was converted into a military hospital in 1773 and now serves as Charles University's teaching hospital.

FAUSTŮV DŮM (FAUST HOUSE)
Although closed to the public, the **Faust House** (Karlovo náměstí 40-41) is associated with so much bizarre history that it's worth a look from the outside. Built in the 14th century, it was first owned by alchemist Prince Václav of Opava, then by famous alchemist Edward Kelley in the 16th century, and Count Ferdinand Mladota in the 18th century. (The count's experiments would oftentimes go awry, resulting in minor explosions and consequent holes in the roof.) Under Rudolf II, an astrologer named Jakub Krucinek lived here with his

© LUCIE ERICKSEN
Emmaus Monastery

May 27, 1942, following the successful assassination of Reinhard Heydrich, the Nazi SS Obergruppenführer and General of Police. Hiding in the cathedral's crypt and betrayed before they could escape, on June 18 the Nationalists found themselves surrounded by hundreds of Gestapo soldiers whose orders were to capture the "criminals" alive. They fought valiantly, though three Czech soldiers died while defending the nave. The remaining four soldiers fought until they were down to their last four bullets, which they then used on themselves.

EMAUZSKÉ OPATSTVÍ (EMMAUS MONASTERY)

Consecrated on Easter Monday in 1372 in the presence of King Charles IV, the **Emmaus Monastery** (Vyšehradská 49, tel. 224 917 662, www.emauzy.cz, May-Sept. Mon.-Fri. 11am-5pm, Apr. and Oct. Mon.-Fri. 11am-5pm, Nov.-Mar. Mon.-Fri. 11am-2pm, 40 Kč) has been through a lot, to say the least. It was first ravaged during the Hussite Wars and then again during the brief French occupation of Prague in the 18th century. By the late 19th century, the church was in such dire condition that it was in danger of being torn down. The worst came during the 1940s and 1950s, however, when both the Nazis and Soviets took turns taking over the premises and brutally killing most of the monks who made their home here. The monastery was finally returned to the Benedictine order after the fall of Communism, and massive efforts to painstakingly restore this wonderful piece of history continue to this day.

two sons, the younger of which killed the other in the name of large amounts of treasure that were purportedly hidden in the house. In the 19th century, Karl Jaenig moved in and proceeded to cover the walls with scribbled funereal texts. He fashioned a working gallows in the home and slept in a wooden coffin. His final wish was to be buried facing the bottom of said coffin. With all the crazy things that have gone down within these walls, perhaps the authorities know what they're doing by not letting the public in. Visit at your own risk.

KOSTEL SV. CYRILA A METODĚJE (ORTHODOX CATHEDRAL OF STS. CYRIL AND METHODIUS)

Built in the 1730s by Kilián Ignáz Dientzenhofer, the baroque **Orthodox Cathedral of Sts. Cyril and Methodius** (Resslova 9a, tel. 224 920 686, http://pravoslavnacirkev.cz, Nov.-Feb. Tues.-Sat. 9am-5pm, Mar.-Oct. Tues.-Sun. 9am-5pm, 75 Kč) is known primarily for being the scene where Czech nationalists took their last stand on

BOTANICKÁ ZAHRADA UNIVERSITY KARLOVY (CHARLES UNIVERSITY BOTANICAL GARDEN)

If you're looking to do something a little different during your stay, try the oft-overlooked **Charles University Botanical Garden** (Na Slupi 16, tel. 221 951 885, www.bz-uk.cz, Feb.-Mar. daily 10am-4pm, Apr.-Oct. daily 10am-5pm, Nov.-Jan. daily 10am-4pm, 50 Kč).

Inaugurated in 1898, it serves as a public garden as well as an educational paradise for students of the university. Outside, there is a fine collection of central European flora, including the valuable *Ginkgo biloba* 'Praga' cultivar—the only specimen of its kind in the world. There are also incredible greenhouses on the premises housing the oldest *Cycas* in the country, along with a collection of cacti, papayas, huge primeval plants, orchids, and a whole lot more.

STARÉ MĚSTO (OLD TOWN)

Staré Město has been the heart and soul of the capital since its founding in 1231. Today, it attracts visitors from all over the world who stare open-mouthed at the staggering beauty accumulated over a millennium's worth of architecture. In Old Town Square alone, one can see Romanesque, Gothic, rococo, and art nouveau buildings blending in nicely with the upsurge of tourism-dependent businesses that have cropped up throughout the district. Trendy restaurants and cocktail bars have replaced old-school eateries and pubs, and the once-quiet cobblestone streets are now filled with large groups of visitors looking to experience a bit of the Bohemian magic that has been immortalized in countless books, plays, and films. Despite the increase in overpriced cafés and upscale shops, Staré Město nevertheless remains as elegant, romantic, and intoxicating as ever.

Celetná ulice (Celetná Street)

Stretching between the Powder Tower (in Nové Město) and Old Town Square is the lively pedestrian lane Celetná, named as such due to the plaited bread rolls (called *calty*) that were baked here in the 13th century. It is one of the city's oldest streets and was part of the royal coronation route of Czech kings that ran all the way to Prague Castle. Lined with picturesque houses as well as numerous shops, cafés, and restaurants, it bustles with activity during the day and reverts to one of Prague's most romantic streets at night. Many of the houses here are of historical significance, including the Pachta

Palace (number 36), which began as a mint in the Middle Ages and became a court building in 1849, employing a then-unknown youngster named Franz Kafka. The House at the Golden Angel (number 29) used to operate as an inn and extended its hospitality to revered guests such as Mozart. And let us not forget the House at the Three Kings (number 3) where Kafka lived between 1896 and 1907.

DŮM U ČERNÉ MATKY BOŽÍ (HOUSE OF THE BLACK MADONNA)

On the corner of Celetná Street and Ovocný trh you'll find one of the world's most striking examples of cubist architecture. The **House of the Black Madonna** (Ovocný trh 19, tel. 224 211 746, www.ngprague.cz, Tues.-Sun. 10am-6pm, 100 Kč) came to be after wholesale merchant František Josef Herbst commissioned respected Czech architect Josef Gočár to design a department store. Built in 1911-1912, the building was a sensitive addition to a historic city center and remains one of Prague's most aesthetically pleasing buildings. It now houses the **Museum of Czech Cubism** (Ovocný trh 19, tel. 224 211 746, Tues.-Sun. 10am-6pm, 100 Kč), which is run by the National Gallery and offers a comprehensive collection of paintings, prints, and sculptures that reflect the 1910-1919 period, cubism's most significant years.

◖ Staroměstské náměstí (Old Town Square)

For most people, entering Old Town Square for the first time is like walking onto a movie set in the 18th century, when colorful facades and architectural styles ranging from Gothic to baroque were par for the course. Not only is it the country's most beautiful square, it is undoubtedly one of the entire continent's as well. It has operated as Prague's economic and political center since the 10th century, acting as marketplace, execution site, and location of nation-changing announcements—including the beginning of the Communist takeover. While its first houses date as far back as the 12th and 13th centuries, the square remains home to some of the city's most spectacular buildings,

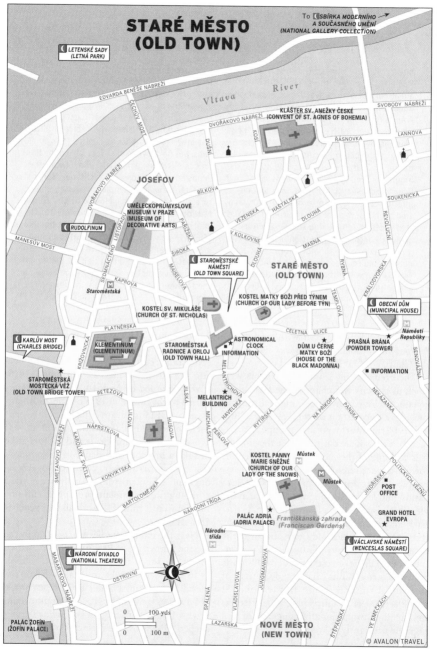

STARÉ MĚSTO (OLD TOWN)

Czech Cubism

Inspired by the work of Georges Braque and Pablo Picasso, four remarkably talented and avant-garde artists—Pavel Janák, Josef Gočár, Josef Chochol, and Vlastislav Hofman—took French cubist principles and adapted them to furniture, decorative objects, and buildings, ignoring the arguments of their predecessors and pushing cubism farther than anyone else dared to. Characterized by sharp points, slicing panes, and crystalline shapes, the Czech cubists believed that the only way an object's internal energy could be properly freed was by smashing the vertical and horizontal surfaces that restrained it. Using the pyramid as the zenith of architectural design and the crystal as the quintessential natural form, they introduced angled planes to everyday objects, giving them a dynamism that transformed them into powerful works of art. The cubist movement was vastly supported by Bohemia's cultural elite, who enjoyed the daring new designs that found their way into their desks, chairs, villas, and offices. Art historian Miroslav Lamac explained the phenomenon: "Prague became the city of cubism with cubist apartment blocks full of cubist flats furnished with cubist furniture. The inhabitants could drink coffee from cubist cups, put flowers in cubist vases, keep the time on cubist clocks, light their rooms with cubist lamps and read books in cubist type." Some of the finer surviving examples of cubist architecture about town are the **House of the Black Madonna** (Ovocný trh 19 in Staré Město), the apartment building at **Elišky Krásnohorské 10-14** in Josefov, and **Adria Palace** (Jungmannovo náměstí 28 in Nové Město). Those interested in learning more about this fascinating movement are strongly urged to visit the Museum of Czech Cubism, housed in the aforementioned House of the Black Madonna.

including Old Town Hall with its famous Astronomical Clock, St. Nicholas Church, and the Church of Our Lady Before Týn.

The ever-growing number of visitors who flock to the city has changed the face of the square, fueling an overt commercialism that includes a line of stalls on the west side selling kitsch to the swarms of tour groups that descend on the square daily. Despite the crowds, it is still one of the most wondrous places in town—a space often filled with smiling faces, people posing for photographs, swing jazz bands, and lovers enjoying the romance in the air, which is as old as it is intoxicating. Cafés, bars, and restaurants have got in on the act, too, setting out tables and chairs that offer the finest views available. Throughout the summer, the square is often the site of world-music concerts, art exhibits, and a wide variety of traditional cultural events. In the winter, it is the setting of Prague's biggest Christmas market, a jolly outdoor affair augmented by a gigantic brilliantly lit tree.

The center of the square is characterized by the **Jan Hus monument,** dedicated to the Protestant reformer who was labeled a heretic and burned at the stake on July 6, 1415. It was designed by Ladislav Šaloun and presented to the public in 1915 on the 500th anniversary of Hus's death. The base of its steps used to be a popular meeting point as well as a perfect place for locals and visitors alike to take a breather and drink in the square's charm. Unfortunately, countless overzealous (and drunken) tourists repeatedly tried climbing the monument, prompting authorities to install a ring of flowerbeds and benches around it.

Near the monument lies a brass strip in the ground known as the **Prague Meridian,** which marks the site of the former Marian Column of 1650. When the column's shadow fell on the meridian at noon, a senior timekeeper in the observation tower of the Klementinum would wave a flag, prompting all of Prague's timekeepers to synchronize their clocks.

PRAGUE

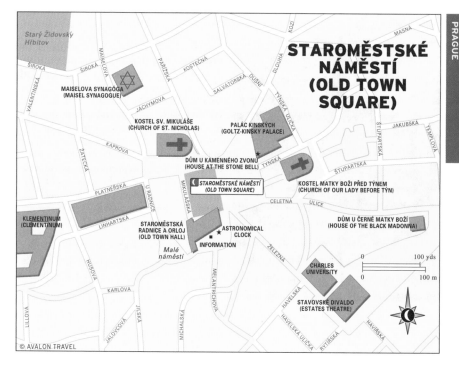

STARÝ ŽIDOVSKÝ HŘBITOV

ŠIROKÁ

MAISELOVA SYNAGÓGA (MAISEL SYNAGOGUE)

MAISELOVA

VALENTINSKÁ

ŽATECKÁ

ŠIROKÁ

JÁCHYMOVA

PAŘÍŽSKÁ

KAPROVA

KOSTEČNÁ

SALVÁTORSKÁ DUŠNÍ

DLOUHÁ KOZÍ

MASNÁ

STAROMĚSTSKÉ NÁMĚSTÍ (OLD TOWN SQUARE)

KOSTEL SV. MIKULÁŠE (CHURCH OF ST. NICHOLAS)

PALÁC KINSKÝCH (GOLTZ-KINSKÝ PALACE)

TÝNSKÁ ULIČKA

JAKUBSKÁ

ŠTUPARTSKÁ

TERHLOVÁ

DŮM U KAMENNÉHO ZVONU (HOUSE AT THE STONE BELL)

TÝNSKÁ

ŠTUPARTSKÁ

PLATNÉŘSKÁ

U RADNICE

MIKULÁŠSKÁ

STAROMĚSTSKÉ NÁMĚSTÍ (OLD TOWN SQUARE)

CELETNÁ

KOSTEL MATKY BOŽÍ PŘED TÝNEM (CHURCH OF OUR LADY BEFORE TÝN)

ULICE

KLEMENTINUM (CLEMENTINUM)

LINHARTSKÁ

STAROMĚSTSKÁ RADNICE A ORLOJ (OLD TOWN HALL)

ASTRONOMICAL CLOCK

INFORMATION

DŮM U ČERNÉ MATKY BOŽÍ (HOUSE OF THE BLACK MADONNA)

Malé náměstí

ŽELEZNÁ

HUSOVA

KARLOVA

LILIOVÁ

JALOVCOVÁ

JILSKÁ

MICHALSKÁ

MELANTRICHOVA

CHARLES UNIVERSITY

STAVOVSKÉ DIVADLO (ESTATES THEATRE)

HAVELSKÁ

HAVELSKÁ ULIČKA

RYTÍŘSKÁ

HAVÍŘSKÁ

0   100 yds

0   100 m

© AVALON TRAVEL

STAROMĚSTSKÁ RADNICE A ORLOJ (OLD TOWN HALL AND ASTRONOMICAL CLOCK)

One of the most striking and popular buildings of Old Town Square is the **Old Town Hall and Astronomical Clock** (Staroměstské náměstí, tel. 775 443 438, Mon. 11am-10pm, Tues.-Sun. 9am-10pm, 100 Kč). The Town Hall was established in 1338 and is actually an amalgamation of neighboring buildings that were joined together over the years, resulting in a mixture of Renaissance and Gothic architectural styles. There is a nearly 200-foot-tall viewing tower inside the building, well worth the time and money as it affords remarkable views of the square and Old Town in general.

The most intriguing feature of Town Hall is, of course, the Astronomical Clock that was incorporated into the structure in 1490.

Legend has it that Master Hanuš, the clock's maker, was blinded by the town's council in order to prevent him from recreating his marvelous achievement elsewhere in Europe. Seeking revenge, Hanuš is purported to have stuck his hands in the machinery, thereby ending his life and damaging the clock (for the time being at least). The clock itself is an intricate piece of machinery and consists of three main components: an astronomical dial showing the position of the sun and moon in relation to the zodiac; a calendar dial with medallions representing the months of the year; and the crowd favorite, *The Walk of the Apostles*—an hourly (9am-9pm) show where wooden statuettes appear from mini trapdoors and move from left to right while a skeletal figure signifying Death pulls a rope to the rhythm of the chimes. In actual fact, the "puppet show" is a rather anticlimactic affair but

© LUCIE ERICKSEN

PRAGUE

Prague Meridian in Old Town Square

worth a look should you happen to be in the square at the top of the hour.

KOSTEL MATKY BOŽÍ PŘED TÝNEM (CHURCH OF OUR LADY BEFORE TÝN)

The **Church of Our Lady Before Týn** (Staroměstské náměstí 604, tel. 222 318 186, mass Tues.-Sat. 10am-1pm and 3pm-5pm, Sun. 10:30am-noon, free) is the grand Gothic building dominating one side of Old Town Square, characterized by its twin towers capped by four small spires. Impressive by day, it adds to the overall fairy-tale feel of "Magic Prague" when lit up at night, causing many visitors to stop in mid-step and simply admire it in silence. It was founded in 1385 during the reign of Charles IV and possesses one of the most remarkable baroque interiors to be found in the city. Brightly stained glass, a rococo altar on the northern wall, and a black-and-gold organ are just some of its features, with the most interesting being the tomb of famed astronomer Tycho Brahe, who served as Rudolf II's "personal consultant."

KOSTEL SV. MIKULÁŠE (CHURCH OF ST. NICHOLAS)

Designed by Kilian Ignaz Dientzenhofer, the **Church of St. Nicholas** (Staroměstské náměstí, daily 10am-4pm, free), not to be confused with the one in Malá Strana, is a gorgeous baroque building on the corner of Old Town Square. It was completed in 1735 and is a favorite with tour groups and visitors in general as it hosts a number of classical music concerts every day of the week. Tickets can be bought in front of the church, which is also the site of the occasional busker or two, including a crowd-pleasing, well-dressed elderly man who plays jazz standards on the saxophone.

PALÁC KINSKÝCH (GOLTZ-KINSKY PALACE)

Standing on a site that was previously occupied by two medieval dwellings, **Goltz-Kinsky Palace** (Staroměstské náměstí 12, tel. 224 810 758, Tues.-Sun. 10am-6pm, 120 Kč) is a late-baroque building with a gorgeous pink-and-white rococo facade that does much to add to the square's overall beauty. It was built between 1755 and 1765 by Anselmo Lurago based on the designs of Kilian Ignaz Dientzenhofer. The palace operated as a German grammar school, and a quiet student named Franz Kafka was enrolled here between 1893 and 1901. His father, Hermann, was around as well, running a haberdashery on the main floor. A chilling historical event occurred on the palace's balcony on February 25, 1948, when then Communist leader Klement Gottwald informed the crowds below that the Communist era had officially begun. Today, the palace hosts various collections of the National Gallery, including one permanent exhibit detailing the Art of Asia and the Ancient Mediterranean.

DŮM U KAMENNÉHO ZVONU (HOUSE AT THE STONE BELL)

Dating back to the second half of the 13th century and recognized as Prague's oldest Gothic building, the **House at the Stone Bell** (Staroměstské náměstí 13, tel. 224 828 245, www.ghmp.cz, Tues.-Sun. 10am-8pm, 120 Kč)

© DOMINI DRAGOONE

a detail of the Astronomical Clock in the Old Town Hall

was painstakingly restored in the late 1980s and now boasts an enchanting baroque courtyard along with three floors of exhibitions run by the City Gallery of Prague. It is the site of occasional concerts and various artistic events as well.

On the Way to Charles Bridge

The easiest and most popular way to reach Charles Bridge is via the twisting cobblestone street known as Karlova. Numerous baroque and Renaissance facades line the way, including the former residence of famed astronomer Johannes Kepler, who lived at number 4. Countless shops on either side of the narrow street offer the usual tourist grab bag of T-shirts, marionettes, and glass, making for a jam-packed route that can become rather frustrating at times. To fully appreciate Karlova, try taking a stroll during the early hours of the morning or late at night when the street is nearly empty and at its most enchanting.

Malé náměstí (Little Square) marks the beginning of Karlova just past Old Town Hall. At its center is a Renaissance fountain protected by a pretty wrought-iron grill from the 16th century. The small square is surrounded by expensive shops, like the colorful Rott Building, as well as hotels, taxis, and antique cars offering hour-long tours of the area at inflated prices.

KLEMENTINUM (CLEMENTINUM)

The **Clementinum** (Mariánské náměstí 5, tel. 222 220 879, www.klementinum.com, tours daily, times vary, 220 Kč) is a massive baroque complex located right by the Charles Bridge that can be accessed from Mariánské náměstí or Karlova Street. It is now home to the National Library of the Czech Republic and holds over six million volumes, including the surviving remnants of Tycho Brahe's library, as well as collections from Count Kinsky and the Lobkowicz family.

On the premises is a pretty Mirror Chapel that was built around 1720. It boasts slick marbled walls and floors, gorgeous ceiling frescoes, and murals depicting the life of the Virgin

Jan Hus: Bohemia's Early Church Reformer

Jan Hus, the man immortalized in the large statue characterizing Old Town Square, was born to poor Czech parents in the town of Husinec in 1369. He became an ordained priest in 1400 and was appointed preacher of Prague's Bethlehem Chapel a mere two years later. It was around this time that relations with England grew stronger thanks to Anne of Bohemia's marriage to Richard II. As a result, the writings of John Wycliffe, otherwise known as "the Morning Star of the Reformation," became available to Hus, whose dissatisfaction with the Roman Catholic Church's corruption and abuse matched Wycliffe's.

In 1410, Archbishop Zbyněk Zajíc confiscated Wycliffe's books and ordered them burned. Hus protested and was excommunicated in 1412 for his efforts. The Bethlehem Chapel was closed and the city of Prague placed under an interdict, meaning it was to be denied all sacraments. No religious services, not even those related to burying the dead, were allowed. Hus left Prague and sought refuge with a variety of noble families who populated Bohemia at the time.

Between 1414 and 1418, the Council of Constance was called on to deal with the increasing problem of heresy and corruption in Europe. King Sigismund of Hungary, brother of King Václav, was the motivating force behind the Council. In the spring of 1415, he invited Hus to attend, promising him safe conduct. Hus agreed to come and planned to defend his position before the Church's highest authorities. He was arrested on his arrival, however, and all his books, including his Bible, were taken from him. He was charged with heresy and refused the chance to defend himself. It quickly became clear that his sentence was a foregone conclusion unless he recanted his position, which he steadfastly refused to do.

Jan Hus was burned at the stake on July 6, 1415. When news of his death reached Bohemia, the nobles—some of whom had sheltered him, and who supported reform—sent a protest, the protestatio Bohemorum, to the Council of Constance. King Sigismund responded by threatening to drown any and all Wycliffe and Hus supporters.

On July 30, 1419, priest Jan Želivský led a Hussite group through the streets of Prague, which resulted in anti-Hussites throwing rocks at them from the New Town Hall. The infuriated crowd stormed the building, seized the burgomaster as well as six town councilors, and threw them all from the windows onto the spears below, marking the "First Defenestration of Prague." A truce was declared on November 13, but not before much of the city had been destroyed.

There were three anti-Hussite crusades in total, all of which involved much of Europe. It wasn't until the late 15th century that the fighting ground to a merciful halt.

© LUCIE ERICKSEN

Jan Hus monument, with the Church of St. Nicholas in the background

Mary. Mozart used to play here occasionally and the chapel continues to host classical music concerts on a daily basis. There is also a breathtaking baroque Library Hall, finished in 1722, with a tremendous trompe l'oeil ceiling symbolizing antique wisdom with a Dome of Wisdom acting as its centerpiece. The hall has remained virtually untouched over the years and is as good an example of an authentic baroque library as you're going to get. Finally, the Astronomical Tower, which was built around the same time as both the chapel and library hall, served as an astronomical observatory that was fitted out by Jesuit Jan Klein with the latest devices of the era. It was from here that the Prague Meridian was determined and a signal, followed by a cannon shot, was fired every noon to let the entire city know that the middle of the day had arrived. Tours of all three sights are offered daily.

🄲 Karlův most (Charles Bridge)

Apart from Prague Castle, Charles Bridge is the city's most popular attraction and synonymous with Prague's world-renowned beauty and mystique. Thousands of visitors cross the bridge daily, stopping to get their portrait painted, posing for one-of-a-kind photographs, and taking slow, romantic strolls hand in hand. Adding to the historic atmosphere are buskers, artists, and vendors selling everything from panoramic pictures of the bridge to handcrafted souvenirs and jewelry. Though packed in the summertime (so much so that it makes it almost impossible to enjoy the bridge's beauty), the crowds do thin out a bit come evening time. The most magical moments to enjoy the glorious view are at night when the castle and near mystical surroundings are brilliantly lit. The truly lucky may even get the entire bridge to themselves, though it'll have to be very late at night or early in the morning before the professional photographers appear hoping for the day's best and brightest light.

It is interesting to note that the Charles Bridge was not the first bridge to stand in its present location. That was the Judith Bridge,

built in 1172, and it served the capital until its unfortunate collapse in 1342 due to heavy flooding. Holy Roman Emperor Charles IV laid the foundation stone of the Charles Bridge on July 9, 1357, at exactly 5:31am. The date and time are of numerological significance as several odd numbers were aligned. Starting with the year then taking the date, month, and time, the numbers read 1-3-5-7-9-7-5-3-1. Head of the bridge's construction was architect extraordinaire Petr Parléř who was also responsible for the majestic St. Vitus Cathedral at Prague Castle. The story goes that he mixed egg yolks into the mortar in an effort to strengthen the bridge's construction.

The bridge itself is 1,692 feet long, 31 feet wide, has 16 spans with radiuses ranging 54.5 to 77 feet, and is situated 43 feet above the river's surface. Although now strictly a pedestrian zone, horse-drawn buggies ran across it from 1883. They were then replaced by trams in 1905, along with buses and cars that drove across the bridge all the way up to 1965.

One of the most beautiful aspects of the bridge is its gorgeous baroque statues, which total 30 in all (plus one just beyond the railing). Most are replicas, though many of the originals can be viewed at the Lapidárium. One thing to look for is the archbishop's five-star brass cross, located on the bridge's balustrade near the statue of St. John the Baptist. Superstition dictates that those who put their hands on the cross so that each of their fingers touches one of the stars will be rewarded by having their most secret desire come true.

STAROMĚSTSKÁ MOSTECKÁ VĚŽ (OLD TOWN BRIDGE TOWER)

At the eastern end of the Charles Bridge on the Staroměstská side is the blackened but beautiful **Old Town Bridge Tower** (Křížovnické náměstí/Charles Bridge, tel. 224 220 569, www.prazskeveze.eu, Nov.-Feb. daily 10am-8pm, Mar. and Oct. daily 10am-8pm, Apr.-Sept. daily 10am-10pm, 75 Kč). It was designed by Petr Parléř in the Gothic style and completed in 1380, serving as both watchtower and part of Prague's

PRAGUE

© LUCIE ERICKSEN

Charles Bridge and the Old Town Bridge Tower

defense system. There is a relatively uninspiring exhibition on the tower's history, but don't miss the opportunity to climb all the way up for a fantastic view of the city center.

On the other end of the bridge is the Lesser Town Bridge Tower, which marks the entrance into Malá Strana.

STATUES

The following is a list of statues found on the Charles Bridge. The statue's sculptor and the date it appeared on the bridge are given in parentheses. The list starts on the Old Town side, with statue number 1 being the first statue on your left, statue number 2 the first on your right, statue number 3 the second on your left, and so on.

1. St. Ivo (M. B. Braun, 1711). Notable 11th-century bishop of Chartres, France. Counselor to King Philip, he fought against the greed of his contemporaries and was imprisoned for a time for opposing King Philip's plans to leave his wife, Bertha, to marry Bertrade of Anjou.

2. St. Bernard (M. V. Jackel, 1709). Founding abbot of Clairvaux Abbey in Burgundy, he was one of the most important church leaders of the first half of the 12th century as well as a powerful propagator of Cistercian reform.

3. Sts. Barbara, Margaret, and Elizabeth (J. Brokoff, 1707). St. Barbara was the extremely beautiful daughter of wealthy Dioscorus, who, fearing his daughter would be demanded in marriage, shut her in a tower to protect her from the outside world. She gradually came to accept the Christian faith, which outraged her father. The prefect of the province sentenced her to death by beheading, a task Dioscorus happily volunteered for. On his way home to do the dirty deed, he was struck by lightning, which is the reason that Barbara is today considered the patron saint in times of danger, thunderstorms, fires, and sudden death.

While watching the flocks of her mistress, St. Margaret was approached by Roman prefect Olybrius, who was determined to make her his concubine or wife. When she resisted and it became clear she wouldn't back down,

Olybrius had her brought before him in a public trial. Threatened with death unless she renounced her Christian faith, Margaret stuck to her guns. Set on fire, the flames that were meant to burn her fizzled out. Bound hand and foot and then thrown into a cauldron of boiling water, her bonds broke and she stood up unharmed. Having had enough, the prefect did the only thing he could think of: Off with her head, he ordered, and that was that. Nobody knows why, exactly, but this eternal virgin is now widely considered to be the patron saint of pregnant women.

Born in Hungary in 1207, St. Elizabeth married into royalty but led a simple, pious life, devoting her time to works of charity. After her husband's death, Elizabeth left the royal court for good, denounced the world, and devoted herself to the care of sick children until her death. She is the patron saint of bakers, children, widows, young brides, the homeless, and the falsely accused.

4. The Madonna with St. Dominic and Thomas Aquinas (M. V. Jackel, 1708). Founder of the Order of Preachers (the Dominicans), St. Dominic traveled all over Italy, Spain, and France preaching the word and attracting numerous followers due to his harmonization of intellectual life with the needs of the people. He is the patron saint of astronomers.

A member of the Dominican order, Thomas Aquinas is perhaps best known for his synthesis of Christianity with Aristotelian philosophy, which became the Roman Catholic Church's official doctrine in 1879.

5. The Lamenting of Christ (E. Max, 1859). Depicts Jesus lying in the Virgin Mary's lap with St. John in the center and Mary Magdalene on the right.

6. Crucifixion (W. E. Brohn, J. J. Heermann, E. Max, 1696, 1861). The Hebrew inscription in gold reads, "Holy, Holy, Holy, Lord God Almighty." It was paid for by a local Jewish person as punishment for allegedly blaspheming in front of the statue in 1696.

7. St. Joseph (E. Max, 1854). Well-known husband of Mary and father of Jesus of Nazareth.

8. St. Anne (M. V. Jackel, 1707). Mother of Mary and grandmother to Jesus.

9. St. Francis Xavier (F. M. Brokoff, 1711). Pioneering missionary who cofounded the Jesuit Order, St. Francis Xavier is the patron saint of Navarre, Spain, as well as missionaries. He is considered by the Roman Catholic Church to have converted more people than anyone except St. Paul.

10. Sts. Cyril and Methodius (Karel Dvořák, 1928). The two saints who were responsible for bringing Christianity to the Slavs in the 9th century.

11. St. Christopher (E. Max, 1857). One of the 14 Holy Helpers, St. Christopher wandered the world and one day came upon a hermit who served others by guiding them to places that were safe to cross. Christopher took over for the hermit but instead of doling out advice, he'd carry travelers safely across the stream he lived by. One day, he carried a child across who was so heavy the weight nearly crushed him. It turned out to be Jesus, who bore the weight of the world upon himself. Christopher is the patron saint of travel and travelers.

12. St. John the Baptist (J. Max, 1857). Widely considered the forerunner of Jesus Christ, St. John the Baptist was a preacher and ascetic who is regarded as a prophet by Christianity, Islam, Mandaeanism, and the Baha'i faith.

13. St. Francis Borgia (F. M. Brokoff, 1710). A duke at the relatively young age of 33, St. Francis Borgia lived happily with his wife and eight children. Upon his wife's death, he gave it all up and became a Jesuit priest, humbling himself continuously and without argument to his superiors. He was eventually made Superior General of the Jesuits and was an instrumental force in the spread of the Jesuit faith.

14. St. Norbert (J. Max, 1853). Dionysian in nature while growing up, St. Norbert faced certain death one day when he was caught in a horrendous thunderstorm. He managed to utter the question, "Lord, what do You want me to do?" The answer that came back from above was, "Turn from evil and do good. Seek peace and pursue it." And that's what he did, fighting the prejudices of those who didn't believe his sudden change of heart and eventually climbing the ecclesiastical ladder all the way up to archbishop.

15. St. Ludmilla (M. B. Braun, 1784). Grandmother of St. Wenceslas and patroness of Bohemia.

16. St. John of Nepomuk (M. Rauchmiller, J. Brokoff, W. H. Herold, 1683). The oldest and most popular statue on the bridge depicts the patron saint of Czechs who, legend has it, was thrown off the bridge after refusing to reveal the secrets of the queen's confession. More likely is that he simply got caught up in one of King Wenceslas IV's rages against the church. A bronze relief below the statue details his unfortunate story and the belief is that if you rub it, you'll not only receive good luck, but return to Prague again as well.

17. St. Francis of Assisi (E. Max, 1855). Founder of the Franciscan order and famed patron saint of ecology and animals, many of which he preached the word of God to.

18. St. Anthony of Padua (J. O. Mayer, 1707). Made a Doctor of the Church by Pope Pius XII in 1946, St. Anthony was known for his dedication and ability to teach the word of God to the uneducated and inexperienced. Much beloved, he was canonized a mere year after his death, which came at the tender age of 36.

19. Sts. Vincent Ferrer and Procopius (F. M. Brokoff, 1712). Patron saint of builders, St. Vincent Ferrer became that due to his uncanny ability to strengthen the church through his inexhaustible preaching, teaching, and missionary work.

Born in Jerusalem, St. Procopius was a reader in Scythopolis. It was during this time that he was arrested by the Roman authorities and martyred when he became the first victim of the persecution of the Church in Palestine by Emperor Diocletian.

20. Bruncvik (L. Simek, 1884). Located beyond the railing, he is the hero of the 11th-century epic poem *Song of Roland.*

21. St. Jude Thaddeus (J. B. Kohl, 1708). A disciple of Jesus, St. Jude Thaddeus is "the miraculous saint" and patron saint of lost causes. He is the one to call on when all hope is lost.

22. St. Augustine (J. B. Kohl, 1708). St. Augustine is the patron saint of brewers due to his conversion from a life full of Old World sex, drugs, and worldly ambitions to the respected positions of bishop and revered saint. He continues to inspire those who struggle to remain on the wagon.

23. St. Nicholas of Tolentino (J. B. Kohl, 1708). A 13th-century pastor who ministered to the poor and criminal, he gained a reputation as a wonder worker after curing the sick with bread that was blessed by Mary, who had answered his prayers.

24. St. Luthgard (M. B. Braun, 1710). A highly esteemed mystic of the Middle Ages, St. Luthgard was a Cistercian nun who envisioned Christ, levitated, and had the sign of stigmata before going blind near the end of her life.

25. St. Cajetan (F. M. Brokoff, 1709). Fighting the good fight against corruption and licentiousness, St. Cajetan established the Theatine order and remains the saint people pray to when the church troubles them and causes doubt.

26. St. Adalbert (F. M. Brokoff, 1709). Became the bishop of Prague in 982. Disliked by the nobility and facing mounting unpopularity, he left for Rome and became a Benedictine monk. Pope John XV sent him back to Prague where he founded Břevnov Monastery.

27. St. Philip Benitius (M. B. Mandel, 1717). General of the Servite order. The papal tiara lying at his feet symbolizes his refusal of the papacy in 1268.

28. Sts. John of Matha, Felix of Valois, and Ivo (F. M. Brokoff, 1714). Both John of Matha and Felix of Valois lived in a hermitage at Cerfroid. They founded the Order of the Most Holy Trinity (the Trinitarians) upon receiving the blessing of Pope Innocent III. Ivo was a notable 11th-century bishop of Chartres, and the counselor to King Phillip of France.

29. St. Vitus (F. M. Brokoff, 1714). One of the 14 Holy Helpers, St. Vitus is the patron

Jewish Prague

The first Jewish settlers came to Prague in the 9th century, most probably from what is now modern-day Iraq. These original settlers were merchants and were invited by Bohemian kings to bolster trade links. By the late 11th century, a Jewish town began to form in Old Town, most likely as a means of defense against anti-Semitic attacks, which were not uncommon. In the 13th century, Rome announced that Jews and Christians were to live separately and went about walling in the ghetto.

Life in the ghetto was closely controlled: Jews were forced to wear identifying caps or badges, were only allowed to work as lowly usurers or rag merchants, and were strictly forbidden from owning land. Attacks on the ghetto became commonplace and culminated in the horrific Pogrom of 1389, which saw the slaughter of approximately 3,000 Jews by their Christian neighbors during Easter weekend.

Things eased up under the reign of Rudolf II (1576-1612) thanks to his tolerance of religion, resulting in the building of the Jewish Town Hall, Maisel Synagogue, and High Synagogue with the generous donations of the ghetto's wealthiest son, Minister of Finance Mordechai Maisel. In 1648, the Jewish community scored big points with Ferdinand III when they repelled the invading Swedish army on the Charles Bridge. Ferdinand enlarged the ghetto as a token of his gratitude. A century later, however, Maria-Theresa (reigned 1740-1780) sent the entire Jewish population of Prague into exile, only to welcome them back three years later when her ministers noticed a worrisome deficit in the tax system.

Enlightened Emperor Joseph II (reigned 1780-1790) took the biggest step toward granting equal rights to Jewish people by issuing his Edict of Tolerance in 1781, which granted non-Roman Catholics the right to education, ended the compulsory dress code, and opened the ghetto's gates. A century later the Jewish community honored Joseph by renaming the ghetto Josefov. As richer Jewish families left the ghetto, Prague's poorest inhabitants moved in. The area became a slum, and in 1893 the city authorities razed most of the ghetto and constructed the art nouveau-influenced Josefov we enjoy today.

saint of epileptics, dancers, and actors as well as being a protector against storms. The remarkable cathedral at Prague Castle is named after him as well.

30. St. Wenceslas (J. Fuhrich, J. K. Bohm, 1858). The one and only martyr, prince of Bohemia, and patron saint of the Czech Republic.

31. Sts. Cosmas and Damian (J. O. Mayer, 1709). Sts. Cosmas and Damian were twin brothers who excelled in the practice of medicine in the 4th century and preached the word of Jesus to their patients while never accepting a dime for their services.

Josefov

Situated between Old Town Square and the Vltava River, Josefov's main street is Pařížská—a chic, pricey avenue full of designer boutiques, swanky restaurants, and trendy cafés. Packed with visitors and the city's fashion-conscious, it is a far cry from the Jewish quarter of the 13th century, when Jewish residents were ordered to vacate their homes and move into their new (and walled) neighborhood. It wasn't until 1781 that the Toleration Edict was issued by Emperor Joseph II of the Austrian Empire, granting civil rights to Prague's Jews. The former ghetto was named Josefstadt and was incorporated into the city in 1850. A vast redevelopment of the area was undertaken during 1893-1913, giving it the look that remains to this day. Six synagogues survived, as did the Jewish Town Hall and Old Jewish Cemetery. Most historical sights fall under the jurisdiction of the Jewish Museum, which offers ticket packages allowing you to visit any and all of them.

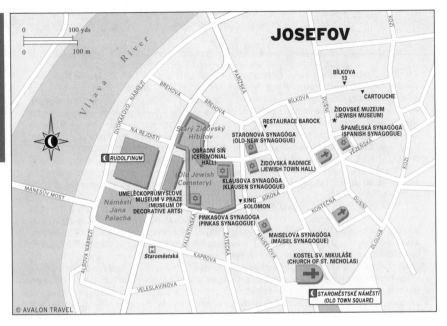

STARONOVÁ SYNAGÓGA (OLD-NEW SYNAGOGUE)

The **Old-New Synagogue** (Červená 2, tel. 222 317 191, Jan.-Mar. daily 9am-4:30pm, Apr.-Oct. daily 9am-6pm, Nov.-Dec. daily 9am-4:30pm, 200 Kč) is without a doubt the heart and soul of the Jewish community. Built in about 1270, this remarkable Gothic building is Europe's oldest active synagogue and consequently one of its most valuable. Over 700 years of continuous prayer has occurred here, with the only exception being during the Nazi occupation of 1941-1945. This was the synagogue Franz Kafka attended and the site of his bar mitzvah. The legend of the Prague Golem is also connected to the synagogue. According to the story, Rabbi Loew created a monster made of clay that would help the Jews in times of trouble. Unfortunately, the Golem got a little too big for his britches, growing increasingly aggressive and violent until it became necessary to put him down. It is said that pieces of the Golem are still kept in the synagogue today and that he can be "awakened" again should the need arise.

ŽIDOVSKÁ RADNICE (JEWISH TOWN HALL)

Located next to the Old-New Synagogue, the **Jewish Town Hall** (Maiselova 18) was built by Pankras Roder in the 1560s and financed by the district's mayor and patron, Mordecai Maisel. Its pretty-in-pink rococo facade was added in the 18th century, but the building's most famous characteristic is the Hebraic clock up on the roof, which is decorated in Hebrew and has hands that turn counterclockwise.

Attached to the Town Hall is the High Synagogue, which got its name due to having its prayer room located on the second floor—a bit of a novelty back in the 16th century when it was built. Also partly financed by Mayor Maisel, the synagogue continues to provide services to non-Orthodox Jews but is closed to visitors and the general public. There is, however, a **Jewish Museum Shop** (tel. 221 711 511, Nov.-Mar. Sun.-Fri. 9am-4:30pm, Apr.-Oct.

Jewish Museum

Sun.-Fri. 9am-6pm, closed Sat. and Jewish holidays) on the main floor.

ŽIDOVSKÉ MUZEUM (JEWISH MUSEUM)

The original mission of the **Jewish Museum** (U Staré školy 1, tel. 222 749 211, www. jewishmuseum.cz, Nov.-Feb. 9am-4:30pm, Mar.-Oct. 9am-6pm, closed Sat. and Jewish holidays, 300 Kč) was to preserve artifacts from the synagogues that were demolished during the district's great renovation at the turn of the 20th century. The museum's exhibitions are located in six different historical sights: Maisel Synagogue, Spanish Synagogue, Pinkas Synagogue, Old Jewish Cemetery, Klausen Synagogue, and Ceremonial Hall.

Maiselova synagóga (Maisel Synagogue): Like most of the district at the time, Maisel Synagogue (Maiselova 10) was built by the mayor of the same name. Established in 1592, it is said to have been the finest of all synagogues in the area until a terrible fire in 1689 destroyed it, along with over 300 houses and

a further 10 synagogues. A neo-Gothic synagogue was built between 1893 and 1905 during a massive reconstruction of the entire district. Today, it houses an interesting collection of Jewish books, textiles, and silver.

Klausova synagóga (Klausen Synagogue): The fire of 1689 destroyed the original Klausen Synagogue (U Starého hřbitova 3A, tel. 222 310 302) but it was rebuilt in 1694 by the same craftspeople responsible for many of Prague's baroque churches. Built by the omnipresent Maisel in honor of a visit paid to the ghetto by Emperor Maximilian II in 1573, it takes its name from the German word "Klausen," meaning "small buildings," as it used to comprise three small buildings. Currently, the synagogue houses a thorough and rather interesting exhibition outlining many Jewish traditions and customs, including bar mitzvahs, weddings, and the everyday Jewish household.

Španělská synagóga (Spanish Synagogue): Considered by many to be Prague's most beautiful synagogue, the Spanish Synagogue (Vězeňská 1, tel. 224 819 464) was built in

1868 on the former site of the oldest Prague Jewish house of prayer—"the Old Shul." Designed in the Moorish style by Vojtěch Ignátz Ullmann, its large dome and incredibly colorful interior includes stained glass windows, stylized Islamic motifs, and gorgeous floral designs in red, gold, and green. Closed for over 20 years, it reopened again on its 130th anniversary and currently houses a permanent exhibition outlining the history of Jewish people in Bohemia and Moravia titled "From Emancipation to the Present."

Pinkasova synagóga (Pinkas Synagogue): Founded by Rabbi Pinkas in 1479, the Pinkas Synagogue (Široká 3) was turned into a memorial after World War II commemorating the Jews in Bohemia and Moravia who were killed in the Holocaust. Over 80,000 names are inscribed on its walls, along with the victims' personal data and name of the community they belonged to. There is also a remarkably moving exhibition of drawings done by children who were held at Terezín before being shipped off to the death camps of the east.

Starý Židovský Hřbitov (Old Jewish Cemetery): Established in the first half of the 15th century, the Old Jewish Cemetery (Široká 3) is a haunting, solemn reminder of what was once a thriving and vibrant community. The cemetery contains roughly 12,000 tombstones, but it is estimated that over 100,000 people are actually buried here. The inconsistency arises due to the fact that the Jews were not allowed to expand the grounds when the cemetery was full. They were consequently forced to bury their dead one on top of the other, resulting in some areas having graves layered 12 deep. The oldest grave on the premises dates back to 1439 and belongs to poet and scholar Avigdor Karo. By far the best-known person buried here is Rabbi Loew, famously associated with the story of the Golem. Mordecai Maisel, Josefov's former influential mayor, is also buried here, about 30 feet southwest of Rabbi Loew's grave. For those who may be wondering, Franz Kafka is not buried here, as the last burial took place in 1787, long before the great writer died. At the cemetery's exit you'll find the **Obřadní**

síň, or Ceremonial Hall (U Starého hřbitova 3A, tel. 222 317 191). Built in 1911-1912 in pseudo-Romanesque style by J. Gerstl, it was initially used by the Prague Burial society but was soon converted into an exhibition venue. Today, one can enjoy displays and presentations outlining a number of Jewish customs and traditions.

Northern Staré Město
As you walk past the Church of St. Nicholas with Old Town Square at your back, you'll come upon Kaprova Street, which leads toward the river. Here, along the banks of the Vltava, is Náměstí Jana Palacha (Jan Palach Square), named after the student who lit himself on fire in protest of the Soviet invasion. Crossing the bridge (Mánesův most) will take you to Malostranská, but it's the grandiose neoclassical Rudolfinum in the middle of the square that everyone stops to gawk at.

◖ RUDOLFINUM
Built between 1876 and 1884, **Rudolfinum** (Alšovo nábřeží 12, tel. 227 059 205, www.galerierudolfinum.cz, www.ceskafilharmonie.cz, gallery and box office Tues.-Wed. and Fri.-Sun. 10am-6pm, Thurs. 10am-8pm, admission varies) now serves as home stage to the Czech Philharmonic Orchestra in what has to be one of the most stunning concert halls on the continent. Rudolfinum also houses a gallery that features some of the city's most interesting and imaginative retrospectives, focusing on contemporary Czech and international artists. The beautiful building is decorated with statues of the world's most famous composers—it was the one of Jewish composer Felix Mendelssohn that was particularly bothersome to the Nazis during their occupation of the city. With the order to remove the statue, the job was given to a couple of Czech laborers who unfortunately had no idea what Mendelssohn looked like. Remembering their lessons in "racial science," they decided to get rid of the statue that had the biggest nose. It was only after they had finished the job that they realized the statue they had pulled down was Richard Wagner's.

© LUCIE ERICKSEN

Rudolfinum is the home of the Czech Philharmonic Orchestra.

KLÁŠTER SV. ANEŽKY ČESKÉ (CONVENT OF ST. AGNES OF BOHEMIA)

The **Convent of St. Agnes of Bohemia** (U Milosrdných 17, tel. 224 810 628, www.ng-prague.cz, Tues.-Sun. 10am-6pm, 150 Kč) was founded in 1231 by Přemyslid Princess Anežka (Agnes), the sister of King Václav I. It was Prague's first Gothic building and operated as a convent as well as the Přemyslid burial grounds. It was renovated in 1963 to serve the National Gallery and now holds an excellent exhibition of Bohemian and Central European medieval and early Renaissance art.

UMĚLECKOPRŮMYSLOVÉ MUSEUM V PRAZE (MUSEUM OF DECORATIVE ARTS)

Designed by Josef Schulz and built in 1897-1899, the neo-Renaissance **Museum of Decorative Arts** (17. listopadu 2, tel. 251 093 111, www.upm.cz, Tues. 10am-7pm, Wed.-Sun. 10am-6pm, permanent and temporary exhibitions 120 Kč, temporary exhibitions 80 Kč) is a veritable feast for the eyes. The facades alone are worth a few moments. Above the first-floor windows are various reliefs depicting a number of crafts and trades, including weaving, jewelry-making, wood-carving, and stone masonry. Above the second-floor windows you'll find the emblems of various Czech towns like home team Staré Město, Hradec Králové, Kutná Hora, and Plzeň. The interiors are just as lavish, with stained glass windows reflecting allegories of the decorative arts and trade, ornately decorated halls, and a second-floor balustrade made from exquisite Carrara and Slivenec marble. The actual exhibitions are fascinating, spanning four halls and detailing 16th- to 19th-century artifacts, including tapestries, pottery, clothing, ceramics, and glass. Anyone with even the slightest interest in this field should put this at the top of their to-do list.

MALÁ STRANA (LESSER TOWN)

Located at the foot of Prague Castle, Malá Strana has long been home to the country's poets, drunkards, politicians, and foreign ambassadors, striking a seemingly impossible balance between the Dionysian and diplomatic. Characterized by quiet cobblestone streets filled with Old World buildings and charming art galleries, it is arguably Prague's prettiest district and one of its busiest as well. Despite its growing number of overpriced souvenir, crystal, and jewelry shops, it has somehow managed to maintain an intimate neighborhood feel about it thanks to its charming restaurants, lively nightlife, and well-preserved churches and historical buildings.

Malostranská mostecká věž (Lesser Town Bridge Tower)

On the Malá Strana side of Charles Bridge, two towers (Nov.-Feb. daily 10am-6pm, Mar. and Oct. daily 10am-8pm, Apr.-Sept. daily 10am-10pm, 75 Kč) stand that used to fortify the bridge's predecessor, the Judith Bridge. The southern tower (on the left as seen from the bridge) was reconstructed in the Renaissance style in 1591, while the tower next to it reflects the Gothic style and was built in the late 15th century. The gateway located between the two towers dates back to the 15th century as well.

Mostecká ulice (Mostecká Street)

Leading up to Malostranska Square from Charles Bridge is Mostecká Street, a short bustling strip filled primarily with souvenir shops, restaurants, and currency exchange outlets. In the summer, you're bound to sidestep visitors munching on snacks, pointing at buildings, or simply crashed out on the sidewalk in dire need of a break.

The first street on the right is Josefská; at the end of it, on the right side, is the small and intimate **Church of St. Joseph** (Josefská 8, Wed.-Fri. 1pm-4pm, free). Built between 1686 and 1692, it has a Dutch baroque exterior while the interior is comparatively plain, apart from a series of baroque altars. Mass is performed here in French on Sunday at 11am.

Across the street, on the other side of the tram tracks, is the decidedly more impressive

Church of St. Thomas (Josefská 8, tel. 257 530 556, www.augustiniani.cz, Mon.-Sat. 11am-1pm, Sun. 9am-noon and 4:30pm-5:30pm, free), still a very active church performing mass on Sunday in English, Spanish, and Czech. Originally a Gothic church founded for the Order of Augustinian Hermits in 1285 and completed in 1379, it was accompanied by an Augustinian Monastery and St. Thomas' Brewery. Inside are copies of two Peter Paul Rubens paintings (the originals of which can be found in the National Gallery's Collection of European Art in Šternberg Palace) as well as the skeletal remains of St. Boniface and St. Just, dressed in costumes of the period and kept in glass-fronted coffins.

Back on Mostecká, at the top of the street, is a McDonald's, which, despite sticking out like a sore thumb, is usually packed with those desperate for a fast-food fix or timid souls not yet ready to try out the local cuisine. Opposite the Golden Arches is majestic Malostranska Square, the lifeblood of all things Malá Strana.

Malostranské náměstí and Vicinity (Malostranska Square)

Founded in 1257, Malá Strana's main hub of activity from day one has been Malostranska Square, which began life as a large marketplace on the outskirts of Prague Castle. Brimming with shops, restaurants, pubs, and palaces, it's easy to see that little has changed over the centuries, as many of the Renaissance and baroque buildings remain virtually untouched.

CHRÁM SV. MIKULÁŠE (ST. NICHOLAS CHURCH)

Dominating Malostranska Square is the remarkable **St. Nicholas Church** (Malostranské náměstí 1, tel. 257 534 215, www.stnicholas.cz, Mar.-Oct. daily 9am-5pm, Nov.-Feb. daily 9am-4pm, 70 Kč), considered by many to be the finest example of high baroque architecture in Prague, if not the country. Completed in 1752, it was the masterpiece of father-son architect team Christoph and Kilian Ignaz Dientzenhofer, the latter being responsible for

PRAGUE

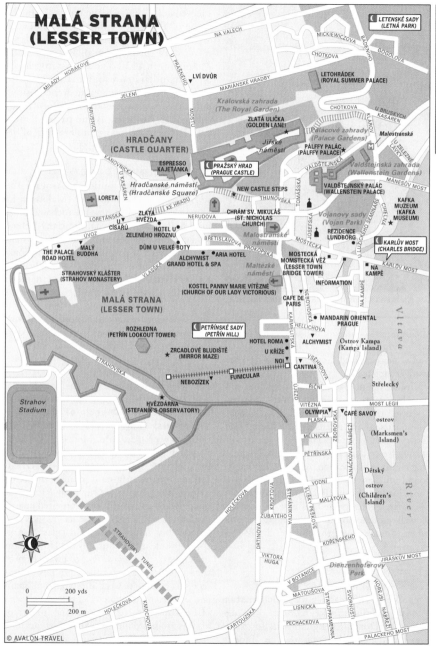

MALÁ STRANA
(LESSER TOWN)

NA VALECH

LETENSKÉ SADY
(LETNÁ PARK)

MICKIEWICZOVA

CHOTKOVA

BADENIHO

GOGOLOVA

MILADY HORÁKOVÉ

U PRÁŠNÉHO

LVÍ DVŮR

MARIÁNSKÉ HRADBY

LETOHRÁDEK
(ROYAL SUMMER PALACE)

JELENÍ

CHOTKOVA

U BRUSKÝCH
KASÁREN

KLÁROV

BRUSNICE

Královská zahrada
(The Royal Garden)

ZLATÁ ULIČKA
(GOLDEN LANE)

Palácové zahrady
(Palace Gardens)

Malostranská

HRADČANY
(CASTLE QUARTER)

Jiřské
náměstí

PÁLFFY PALÁC
(PÁLFFY PALACE)

U ŽELEZNÉ
LÁVKY

KÁNOVNICKÁ

U KASÁREN

ESPRESSO
KAJETÁNKA

PRAŽSKÝ HRAD
(PRAGUE CASTLE)

VALDŠTEJNSKÁ

Valdštejnská zahrada
(Wallenstein Gardens)

MÁNESŮV MOST

LORETA

Hradčanské náměstí
(Hradčanské Square)

NEW CASTLE STEPS

THUNOVSKÁ

TOMÁŠSKÁ

VALDŠTEJNSKÝ PALÁC
(WALLENSTEIN PALACE)

KAFKA
MUZEUM
(KAFKA
MUSEUM)

LORETÁNSKÁ

ZLATÁ
HVĚZDA

KE HRADU

NERUDOVA

CHRÁM SV. MIKULÁŠ
(ST. NICHOLAS
CHURCH)

JOSEFSKÁ

CIHELNÁ

U
CÍSAŘŮ

HOTEL U
ZELENÉHO HROZNU

Vojanovy sady
(Vojan Park)

UVOZ

DŮM U VELKÉ BOTY

BŘETISLAVOVA

Malostranské
náměstí

MOSTECKÁ

REZIDENCE
LUNDBORG

U LUŽICKÉHO SEMINÁŘE

KARLŮV MOST
(CHARLES BRIDGE)

THE PALACE
ROAD HOTEL

MALÝ
BUDDHA

ALCHYMIST
GRAND HOTEL & SPA

ARIA HOTEL

PROKOPSKÁ

Maltézké
náměstí

MOSTECKÁ
MOMSTECKÁ VĚŽ
(LESSER TOWN
BRIDGE TOWER)

KARLŮV MOST

NA
KAMPĚ

VLAŠSKÁ

STRAHOVSKÝ KLÁŠTER
(STRAHOV MONASTERY)

KOSTEL PANNY MARIE VÍTĚZNÉ
(CHURCH OF OUR LADY VICTORIOUS)

CAFE DE
PARIS

INFORMATION

NA KAMPĚ

MALÁ STRANA
(LESSER TOWN)

NEBOVIDSKÁ

MANDARIN ORIENTAL
PRAGUE

Vltava

ROZHLEDNA
(PETŘÍN LOOKOUT TOWER)

PETŘÍNSKÉ SADY
(PETŘÍN HILL)

HELLICHOVA

KARMELITSKÁ

ALCHYMIST

Ostrov Kampa
(Kampa Island)

ZRCADLOVÉ BLUDIŠTĚ
(MIRROR MAZE)

HOTEL ROMA

U KŘÍŽE

VŠEHRDOVA

NOI

CANTINA

NEBOZÍZEK

FUNICULAR

ÚJEZD

ŘÍČNÍ

Střelecký

HVĚZDÁRNA
(STEFANÍK'S OBSERVATORY)

VÍTĚZNÁ

MOST LEGII

Strahov
Stadium

OLYMPIA

CAFÉ SAVOY

ZBOROVSKÁ

JANÁČKOVO NÁBŘEŽÍ

ostrov

STRAHOVSKÁ

PLÁSKÁ

(Marksmen's
Island)

MĚLNICKÁ

PETŘÍNSKÁ

Dětský

VODNÍ

ostrov

River

MALÁTOVA

(Children's
Island)

HOLEČKOVA

KROFTOVA

ŠTEFÁNIKOVA

ELIŠKY PEŠKOVÉ

ZUBATÉHO

KOŘENSKÉHO

STRAHOVSKÝ TUNÉL

DRTINOVA

VIKTORA
HUGA

JIRÁSKŮV MOST

Dienzenhoferovy
Park

0   200 yds

0   200 m

HOLEČKOVA

KMOCHOVA

V BOTANICE

MATOUŠOVA

LISNICKÁ

STAROPRAMENNÁ

SVORNOSTI

HOŘEJŠÍ NÁBŘEŽÍ

KARTOUZSKÁ

PECHÁČKOVA

PALACKÉHO MOST

© AVALON TRAVEL

© TOM DIRLIS

St. Nicholas Church on Malostranska Square

the immense dome and bell tower that is now an integral part of Prague's left bank skyline. Sadly, neither lived long enough to see their work completed.

Inside, the myriad of statues, frescoes, and paintings continue on in flamboyant style, representing the astounding work of the epoch's finest artisans and artists. It's the Main Nave, however, whose vault is covered by an awe-inspiring fresco depicting the life of St. Nicholas that commands attention. An art gallery can be found on the second level of the church, and those interested can climb the bell tower for a small fee. Concerts are held here on occasion as well, commemorating, no doubt, the time when Mozart played the church's 2,500-pipe organ in 1787.

LICHTENŠTEJNSKÝ PALÁC (LICHTENSTEIN PALACE)

Opposite St. Nicholas Church is **Lichtenstein Palace** (Malostranské náměstí 13), designed by Domenico Egidio Ross for Karel von Lichtenstein, better known as "Bloody

Lichtenstein." He was the one who, in the name of Emperor Ferdinand II, sentenced and executed 27 Protestant leaders that dared revolt after their loss on Bilá Hora (White Mountain) in 1621. The 27 cast-iron heads on stone pillars now found at the front of the palace commemorate the event. Visitors don't have to worry about losing their heads these days, however, as the palace is now used by the peace-loving music faculty of the Academy of Performing Arts.

OTHER BUILDINGS OF NOTE

Other noteworthy buildings around the square include **Old Town Hall** (Malostranské náměstí 21), which is now the rock and blues joint Malostranská beseda; **Smiřický Palace** (Malostranské náměstí 18), with its unmistakable turrets and hexagonal towers, now housing the Parliament of the Czech Republic; and **Kaiserstein Palace** (Malostranské náměstí 23), which used to be the former home of great Czech soprano Emmy Destinn. Today it hosts numerous banquets and conferences with the occasional classical concert performed in Emmy Destinn Hall on the second floor.

SOUTH OF THE SQUARE

Following the tram lines south of Malostranska Square is the world-famous **Kostel Panny Marie Vítězné (Church of Our Lady Victorious)** (Karmelitská 9, tel. 257 533 646, www.pragjesu.info, Mon.-Sat. 8:30am-7pm, Sun. 8:30am-8pm, free). Built in 1613 by Giovanni Maria Filippi for the German Lutherans and originally named the Holy Trinity, the Church of Our Lady Victorious not only houses one of the most revered images in Catholicism, it also represents Prague's first baroque building. Enshrined in a glass case on the right side of the church is the Holy Infant of Prague *(Il Bambino di Praga)*, a wax effigy of the Infant Jesus that is believed to possess miraculous healing powers. Brought from Spain and donated to the church by Princess Polyxena of Lobkowitz in 1628, it continues to attract visitors from around the world—so much so that the church has not been able to hold a regular service there in years. A tiny museum adjacent to the church traces the wunderkind's history, while a gift shop full of baby replicas, books, and handmade crafts addresses all your religious needs.

Northern Malá Strana

Adjacent to Malostranska Square is picturesque Nerudova Street, which stretches all the way up to the Castle grounds. At the foot of Nerudova is Zámecká Street, which ends on Thunovská. A quick left on Thunovská will bring you in front of the **Nové zámecké schody (New Castle Steps)**—a peaceful route up to the Castle proper that is a little less trying than taking Nerudova Street.

VALDŠTEJNSKÝ PALÁC (WALLENSTEIN PALACE)

While one end of Thunovská Street brings you to the New Castle Steps, the opposite end leads to Sněmovní Street, a left onto which will bring you face to face with Czech parliament buildings as well as the Venezuelan embassy. Following Sněmovní down and to the right will bring you out to **Wallenstein Palace** (Valdštejnské náměstí 4, tel. 257 071 111, www.senat.cz, Nov.-Mar. first Sat.-Sun. of the month 10am-4pm, Apr.-May. and Oct. every Sat.-Sun. 10am-5pm, June-Sept. every Sat.-Sun. 10am-6pm, free), which is also the seat of the Czech Senate. Built by Andrea Spezza in 1624-1630 for General Albrecht of Wallenstein, Commander of the Catholic forces during the Thirty Years' War, the palace's sheer size is enough to make your jaw drop. The main hall alone measures roughly two stories in height, and its ceiling is adorned with a fresco of Wallenstein portrayed as Mars, Roman god of war.

PÁLFFY PALÁC (PÁLFFY PALACE)

Pálffy Palace (Valdštejnská 14, daily 10am-6pm, free) is one of the more significant contributors to Prague's baroque architecture. More or less identical to how it looked after its restoration in 1853, the palace has a rather unconventional design, with its first floor acting as the mezzanine and the second floor boasting a richly gilded stucco mirror hall, high-brow restaurant, private room, and terrace.

PALÁCOVÉ ZAHRADY POD PRAŽSKÝM HRADEM (PALACE GARDENS BELOW PRAGUE CASTLE)

Located on the southern slope of Prague Castle hill are the **Palace Gardens Below Prague Castle** (Valdštejnská 12, tel. 274 008 143, www.palacove-zahrady.cz, Apr. and Oct. daily 10am-6pm, May and Sept. daily 10am-7pm, June-July daily 10am-9pm, Aug. daily 10am-8pm, 80 Kč), a stunning, intertwining collection of five gardens: Ledebourk Garden, Small Pálffy Garden, Great Pálffy Garden, Kolowrat Garden, and Small Fürstenberg Garden. The gardens are decorated with baroque statues, fountains, water jets, and small pavilions. No visitor should miss the opportunity to enjoy the nearly 30 garden terraces open to the public, each of them offering their own unique layout and view.

Farther down the road you'll find the double-winged late baroque **Kolovratský palác (Kolowrat Palace)** (Valdštejnská 10), the Czech Senate's second home, which is closed to the public. Farther still, you'll come across the delightful **Fürstenbersk Gardens** (Apr. and Oct. daily 10am-6pm, May and Sept. daily 10am-7pm, June-July daily 9am-9pm, Aug. daily 10am-8pm, 50 Kč), which reopened in 2009 to the delight of all.

VALDŠTEJNSKÁ JÍZDÁRNA (WALLENSTEIN RIDING SCHOOL)

At the end of Valdštejnská Street is the Malostranská subway station, where you'll find the entrance to **Wallenstein Riding School** (Valdštejnská 1, tel. 257 073 136, www.ng-prague.cz, Tues.-Sun. 10am-6pm, admission varies), which served as Prague's largest riding school until the end of the 17th century. Nowadays, its space is used to display various short-term art exhibits that are rather hit and miss.

Walking Nerudova Street

Bearing the name of Jan Neruda, Malá Strana's most famous poet and journalist, Nerudova Street is a breathtaking (literally—it's steep) cobblestone street leading up to Prague Castle as the final leg of the Royal Route. Jam-packed with souvenir shops, art galleries, cafés, and restaurants, it does what it can to coax your hard-earned dollars out of your pocket and into the local economy.

A word to the wise: While dodging traffic and ducking out of countless photographs, you may be tempted to dine in one of the many establishments advertising "traditional" Czech cuisine like goulash (which is Hungarian, by the way). Sadly but truly, these restaurants are infamous for serving subpar food at inflated prices, preying on tourists who walk through their doors with the hope of experiencing something authentic. For a true Czech dining experience, you're far better off trusting one of the Czech restaurants listed in this guide than any of the many who stand outside of these "genuine" restaurants and try to lure you in.

Of course, it would be remiss not to mention the magnificent architecture that abounds. A fine example is the beautiful Church of Our Lady of Unceasing Succor and St. Kajetan on Nerudova 22, which now recreates Mozart's illustrious time in Prague by putting on professional performances of his work with musicians dressed in original costumes from the 18th century. Nearby are two stunning examples of baroque architecture: Thun-Hohenstein Palace (1714), at Nerudova 20, which houses the Italian Embassy, and Morzin Palace (1721), at Nerudova 5, home to the Romanian embassy.

Another unique feature on Nerudova is the way many of its buildings are marked with interesting symbols. Up until the introduction of numbers for addresses in 1770, all the houses were distinguished by signs. As you make your way up or down the street, keep an eye out for some of the more interesting ones, like At the Red Eagle (U červeného orla), at Nerudova 6, and At the Two Suns (U dvou sluncŭ), Jan Neruda's previous residence, up near the top at Nerudova 47. The following is a full list of all the signs:

- **5/256**–At the Black Stag (U mouřenínŭ)
- **6/207**–At the Red Eagle (U červeného orla)
- **11/253**–At the Red Ram (U červeného beránka)
- **12/210**–At the Three Fiddles (U tří houslíček)
- **15/249**–At the Golden Crown (U zlaté koruny)
- **16/212**–At the Golden Cup (U zlaté číše)
- **18/213**–Of St. John of Nepomuk (U sv. Jana Nepomuckého)
- **23/245**–At the White Pigeon (U bílé holubice)
- **27/243**–At the Golden Key (U zlatého klíče)
- **28/217**–At the Golden Wheel (U zlatého kola)
- **34/220**–At the Golden Horseshoe (U zlaté podkovy)
- **35/239**–Of the White Angel (U bílého anděla)
- **39/237**–At the White Beet (U bílé řepy)
- **40/223**–At the Prison of St. John (U žaláře sv. Jana)
- **41/236**–At the Red Lion (U červeného lva)
- **42/224**–At the Three Steps (U tří stupňů)
- **43/236**–At the Green Lobster (U zeleného raka)
- **47/233**–At the Two Suns (U dvou sluncŭ)
- **49/232**–At the White Swan (U bílé labutě)
- **51/231**–At the Green Stag (U zeleného jelínka)

PRAGUE

© LUCIE ERICKSEN

Wallenstein Gardens

VALDŠTEJNSKÁ ZAHRADA (WALLENSTEIN GARDENS)

Facing the Malostranská subway station entrance, you'll find the entrance to **Wallenstein Gardens** (Apr.-Oct. Mon.-Fri. 7:30am-6pm, Sat.-Sun. 10am-6pm, June-Sept. Mon.-Fri. 7:30am-7pm, Sat.-Sun. 10am-7pm, free) on the left. Built in the baroque style at the same time as Wallenstein Palace, the gardens are arguably the best kept in the city and are often full of locals enjoying their lunch, reading a book, or simply basking in the refuge from Malá Strana's merry madness. Many of the statues and fountains are copies of Dutch artist Adriaen de Vries's works, a necessity since the originals were plundered by the Swedes in 1648. At the far end of the grounds is the pretty Sala Terrena, which figured prominently in the film *Amadeus* and occasionally holds classical concerts of its own. Close by you'll find a wall built from artificial stalactites as well as an aviary for exotic birds.

MALOSTRANSKÁ SUBWAY STATION AND VICINITY

The courtyard of the Malostranská subway station is a favorite meeting place for tour groups, students, and folks who simply need to take a load off. Outside the station, head for the streetlights. To the left is Mánesův Bridge, which leads to Old Town Square. To the right is Letenská Street, which winds its way back to Malostranska Square. (It also offers a second entrance to Wallenstein Gardens.) Straight ahead, however, is U Lužického semináře Street. Crossing the lights and coming onto the street itself, you will soon come to a fork in the road. On the left are a number of benches offering a wonderful view of Charles Bridge on the right, and Rudolfinum on the left. This is a wonderful place to relax, drink in the view, and, if you're lucky, hang out with some of the neighborhood's swans. This entire area was submerged under water during the flood of 2002 but was rebuilt quickly to the delight and relief of both residents and visitors.

Franz Kafka: Son of the Surreal

Perhaps no other writer managed to capture the debilitating atmosphere of 20th-century alienation better than Franz Kafka (1883-1924). His nightmarish worlds of dehumanization, totalitarianism, and bureaucratic catch-22s captured the imagination of millions of readers and remain as relevant today as when they were first published. Born in Prague on July 3, 1883, he was the son of domineering Hermann Kafka and delicate mother Julie (Löwy). Kafka also had three sisters, all of whom went on to die in Nazi concentration camps. Kafka's father in particular was the impetus for a large part of his writings, as he explained once in a letter to him: "My writing was all about you; all I did there, after all, was to bemoan what I could not bemoan upon your breast. It was an intentionally long, drawn out leave-taking from you."

Educated at both the German National and Civic Elementary School and the German National Humanistic Gymnasium, he entered Ferdinand-Karls University in 1901 and received a doctorate in law in 1906. It was during this time that Kafka began keeping company with a small circle of Prague intellectuals that included Franz Werfel, Oskar Baum, and close friend Max Brod, who encouraged him to write as much as possible.

Kafka's best-known works include the bizarre *Metamorphosis* (1915), where he famously turns into a despicable bug, as well as his novels *The Trial* (1925) and *The Castle* (1926), both of which were published posthumously and deal with the darker side of the law where crimes are doled out freely and anonymously. His unfinished novel *Amerika* (1927) was also published after his death and portrayed a young Karl Rossmann, who enters New York Harbor and sees the Statue of Liberty brandishing a sword instead of her famous lamp. A mere six chapters were all that Kafka managed to complete before dying of tuberculosis on June 3, 1924. Despite Kafka's wishes to have all of his work destroyed upon his death, longtime friend Max Brod ignored the request and made public all of Kafka's unpublished work, a gift that all lovers of literature continue to be most thankful for.

FRANZ KAFKA MUZEUM (FRANZ KAFKA MUSEUM)

You'll find the **Franz Kafka Museum** (Cihelná 2b, tel. 257 535 373, www.kafkamuseum.cz, daily 10am-6pm, 160 Kč) where U Lužického semináře Street turns into Cihelná. On display are many first editions of Kafka's works, along with his diaries, manuscripts, photographs, and letters. For those who want to take a little piece of the famed writer home with them, the gift shop offers all of his works, as well as postcards, calendars, mugs, mouse pads, and a whole lot more. The pretty courtyard in front of the shop is decorated with a quirky statue of two naked men, complete with shifting torsos, urinating into a fountain. Many take a moment to photograph the amusing piece but don't realize that nearby are some stairs that, if you follow them down, will bring you to a small clearing with a couple of secluded park benches. This is a great, somewhat secret place to rest your feet and enjoy another wondrous view of Charles Bridge.

VOJANOVY SADY (VOJAN PARK)

A tranquil oasis in the heart of the city, **Vojan Park** (U Lužického semináře 17, tel. 257 531 839, winter daily 8am-5pm, summer daily 8am-7pm) is one of Prague's oldest parks, dating back to around 1300. In the 17th century it belonged to the Convent of Barefoot Carmelites, but today it functions as a perfect spot for a picnic, a game of Frisbee, or a leisurely stroll. Two chapels can be found here—the Chapel of Elijah and another dedicated to St. Theresa. In the depths of the park is a staircase leading up to a tiny park where, on a good day, you just might come across a couple of peacocks out for a pleasant walk of their own.

Upon exiting Vojan Park, you can either turn left and head back to Malostranská subway or head right and continue toward Charles Bridge and the beginning of Kampa Square. Before you reach it, however, turn right on a tiny street named **Mišenská.** Here you'll find one of the film industry's favorite streets; it has been well preserved and can easily be made to look like any European city from a few centuries ago. (Indeed, this entire area is oftentimes filled with movie types.) A few intimate cafés are located here, including local haunt Veronský Dům, which serves delicious wine and dessert to neighborhood artists. When done, follow the street to its end and voilà! You're back at Mostecká.

MALTÉZSKÉ NÁMĚSTÍ (MALTESE SQUARE)

To the south of Malostranska Square is tiny and peaceful Maltese Square, which took its name from the Priory of the Knights of Malta who used to occupy this part of Malá Strana. It is characterized by a statue of St. John the Baptist—part of a fountain that was built in 1715 to mark the end of the plague epidemic. Opposite the square rests the striking Church of Our Lady beneath the Chain, complemented by two large towers that remind passersby of its previous function as a fortified priory. Founded in the 12th century, it remains Malá Strana's oldest church and was originally used to guard the approach to the old Judith Bridge, precursor to the Charles Bridge. The Hussite Wars led to the abandonment of further construction, which is why an ivy-covered courtyard exists today in place of a nave. For those who may be wondering, the church's odd name refers to the chain used during the Middle Ages to close the monastery's gatehouse. Classical concerts are held here regularly, affording the opportunity to enjoy the well-preserved interior that is otherwise closed to the public.

Nearby, at Maltézké náměstí 1, is the beautiful baroque **Nostický palác (Nostitz Palace),** which was built in 1658-1660 and now houses both the Ministry of Culture and the Dutch embassy. Concerts are often held here in the summertime and tend to be rather popular affairs. A few steps past the palace marks the beginning of Nosticova Street, which leads to an unassuming little park frequented mostly by dog walkers, young lovers, and the occasional homeless person. Most don't stay long in the park; instead they walk right through it to enter a bigger, far more impressive piece of property: Kampa Island.

Ostrov Kampa and Vicinity (Kampa Island)

Roughly two-thirds of the way down Charles Bridge (en route to Malá Strana), you'll notice a divided stairway on the left. At the bottom of these stairs, **Na Kampě (Kampa Square)** officially begins. Lined with restaurants, inns, park benches, and acacia trees, it is one of the more picturesque parts of the city and often hosts fairs and outdoor exhibits during the summer months.

Kampa Island lies directly ahead. Before entering, take the tiny street on the right named Hroznová and follow it as it curves left. It will lead you to a small opening where, on the right, you'll spot a little bridge that carries pedestrians over **Čertovka (Devil's Stream),** a burbling offshoot of the Vltava River. You'll also see the Grand Prior's Millwheel, which continues to turn despite the termination of the mill in 1936.

Over the little footbridge, you come out onto Velkopřevorské náměstí (Grand Priory Square). On the right is the colorful and historically poignant **John Lennon Peace Wall.** On the left is **Buquoy Palace** (Velkopřevorské náměstí 2), yet another beautiful baroque building that has operated as the French embassy for many years. Continuing straight ahead will take you to Maltese Square, but if you head back to Hroznová and continue to the right, you'll end up directly in front of the entrance to Kampa Island.

Back in the day (think the Middle Ages), Kampa Island comprised primarily gardens and was mainly used for washing clothes or bleaching linens. These days, Kampa has little to do with laundry and everything to do

John Lennon Peace Wall

© LUCIE ERICKSEN

On December 8, 1980, Mark David Chapman walked calmly up to John Lennon and shot him dead in front of his wife, Yoko Ono. The murder of the former Beatle sent shock waves around the world, including in Prague, where simply singing his songs in public could land one in jail for perpetrating "subversive activities against the state." Risking capture and severe punishment, an anonymous group of youths stole away in the still of the night and set up a mock grave to honor their underground hero. This simple yet dangerous act of defiance caught the attention of the Communist secret police and captured the imagination of the population at large.

Despite repeated warnings from the state, fans of Lennon's music, as well as believers of his message of peace, would slip into the square unnoticed to write down their own "rebellious" thoughts on the subject. The wall was whitewashed over and over again, but paintings of the icon, along with his lyrics of love and hope, continued to appear. Within a short period of time, the wall became an informal political forum for those daring enough to voice their grievances against the Communist regime.

Shortly after the Velvet Revolution in 1989, the wall was returned to its original owners, the Knights of Malta, as part of a generous restitution package. Proving to be no more understanding than their predecessors, the Knights were on the verge of whitewashing the wall yet again when an unlikely savior in the form of the French ambassador, whose office looked directly onto the graffiti-covered wall, called up the municipal authorities and asked them to leave it as it is. The event sparked a minor diplomatic incident, but the wall remained.

New messages continued to appear in the 1990s, but most were in the form of lightweight (and at times crude) thoughts scrawled down by tourists who knew little, if anything, of the wall's original significance. In 1998, the Prague-based John Lennon Peace Club joined forces with the Knights of Malta and began reconstructing the crumbling facade. The wall's original plaster had been ravaged by tourists who wanted to take a "piece of peace" home with them and was consequently replaced by a solid white surface. The two groups then threw a "happening" where local hipsters, backpackers, and anyone else who wanted to join in were invited to add their opinions on all things John. Not surprisingly, none of the new messages packed the punch of the old. Anti-Communist and pro-freedom slogans were replaced with flowers, butterflies, and tiresome clichés—all of which were put down for posterity with brushes and paint provided by the church.

The Knights of Malta have, at times, painted over slogans they deemed to be either too large or not in line with their own beliefs. This has caused concern amongst some who feel the wall has lost its value as a venue for free speech. If you look hard enough, however, you can still find the occasional heartfelt message from somebody somewhere who continues to imagine all the people living life in peace.

© TOM DIRLIS

The area along the Čertovka canal is considered Prague's "little Venice."

with fun and relaxation. Pull up a seat on one of the benches overlooking the Vltava and let the river lull you into a state of happiness and relaxation. This is a perfect place to read a book, whisper sweet nothings into your lover's ear, or daydream about quitting your job and staying here for good. Filled in the summertime with neighborhood dogs, students with guitars, tourists, picnickers, and sunbathers, Kampa Island is the kind of place you want to stroll through slowly, paying close attention to its quiet simplicity. Do that and the chirping of the birds, the laughter of young and old, and the hushed flow of the mighty Vltava will stay with you forever.

Kampa Island is also the setting of **Kampa Museum** (U Sovových Mlýnů 2, tel. 257 286 147, www.museumkampa.cz, daily 10am-6pm, 160 Kč), which houses international contemporary art and a private collection of important Czech modernist works. Highlights include selections of seminal Czech abstractionist Frantisek Kupka's work as well as 18 bronze sculptures by Czech artist Otto Gutfreund, one of Eastern Europe's first cubists.

Walking through the museum grounds or past them and turning left brings you up close and personal with the Vltava. A few benches are scattered around for your convenience, providing an even quieter place to reflect upon all things Bohemian. Further along, near the southern end of the island, is the 13th-century **Kaple sv. Jana Na Pradlé (Chapel to St. John of the Laundry)**—a testament to the area's previous function.

Střelecký ostrov (Marksmen's Island)

Located in the middle of the Vltava River, opposite Kampa and near the National Theater, the island is accessible from Legií Bridge via a large stone stairway. It is the perfect place to take a romantic stroll and have a pleasant dinner or drink at the Střelecký Ostrov Restaurant and Terrace. Concerts are held here during the warmer months, and there's even an outdoor cinema screening movies once a week

June-September. This shaded oasis is an excellent way to escape the bustle of the center or enjoy a variety of cultural events.

Dětský ostrov (Children's Island)

Those traveling with children will not want to miss this pretty island dedicated to the little darlings. Sitting opposite Střelecký ostrov, next to the big lock full of boats traveling up and down the river, it is easily accessible from the left bank of the Vltava via a small bridge. A large playground offers plenty of things for the kids to do, including sandpits, swings, and ramps. The play area is fenced in, and there's a supervisor present to make sure everyone is playing nicely. This is a wonderful way to keep the kids entertained after they inevitably grow tired of sightseeing.

◖ Petřínské sady (Petřín Hill)

Located west of Malá Strana and stretching up to a height of 1,043 feet is Petřín Hill, a loose network of eight different parks offering visitors a haven from the hectic goings-on down below as well as a jaw-dropping panoramic view of the entire city. In the 12th century the area was covered with vineyards that were later transformed into gardens and orchards. It is also interesting to note that much of the stone used to build various sites around Prague came from the quarry that originally operated here. Extremely popular in the spring when the fruit trees begin to bloom, the hill attracts scores of young lovers, some of whom come to lay flowers on the monument dedicated to Karel Hynek Mácha, the Czech Republic's most famous Romantic poet.

A leisurely walk up the hill is a particularly rewarding experience, but most prefer to save their energy and take the **funicular** (daily 9am-11pm, 26 Kč), reached via Újezd Street. Halfway up the hill, the funicular stops close to Restaurant Nebozízek, a rather touristy establishment that nonetheless offers its patrons a magnificent view of the city, not to mention an eye-level view of Prague Castle.

Traversing the southern edge of the hill is the **Hladová Zed' (Hunger Wall)**, built in 1360-1362 by order of Charles IV, whose purpose, it is argued, was not strategic as was once believed, but rather to feed the city's poor by offering them a way to make some much-needed money.

ROZHLEDNA (PETŘÍN LOOKOUT TOWER)

Built out of recycled railroad tracks in 31 days for the 1891 Jubilee Exhibition, **Petřín Lookout Tower** (tel. 257 320 112, Mar. and Oct. daily 10am-8pm, Nov.-Feb. daily 10am-6pm, Apr.-Sept. daily 10am-10pm, 105 Kč) has managed to survive all these years despite an order issued by Adolf Hitler to have it removed, as well as the Communist regime's utter lack of interest in it during their 40-year run. Modeled after the Eiffel Tower, it was renovated following the Velvet Revolution and now serves as a symbol of Czech independence. The tower itself is only 197 feet in height, but factor in its location on top of Petřín Hill and you start to understand why, on a clear day, you can see as far as Sněžka Mountain, the Czech Republic's highest peak, located roughly 93 miles away.

ZRCADLOVÉ BLUDIŠTĚ (MIRROR MAZE)

Next to Petřín Lookout Tower stands a mock medieval castle that is home to the **Mirror Maze** (tel. 257 315 212, Mar. and Oct. daily 10am-8pm, Nov.-Feb. daily 10am-6pm, Apr.-Sept. daily 10am-10pm, 75 Kč), another leftover of the 1891 Jubilee Exhibition. Although small, the maze still manages to delight children of all ages. There is also a marvelous diorama depicting one of the Czech Republic's proudest moments in history: their defending of the Charles Bridge during the Swedish invasion of 1648.

HVĚZDÁRNA (STEFANIK OBSERVATORY)

Stefanik Observatory (tel. 257 320 540, www.observatory.cz, Nov.-Feb. Tues.-Fri. 6pm-8pm, Sat.-Sun. 11am-8pm, Mar. and Oct. Tues.-Fri. 7pm-9pm, Sat.-Sun. 11am-6pm and 7pm-9pm,

Apr.-Aug. Tues.-Fri. 2pm-7pm and 9pm-11pm, Sat.-Sun. 11am-7pm and 9pm-11pm, Sept. Tues.-Fri. 2pm-6pm and 8pm-10pm, Sat.-Sun. 11am-6pm and 8pm-10pm, Tues.-Fri. 6pm-8pm, Sat.-Sun. 11am-8pm, 65 Kč) dates back to 1928 and was completely reconstructed in the 1970s, giving it the appearance it maintains today. Mostly used as an incentive to get people hooked on astronomy, the observatory allows visitors to catch glimpses of sunspots and solar flares by day and the moon, stars, and planets by night.

HRADČANY

Founded in the year 1320 during the reign of John of Luxembourg, Hradčany is a picturesque, mostly residential area that stretches north across the hilltop and west to Strahov Monastery. It is, of course, home to Prague Castle, easily the most famous of Prague's sights, as well as its most visited. While a tour of the castle grounds is mandatory for any visitor, the district's surrounding streets are also worth a look for they are tiny, twisting pockets of the past: a blend of Gothic, Renaissance, and the baroque that stirs the heart and captivates the imagination.

◖ Pražský hrad (Prague Castle)

High atop a hill on the left bank of the Vltava River sits Prague Castle—the most recognizable structure in the entire Czech Republic. It is not only a grandiose fixture on an already bewitching skyline but also a great source of national unity and pride. Constructed by Prince Bořivoj in the second half of the 9th century, it began as a wooden fortress and underwent four major reconstructions before reaching the form we recognize today. Its biggest development came during the 14th century when Charles IV made the grounds his residence and ordered the building of the awe-inspiring St. Vitus Cathedral. Each ruler who sat here made changes to suit his own personal tastes, and the result is a marvelous mixture of architectural styles ranging from Romanesque to

© LUCIE ERICKSEN

walking through Hradčany toward Prague Castle

PRAGUE

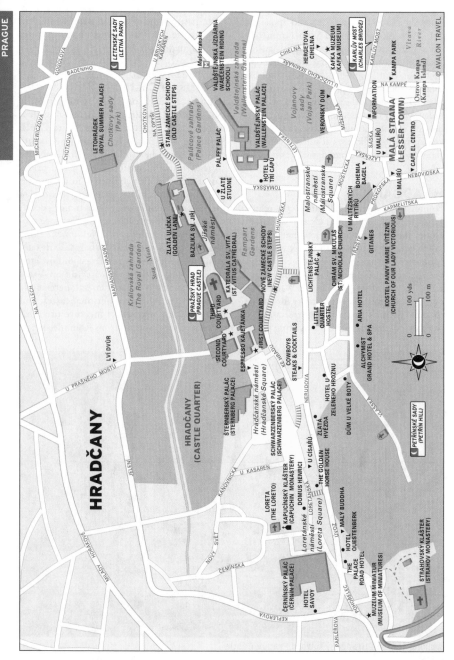

HRADČANY

HRADČANY
(CASTLE QUARTER)

MALÁ STRANA
(LESSER TOWN)

© AVALON TRAVEL

LETNÉ SADY
(LETNÁ PARK)

LETOHRÁDEK
(ROYAL SUMMER PALACE)

Chotkovy sady
(Park)

Královská zahrada
(The Royal Garden)

STARÉ ZÁMECKÉ SCHODY
(OLD CASTLE STEPS)

Palácové zahrady
(Palace Gardens)

VALDŠTEJNSKÁ JÍZDÁRNA
(WALLENSTEIN RIDING SCHOOL)

Valdštejnská zahrada
(Wallenstein Gardens)

VALDŠTEJNSKÝ PALÁC
(WALLENSTEIN PALACE)

PÁLFFY PALÁC

HERGETOVA CIHELNA

KAFKA MUZEUM
(KAFKA MUSEUM)

KARLŮV MOST
(CHARLES BRIDGE)

KAMPA PARK

Vltava River

NA KAMPĚ

Ostrov Kampa
(Kampa Island)

Vojanovy sady
(Vojan Park)

VERONSKÝ DŮM

INFORMATION

CAFE EL CENTRO

VERONSKÝ DŮM

HOTEL U TŘÍ ČÁPŮ

U ZLATÉ STUDNĚ

Malostranské náměstí
(Malostranské Square)

BOHEMIA BAGEL

U MALÍŘŮ

U MALTÉZSKÝCH RYTÍŘŮ

GITANES

CHRÁM SV. MIKULÁŠ
(ST. NICHOLAS CHURCH)

LICHTENŠTEJNSKÝ PALÁC

ZLATÁ ULIČKA
(GOLDEN LANE)

BAZILIKA SV. JIŘÍ

Jiřské náměstí

KATEDRÁLA SV. VÍTA
(ST. VITUS CATHEDRAL)

Rampart Gardens

NOVÉ ZÁMECKÉ SCHODY
(NEW CASTLE STEPS)

PRAŽSKÝ HRAD
(PRAGUE CASTLE)

THIRD COURTYARD

SECOND COURTYARD

FIRST COURTYARD

ESPRESSO KAJETÁNKA

COWBOYS STEAKS & COCKTAILS

LITTLE QUARTER HOSTEL

ARIA HOTEL

KOSTEL PANNY MARIE VÍTĚZNÉ
(CHURCH OF OUR LADY VICTORIOUS)

ALCHYMIST GRAND HOTEL & SPA

HOTEL U ZELENÉHO HROZNU

DŮM U VELKÉ BOTY

STERNBERSKÝ PALÁC
(STERNBERG PALACE)

SCHWARZENBERSKÝ PALÁC
(SCHWARZENBERG PALACE)

Hradčanské náměstí
(Hradčanské Square)

ČERNÍNSKÝ PALÁC
(ČERNÍN PALACE)

HOTEL SAVOY

LORETA
(THE LORETO)

KAPUCÍNSKÝ KLÁŠTER
(CAPUCHIN MONASTERY)

DOMUS HENRICI

Loretánské náměstí
(Loreta Square)

U CÍSAŘŮ

THE GOLDEN HORSE HOUSE

ZLATÁ HVĚZDA

HOTEL MALÝ BUDDHA

THE PALACE ROAD HOTEL

QUESTENBERK

MUZEUM MINIATUR
(MUSEUM OF MINIATURES)

STRAHOVSKÝ KLÁŠTER
(STRAHOV MONASTERY)

PETŘÍNSKÉ SADY
(PETŘÍN HILL)

0   100 yds
0   100 m

baroque. It is the largest ancient castle in the world, measuring 1,870 feet long and an average of 420 feet wide, with a total area of roughly 18 acres. It has operated as the official seat of Czech presidents since 1918 and is by far the most visited site in the country. A tour of the grounds requires half a day (not including museum visits), and you can expect it to get pretty crowded during the summer season. If you'd like a little more elbow room, try coming early in the morning or late in the afternoon, or, if entering the actual sights doesn't particularly interest you, do as the natives do and come late at night, when the grounds are nearly empty and the air electric with magic and romance.

Admission to the castle grounds is free, but you will need a ticket for many of the main sights. These can be bought at the **Tourist Information Center** (Second Courtyard: tel. 224 372 423, Third Courtyard: tel. 224 372 434, tourist.info@hrad.cz, Apr.-Oct. daily 9am-5pm, Nov.-Mar. daily 9am-4pm), which

can also arrange guided and audio tours. A regular "long visit" ticket costs 350 Kč and allows access to St. Vitus Cathedral, the Old Royal Palace, the permanent exhibition "The Story of Prague Castle," St. George's Basilica, the Convent of St. George and its National Gallery exhibit, Golden Lane with Daliborka Tower, the Prague Castle Picture Gallery, and Rosenberg Palace. A "short visit" ticket costs 250 Kč and gets you into St. Vitus Cathedral, the Old Royal Palace, St. George's Basilica, and Golden Lane with Daliborka Tower.

During the high season (Apr.-Oct.), the castle complex is open daily 5am-midnight, while those sights requiring a ticket are generally open daily 9am-5pm. The castle's gardens and Stag Moat are open April and October daily 10am-6pm, May and September daily 10am-7pm, June-July daily 10am-9pm, August daily 10am-8pm. In the winter (Nov.-Mar.), sights requiring tickets are open daily 9am-4pm, while the castle gardens and Stag Moat are closed.

© TOM DIRLIS

the entrance to Prague Castle

FIRST COURTYARD

The official and most impressive entrance to the castle grounds is the main gate on Hradčanské náměstí, characterized by Ignatz Platzer's enormous 18th-century baroque **statues of battling Titans.** The two statues tower over the castle guards standing beneath them and are a favorite of professional and amateur photographers alike. There is a **changing of the guard** every hour on the hour 5am-10pm, the most impressive of which occurs at noon when the change is accompanied by a brass band playing from Plečníkova síň (Plečnik Hall) overlooking the First Courtyard. The Second Courtyard is reached via Matyášova brána (Matthias Gate), Bohemia's earliest baroque work, dating all the way back to 1614.

SECOND COURTYARD

Passing through Matthias Gate, you can't help but notice the Second Courtyard's centerpiece—a beautiful 17th-century baroque **fountain.** You'll often find visitors taking a break here or dousing themselves with water

St. Vitus Cathedral

© LUCIE ERICKSEN

on a particularly hot day. To the right is **Kaple svatého Kříže (Chapel of the Holy Cross),** which was built in 1736. Formerly the treasury of St. Vitus Cathedral, it now operates as a gift shop and the castle's box office.

In the northern wing of the courtyard stands the great gold-and-white **Španělský sál (Spanish Hall),** named as such after Rudolf II's popular Spanish horses, which were kept in the stables below the hall. Decorated lavishly with large mirrors and golden chandeliers, as well as sculptures by Adriaen de Vries representing allegories of the Arts, Science, Commerce, and Industry, it is now used primarily for state receptions and rare concerts. It is open to the public only twice a year: May 8, which marks Czech liberation from Germany at the end of World War II, and October 28, which was the date an independent Czechoslovak state was established.

THIRD COURTYARD

A passage on the Second Courtyard's eastern side leads to the castle's third and most important courtyard. At its center is the monumental St. Vitus Cathedral, which never fails to leave an indelible impression.

Katedrála sv. Vita (St. Vitus Cathedral) is without a doubt the religious heart and soul of the country. Not only is it one of the Czech Republic's finest examples of Gothic architecture, it's also the lifeblood of the nation's spirit, where coronations of kings were held and the land's patron saints buried.

In 1344, Charles IV secured an archbishopric for his beloved Prague and construction on the cathedral began under the watchful eye of French architect Matthew of Arras. Petr Parléř took over the reins in 1352 on Matthew's death, but the masterwork remained unfinished for centuries despite the tremendous efforts of sovereigns to continue construction. It wasn't until the late 19th century when the unimaginatively named Union for the Completion of the Building of St. Vitus Cathedral took control and finally realized Parléř's original plans. The cathedral was finally consecrated in 1929.

St. Vitus's exterior is characterized by the

prominent **Great Tower,** topped with a baroque dome and home to Sigismund, Bohemia's largest bell, which was made in the mid-16th century and weighs well over 33,000 pounds. To the right of the tower you'll find the cathedral's **southern doorway,** which formerly operated as the main entrance. Known as the Golden Gate, it is unmistakable due to the large multi-colored Venetian-glassed mosaic depicting the Last Judgment.

The **western door** of the cathedral, found opposite the passageway connecting the Second and Third Courtyards, now serves as the main entrance and is decorated with reliefs depicting various stories and legends of St. Wenceslas and St. Adalbert. This entire section of St. Vitus is in fact its newest addition, dating back to the late 19th and early 20th centuries.

Inside, the massive **nave** is almost overwhelming at first, and the beautiful stained glass windows on the left add an ethereal quality to an already otherworldly atmosphere. Looking closely, the third window stands out in both color and style. No wonder, seeing as it was done by Alfons Mucha, one of the country's most famous artists.

On the far right of the cathedral is the awe-inspiring **Chapel of St. Wenceslas.** It is located directly on the site where Wenceslas was buried and was built in 1345 by Charles IV in honor of the saint. Although closed to the public, visitors can still crane their necks at the chapel's entrance and admire the ornate frescoes, covering an area of nearly 2,500 square feet, which portray scenes from both the Bible and St. Wenceslas's life. The chapel is also decorated with over 1,300 priceless gems and contains the decorated tomb of the saint himself in the middle of the chapel, along with some of his belongings, including his armor and helmet. It is interesting to note that every coronation in Czech history took place here, with kings often coming to pray as well. Today, mass is held every year on September 28—St. Wenceslas Day. In the southwestern corner of the chapel stands a door leading to a chamber containing the heavily protected crown jewels. The door is locked with the help of seven keys

that are kept separately by seven different state and church officials.

A further note of interest is the **tombstone of St. John of Nepomuk,** whose pedestal and statue contain a mind-boggling two tons of silver. Nearby, in front of the high altar, is the entrance to the cathedral's **underground mausoleum and royal crypt,** which contains the graves of various Czech sovereigns and patron saints, including Rudolf II and Charles IV.

Starý Královský palác (Old Royal Palace): In the courtyard's eastern end is the Old Royal Palace, which was founded in the late 9th century as nothing more than a wooden building with a stone foundation wall. It was rebuilt into a Romanesque palace made of stone by Prince Sobeslav in the early 12th century. A number of kings used it as their residence during the course of the next 600 years, each of them converting the premises to fit their own tastes and style of their respective periods.

The jewel of the palace is beyond a doubt the impressive **Vladislav Hall,** which was designed by Benedict Reid at the turn of the 16th century. It boasted the largest secular space in the city at the time and was arguably the grandest late Gothic hall in all of central Europe. Back then, the hall was used primarily for coronations, balls, and markets, as well as indoor jousting tournaments, which explains the presence of the Jezdecké schody (Rider's Steps) that allowed knights to enter the area while remaining on horseback. Note the difference in architectural styles when comparing its fantastic vaulted ceiling representing Gothic's last gasp with the large square windows exemplifying the beginning of the Renaissance. Today, the hall is where the National Assembly elects its new president and was the setting for the swearing in of Václav Havel in 1990—the country's first president after over 40 years of Communist rule.

At the eastern end of the hall is a balcony that overlooks **All Saints Church,** which was built by Petr Parléř during the second half of the 14th century. It was destroyed by fire in 1541, leaving only its peripheral walls intact, and was redone in the Renaissance style near

PRAGUE

© CRAIG ERICKSEN

St. George's Basilica, as seen from the top of St. Vitus Cathedral

Bazilika sv. Jiří (St. George's Basilica): Founded by Prince Vratislav in 921, St. George's Basilica is Prague's second-oldest church. Its eye-catching red-and-cream baroque facade marks a stark contrast from its austere Romanesque interior, which houses the tombs of some of the Přemyslid dynasty of princes in its main nave. The church concert hall with excellent acoustics. Left of the basilica is the sober-looking Convent of St. George, now serves as a classical music which was established in 973 by Boleslav II. Today it acts as a branch of the National Gallery and offers an interesting exhibit of Renaissance and baroque works.

Zlatá Ulička (Golden Lane): Down the hill from St. George's is Golden Lane: a tiny, colorful street comprising 11 historic homes that came to be after the northern wall of Prague Castle was constructed. Dating to the 16th century, it was originally the residence of castle servants (likely goldsmiths and castle marksmen), with most homes remaining occupied until World War II. Its most famous resident was the one and only Franz Kafka, who stayed at number 22 with his sister Ottla, although, judging by the minute size of the home, one has to wonder how. These picturesque, pint-size houses are charming to say the least. However, when seen by day, one hardly has a chance to appreciate them as the narrow street is choked with visitors craning their necks to get a better look. What's more, the interiors of the homes have all gone the way of souvenir shops, causing an even more beleaguering bustle. For those who would truly like to enjoy the atmosphere of this marvelous little street, pay a visit during the evening when the castle grounds are nearly empty. The result is an atmospheric, romantic experience you won't soon forget.

At the eastern end of the lane are stairs that lead you under the last house to **Daliborka (Dalibor Tower).** A former prison, it took its name from the knight Dalibor of Kozojedy, who was held here as punishment for providing shelter to peasants who were part of a local uprising. Legend has it that he passed his time while awaiting execution by playing the violin.

the end of the 16th century. The church is only open to the public during religious services and for the occasional concert.

Above the hall is the **Bohemian Chancellery,** site of a major turning point in Czech history; in 1618 it was where Protestant nobles rebelled against the Habsburg emperor and promptly threw two governors and their secretary out the window. This bold move sparked what was to become the Thirty Years' War.

The **Diet Chamber,** which can be accessed via a stairway to the right of the Rider's Steps, is also worth a look. It also possesses a wonderfully vaulted ceiling, along with crests from all of Bohemia's most important families and volumes from the court library.

JIŘSKÉ NÁMĚSTÍ AND VICINITY (GEORGE SQUARE)

Just east of St. Vitus Cathedral is George Square, the center of the castle complex. Its main street, Jiřská, stretches from St. George's Basilica to the castle's eastern gate.

The music was apparently so beautiful that it enchanted all who heard it. Well-known classical composer Bedřich Smetana's 1868 opera *Dalibor* pays tribute to the man and his story.

Muzeum Hraček (Toy Museum): Covering two floors and seven rooms of exhibits, the Toy Museum (Jiřská 6, tel. 224 372 294, daily 9:30am-5:30pm, 60 Kč) is the second largest of its kind in the world, showcasing toys from ancient Greece to modern-day Barbie. Kids will either love or hate this place, as most toys are kept well out of reach.

Královská zahrada (The Royal Garden)

Founded in 1534 by Ferdinand I, the Royal Garden was originally designed in the Renaissance style and intended as a gift for his wife, Queen Anne. Sadly, the queen never had a chance to enjoy the lovely grounds as she died while giving birth to her 15th child. Over the years, the garden gained an enviable reputation across the continent due to its collection of rare and exotic plants, which then included orange, lemon, and fig trees. It went through a couple of transformations, including being designed in the baroque style during the first half of the 18th century, then later taking on the form of an English-style park, which it continues to resemble today. There are still plenty of baroque and Renaissance reminders, however, including a lovely little garden. Closed to the public for centuries, the garden is now open (except during winter) and can be accessed via U Prašného mostu, as well as through the castle's second courtyard.

LETOHRÁDEK (ROYAL SUMMER PALACE)

At the eastern end of the garden is the beautiful Belvedere, or Royal Summer Palace. It is Prague's finest example of Italian Renaissance architecture and sports a green copper roof, Ionic columns, and arcades. Designed by Paolo della Stella, it was built between 1538 and 1564. In front of the building is the Singing Fountain, built between 1562 and 1568 by Master Jaroš. Made of bronze and bell metal, its

© LUCIE ERICKSEN

the Royal Summer Palace in the Royal Garden

jets produce a "musical" sound when the water hits the fountain's resonating bronze plate.

MÍČOVNA
(BALL GAME COURT)

On the garden's southern side, overlooking the Stag Moat, is the elegant Míčovna or Ball Game Court, easily recognized by its black-and-white sgraffito. Built by Bonifac Wohlmut in 1567-1569, it was used by the emperor's courtiers for various sports activities and competitions and also served as a riding school and stable. Today it is mainly used for a variety of art exhibitions, concerts, and state social events.

JELENÍ PŘÍKOP
(STAG MOAT)

Below the ramparts of the castle is the wonderful and peaceful getaway known as the Stag Moat. Rudolf II kept a choice selection of animals here, including deer, lions, and tigers, although there hasn't been a stag sighting since the 17th century. Closed for years and reopened by Havel during his presidency, this shady and secluded natural path stretches all the way to Malá Strana and is perfect for those looking to avoid the castle's crowds.

Hradčanské náměstí
(Hradčany Square)

Opposite the entrance to the Prague Castle grounds is Hradčany Square, characterized by grand buildings and offering the finest views of Prague proper. Originally kept separate from the castle grounds by a system of fortifications and moats, the area's houses were burned to the ground during the great fire of 1541 and later rebuilt into magnificent palaces by church dignitaries and the town's elite. Little has changed since then, allowing visitors the opportunity to marvel at various architectural styles that have come and gone including Renaissance, baroque, and rococo.

On the north side of the square is the **Arcibiskupský palác (Archbishop's Palace)** (Hradčanské náměstí 16), a wonderful example of rococo that came into the hands of Archbishop Anton Brus in 1562 and has served

as the seat of Prague's archbishop and the archdiocese ever since. It consists of four wings and just as many courtyards; unfortunately it is closed to the public.

ŠTERNBERSKÝ PALÁC
(STERNBERG PALACE)

Built between 1697 and 1707 for Count Vaclav Vojtech of Sternberg, **Sternberg Palace** (Hradčanské náměstí 15, tel. 233 090 570, www.ngprague.cz, Tues.-Sun. 10am-6pm, 150 Kč) is located next to the Archbishop's Palace and is a fine example of baroque architecture. Currently owned by the National Gallery, its last exhibition featured German and Austrian masterpieces from the 19th century. Art fans are encouraged to check the website to see what remarkable works of art will be on display during their visit.

SCHWARZENBERSKÝ PALÁC
(SCHWARZENBERG PALACE)

Opposite Prague Castle and Sternberg Palace is **Schwarzenberg Palace** (Hradčanské náměstí 2, tel. 223 081 713, www.ngprague.cz, Tues.-Sun. 10am-6pm, 150 Kč), one of the city's most beautiful Renaissance buildings and easily recognizable by its decorative sgraffito. It was built between 1545 and 1563 by Agostino de Galli and used to house the Military Museum. The palace was acquired by the National Gallery in 2002, and a massive 260-million-crown renovation of the premises was completed in early 2007. Art lovers are well advised to check the website for details of upcoming exhibitions and plan their visit accordingly.

Loretánské náměstí
(Loreta Square)

A short walk west from Hradčany Square will lead you to Loreta Square, which was created in the 18th century while construction of Černín Palace was underway. The builders at the site were shocked to uncover a strange pagan cemetery full of headless skeletons. The bones were never identified, and the earth that was dug up remained untouched until it was eventually used to form the embankment that divides

© LUCIE ERICKSEN

Angel statues adorn the entrance to the Loreto.

the square into two levels today. The square's main attractions are Černín Palace and the Loreto, but make sure to stroll through Nový Svět (New World) as well. Located behind the square, it is a charming little neighborhood full of some of the most romantic homes and streets Prague has to offer.

ČERNÍNSKÝ PALÁC
(ČERNÍN PALACE)
Located between Prague Castle and Strahov Monastery, **Černín Palace** (Černínská 5) is yet another example of early baroque architecture. Built between 1669 and 1682, it was designed by Francesco Caratti for Count Humprecht Jan Černín of Chudenice, one of Bohemia's richest and most powerful men at the time. It is Prague's third-largest palace and boasts an impressive 492-foot-long facade punctuated by 30 continuous semicolumns. Gestapo interrogations were held here during the Nazi occupation, but the palace is better known for being the site of Jan Masaryk's death in March 1948. The son of the first Czech president, he died

mysteriously two weeks after the Communists gained power. Originally thought to be a suicide, police finally confirmed in 2004 that he had indeed been murdered. Today, the palace serves as the Ministry of Foreign Affairs and is occasionally open to the public during the summer.

LORETA
(THE LORETO)
The Loreto (Loretánské náměstí 7, tel. 220 516 740, www.loreta.cz, Nov.-Mar. daily 9am-12:15pm and 1pm-4pm, Apr.-Oct. daily 9am-12:15pm and 1pm-5pm, 130 Kč) is a remarkable baroque pilgrimage site containing beautiful chapels and chambers dating back to 1626. Its central point is the Santa Casa, modeled after the original building that stood in the town of Nazareth—purportedly the site of the famed Incarnation where Archangel Gabriel announced to the Virgin Mary that she would give birth to the son of God. Legend has it that this Santa Casa was miraculously transported by angels to the small town of Loreto in Italy,

spawning a rash of knockoffs of the building across Europe. This particular version was built on the orders of Kateřina of Lobkowicz as part of the Roman Catholic campaign after the Czech Protestants were defeated at the Battle of White Mountain. Other buildings of note are the Church of the Nativity, which holds the fully clothed, skeletal remains of two Spanish saints, St. Felicissimus and St. Marcia, as well as the Chapel of Our Lady of Sorrows. This latter building is home to a painting of a bearded woman (St. Starosta) hanging from a cross. Apparently she had taken a vow of virginity, which was threatened by her father's announcement of her marriage to the king of Sicily. God took pity on the woman and helped her grow a beard in an effort to make her undesirable. Horrified, her father had her crucified, and she now has the dubious honor of being the saint of unhappily married women. Also worth a visit is the treasury, where you'll be dazzled by the amazing Prazske slunce (Prague Sun), a diamond monstrance made of solid silver and gold that's studded with 6,222 stones.

KAPUCÍNSKÝ KLÁŠTER (CAPUCHIN MONASTERY)

At the northern end of Loretánské náměstí stands the **Capuchin Monastery** (Loretánské náměstí 6, tel. 233 103 334, www.kapucini.cz). Built in 1600, it is the oldest monastery of its kind in the country. Unfortunately, it is closed to visitors except for special occasions, and even then certain areas are still off-limits. There is, however, a pretty life-size nativity scene erected every Christmas that adds to its rather mystical charm.

STRAHOVSKÝ KLÁŠTER (STRAHOV MONASTERY)

The Premonstratensians are a Roman Catholic order founded in 1120 by St. Norbert, and they have been at **Strahov Monastery** (Strahovské nádvorí 1, tel. 233 107 711, www.strahovsky-klaster.cz, daily 9am-noon and 1pm-5pm, 90 Kč) ever since it was founded in 1143, making it one of the oldest monasteries of the Premonstratensian order in the world. All the

monastery buildings have something interesting to offer visitors, starting with Strahov Church, otherwise known as The Basilica of Our Lady. Dedicated to St. Norbert, it is beautifully adorned with frescoes by Neunhertz depicting the Virgin Mary and life of the order's founder. The church's organ is of particular significance as it was played by Mozart during his visit here in 1787. There is also Strahov's famous library, a collection of roughly 200,000 books that is located in both the Theological and Philosophical Halls and includes works from famous printers like influential Renaissance humanist Christoffel Plantin from Antwerp. The Cabinet of Curiosities, meanwhile, houses a fascinating natural science collection whose prize possession is the remains of the now-extinct dodo bird. Finally, the ancient printing presses located downstairs are also worth visiting, as are the remains of St. Norbert himself, which were brought here in 1627 upon his becoming an official patron saint of Bohemia.

MUZEUM MINIATUR (MUSEUM OF MINIATURES)

Generally unknown and rarely advertised, the **Museum of Miniatures** (Strahovske Nádvoři 11, tel. 233 352 371, daily 9am-5pm, 80 Kč) is tucked away in the courtyard of Strahov Monastery and houses the remarkable work of Siberian-born Anatolij Koněnko. Using the provided magnifying glasses and lenses, visitors are stunned to see the portrait of Anton Chekhov designed on half a poppy seed, the Lord's Prayer written on a human hair, and a three-dimensional miniature replica of the Eiffel Tower in the eye of a needle. You'll also find mini copies of famous paintings by masters such as Salvador Dalí, Henri Matisse, and Leonardo da Vinci, as well as the world's smallest book—a 30-page recreation of *Chameleon* by Anton Chekhov.

DEJVICE

To the north of Hradčany lies Dejvice, a sprawling neighborhood characterized by embassies, ambassadors' villas, university campuses, and residential areas of the middle-class and upwardly mobile. This was an area that radiated plenty of prestige in the first half of the 20th century and still carries that tradition today with high-profile businesspeople and politicians making their homes here. While admittedly registering low on the sights-to-see scale, a walk through Dejvice can be a very relaxing and pleasant experience, not to mention one that's well away from the throngs of visitors found elsewhere. The easiest way to reach the area is by taking the A (green) subway line and getting off at Dejvice station.

Divoká Šárka

Just off Evropská Street, on the way to Václav Havel Airport, is the wild and wonderful **Divoká Šárka,** Prague's best-known and favorite park. The easiest way to get there is to take tram number 20 or number 26 to the Divoká Šárka tram stop (hard to miss thanks to the large McDonald's looming over it). Named after the legendary warrior Šárka, who is said to have thrown herself off the cliffs in despair, this vast valley offers hiking and biking trails, climbing, golfing, and, of course, swimming. Hordes of people young and old make their way to Džbán Reservoir in the west end of the park to cool off with a refreshing swim before sprawling out against the rocks to work on their tan. There is also a public pool open on hot days; it is stream-fed, so be prepared for the water to be cold! Although you won't be able to get any swimming in, Divoká Šárka is also a great place to visit in the wintertime. Blanketed by snow and quiet to the point of eeriness, it's a perfect place to clear your head, get in touch with nature, or do a bit of cross-country skiing before entering the real world again.

Břevnovský klášter (Břevnov Monastery)

Břevnov Monastery (Markétská 1/28, tel. 220 406 111, www.brevnov.cz, tours Apr.-Oct. Sat.-Sun. 10am, 2pm, and 4pm, Nov.-Mar. Sat.-Sun. 10am and 2pm, 80 Kč) was founded by Bishop Vojtech and King Boleslav II in 993 and bears the honor of being Bohemia's very first monastery. Its current baroque form owes to prolific father-son architect team Christoph and Kilian Ignaz Dientzenhofer and dates back to the early 18th century. Its altarpieces, sculptures, woodcarvings, and ceiling frescoes represent the delightful handicraft of the period, while the crypt, located in the choir of the church, dates back to its original Romanesque beginnings. Comprising the Church of St. Margaret, the convent and prelature, outbuildings, the entrance gate, and the garden, the monastery is now home to 13 Benedictine monks who go about their business peacefully—something that wasn't possible during the Communist years, 1948-1989, when some of the grounds were used by the secret police.

Letohrádek Hvězda (Hvezda Summer Palace)

Designed by and built for Archduke Ferdinand of Tyrol in the 1550s, **Hvezda Summer Palace** (Liboc 25, tel. 235 357 938, Apr. and Oct. Tues.-Sun. 10am-5pm, May-Sept. Tues.-Sun. 10am-6pm, 70 Kč) is a three-story Renaissance summer palace in the shape of a six-pointed star—a design that apparently reflected the archduke's beliefs on the construction of the universe. If that sounds confusing, don't worry; nobody to this day has been able to figure out what he was thinking either. Now functioning as the rather modest Museum of Czech Literature, the palace also has a permanent exhibition outlining the history of this interesting building, a model of the historic Battle of White Mountain that was fought here, and a lovely wooded park.

Crowne Plaza Hotel

Officially declared a national monument, the **Crowne Plaza Hotel** (Koulova 15, tel. 296 537 111, www.crowneplaza.cz) is a triumphant example of Marxist-Leninist decor and an imposing reminder of the not-too-distant past. Built in the 1950s, it was originally called the Hotel International and was inspired by the design of Moscow University's Tower. Today, the facade above the entrance depicting Russian war heroes being greeted by Czech peasants seems rather absurd considering the droves of businesspeople and nouveau riche who now occupy the hotel's bars.

Baba Settlement

On the hill above the Crowne Plaza Hotel is an interesting collection of private residences known as the Baba Settlement, which was built in the 1930s. Designer and prominent Czech architect Pavel Janák invited three generations of fellow architects to help him present various aspects of modernism. Predominantly functionalist, the settlement includes houses suitable for newlywed couples all the way up to large families. Soon after its construction, the settlement was recognized as a stellar example of Czech modernism and remains a proud part of Czech cultural history to this day.

HOLEŠOVICE

In the past, Holešovice was primarily known as a bustling industrial zone that was also home to Prague's main harbor and docklands. Over the years, however, the area experienced a decline that saw the closing of numerous factories and a

once lively port turn to a sleepy backwater. The flood of 2002 didn't help matters as Holešovice was one of the hardest-hit districts.

Things have begun to change. An ambitious new building development aims to revitalize the area by creating a massive new 1.5-million-square-foot embankment that will include large sections of residential housing, state-of-the-art office buildings, and modern retail outlets. There are also tentative plans to build a new harbor that will make room for yachts and pleasure boats. Add the fact that Praguers have been steadily buying up property here over the last few years, and one quickly begins to see that this former blue-collar neighborhood may soon become the city's hottest "new" district.

Výstaviště

Built to house the Jubilee Exhibition of 1891, **Výstaviště** (U Výstaviště 1, tel. 220 103 111, www.incheba.cz, daily 10am-midnight, free), in all its wrought-iron glory, is a 3.4-million-square-foot multifunctional area that nowadays

Výstaviště, built to house the Jubilee Exhibition of 1891

© LUCIE ERICKSEN

plays host to trade fairs ranging from the literary to the pornographic. On its grounds you'll also find Křižíková Fontána, the Lapidárium, Lunapark, and Sea World (Mořský svět).

KŘIŽÍKOVÁ FONTÁNA
(KRIZIK'S FOUNTAIN)

If you're still at the exhibition grounds by the time dusk settles in, stick around and watch the water and light show at **Krizik's Fountain** (U Výstaviště 1, tel. 723 665 694, www.krizikova-fontana.cz, Mar. daily on the hour 7pm-9pm, Apr.-Oct. daily on the hour 8pm-10pm, 200 Kč). Spinning, spraying, gurgling, and gushing to both popular and classical music, including Michael Jackson and *Swan Lake,* the Fountain entertains die-hard fans and curious onlookers daily. Tip: If possible, stay for the late show, when it's properly dark and the lights can do their thing to the fullest.

LAPIDÁRIUM

If you manage to make it to the exhibition grounds for a visit, do not miss the opportunity to check out the **Lapidárium** (Výstaviště 422, tel. 233 375 636, www.nm.cz, Tues.-Sun. noon-6pm, 50 Kč). Housing over 400 stone sculptures dating from the 11th-19th centuries, this wonderful museum is a crash course in monuments long gone (but not forgotten). Included in this fascinating exhibition are 10 of Charles Bridge's original statues, the *Lions of Kouřim* (Bohemia's oldest surviving stone sculpture), parts of the Renaissance Krocín Fountain that once stood proudly in Old Town Square, and equestrian statues of past Austrian emperors, to name just a few.

LUNAPARK

Popular with kids of all ages is Prague's version of **Lunapark** (U Výstaviště 1, tel. 220 103 111/484, www.incheba.cz, Tues.-Fri. 2pm-9pm, Sat.-Sun. 10am-9pm, free admission, rides paid separately). Rides include a Ferris wheel, a roller coaster, a haunted house, and any number of vomit-inducing attractions for all those brave enough to hop aboard. St. Matthew's Fair is held here every year as well,

which brings in an additional 130 rides for fun-lovers of all ages.

MOŘSKÝ SVĚT
(SEA WORLD)

Sea World (Výstaviště 422, tel. 220 103 275, www.morsky-svet.cz, daily 10am-7pm, 280 Kč) is the Czech Republic's largest aquarium and has been a hit with locals and visitors ever since it opened in the summer of 2002. Sporting an exhibition space of over 10,000 square feet, Sea World's state-of-the-art aquariums simulate the sea's natural environment, including high and low tide, natural sunlight, and the moon's phases when night falls. Some of the aquarium's well-taken-care-of inhabitants include a sand tiger shark, barracudas, whitefish, zebra fish, lobsters, crabs, and numerous colorful corals and coral fish that can be observed in an 82-foot-long submarine cave.

Stromovka

Next to Výstaviště is sprawling Stromovka Park, whose origins began in 1268 when Czech King Přemysl Otakar II developed it into his royal hunting grounds. It has managed to survive numerous disasters over the years, the last of which was the flood of 2002, when over 600 trees were lost. It was renovated and opened once again in April 2003 and remains as popular as ever. You'll find plenty of people in-line roller-skating, walking the dog, strolling hand in hand, and spending quality time with the kids by the pond.

PLANETÁRIUM PRAHA
(PRAGUE PLANETARIUM)

Tucked inside Stromovka Park, just west of Výstaviště, is **Prague Planetarium** (Královská obora 233, tel. 220 999 001, www.planetarium. cz, Mon.-Thurs. 8:30am-noon and 1pm-8pm, Sat.-Sun. 9:30am-noon and 1pm-8pm, show prices vary). Its main room, Cosmorama Hall, accommodates up to 210 people and boasts the country's largest projection screen at 9,074 square feet. Most programs are in Czech but there are three that can be heard in English: *Astrology and Alchemy in the Court of Rudolph*

II, which takes audiences back to 1600 and delves into all things alchemic, *The Night Sky,* a journey through stars, constellations, and celestial highlights that comes complete with laser effects, and *Wanderers through Space and Time,* which is dedicated to the Pioneer and Voyager space probes.

Sbírka moderního a současného umění (National Gallery Collection of 19th-, 20th-, and 21st-Century Art)

Veletržní palác (Trade Fair Palace) was built in 1929 and hosted countless trade fairs before becoming home to the **National Gallery Collection of 19th-, 20th-, and 21st-Century Art** (Veletržní palác, Dukelských hrdinů 47, tel. 224 301 111, www.ngprague.cz, Tues.-Sun. 10am-6pm, 180 Kč) in 1996, following a heavy face-lift. The first floor is where you'll find various temporary exhibitions, along with foreign artists like Gustav Klimt, Max Ernst, and Pablo Picasso. The second floor is dedicated to 1930-2000 Czech art, including a very interesting screening room showing short silent films made between the world wars and showcasing the beginning of Czechoslovakia's experimental movement. Some of the films are of particular interest as they depict a Prague now long gone, including images of old trams that used to cross over the Charles Bridge. The third floor is where some of the country's biggest names, such as František Kupka and Josef Čapek, are to be found. There is also a very interesting wing exhibiting French art that displays works by Auguste Rodin, Claude Monet, Edgar Degas, and Pierre-Auguste Renoir, to name but a few. The fourth floor is where the 19th-century art is kept, along with a healthy collection of famed Czech sculptor Josef Václav Myslbek's grander works, including his most famous piece, *Hudba* (Music). A couple of other paintings to look for here are Gabriel Max's *A Prevorst Prophetess in Ecstasy* and E. K. Liška's *Cain.* If you plan on visiting, make sure to set aside at least two hours for unrushed gawking.

Letenské sady (Letná Park)

The weekend of the Velvet Revolution was a cold, wintry affair, but that didn't stop nearly one million people from gathering at Letná Park to celebrate national sovereignty and the return of democracy. Situated on a plateau high above the city proper, the park today is a hot spot for in-line roller-skaters, kite flyers, skateboarders, and just about anybody else wishing to enjoy a sunny afternoon or warm summer evening. In the center of the park is **Letenský zámeček** (Letenské sady 341, daily 11am-11pm), an excellent outdoor beer garden where you'll find Czechs and foreigners chilling with an ice-cold beer under chestnut trees and enjoying a postcard-perfect view of Prague. A leisurely stroll down any of the park's wide walkways will inevitably lead you to a marble plateau, now the stomping grounds of skateboarders and their groupies. From 1955 to 1962, however, it was the spot where Stalin's Monument—a monstrous 51-foot-high, 72-foot-long statue—used to stand, overlooking the city. A giant metronome was installed in its place in 1991 to symbolize the passage of time.

Národní technické muzeum (National Technology Museum)

Although its name might not inspire immediate interest, the **National Technology Museum** (Kostelní 42, tel. 220 399 111, www.ntm.cz, Tues.-Fri. 9am-5:30pm, Sat.-Sun. 10am-6pm, 170 Kč) is a fascinating look at the role science and technology played in Czechoslovakia. Filled to the brim with steam trains, antique motorcycles, gleaming old planes, bicycles, and cars, this collection reminds visitors how advanced Czechoslovak society was in the early 20th century before Communism put a big red stop to it. A realistically reconstructed coal mine offers tours in English and the chance to see just how claustrophobic you may or may not be. Rounding out the collection is an impressive photography and cinematography section, a mock TV studio, rare astronomical instruments, and timekeeping technology.

© LUCIE ERICKSEN

Take in the view at Letná Park.

ŽIŽKOV

Named after one-eyed Hussite hero Jan Žižka, working-class Žižkov has always been one of Prague's more notorious districts, characterized by lively 24-hour bars and bordellos. While some of its buildings close to the center are getting much-needed makeovers, a significant portion of the district remains old and run-down, with abandoned buildings and spotty streets serving as reminders that not all of Prague is as perfect as it may seem. Nevertheless, it is a part of town where one can get a true feeling of Prague's rarely publicized underbelly, a place where the city's upscale stores and Western European influences are replaced with mom-and-pop eateries, neighborhood shops, and local watering holes that care little, if at all, about catering to the tourist trade.

Kostel Nejsvětějšího Srdce Páně (Church of the Most Sacred Heart of Our Lord)

Proudly sporting Prague's largest clock, the **Church of the Most Sacred Heart of Our Lord** (Náměstí Jiřiho z Poděbrad 19, tel. 222 727 713, www.srdcepane.cz, mass Mon.-Sat. 8am and 6pm, Sun. 9am, 11am, and 6pm) is also one of the more interesting and inspiring pieces of 20th-century architecture to be found in the city. Built between 1928 and 1932 by Slovenian architect Jozef Plečnik, who was also responsible for some of the additions to Prague Castle, the Church still triggers debates among the locals, half of whom find it to be an eyesore while the other half couldn't imagine the neighborhood without it.

Žižkovská televizní věž (Žižkov TV Tower)

Arguably the most dominant structure in Prague 3 and, according to your taste, either the most striking or ugliest building in the district, the **Žižkov TV Tower** (Mahlerovy sady 1, www.towerpark.cz, daily 8am-midnight, 150 Kč) stands proudly as the Czech Republic's highest structure at 709 feet. Its completion in 1992 was met with immediate criticism, among which were concerns of it giving

Paneláky: Prefab Architecture

Though Prague is known throughout the world for its breathtaking architecture that managed to survive the continent-wide devastation of World War II, there is another form of architecture that rarely gets any attention. The *panelák* or *paneláky* (plural) are what we would call "tenements" in American English or a "block of flats" in British English. Essentially, *paneláky* are a series of high-rise apartment blocks made from prefabricated, reinforced concrete panels. Each apartment block contains hundreds of identical apartments, and each complex comprises a handful to a dozen identical apartment buildings. The result is a veritable concrete jungle: dull gray suburban communities with zero aesthetic appeal. The apartments themselves are nothing to write home about either. Boxy, poorly laid-out, and separated by flimsy partition walls, they are a claustrophobic's nightmare and an eavesdropper's dream come true.

Built during the Communist period to champion uniformity and raise a disparaging eye toward individualism, *paneláky* remained a cheap housing option for many years after the Velvet Revolution. Today, however, many of these unimaginative apartments are getting makeovers, with owners rebuilding walls, laying down proper floors, and replacing bathrooms and kitchens with modern designs in mind. The result is a far more comfortable living arrangement that has begun to attract a wide array of tenants, ranging from students to doctors, all of whom find the still reasonable rent and contemporary design much to their liking.

You'll find *paneláky* all over the outer parts of town, but the biggest collection of them is in Jižní Město, located at the southeastern edge of the city. To get there, take the subway to Háje, Opatov, or Chodov (all located on the red line) and head for the huge gray buildings dotting the skyline.

children cancer. The tower stuck it out, however, and is now considered the area's defining landmark. Recent renovations afford visitors fantastic views of the city, as well as various videos and interactive activities to keep the curious informed and entertained.

Národní památník na Vítkově (National Memorial)

The **National Memorial** (U památníku 1900, tel. 222 781 676, www.nm.cz, Apr.-Oct. Wed.-Sun. 10am-6pm, Nov.-Mar. Thurs.-Sun. 10am-6pm, 110 Kč) on Vítkov Hill in Žižkov is hard to miss. It is a somber building devoid of windows and accompanied by a massive equestrian statue featuring Czech military commander Jan Žižka astride his horse. Designed in the late 1920s by Jan Zázvorka, its original purpose was to honor the remains of Czech legionnaires who battled against the Austro-Hungarian Empire during World War I. When the Communists took over, it became the resting place of state and party leaders.

There was speculation after the revolution in 1989 as to what the grounds should function as, but nobody could come up with a viable answer. In 2000, however, management duties fell to the National Museum, which revamped the grounds into the symbol of Czech sovereignty it now represents.

Olšanské Hřbitovy (Olšany Cemetery)

Built in an effort to handle the escalating number of plague victims who began dying en masse in 1680, **Olšany Cemetery** (Vinohradská 153, tel. 272 011 113-17, www.hrbitovy.cz, Nov.-Feb. daily 8am-5pm, Mar.-Apr. and Oct. daily 8am-6pm, May-Sept. daily 8am-7pm) is Prague's largest burial ground. When the plague reared its diseased head once again in 1787, Emperor Joseph II banned the burial of bodies within the city limits and declared Olšany the city's central graveyard for hygienic purposes. Two very famous faces from Communism lay buried here. The first is Jan Palach, the country's most famous anti-Communist martyr who set himself ablaze on Wenceslas Square in 1969 in protest of the Soviet invasion. The second is first Communist president Klement Gottwald, who, ironically, died shortly after catching a cold at Stalin's funeral in March 1953.

Nový Židovský Hřbitov
(New Jewish Cemetery)

Not to be confused with the Old Jewish Cemetery in Old Town Square, the **New Jewish Cemetery** (Izraelská 1, tel. 226 235 248, www.kehilaprag.cz, Oct.-Mar. Sun.-Thurs. 9am-4pm, Fri. 9am-2pm, Apr.-Sept. Sun.-Thurs. 9am-5pm, Fri. 9am-2pm, closed Sat. and Jewish holidays) is located opposite the Želivského subway station at the tail end of the green subway line. At the top of the escalator, follow the exit straight ahead marked "Židovské Hřbitovy." When you emerge from the station, the cemetery will be on the immediate right. Franz Kafka is buried here; you'll find his grave by taking the first path on the right and following it four entrance gates down to lot 21. His rather unassuming tombstone is decorated with the occasional bouquet of flowers, and some have left coins on the rocks directly in front of his grave with what seem to be messages hidden underneath. Many make the pilgrimage to this very spot every June 3—the day the great writer died.

VINOHRADY

Literally meaning "vineyards" because the entire area was once covered with them, Vinohrady today is a popular residential area that has seen an increase in small-to-medium independent (and oftentimes artistically oriented) businesses. Beautiful art nouveau buildings complement tree-lined neighborhoods including prominent Peace Square and Riegrovy Park, one of Prague's premier outdoor drinking spots. Located a few minutes from the center and home to a myriad of excellent restaurants, bars, and shopping facilities, Vinohrady remains one of Prague's most attractive and desirable districts.

Kostel sv. Ludmily
(Church of St. Ludmilla)

The centerpiece of Náměstí Míru (Peace Square) and Vinohrady proper, the Church of St. Ludmilla is an impressive, neo-Gothic, two-spire basilica that was built between 1888 and 1893 based on the designs of Josef Mocker. Above the main entrance is a relief of Christ with St. Wenceslas and St. Ludmilla on either side. Open only mass, the church now acts mostly as a popular meeting place for the many in town who prefer to soak up the scene on the neighboring benches than engage in any ecclesiastical activities.

Divadlo na Vinohradech
(Vinohrady Theater)

Opposite Peace Square is the gorgeous art nouveau building better known as the **Vinohrady Theater** (Náměstí Míru 7, tel. 224 257 601, www.dnv-praha.cz, box office Mon.-Fri. 11am-7pm, Sat. 1pm-7pm). Opened in 1907, it stands as one of Prague's oldest theaters and has managed to remain one of the premiere venues for Czech theater and ballet.

Muzeum Antonína Dvořáka
(Antonín Dvořák Museum)

Classical composer Antonín Dvořák (1841-1904) is arguably the Czech Republic's most widely known personality abroad and is a national hero at home. An exhibition of his memorabilia is on display at the **Antonín Dvořák Museum** (Villa Amerika, Ke Karlovu 20, tel. 224 923 363, www.antonindvorak2004.cz, Tues.-Sun. 10am-5pm, 40 Kč), tucked behind the wrought-iron gates of Villa Amerika—a pretty 18th-century palace that served as a cattle market and restaurant in the past. Concerts are held here regularly and tend to fill up quickly.

Riegrovy sady
(Riegrovy Park)

Located behind the National Museum off Italská Street, Riegrovy Park was completed in 1908 and now serves as a fantastic outdoor beer garden populated by locals and expats

A Visit to Vyšehrad

South of Nové Město, you'll find historic Vyšehrad, whose slightly mysterious-looking outline of spires is an indelible part of Prague's skyline. Steeped in legend, it is the site of Princess Libuše's foretelling of Prague's future glory, a vivid vision that prompted her to send her horse out to find Přemysl the Ploughman, the man she would eventually take as husband and king before founding the capital and the Přemysl dynasty. What actually happened was that a fortified castle was built here in the middle of the 10th century and enjoyed a brief period as the seat of ultimate political power under King Vratislav II before the Přemyslid rulers decided to pack up and head to Prague Castle.

To see all that Vyšehrad has to offer, take the subway (red line) to Vyšehrad station. Walk past the rather ugly-looking Congress Center and through the baroque gateway into the park proper. As you enjoy your leisurely stroll through the peaceful surroundings, you'll come upon the **Rotunda of St. Martin.** This is Prague's oldest surviving Romanesque building, and though it dates all the way back to the 11th century, it still holds evening mass to this day. Continuing on, the next sight of interest is the neo-Gothic **Church of Sts. Peter and Paul.** Built during the beginning of the 20th century, it was based on the designs of Joseph Mocker and boasts an exquisite art nouveau interior. Next door is **Slavin,** Vyšehrad's famous cemetery, which is home to some of the country's most important cultural and political figures. Among the arcades and pretty memorials rest such giants as Antonín Dvořák, Bedřich Smetana, Karel Čapek, Jan Neruda, and Josef Václav Myslbek.

happily quenching their thirst. Leading up to the drinking area are pretty gardens lined with benches often filled with couples seeking a bit of privacy. The beer garden itself consists of a few hundred people seated at long tables pounding back beers and catching up with old friends. A large screen occasionally projects various sporting events while a kiosk offers up sausages, chips, and peanuts, should all that drinking make you hungry. This is a great place to experience a relaxed and authentic side of Prague.

Entertainment and Events

Prague has been one of Europe's cultural capitals for centuries and doesn't look to be slowing down any time soon. There is always something going on in the Golden City to keep its visitors and residents occupied, whether it's letting one's hair down at one of the countless pubs or cocktail bars, or rubbing shoulders with revelers and rabble-rousers at any number of swanky yet welcoming clubs.

Those looking for a more cultivated level of entertainment will certainly find no shortage of ballets, symphonies, and operas to keep them occupied, while theater and film fans have an inexhaustible selection to choose from thanks to the wide variety of homegrown and imported talent gracing the city's stages and silver screens.

BARS

Prague's nightlife is legendary, satisfying the entire spectrum of nocturnal tastes from smoky cellar bars to upscale lounges. No matter what your poison or pleasure, you can rest assured you'll find it here.

Nové Město

Everybody has ended their night of debauchery at **Batalion Hard Rock Café** (28. října 3, tel. 220 108 147, www.batalion.cz, daily 24 hours) at one point or another. Popular with off-the-clock bar staff, not-ready-to-pack-it-in-yet tourists, and natives going the extra mile, this bare-bones, two-floor, rowdy yet friendly bar will happily ply you with beer until you pay up or pass out. It's a true rite of passage.

Located near the National Theater, **Propaganda** (Pštrossova 29, tel. 602 975 083, www.propagandabar.cz, Mon.-Fri. 11am-2am, Sat.-Sun. 5pm-2am) is a small, intimate, and lively bar that packs in local students, artists, and the occasional celebrity. Cheap beer, a decent array of cocktails, and flexible closing times make this a fun and affordable time for all.

Kavárna Velryba (Opatovická 24, tel. 224 931 444, www.kavarnavelryba.cz, daily 11am-midnight, gallery Mon.-Fri. 11am-midnight, Sat. 5pm-midnight) is a time-honored student pub with cheap beer and a no-frills, laid-back attitude to match. It's a perfect pit stop during the middle of the day and an excellent place to start your evening of carousing. Check out the small gallery in the back, which holds regular exhibits of up-and-coming local artists.

Nebe (V Celnici 4, tel. 608 644 784, http://nebepraha.cz, Mon. 2pm-2am, Tues.-Wed. 2pm-3am, Thurs. 2pm-4am, Fri. 2pm-5am, Sat. 6pm-5am, Sun. 6pm-2am) is a cocktail-music bar that continues to pack them in on the weekends thanks to the extensive drinks menu and overall fun vibe that will get you drinking and dancing in no time.

Red Room (Myslíkova 28, tel. 222 520 084, www.redroom.cz, Tues.-Thurs. 6pm-1am, Fri. 6pm-2am, Sat. 7pm-2am, Sun. 7pm-1am) opened in 2009 and caught on quickly with students, teachers, and overall fun-seekers thanks to its friendly chilled-out vibe. Its blood-red walls are adorned with local art, while its tiny stage plays home to local talent, making this an ideal place to visit should you want to rub elbows with . . . well, locals. Oh, and it's the only place where you'll find pitchers of beer readily available. Go. Drink. Enjoy.

Notorious for its spotty service and less than gregarious bouncers, **Solidní jistota** (Pštrossova 200/21, tel. 725 984 964, www.solidnijistota.cz, Tues.-Thurs. 6pm-2am, Fri.-Sat. 6pm-4am, Sun. 4pm-1am) nevertheless fills up with glamorous-looking 20-somethings yearning to be seen and perhaps meet someone whose pockets are deeper than their personalities. Fun can certainly be had here, although ignoring the overall self-important vibe is of the utmost necessity.

Staré Město

Bar and Books (Týnská 19, tel. 224 815 122, www.barandbooks.cz, Sun.-Wed. 11am-3am, Thurs.-Sat. 11am-4am) adds a splash of class and romance to Old Town thanks to its red leather seats, formally attired waitstaff, and dimly lit ambience. Come on in and join business folk, artists, and lovers who while away

Bar and Books adds a splash of class to Old Town.

the wee hours with expensive brandy, top-notch cocktails, and the world's finest cigars.

If you're looking to bump and grind alongside an international fun-loving crowd, **Bombay Cocktail Bar** (Dlouha 13, tel. 222 324 040, www.bombay-bar.cz, Sun.-Wed. 7pm-4am, Thurs. 7pm-5am, Fri.-Sat. 7pm-6am) is the place to be. The bar itself stretches all the way down one side of the room, which makes getting served a relatively painless affair no matter how packed the place gets. So order up a margarita or one of the many exotic beers on offer and dance the night away in one of the looser atmospheres the city has to offer.

Finding the entrance to **2. Patro** (Dlouhá 37, www.2patro.cz, Mon.-Thurs. 5pm-2am, Fri.-Sat. 5pm-4am, cover charge varies) can be tricky the first time. Head into the courtyard, go through the unmarked doors, and walk up two flights of stairs. Then ring the bell, and voilà! Inside you'll find hipsters and artist types grooving to all kinds of classic and contemporary music. Though not much more than a

large high-ceilinged room, there's something about the fun and friendly vibe here that packs them in every weekend.

If you'd like a taste of Prague's seedier side, then **Chapeau Rouge** (Jakubská 2, tel. 222 316 328, www.chapeaurouge.cz, Mon.-Thurs. noon-3am, Fri. noon-4am, Sat. 4pm-4am, Sun. 4pm-2am) is the place for you. Wild, grungy, and one of the most popular and happening hangouts since the day it opened, it also offers the latest in electronic music in the downstairs **Enfer Rouge** bar, where things just get seedier.

Located a minute away from Charles Bridge and yet miraculously devoid of tourists, **Duende** (Karoliny Světlé 30, tel. 774 486 077, www.barduende.cz, Mon.-Fri. 1pm-midnight, Sat. 3pm-midnight, Sun. 4pm-midnight) may just be Prague's best-kept secret. Uniquely decorated (life preservers and wooden tigers), this Latin-themed café-bar fills up nightly with a free-spirited artistic crowd looking for a laid-back place to sip a glass of wine or two. Make sure to try the Ořechovka walnut liqueur.

If you're aching for a dose of Southern rock-style Americana, head to **Harley's Bar** (Dlouhá 18, tel. 602 419 111, www.harleys.cz, Sun.-Tues. 8pm-4am, Wed.-Thurs. 8pm-5am, Fri.-Sat. 8pm-6am) and join resident mascot Jack Daniels for one bourbon, one scotch, and one beer. A fun, loose atmosphere and pleasant bar staff keep this stylish biker bar packed with locals and tourists well into the night.

Right in the heart of Old Town, **Kozička** (Kozí 1, tel. 776 304 876, www.kozicka.cz, Mon.-Thurs. noon-4am, Fri. 5pm-4am, Sat. 6pm-4am, Sun. 7pm-3am) is a spacious basement bar that fills up with locals and tourists on a nightly basis. Popular and unpretentious, this homey hangout is a breath of fresh air in what has become a heavily tourist-centric area.

Celebrating South and Central American culture on the outskirts of Old Town Square, **La Casa Blu** (Kozí 15, tel. 224 818 270, www.lacasablu.cz, Mon.-Sat. 11am-11pm, Sun. 2pm-11pm) is a brightly lit, smoke-free bar that's a

© TOM DIRLIS

Bombay Cocktail Bar

Harley's Bar

big hit with students, tourists, and just about anybody else who winds up here. Tasty burritos, cool mojitos, and a lively atmosphere are just a few of the reasons why this place should not be missed.

M1 Secret Lounge (Masná 1, tel. 227 195 235, www.m1lounge.com, Sun.-Thurs. 7pm-3am, Fri.-Sat. 7pm-5am) established itself early on as one of the trendier places to be seen in Prague, and things haven't changed much. Amid the soft lights and long red couches, expats mix with models who mix with film people who mix with fat cats on the rise. Jam-packed on weekends, M1 is also a great place to visit midweek as it's one of the few places in Old Town that serve up cocktails and ambience until the wee hours.

Known for years as Molly Malone's, **James Joyce Irish Pub** (U obecního dvora 4, tel. 224 818 851, www.jamesjoyceprague.cz, Sun.-Thurs. 11pm-midnight, Fri.-Sat. 11am-1am) carries on the tradition by offering a warm, friendly, and genuine Irish pub experience with 52 different types of Irish whiskey to boot.

Friendly staff, warm rustic decor, and the best pint of Guinness in town make this an excellent bet during its quiet afternoons or rowdier evenings.

Soaked in both beer and tradition, **U Zlatého tygra** (Husova 17, tel. 222 221 111, www.uzlatehotygra.cz, daily 3pm-11pm) is a must for those interested in seeing where some of the country's greatest writers, like the late great Bohumil Hrabal, used to get inebriated. Václav Havel and Bill Clinton also raised their glasses here, and one never knows who else might walk through the door. Keep in mind that the two medium-size rooms start filling up as soon as the doors open, so make sure to get here early.

PAPAS bar/lounge (Betlémské náměstí 8, tel. 222 222 229, www.papasbar.cz, Mon.-Thurs. 4pm-1am, Fri.-Sat. 4pm-2am, Sun. 4pm-midnight) is a friendly, centrally located cocktail bar with over 150 tasty concoctions to choose from. Excellent music, a warm atmosphere, and attentive bar staff make it a solid choice for any occasion.

Malá Strana

Tucked away a little farther up from the U.S. embassy, **Baráčnická rychta** (Tržiště 23, tel. 257 532 461, www.baracnickarychta.cz, Mon.-Sat. 11am-11pm, Sun. 11am-9pm, cover charge varies) is a refreshing authentic change from establishments catering specifically to tourists. A small beer hall filled with students and laborers is what you'll usually find on the ground floor, but those who venture downstairs will find a large Communist-era music hall that stages local rockers and swing bands on any given night. This is the place to be when you've had your fill of sightseeing and shopping and want a taste of what used to be like in Malá Strana.

Located on an unassuming street just past Charles Bridge, **Blue Light** (Josefská 1, tel. 257 533 126, www.bluelightbar.cz, daily 7pm-4am) is a small bar that's a big hit with just about anybody who passes through its doors. Ice-cold cocktails are served up by friendly staff to an attractive clientele that's ready to party till the sun comes up. Get here early if you want one of the few tables available, or sidle up to the bar and make some new friends; it's that kind of place. Just down the street from the U.S. embassy, **J.J. Murphy's** (Tržiště 4, tel. 257 535 575, www.jjmurphys.cz, daily 9am-1am) is a friendly and spacious Irish pub where locals and tourists regularly settle in for a delicious pint of Guinness. Perfect for lunch, dinner, or a drink or two with friends, J.J.'s also offers sports fans an upstairs lounge that showcases the day's main matches.

Though often criticized for its spotty service, **Zanzibar** (Lázeňská 6, tel. 257 530 762, www.zanzi.cz, daily 5pm-3am) continues to pack in tourists and locals alike thanks to its late hours and impressive cocktail list. It's pink, red, and neon decor feels more Mexican-restaurant than anything African-related, but no one seems to mind, especially after downing a couple of their tasty mojitos. It's a fine choice for the wee-hours drinker, though sitting at the bar to avoid being ignored by the hit-or-miss waitstaff is highly recommended.

BarBar (Všehrdova 17, tel. 257 312 246, www.bar-bar.cz, daily noon-midnight) is a friendly neighborhood bar that underwent massive reconstruction in 2012. The rustic Czech vibe was replaced with a sparser, more modern decor that has been criticized by local purists. The drinks, small-food menu, and service are still top-notch, however, making it a solid choice this side of the Vltava despite all the changes.

PopoCafePetl Music Club (Újezd 19, tel. 739 110 021, www.popocafepetl.cz, Mon.-Sat. 6pm-2am) is yet another subterranean affair, packed for the most part with students and music lovers who enjoy hearing something more than just techno or drum and bass. The drinks are cheap, the music varied (ranging from pop to hip-hop), and the utter lack of attitude will keep you here till the staff politely informs you it's time for beddy-bye.

Shadow Cafe (Újezd 16, tel. 774 742 369, www.shadowcafe.cz, Sun.-Thurs. 1pm-1am, Fri.-Sat. 4pm-2am) consists of three small but cozy rooms featuring some fantastic (if a bit grim) figures painted on its red walls. It's one of the better places to chill on this side of the river thanks to its affordable prices and laid-back clientele. It's an excellent choice for those looking to enjoy a couple of drinks while avoiding the neighborhood's numerous tourist traps.

Don't let the name throw you: **Mad Bar** (Plaská 5, tel. 257 219 855, www.madbar.cz, Mon.-Fri. 11am-midnight, Sat.-Sun. 3am-midnight) is actually a well-behaved local bar boasting modern well-lit decor and some of the finest staff in the city. Well-made drinks and a friendly easygoing vibe are two more reasons to visit this fine establishment. Reservations are strongly recommended.

Back in the day, dreadlocks, dogs, and dime bags were all you needed to enjoy a night at **Klub Újezd** (Újezd 18, tel. 251 510 873, www.klubujezd.cz, daily 2pm-4am). Things have calmed down quite a bit since then, but if you want a true Prague experience, put this on your "to-drink" list. Don't let its rough, unrefined appearance sway your opinion. It may not look like much, but Újezd has been a hit with both locals and tourists for as long as anyone can remember.

U Malého Glena (Karmelitská 23, tel. 257 531 717, www.malyglen.cz, daily 10am-2am, live music cover charge varies) or "Little Glen's" is a smallish, typical-looking pub that has been serving up tasty soups, sandwiches, and Tex-Mex to both expats and Czechs since the early 1990s. Fun, friendly, and easygoing, this is a place worth visiting when you're in need of a break from the Malá Strana madness. If you visit in the evening, make sure to check out the tiny jazz cellar located downstairs, which regularly features some of Prague's hottest talent.

Holešovice

Barrel (Šmeralova 12, tel. 777 608 104, Mon.-Sat. 6pm-4am, Sun. 6pm-3am) is a simply furnished, inconspicuous little bar not far from Letná Park. It's one of the few places in the neighborhood open late, so you can always expect to find a local or two sipping drinks or dozing off at the tables. Quiet, friendly, and

Do You Really Want to Try Absinthe?

In the mid-to-late 19th century, there was hardly an artist anywhere who didn't cite absinthe as their drink of choice. Picasso, Van Gogh, Wilde, Toulouse-Lautrec, Baudelaire, Poe, and Hemingway were but a few of the Bohemian bourgeoisie who enjoyed a glass or two of "The Green Muse." Their extravagant descriptions of the drink's mind-altering effects went a long way in shaping its popularity and mystique, though closer inspection and study have shown that those claims were largely exaggerated and based on little more than a tipsy imagination.

The mythic drink's origins can be traced back to the end of the 18th century when French doctor Pierre Ordinaire began using wormwood (*Artemisia absinthium*) together with anise, fennel, hyssop, and numerous other herbs distilled in an alcoholic base as an herbal remedy for his patients. The curious concoction eventually ended up in the hands of Henri-Louis Pernod, who, upon opening his first distillery in 1805, went on to produce Extrait d'Absinthe, sparking the Pernod dynasty and a national phenomenon. Numerous reports regarding the drink's harmful effects began to emerge, though most, if not all, were alarmist and

reflected the opinions of the rich and powerful who were either for the banning of alcohol or wanted to eliminate the competition absinthe had brought to France's wine industry. "The Green Fairy," as it was known in some circles, was banned in France in 1914 due to mounting reports of its dangerous side effects, which we now know were the result of cheap knockoff brands produced to make a quick franc. Nevertheless, it was the end of an era, and Pernod's plant, which was home to 110 years of profitable production, served as a field hospital during World War I before being sold on December 31, 1917, to Nestlé.

Today, absinthe is still banned in most countries, but you'll find it readily available in plenty of Prague bars, who play up the drink's magical history. If you decide to give it a whirl, it will be served to you in a small glass, along with a teaspoon and packet of sugar. Pour some sugar onto the spoon, then soak the spoonful with absinthe and light it in order to caramelize the sugar. When the flame goes out, stir the sugar into your drink, buck up, and drink down. You'll soon realize why most bars have a two-absinthe maximum.

relaxed, this is the place to visit when you're looking to wind down with a nightcap.

Popular from the get-go, **Fraktal** (Šmeralova 1, tel. 777 794 094, www.fraktalbar.cz, daily 11am-midnight) is a cozy, cheerful bar full of expats and Czechs who are serious about having a good time. Few visitors make it out here, but if you find yourself weary of the downtown core, make the trip out to Holešovice and join in the fun. It's also known as one of the few places in town where you can get a proper North American-style hamburger.

Laid back and refreshingly unpretentious, **Wakata** (Malířská 14, tel. 777 097 196, www. wakata.eu, Mon.-Thurs. 5pm-3am, Fri. 5pm-5am, Sat. 6pm-5am, Sun. 6pm-3am) is a small and intimate DJ lounge that delivers excellent jungle, hip-hop, dub, and drum and bass in a

small and intimate DJ lounge. It's cheap, fun, and a fave with the underground set.

Žižkov

Bukowski's (Bořivojova 86, tel. 774 530 689, daily 6pm-3am) was an instant hit with both expats and Czechs when it opened in 2009, and it has not looked back since. One reason is that it serves as a welcome alternative to the area's large number of unimaginative beer pubs, while another is the winning combination of friendly service, laid-back ambience, and wide range of delicious cocktails. Good times are all but guaranteed.

Long a neighborhood staple, **U Sadu** (Škroupovo náměstí 5, tel. 222 727 072, www.usadu.cz, Sun.-Wed. 8am-2am, Thurs.-Sat. 8am-4am) is well worth going out of your way to visit. Decorated with Socialist-era relics that include meat grinders and gas masks, this institution has "traditional" written all over it. Whether it's copious amounts of beer you're looking to consume or the stinky yet delicious *nakladany hermelin* (pickled cheese) you've come to relish, U Sadu will convince you to stay longer than you had originally intended.

U vystřelenýho oka (U Božích bojovníků 3, tel. 222 540 465, www.uvoka.cz, Mon.-Sat. 4:30pm-1am) or "At the Shot-Out Eye" is named in honor of the one-eyed Hussite General Jan Žižka, whose statue is located atop the hill behind the pub. Cheap beer, loud tunes, eclectic art on the walls, and a general sense of idiosyncratic merriment is what you can expect at this local watering hole.

CLUBS

The club scene in Prague is a vibrant and varied affair that ranges from the down-and-dirty vibe of Palac Akropolis to swank and trendy institutions like Radost FX. Club attire is just as diverse. It's common to see anything from the completely casual to the bluntly provocative, often in the same group of friends. Clubs tend to get busy around midnight and stay that way till the wee hours, with most clubbers heading home as others begin their day. Most offer different musical programs depending on the night of the week, so check the local listings to find the right fit for you.

Cross Club (Plynární 23, tel. 775 541 430, www.crossclub.cz, daily 6pm-6am) is the artistically bent locals' club of choice thanks to its hip yet unpretentious vibe. Its numerous subterranean levels are decked out with rotating sculptures, welded tables adorned with engine parts, and trippy lighting, which makes for a unique partying experience. DJs spin anything from punk to drum and bass, and live shows are just as varied. This is the place to come to when you feel like clubbing but could do without the steep prices and cooler-than-thou attitude.

Karlovy Lázně (Novotneho Lavka 5, Staré Město, tel. 222 220 502, www.karlovylazne. cz, daily 9pm-5am, 180 Kč) is advertised as Central Europe's largest dance club. Very touristy and rather pricey, it nevertheless boasts four lively floors and five clubs playing anything from house to hip-hop. Get here early (around 10pm) if you want to avoid the long line.

Infinity (Chrudimská 2a/2526, Vinohrady, tel. 272 176 580, www.infinitybar.cz, Tues. 6pm-3am, Wed.-Thurs. 6pm-4am, Fri.-Sat. 6pm-4:30am, cover charge varies) is one of the more popular pickup joints in Prague, with hedonistic hopefuls getting their game on in a loose and friendly environment characterized by a huge bar and tiny dance floor. Do your hair, iron your shirt, and come rub shoulders with Prague's beautiful people.

A veritable institution and still the most-popular bar in the district, **Palac Akropolis** (Kubelíkova 27, Žižkov, tel. 296 330 911, www.palacakropolis.cz, daily 11:30am-3am, no cover charge) is a bar, club, and concert venue all rolled into one. Beer flows freely upstairs, but it's downstairs where all the action happens with travelers and artsy types shooting the breeze over battered tables and blazing beats. This is the place to be if a night of bona fide Bohemian behavior is what you're after.

Radost FX (Belehradská 120, Vinohrady, tel. 224 254 776, www.radostfx.cz, daily 7pm-5am, cover charge varies) is where Prague's in-crowd parties most nights of the week. The space itself is an appealing mix of nightclub, cocktail bar, art gallery, and vegetarian café, all of which are top-notch. Lush decor, sexy clientele, and stylish bar staff have helped make Radost one of Prague's premiere nightspots for many years.

Plagued for years by rumors that it would be shut down due to neighbors complaining about the constant noise, the **Roxy** (Dlouhá 33, Staré Město, tel. 224 826 296, www.roxy.cz, daily 7pm-5am, cover charge varies) has nevertheless managed to stay open and remains as popular as ever. Some of the world's top DJs and live acts have performed here, and the slightly dilapidated interior, along with a relaxed and tolerant vibe, makes this a big hit with locals, expats, tourists, and just about anybody else who likes their drum and bass, jungle, and techno. This is arguably Prague's most famous nightspot and not to be missed by any serious clubber.

Le Clan (Balbínova 23, Vinohrady, www. leclan.cz, Tues.-Sat. 2am-noon, cover charge varies) is a laid-back and well-lit after-hours club that attracts all walks of life, most of them looking for any type of chemical to delay their inevitable comedown. It's pricey and can feel a little cliquey at times, but it's also one of the few places in town that rages on till lunch time.

LIVE MUSIC

Considering the sheer volume of bars and clubs in the capital, it should come as no surprise that the live music scene is a thriving one. Whether it's international acts playing smaller, more intimate venues or established local bands rocking the Kasbah, there's always something to take in on any given night. The handful of jazz clubs in town hosts some of the finest musicians in the country for a relative pittance, while other music clubs hold a wide variety of concerts ranging from funk and reggae to straight-out rock, punk, and thrash. There are also a whole host of cover bands (called "revivals") that add an element of amusement to an already enjoyable show. Cover charges are low, crowds are laid-back, and the air is always thick with smoke and sweat. Make sure to keep an eye out for the weekly music schedules posted all over town to see who will be performing during your stay.

Jazz lovers will definitely want to check out the hip and friendly **Jazz Dock** (Janáčkovo nábřeží 2, Smíchov, tel. 774 058 838, Apr.-Sept. Mon.-Thurs. 3pm-4am, Fri.-Sat. 1pm-4pm, Sun. 1pm-2am, Oct.-Mar. Mon.-Fri. 5pm-4pm, Sat. 3pm-4am, Sun. 3pm-2am, cover charge varies). An excellent range of live acts as well as fantastic cocktails and a unique view of the city thanks to its location on the riverbank all make this a fun and dependable choice.

One of the better midsize venues in town is **Lucerna Music Bar** (Vodičkova 36, Nové Město, tel. 224 217 108, www.musicbar.cz, daily 7pm-3am, cover charge varies), which

Jazz Dock

boasts a long list of famous and eclectic artists who've graced its stage. Weekends give way to tremendously popular 1980s DJ nights, where locals who are way too young to remember the decade get down and do "The Safety Dance." Smack-dab in the center of town is **Rock Café** (Národní 20, Nové Město, tel. 224 933 947, www.rockcafe.cz, Mon.-Fri. 10am-3am, Sat. 5pm-3am, Sun. 5pm-1am, cover charge varies), proud bringer of lesser-known alternative and punk bands to Prague. Albeit lacking in ambience and service, it does offer weekly movie screenings and more cover bands than you can shake a Stratocaster at. Your best bet is to check out the music program in advance and take it from there.

XT3 (Rokycanova 29, Žižkov, tel. 222 783 463, www.xt3.cz, Mon.-Thurs. 11am-2am, Fri. 11am-5am, Sat. 2pm-5am, Sun. 2pm-2am, cover charge varies) is one of the better-known clubs in town, housing a lively bar at street level as well as a cavernous club housing local DJs and live music that's as eclectic as the crowd that packs the place.

Located conveniently close to Old Town Square is **Agharta Jazz Centrum** (Železná 16, Staré Město, tel. 222 211 275, www.agharta. cz, daily 7pm-1am, 250 Kč), one of the better venues in town to enjoy homegrown jazz. Featuring well-known live acts in a warm, cozy environment, Agharta fills up early, so you may want to book seats in advance. Don't forget to check out their record store, where you'll find plenty of local (and affordable) recordings.

One of the finer places to catch modern, contemporary, and Latin jazz is **U Staré Paní Jazz Club** (Michalská 9, Staré Město, tel. 605 285 211, www.jazzstarapani.cz, daily 7pm-2am, admission varies), where most of the hottest players in town come to swing. Jams will last all night if the mood is right, and if you get the munchies between sets, this is the only jazz club in town that'll be able to come to your rescue.

Founded in 2000, **Ungelt Jazz & Blues Club** (Týn 2, Staré Město, tel. 224 895 787, www.jazzungelt.cz, daily 8pm-1am, admission varies) is located mere steps from Old Town Square and is home to some of the finest jazz,

blues, and funk you're liable to hear. Situated in cellar rooms dating back to the 15th century, the club attracts many tourists who come to enjoy the nation's top musicians. This is the most expensive jazz club in Prague but still quite reasonable by Western standards.

THE ARTS

The arts scene in Prague strikes a balance between the time-honored and cutting-edge, much to the delight of theater, music, and film fans. From standards like *Pygmalion* and *La Traviata* to groundbreaking domestic dance troupes and avant-garde filmmakers, artistic expression is alive and well in the bosom of Bohemia. What else could one expect from a country whose former president was a dissident playwright?

Theater

Sitting majestically alongside the banks of the Vltava River is **Národní divadlo (National Theater)** (Ostrovní 1, Nové Město, tel. 224 901 448, www.narodni-divadlo.cz, box office daily 10am-6pm), one of Prague's most important cultural landmarks. Built between 1868 and 1881, this neo-Renaissance building with the gleaming golden roof plays host to some of the city's finest ballet and opera performances. If *Carmen* or *Swan Lake* isn't your thing, a tour of this magnificent building is still worth your time.

At the forefront of contemporary theater, dance, and music is the critically acclaimed **Divadlo Archa (Archa Theater)** (Na Poříčí 26, Nové Město, tel. 221 716 333, www.archatheatre.cz, box office Mon.-Fri. 10am-6pm). Its versatile space attracts rather avant-garde productions and has hosted such well-known artists as David Byrne, Allen Ginsberg, and The White Stripes.

The odd-looking glass building next to the National Theater is **Laterna Magika (Magic Lantern)** (Národní 4, Nové Město, tel. 224 931 482, www.laterna.cz, box office daily 10am-6pm), a black-light theater that has been delighting audiences for decades. Not knowing the Czech language doesn't affect one's enjoyment of the performance as there are no words spoken; rather, performances rely on a combination of film projection, dance, sound, lights, and pantomime.

Popular with tourists and children alike is the **Národní divadlo marionet (National Marionette Theater)** (Žatecká 1, Staré Město, tel. 224 819 322, www.mozart.cz, box office daily 10am-8pm), which has been entertaining audiences with its unique portrayal of Mozart's *Don Giovanni* since 1991. There are no humans on stage here, just classically carved marionettes. While relying more on cuteness than anything else, these performances are nevertheless skillful adaptations of the original masterpiece by some of the country's top puppeteers.

Located on trendy Pařížská Street is another black-light endeavor—the **Divadlo Image (Image Theater)** (Pařížská 4, Staré Město, tel. 222 314 448, www.imagetheatre.cz, box office Mon.-Fri. 9am-8pm, Sat.-Sun. 10am-8pm). Focusing mainly on contemporary dance and music, the theater puts on three or four productions a month as well as a medley of their more successful bits in a production titled *Best of Image.*

In December 2002, **Švandovo divadlo (Švanda Theater)** (Štefánikova 57, Smíchov, tel. 257 318 666, www.svandovodivadlo.cz, box office Mon.-Fri. 11am-7pm, Sat.-Sun. 5pm-7pm) opened its doors to the public again after a lengthy period of reconstruction and hasn't looked back since. Theater lovers will find much diversity here, ranging from Chekhov to Shakespeare to Molière. Most performances offer English subtitles—a relief to non-Czech-speaking foreigners who have few opportunities to enjoy a night at the theater. The suburb of Smíchov is located just south of Malá Strana and can be easily reached by taking the subway's yellow line to Anděl station. A number of trams serve the area as well, the most popular of which are the 4, 9, 10, 12, and 20.

Classical Music and Dance

Next door to Radio Free Europe is the elegant **Státní Opera Praha (Prague State Opera)** (Wilsonova 4, Nové Město, tel. 224

227 266, www.sop.cz, box office Mon.-Fri. 10am-5:30pm, Sat.-Sun. 10am-noon and 1pm-5:30pm), where classics are performed by artists hailing from all around the world. Overshadowed a little by the magnificence of the National Theater, the State Opera is nevertheless an excellent venue to watch top-notch performances of all the master works.

The **Municipal House** (Náměstí republiky 5, Nové Město, tel. 222 002 101, www.obecnidum.cz, box office daily 10am-7pm) is home to the Prague Symphony as well as the main venue of the very popular Prague Spring International Music Festival. A stunning example of art nouveau, it is the center of cultural life in Prague thanks to the numerous conferences, balls, and concerts held in its elaborately decorated rooms.

Standing proudly at the edge of Staré Město is the neoclassic **Rudolfinum** (Alšovo nábřeží 12, tel. 227 059 227, www.ceskafilharmonie.cz, box office Mon.-Fri. 10am-6pm), arguably one of Europe's most beautiful concert halls. Home to the Czech Philharmonic Orchestra as well as to world-class musicians from all over the globe, this magnificent building is well worth visiting for its sublime interior alone.

Built in 1783, the **Stavovské divadlo (Estates Theater)** (Železná 11, Staré Město, tel. 224 228 503, www.stavovskedivadlo.cz, box office daily 10am-6pm) is not only a breathtaking example of late baroque architecture but Prague's oldest theater as well. The Czech national anthem was first performed here, as was *Don Giovanni,* conducted by Mozart himself in 1787. Today, *Don Giovanni* continues to play to a packed house of people eager to relive a time long gone.

Cinemas

Offering up a mix of new releases and offbeat independent films, **Světozor** (Vodičkova 41, Nové Město, tel. 224 946 824, www.kinosvetozor.cz) attracts a wide range of people, from popcorn-munching filmgoers to all-out cinephiles. It also hosts a variety of film festivals throughout the year, so make sure to check the

© TOM DIRLIS

The Estates Theater is Prague's oldest theater.

cinema's schedule if you're interested in taking in a film while here.

Lucerna (Vodičkova 36, Nové Město, tel. 224 216 972, www.lucerna.cz), is a beautiful old-fashioned European cinema complete with a coat check and a balcony. Hollywood films have been slowly giving way to foreign works from around the globe, with the occasional Czech film accompanied by English subtitles shown as well. This is a great place to see a movie if you'd like a change of pace from the usual multiplex experience.

Straddling the border between Old Town and New, **Cinema City Slovanský Dům** (Na Příkopě 22, Nové Město, tel. 255 742 021, www.cinemacity.cz) boasts 10 screens showing the latest films from Hollywood and around the world. Its slick, modern interior and excellent sound system make for an enjoyable film-going experience, and you can reserve tickets in advance either online or in person.

True film aficionados will want to have a look at what **Kino Aero** (Biskupcova 31, Žižkov, tel. 271 771 349, www.kinoaero.cz)

is offering during their stay. A retro theater with rough-around-the-edges charm, it manages to secure showings of films no other theater in town seems to even consider, let alone pursue. There is also a popular and extremely comfortable café-bar to add to your evening's enjoyment.

FESTIVALS AND EVENTS
Unlike other cities, where the festival season tends to center around the summer months, Prague's calendar is full of culture and fun all year round. Whether it's classical music or contemporary dance, Shakespeare, or the latest in European cinema, fans of all artistic media and disciplines are sure to find something that will both entertain and enlighten.

Spring
Originally scheduled in January, **Febiofest** (Růžová 13, tel. 221 101 111, www.febiofest. cz) now runs annually during late March and features roughly 300 films from over 60 countries. Some of contemporary cinema's most

important films are screened at various venues around the city, as are debut and sophomore efforts of Europe's up-and-coming filmmakers. A favorite of the festival is its retrospective series, which in the past has featured such high-profile names as Pier Paolo Pasolini and Michelangelo Antonioni.

Continuing a tradition that dates way back to 1595 is **Matějská pout' (St. Matthew's Fair)** (U Výstaviště, tel. 220 103 204, late Feb.-mid-Apr. Tues.-Fri. 2pm-9pm, Sat.-Sun. 10am-9pm), held annually at Prague's Exhibition Grounds in Holešovice. Kids of all ages are invited to take part in the over 120 attractions on hand. The rides are pretty cheesy, but it's the laid-back heralding of warmer weather that most people seem to enjoy.

Marking the death of winter and the birth of spring is **Pálení čarodějnic,** better known as **Witches' Night** (April 30). In an effort to purge the land of winter spirits, faithful citizens light bonfires around the country and burn an effigy of a hag (or witch). Some of the more daring participants will even try to jump over the flames. This is always a fun night in the Czech Republic that comes complete with loud music, good food, and, you guessed it—beer. This tradition is alive and well in most Czech villages. In Prague, you can usually hear a witch's death screams coming from Petřín Hill or near the student dorms in Strahov.

One of the more romantic days in Prague occurs on May 1, or **May Day.** Lovers of all walks of life make the trek to Petřín Hill, locate the statue of 19th-century Romantic poet Karel Hynek Mácha, and kiss under the cherry tree next to it. A kiss under the tree ensures a year full of love, and judging by all the smooching that goes on, there'll be plenty of love to last decades. A recent development worth noting is the expat chicken party—an all-day affair where anyone is welcome to bring their own chicken dish and partake in all the other tasty poultry-based delights prepared by fellow foreigners. It's very informal, lots of fun, and a great way to meet people in the expat community; just look for the large group on the hill devouring chicken wings.

Growing steadily in numbers every year is the **Prague International Marathon** (various routes throughout the city, tel. 224 919 209, www.pim.cz, mid-May), which takes runners through a mostly flat course that includes some of the city's most beautiful buildings. There's also a six-mile race whose route is no less picturesque. A massive street party is held afterward where runners, organizers, and beer lovers refresh themselves with Bohemia's finest brews.

Literature lovers are treated to readings and Q&A sessions with some of the world's best-known writers during the **Prague Writer's Festival** (various venues, tel. 224 241 312, www.pwf.cz, mid-April). Past guests include Martin Amis, Harold Pinter, Margaret Atwood, and Salman Rushdie.

One of Prague's more unique festivals is **Mezi ploty** (Ústavní 91, tel. 603 576 635, www.meziploty.cz, last weekend in May), a two-day festival showcasing professional, amateur, and mentally or physically disabled artists, dancers, and musicians. Very popular and loads of fun, the weekend's events are held on the grounds of Bohnice Psychiatric Hospital.

Lovers of classical music would be wise to attend Prague's most popular music festival—**Prague Spring** (various venues, tel. 257 312 547, www.festival.cz, mid-May-early June). The festivities kick off on the anniversary of the death of Czech composer Bedřich Smetana with a rousing performance of his tone poem *Má Vlast* (My Country). Showcasing some of the world's most outstanding performing artists, symphony orchestras, and chamber music ensembles, Prague Spring is not to be missed. Booking in advance is essential.

Summer

Fans of traditional Gypsy music, as well as those interested in learning more about Roma culture, should definitely check out **Khamoro** (various venues, tel. 222 518 554, www.khamoro.cz, last week in May). This is a lively festival that holds concerts at venues around the city and offers numerous informative and entertaining workshops and seminars.

Growing in prestige and popularity year by

year is the modern dance festival **Tanec Praha** (various venues, tel. 224 817 886, www.tanec-pha.cz, throughout June). Offering a development prize for Dance Discovery of the Year, Tanec Praha is an exciting event and a wonderful opportunity to see the world's finest performers in some of the city's better theaters.

The quiet Vltava riverfront turns into a nonstop concert during the **United Islands of Prague** (various venues, tel. 257 325 041, www.unitedislands.cz, throughout June), a high-energy festival that offers fans the opportunity to enjoy a multitude of musical genres such as world, ethno, folk, jazz, blues, and rock. Some of the festival's past artists include Fishbone, Placebo, and Medeski Martin and Wood.

Even though all the performances are in Czech, lovers of Shakespeare will want to attend Prague's annual **Summer Shakespeare Festival** (Burgrave Palace, Prague Castle, tel. 220 514 275, www.shakespeare.cz, late June-early Sept.). Originally initiated by former president and playwright Václav Havel, a handful of the Bard's works are put on every year to the delight of all. Language barriers aside, it truly is a memorable experience watching a masterpiece under a warm, summer sky with Prague Castle serving as backdrop.

Fall

Since its inception, the **Prague Autumn Festival** (various venues, tel. 222 540 484, www.pragueautumn.cz, mid-Sept.-early Oct.) has focused on major classical works dating from the 18th century to the present. Russian, German, and Czech orchestras and choirs perform regularly in some of Prague's most beautiful venues. Recent years have added surprises such as Chinese opera and the Xalapa Guitar Orchestra from Mexico. This event has been growing in popularity over the years, making the advance booking of tickets essential.

Despite the fact that the country no longer exists, the **Anniversary of the Birth of Czechoslovakia** (Oct. 28) continues to be observed. Fireworks displays and the consumption of large amounts of beer are usually on the menu. If the holiday falls near a weekend, the city empties as most Czechs and locals head for cottage country.

Celebrating the fall of Communism and the ushering in of a new era, the **Anniversary of the Velvet Revolution** (Nov. 17) is a surprisingly subdued affair. Flowers are laid and candles are lit at both the top of Wenceslas Square and Národní třída, but one gets the feeling that most people are too busy enjoying their Westernized lifestyles to remember the way things used to be.

Winter

One of the more charming and colorful traditions in Prague is **Mikuláš** (all over town, particularly Old Town Square, Dec. 5), a sort of judgment day for kids. Typically, a group of three characters—St. Nicholas, an Angel, and a Devil—roam the streets and stop kids randomly, asking them whether they've been naughty or nice. Most kids admit to having been good and sing a song or recite a short poem to prove it. They are then rewarded with a piece of candy by the Angel. The "bad" kids are supposed to get a sack of coal or potatoes instead of sweets, but you'll be hard-pressed to find that happening these days.

When people hear of carnivals or masquerades, most think of New Orleans or Rio de Janeiro. **Masopust** (various venues in Žižkov, www.praha3.cz, mid-Feb.), while nowhere nearly as large in scope or international attention, is a whole lotta fun nonetheless. Faces are painted, meat is grilled, and merrymaking rings loudly throughout the city. Events, parades, and nighttime activities revolve around the borough of Žižkov, which happily brings this colorful tradition to life year after year.

Shopping

The beginning of Prague's burgeoning tourist industry brought with it an increased exposure to Western styles and habits, which, when coupled with a slow but steady increase in wages, helped shape the average Czech's approach to shopping and created a consumer savvy unseen in these parts before. The inevitable result was a tremendous and seemingly overnight growth of designer boutiques, multinational brands, and sprawling shopping malls. Although they may hesitate to admit it, today's Czech is just as liable to spend a weekend out shopping as they are relaxing at the cottage—something that was unthinkable a mere decade ago. Increased consumer awareness has led to increased spending, resulting in Prague reaching a level of sophistication that now rivals the same Western markets that were once on the other side of the curtain.

SHOPPING DISTRICTS

The first of the city's central shopping districts is the mighty **Wenceslas Square,** starting at the top of Muzeum and stretching all the way down to the bottom of Můstek. Along the way are bookshops, clothing stores, jewelry dealers, department stores, and arcades brimming with well-known brands and typically hefty price tags. There are a handful of souvenir shops kicking around as well, hawking the same cheaply manufactured kitsch one can easily find in Old Town Square or Malá Strana. At the bottom of the square on the right is the beginning of **Na Příkopě Street.** Home to all things multinational and fashionable, it was recently ranked 18th in a survey called "Main Streets of the World," behind Manhattan's Fifth Avenue and London's Oxford Street.

Two streets dominate the shopping scene in Old Town Square: **Pařížská** and **Celetná.** The first is home to trendy, expensive, and well-known designer boutiques that include Louis Vuitton, Boss, and Dior. The second is full of crystal, Bohemian glass, and souvenir shops that range from the elegant and appropriately expensive to the crappy and overpriced. The rest of the common pedestrian areas are dominated by shops selling tacky souvenirs like "Czech me out!" T-shirts and cheaply made beer mugs. There are, however, a small number of tiny shops selling antiques, old books, and prints that are tucked away down side streets and require hunting down.

Crossing the Charles Bridge and into Lesser Town will bring you face to face with two main shopping drags. The first is **Mostecká,** which runs from the end of the bridge to Malostranska Square and is packed with jewelry, crystal, glass, and souvenir shops. The second is **Nerudova,** which offers more of the same. Prices are typically higher on this side of the river, but a bit of legwork and comparison shopping should help you find a few reasonably priced items.

NOVÉ MĚSTO
Antiques

Unfortunately, **Antic Aura** (Vyšehradská 27, tel. 224 922 575, Mon.-Fri. 11am-6pm) is only open during weekdays, but if you've got some time to browse and need a new purse or some swanky jewelry, look no further. Ceramics and art pieces are also available.

Books and Music

Long an expat haven and institution, **The Globe Bookstore & Coffeehouse** (Pštrossova 6, tel. 224 934 203, www.globebookstore. cz, Mon.-Thurs. 9:30am-midnight, Fri.-Sun. 9:30am-1am) has been serving up books and bites since its original location in Holešovice. Now operating in New Town, it remains one of the best places in Prague to pick up new releases, meet fellow foreigners, grab a snack, or simply catch up on email. Furthermore, its live music, movie nights, and a whole host of other events keep the Globe as lively as it ever was.

One of the wider selections of books in

English can be found at **Palác knih Luxor** (Václavské náměstí 41, tel. 296 110 370, www. neoluxor.cz, Mon.-Fri. 8am-8pm, Sat. 9am-7pm, Sun. 10am-7pm) on Wenceslas Square. New arrivals can be found on the main floor, along with a healthy variety of popular magazines like *National Geographic* and *Rolling Stone*. Literature that includes classics, crime, and contemporary best-sellers is located downstairs in a spacious setting supervised by helpful English-speaking staff.

Located on busy Wenceslas Square, **Kanzelsberger** (Václavské Náměstí 42, tel. 224 219 214, www.dumknihy.cz, daily 9am-8pm) offers a modest collection of English fiction and nonfiction, though their selection of art books dealing with painting, architecture, photography, and interior design is definitely worth a peek.

Oxford Bookshop (Opletalova 5/7, tel. 224 220 521, www.oxfordbookshop.cz, Mon.-Thurs. 10am-6pm, Fri. 10am-4pm) offers one of the largest selection of books in English and foreign languages, including French, Spanish, German, Italian, and Russian. Fiction, nonfiction, art books, children's books, and stationery supplies are all available here.

Department Stores

Kotva (Revoluční 1/655, tel. 224 801 111, www.od-kotva.cz, Mon.-Fri. 9am-8pm, Sat. 10am-7pm, Sun. 10am-6pm) underwent renovations in an attempt to remain competitive with the Palladium, located across the street. Despite the new coat of paint and design, however, the same run-of-the-mill reasonably priced goods are still on offer. Jewelry, perfume, and snacks remain on the ground level, while men's and women's clothing, sporting goods, furniture, and more await on higher floors. There's also a supermarket where you can stock up on rations before hitting the sightseeing trail again.

Twelve million people pass through **Tesco** (Národní třída 26, tel. 222 003 111, www. tesco-shop.cz, department store and supermarket Mon.-Sat. 7am-9pm, Sun. 8am-8pm) every year, which explains why it oftentimes

resembles a zoo. There's a decent-size supermarket downstairs, while the newly renovated department store offers four floors of affordably-priced wares that include cosmetics, fashion, and electronic goods.

Popular British department store **Debenhams** (Václavské náměstí 21, tel. 221 015 026, www.debenhams.cz, Mon.-Sat. 9am-8pm, Sun. 10am-8pm) offers visitors a supermarket in the basement; designer cosmetics, footwear, and leather on the main floor; and women's and men's fashions above that. The prices are what you would expect them to be seeing as it's located in the heart of Wenceslas Square.

Fashion

Fashionistas will want to check out inventive Czech fashion label **Chi-Chi** (Senovážné Náměstí 10, tel. 777 094 421, www.chi-chi. cz, Mon.-Fri. 11am-7pm, Sat. 11am-5pm). Developed by hip avant-garde designer Josefina Bakošová, her bold colors, asymmetric shapes, and an overall sporty vibe lend her collections a trendy street-smart chic that's a hit with fashion fans both here and abroad.

La femme Mimi (Štěpánská 51, tel. 224 214 106, www.lafemmemimi.cz, Mon.-Fri. 10am-7:30pm) is a wonderful little shop specializing in colorful cotton and silk shirts, skirts, handbags, and dresses, all of which are intricately handwoven and inspired by Asian designs and the environment. This is a true original in the heart of New Town.

If... (Mezibranská 9, tel. 222 211 357, www. ivanafollova.com, Mon.-Fri. 9am-2pm) offers unique ready-to-wear clothes and accessories for women who prefer a touch of the pampered and luxurious. Founded by Ivana Follová, whose credits include designs for rock bands, operas, and a host of local celebrities, this boutique has made a name for itself thanks to its exciting and original contemporary designs.

Galleries

At the forefront of showcasing independent art is **Gallery Art Factory** (Václavské náměstí 15, tel. 224 217 585, www.galleryartfactory.

cz, Mon.-Fri. 10am-6pm). Its 5,382-square-foot exhibition space serves internationally respected artists as well as the hungrier ones who are just coming up. The gallery's biggest triumph is its annual "Sculpture Grande" event, where large thought-provoking sculptures are exhibited publicly all up and down Wenceslas Square.

The **Jiří Švestka Gallery** (Biskupský dvůr 6, tel. 222 311 092, www.jirisvestka.com, Tues.-Sat. 11am-6pm) is the Czech Republic's first and foremost private gallery, showcasing internationally known Czech artists like Krištof Kintera and Jiří Černický as well as young artists looking to carve their niche in the global art scene. Modern contemporary art is the gallery's focus, with a particular taste for the unapologetically innovative.

Gifts

If you yearn for a time when people wrote letters instead of typed them, then **Papelote** (Vojtěšská 9, tel. 774 719 113, www.papelote.cz, Mon.-Fri. 11am-7pm, Sat. noon-6pm) is the place for you. Specializing in environmentally friendly paper products, they offer uniquely artistic stationery and supplies, including notebooks, postcards, and wrapping paper, to name just a few.

Hard-de-core (Senovážné náměstí 10, tel. 777 094 421, www.harddecore.cz, Mon.-Fri. 11am-7pm, Sat. 11am-5pm) is an art workshop, design studio, and boutique all in one. You'll find plenty of original clothing as well as accessories, ceramics, jewelry, books, and a whole lot more. Art classes are also held on the premises, allowing aspiring artists or mere hobbyists to take a variety of classes, including pottery, painting, and interior design.

Silver-screen aficionados ought to check out **Terry Posters** (Vodičkova 41, tel. 224 946 829, www.terry-posters.com, Mon.-Fri. 10am-8pm, Sat. noon-5pm), located inside Svetozor Cinema. Its large selection of vintage Czechoslovak movie posters from 1930 to 1989 as well as over 8,000 original posters representing films of every decade and genre makes this a must for any film buff.

Glass

One of the few interesting shops in Černa růže shopping center is **Moser Praha** (Na Příkopě 12, tel. 224 211 293, www.moser-glass.com, Mon.-Fri. 10am-8pm, Sat. 10am-7pm, Sun. 11am-7pm). Established by Ludwig Moser in Karlovy Vary in 1857, Moser went on to become one of the most respected glassmakers in the world. Known for its elegant beauty and extravagant designs, Moser Glass always makes for a unique, if slightly expensive, gift.

Jewelry

"An exceptional store for exceptional people" is the motto of **Klenotnictví Dušák** (Na Příkopě 1047/17, tel. 224 213 025, www.dusak.cz, Mon.-Fri. 10am-7pm, Sat. 10am-6pm, Sun. 1pm-6pm) and their selection of 31 renowned brands of watches, clocks, and jewels offers just that. Breitling, Omega, Rado, and Montblanc are but a handful of the top-tier manufacturers you'll find here at the flagship store.

Founded in Germany in 1978, **Halada** (Na Příkopě 16, tel. 224 218 643, www.halada.cz, Mon.-Sat. 9am-7pm, Sun. 10am-6pm) serves up innovative designs at the highest possible quality. All kinds of gold and silver are on offer, as well as diamonds, pearls, wedding rings, and colorful gems. It's as classy and as expensive as you'd expect.

Markets

Market at the Fountain (Spálena 30, daily 7:30am-7pm) is a congregation of kiosks located right behind Tesco. Out-of-town farmers come in to peddle their fruit and vegetables, most of which are both cheaper and taste better than what you'll find at, well, Tesco, for example. Various snacks, knickknacks, and weather-appropriate clothing are also sold here at reasonable prices.

Shopping Centers

The **Palladium** (Náměstí republiky 1, tel. 225 770 250, www.palladiumpraha.cz, Sun.-Wed. 9am-9pm, Thurs.-Sat. 9am-10pm) opened in October 2007, reviving the commercial area surrounding Náměstí republiky. Designed

© TOM DIRLIS

the Palladium

with a sense of both the traditional and modern in mind, its fountains, natural lighting, and shopping pavilions have been a hit with shoppers, who have roughly 180 stores and 20 restaurants, cafés, and bars to choose from. With popular shops like Sony, Body Shop, Puma, and Marks & Spencer on the premises, as well as restaurants representing the most popular cuisines from around the world, odds are the Palladium will be a strong commercial contender for a long time to come.

Rather uninspired, despite a couple of name brands like Adidas and Pierre Cardin, **Černá růže** (Na Příkopě 12, tel. 221 014 111, www. cernaruze.cż, Mon.-Fri. 10am-8pm, Sat. 10am-7pm, Sun. 11am-7pm) leaves most of its visitors feeling like spending their money elsewhere. It's worth taking a peek on the off-chance you'll find a bargain, but don't say you weren't warned.

Myslbek Center (Na Příkopě 19-21, tel. 226 209 131, www.myslbek.com, Mon.-Sat. 8:30am-8:30pm, Sun. 9:30am-8:30pm) bustles from the opening bell, with visitors and locals darting in and out of name-brand stores looking for the day's best deal. Pizza Coloseum and Sushi Point are located on the ground floor and first floor, respectively, giving shoppers and nonshoppers at least two solid reasons to come here.

Slim overpriced pickings in the fashion department does not a successful mall make, which is why a visit to **Slovanský Dům** (Na Příkopě 22, tel. 604 904 081, www.slovanskydum.com, daily 10am-8pm) only makes sense if you are visiting the excellent Kogo Ristorante or Ambiente Brasileiro. There is a Cinema City Multiplex, too, which makes for an entertaining and air-conditioned option should you need a break from the crowds or summer heat. Matinee, anyone?

STARÉ MĚSTO
Antiques
If you're looking for accessories that date back to the 1920s or 1930s, **Art Deco** (Michalská 21, tel. 224 223 076, www.artdecogaleriemili.com, Mon.-Fri. 2pm-7pm, Sat. by prior

arrangement) is your best bet. This fun, swingin' store has tons of interesting clothing and bric-a-brac from Prague's golden age, so take your time sifting through everything until you find that treasure you've been looking for all these years. Open since 1990, **Antique V. Andrle** (Křížovnická 1, tel. 222 311 625, www.antiqueandrle.cz, Mon.-Sat. 10am-7pm, Sun. 10am-6pm) continues to offer a highly sophisticated line of antiques that includes necklaces, earrings, paintings, sculptures, ceramics, and grandfather clocks. Serious and novice antiques hunters alike would be wise to check out this well-established dealer during their visit.

Lovers of art deco design will do themselves a great service by paying a visit to **Kubista** (Ovocný trh 19, tel. 224 236 378, www.kubista.cz, Tues.-Sun. 10am-6:30pm). Located on the ground floor of Dům U Černé Matky Boží (House of the Black Madonna), the shop provides visitors with the opportunity to buy exclusive reproductions of original designs by Czech art deco masters like Pavel Janák and Josef Gočár. Original furniture from the period as well posters, postcards, and books are also available.

Cinolter Antiques (Maiselova 9, tel. 222 319 816, www.antiquesprague.cz, daily 9:30am-7pm) was established in 2001 and quickly became one of the city's most respected establishments thanks in part to its relationships with the National Gallery and the Jewish Museum. Antique jewelry, clocks, porcelain, and much more are offered in a pleasant environment by friendly English-speaking assistants happy to help you pick out that elusive piece you've been searching everywhere for.

Books and Music

Music Antiquariat (Týnská 8, tel. 222 317 231, www.musicantiquariat.cz, Mon.-Sat. 10:30am-7pm) lends credence to the belief that vinyl ain't dead. Rare and hard-to-find LPs, 45s, and 12-inch remixes spanning every genre you can think of can be found here, along with tour posters, promotional stills, and funky memorabilia.

Conveniently located between Náměstí republiky and Old Town Square is **BigBen Bookshop** (Malá Štupartská 5, tel. 224 826 565, www.bigbenbookshop.com, Mon.-Fri. 9am-8pm, Sat. 10am-8pm, Sun. 11am-6pm), where you'll find an excellent selection of new titles, classics, children's books, and nonfiction. The shop's friendly staff is always ready to lend a helping hand and will also order any book you're desperately trying to track down.

Disko Duck (Karlova 12, tel. 222 221 696, www.diskoduck.cz, daily 12:30pm-6:30pm) is situated a stone's throw from the Charles Bridge and offers pretty much everything today's hip DJ needs. New 12-inch vinyl and CDs from around the world are imported regularly, adding to their already 5,000-strong record collection that includes house, hip-hop, techno, and jungle. DJ equipment such as turntables, mixers, needles, and headphones are also available.

Maximum Underground (Jilská 22, tel. 724 307 198, www.maximum.cz, Mon.-Sat. 11am-7pm) has something for all music lovers, be it indie, dancehall, dubstep, or ska. Plenty of hard-to-find releases are here, as well as an interesting assortment of independent films on DVD.

Fashion

Timoure et Group (V Kolkovně 6, tel. 222 327 358, www.timoure.cz, Mon.-Fri. 10am-7pm, Sat. 11am-5pm) is a well-known Czech fashion design duo that is popular with local celebrities. Creating minimalist ready-to-wear collections in their own distinct, downplayed style, TEG offers a sophisticated line of clothing and accessories perfect for any occasion.

The Item (Žatecká 8, tel. 777 273 238, www.theitem.cz, Mon.-Fri. 11am-7pm, Sat. 11am-6pm, Sun. noon-5pm) is an eclectic boutique specializing in funky clothes, retro costume jewelry, and vibrant accessories for fashion lovers of all ages. Designs from bygone eras combined with the latest in international fashion make this an excellent choice for anyone with a playful sense of life.

Jozef Sloboda (Rytířská 11, tel. 224 248 971, www.jozefsloboda.cz, daily 11am-7pm) is a boutique for men owned and operated by the famous Czech designer and trendsetter of the same name. Whether it's hip leisurewear you're looking for or something a little more formal for those special nights out, odds are you'll find it here. **Atelier Tatiana** (Dušní 1, tel. 224 813 723, www.tatiana.cz, Mon.-Fri. 10am-7pm, Sat. 11am-4pm) showcases respected designer Tatiana Kováříková's stylish work, which has been worn by actors, singers, and international models. You'll find elegant, funky, and practical formal and casual wear, all at relatively affordable prices.

Galleries

Galerie Jakubská (Jakubská 4, tel. 224 827 926, www.galeriejakubska.cz, daily 10am-8pm) revolves around the bold work of Ukrainian-born impressionist painter Alexandr Onishenko. Exhibited all over the world, his vibrant paintings depict lush landscapes, lifelike animals, and a haunting Gothic view of Prague. Many of the paintings available here will stay with you long after you've left.

Galerie Art Praha (Staroměstské náměstí 20, tel. 224 211 087, www.galerieartpraha.cz, Mon.-Fri. 10:30am-6pm, Sat. 10:30am-5pm) has an extensive collection of paintings from some of the more daring and innovative Czech and Slovak artists of the 20th century. The staff is extremely helpful and knowledgeable and will be more than happy to help you find what you're looking for, even if you're unable to properly express what exactly that is.

Gagik Manoukian's Gallery of Modern Art (Jilská 9, tel. 608 557 679, www.gagik-gallery.com, daily noon-7pm) was founded by Armenian-born Gagik and offers striking work influenced by cubism, expressionism, and the avant-garde. Dynamic colors, sharp contrasts, and playful textures of light abound in this warm and welcoming shop. (There is also a second location at Husova 8, with the same contact details and business hours.)

The finest painters and sculptors in the country are regularly exhibited at **Galerie Gambit** (Řetězová 7, tel. 602 277 210, www.

gambitgalerie.cz, Tues.-Fri. noon-6pm). Anything goes, from more traditional works inspired by the streets of Prague to airy, metallic installations that bend perspectives and meaning. This is an excellent choice for art aficionados.

Gifts

Just off Na Příkopě is **Dům Hraček Sparkys** (Havířská 2, tel. 224 239 309, www.sparkys.cz, daily 10am-7pm). Three colorful floors are filled with toys ranging from stuffed animals to board games and action figures. Affordable and centrally located, this is the place to come to when it's time to pick up something for the kids.

Growing all the necessary ingredients on their organic Gardens Complex in the tiny village of Ostrá, **Dr. Stuart's Botanicus Shops** (Týn 3, tel. 234 767 446, www.botanicus.cz, daily 10am-6:30pm) offer health and beauty products with a natural touch. Whether it's cosmetics, soaps, teas, spices, or candles you're looking for, you'll be able to buy it here and feel good about not hurting Mother Earth in the process.

Traditional (Haštalská 7, tel. 222 316 661, www.traditional.cz, daily 10am-6pm) is a small shop selling one of the few remaining collections of antique print blocks for textile printing. All blocks are beautifully hand-carved, functional antiques dating as far back as 1800 and offer an excellent opportunity to own a truly authentic piece of Czech history.

Glass

Named after a group of Bohemian artisans from the early 1900s, **Artêl Style** (Celetná 29, tel. 224 815 085, www.artelstyle.com, daily 10am-7pm) offers elegant handmade crystal pieces meant to last a lifetime. From hand-blown molten crystal to whimsically innovative collector's items, Artêl has something for every glassware enthusiast.

Bořek Šípek (Valentinská 11, tel. 602 322 169, www.boreksipek.com, Mon.-Fri. 10am-6pm, Sat.-Sun. 11am-5pm) offers top-of-the-line glass products, including vases, bowls,

Cristallino offers one of Prague's largest selections of glassware.

© TOM DIRLIS

tables, and chandeliers, all of which echo a classy neo-baroque design. Those wishing to begin a collection or complement an already existing one would be wise to begin here.

Cristallino (Celetná 12, tel. 224 225 173, www.cristallino.cz, Jan.-Mar. daily 9am-7pm, Apr.-Dec. daily 9am-8pm) is a huge shop near Old Town Square offering one of Prague's largest selections of both traditional and modern glassware. Bohemian crystal, porcelain, and jewelry can be found as well, not to mention gorgeous chandeliers and unique folk art that make for memorable gifts. The friendly and knowledgeable service is a breath of fresh air compared to other, stuffier establishments.

Located right in the heart of Old Town Square, **Erpet Bohemia Crystal** (Staroměstské náměstí 27, tel. 224 229 755, www.erpetcrystal.cz, daily 10am-11pm) is home to a large variety of gorgeous hand-cut lead crystal, color-cut crystal, chandeliers, lamps, and all kinds of handmade glass and jewelry. Easily one of the best-known shops in Prague, it is also one of the priciest.

Housed in a lovely Renaissance building in the historic Ungelt courtyard, **Material** (Týn 1, tel. 608 664 766, www.i-material.com, daily 10:30am-8pm) features the work of owner and avant-garde artist Tomáš Kysela. Glass beads, chandeliers, drinking glasses. and more are on display, as are his hugely popular and eye-catching vases that change color according to how they're backlit. It's well worth a look.

Preciosa (Jáchymova 26/2, tel. 488 118 106, www.preciosa.com, Mon.-Fri. 10am-7pm, Sat. 11am-6pm, Sun. 11am-5pm) specializes in finely cut crystal shaped into jewelry, chandeliers, figurines, and decorative light fixtures. This is the place to visit for authentic top-of-the-line Czech craftsmanship.

Jewelry
Klenotnictví Köttner (Havířská 5, tel. 222 212 484, www.kottner.cz, Mon.-Fri. 10am-6pm, Sat. 10am-6pm) was originally opened in 1919 and has been at the forefront of upscale traditional jewelry ever since. Pearls, wedding rings, diamond bracelets, and luxury earrings await at one of the city's most trusted and respected jewelers.

Markets
Melantrichova Street picks up where Wenceslas Square leaves off, connecting it with Old Town Square. Halfway to the Old Town, you'll come upon open-air **Havelský Market** (Havelská ulice, Mon.-Fri. 7:30am-6pm, Sat.-Sun. 8:30am-6pm). This is an excellent place to get fresh fruit and vegetables, although many of the stalls have given themselves over to the tourist trade, hawking anything from subpar paintings to fragile wooden knickknacks. Careful browsing should land you a decent deal or two, however.

Specialty Shops
Qubus (Rámová 3, tel. 222 313 151, www.qubus.cz, Mon.-Sat. 11am-7pm) is undoubtedly one of Prague's coolest home-decor boutiques. Selling conceptual pieces by Czech designer

Maxim Velčovský as well as a diverse selection of European furnishings, the shop is full of sleek and modern furniture, cute utensils, accessories, and popular gift items like flower vases shaped like white porcelain boots. **De.co by de.fakto** (Vejvodova 447/3, tel. 224 233 815, www.defakto.cz, Mon.-Fri. 9:30am-6pm, Sat. 9:30am-4pm, closed Sat. July-Aug.) is a funky boutique specializing in decorations for the home and designer kitchenware. There are loads of interesting gift ideas, from subtle silver clocks to brightly colored cutlery, glasses, and bowls.

MALÁ STRANA
Antiques
Ahasver (Prokopská 3, tel. 257 531 404, www.ahasver.com, Tues.-Sun. 11am-6pm) is a charming little shop in the prettiest part of town, and it deals primarily with antique and folk clothing. A wide range of gowns and accessories are available, including purses, brooches, jewelry, and lace. This is a step back in time if ever there was one.

Vetešnictvi (Vítězná 16, tel. 257 310 611, Mon.-Fri. 10am-5pm) is a veritable grab bag of antiques, historically significant items, and good old-fashioned junk. Dig around and you'll find just about anything here, including furniture, tools, medals, postcards, beer mugs, and who knows what else. A lot of this stuff is from the Communist era, which might explain the bust of Lenin overseeing the shop.

Books and Music
Shakespeare & Sons (U Lužického semináře 10, tel. 257 531 894, www.shakes.cz, daily 11am-7pm) does little to curb the exorbitant prices locals are forced to pay in order to remain literate, but you will find an excellent selection of books ranging from cookbooks to gender studies to psychology and sci-fi. Expect lots of Czech authors and high lit as well, all of which makes for a pleasant afternoon of reading in nearby Kampa Park.

Galleries
Located near the Old Castle Steps, **ArtSen** (Thunovská 19, tel. 776 070 703, www.artsen.cz, daily 10:30am-6pm) is a small gallery offering authentic paintings of Prague and its tourist-friendly environs. There's nothing mind-blowing here, but it's a good place to pick something up if your taste leans toward a more conventional palette.

Galerie Kodl (Vítězná 11, tel. 251 512 728, www.galeriekodl.cz, Mon.-Fri. 10am-1pm and 2pm-6pm) is a family tradition that dates back over 100 years. Both an auction house and a gallery, this is a must for art lovers looking to expand their collections. The paintings, drawings, graphics, and sculptures on display represent some of the finest talent working in the country today. The gallery is known throughout the continent for its professionalism and expertise.

Not far from Charles Bridge is the excellent **Gallery U Zlatého Beránka** (Míšeňská 67/10, tel. 257 534 940, www.jstastny.com, daily noon-7pm) which is owned and operated by resident painter Jiří Šťastný. Eye-catching art reflecting Prague's breathtaking architecture as well as thought-provoking abstract and representational work by Šťastný and other Eastern European artists make this charming gallery essential for both the educated and amateur art fan.

Galerie Peron (U Lužického semináře 12, tel. 257 533 419, www.peron.cz, Mon.-Fri. 11am-6pm, Sat.-Sun. noon-6pm) is one of the neighborhood's longest-running galleries, and with good reason. Specializing in superb late-20th-century Czech fine arts and design, it also keeps art fans and collectors satisfied by hosting regular auctions of its paintings, sculptures, furniture, and glass. It's well worth a look.

Gifts
Blue Praha (Mostecká 12, tel. 257 533 716, www.bluepraha.cz, daily 10:15am-7:15pm) offers a wide variety of gift items, including books, T-shirts, and random knickknacks that make for small inexpensive gifts. There are also a number of traditional glass works available in both classic and modern styles.

© TOM DIRLIS

The Czech Beer Shop sells the country's most popular product.

A gift from Prague that never fails to make an impression is a handcrafted marionette, which is exactly what you'll find next to Charles Bridge at **Marionety Truhlář** (U Lužického semináře 5, tel. 602 689 918, www.marionety.com, daily 10am-7pm). A far cry from the mass-produced miniature examples found on any heavily touristed street, this shop takes special care preserving the unique quality any fine doll should have. Sure, it's a little

pricey, but it'll remind you of magical Prague for the rest of your life.

Kunstkomora (Lázeňská 9, tel. 246 028 019, www.kunstkomora.cz, Tues.-Sat. 11am-7pm) is one of the more interesting shops in town thanks to its impressive collection of art, antiques, and curiosities hailing from all around the world. You'll find fantastic collections inspired by Rudolf II and Peter the Great as well as remarkable historical, geological, religious, and ethnographical objects that'll boggle the mind and bruise the wallet.

From teddy bears to bedroom sets, **L'Architecte de l'Enfant** (Karmelitská 18, tel. 257 530 421, www.vibel.com, Tues.-Fri. 10am-7pm, Sat. 10am-6pm) has got everything your adorable young son or daughter might need. Vibrant colors and imaginative themes such as Space, Fish, and Cat create a warm, affectionate environment any parent would envy. Buying the heavy furniture on display certainly isn't practical, but you're bound to find some very pretty accessories that might not be available back home.

If you take the first left coming off Charles Bridge, you'll find the **Czech Beer Shop** (Lázeňská 15, tel. 257 532 687, www.czechbeershop.com, daily 10am-6pm), selling bottles and cases and kegs, oh my! A decent selection of domestic brews are available here, and you'll be wise to inform yourself of whatever customs laws apply to you before making a large impulsive purchase. Then again, you could always take your haul to nearby Kampa Park and imbibe it there.

Sports and Recreation

Keeping active and fit is a national pastime in the Czech Republic, which explains why the problem of obesity that has plagued North America hasn't reared its ugly head here. Traditional activities like hiking and swimming are de rigueur on the weekends as Czechs head for their cottages and spend countless hours in their beloved forests and rivers. Cycling and

in-line roller-skating are also very popular, with countless couples and groups of friends suiting up and hitting the trails. The upwardly mobile and business-oriented have gotten in on the act as well, generating an interest in golf and squash that was practically nonexistent a few years ago. Interest in sports has continued to grow, bringing with it both an increase and improvement in facilities that have made it easier than ever for visitors to maintain a healthy lifestyle during their stay.

BILLIARDS

Billiard-Centrum V Cípu (V Cípu 1, Nové Město, tel. 725 857 458, www.billiardcentrum. cz, daily 11am-2am) is a dilapidated yet grandiose pool hall hidden down an alley not far from Wenceslas Square. High ceilings, crystal chandeliers, and cavernous surroundings are what you can expect, along with plenty of well-maintained billiard and snooker tables. There's a bowling alley, a table-tennis room, and plenty of dart boards as well, making this an excellent choice for anyone in a playful frame of mind.

Akademie Billiard Club (Šmeralova 5, Holešovice, tel. 233 375 236, daily 4pm-4am) is a medium-size pool hall where billiards enthusiasts and first-timers play until well past midnight. Cheap beer, decent tables, and a jukebox full of hard rock and cheesy pop songs complete the picture.

BOWLING

Located near the Masarykovo train station, **Bowling Celnice** (V Celnici 10, Nové Město, tel. 221 033 020, www.bowlingcelnice.cz, Sun.-Thurs. noon-midnight, Fri.-Sat. noon-2am) is a modern bowling alley offering visitors the finest amenities in town as well as top-of-the-line pool tables and dart boards. Reserving a lane in advance is strongly recommended, as birthdays and office parties are held here on a regular basis.

CLIMBING

Adrenaline Pit (Václavské náměstí 835/15, Nové Město, tel. 224 232 752, www.adrenalinepit.cz, Mon.-Thurs. 7am-11pm, Fri. 7am-10pm, Sat. 9am-10pm, Sun. 9am-11pm) is a modern, centrally located indoor climbing environment featuring a 36-foot climbing wall, 22 climbing lanes, and an overhang of approximately 30 feet. You'll also find squash courts, massage and sauna facilities, and a bar to cool off at after your body's had enough healthy activity for one day.

CYCLING

One fun way to travel around Prague is by bicycle, and **City Bike** (Králodvorská 5, Staré Město, tel. 776 180 284, www.pragueonline. cz/citybike, Apr.-Oct. daily 9am-7pm, tours 10am, 2pm, and sunset) is the place to go should you feel the same way. Their rental rates are affordable, and they offer free group rides three times a day led by locals who know their way around.

FITNESS CENTERS

Delroy's Gym (Zborovská 4, Smíchov, tel. 776 373 322, www.delroys-gym.cz, Mon.-Fri. 10am-6pm, Sat. 10am-4pm) has been the martial-arts center of choice for Czechs, foreigners, politicians, and visiting celebrities since Delroy Scarlett established it in 1993. Friendly, affordable, and relatively near the center, this is a great place to go if you need to take out some frustration on a punching bag or simply hit the weights in a friendly environment.

Renovated in 2009, the **Health Club and Spa InterContinental** (Náměstí Curieových 43, Staré Město, tel. 296 631 525, www.intercontinental.com/prague, Mon.-Fri. 6am-11pm, Sat.-Sun. 8am-10pm), features 10,000 square feet of top-notch cardio and workout facilities as well as saunas, solariums, a whirlpool, and a swimming pool. It's a little on the upscale side, as you might expect, but the state-of-the-art machines and exceptional trainers make it worth the extra expense.

If all that heavy Czech food is starting to make you feel sluggish, head for **Sportcentrum YMCA** (Na Poříčí 12, Nové Město, tel. 224 875 811, www.scymca.cz, Mon.-Thurs. 6:30am-10pm, Fri. 6:30am-9pm, Sat. 9am-7pm, Sun. 10am-9pm). You'll find the same services that people have come to expect from the YMCA elsewhere, including a weight room, a swimming pool, a sauna, and massages. Less busy than most gyms and more affordable to boot, the Y is a reasonable alternative when you're looking for a simple workout without the frills.

Certainly the most central and arguably the

Aye, That's the Rub!

Prague's Asian population continues to grow steadily, as evidenced by the vast array of restaurants, textile shops, convenience stores, and fruit and vegetable stands that continue to pop up across the city. Thai massage is the latest import from the Far East to have caught on here, with new studios opening in the choicest parts of town on a regular basis.

It's believed that Thai massage was developed over 2,500 years ago in India before it made its way to Thailand, where Ayurvedic techniques and principles were gradually influenced by traditional forms of Chinese medicine. The result is a form of massage wherein the therapist uses their hands, knees, legs, and feet to move you into a series of yoga-like stretches, which is why Thai massage is also commonly referred to as "Thai yoga massage." Muscle compression, joint mobilization, and acupressure are also used during treatment, which can last one to two hours and leave you feeling both relaxed and energized at the same time.

Here's a short list of some of the more popular massage studios in town that can help take the aches and pains away after a long day of sightseeing. Make sure to pay their websites a visit before visiting to see which massage

and price range is most suited to your needs and budget.

· **Nam Jai** (Kaprova 11, tel. 222 328 747, www.namjai.cz) is located just off Old Town Square in Josefov and offers traditional back and head massage, full-body hot-stone massage, foot reflexology massage, and a whole lot more.

· **Mystic Temple** (Politických vězňů 1599/25, tel. 221 779 510, www.mystic-temple.cz) is located near the National Theater and offers a variety of massages with alluring names such as Spirit of Siam and Dark Side of the Moon.

· **Thai Fit** (Vodičkova 41, tel. 224 152 016, www.thaifit.cz) can be found near Wenceslas Square and has the honor of being Prague's oldest Thai massage studio. It offers traditional Thai massage, lava stone massage, and a romantic massage for two.

· **Thai World** (Na Můstku 1, tel. 224 225 710, www.thai-world.cz) is one of Prague's largest and best known studios, conveniently located a stone's throw from the Můstek subway station. Reasonable prices and expertise in a number of traditional massages are what you can expect here.

most fashionable, **World Class Fitness Center Prague** (Václavské náměstí 22, Nové Město, tel. 224 282 899, www.worldclass.cz, Mon.-Fri. 6am-10:30pm, Sat. 7am-10pm, Sun. 9am-10pm) is an enormous multilevel health club spanning over 19,000 square feet and offering everything any health nut could want. Whether it's aerobics, weights, saunas, tanning beds, or a wide range of cardio machines you're looking for, look no further.

GOLF

Golf has started to catch on in the Czech Republic, and the **Erpet GolfCentrum** (Strakonická 2860/4, Smíchov, tel. 296 373 111, www.erpetgolfcentrum.cz, daily

8am-11pm) has established itself firmly as *the* indoor golf center in town. The center comes complete with a two-story driving range, four golf simulators offering players more than 30 world-renowned courses to choose from, and the Astar Learning system, which helps users perfect their swing. Reservations are recommended.

Golf Club Praha (Plzeňská 401/2, Smíchov, tel. 257 216 584, www.gcp.cz, daily 7am-sunset) is Prague's only outdoor course, a nine-hole affair that also includes a training area, a clubhouse, and a restaurant. Falling short of most golf enthusiasts' expectations, the course may cure your immediate itch to get a game in, but it won't satisfy it completely.

IN-LINE ROLLER-SKATING

Arguably the best place for in-line roller-skating in Prague, **Ladronka In-Line Park** (Ladronka Park, Ke Kotlářce St. and Plzeňská St., Dejvice, tel. 775 082 858, www.ladronka.cz, daily noon-9pm) provides a flat, perfectly refurbished, 2.4-mile-long surface completely devoid of pedestrians, dogs, or baby carriages (they have their own path). Admittedly, Ladronka is a little off the beaten path, but many flock to it, having tired of the incessant crowds at both Letná and Stromovka Parks.

SQUASH

Squash-Haštal (Haštalská 20, Nové Město, tel. 224 828 561, www.squash-hastal.cz, Mon.-Thurs. 7am-11pm, Fri. 7am-9pm, Sat.-Sun. 9am-9pm) is an excellent choice located in the heart of downtown. Six climate-controlled courts are available, as is a fitness bar, a sauna, and a cardio-centric gym. Reservations are recommended.

Squash and Fitness Centrum Arbes (Arbesovo náměstí 15, Smíchov, tel. 257 326 041, www.squasharbes.cz, Mon.-Fri. 7am-11pm, Sat.-Sun. 9am-11pm) offers visitors four squash courts that unfortunately always seem to be reserved before normal working hours begin (7am-9am) as well as after they end (5pm-7pm). Your best bet is to try your hand—or racket—during the middle of the day. Reservations are recommended, however, as the place does steady business thanks to its relatively central location.

SWIMMING

Prague's outdoor pools tend to fill up quickly during the summer, but if crowds aren't your thing, opt for the indoor pool at **Hotel Axa** (Na Poříčí 40, Nové Město, tel. 222 323 967, www.bazenaxa.cz, daily 7am-9pm and 5pm-10pm). Rarely occupied and open year-round to both guests and the public, this 82-foot-long pool is a great place to get in a good swim either at the beginning or the end of the day.

A veritable landmark in the field of sports facilities, **Plavecký Stadion Podoli** (Podolská 74, Podoli, tel. 241 433 952, www.pspodoli. cz, daily 6am-9:45pm) hasn't changed much over the decades yet remains as popular as ever. The large outdoor pool is jam-packed during the warmer months, while the Olympic-size indoor pool attracts a more dedicated and athletic group. You'll also find a weight room, a sauna, and a fitness shop on the premises, along with a huge lawn for soaking up rays during the summer.

Should you find yourself in Dejvice, check out the excellent outdoor swimming pool in the middle of **Divoká Šárka** (June daily 10am-6pm, July-Aug. daily 9am-7pm, Sept. if weather permits, 50 Kč over age 10, 20 Kč ages 5-10, free under age 5, 40 Kč seniors).

TENNIS

Founded in 1893, **ČLTK** (Štvanice 38, Holešovice, tel. 222 316 317, www.cltk.cz, daily 7am-midnight) is easily the Czech Republic's oldest and most prestigious tennis club. Located on Štvanice Island in Holešovice, the complex offers 14 outdoor clay courts as well as 6 indoor courts. The central court hosts up to 8,000 spectators and is the annual scene of various Association of Tennis Professionals and Women's Tennis Association tournaments. Reservations are absolutely necessary.

Neighboring the Letná Beer Garden is **Tenisový Klub Slavia Praha** (Letenské sady 32, Holešovice, tel. 233 374 033, www.volny.cz/tkslavia, indoors Nov.-Mar. daily 7am-9pm, outdoors Apr. 15-Oct. 15 daily 7am-9pm). Equipped with eight outdoor clay courts along with a tennis bubble for the colder months, this well-respected tennis club also offers tennis lessons and hosts year-round tournaments.

YOGA

Not far from Wenceslas Square is **YogaJoga Studio** (Školská 12, Nové Město, tel. 775 237 930, www.yogajoga.cz). Reservations must be made online in advance for classes, which include Iyengar, Vinyasa Flow, Power Yoga, Dynamic Yoga, Hatha Yoga, Prana Vashya Yoga, Ashtanga Vinyasa Yoga, and Kundalini Yoga. Private lessons and pregnancy yoga are also available.

Kundalini Yoga Center (Jindřišská 10, Nové Město, tel. 733 512 906, www.kundaliniyoga.cz) is an intimate studio located in the center of Prague that has been keeping Czechs and foreigners healthy since its opening in 2010. Modern changing rooms, showers, and a tea bar make sessions here both a pleasant and invigorating experience. Check the website for the current class schedule.

SPECTATOR SPORTS

If you ask a Czech what the national sport is, odds are they'll shrug their shoulders and tell you it's a toss-up between ice hockey and soccer. When it comes to the former, the Czech Republic has plenty to boast about. Not only have they consistently placed near the top of every important international tournament, including winning the gold medal at the 1998 winter Olympics, they also have a remarkable number of superstars dominating North America's National Hockey League. And while their soccer team isn't quite as impressive, world-famous players like Pavel Nedvěd have kept World Cup hopes alive and fans riveted to their TV sets. Most players who demonstrate excellence in either sport tend to head for larger markets and bigger paychecks, but that doesn't stop Czechs from following both sports religiously, filling up hockey rinks and soccer stadiums every time play-off season arrives. Tickets are very affordable, and the possibility of seeing tomorrow's stars play their hearts out today adds an element of excitement to the games that is often lacking in more established leagues.

Ice Hockey

Having settled in nicely at O2 Arena, **HC Slavia Praha** (O2 Arena, Ocelářská St. 2, Českomoravská, www.hc-slavia.cz) finally won its first championship in 2003. The team's die-hard fans make going to any game a unique experience, but if you really want to see them go rabid with emotion, make sure to get a ticket when they play longtime rivals HC Sparta Praha.

HC Sparta Praha (Tipsport Arena, Za Elektrárnou 419, Holešovice, tel. 266 727 454, www.hcsparta.cz) is Prague's most popular hockey team. Well financed and well managed, they dominate during the regular season and are consistently a force to be reckoned with during the play-offs. Tickets are always available for home games, though you might want to think about reserving in advance when it comes to postseason play.

Soccer

AC Sparta Praha (Toyota Arena, Milady Horákové 98, Holešovice, tel. 296 111 400, www.sparta.cz) is without a doubt the most successful soccer team in the country and well-known for its rowdy and faithful followers. They won their 35th Czech championship in 2010 and continue to be a thorn in the side of larger, better-known teams during international tournaments. A trip to one of their matches will prove a memorable experience for even less serious fans of the game.

Playing in a modest stadium to fans who for the most part look like they cashed their pension checks on the way to the game, **FK Viktoria Žižkov** (Stadion FK Viktoria Žižkov, Seifertova třída, Žižkov, tel. 221 423 427, www.fkvz.cz) is the city's underdog, to say the least. Nobody expects much from this team, especially since they were relegated in 2003 and nailed for match-fixing in 2004. Back in the first division, nobody considers them to be a challenge for the league title, but that doesn't stop their loyal fans from coming out and enjoying the day.

Despite its devoted fans and ability to occasionally overcome unbeatable odds, **SK Slavia Praha** (Eden Arena, Vladivostocká 2, Vršovice, tel. 233 081 751, www.slavia.cz) continues to place second in the division standings behind cross-town rivals Sparta Praha. They are certainly worth a shot should you happen to find yourself in tourist-free Prague 10.

Horse Racing

Running April-October, **Chuchle** (Radotínská 69, Radotín, www.velka-chuchle.cz) offers flat racing every Sunday starting at 2pm. The

Czech Derby is held here in June, giving fans one last opportunity to enjoy a day at the track before shutting down till the end of August. Those interested in betting on the ponies should take note that bookmakers are not allowed at the track. Rather, a tote betting system is in place that pools all bets and shares the total among the winning tickets. There is also a very unpopular 5 percent betting tax added to all bets.

Accommodations

Rates keep climbing as Prague establishes itself as one of Europe's hottest travel destinations. Great deals can still be found online, however, with many hotels offering package deals and holiday specials. Booking in advance will save you some cash, as will having your meals and drinks away from the hotel's premises, where considerably cheaper prices can be found.

NOVÉ MĚSTO

New Town is the hub of all things commercial and tourist-oriented, which means staying here guarantees you a wide selection of hotels, restaurants, and shops. It also means you'll be right in the thick of things, part of the mass that moves up and down Wenceslas Square and the surrounding area. Many like the energetic feel of the district, while others tire quickly of the bustle and late-night antics of drunken revelers. Its proximity to Old Town, as well as Vinohrady and Žižkov, make staying here a strategically wise choice if you plan on doing some exploring outside the downtown core.

1,000-2,000 Kč

What **AZ Hostel** (Jindřišská 5, tel. 224 241 664, www.hostel-az.com, 1,980 Kč d) lacks in character, it more than makes up for in location. Within spitting distance of Wenceslas Square, it's about as central as it gets and guarantees you will see all of what downtown has to offer without ever having to step foot on a subway or tram. The 1- to 7-bed rooms plus a dormitory are clean and spacious, and the staff is on call 24 hours a day should you need assistance. Although it may not have the charm of some of the more colorful hostels in town,

you'll get maximum value in terms of price and convenience.

The centrally-located **Bontour Hostel** (Myslíkova 22, tel. 224 922 097, http://bontour.prague-hostels.cz, 1,600 Kč d) offers double, triple, and quadruple rooms that are as Spartan as they are clean. Tea and coffee are on the house, as is a storage room should you need to stow away any heavy luggage. The service can be awfully spotty, but the reasonable price and proximity to all of Prague's major sights more than makes up for it.

Another affordable option just minutes from both Wenceslas Square and Old Town Square is **Prague Hostel Rosemary** (Růžová 5, tel. 222 211 124, www.praguecityhostel.cz, 1,700 Kč d). On offer are dormitory beds, 1- to 6-bed rooms with private baths and kitchens, and less-expensive 2- to 6-bed private rooms that share a bath. Clean and friendly, there are also two computers available that offer free Internet as well as a common room where you can meet other like-minded travelers. It's pretty basic fare, but the price is right and the location is top-notch.

Hostel City Center (Ječná 12, tel. 266 315 266, www.hostel-citycenter.cz, 1,800 Kč d) is just a few minutes' walk to Wenceslas Square and all things central. Free Internet, Wi-Fi, and storage complement single, double, triple, and quadruple rooms which are clean, quiet, and serviced by a helpful and friendly staff. It's a solid choice for the no-frills traveler.

2,000-3,000 Kč

Pension Museum (Mezibranská 15, tel. 296 325 186, www.pension-museum.cz, 2,500 Kč d) is located mere steps from the National

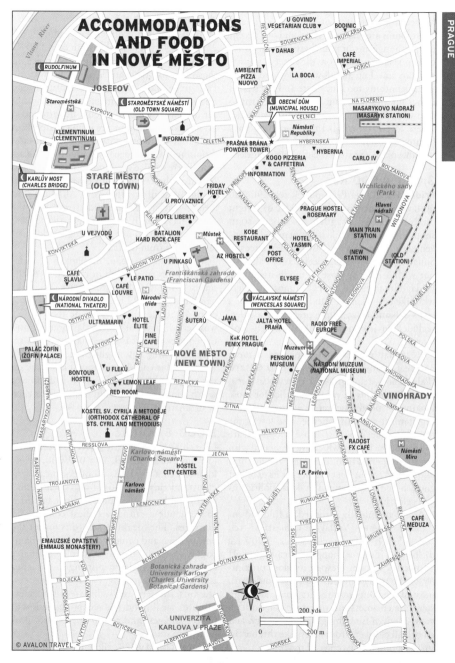

ACCOMMODATIONS AND FOOD IN NOVÉ MĚSTO

Vltava River

RUDOLFINUM

JOSEFOV

Staroměstská

KAPROVA

STAROMĚSTSKÉ NÁMĚSTÍ (OLD TOWN SQUARE)

KLEMENTINUM (CLEMENTINUM)

INFORMATION

CELETNÁ

MELANTRICHOVA

KARLŮV MOST (CHARLES BRIDGE)

STARÉ MĚSTO (OLD TOWN)

PERLOVÁ

U PROVAZNICE

HOTEL LIBERTY

U VEJVODŮ

KONVIKTSKÁ

BATALION HARD ROCK CAFE

Můstek

NÁRODNÍ TŘÍDA

U PINKASŮ

CAFÉ SLAVIA

LE PATIO

CAFÉ LOUVRE

Františkánská zahrada (Franciscan Gardens)

NÁRODNÍ DIVADLO (NATIONAL THEATER)

Národní třída

OSTROVNÍ

ULTRAMARIN

HOTEL ÉLITE

VLADISLAVOVA

U ŠUTERŮ

JÁMA

FINE CAFÉ

JUNGMANNOVA

PALÁC ŽOFÍN (ŽOFÍN PALACE)

OPATOVICKÁ

SPÁLENÁ

LÁZARSKÁ

MASARYKOVO NÁBŘEŽÍ

DITTRICHOVA

BONTOUR HOSTEL

MYSLÍKOVA

U FLEKŮ

LEMON LEAF

RED ROOM

NOVÉ MĚSTO (NEW TOWN)

ŠTĚPÁNSKÁ

REZNICKÁ

RAŠÍNOVO NÁBŘEŽÍ

TROJANOVA

NA MORÁNI

KOSTEL SV. CYRILA A METODĚJE (ORTHODOX CATHEDRAL OF STS. CYRIL AND METHODIUS)

ŽITNÁ

VE SMEČKÁCH

KRAKOVSKÁ

RESSLOVA

KARLOVO

Karlovo náměstí (Charles Square)

HOSTEL CITY CENTER

JEČNÁ

VYŠEHRADSKÁ

Karlovo náměstí

U NEMOCNICE

LIPOVÁ

KATEŘINSKÁ

EMAUZSKÉ OPATSTVÍ (EMMAUS MONASTERY)

TROJICKÁ

SLOVANY

POD SLOVANY

PODSKALSKÁ

NA STUPNI

BOTIČSKÁ

VLASTOU

Botanická zahrada University Karlovy (Charles University Botanical Gardens)

VINIČNÁ

BENÁTSKÁ

APOLINÁŘSKÁ

KE KARLOVU

UNIVERZITA KARLOVA V PRAZE

ALBERTOV

HLAVOVA

STUDNIČKOVA

HORSKÁ

0   200 yds
0   200 m

U GOVINDY VEGETARIAN CLUB

BODINIC

REVOLUČNÍ

SOUKENICKÁ

TRUHLÁŘSKÁ

DAHAB

AMBIENTE PIZZA NUOVO

LA BOCA

CAFÉ IMPERIAL

NA POŘÍČÍ

KRÁLODVORSKÁ

OBECNÍ DŮM (MUNICIPAL HOUSE)

Náměstí Republiky

NA FLORENCI

MASARYKOVO NÁDRAŽÍ (MASARYK STATION)

V CELNICI

PRAŠNÁ BRÁNA (POWDER TOWER)

HYBERNSKÁ

KOGO PIZZERIA & CAFFETERIA

HYBERNIA

CARLO IV

BOLZANOVA

INFORMATION

FRIDAY HOTEL

NA PŘÍKOPĚ

PANSKÁ

NEKÁZANKA

SENOVÁŽNÁ

Vrchlického sady (Park)

JINDŘIŠSKÁ

PRAGUE HOSTEL ROSEMARY

OPLETALOVA

WILSONOVA

Hlavní nádraží

KOBE RESTAURANT

HOTEL YASMIN

RŮŽOVÁ

MAIN TRAIN STATION (NEW STATION)

AZ HOSTEL

POST OFFICE

POLITICKÝCH

ELYSEE

VÁCLAVSKÉ NÁMĚSTÍ (WENCESLAS SQUARE)

OPLETALOVA

OPLETALOVA VEZNI

WASHINGTONOVA

WILSONOVA

(OLD STATION)

ŠPANĚLSKÁ

JALTA HOTEL PRAHA

RADIO FREE EUROPE

K+K HOTEL FENIX PRAGUE

Muzeum

NÁRODNÍ MUZEUM (NATIONAL MUSEUM)

POLSKÁ

MÁNESOVA

PENSION MUSEUM

MEZIBRANSKÁ

LEGEROVA

RUBEŠOVA

BĚLEHRADSKÁ

VINOHRADSKÁ

VINOHRADY

BALBÍNOVA

RÍMSKÁ

ANGLICKÁ

HÁLKOVA

RADOST FX CAFÉ

Náměstí Miru

I.P. Pavlova

RUMUNSKÁ

LUBLAŇSKÁ

ŠAFAŘÍKOVA

LONDÝNSKÁ

AMERICKÁ

TYRŠOVA

SOKOLSKÁ

KOUBKOVA

BRUSELSKÁ

BĚLGICKÁ

CAFÉ MEDUZA

LEGEROVA

WENZIGOVA

ZÁHŘEBSKÁ

BĚLEHRADSKÁ

FRIČOVA

© AVALON TRAVEL

Museum and the top of Wenceslas Square. Most rooms are relatively clean and of a decent size, although it's in your best interest to request one facing away from the street as tourists and cars travel up and down it day and night. There's nothing too fancy here and the staff is rather hit and miss, but if you don't want to deal with taxis or it's important to have somewhere to put down all those shopping bags before going out to dinner, then this is one affordable place you should definitely consider.

3,000-4,000 Kč

Friday Hotel (Na Příkopě 13, tel. 296 200 300, www.fridayhotel.cz, 3,100 Kč d) is right on Na Příkopě, Prague's busy pedestrian shopping area, which just happens to be conveniently close to Old Town and Wenceslas Square. Focusing on classical luxury balanced out with a healthy dose of modernism, the Friday Hotel should appeal to most travelers who like being smack-dab in the middle of a city's ebb and flow. Those preferring a quiet, secluded environment should definitely look elsewhere.

Reasonably priced and located a mere 330 feet from Wenceslas Square, **U Šuterů** (Palackého 4, tel. 224 948 235, www.usuteru.cz, 3,300 Kč d) is an excellent choice for those looking to spend moderately without sacrificing comfort and convenience. The loft at the top of the hotel's spiral staircase is lovely, as are the rest of the rooms, which are decorated with traditional period furniture. Their restaurant is also known throughout the city for its excellent goulash and is frequented by local politicians and celebrities.

Many are initially surprised to find the entrance to **Elysee** (Václavské náměstí 43, tel. 221 455 111, www.hotelelysee.cz, 3,900 Kč d) located inside a shopping arcade just off Wenceslas Square. Despite its close proximity to the unceasing bustle of the boulevard, most of the 70 rooms are very quiet, although some are enclosed and therefore don't offer a view. Modern furnishings, tight security, and an overall clean environment make this hotel a smart option in the center of town.

4,000-5,000 Kč

◖ **Hotel Yasmin** (Politických vězňů 12, tel. 234 100 100, www.hotel-yasmin.cz, 4,900 Kč d) has been the accommodations of choice for those who like their hotels modern yet warm. Pale green walls, big hairy sculptures, and floating trees and ornaments are just some of the decorative curiosities you'll be surrounded by. All rooms and suites are immaculately kept and come equipped with minibars, air-conditioning, LCD-screen TVs, and Internet access. There's a nice gym and sauna as well, and Noodles, the restaurant-café-bar, offers tasty cuisine from all over the world. Although situated on a relatively quiet side street, take the extra precaution if you're a light sleeper and request a room on one of the higher floors or facing away from traffic.

You'll find 94 clean, modern, and functional rooms smack-dab in the center of the tourist town at **Jalta Hotel Praha** (Václavské náměstí 45, tel. 222 822 111, www.hoteljalta.com, 4,950 Kč d). Some of the rooms offer wonderful views of Wenceslas Square, and the courteous staff is more than happy to arrange anything you might need. The trendy and reputable COMO restaurant is located on the ground floor as well, and it is definitely worth a meal or two should you have the time or inclination.

5,000-6,000 Kč

Like all K+K Hotels, the ◖ **K+K Hotel Fenix** (Ve Smečkách 30, tel. 225 012 000, www.kkhotels.com, 5,150 Kč d) offers guests spacious and tidy communal areas, clean and comfortable rooms, and excellent facilities that include a sauna, a fitness center, and massages. The breakfast served is one of the best in town and comes complete with champagne. Its location near a couple of cabaret clubs may be a little off-putting to some but is in no way threatening. Plenty of shops, restaurants, theaters, and sights are within a few minutes' walk, and the reception desk will happily suggest and set up any type of program you want.

Hotel Liberty (28. října 11, tel. 221 181

Over 6,000 Kč

Opulent, elegant, and unforgettable are just some of the words visitors use to describe **C Carlo IV** (Senovážné náměstí 13, tel. 224 593 111, www.boscolohotels.com, 6,100 Kč d), located in a neoclassical building just a short walk from the Powder Tower. From its grand reception hall to its very comfortable (although sometimes small) rooms, one is immediately and completely immersed in Old World charm and style. The fantastic spa and pool area boasts subdued lighting as well as fruit and drinks, making it the perfect spot for some well-deserved rest and relaxation.

STARÉ MĚSTO

From humble hostels to Old World luxury, Old Town's got it all. Unlike Nové Město's commercial vibe, the streets here radiate history, the architecture makes you feel like you're on the set of a fairy tale, and the nightlife is arguably the finest the city has to offer. Most of your time will probably be spent in and around Old Town anyway, so why not set up camp here as well?

1,000-2,000 Kč

If you're planning on staying in one of the dorms, you can forget about getting much sleep at **Travellers' Hostel** (Dlouhá 33, tel. 224 826 662, www.travellers.cz, 1,900 Kč d). People come and go at all hours, and the aftermath of any given night looks like a frat party gone wrong. Opt instead for one of the rooftop apartments, which are simple but clean, comfortable, and spacious. Being a block away from Old Town Square has its obvious advantages, as does staying next to the Roxy—one of Prague's biggest and best clubs. Keep in mind that there tends to be a very long waiting list here, so make sure you book well in advance, particularly during the high season.

Relatively new to the scene, **Old Prague Hostel** (Benediktská 2, tel. 224 829 058, www.oldpraguehostel.com, 2,000 Kč d) is one minute's walk from Old Town Square and all the restaurants, bars, and sights that come with it. Free breakfast, linens, lockers, and Internet

© TOM DIRLIS

the opulent and elegant Carlo IV

149, www.hotelliberty.cz, 5,100 Kč d) offers 32 colorful and luxurious rooms and suites that come complete with antiques, chandeliers, and all the modern amenities one looks for in a boutique hotel. Some rooms offer a balcony or terrace, affording guests pretty views of Prague Castle. Their motto, loosely translated, is "Our rooms don't only have numbers, they have souls as well," and one does sense that their stylish, spacious rooms are indeed living things as opposed to the often stark, characterless accommodations of the bigger chains.

Housed in a 14th-century building on a quiet side street located minutes from Wenceslas Square, Old Town, New Town, Malá Strana, and more, the **Hotel Élite** (Ostrovni 32, tel. 224 932 250, www.hotelelite.cz, 5,500 Kč d) is what you'd expect from a typical quaint European hotel. The rooms are small but clean, and the staff is helpful and friendly. Try to get a room overlooking the courtyard or splurge for the junior suite if romance is the reason you're in town.

PRAGUE

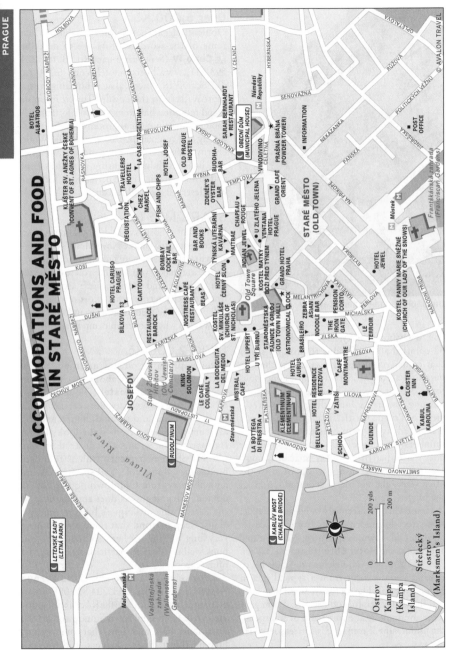

ACCOMMODATIONS AND FOOD IN STARÉ MĚSTO

Travellers' Hostel offers cheap accommodations in Old Town.

© TOM DIRLIS

access are definite pluses here, as is the availability of nonsmoking rooms—always hard to find in Prague. There are rooms with 2-8 beds along with a suite that accommodates five. The staff has never been accused of being the friendliest, but that's a common enough complaint. One tip is to make sure you don't get a room that's attached to the common room—not if you want to get any sleep, that is.

2,000-3,000 Kč
Simple yet tasteful rooms are what you get at **Pension Corto** (Havelská 15, tel. 224 235 779, www.corto.cz, 2,000 Kč d), a very affordable and centrally located boutique-style bed-and-breakfast. First-floor rooms look out onto outdoor market Havelská Tržnice, while those wishing to stay on the top floor (the fifth) should be aware that there is no elevator due to the building's historic and heritage-protected status. As a result, the reconstructed attic rooms up top come at a slightly cheaper price. All rooms come with satellite TV, Wi-Fi,

and a kettle. Excellent value is what you can expect here.

If it's an unconventional holiday you're after, try staying at the **Botel Albatros** (Nábřeží Ludvíka Svobody, tel. 224 810 547, www.botelalbatros.cz, 2,500 Kč d), a boat-hotel situated on the tranquil Vltava River that offers 82 rooms and four apartments. While the boat's quarters may not be the most spacious and luxurious you've ever seen, its summer terrace and bar offer outstanding views of Hradčany and Prague Castle, which more than makes up for it. Located away from the hustle and bustle, though only a 5- to 10-minute walk away from it, this is a great option for those seeking something a tad more adventurous than the usual fare.

While certainly not a luxurious hotel, the **Cloister Inn** (Konviktská 14, tel. 224 211 020, www.cloister-inn.com, 2,600 Kč d) offers excellent value for the money. A very helpful and efficient staff keep the large, spacious rooms clean as a whistle and are more than willing to advise you on the large number of restaurants, bars, and shops in the vicinity. Being minutes away from Old Town Square, Wenceslas Square, and the Vltava River makes this a very practical and convenient choice.

Hotel Černý slon (Týnská 1, tel. 222 321 521, www.hotelcernyslon.cz, 2,700 Kč d) is a Gothic building that was built in 1330-1340 and is UNESCO-listed and protected. Sixteen big rooms with wooden floors are available, some of which look out onto charming Old Town streets where one can lose hours watching the people pass by. Quaint, cozy, and competitively priced, it fills up fast, so make sure to reserve well in advance. Keep in mind that there is no elevator, so book accordingly.

3,000-4,000 Kč
Hotel Aurus (Karlova 3, tel. 222 220 262, www.aurushotel.cz, 3,200 Kč d) is located in a beautiful UNESCO-protected building whose history can be traced back to the 16th century. There is lots of charm here with wooden beams, antique furniture, and the occasional hand-painted ceiling, providing guests with a sense of

PRAGUE

© TOM DIRLIS

Sleep on the Vltava River, care of Botel Albatros.

history and culture that eludes the international chains. Its location in the heart of Old Town's busy pedestrian area will either have you lauding its proximity to everything or cursing the human traffic. Choose wisely.

❮ **U Zlatého jelena** (Štupartská 6/Celetná 11, tel. 257 531 925, www.goldendeer.cz, 3,300 Kč d) is a charming little hotel whose lack of pretension gives guests that "home away from home" feeling. The staff is pleasant, the rooms are large and decorated with antique furnishings, the baths are luxurious, and the breakfast is generous. Being located about 100 paces from Old Town Square doesn't hurt either. This is where you want to be if you favor the down-home and authentic over the slick, plastic, and contrived.

Built in the 15th century and located just 300 feet from Old Town Square is **U Tří Bubnů** (U radnice 8 and 10, tel. 224 214 855, www. utribubnu.cz, 3,500 Kč d). There is a very strong sense of the traditional and unspoiled here, with large, tastefully decorated rooms providing a much warmer atmosphere than

most of the slick new hotels springing up these days. Part of its traditional atmosphere includes the lack of an elevator, however, so those not interested in climbing the original stone staircase every day should arrange for a room on one of the lower floors.

Hotel Jewel (Rytířská 3, tel. 224 211 699, www.hoteljewelprague.com, 3,200 Kč d) is a small, three-star, family-run operation located a few steps from Wenceslas Square and a couple of minutes from Old Town Square. There are 11 tastefully furnished, air-conditioned rooms available, and the friendly staff is always willing to advise on nearby restaurants or help you plan a daily trip out of the city. Those not insisting on or looking for the luxury that comes with five-star hotels will be more than happy here. One note: There is no elevator, and climbing a healthy number of steps every day can be a rather trying experience for some.

Built in the second half of the 14th century, the building now housing **Hotel Lippert** (Mikulášská 2, tel. 224 232 250, www.ho-tel-lippert.cz, 3,600 Kč d) has survived some

© TOM DIRLIS

the hip Hotel Josef

hairy times, including a fire in 1945 during the Prague uprising. Today it offers 12 lovely rooms, most of which overlook Old Town Square all the way across to Týn Church. The rooms are comfortable and spacious, blending modern touches with Old World design like wooden beams and beautiful painted ceilings. Some may not like the fact that staying here means you're right in the thick of things tourist-wise, while others will find it a godsend.

Originally a residential building, the **Hotel Caruso Prague** (U Milosrdných 2, tel. 224 815 768, www.hotelcarusoprague.cz, 3,700 Kč d) was completely rebuilt in 2002-2003 and is now a boutique hotel offering 47 charming rooms in the heart of Josefov. Designed in a warm traditional style, the hotel goes out of its way to make you feel at home with some of the most helpful and pleasant staff you'll find anywhere. Another plus is that its location is not in the middle of all the nonstop activity of Old Town and Wenceslas Square. However, those sights, as well as a number of restaurants, museums, shops, and bars, are only a few minutes'

walk away. Large enough to warrant its four-star rating yet small enough for it to be personal and relaxed, the Caruso continues to make its guests' stay a memorable one.

4,000-5,000 Kč

Arguably the hippest boutique hotel in Old Town, the **Hotel Josef** (Rybná 20, tel. 221 700 111, www.hoteljosef.com, 4,100 Kč d) offers 109 stylish, soundproof rooms, many of which are nonsmoking and overlook a pretty and rather large courtyard. Complimentary bathrobes, slippers, bath products, and mineral water are just a few of the perks that come with staying here, and the famous glass-walled baths (found in the Superior rooms) are something you won't forget any time soon. Rooms 704 and 801 are especially luxurious and come with impressive views of Prague Castle and the countless spires of Old Town Square.

Located in Old Town in a building well over 600 years old, the **Hotel Residence Retezova** (Retezova 9, tel. 222 221 800, www.retezova. com, 4,600 Kč d) offers nine elegant apartments ranging from Studios to Attic Family Apartments. All rooms come with satellite TV, DVD players, and free Internet access, and while some rooms don't have air-conditioning, the unfailingly helpful staff will be happy to provide you with a fan. Beautifully painted wooden beams, Gothic vaulted ceilings, and fireplaces here and there make this hotel one of the more charming and aesthetically pleasing options in town.

Comfortable beds, helpful staff, and a hearty breakfast are just a few reasons to consider staying at the **Ventana Hotel Prague** (Celetna 7, tel. 221 776 600, www.ventana-hotel.net, 4,800 Kč d). Offering 29 spacious, modestly decorated rooms in the heart of Old Town Square, this elegant boutique hotel scores consistently high with visitors of all tastes and backgrounds.

5,000-6,000 Kč

Directly opposite the Astronomical Clock is the fantastic **Grand Hotel Praha** (Staroměstské náměstí 22, tel. 221 632 556, www.

the centrally located Ventana Hotel Prague

remarkable wooden painted ceilings and frescoes dating back to the 14th century, it provides guests with that old European charm many pay top dollar to experience. Rooms range in size from the Deluxe Room (410 square feet) to the stunning Tower Suite (764 square feet), which spans three floors and has a heart-shaped bedroom. Excellent and omnipresent staff members do everything they can to make your stay as comfortable as possible, including leaving chocolates on pillows and Evian water on the table. It's pricey but memorable.

MALÁ STRANA

The hotels are a little pricier in Lesser Town, but considering Charles Bridge, Kampa Park, Petřín Hill, and Prague Castle are all close by, that little extra goes a long way. Smaller in size than either Nové Město or Staré Město, the neighborhood is characterized by narrow winding side streets that provide intimacy and comparative quiet when night comes, as stag parties and pleasure seekers retreat to the other side of the Vltava.

1,000-2,000 Kč

Halfway up Nerudova on the way to Prague Castle, **Little Quarter Hostel** (Nerudova 21, tel. 257 212 029, www.littlequarter.com, 1,200 Kč d) offers clean 2- to 5-person rooms and private rooms to younger and budget-conscious travelers. Unforgettable views of Prague Castle and Petřín Hill are complemented by friendly 24-hour reception service as well as free Internet and Wi-Fi.

2,000-3,000 Kč

Spanning three buildings on Nerudova and two a little higher up on Úvoz, **The Palace Road Hotel** (Nerudova 7, tel. 257 531 941, www.palaceroad.com, 2,300 Kč d) is perfect for the frugal-class traveler. Visitors can choose from rooms and apartments, most of which are spacious, Spartan, and clean. The drawback for some guests might be sharing a bath with another room. The apartments are bigger and boast private baths, fridges, and kettles; some even have their own kitchen. Considering its

grandhotelpraha.cz, 5,100 Kč d). The large and immaculate rooms are furnished with antiques and sport luxurious baths that are very well appointed. Those with money to burn should opt for the impressive attic apartment, which consists of two bedrooms linked by a spiral staircase with en suite baths. It also boasts soaring ceilings, huge beams, and oak floors, not to mention an incredible view of the Astronomical Clock and the people that gather on an hourly basis to watch its mini puppet show. The noise of drunkards spilling out onto the square at the end of the night might bother some, so make sure your room has double glazing, or bring earplugs. If you're a particularly light sleeper and don't mind sacrificing the tremendous view, ask for room 205, which overlooks a quiet courtyard.

Over 6,000 Kč

The Iron Gate (Michalská 19, tel. 225 777 777, www.irongate.cz, 6,300 Kč d) is located on a quiet side street just off Old Town Square away from the throngs of tourists. Decorated with proximity to the castle and Malá Strana, there really is no better value around. Two things to keep in mind, however: The steps are numerous (as the hotel's name implies), so if you're not that mobile, don't bother staying here. Secondly, the breakfast that is included in the rates is vegan, which may or may not interest you. Should you decide to go with this place, make sure to book early, as all five buildings fill up rather quickly.

For excellent value at the foot of Petřín Hill, try **U Kříže** (Újezd 20, tel. 257 313 272, www. ukrize.cz, 2,300 Kč d). Reliable, friendly service and a peaceful atmosphere is what you can expect here, with Kampa Park, Charles Bridge, and the National Theater only minutes away. The 16 rooms and suites are furnished simply and kept extremely clean. Some overlook Petřín, which makes for a pleasant view, but light sleepers might be kept up at night due to the trams that run past. If that's the case, ask for a room overlooking the atrium.

3,000-4,000 Kč

Hotel U Zeleného hroznu (Jánský vršek 11, tel. 725 405 015, www.uzelenehohroznu.cz, 3,200 Kč), is located on a quiet side street near the foot of Prague Castle. Its eight clean, comfortable, and unique suites reflect the personalities of eight distinct historical Czech figures, including Alfons Mucha, Tycho Brahe, and Franz Kafka. There's plenty of excellent value and service. One slight drawback to consider is that the walls are a little on the thin side, so fingers crossed for a quiet neighbor.

If you like family-run hotels that offer professional service and care, then **Dům U velké boty** (Vlašská 30, tel. 257 532 088, www. dumuvelkeboty.cz, 3,150 Kč d) is for you. This 12-room bed-and-breakfast is operated by the very hospitable Rippl family and is one of the best-kept secrets (until now) that Malá Strana has to offer. Large, clean rooms furnished with comfortable beds and lovely antiques await. While there are no TVs in any of the rooms, you'll hardly miss it. Being minutes away from Charles Bridge and Petřín

Hill makes the location hard to beat, and the hotel's peaceful surroundings will help you enjoy the kind of sleep you look forward to when on vacation. If a friendly personal touch coupled with simple yet elegant surroundings is what you're looking for, look no further.

Situated at the foot of lovely Petřín Hill stands the 【 **Hotel Roma** (Újezd 24, tel. 222 500 120, www.hotel-roma-prague.com, 3,300 Kč d), featuring 25 gorgeous suites and 62 spacious double rooms. The hotel's lovely reception area houses a bar, offers free Internet, and is home to a terrific aquarium that includes an impressive-looking and mostly friendly shark. Close to many sights, including Charles Bridge, Kampa Park, and the National Theater, the hotel is also near many excellent restaurants, such as Cantina and Le Bastille. A tip for those who appreciate a good balcony: Make sure to ask for room 310.

At the top of Nerudova Street, you'll find **Zlatá hvězda** (Nerudova 48, tel. 257 532 867, www.hotelgoldenstar.cz, 3,650 Kč d), whose building dates back to 1372, when it functioned as the Mayor of Hradčany's residence. Located a convenient two-minute walk from Prague Castle and St. Vitus Cathedral, its rooms are bright, high-ceilinged, and well furnished. Do yourself a favor and request a room on the fourth floor, where the views are simply mesmerizing. Friendly and helpful staff top off this excellent choice.

Located on a quiet side street a mere stone's throw from Malostranska Square is the **Hotel U Tří Čápů** (Valdštejnské náměstí 8, tel. 257 210 779, www.hotelthreestorks.cz, 3,900 Kč d). Boasting 10 deluxe double rooms, eight standard double rooms, and two single rooms, the hotel is one of the neighborhood's most impressive examples of luxury accommodations. All rooms are equipped with air-conditioning, minibars, safes, phones, LCD TVs, and DVD players, with a wide array of films available. Spacious, clean, and sporting one of the friendliest hotel staffs in town, the Hotel U Tří Čápů is an excellent choice for those looking to spoil themselves.

4,000-5,000 Kč

Rezidence Lundborg (U Lužického semináře 3, tel. 257 011 911, www.lundborg.se, 4,600 Kč d) is a luxurious baroque hotel housed in a 700-year-old building offering 13 apartments and suites (no rooms) that are located at the end of Charles Bridge. All suites come fully equipped with TVs, free Internet, whirlpool tubs, kitchens, sound systems, original wooden Renaissance ceilings, and magnificent views overlooking the bridge. Suites range from the Junior Suite (323 square feet) to the Imperial Suite (1,500 square feet), all of which are the epitome of quality and comfort, making this one of the better places in town to rest your weary head.

5,000-6,000 Kč

If you're a lover of music, start saving your money now for a stay at the incomparable ◖ **Aria Hotel** (Tržiště 9, tel. 225 334 111, www.ariahotel.net, 5,300 Kč d). Each of its four floors is dedicated to a particular genre of music, with every stylishly decorated room honoring an artist in that genre. From The Beatles to Vivaldi, all rooms are stocked with original artwork, books, and music that pay tribute to the artist in question. Apart from the beautiful modern decor, this boutique hotel also boasts an executive conference room, a private screening room for up to 40, a music salon, a winter garden, a fitness center, and much, much more. All rooms also have a computer and DVD hookup with an extensive library of movies and music available at your fingertips. Exceptional staff, along with complimentary fruit bowls, dressing gowns, slippers, and designer toiletries, enhance an already superb experience.

Over 6,000 Kč

While considerably more expensive than most, the **Mandarin Oriental Prague** (Nebovidska 459/1, tel. 233 088 888, www.mandarinoriental.com/prague, 7,800 Kč d) is nevertheless one of the more remarkable and luxurious hotels in town. Spacious, comfortable, and spotless rooms ranging from the contemporary to the historical await, as does the only spa in the world that's located in a former Renaissance chapel. Helpful staff, top-notch food, a fitness center, and a massage suite are a few more reasons why the Mandarin is a superb choice for those able to afford it.

Depending on your point of view, being located next to the guarded U.S. embassy makes the **Alchymist Grand Hotel & Spa** (Tržiště 19, tel. 257 286 011, www.alchymisthotel.com, 8,400 Kč d) either the safest or most dangerous location in Prague. This remarkable boutique hotel showcases Italian opulence at its finest with an abundance of rococo, art deco, and gold mirrors decorating its premises. An incredible spa and steam room are available, as is a gorgeous swimming pool that comes complete with an overhanging chandelier. For those who like to mingle, there's a gathering every evening at 5:30pm with complimentary wine and cheese. A few of the amenities to be found in the Deluxe Rooms (which are the smallest) are plasma TVs, DVD/CD players, safes, Internet access, and gorgeous marble-floored baths. The suites, meanwhile, are in a class of their own. Although one of the more expensive hotels in town, the Alchymist is also one of the finest you'll find in Europe.

HRADČANY

Accommodations in the castle district are going to cost you, but most would argue that a stay in this peaceful, historic, and incredibly romantic part of town is absolutely priceless. Slightly removed from the action yet close enough to all the main sights and districts, Hradčany is an excellent choice for families or couples looking for a quieter type of getaway.

1,000-2,000 Kč

The Golden Horse House (Úvoz 8, tel. 603 841 790, www.goldenhorse.cz, 1,550 Kč d) is the perfect choice for the unpretentious budget traveler. Two simple, self-contained apartments are offered, each with their own bath, TV, and Internet connection. Clean, simple, and two minutes from the Castle, this is easily the best deal in the district. Book well in advance.

3,000-4,000 Kč

Domus Henrici (Loretánská 11, tel. 220 511 369, www.domus-henrici.cz, 3,300 Kč d) is hidden down a quiet street in the middle of Prague Castle, Strahov Monastery, and the Loreto, offering its guests a warm neighborhood-type feel away from the hordes of tourists that dominate the city's center. Redesigned in 2006, it boasts four double rooms, three deluxe doubles, and a suite, all of which come equipped with HDTVs, surround-sound stereos, and corner baths. Room 6 has a magnificent view of the city, while a leisurely stroll downhill will take you into Malá Strana and beyond. Those who shudder at the thought of walking back uphill, fear not. Prague's excellent public transportation system will whisk you right up and deposit you just up the road from the hotel. Excellent value for the money means you have to book well in advance.

4,000-5,000 Kč

The **Romantik Hotel U Raka** (Černínská 10, tel. 220 511 100, www.romantikhotel-uraka. cz, 4,000 Kč d) is a charming, unique, and comfortable hotel located within walking distance of the Palace Gardens. Designed and run by photographer Alexandr Paul and his daughter Aneta, guests are made to feel welcome immediately upon arrival—so much so that they come to feel they are staying at a five-star hotel rather than an intimate rustic inn. Once settled, take a stroll through picturesque Nový Svět, a street well known for its ability to spark romance, located just 10 minutes from Prague Castle. After the day's sightseeing is over, return to the hotel and relax in its peaceful garden with a glass of champagne and wonder why anyone would want to stay anywhere else. This is a perfect place for romantic couples—not so much for families or party animals. Book early.

5,000-6,000 Kč

Situated a few steps away from Prague Castle between Strahov Monastery and Loreta Square is **Hotel Questenberk** (Úvoz 15, tel. 220 407 600, www.questenberk.cz, 5,000 Kč d). A beautiful baroque building that resembles a church more than an upscale hotel, it sports 26 double rooms with four king suites that are tastefully furnished. The hotel's finest room is room 406, which is set in the attic with original wooden beams, has two windows offering panoramic views of golden Prague, and boasts a superb en suite bath. Book well in advance.

Over 6,000 Kč

Originally the residence of Roman emperor and Bohemian King Rudolf II, as well as famous astronomer Tycho Brahe, **U Zlaté studně** (U Zlaté studně 166, tel. 257 011 213, www.goldenwellhotel.cz, 6,300 Kč d) is drenched in history and offers all the modern amenities one looks for in a hotel without sacrificing any of its Old World charm. Four floors house 18 rooms and two suites, all designed with beautiful reproductions of antique pieces from the 17th, 18th, and 19th centuries. The service is courteous and professional, starting with a champagne reception on each guest's arrival. Make sure to check out their pillow menu—one more detail to help make your stay as comfy as possible. And consider this fair warning: The view of Prague stretching out before you while having breakfast or coffee on their terrace will make you think twice about getting to the airport on time.

Charming, old fashioned, and swanky enough for the likes of Madeleine Albright, Sean Connery, and the Red Hot Chili Peppers, **Hotel Savoy** (Keplerova 6, tel. 224 302 430, www.hotel-savoy.cz, 7,200 Kč d) is a five-star hotel with a price tag to match. Large comfortable rooms with luxurious baths and excellent views (particularly on the eighth floor) are topped off with complimentary robes, slippers, and a minibar. Top-of-the-line facilities include a whirlpool tub, a fitness center, a sauna, and a more-than-competent masseuse who can always be found in the hotel's "Relax Center." Located in Prague's diplomatic quarter, the Savoy makes for a quiet, elegant, and rather extravagant choice.

PRAGUE

DEJVICE

Primarily a residential district, Dejvice is also home to gorgeous Divoká Šárka and a large number of beautiful ambassadors' villas. The airport and city center are a mere 20 minutes away by both bus and subway, making this area a favorite with those who prefer some distance between where they play and where they stay.

Under 1,000 Kč

They certainly aren't much, but the rooms offered at Strahov college student dorm **Hostel SPUS Strahov** (Chaloupeckeho ul. Block 4, tel. 220 513 419, July 1-Sept. 20, 900 Kč d) are easily the best deal around. As Spartan as they come, each room has two simple beds, while shared shower and toilet facilities are located on each floor. There are a couple of bars on campus as well as a small shop, and Prague Castle is only a 10- to 15-minute walk away. This is an ideal choice for the backpacker on a tight budget who needs a no-frills yet clean place to crash.

2,000-3,000 Kč

The **Diplomat Hotel Prague** (Evropská 15, tel. 296 559 111, www.diplomathotel.cz, 2,900 Kč d) is the last stop on the airport bus's route and is located next to the Dejvicka subway station. This may explain why vast numbers of tour groups regularly fill its 398 rooms and suites. The decor is dated, and the service, while good, may not live up to some peoples' Western standards, but the rooms are spacious, clean, and more than adequate. Depending on your tastes, you'll find its distance from the city center either a plus or a minus. However, Malá Strana is a mere two subway stops away, Old Town Square is three, and Wenceslas Square is four. All can be reached within minutes, as can lovely Divoká Šárka, one of Prague's largest and finest parks.

3,000-4,000 Kč

Deep in Dejvice lies **Hotel Villa Schwaiger** (Schwaigerova 59/3, tel. 233 320 272, www.villaschwaiger.com, 3,000 Kč d), a pretty villa offering 22 luxurious rooms among ambassadors'

residences and sprawling, soothing Stromovka Park. The specialty rooms, including the Zen-like "Chinese Room" or the "Provençal Room," with its southern flavor and flair, are interesting additions to this very well-kept and professional hotel. One drawback to this otherwise lovely place is its distance from public transportation, forcing guests to either learn the bus and subway system quickly or shell out for a cab. On the other hand, the excellent restaurant-pub Na Slamníku is located directly across the street.

HOLEŠOVICE

Slightly off the beaten path, Holešovice is nevertheless a good choice for those who want to throw themselves into an authentic Prague environment. Small, locally-owned businesses are what you'll find here, along with a healthy mixture of hip natives and expats who populate the area's bars and restaurants. Letná and Stromovka parks are nearby, enabling pleasant afternoon walks and hours of beer garden goodness.

1,000-2,000 Kč

Sir Toby's Hostel (Dělnická 24, tel. 246 032 610, www.sirtobys.com, 1,800 Kč d) is hands down one of the finest hostels in town. The rooms are quiet, clean, bright, and spacious, complete with rolling lockers found under the bed and loads of hot water. The staff is friendly and helpful, and there's free Wi-Fi, coffee, and tea to boot. Its location away from the center may not appeal to some, but it's just a quick 10-minute tram ride away, and most people come to appreciate the distance from the maddening crowds. This is a perfect place for those on a budget not interested in the typical drink-till-you-drop hostel atmosphere.

2,000-3,000 Kč

It ain't fancy, but the **Hotel Belvedere** (Milady Horákové 19, tel. 220 106 111, www.hotelbelvedereprague.cz, 2,300 Kč d) gets the job done at a relatively reasonable price. The rooms are basic but clean and come with all the essentials: comfortable beds, safes, writing desks, coffeemakers, and decent-size baths. Although a little far from the center, Strossmayerovo náměstí is just down the street, and all sorts of trams and buses can get you over the river and into Old Town in 10 minutes. You won't see any monuments or tourist-filled squares here, but you'll be close and spend a fraction of the cost. It's ideal for the frugal traveler who likes staying local and doesn't mind a lack of frills.

ŽIŽKOV AND VINOHRADY
Both districts are known for their numerous restaurants, pubs, and wine bars as well as loyal residents who wouldn't change their location for the world. Close to the center yet far enough to not be overwhelmed by it, both areas are perfect for those seeking vibrant surroundings and local character.

1,000-2,000 Kč
The trek up the hill to get to **Clown & Bard** (Bořivojova 102, tel. 222 716 453, www.clownandbard.com, 1,500 Kč d) is not an enviable one, especially if your backpack is on the heavy side or you're stumbling home after having a little too much to drink. Nevertheless, its relaxed, open, and extremely friendly atmosphere continues to attract travelers of all walks of life. The 32-bed dorm up top is as noisy as you'd expect it to be, but the smaller suites are considerably quieter. Cheap Internet, 24-hour reception, and a large breakfast are a few pluses, as is its location, 15 minutes from the center.

Located a breezy 15-minute walk from the center is **Hostel Elf** (Husitská 11, tel. 222 540 963, www.hostelelf.com, 1,400 Kč d), a friendly, colorful environment that attracts a wide variety of international guests. Free Internet, breakfast, coffee, and tea are available, and the 24-hour staff is always happy to help you find whatever it is you might need. There is also a common area that includes comfy couches and outdoor benches, which are ideal for making new friends. The baths could be a bit cleaner and it can get noisy at night, but those staying for a relatively short time will hardly notice or care.

If a hostel exists out there that can be described as upscale, ◖ **Miss Sophie's Prague**

(Melounova 3, tel. 246 032 621, www.misssophies.com, 2,000 Kč d) is it. Modern art and furniture evoke a cool, trendy setting where you can casually put your feet up and relax in style. The beds are soft, the pillows fluffy, the rooms spotless, and the staff polite. Truth be told, Miss Sophie's is better than some of the higher-priced, overrated hotels in the center trying to pass themselves off as comfortable lodgings. It's a tad more expensive than other hostels, but you'll immediately notice where that extra little bit went.

2,000-3,000 Kč
Its central location just 1.5 blocks from busy I. P. Pavlova and its corresponding subway station make **Hostel Advantage** (Sokolská 11, tel. 224 914 062, www.advantagehostel.cz, 2,200 Kč d) a very convenient and strategic choice. Rather large, it offers clean and spacious shared and private rooms as well as cheap beer and free Internet access (although you'll have to fight for computer time). There is also a *jídelna* across the street with cheap, tasty food—perfect for a backpacker's budget.

3,000-4,000 Kč
The **Hotel Seven Days** (Žitná 46/572, tel. 222 923 111, www.hotelsevendays.com, 3,000 Kč d) is housed in a building that dates to 1888 and is now protected by the UNESCO Heritage List. Its 50 air-conditioned, tastefully furnished rooms come complete with cable and pay TV and Internet access, along with sufficiently spacious, clean baths. Located within a couple of minutes' walk from the National Museum and Wenceslas Square, you'll save a bundle on taxis and drop a few pounds in the process.

5,000-6,000 Kč
Although it advertises itself as a four-star hotel, the **Ametyst** (Jana Masaryka 11, tel. 222 921 921, www.hotelametyst.cz, 5,700 Kč d) may fall short of some guests' Westernized expectations. Nevertheless, its 84 rooms are clean and comfortable and come with all the amenities one looks for while on vacation. Located

in the heart of Vinohrady, it's a little farther away from the city's sights than other hotels, but the nearest subway stop is a 5-minute walk, and Wenceslas Square is just 15 minutes away. There are not enough superlatives to describe the experience at **Le Palais** (U Zvonařky 1, tel. 234 634 111, www.palaishotel.cz, 6,000 Kč d), a boutique hotel with 60 gorgeous rooms and 12 deluxe suites. It's the small touches that set this fantastic hotel apart. From the warm welcome and hotel tour on arrival to the free mini-bar, turn-down service, chocolate on the pillow, and surprise rose petals and candles lining your bathtub, Le Palais goes out of its way to make you feel like royalty. The staff's kindness and attention to detail are unparalleled—so much so that you'll wish you had booked a longer stay. It's highly recommended.

Food

Prague's restaurant scene has evolved dramatically over the last decade from dreary to diverse, resulting in a wide variety of cuisines and gourmet dining options. Apart from traditional Czech establishments serving classic mains like goulash, *svíčková* (beef in cream sauce), and pork, dumplings, and cabbage, diners can now gorge on any number of international dishes hailing all the way from Afghanistan to Zagreb. Service continues to improve as well, though it still has a way to go before reaching the friendly and prompt attention Westerners are used to. Nevertheless, what was once a barren wasteland of unimaginative meat-heavy dishes and bland brown sauces has flourished into a tantalizing terrain of culinary sophistication even the choosiest of palates can appreciate.

NOVÉ MĚSTO
American
[C] **Jáma** (V Jámě 7, tel. 224 222 383, www.jamapub.cz, Mon.-Sat. 11am-1am, Sun. 11am-midnight, mains 109-490 Kč) is a friendly American-run pub that has been a staple of the expat community since 1994. Serving up hearty hamburgers and tasty Tex-Mex with a smile, this is a good place to visit if you want to meet locals and expats or simply need a healthy dose of home.

Asian
Lemon Leaf (Myslíkova 14, tel. 224 919 056, www.lemon.cz, Mon.-Thurs. 11am-11pm, Fri. 11am-midnight, Sat. noon-midnight, Sun. noon-11pm, mains 159-299 Kč) has won over some pretty loyal customers over the years, and with good reason. The menu includes standard steak and pasta dishes, but it's the Thai food people come for. Crisp spring rolls and spicy chicken meatballs make for unbeatable appetizers, while the Panang curry pork with coconut milk, chili, lemon leaves, and rice seems to put smiles on faces as well. Elegant without being stuffy, this is a popular expat hangout and is the perfect place for a dinner date. Very affordable lunch specials are offered on weekdays and include a main course, soup, and rice.

Sansho (Petrská 25, tel. 222 317 425, http://sansho.cz, Tues.-Thurs. 11:30am-3pm and 6pm-11pm, Fri. 11:30am-3pm and 6pm-11:30pm, Sat. 6pm-11:30pm, lunch mains 125-225 Kč, tasting menu 850 Kč) offers excellent lunch specials, such as their famous Jungle Curry Rabbit, as well as one of the finer tasting menus in town, which includes mouthwatering dishes like salmon sashimi, soft-shell crab, and beef rending. While the tasting menu is a tad pricey, the lunch specials are very affordable and well worth a try.

Located next to Café Louvre, **Le Patio** (Národní 22, tel. 774 539 301, www.lepatio.cz, Mon.-Fri. 9am-11pm, Sat.-Sun. 10am-11pm, mains 155-365 Kč) offers an Asian fusion menu in a warm and friendly rustic environment. Pho duck, prawn noodles, and hot-and-sour beef are reliable choices, as is their excellent and reasonably-priced tasting menu.

Cafés

The 🗲 **Cafe Imperial** (Na poříčí 15, tel. 246 011 440, www.cafeimperial.cz, daily 7am-11pm, mains 229-375 Kč) was the place to be if you were a part of the Bohemian elite in the 1940s. Lucky for us, it has managed to maintain its elegance through the decades. Spacious surroundings, coupled with intricately tiled mosaics on both the walls and ceilings, transport you to another era, as does the exceptional and well-mannered service. The veal schnitzel has been hailed as the finest around, and those watching their weight ought to consider the light yet delicious tagliolini. Don't forget to leave room for dessert, particularly the crème brûlée and chocolate bomb "surprise."

Café Louvre (Národní 22, tel. 224 930 949, www.cafelouvre.cz, Mon.-Fri. 8am-11:30pm, Sat.-Sun. 9am-11:30pm, mains 129-329 Kč) is a spacious Parisian-style café right in the heart of downtown. Founded in 1902, it has seen the likes of Kafka and Einstein pass through its doors and is now regularly filled with tourists, local artists, and the business class. This is a perfect place to take a break from the bustling streets and unwind with a cup of coffee in elegant surroundings. The food is hit and miss, however, as are the desserts, so be warned. Five pool tables in the back can be rented by the hour as well, should you feel like getting a game in before hitting the streets.

Opposite the National Theater sits **Café Slavia** (Smetanovo nábřeží 1012/2, tel. 224 218 493, www.cafeslavia.cz, Mon.-Fri. 8am-midnight, Sat.-Sun. 9am-midnight, mains 139-359 Kč), a pleasant art deco café that used to be the unofficial meeting place of the city's artists and intellectuals, including former President Václav Havel, who was a regular during his dissident years. These days it's usually frequented by tourists during the day and the after-theater crowd at night. Try securing one of the window tables that offer gorgeous views of either the National Theater or Prague Castle.

Continental

Carnivores beware! **Kobe Restaurant** (Václavské náměstí 11, tel. 224 267 248, www.

koberestaurant.cz, daily noon-midnight, mains 250-590 Kč) boasts some of the finest Kobe steak you'll ever taste, as well as a number of meat specialties like roasted lamb chops that are guaranteed to have you coming back for more. Efficient service, an exceptional wine list, and reasonable prices make this a choice you won't regret.

Offering generous portions of Czech and international dishes at modest prices has earned **Hybernia** (Hybernská 7, tel. 224 226 004, www.hybernia.cz, Mon.-Fri. 8am-midnight, Sat.-Sun. 11am-midnight, mains 135-295 Kč) a very loyal customer base, particularly at lunchtime. Businesspeople, locals, and heads of state all drop in regularly, filling up its three rooms and (during the warmer months) quiet outdoor courtyard. Popular dishes include the chicken skewer and grilled pork ribs.

Czech

U Vejvodů (Jilská 4, tel. 224 219 999, www.restauraceuvejvodu.cz, Mon.-Sat. 10am-4am, Sun. 11am-3am, mains 150-600 Kč) continues to be a hit with small and large groups alike thanks to its enormous though comfortable size, large and reasonably priced Czech dishes, and thirst-quenching draft beer. Whether it's the roast duck, goulash, or pork knee you go for, odds are you won't be disappointed. Evenings often offer live music, so plan accordingly.

Housed in a building that dates all the way back to 1499, 🗲 **U Fleků** (Křemencova 11, tel. 224 934 805, www.ufleku.cz, daily 10am-11pm, mains 149-389 Kč) is a pub, restaurant, and microbrewery all in one. A large complex of rooms designed in true beer hall fashion is packed to the gills daily with tour groups and visitors looking for a taste of the authentic. The menu favors meat and wild game dishes that can (and should) be washed down with a glass of their home-brewed dark beer. The waiters can leave a lot to be desired as some of them can seem grumpy or as though they have a chip on their shoulders. Do your best to ignore them and turn your attention instead to

PRAGUE

© TOM DIRLIS

U Fleků is a pub, restaurant, and microbrewery all in one.

the lively accordion shows performed intermittently throughout the day.

Beer aficionados will be wise to mark down **U Pinkasů** (Jungmannovo náměstí 16, tel. 221 111 150, www.upinkasu.cz, restaurant daily 11:30am-11pm, cellar pub daily 4pm-2am, mains 159-329 Kč) on their must-see list. Legend has it that in 1843 this very same establishment was the first to serve Pilsner Urquell to its happy customers, and the suds have been flowing ever since. It is one of the few places in Prague that serve the brew unpasteurized, and you'll notice the difference in taste immediately. The menu is chock-full of traditional Czech dishes and wild game delicacies that include duck, hare, and boar—all of which come in very generous portions. Centrally located yet remarkably cheap, this place is highly recommended for those looking for a taste of the unpolished and authentic.

If you're looking to mingle with locals while sampling some traditional Czech fare, then **U Provaznice** (Provaznická 3, tel. 224

232 528, www.uprovaznice.cz, daily 11am-midnight, 189-359 Kč) is definitely for you. Grab a large wooden table and go with the duck, ribs, and mixed grill for two, which are absolutely delicious—all the more so when washed down with an ice-cold Pilsner Urquell. Generous portions and reasonable prices are two more reasons to visit.

Latin American

Located inside the Hotel Salvator is the warm and inviting **La Boca** (Truhlářská 10, tel. 222 312 073, www.laboca.cz, daily 9am-11pm, mains 249-398 Kč). The internal terrace garden is the focal point, with a few booths and even a children's play area rounding out the rest of the space. The tomato soup and caesar salad make for excellent starters, while just about any of the pastas, tapas, or salads (most of which are too large to finish) will leave you more than satisfied.

Mediterranean

Homemade pastas, fresh seafood, and excellent pizza are what you can expect from **Ambiente Pizza Nuova** (Revoluční 1, tel. 221 803 308, www.ambi.cz, daily 11:30am-11:30pm, mains 168-450 Kč). Popular with families, expect plenty of hustle and bustle, particularly in the kid-friendly indoor playground on the premises. The wine selection is plentiful, the waitstaff friendly, and the location close to everything you could possibly want to see, making it an easy and always reliable choice.

Inside Slovanský Dům, **Kogo Pizzeria & Caffeteria** (Na Příkopě 22, tel. 221 451 259, www.kogo.cz, daily 11am-11pm, mains 245-680 Kč) fills up regularly with families, businesspeople, and couples who can't wait to sink their teeth into the excellent Mediterranean menu. The risotto alla pescatora is particularly popular, as is the linguine with lobster, shrimp, and zucchini. Brightly lit, full of energy, and very affordable considering the portions and location, Kogo is one of the surer bets in town.

La Terrassa (Janáčkovo nábřeží-Dětský ostrov, tel. 725 161 616, www.laterrassa.cz, daily 11am-midnight, mains 195-595 Kč) has restaurant owned and operated by Prague's Hare Krishna community. Diners share tables and floor cushions, although more conventional seating is available upstairs. All of the food served is grown on their organic farm outside the city, making it one of the healthier options in town.

STARÉ MĚSTO
Asian

Buddha-Bar (Jakubská 8, tel. 221 776 400, www.buddha-bar.cz, Tues.-Sat. 6pm-3am, mains 390-795 Kč) is located underneath Prague's version of the international Buddha-Bar hotel chain. It's dark and romantic and not for everyone's budget, but if you feel like splurging, you won't regret such tasty dishes as the seared tuna and lamb curry. Attentive service and a decadent atmosphere complete this upscale yet elegant scene.

Zebra Asian Noodle Bar (Melantrichova 5, tel. 777 873 333, www.zebranoodlebar.cz, daily 11am-11:30pm, mains 189-279 Kč) is a bright and modern restaurant with an open kitchen that has won over plenty of die-hard fans lately. Their pad thai with shrimp, massman curry with beef, and range of sushi and dim sum selections are all excellent choices when winding down from a full day of shopping and sightseeing.

Cafés

Despite its proximity to the Charles Bridge, **Café Montmartre** (Řetězová 7, tel. 222 221 244, Mon.-Fri. 8am-11pm, Sat.-Sun. noon-11pm, mains 58-120 Kč) has somehow managed to stay relatively tourist-free. It has been around since the first republic and was once a favorite watering hole of the town's literati. You'll now find students, artists, and office workers kicking back with a drink or enjoying a sandwich or dessert. This place is a true survivor.

Tucked away on tiny Týnská Street, **Týnská literární kavárna** (Týnská 6, tel. 224 827 807, www.knihytynska.cz, Mon.-Fri. 10am-11pm, Sat.-Sun. noon-11pm, mains 85-105 Kč) is where you'll find local writers and

U Pinkasů, home of the first Pilsner Urquell

© TOM DIRLIS

quickly become one of Prague's best places for tapas thanks to tasty offerings like Jamon Iberico, baked tiger prawns with garlic and chili, and their perfect tortilla de patatas. Mains such as the pork steak de Salamanca and sea bass with stuffed peppers round out an authentic and continuously evolving menu.

High ceilings, shiny copper, and a brightly lit kitchen all give **Fine Café** (Vladislavova 17, tel. 224 054 070, www.finecafe.cz, Mon.-Sat. 11am-11pm, mains 165-375 Kč) a brasserie-type feel that complements its creative menu. From corn-fed chicken with pistachio pesto and polenta to soft-shell crab with saffron risotto, this friendly and modern eatery has established itself quickly as one of Nové Město's more reliable options.

Vegetarian

Cheap, simple, and extremely popular, ◖ **U Govindy Vegetarian Club** (Soukenická 27, tel. 605 700 871, www.govindarestaurace.cz, Mon.-Fri. 11am-6pm, Sat. noon-4pm, mains 96-110 Kč) is a self-service vegetarian

Tea Time

Prague may be known the world over for its tasty and refreshing beer, but there's a popular and far healthier indulgence few talk about. The first official tearoom or *čajovna* opened in the Lucerna building in 1912 but shut down just a few months later. Things didn't pick up again until after the Communist regime had been replaced, which is when the country's largest chain, Dobrá Čajovna, opened its first tearoom on Wenceslas Square on June 1, 1993.

Unlike most modern brightly lit establishments, Czech tearooms tend to favor subdued lighting and music, coupled with a relaxed and informal setting. Extensive menus offering black, green, oolong, white, and rooibos teas, among others, are the norm, as is a completely smoke-free environment. Many tearooms also sell tea in bulk as well as corresponding accessories such as traditional teapots, cups, filters, and more.

Here's a small sampling of tea rooms that have cemented their popularity with locals and visitors alike.

- **Dobrá Čajovna** (Václavské náměstí 14, tel. 224 231 480, www.tea.cz/cajovna) offers one of the widest varieties of teas in the Czech Republic, and their flagship establishment is arguably one of the most famous in the country.

- **Siva** (Masná 8, tel. 222 315 983, www.cajiky. cz) is an Arabian-themed tearoom with over one hundred types of tea on offer. Hookahs are available with flavored tobacco, and belly dancing is performed on Wednesday, Friday, and Saturday.

- **Čajovna pod Stromem Čajovým** (Mánesova 38, tel. 223 011 050, www.cajovnapodstromem.cz) is located in Prague 2 not far from the National Museum. Friendly service as well as Czech mead, water pipes, and over 130 types of tea on offer have solidified this intimate room's reputation as one of the better spaces around.

- **Růžová Čajovna** (Růžová 8, tel. 222 245 894, www.pangea-tea.cz) breaks tradition by offering wine, coffee, and even ice cream sundaes alongside its extensive tea selection, a fact its customers don't seem to mind, considering how often most come back.

- **Amana Tearoom** (Záhořanského 6, tel. 224 922 591, www.amana.estranky.cz) is somewhat bare-bones and slightly off the beaten path but popular nevertheless with locals who can't seem to get enough of what could very well be the largest selection of teas in town.

students sipping on wine or devouring pub food like fried cheese or pickled fish. A large patio is open during the summer months, while the winter offers a more intimate setting inside the café's series of arched rooms. Somehow managing to stay tourist-free despite it being located mere yards from Old Town Square, Týnská literární kavárna is a wonderful place to put a few drinks away before rejoining the masses.

Located in the House of the Black Madonna, the █ **Grand Café Orient** (Ovocný trh 19, tel. 224 224 240, www.grandcafeorient.cz, Mon.-Fri. 9am-10pm, Sat.-Sun. 10am-10pm, mains 95-210 Kč) is a cheerful and relaxing cubist-influenced café that's perfect for a light meal or a coffee break. Most of the food on offer is of the sandwich and baguette variety, but there are a number of desserts available, including crepes, pies, cakes, and fruit cups. This is a wonderful way to spend an hour or two.

Continental

Mistral Cafe (Valentinská 11/56, tel. 222 317 737, www.mistralcafe.cz, daily 10am-11pm, mains 139-294 Kč) is a modern, artsy, and spacious restaurant offering a vastly richer dining experience than the usual tourist traps that dot the area. Sandwiches, meat dishes, and a few Czech classics make up the menu, all of which

© TOM DiRLIS

the Nostress Café Restaurant

are carefully prepared and served by a friendly and efficient staff. This is a fine and affordable alternative to the rather predictable and over-priced fare nearby.

Competing for the finest dining experience in Prague is **Bellevue** (Smetanovo nábřeží 18, tel. 222 221 443, www.zatisigroup.cz, daily noon-3pm and 5:30pm-11pm, mains 490-790 Kč), whose window seats provide a picture-perfect view of Charles Bridge and Prague Castle. Live piano music in the evenings provides a romantic backdrop as diners dig in to all kinds of beef, fish, pasta, and duck dishes and wash it all down with a bottle chosen from the rather comprehensive wine list. Many opt for the "Best of Bohemia Menu," and some of the braver souls spoil themselves with the extraordinary fillet of fallow deer. Sunday brunch has live jazz and all the Bohemia Sekt you can drink. This restaurant is highly recommended, and reservations are advised.

While certainly not cheap, **Le Terroir** (Vejvodova 1, tel. 222 220 260, www.leterroir.cz, Tues.-Sat. 11am-11pm, 3-course menu

1,320 Kč, 5-course menu 1,650 Kč) is nevertheless an excellent option should you feel like celebrating or impressing that special someone in your life. Delicious meat and seafood options like veal, lamb chops, scallops, and lobster are available, as are a number of fine wines. If money is not an issue, do yourself a favor and head to this charming and romantic cellar restaurant tonight.

The **Nostress Café Restaurant** (Dušní 10, tel. 222 317 007, www.nostress.cz, daily 10am-midnight, mains 260-490 Kč) is a category-defying space that operates as an art gallery, lifestyle shop, and fusion restaurant all at once. Simple tables rest amid antiques and towering works of art, while business folk, shoppers on a lunch break, and high-end tourists from the ritzier hotels dive into delicious helpings of chicken curry panang and grilled salmon steak. This is a great place to have a relaxing lunch in one of Prague's busiest restaurant districts. You may even find yourself picking up some wrought-iron furniture on the way out.

V Zátiší (Liliová 1, tel. 222 221 155, www.vzatisi.cz, daily noon-3pm and 5:30pm-11pm, mains 495-795 Kč) was one of the first restaurants in town to open its doors after the Velvet Revolution of 1989. It won the Best Restaurant in Central and Eastern Europe award in 1996 and the Best Restaurant in Prague award in 2001, solidifying its reputation as one of the finer establishments about town. Intimate and elegant, its four rooms are decorated in unique style, including artists' easels placed randomly about the premises and paintings from the country's finest artists gracing the walls. The service can be spotty (always a problem in Prague) and the menu changes often, but meals typically revolve around creative examples of French, Asian, and Czech cuisines. A big hit with celebrities, foodies, and the town's elite, this is an experience no diner forgets soon.

Cuban

Modeled after Papa Hemingway's old stomping grounds in Havana, **La Bodeguita del Medio** (Kaprova 5, tel. 224 813 922, www.bodeguita.cz, Sun.-Mon. 11am-2am, Tues.-Sat.

11am-4am, mains 199-599 Kč) is a little slice of salsa just off Old Town Square. Begin the evening with one of the mouthwatering Cuban dishes on offer and an ice cold mojito; the bar claims to serve over 300 on any given day. Dance shows every night starting at 8pm feature Tradicion, a lively group of scantily clad salsa dancers who always manage to drive diners out of their seats and onto their tables or the bar, turning La Bodeguita into a writhing free-for-all before the night's done. "Fun" is the key word here.

Czech

Brought to you by the Ambiente group, **La Degustation** (Haštalská 753/18, tel. 222 311 234, www.ambi.cz, daily 6pm-midnight, menu 2,150-3,150 Kč) is nothing short of a gastronomic miracle right in the heart of Old Town. Two tasting menus, the Dégustation Bohême Bourgeoise and Dégustation du Chef, offer seven carefully prepared mouthwatering courses, plus seven more *amuse-bouches* before and between courses. The former concentrates on Czech culinary art at the end of the 19th century, while the latter presents traditional Czech meals fused with a distinctly French style. Simply put, this is a restaurant like no other in the city, one that treats the entire dining process as a feast for the eyes and theater of the palate; it's highly recommended.

Cartouche (Bílkova 14, tel. 222 317 103, www.cartouche.cz, daily 11:30am-11pm, mains 249-599 Kč) is an atmospheric and increasingly popular throwback. Located in a cellar that's decorated with red bricks, massive oak tables, and a ton of burning candles, you can't help but feel you've traveled back in time. Mouthwatering dishes like roast duck, rib-eye steak, and medieval meat platter are offered at reasonable prices and with friendly service. It's a great choice.

Le Café Colonial (Široká 6, tel. 224 818 322, http://colonialpub.cz, Mon.-Fri. 8am-midnight, Sat.-Sun. 9am-midnight, mains 146-395 Kč) offers diners a light, pleasant atmosphere and a large varied menu that includes

such tantalizing treats as schnitzel, pork ribs, and goulash. This is an excellent place to have brunch or dinner, either before or after strolling through lovely Josefov.

French

A longtime favorite with the French expat crowd, **Chez Marcel** (Haštalská 12, tel. 222 315 676, www.chezmarcel.cz, daily 11:30am-1am, mains 190-420 Kč) is a popular café-bar whose quiche and authentic bistro dishes like rabbit in mustard sauce keep customers coming back for more. By day, the place affects a lazy kind of charm, making it a perfect spot to unwind with a cup of coffee and the day's *Le Monde*. At night, hipsters and couples start filing in, ordering up carafes of wine and adding to the overall joie de vivre.

Located in the Hotel Paris Praha, the **Sarah Bernhardt Restaurant** (U Obecního domu 1, tel. 222 195 195, www.hotel-paris.cz, daily 6:30am-11pm, mains 380-590 Kč) is a beautifully appointed art nouveau space characterized by art deco fixtures, inlaid wood paneling, and gilded stucco work. The menu, as elegant as the restaurant's interiors, offers such specialties as grilled tuna fillet and roasted veal medallions, both of which are best enjoyed with a bottle chosen from the extensive wine list. Reservations are recommended.

Indian

Indian Jewel (Týn 6, tel. 222 310 156, www.indianjewel.cz, daily 11am-11pm, mains 180-490 Kč) is a relatively recent addition to the Indian food scene in Prague, and it consistently delivers the goods. From its traditional decor to its authentic dishes like *machi tikka, jhinga* pepper masala, and *dhingri mattar,* you'll enjoy meat, fish, and vegetarian delights served by attentive staff that provides the same care and hospitality Indians are renowned for throughout the world.

If you're in Old Town Square and don't feel like spending 250 Kč and up for something to eat, try **Beas** (Týnská 19, tel. 608 035 727, www.beas-dhaba.cz, Mon.-Fri. 11am-8pm, Sat. noon-8pm, Sun. noon-6pm, mains 89-149

© TOM DIRLIS

Chez Marcel

Kč), arguably the city's best Indian food for the price. Specializing in vegetarian cuisine, they offer a handful of daily specials and a couple of sides, all of which are cooked fresh and richly spiced. There isn't much to the decor or atmosphere of the place, but if you're looking for something quick and tasty, you won't find a better deal nearby.

International

Pařížská is one of the trendier streets in Prague, and **Restaurace Barock** (Pařížská 24, tel. 222 329 221, www.barockrestaurant.cz, daily 10am-1am, mains 295-635 Kč) does its best to fit in. Large, stylish, and sleek, it attracts the ultracool and wannabe set, complete with pouty looks and Versace sunglasses. Owned by Tommy Sjoo and Nils Jebens, who also operate the flawless Kampa Park restaurant, the international menu does have its moments, particularly the sushi, as well as other more imaginative Asian fusion dishes. In the end, some will like the high-end attitude that overflows here, while others will be turned off completely.

Bílkova 13 (Bílkova 13, tel. 224 829 254, www.bilkova13.cz, daily 11am-11pm, mains 165-528 Kč) is a large yet intimate space that has continued to improve steadily both in service and menu offerings. Its international dishes change regularly and can be hit or miss, although you can't go wrong with the excellent seafood options such as the seared tuna steak and sea bass fillets.

School (Smetanovo nábřeží 22, tel. 222 222 173, www.school.cz, Sun.-Thurs. 9am-midnight, Fri.-Sat. 9am-1am, mains 230-450 Kč) is a modern and friendly restaurant offering simple yet delicious meals complemented by a romantic view of Prague Castle. The salmon steak, duck leg, and grilled pork tenderloin are all done expertly, and the homemade apple strudel has been hailed as one of the finest in town.

Jewish and Kosher

Across the street from Pinkas Synagogue sits **King Solomon** (Široká 8, tel. 224 818 752, www.kosher.cz, Sun.-Thurs. noon-11pm, Fri.

© TOM DIRLIS

Indian Jewel

dinner and Sat. lunch by reservation only, mains 510-950 Kč), Prague's oldest and best-known kosher restaurant. Specialties include wiener schnitzel, *holishkes,* roasted duck, and gefilte fish, all of which are served during dining hours that adhere to the Sabbath. There is a long and rather impressive list of Israeli, American, and Moravian kosher wines available as well. Keep in mind that while the food here is generally very good, the prices are quite high.

Latin American

La Casa Argentina (Dlouhá 35/730, tel. 222 311 512, www.lacasaargentina.cz, Sun.-Mon. noon-midnight, Tues.-Sat. noon-2am, mains 350-1,170 Kč) is a theme restaurant complete with fedoras, Maradona soccer jerseys, and sexy tango dancers. The main dining room has been made to resemble a typical Argentine street scene. Another room has water running down its walls and a caged lizard. There's also a bar in the back decked out in a nautical theme. Many will find this to be a little too kitschy for their

taste. Still others will wonder whether the wait-staff could be any more useless. Why then do people insist on coming here? In a word: steak. Imported from Argentina, the steak served will help you quickly come to understand why the country eats more red meat than any other. Be warned: everything about this place, including the menu, is a hit-and-miss affair. But the steak is so good you'll forgive just about anything for one more bite.

Owned by the highly reputable Ambiente group, **Brasileiro** (U Radnice 8, tel. 224 234 474, www.ambi.cz, daily 11am-midnight, 665 Kč all you can eat) is an all-you-can-eat Brazilian bonanza that can do no wrong. Meat is grilled in the *churrasco* style and served by *churasqueros* who are both your waiters and cooks. Winding their way among the tables, they happily offer diners various meats from their skewers, explaining the differences in taste and preparation of each. This is primarily a carnivore's paradise, but vegetarians can pay half price and gorge themselves on the salad bar, which includes sushi, stuffed mushrooms, fresh greens, and marinated peppers. You'll be hard-pressed to find another restaurant in town that offers as much bang for your buck.

Mediterranean

VinoDiVino (Štupartská 769/18, tel. 222 311 791, www.vinodivinopraha.cz, daily noon-10pm, mains 220-490 Kč) is located in the heart of the tourist zone and has the prices to match. An ever-changing menu of meat, fish, and pasta dishes are served up in a brightly lit modern space by friendly staff that's always happy to help. It's a solid choice if you're in the center and feeling like Italian.

The front room of **La Bottega di Finestra** (Platnéřská 11, tel. 222 233 094, www.lafinestra.cz, Mon.-Sat. noon-11pm, Sun. noon-10pm, mains 265-545 Kč) offers display cases full of salads, quiches, pastas, seafood, baked goods, and more, whetting your appetite before you even sit down. Mouthwatering Italian dishes ranging from mushroom risotto to grilled octopus are available, though the menu changes often. Regardless of what's being offered, however, you can rest easy that this superb establishment will not disappoint.

Middle Eastern

Kabul Karolina (Karolíny Světlé 14, tel. 224 235 452, www.kabulrestaurant.cz, daily noon-11pm, mains 170-290 Kč) is a small homey restaurant offering traditional Afghan food as well as a handful of pizzas and Czech dishes for those with less adventurous palates. The meal of mutton and kebabs are first rate, as are the assortment of vegetarian offerings, including the Kabeli and Afghan salad. You can expect warm service and reasonable prices, too.

Seafood

While certainly not cheap, **Zdeněk's Oyster Bar** (Malá Štupartská 5, tel. 725 946 250, http://oysterbar.cz, daily 11:30am-1am, mains 295-695 Kč) is a solid choice for those with a desire for fresh seafood. You'll find a lot of variety here, from shrimp platters to lobster rolls, crab claws to caviar, all imported daily from France, Britain, and beyond.

A relative newcomer to the Old Town restaurant scene, **Fish & Chips** (Dlouhá 21, tel. 606 881 414, http://fishandchipsprague.cz, daily 11am-1am, mains 145-325 Kč) offers exactly what its name says. Enjoy full or half portions of cod, trout, or Scottish salmon along with a selection of fries, onion rings, and other fried and battered delights. Reasonable prices, decent service, and simple, hearty fare are the name of the game.

Vegetarian

Maitrea (Týnská 6, tel. 221 711 631, www.restaurace-maitrea.cz, Mon.-Fri. 11:30am-11:30pm, Sat.-Sun. noon-11:30pm, mains 155-165 Kč) is arguably Prague's finest vegetarian restaurant and most likely its best designed. High ceilings, arched doorways, elongated lamps, and sculptural fountains are just a few of the things that'll tickle your cornea. And the lip-smacking and affordable menu—ranging from pastas to stir-fries to burgers and

burritos—will have you coming back sooner than you'd think. It's highly recommended.

MALÁ STRANA
American

Cowboys Steaks & Cocktails (Nerudova 40, tel. 296 826 107, www.kampagroup.com, daily noon-1am, mains 265-795 Kč), is a steak house that comes complete with all the fixin's. Billing itself as having the biggest, best, and sexiest steaks in town, the focus here is on quality and fun. Friendly waitstaff bedecked in Stetsons and leather vests serve generous portions of steaks, seafood, and poultry dishes to your cowhide-covered booth, or, if the weather's right, to your table on the heated rooftop terrace that offers an exceptional panoramic view of the city. Make sure to leave room for dessert in the form of good old-fashioned American cheesecake or chocolate brownies.

Hearty soups and sandwiches, along with free coffee and soda refills (still a foreign concept here), are just some of the reasons why **Bohemia Bagel** (Lázeňská 19, tel. 257 218 192, www.bohemiabagel.cz, daily 8am-9pm, mains 135-179 Kč) continues to do big business with visitors and locals alike. This is the only place in town where you'll find fresh bagels and cream cheese, and the "Wake and Bake" breakfast specials are a great reason to get out of bed and make it to one of the three central locations by 11am. The second location is at Másna 2, tel. 224 812 560, and the third is at Dukelských hrdinu 48, tel. 220 806 541.

Asian

◖ **Noi** (Újezd 19, tel. 257 311 411, www.noirestaurant.cz, daily 11am-1am, mains 180-290 Kč) has established itself as one of Prague's premier Thai restaurants thanks to its reasonable prices, attentive staff, and consistently delicious dishes. Duck, fish, beef, and chicken are all on offer, and the pad thai and *lab kai* salad are arguably the finest in town. It's highly recommended.

Balkan

As you approach the American embassy on Tržiště Street, tantalizing smells waft through the air, accompanied by the percussive rhythmic sounds of Gypsy music. Follow your nose a little farther and you'll come to **Gitanes** (Tržiště 7, tel. 257 530 163, www.gitanes.cz, daily noon-midnight, mains 185-595 Kč), a jewel of Balkan cuisine in the middle of Malá Strana. Decorated with colorful icons, paintings, and photographs of the former Yugoslavia, its two rooms emanate a warmth and hospitality that's hard to find in Prague. The menu relies heavily on Yugoslavian cuisine but mixes in a few Italian specialties as well. The fried peppers stuffed with cheese make for a wonderful appetizer, and the chef's paella for two might just convince you to return before your trip is over.

Not far from the square in Malá Strana is **Luka Lu** (Újezd 33, tel. 257 212 388, http://lukalu.cz, daily 11am-midnight, mains 145-445 Kč), a colorful Croatian restaurant serving traditional meals with a smile. Grab a seat and dig into seafood dishes such as grilled octopus and calamari as well as a number of inventive pasta and meat options.

Cafés

The family-run **Cafe de Paris** (Maltézské náměstí 4, tel. 603 160 718, www.cafedeparis.cz, daily noon-midnight, mains 169-395 Kč) has remained popular with locals and visitors for years now thanks to its pleasant atmosphere, attentive service, and small, carefully prepared menu. Anyone coming here for the first time must try the Entrecote Cafe de Paris, which is cooked according to a 75-year-old secret recipe, or the fresh sea bass, which is always prepared to perfection. A nice selection of cheeses, desserts, and wines complete the authentic brasserie vibe.

Tucked away down a quiet cobblestone street not far from Charles Bridge, **Vinograf** (Mišenská 8, tel. 604 705 730, www.vinograf.cz, Mon.-Sat. 4pm-midnight, Sun. 2pm-10pm) is a charming little café and wine bar that plays home to thirsty tourists during the day and local artists and residents at night. Its intimate, tastefully decorated space is often the site of lively parties, particularly as the night wears on.

Continental

Although occasionally plagued by stories of poor or rude management, **Pálffy palác** (Valdštejnská 14, tel. 257 530 522, www.palffy.cz, daily 11am-11pm, mains 390-550 Kč) continues to remain at the top of most peoples' lists as one of the best and most romantic dining spots in Prague. Housed in the elegant baroque palace of the same name, tourists, young professionals, and the occasional politician take their time poring over the menu, which offers a delicious assortment of meat, fish, and vegetarian dishes. This is one lunch or dinner you won't soon forget.

Quiet Maltese Square is the home of **U Malířů** (Maltézské náměstí 11, tel. 257 530 318, www.umaliru.cz, daily noon-11pm, mains 420-690 Kč), a highly reputable and very popular vaulted and frescoed tavern that excels on every level. Everything on the menu is good, be it the duck, game, beef, lamb, or fresh seafood flown in daily. Many consider this the finest dining Prague has to offer, and it's a must for those whose budgets allow it.

U Maltézských rytířů (Prokopská 10, tel. 257 530 075, www.umaltezskychrytiru.cz, Mon.-Fri. 11am-11pm, Sat.-Sun. 1pm-11pm, mains 130-360 Kč) is an exceptional restaurant whose specialty is traditional Czech dishes, particularly the roasted duck and marinated pork knee. The main floor is a vaulted Renaissance affair offering three cozy tables, but downstairs is where you'll find the jewel of the place: two romantic Gothic vaults offering intimate lounges that have been the site of many a celebrity party and marriage proposal. Low lighting and jazzy piano music complete the scene. Reservations are a must.

A decadent coffeehouse at the turn of the 20th century, the ◖ **Café Savoy** (Vítězná 5, tel. 257 311 562, www.ambi.cz, Mon.-Fri. 8am-10:30pm, Sat.-Sun. 9am-10:30pm, mains 145-508 Kč) is now an excellent choice

© TOM DIRLUS

You'll find the best brunch in town at Café Savoy.

for settling in with a drink or light meal and soaking up the ambience. The restored ceiling alone—a triumphant trompe l'oeil that interweaves leaves, apples, grapes, and ribbons—is worth a visit, and the dining area on the upper level provides an excellent view of the three enormous crystal chandeliers that light up the main room. The menu consists of decent roast meats, including wiener schnitzel and grilled chicken breast, along with a delicious weekend brunch special.

Czech

Olympia (Vítězná 7, tel. 251 511 080, www. kolkovna.cz, daily 11am-midnight, mains 149-329 Kč) is part of the well-known Kolkovna chain and offers traditional Czech dishes at very affordable prices. Ribs, roast duck, and goulash are a few of the offerings, all of which can be enjoyed with a delicious glass of Pilsner Urquell. Perfect for large groups or families, reservations are recommended.

Located halfway up Petřín Hill, **Nebozízek**

(Petřínské sady 411, tel. 257 315 329, www. nebozizek.cz, daily 11am-11pm, mains 180-290 Kč) offers traditional Czech meat dishes at very affordable prices. The real reason to come here, however, is for the breathtaking views of Prague Castle, Old Town, and Charles Bridge that unfold beneath you. It's a worthwhile hike up the hill should you be in the vicinity.

International

There are many words one can use to describe the interiors at **Alchymist** (Nosticova 1, tel. 257 312 518, www.alchymist.cz, Tues.-Sat. 6pm-11pm, mains 260-510 Kč), and "opulent" is certainly one of them. Relying on a mix of European, Moorish, and baroque styles, you come to feel like you're dining in the 18th-century more than modern-day Malá Strana. The baked duck and tuna fillet are two surefire hits, as is the ever-changing yet always reliable dessert menu, all of which is brought to you by an extremely professional and polite waitstaff.

Opposite the Kafka Museum sits an 18th-century building that originally served as a brick factory, or *cihelna*. Today, it's the home of **Hergetova Cihelna** (Cihelná 2b, tel. 296 826 103, www.kampagroup.com, daily 11:30am-1am, mains 295-595 Kč), a chic restaurant, cocktail bar, café, and music lounge rolled into one. The delicious and well-presented international menu ranges from Asian to Continental to American, offering something for those with even the finickiest of tastes. There's also a large summer terrace overlooking the river providing an unforgettable picture-perfect view of Charles Bridge.

It's not easy to find quality gourmet meals at reasonable prices in Prague, but **Little Whale** (Maltézské náměstí 15, tel. 257 214 703, www. umalevelryby.cz, daily 10am-10pm, mains 340-420 Kč) accomplishes both with ease. It's somewhat small but offers an intimacy that's perfect for dinner with family, friends, or that special someone. The international menu changes on a regular basis, so make sure to check the website and reserve ahead of time.

Mediterranean

Authentic Spanish cuisine served by refreshingly cheerful waitstaff is what you'll find at **Cafe El Centro** (Maltézské náměstí 9, tel. 257 533 343, www.elcentro.czrb.cz, daily noon-midnight, mains 130-399 Kč). Its arched doors, vaulted ceilings, and suspended smoked hams provide an ambience that is part Czech pub, part Spanish bodega, and all culinary comfort. Just about everything on the extensive menu is good and the portions are very generous, particularly two-person dishes like the paella and rabbit *montanesa*.

Ristorante Karmelita (Ujezd 31, tel. 257 312 564, www.restauracecarmelita.cz, daily 11am-midnight, mains 135-397 Kč) is a friendly and reliable pizzeria that serves up a well-balanced variety of pizza, pasta, and meat dishes, all of which are reasonably priced and come in very generous portions. You really can't go wrong with whatever you choose here, particularly the tiramisu, which you should definitely leave room for.

Mexican

Opposite Petřín Hill is **Cantina** (Újezd 38, tel. 257 317 173, www.restauracecantina.cz, daily 11:30am-midnight, mains 180-399 Kč), a veteran of the Mexican restaurant scene that still has patrons waiting at the bar on the off chance somebody's reservations fall through. Though the setting is pseudo-rustic and slightly kitschy (think burlap-covered ceiling and vintage tequila posters), the menu nevertheless impresses time and again. The gorditas are as good as any you'll find back home and the fajitas are usually a sure bet as well. Slightly overshadowed by newer, bigger Mexican restaurants that have recently arrived on the scene, Cantina still manages to hold its own this side of the river. Reservations are a must.

Seafood

Consistently ranking as one of Prague's finest dining establishments, **Kampa Park** (Na Kampě 8b, tel. 296 826 102, www.kampagroup.com, daily 11:30am-1am, mains 525-895 Kč) is an experience you won't soon forget. The selection of fresh seafood, wild game, and contemporary meat dishes is second to none, as is the extensive range of wines on offer, numbering over 150. Excellent service, unbeatable quality, and the most magnificent riverside views of Charles Bridge and beyond are just some of the reasons why locals, tourists, and visiting dignitaries continue to flock here—including Hillary Clinton, who was quoted as saying, "I wanted our last night at Kampa Park to go on forever."

HRADČANY

Asian

Advertising itself as an "Oriental tearoom and restaurant," the extremely popular **Malý Buddha** (Úvoz 46, tel. 220 513 894, www.malybuddha.cz, Tues.-Sun. noon-10:30pm, mains 110-250 Kč) offers diners a serene alternative to the chaos of Prague Castle. Comprising a series of vaulted spaces that culminate in a shrine dedicated to a large orange Buddha, this unique establishment is also one of the few in Prague that is completely non-smoking. The menu boasts over 50 types of tea as well as enticing entrées and very affordable vegetarian and meat-based dishes. It's a highly recommended alternative to the usual fare found in the immediate area.

Czech

Having played host to a number of dignitaries, including George and Barbara Bush, Margaret Thatcher, and Mikhail Gorbachev, it would be accurate to say that **U Císařů** (Loretánská 175/5, tel. 220 518 484, www.ucisaru.cz, daily 9am-1am, mains 270-550 Kč) is a pretty safe bet. The interiors are reminiscent of a small castle, complete with original antiques, arched doorways with wrought-iron gates, and paintings of former Czech rulers gracing each table. Attentive waiters are more than happy to explain the traditional Czech dishes on offer, and a pianist tickles the ivories to ensure a relaxed and pleasurable time is had by all.

Set in the Royal Gardens, **Lví dvůr** (U Prašného mostu 6/51, tel. 224 372 361, www.

lvidvur.cz, daily 11am-11pm, mains 240-590 Kč) manages to combine original period pieces with contemporary touches to create an unforgettable dining experience. The house specialty is traditional Czech food with grilled piglet and roast pork tenderloin just two tasty examples.

The service here is typically excellent, and during the summer months an ample terrace is opened to the public, allowing awe-inspired diners romantic views of St. Vitus Cathedral and the Castle Towers.

Castle tiring you out? Dying for a pit stop? Check out **Espresso Kajetánka** (Hradčanské náměstí 1, tel. 257 533 735, www.espressokajetanka.cz, daily 10am-8pm, mains 239-499 Kč), located near the castle entrance. Reasonably priced meat dishes and salads make up the bulk of the menu, but it's the remarkable views of Malá Strana and New Town that make this one of the more popular choices in the area.

DEJVICE
Czech
Local favorite **Bruska** (Dejvická 20, tel. 222 362 616, www.restaurace-bruska.cz, Mon.-Sat. 11am-11:30pm, Sun. 11:30am-11pm, mains 139-379 Kč) is a laid-back neighborhood restaurant featuring tasty traditional Czech dishes and some of the finest beer in the district. It's well worth a trip if you're interested in trying the local cuisine, and if you happen to be there on a weekend, go for the ribs—you won't be disappointed.

Pod loubím (Evropská 26, tel. 233 326 097, www.podloubim.com, Mon.-Fri. 11am-midnight, Sat.-Sun. noon-midnight, mains 109-269 Kč) is a stylish pub-restaurant that focuses on traditional Czech fare like goulash, beef and dumplings, chicken, and turkey. The beer is fresh, the service adequate, and the daily menu a bargain for those looking to keep costs down. This is one of the more reliable choices in the area.

Located on a residential street, unassuming local favorite **U Kavalíra** (Jaselská 10, tel. 224 322 437, www.ukavalira.com, daily 11am-midnight, mains 149-390 Kč) has kept Prague 6

happily in beer and homemade Czech dishes for many years now. From the traditional decor to the carefully prepared and very affordable meat, fish, and game dishes, the restaurant allows for rubbing elbows with the locals and dining in authentic Dejvice fashion.

Indian
Located a stone's throw from Hradčanská subway station, **Haveli** (Dejvická 6, tel. 233 344 800, www.haveli.cz, daily 11am-11pm, mains 195-495 Kč) serves mouthwatering Indian dishes to delightfully surprised visitors and in-the-know locals who keep coming back for more. The service is excellent and the menu boasts one of the broader vegetarian selections in town. This is one of the finer Indian restaurants in Prague and a must if you're anywhere in the vicinity.

Mediterranean
Kavala (Charlese de Gaulla 5, tel. 224 325 181, www.kavala-praha.cz, daily 11am-11:30pm, mains 160-490 Kč) is a well-reputed Greek restaurant serving up all the traditional dishes you might expect, including souvlaki, lamb, calamari, and more. Friendly service, a delicious wine list, and reasonable prices make this one of the more dependable establishments in Dejvice.

Mexican
Fiesta (Václavkova 2, tel. 224 324 448, www.fiesta-mexickarestaurace.cz, Mon.-Thurs. 10am-11pm, Fri.-Sat. 10am-11:30pm, Sun. 11am-10pm, mains 160-320 Kč) serves up generous portions of some of the finest Mexican food this side of the river. The Azteca soup is delicious, as are the steaks and fajitas. An outdoor patio is erected in the summer and it fills up fast, so get there early and find out why the locals keep coming back for their Fiesta fix.

HOLEŠOVICE
Asian
Located next to the dance club of the same name, **Sasazu** (Bubenské nábřeží 306/13, tel.

284 097 455, www.sasazu.com, Sun.-Thurs. noon-midnight, Fri.-Sat. noon-1am, mains 215-599 Kč) is an exceptional Asian restaurant offering an ever-changing fusion style menu meant to delight, astonish, and amuse all your taste buds. Grab a seat amid the traditional Asian decorations and furnishings and allow yourself to be transported to another dimension. It's well worth the trip to Prague 7.

Czech

Established by Lou Fanánek Hagen, lead singer of legendary Czech rock band Tři Sestry, **Hostinec na Staré Kovárně** (Kamenická 17, tel. 233 371 099, www.starakovarna.cz, Mon.-Sat. 11:30am-1am, Sun. 11:30am-11:30pm, mains 110-349 Kč) is a cross between an old-school table-sharing Czech pub and a modern restaurant, with an emphasis on fun. Ignore the motorcycle dangling from the ceiling and flip through the extensive menu, which offers colorful Czech dishes like the stuffed Bill Gates turkey and roasted pork à la Warren Buffet. Keep in mind that the full menu is only available after 2:30pm, so plan your time accordingly, or get here early and down some of the tastiest beer this side of Holešovice.

Mediterranean

The concept of **Osteria Ai Galli** (Veletržní 71, tel. 775 439 222, http://osteriaaigalli.cz, Mon. 6pm-10pm, Tues.-Thurs. noon-3pm and 6pm-10pm, Fri. noon-3pm and 5pm-10pm, Sat. noon-10pm, mains 195-575 Kč) is simple: The chef comes out and tells you what fresh ingredients are on offer that day and what tasty homemade dishes he can make from them. Don't let the lack of a written menu throw you, though, as dishes ranging from monkfish to clams in a white wine and garlic broth will have you smacking your lips in no time.

ŽIŽKOV AND VINOHRADY
American

Most locals swear ▐ **The Tavern** (Chopinova 26, www.thetavern.cz, Tues.-Fri. 5pm-10pm, Sat. noon-10pm, mains 129-179 Kč) offers the best burgers in town, and they may very well be right. The Blue Smoke Burger, pulled pork sandwich, and vegetarian-friendly Urban Garden Burger are all instant classics, and the intimate 8- or 9-table setup adds to the overall friendly vibe. They have no phone, but you can make reservations via the website. It's highly recommended.

An American menu designed by an American chef gives **Mood** (Koněvova 28/29, tel. 222 517 615, www.restaurantmood.cz, daily 11am-11pm, mains 165-265 Kč) the authenticity sorely lacking in other American-themed restaurants. From buffalo wings to barbecue ribs to one of the finest hamburgers in town, this bright and modern option in the heart of Žižkov is the real red, white, and blue deal.

Asian

Located near the Jiřího z Poděbrad subway station, **Pho Vietnam Tuan & Lan** (Slavíkova 1, tel. 774 167 786, daily 10am-10pm, mains 79-169 Kč) is a no-frills take-out place with a few tables where you can stand and nosh. Excellent soups, spring rolls, and noodle and rice dishes are on offer at very affordable prices, making it the perfect pit stop.

Cafés

Café Meduza (Belgická 17, tel. 222 515 107, Mon.-Fri. 10am-1am, Sat. noon-1am, Sun. noon-midnight, snacks 65-149 Kč) is a very local, very cozy hangout for university students and aspiring artists still looking for that big break. Most come for the coffee or the mulled wine, but there are a number of tasty treats to be had, including a wide array of sweetened pancakes, open-faced sandwiches, and a handful of vegetarian delights—all at very reasonable prices.

Continental

Situated on the right bank of the Vltava River and covering the top two floors of the Dancing Building, **Celeste** (Tančící dům-Rašínovo nábřeží 80, tel. 221 984 160, www.celesterestaurant.cz, Mon.-Sat. noon-2:30pm and 6:30pm-10:30pm, mains 425-745 Kč) is a modern yet elegant restaurant offering tasty Mediterranean fare as well as some of the finest views of the city. The menu changes regularly, so if you're not sure what to order, the helpful and attentive staff will be glad to help you choose correctly. It's pricey but worth it.

Czech

Demínka (Škrétova 1, tel. 224 224 915, www. deminka.com, daily 11am-11pm, mains 150-305 Kč) is one of the original Pilsner Urquell restaurants in town, which means its beer is both fresh and top-notch. Their traditional Czech, fish, and pasta dishes aren't too shabby, either, and can be enjoyed in lovely art deco surroundings. The service can be spotty at times, but that's par for the course in this town. Reservations are recommended.

International

Considered by many resident foreigners to be one of the more romantic dining spots in town, **Mozaika** (Nitranská 13, tel. 224 253 011, www.restaurantmozaika.cz, Mon.-Fri. 11:30am-midnight, Sat. 2pm-midnight, Sun. 4pm-midnight, mains 189-384 Kč) is also known for its wildly changing international menu, which includes what many maintain is the finest burger around. This is a lovely local restaurant whose ambience, service, and cuisine are worth the short trip out of the center.

Located in the building where the great soprano Emmy Destinn was born, **U Emy Destinnové** (Kateřinská 7, tel. 224 918 425, www.uemydestinnove.cz, Mon.-Fri. 11am-11pm, Sat. 6pm-11pm, mains 295-550 Kč, degustation menu 800 Kč) is an elegant restaurant offering high-quality meat and seafood dishes such as wild boar and grilled swordfish. The American owner and chef Steven Trumpfheller also prepares a degustation menu once in a while to change things up so make sure to check the website. Excellent service, a well-thought-out wine list, and live piano music Wednesday and Thursday

are a few more reasons to visit this fine establishment.

Mediterranean

"Simplicity, tradition, passion" is the motto at **Aromi** (Mánesova 78, tel. 222 713 222, www. aromi.cz, Mon.-Sat. noon-11pm, Sun. noon-10pm, mains 275-445 Kč), and they deliver on all three counts. A simply prepared menu dominated by seafood and pasta is what people keep flocking here for, enjoying mouthwatering dishes like octopus with sweet-and-sour tomatoes and potatoes with pumpkin risotto. For dessert, try the chocolate fondant with coconut ice cream and white chocolate sauce, or, if you can't decide what to order, ask any of the very attentive waitstaff, who'll be happy to help. It's highly recommended, and reservations are advised.

Partly hidden down a side street on Karlovo náměstí is **Pizzeria di Carlo** (Karlovo náměstí 30, tel. 222 231 374, www.dicarlo.cz, Mon.-Fri. 11am-10:30pm, mains 115-369 Kč), a local favorite that bustles with brisk business from the moment it opens its doors. Casual, friendly, and offering a vast number of Italian dishes, the generously portioned pastas and brick-fired pizzas win over diners time and time again.

Ristorante Sapori (Americká 20, tel. 222 523 533, www.ristorante-praha.cz, daily 10am-midnight, mains 185-420 Kč) adds a touch of elegance to Vinohrady thanks to its high ceilings, hardwood floors, and tablecloth trimmings. The food is not bad, either, with constantly changing yet always tasty seafood, pasta, and meat dishes available. Reservations are recommended.

Considered by many to be the best Greek restaurant in town, **Olympos** (Kubelíkova 9, tel. 222 722 239, www.taverna-olympos. eu, daily 11:30am-midnight, mains 195-480 Kč) sits high atop Žižkov hill, offering diners traditional Greek delights like souvlaki and gyros along with mouthwatering veal and lamb dishes. Using original ingredients that have been shipped all the way from the mother country, Olympos does a solid job recreating an authentic Greek dining experience.

This is especially true during the warmer months, when the sunny outdoor patio is open for business.

Regularly patronized by Prague's Italian community, **Trattoria Cicala** (Žitná 43, tel. 222 210 375, http://trattoria.cicala.cz, Mon.-Sat. 11:30am-10:30pm, mains 120-590 Kč) is a charming cellar restaurant that delights fans of Italian cuisine. Pretty much everything on offer is delicious, but if you can't decide, feel free to ask the staff for suggestions, or simply allow friendly owner Aldo to cook up something spontaneous for you.

Mexican

The small but comfortable **Las Adelitas** (Americká 684/8, tel. 222 542 031, www.lasadelitas.cz, Mon.-Fri. 11am-1am, Sat.-Sun. noon-1am, mains 115-399 Kč) is one of the finest places in the city to find Mexican food.

The quesadillas and enchiladas are exceptional, and the selection of tequilas is unrivaled. The food is prepared quickly, service comes with a smile, and the premises are strictly nonsmoking; it's highly recommended. There's a second location at Malé náměstí 13, tel. 222 233 247.

Vegetarian

Adjoining one of the best-known clubs in town, the **Radost FX Café** (Bělehradská 120, tel. 224 254 776, www.radostfx.cz, daily 11:30am-3am, mains 130-315 Kč) is usually full of hipsters who can't seem to get enough of the delicious vegetarian menu. With Greek, Indian, Thai, and Mexican fare, this is one of the few places in Prague that serves mouthwatering meals well into the wee hours. Weekends offer a very popular brunch menu as well. It's highly recommended.

Information and Services

VISITOR INFORMATION OFFICES

The **Prague Information Service** (tel. 221 714 444, www.praguewelcome.com, daily 9am-7pm) is the foremost tourist authority on all things Praha. Whether it's basic information regarding the country, culture, transportation, accommodations, cultural events, day trips, or organized tours, you'll find everything you need right here. A number of maps and brochures can be picked up at their four branches: Rytířská 31 (Mon.-Sat. 10am-7pm); Staroměstské náměstí 1 (Mon.-Sat. 9am-8pm, Sun. 10am-7pm); Prague Airport (daily 8am-8:30pm); Lesser Town Bridge Tower, Malá Strana (Apr.-Oct. daily 10am-6pm).

EMERGENCY SERVICES

The main police station, located just a short walk from Wenceslas Square at Jungmannovo náměstí 9, is open 24 hours a day. The police in Prague have a less than stellar reputation, although that has been improving over the last few years, and most can now speak at least a little English. Nevertheless, odds are that whatever you have lost will most likely stay that way. If you somehow lose your passport, report it to your embassy immediately. Keep in mind that knowing your passport number or having it written down somewhere will significantly speed up the process of getting it replaced.

In case of emergency, the numbers to call are:

• Ambulance: 155

• Police: 158

• Fire: 150

• General emergency: 112

• Emergency road service: 1230, 1240

© LUCIE ERICKSEN

Česká spořitelna ATMs are easy to find.

MEDICAL SERVICES

There are plenty of hospitals in Prague, but the two that can provide 24-hour emergency care in English are **Motol Hospital** (V Úvalu 84, tel. 224 431 111, emergency tel. 224 433 681-2, pediatrics tel. 224 433 690-1, www.fnmotol.cz) and **Na Homolce Hospital** (Roentgenova 2, tel. 257 271 111, www.homolka.cz), which is home to the city's best-equipped facilities. Both are located in Prague 5.

The **Canadian Medical Center** (Veleslavínská 1, tel. 235 360 133, after business hours emergency tel. 724 300 301, www. cmcpraha.cz, Mon., Wed., and Fri. 8am-6pm, Tues. and Thurs. 8am-8pm, Sat. 9am-2pm) in Prague 6 is one of the longest-running international clinics in town and consistently voted one of the best by resident foreigners. Opposite the National Theater, the **PolyClinic at Národní** (Národní 9, tel. 222 075 119-120, emergency tel. 777 942 270, www.poliklinika. narodni.cz, Mon.-Fri. 8:30am-5pm) is run by U.S. board-certified physicians and has a variety of specialists available, along with a lab

and physical therapy. The **Unicare Medical Center** (Na Dlouhém Lánu 11, tel. 235 356 553, 24-hour emergency service tel. 608 103 050 or 602 201 040, www.unicare.cz, Mon.-Fri. 8am-8pm, Sat. 9am-4pm) provides highly reputable care in Prague 6 and can be contacted 24 hours a day.

For expert dental care, contact centrally located **Erpet Medical Centrum** (Pštrossova 10, tel. 221 595 000, emergency tel. 724 511 547, www.erpetmedical.cz, Mon.-Fri. 7am-8pm) or **American Dental** (Hvězdova 33, tel. 241 410 001, www.americandental.cz, Mon.-Fri. 8am-8pm).

The Czech word for pharmacy is *lékárna*. Only over-the-counter medicines are available at these pharmacies, and their operating hours are generally Monday-Friday 7:30am-6pm. All **pharmacies** in Prague are required to post contact information for the city's 24-hour pharmacies. A few of the more handy ones are Lékárna Palackého (Palackého 5, tel. 224 946 982) in Prague 1 and Lékárna U Svaté Ludmily (Belgická 37, tel. 222 513 396) in Prague 2. If it's late and the door is locked, simply ring the buzzer and wait. Keep in mind that a small additional fee will be added for after-hour services.

BANKS AND CURRENCY EXCHANGE

Banks in Prague generally offer decent rates of exchange but are only open Monday-Friday 8am-5pm. Most of the big players are found in the center, a few of which are: **Česká spořitelna "Expat Center"** (Rytířská 29, tel. 956 720 000, www.csas.cz/expatcenter); **Komerční Banka** (Na příkopě 33, tel. 800 521 521, www. kb.cz); **GE Money** (Revoluční 8, tel. 224 800 210, www.gemoney.cz); and **Raiffeisen Bank** (Na příkopě 24, tel. 225 374 059, www.rsts. cz). Most banks tend to offer the same rates, but you'll be wise to take advantage of their close proximity to each other and do some comparison shopping.

There are plenty of currency exchange outlets around town, but those in the thick of the tourist trade generally offer terrible rates, oftentimes covered up by their advertising "no commission" on the exchange. Don't be fooled. One of the most reputable exchange offices (Národní 43, daily 10am-7pm) in town these days is an unassuming hole-in-the-wall on Národní Street next to one of the Můstek subway exits.

POSTAL SERVICES
Post offices are scattered throughout the city but have varying business hours and levels of service. If you just need a stamp, you're better off asking at kiosks, newsstands, or anywhere you see postcards being sold. The main post office, **Hlavní Pošta** (Jindřišská 14, tel. 840 111 244, www.cpost.cz, daily 2am-midnight), is your best bet for other services and has a pretty interior you can gaze at while waiting for your number to come up.

INTERNET
Prague is overrun with Internet cafés, and while prices, service, and comfort vary enormously, you can be sure that those located in Malá Strana and Old Town Square will be considerably more expensive than in other areas. Feel free to compare prices, but if time is of the essence, you can't really go wrong with the following: **Click Internet Cafe** (Malé Náměstí 13, tel. 221 423 175, www.clickinternet.cz, daily 10am-11pm, 70 Kč per hour); **Internet Café Opletalova** (Opletalova 28, tel. 224 211 316, www.intera.cz, daily 10am-10pm, 78 Kč per hour); and **Internet Café Spika** (Dlažděná 4, tel. 224 211 521, www.netcafe.spika.cz, daily 8am-midnight, 90 Kč per hour). Free Wi-Fi is sometimes available, while other establishments might charge a nominal fee before giving you the necessary password.

LAUNDRY
There are a handful of launderettes in Prague. The most popular are **Prague Andy's Laundromat** (Korunní 14, tel. 222 510 180, http://praguelaundromat.cz, daily 8am-8pm), near the Náměstí Míru subway station, and **Royal Clean** (Myslíkova 17, tel. 222 710 986, www.royalclean.cz, Mon.-Fri. 7:30am-7pm), in the center of town.

Getting There

BY AIR
Václav Havel Airport (K Letišti 6, tel. 220 111 888, www.prg.aero/en) is located in Dejvice, roughly 12.5 miles northwest of the downtown core. The airport is comparatively small and easy to navigate, as the arrivals and departures halls are next to each other.

The taxi situation in Prague is pretty abominable all around, but most cabs set a fixed fee for service from the airport to anywhere in town. The going rate these days is 700 Kč but is always subject to change. A far cheaper alternative is the **Čedaz** (tel. 220 116 758, www.cedaz.cz, 150 Kč) shuttle bus that leaves the airport every 30 minutes daily 7:30am-7pm and drops passengers off downtown near Náměstí republiky. You can also take the friendly **Prague Airport Shuttle** (tel. 602 395 421, www.prague-airport-shuttle.com), which will take up to four passengers anywhere in town for a fixed fare of 600 Kč, or 5-8 passengers for 900 Kč.

BY TRAIN
All international trains make their final stop at either **Nádraží Holešovice** (Nádraží Holešovice Station, Partyzánská 1, Holešovice, tel. 220 806 790) or **Hlavní nádraží** (Main Station, Wilsonova 8, Nové Město, tel. 972 241 100). Both train stations are on the subway's red line, making them easy to reach and traveling around the city a cinch.

The Main Station is located right down-town, a couple of minutes' walk away from Wenceslas Square. There is an information desk at the station as well as kiosks and shops where you can grab a sandwich or a drink. Be wary of anyone who approaches you offering accommodations or bar tips. The station does attract addicts and the homeless, and while it's relatively safe, there is no reason to stick around the station any longer than you have to.

Stations serving domestic routes include **Masarykovo nádraží** (Masaryk Station, Hybernská 13, Nové Město, tel. 972 246 100), situated in Prague 1 between Náměstí repub-liky and Florenc subway-bus station, which serves a large number of cities and towns in northern and eastern Bohemia. **Smíchovské nádraží** (Smíchov Station, Nádražní, Smíchov, tel. 221 111 122), in Prague 5, serves all major towns and cities in the south and west of the Czech Republic.

Trains from Prague to Budapest leave 5-6 times a day. The trip takes 7-9 hours.

Visit www.idos.cz for schedules and fares of all trains, buses, and planes leaving or criss-crossing the country.

BY BUS

Florenc bus station (Křižíkova 4, Žižkov, tel. 900 144 444, www.csad.cz) is where all do-mestic and international buses come and go. As with the train station, spending any more time here than absolutely necessary is not rec-ommended. Pickpockets, drunks, and vari-ous odds and ends lurk around, so take care of business and keep on moving. Luckily, the station is served by two subway lines that will quickly take you pretty much anywhere you need to go. On the premises is a **Eurolines office** (Křižíkova 2b, tel. 245 005 245, www. eurolines.cz, Sun.-Fri. 6:30am-10:30pm, Sat. 6:30am-9pm), which can help you reserve a seat on any of their numerous buses connect-ing Prague with the rest of the continent.

Buses leave Prague for Budapest 3-4 times a week. The trip lasts 7.5 hours, and a round-trip ticket costs approximately 1,000 Kč.

BY CAR

A valid UK, U.S., or Canadian license is re-quired for you to lawfully drive in the Czech Republic. The country's highways are continu-ally being upgraded, which means that traffic jams and various delays are not out of the ordi-nary. For travel on the highways, you have to buy a sticker at a border crossing, gas station, or post office and affix it to your windshield. The validity of coupons is as follows: "R" is valid for one year, "M" for one month, and "D" for one week.

If you're approaching Prague from the east, you'll cross through Zilina, Slovakia. Drivers from the south will pass through Linz, Austria. Coming from the west, Waldhaus-Rozvadov serves as the border, and Reitzenhain-Pohranicí greets those coming from the northwest.

While Prague boasts highway connec-tions from five major directions, the coun-try's highway network leaves plenty to be desired as it is incomplete and suffers from poor upkeep. Nevertheless, two major high-ways lead to the Czech border: the D5 (or international E50) stretches southwest past Plzeň and on to Germany, while the D1 (or international E65) heads to Brno and contin-ues on to Slovakia.

With regard to distances to Prague, Budapest is 347 miles, Vienna is 194 miles, Warsaw is 320 miles, and Berlin is 220 miles.

Driving from Budapest to Prague takes 5-6 hours and is quite simple. Take the M1 out of Budapest toward Bratislava. Take the Bratislava exit, continuing along the D2/E65 into Slovakia. Follow the D2/E65 through Slovakia and into the Czech Republic toward Brno. As you approach Brno, take the D1/E65 toward Prague. Continue along the D1/E65 until you reach Prague.

PRAGUE

Getting Around

Prague's excellent public transportation system connects all the city's major hubs and hot spots by either tram or subway. Taxi rides are a little risky, as plenty of drivers are looking for the next great sucker, but it beats driving around town, which is a remarkably frustrating experience. When all is said and done, the best way to get around this beautiful capital is the old-fashioned way—walking.

BY PUBLIC TRANSPORTATION

Early birds and night owls will both be happy to know that Prague's public transportation system runs 24 hours a day. Regular service typically starts around 4:30am and stops 10 or so minutes after midnight. Night trams (all numbered in the 50s) and buses (all numbered in the 500s) continue on through the wee hours, whisking the tired and the tipsy to

© LUCIE ERICKSEN
a Prague tram

their final destinations. Many visitors stand confused at bus and tram stops trying to decipher the timetables. It's quite easy, really. The stop you are currently waiting at will be highlighted. Look for the stop you are headed to. If it's located below the one you are currently at, then you're going the right way. If it's located above your current position, cross the street and take the bus or tram heading in the opposite direction.

Prague's subway system consists of three lines that cover pretty much the entire city and easily get you to any and all of the major sights and squares. They run every two minutes during peak times and roughly every seven or eight minutes in the evening. Trams are also an excellent way to get around the city, particularly the number 22, which leads up to the castle. They run every 5-8 minutes during peak hours and every 10-20 minutes as the day unfolds. Buses are rarely used by visitors as they tend to serve the outer districts, and everything worth seeing can be reached by either subway or tram. They run approximately every 5-15 minutes during the busier hours and every 20-30 minutes when things slow down.

Dopravní podnik hl. m. Prahy (Prague Public Transit Company) (www.dpp.cz) runs Prague's public transportation system. For more information on public transportation, check out their website.

Tickets

Tickets are bought in advance at kiosks and newsstands as well as from ticket machines located at various stops and at all subway stations. There is a wide variety of tickets available, but most people need only concern themselves with two types. The first is the 24 Kč ticket, which is good for a 30-minute ride on any form of transportation. The second is a 32 Kč ticket that lasts 90 minutes and allows unlimited travel within the city, including transfers among subways, buses, and trams.

If you are planning on sticking to the center of Prague, a pass of any kind will not be necessary, as most sights are easily reached on foot. For longer trips to the castle or outlying neighborhoods, odds are you'll save money by simply purchasing individual tickets. Should you plan on doing a lot of traveling in and around the city, however, or you're not able or interested in doing much walking, a pass will definitely come in handy. The current rates for passes are 110 Kč for a 24-hour pass and 310 Kč for a three-day pass.

All tickets must be validated when you board a bus or tram or on entering the "ticket holders only" area of the subway. Stamp your ticket (face up) in the yellow ticket machines found on buses and trams, as well as at the entrances of all subway stations. There are plenty of ticket inspectors patrolling all forms of transportation and it's no secret that they prey on tourists, heading immediately toward large groups speaking foreign languages that may or may not have bothered to pay their way.

BY TAXI

Prague's reputation for having some of the most corrupt cab drivers on the continent remains true, so you'll be wise to follow a few simple steps to avoid any unfortunate incidents. First of all, never approach taxis that are waiting in line at any of the city center's sights. Rather, approach the ones at designated "Taxi Fair Place" stands. The most central ones are located at Václavské náměstí, Staroměstské náměstí 5, Národní třída, Náměstí Republiky, and Malostranské náměstí. Secondly, don't flag down a cab unless absolutely necessary. They aren't all out to get your money, but many are, and those sitting on the fence won't think twice once they realize you're a tourist. If you can't get to a Taxi Fair Place stand, the next best thing to do is simply call ahead and request a cab from any of the following cab companies: **AAA** (tel. 222 333 222, www.aaataxi.cz), **City Taxi** (tel. 257 257 257, www.citytaxi.cz), or **Modrý Anděl** (tel. 737 222 333, www.modryandel.cz). Doing this will dramatically cut down on the possibility of you being ripped off and having to deal with what can quickly escalate into an ugly situation.

Rates in Prague tend to change often. Currently, a flat fee of 40 Kč is applied on entering the taxi, and a maximum of 28 Kč can be charged for every kilometer traveled.

BY CAR

Driving is by far the worst way to get around the city as the central areas that typically attract visitors are either pedestrian zones or clogged with endless traffic. Roads leading out of the city on Friday and Saturday are equally terrible, as are the roads leading back into the city on Sunday.

Parking

Parking in Prague can be a nightmare thanks to a limited number of spaces and a relatively high rate of auto theft. Remain patient while searching for a spot and, if possible, never leave anything of value in the car.

Tickets, which should be displayed face-up on your dashboard and made plainly visible through the windshield, can be purchased from coin-operated parking meters located on the respective street or lot.

The streets in Prague's center break down into three distinct types of parking zones: blue, orange, and green. The blue zones are reserved for local residents and companies. (This law is strictly enforced, so avoid these spots no matter how tempting they may look.) The orange zones accommodate parking for a maximum of two hours. The current rate is 40 Kč an hour. Green zones are for those looking to park for up to six hours, and the current charge is 30 Kč per hour.

If you're not sure where to park, eliminate the guesswork and use the underground garage at the **Palladium Shopping Center** (Náměstí Republiky 1, tel. 225 770 310, www.palladiumpraha.cz). Open daily 24 hours and offering 900 spaces, it's both the biggest and arguably safest lot in town. Current rates are 50 Kč for the first two hours and 45 Kč for each subsequent hour. A 24-hour ticket costs 700 Kč, while a 3-day ticket runs 1,800 Kč.

Car Rental

The car rental scene in Prague can be both an expensive and frustrating one, with rates climbing year after year and service—particularly in regard to choice of cars and management of reservations—still leaving something to be desired. Nevertheless, the overall situation is improving, and the companies below tend to be hits more than misses.

Avis (Klimentská 46, tel. 221 851 225, www.avis.cz, Mon.-Fri. 8am-4:30pm, from 2,250 Kč per day) is internationally known and rather reliable. **Alimex** (Aviatická 1048/12, tel. 220 114 860, www.alimex. eu, Mon.-Fri. 8am-5pm, from 350 Kč per day) gives you the best bang for your buck, though reservations ahead of time are essential. **Budget** (Wilsonova 300/8, tel. 222 319 595, www.budget.cz, daily 8am-8pm, from 1,100 Kč per day) and **Hertz** (Evropská 15, tel. 225 345 041, www.hertz.cz, daily 8am-8pm, from 2,600 Kč per day) have also earned decent reputations in town. These companies also have offices at the airport.

Try to arrange your car rental a few days ahead of time for the best possible results, and don't forget to bring your international driver's license, passport, and credit card with you.

BOHEMIA

Bohemia is characterized by its majestic castles, well-preserved towns, rolling hills, and lush river valleys. Located smack-dab in the heart of Europe, it attracts visitors from all over the continent who are stunned time and again by the multitude of sights and scenery on offer as well as by the difference in attitude and traditions of Czechs not interested in living in their country's

© TOM DIRLIS

HIGHLIGHTS

LOOK FOR **◖** TO FIND RECOMMENDED SIGHTS, ACTIVITIES, DINING, AND LODGING.

◖ Hrad Karlštejn (Karlštejn Castle):
Located in the pretty Český kras region, the castle is one of the country's most popular destinations thanks to its picture-perfect exterior and close proximity to Prague (page 156).

◖ Hrad Křivoklát (Křivoklát Castle):
This castle is a local favorite boasting Central Europe's second-largest late-Gothic hall. Its location in the pretty Berounka River Valley offers the perfect backdrop for a romantic walk or drive (page 161).

◖ Kostnice Sedlec (Sedlec Ossuary):
Built from the bones of over 40,000 people, this macabre chapel's interior gives new meaning to the phrase "waste not, want not" (page 168).

◖ Zámecké divadlo (Castle Theater):
Český Krumlov's baroque theater is one of the best preserved in the world and comes complete with gorgeous costumes and functional machinery (page 173).

◖ Vřídla (The Springs): The peaceful, picturesque surroundings and curative waters of the Czech Republic's largest spa have helped everyone from Casanova to Kafka. Why not you, too (page 177)?

famed capital. The proximity of majestic castles like Karlštejn, Konopiště, and Křivoklát make for leisurely and enchanting day trips back in time and away from the hordes that regularly swarm Prague's center. Those interested in the darker side of things can't miss the opportunity to visit Kutná Hora's macabre Ossuary, and history buffs will learn plenty from Terezín's memorial to one of the 20th century's darkest chapters. To the west lies Karlovy Vary, site of the country's renowned international film festival and the mother of all spa towns, whose

wide array of hotels, restaurants, and curative services blend peacefully with its graceful hilly surroundings. To the south, one finds the unbelievably romantic Český Krumlov, home to the country's second-largest castle and a perfectly preserved medieval town center. Beer and Becherovka are the region's poisons of choice, and you'll find no shortage of either in the endless number of pubs that happily offer the world's best brew to anyone who walks through their doors. With all major destinations easily reached by either bus or train, it is now easier

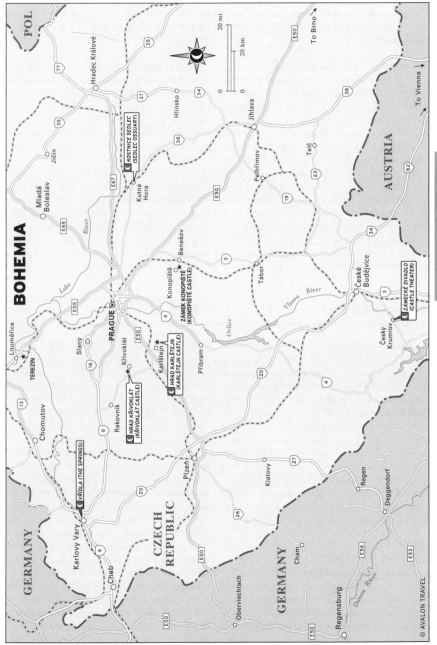

BOHEMIA

POL

20 mi

20 km

Hradec Králové

35

77

37

Hlinsko

34

Jihlava

E50

To Brno

38

To Vienna

AUSTRIA

B2

Telč

35

Jičín

E67

KOSTNICE SEDLEC
(SEDLEC OSSUARY)

38

23

Pelhřimov

19

Mladá
Boleslav

E65

Kutná
Hora

E50

River

BOHEMIA

Litoměřice

TEREZÍN

E55

Labe

PRAGUE

Benešov

3

Tábor

České
Budějovice

3

ZÁMECKÉ DIVADLO
(CASTLE THEATER)

Konopiště

ZÁMEK KONOPIŠTĚ
(KONOPIŠTĚ CASTLE)

Vltava River

Orlice

Český
Krumlov

Slaný

16

Křivoklát

E50

Karlštejn

HRAD KARLŠTEJN
(KARLŠTEJN CASTLE)

Příbram

20

4

13

Chomutov

6

Rakovník

HRAD KŘIVOKLÁT
(KŘIVOKLÁT CASTLE)

VŘÍDLA (THE SPRINGS)

Plzeň

Klatovy

27

Regen

Deggendorf

Karlovy Vary

6

20

26

CZECH
REPUBLIC

GERMANY

Cham

E56

E53

Cheb

E50

Oberviechtach

GERMANY

E50

Donau River

Regensburg

E50

© AVALON TRAVEL

BOHEMIA

than ever for visitors to escape Prague's maddening crowds to enjoy a truly authentic Bohemian experience.

PLANNING YOUR TIME

Due to the close proximity of most locations to Prague, many visitors opt for day trips to a town or sight, and then return to the capital for dinner and a nightcap. This is definitely the easiest way to take in as much as possible, but should you want to leave the magic city behind and travel the Bohemian countryside at a leisurely pace, a week ought to be enough to cover everything. Distances between the sights described are short by North American standards, which means less time in the car and more time to explore the region's history and beauty.

Karlštejn, Konopiště, Křivoklát, and Terezín can each be visited in a morning or afternoon, as there is little else to see other than the specific sights they are known for. Traveling from one destination to another, however, is neither convenient nor practical, so plan on doing them as separate day trips.

Kutná Hora can also be covered in a day, but offers a charming selection of bars, restaurants, and shops that can, according to your tastes, twist your arm into staying overnight. Český Krumlov and Karlovy Vary, meanwhile, definitely deserve overnight stays. While they can each be done in a day, their charm and overall atmosphere are infectious, and many who leave the same day they arrived do so wishing they had planned for an extra day's visit. So do yourself a favor and leave enough time to properly absorb and appreciate the grandeur of Český Krumlov's castle and magical town square as well as the spas of Karlovy Vary, which will have you feeling as good as new after a peaceful and relaxing couple of days.

Karlštejn

Karlštejn village is situated along the banks of the Berounka River in the picturesque region of Český kras. It is located roughly 20 miles southwest of Prague and is home to the country's second-most popular tourist destination, Karlštejn Castle. Open longer throughout the year than any other sight in the country, the castle is typically overrun by busloads of tourists from all around the world, which brings an onslaught of souvenir stalls, ice cream vendors, and inflated prices. A visit to this beautiful castle makes an excellent day trip, and it's close enough to Prague that you can easily be back for dinner.

SIGHTS
◖ Hrad Karlštejn (Karlštejn Castle)
Constructed by Charles IV in order to keep the royal treasures safe—particularly his collection of holy relics and coronation jewels of the Roman Empire—**Karlštejn Castle** (tel. 311 681 617, www.hradkarlstejn.cz) took nine

years to build and was ultimately finished in 1365. Situated on a rocky outcrop surrounded by forests, vineyards, and hills, it is not only a stronghold against potential danger but a thing of remarkable beauty as well. As a matter of fact, the King and son Wenceslas oftentimes used the castle as their summer home and royal palace. Besieged on a number of occasions, the worst of it coming at the hands of the Hussites in 1422, the castle has nevertheless survived one way or another through the years. A major renovation took place in the 19th century, giving us the majestic exterior we admire today.

In order to see the interior of the castle, visitors can choose from two tours. The first tour (270 Kč) runs for 50 minutes and takes you through the Courtier's Hall, the Hall of Knights with the chapel of St. Nicolas, the Chapter Deanery, the Royal Bedroom, the Audience and Banquet Halls, the Hall of Ancestors, the Treasury and Jewels Hall, and the former castle prison. The second tour (advance booking required, 300 Kč) lasts 100

A Short History of Bohemian Crystal

Glassmaking in the region dates all the way back to the 13th century, when glass was produced in northern Bohemia's Lusatian Mountains and used in monastery windows. The proliferation of chalk and potash, which enabled the production of a more stable product than that of their Italian counterparts, allowed the industry to thrive, and by 1414 the world's first glass factory was founded in Chřibská.

In the 17th century, Emperor Rudolf II's gem cutter Caspar Lehmann invented the process of glass engraving, a startling discovery that sent Bohemian crystal soaring in popularity and excellence. By the time the 18th century rolled around, Bohemia had become the world's leader in crystal production, with factories popping up all over Europe as well as in Cairo, Beirut, New York, and Mexico.

The Industrial Revolution in the 19th century allowed for the mass production of Czech crystal, and it wasn't long after that it was being exported en masse to the entire world. Glassmaking schools were also established so that the time-honored craft could be handed down to coming generations.

Two world wars and the suffocating grip of Communism interfered with production in the 20th century, but artisans and manufacturers persevered, turning out beautiful hand-cut pieces that maintained the artistic integrity they'd inherited from their predecessors. Their determination paid off in large dividends in 1989 when Communism fell and the world at large was reintroduced to the very thing that had enchanted kings and queens for centuries.

Today, Bohemian crystal is one of the most sought-after gift items in the Czech Republic thanks in large part to its eye-catching beauty and relatively reasonable price tag. It comes in a staggering number of forms, including glasses, candlesticks, decanters, vases, and chandeliers, to name just a few.

BOHEMIA

minutes and visits the Church of Our Lady, the Chapel of St. Catharine, the former Sacristy, the wooden bridge, the Lapidary Museum, the castle's picture gallery, the library, and Holy Cross Chapel. There is an additional 30 Kč fee for reservations made in advance.

The castle's hours change frequently; therefore, it's strongly recommended that you check the website for up-to-date information before your visit.

ENTERTAINMENT AND EVENTS
Karlštejn Vintage

For two whole days in late September, both the village and the castle grounds of Karlštejn are transformed into one large medieval experience called **Karlštejn Vintage** (www.hrad-karlstejn.cz, 100 Kč on Sat. good for both Sat. and Sun., 80 Kč Sun., free under age 16). Performances abound, including a number of traditional music concerts along with those by royal trumpeters and jesters. There is so much

to see that one doesn't know whether to begin with the grand royal joust, the fencing performances, the Gothic and Renaissance fashion show, or the fire-eating and magic demonstrations. A huge medieval fair in the village offers delicious, meat-heavy culinary delights from the period, and there is plenty of local wine to imbibe as well. For those who would like to live in a completely different dimension of time for a day or two, make sure to circle this event, as it's one that always attracts a large, fun-seeking crowd.

SHOPPING

The tiny souvenir shops and stalls located all around the castle and village sell typical fare that can be found just about anywhere in the country. Products include Czech garnet, Bohemian crystal, handicrafts, and tacky T-shirts. If you're considering some of the more expensive items as gifts, a good plan is to have an idea of what the prices are in Prague and compare. You may be surprised to find that some products are actually cheaper in the capital. This is due to the massive influx of tourists that arrive daily and are eager to buy. Another tip is to bring snacks or water from Prague, as the shops at the base of the village tend to sell these items at heavily inflated prices.

SPORTS AND RECREATION

Although still very much a new and growing sport in the Czech Republic, golf has begun to catch on and **Golf Resort Karlštejn** (Běleč 272, Liteň, tel. 311 604 999, www.karlstejn-golf.cz, May-Aug. daily 7am-9pm, Sept. daily 8am-7pm, Apr. and Oct. daily 8am-6pm) is one of the finer courses around. Opened in 1993 and designed by Canadians Les Furber and Jim Eremko, the course's hilly landscape, gorges, lakes, and multiple sand traps combine to make these 18 holes an "easy bogey but difficult birdie" kind of place. Albeit not of the same caliber as some of the more famous courses in the world, there is something to be said about enjoying an afternoon of golf with majestic Karlštejn Castle in the background. Greens fees are 2,000 Kč Monday-Friday (1,350 Kč Mon.-Wed. until 11am) and 3,000 Kč Saturday-Sunday.

ACCOMMODATIONS

The **Romantic Hotel Mlýn Karlštejn** (Karlštejn 329, tel. 311 744 411, www.hotelmlynkarlstejn. cz, 2,300 Kč d) sits on the Berounka River next to the castle. Its 21 tastefully furnished rooms have all the modern amenities a traveler could want, and its warm down-home friendly restaurant makes for an excellent place to enjoy a tasty traditional meal. Plenty of sporting opportunities are available as well, including a fitness center on the premises and a professional golf course a mere five minutes away.

Situated quite close to the castle is the **Hotel Koruna Karlštejn** (Karlštejn 13, tel. 311 681 465, www.korunakarlstejn.cz, 1,300 Kč d). Sporting 14 rooms with basic amenities, it is a comfortable and affordable choice should you want to spend the night and explore the region. The staff is helpful, and the hotel's restaurant, lounges, and summer terrace are wonderful spots to enjoy a meal, morning coffee, or after-dinner cocktail.

FOOD

The **Koruna Restaurant** (Karlštejn 13, tel. 311 681 465, www.korunakarlstejn.cz, daily 10am-10pm, mains 89-310 Kč) is part of the hotel of the same name, serving up traditional meals in traditional surroundings and on a lovely summer terrace that seats 120. Those who like wild game will be happy to learn that the venison dishes tend to be top of the line.

U Janů (Karlštejn 28, tel. 311 681 210, www.ujanu.cz, daily 11am-10pm, mains 170-280 Kč) is another restaurant in the vicinity that serves up authentic Czech fish and turkey dishes, not to mention a mouthwatering mixed-grill plate. The setting is traditional, the service friendly, and the prices affordable.

INFORMATION AND SERVICES

There is no official visitor information office, but any and all information regarding Karlštejn can be found either online at the castle's website or from any information center in Prague. Joining one or both tours of the castle will provide you with additional information.

GETTING THERE

By Train

Most people prefer to travel to the castle by train. Trains leave from either Prague's Hlavní nádraží or Smíchovské nádraží roughly every hour, and the trip takes a pleasant 40-45 minutes along the Berounka River. A second-class ticket with return costs 52 Kč. The village and castle are about a 15-minute walk from the station.

By Car

Karlštejn is 19 miles from Prague. If you have a car and would like to drive through the Czech countryside, there are two ways to get to the castle. The first and more scenic route is to leave Prague in a southwesterly direction along Highway 4 in the direction of Strakonice. Take the Karlštejn cutoff and follow the signs. The second route follows Route 5 out of Prague toward Plzeň. You'll find the Karlštejn cutoff about 20 minutes into your trip. Both routes take about half an hour.

The main parking lot is located in the center of town, approximately 1.2 miles from the castle. The cost is 80 Kč (flat rate).

Konopiště

The Posázaví Region is a peaceful, picturesque area that has been a favorite with Praguers desperately looking to escape the rigors of the big city. It seems like there are woods, castles, churches, and charming little towns everywhere you turn, and a drive or train ride through these parts remind one of the curative powers of both travel and nature. There is no question that Konopiště Castle, near Benešov, is the region's most famous attraction, second only to Karlštejn in popularity. Located a mere 30 miles from Prague, a visit to the castle makes for an easily managed and enjoyable day trip—a remarkable step back in time you won't soon forget.

SIGHTS
Zámek Konopiště
(Konopiště Castle)

Konopiště Castle (tel. 317 721 366, www. zamek-konopiste.cz, Apr.-May and Sept. Tues.-Sun. 10am-4pm, June-Aug. Tues.-Sun. 10am-5pm, Oct.-Nov. Sat.-Sun. 10am-3pm) was originally founded as a Gothic fortress in 1300 in the Sázava River valley. It went through a handful of architectural changes before undergoing extensive reconstruction in the 19th century. In 1887 the castle came under the ownership of Archduke Franz Ferdinand, whose eventual assassination in 1914 triggered World War I. In the 1890s, St. George renovated the castle, adding such modern touches as flush toilets, electricity, and an elevator. There is no doubt that the Archduke lived luxuriously here with his Czech wife, Sophie, entertaining nobility and constantly feeding his one great obsession—hunting.

According to his records, the archduke shot roughly 300,000 creatures in his lifetime, including foxes, deer, tigers, bears, wild boar, and birds. To put that in perspective, that means he shot 20 animals every day for roughly 41 years. More than 100,000 of these animals decorate the walls at Konopiště, making a tour through the trophy and antler rooms a rather overwhelming and somewhat spooky experience.

There are three guided tours available, all of which require a separate ticket. Tour 1 (50 minutes, 220 Kč) takes you through Ferdinand's remarkable hunting collection on display, which, despite only representing roughly 1 percent of his entire collection, still ranks as one of Europe's largest. Visitors are also treated to the castle's parlors, which have been meticulously restored. Tour 2 (55 minutes, 220 Kč) deals with the Great Armory, which boasts one of the largest and most impressive collections of weapons, along with the chapel and the Gentlemen's Club, which was out of bounds to women at the time. Tour 3 (60-70 minutes, 320 Kč) is considerably more expensive, but allows guests to visit the private apartments used by the archduke and his family; the apartments have been left virtually untouched since the state took possession of the castle in 1921.

Before leaving, make sure to allow yourself enough time to stroll through the well-kept gardens, still home to a number of quail, pheasant, and peacocks. There are several open areas that make perfect spots for a romantic picnic as well. Should you feel like picnicking, however, make sure to do your shopping beforehand, as there aren't any grocery stores near the castle.

SHOPPING

There aren't too many shopping opportunities available, except at the castle courtyard and terrace, where you'll find a small array of souvenirs, postcards, books, and classical music CDs.

BOHEMIA

Konopiště Castle

© TOM DIRLIS

SPORTS AND RECREATION

If you're staying overnight and love golf, you cannot miss the opportunity to tee off at **Golf and Spa Resort Konopiště** (Tvoršovice 27, Benešov, tel. 317 784 044, www.gcko.cz, Mar.-Oct. daily 8am-dusk, greens fees for 18 holes 1,750 Kč Mon.-Thurs., 2,100 Kč Fri.-Sun.). Two 18-hole master courses await, as do a driving range, various short-game areas, and a 9-hole public course for beginners. There's even an indoor facility should you visit during the winter. Their château—complete with a clubroom, a pro shop, a restaurant, and a hotel—has thus far been raved about.

ACCOMMODATIONS

The **Hotel Benica** (Ke Stadionu 2045, Benešov, tel. 317 725 611, www.benica.cz, 1,790-2,490 Kč d) is located about 0.5 mile from Konopiště Castle in tranquil countryside surroundings. There are 67 rooms and three suites in all, along with a pretty, well-maintained outdoor swimming pool. Comfortable and close to any and all sights and shops, the hotel also boasts

an excellent trattoria known for cooking up Czech favorites, Italian specialties, and fantastic pizza.

Situated right by the Konopiště Castle, the **Hotel Nová Myslivna** (Konopiště 22, tel. 317 722 496, www.e-stranka.cz/novamyslivna, 800 Kč d) offers its guests modern facilities in warm friendly surroundings, along with excellent traditional meals at a quarter of the price you'd pay in Prague. If you plan on staying in town overnight, this place is hard to beat.

FOOD

The name of **Restaurace Stará Myslivna** (Konopiště 2, tel. 317 700 280, www.staramyslivna.com, daily 10am-10pm, mains 158-345 Kč) means "Old Gamekeeper's Lodge"—a fitting name for this homey, rustic restaurant. Traditional, meat-heavy meals that include venison specialties are on offer and go very well with a glass of ice-cold Pilsner Urquell beer.

Located just under the castle, **Restaurace Nova Myslivna** (Konopiště 22, tel. 317 722

496, www.e-stranka.cz/novamyslivna, daily 11am-11pm, mains 140-270 Kč), or "New Gamekeeper's Lodge," offers excellent traditional Czech food in elegant surroundings. Known for its social events, it is oftentimes the setting of huge parties that include barbecues on the terrace, sword-fighting shows, and nights filled with folk and dance music. Make sure to check out the website for listings or simply pay a visit and enjoy the fantastic fare.

INFORMATION AND SERVICES

There is no official information center per se. Any questions you might have can be answered at the castle ticket window or online at the castle's official website.

GETTING THERE
By Bus

Buses leave Prague's Florenc station roughly every 45 minutes and stop in Benešov. The two-mile walk to the castle from Benešov is clearly marked. A round-trip ticket costs 56 Kč.

By Train

Trains leave hourly from Prague's main train station, Hlavní nádraží, and tickets cost 72 Kč. There is no train station in Konopiště, however, so you have to get off at Benešov station and then either catch one of the infrequent local buses headed for the castle or walk 1.25 miles. If walking, turn left as you leave the station, then left across the bridge over the railroad, and follow Konopištská Street west.

By Car

Konopiště is 30 miles from Prague. Take the D1 expressway heading south and exit near Benešov, following the signs for Konopiště. The trip takes about 45 minutes. The parking lot near the castle costs 85 Kč and is the best, and pretty much only, option.

Křivoklát

Křivoklát is located roughly 28 miles west of Prague in the lush and peaceful Berounka River Valley. Apart from the castle's wooded, hilly surroundings being a thing of remarkable natural beauty, they are also a UNESCO biosphere preservation area, making Křivoklát an exceptional place to visit for a walk or a hike. The castle dates back to the 12th century and was a favorite of King Wenceslas IV, who preferred it to his father's Karlštejn lodgings. During the course of its history, it served both as a fortress and as a prison that once held English alchemist Edward Kelly, who was kept here after Rudolf II grew tired of waiting for him to turn base metals into gold. Less crowded and nowhere near the tourist attraction its upstream neighbor Karlštejn is, Křivoklát is a wonderful reason to escape the modernity and bustle of the city and enjoy one of the oldest and best-known castles in the country.

SIGHTS
◖ Hrad Křivoklát (Křivoklát Castle)

Largely unknown to tourists, **Křivoklát Castle** (Křivoklát 47, tel. 313 558 440, www.krivoklat.cz, 110-240 Kč) nevertheless boasts one of the finest interiors to be found in the country. A tour of the grounds includes the late Gothic **Royal Chapel,** affectionately dubbed the "pearl" of the castle, which was originally open only to royalty and nobility. It is characterized by a 15th-century altar to the Virgin Mary, which looks to the right in the direction of where the king sat with his family. The intricate carvings decorating the pews are both beautiful and slightly unnerving, as they are of angels holding medieval torture instruments. If the chapel is the pearl of the castle, the magnificent **Great Royal Hall** is its heart. Measuring an impressive 79 feet long, it is Central Europe's second-largest late-Gothic

BOHEMIA

© TOM DIRLIS

Křivoklát Castle

hall and features remarkable Gothic ribbing as well as a replicated throne and a collection of statues that gives the feeling of somehow being transported back in time to an audience with the King. The **Knight's Hall** is equally magical with its fantastic collection of late Gothic art, and the **Furstenberg Picture Gallery** has the distinct honor of being one of the Czech Republic's largest castle libraries, with a collection numbering well over 50,000 volumes. Finally, there are the **castle's dungeons,** as well as those of **Huderka Tower,** which have preserved various torture devices, including a rack and an iron maiden. A walk through here chills the blood and serves as a reminder of the period's shocking cruelty, offering a very different picture from the majesty distinguishing the rest of the grounds.

Tours of the castle are offered January 1-March 22 Saturday 10am-3pm; March 23-April 30 and October Tuesday-Sunday 10am-4pm; May Tuesday-Sunday 10am-5pm; June and September Tuesday-Sunday 9am-5pm; July-August Tuesday-Sunday 9am-6pm; November-December Saturday-Sunday 10am-3pm.

ENTERTAINMENT AND EVENTS

The annual **Křivoklání Festival** (mid-Oct.) is a step back in time and then some. Held at the castle, the festival focuses on all things medieval, including fencing tournaments, medieval music concerts, jugglers, and a harrowing presentation of what is politely called "The Executioner's Art." The festival is also accompanied by a fun-filled fair where visitors can try their hand at archery or taste the Czech specialty known as *medovina* (hot mead).

ACCOMMODATIONS

Penzion Nad Hradem (Lánská 27, tel. 313 558 716, www.restauracenadhradem.cz, 900 Kč d) offers four double rooms and a suite above its restaurant of the same name. The rooms are simple but clean, and the hotel staff and wait-staff are friendly and helpful in answering any questions you might have. It's a smart, affordable choice if you're looking for somewhere basic to lay your head for a night.

Perfect for the budget traveler, the **Hotel Roztoky** (Roztoky u Křivoklátu 14, tel. 607 854 425, www.hotelroztoky.cz, 870 Kč d) offers clean and comfortable dorm-type single, double, and triple rooms. The attached restaurant serves traditional Czech cuisine at very affordable prices (mains 80-150 Kč) and the location, a mere 0.5 mile away from the castle, is not too shabby, either.

FOOD

Seating 60 and serving up traditional Czech dishes just like grandma used to make is **Penzion a Restaurace U Jelena** (Hradní 53, tel. 313 558 529, www.ujelena.eu, Sun.-Thurs. 10am-10pm, Fri.-Sat. 10am-midnight, mains 145-320 Kč). A common location for banquets, wedding receptions, and the like, it has earned a decent reputation for its venison, fish, and poultry dishes.

INFORMATION AND SERVICES

There is no official information center per se. Any questions you might have can be answered at the castle ticket window or online via the castle's official website.

GETTING THERE
By Train

Trains heading directly to Křivoklát are rare. The best thing to do is to catch one of the regularly departing trains for Beroun from either Prague's Smíchovské nádraží or Hlavní nádraží. Then change trains at Beroun for Křivoklát. The whole trip takes a little over 1.5 hours and costs approximately 110 Kč. The train station is about 0.5 mile (a 15-minute walk) from the castle.

By Car

Křivoklát is 28 miles from Prague. Follow the E50/D5 in the direction of Beroun. Turn off at junction 14 and take the Berounka Valley west in the direction of Rakovník.

Parking is located under the castle. The cost is 60 Kč (flat rate).

BOHEMIA

Terezín

Knowing his empire was under threat of attack by Prussian forces, Emperor Joseph II had a fortress town built here in 1780. Roughly 160 years later, Nazi forces took command of the area, establishing a terrifying transit camp that held approximately 140,000 people in total, over half of whom were shipped off to Auschwitz and Treblinka. Terezín is also remembered as the site where the Nazis fooled the world. On June 23, 1944, foreign visitors, including two from the Red Cross, came to inspect the grounds in order to ascertain whether the rumors of atrocities committed against Jewish people were true. What they found instead was children studying at schools, shops stocked with goods, and a thriving cultural life that even included a jazz band. Convinced by the carefully choreographed stunt, the visitors left satisfied that everything was aboveboard. By the time Russian forces liberated Terezín on May 10, 1945, over 35,000 Jewish people had died here due to disease, starvation, or suicide.

SIGHTS
Terezín Memorial
HLAVNÍ PEVNOST (MAIN FORTRESS)

An eerie silence hangs heavily in the air on entering the **Main Fortress**, one that envelops the town's gloomy grid-pattern streets. **The Ghetto Museum,** the main sight, lies just off the main square. Opened in 1991 in

BOHEMIA

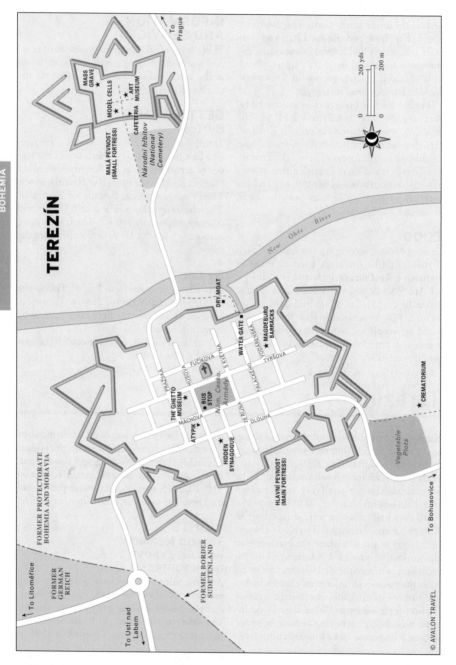

TEREZÍN

To Prague

MASS GRAVE

MODEL CELLS

ART MUSEUM

CAFETERIA

MALÁ PEVNOST (SMALL FORTRESS)

Národní hřbitov (National Cemetery)

200 yds
200 m

New Ohře River

DRY MOAT

WATER GATE

MAGDEBURG BARRACKS

PRAŽSKÁ

HUSOVA

FUČÍKOVA

5. KVĚTNA

Nám. Česko. Armády

VODÁRENSKÁ

TYRŠOVA

PALACKÉHO

THE GHETTO MUSEUM

BUS STOP

MÁCHOVA

ATYPIK

28. ŘÍJNA

DLOUHÁ

HIDDEN SYNAGOGUE

HLAVNÍ PEVNOST (MAIN FORTRESS)

★ CREMATORIUM

Vegetable Plots

To Bohušovice

FORMER PROTECTORATE BOHEMIA AND MORAVIA

To Litoměřice

FORMER GERMAN REICH

FORMER BORDER SUDETENLAND

To Ústí nad Labem

© AVALON TRAVEL

BOHEMIA

© LUCIE ERICKSEN

the National Cemetery in Terezín

the town's former school, it chronicles the rise of Nazism in Czechoslovakia as well as daily life in the ghetto. The exhibitions have been arranged with the help of those who survived the ghetto.

The **Magdeburg Barracks** is the Ghetto Museum's second branch. Opened in 1997, it features a reconstructed prison dormitory from the period as well as exhibits detailing the remarkable music, art, literature, and theater that somehow managed to develop here under such terrible conditions.

MALÁ PEVNOST (SMALL FORTRESS)

During 1940-1945, the **Small Fortress** served as the Prague Gestapo's prison. In front of the fortress is the **Národní hřbitov (National Cemetery),** where the bodies of 10,000 victims are buried and overseen by a gigantic wooden cross. Above the fortress gate hangs a chilling sign that reads Arbeit Macht Frei ("Work Sets One Free"). There are workshops and isolation cells, prison barracks and execution grounds, each one harder to comprehend and absorb.

PRACTICALITIES

The Ghetto Museum and Magdeburg Barracks are open November-March daily 9am-5:30pm, April-October daily 9am-6pm. The Small Fortress is open November-March daily 8am-4:30pm, April-October daily 8am-6pm. Tickets for the Ghetto Museum and Magdeburg Barracks or the Small Fortress are 170 Kč, while a combined entrance ticket costs 210 Kč.

Further information about the memorial (tel. 416 782 225) can be found at www.pamatnik-terezin.cz. There's an on-site **information center** (Ghetto Museum, tel. 416 782 616, Mon.-Thurs. 8am-5pm, Fri. 8am-1:30pm, Sun. 9am-3pm).

ENTERTAINMENT AND EVENTS

There are no set cultural events that happen annually or on a regular basis at Terezín.

However, there are competitions, concerts, and plays performed on occasion. The Attic Theater in the Magdeburg Barracks has been known to put on both musical and dramatic performances from children's theaters in the Czech Republic and abroad. Well-known Jewish classical musicians visit and perform here on occasion as well. Check Terezín's official website (www.pamatnik-terezin.cz) for current details.

FOOD

Terezín isn't exactly a town known for its restaurant scene, as most visitors prefer to leave soon after they've done the rounds. However, if you're feeling a tad hungry, try the goulash or other Czech standards at **Atypik** (Máchova 91, tel. 416 782 780, Mon.-Fri. 9:30am-9pm, Sat. 11am-9pm, Sun. 11am-6pm, mains 130-185 Kč). It's a standard café on the main square and as good a place as any to have a coffee or bite to eat while absorbing what you've just seen.

INFORMATION AND SERVICES

Find everything you need to know about Terezín and its history at the **Tourist Information Center** (Náměstí ČSA 179, tel. 416 782 616, Mon.-Thurs. 8am-5pm, Fri. 8am-1:30pm, Sun. 9am-3pm).

GETTING THERE
By Bus

Buses leave Prague's Florenc station hourly, with the journey taking roughly an hour. Tickets cost approximately 90 Kč. The bus makes two stops, at the small fortress and at the large fortress—you get off the bus depending on where you'd like to begin your visit.

By Car

Terezín is located 31 miles northwest of Prague. At Holešovice, join Route 8 or the E55 via Veltrusy and follow it all the way to Terezín.

There is a large parking lot near the small fortress. The cost is 60 Kč (flat rate).

Kutná Hora

The discovery of rich silver ore deposits in the second half of the 13th century sparked an economic boom in Kutná Hora that turned this sleepy mining settlement into the second-most important town in Bohemia, rivaling Prague in terms of economic, political, and cultural importance. King Wenceslas II declared it a royal town in 1307, and the Royal Mint, established in Kutná Hora a year later, went on to produce roughly one-third of Europe's total production of silver. As the town's wealth grew, so did the number of grandiose palaces and churches, forming one of the continent's most beautiful city centers. Things started taking a turn for the worse at the beginning of the 16th century, however, when Germany's dramatic increase of silver production, coupled with huge amounts of silver being imported from the Americas, began weakening Kutná Hora's power significantly.

The gradual depletion of ore deposits and the destruction caused by the Thirty Years' War were the industry's final death blows, leading to the closing of the Royal Mint in 1727 and marking the end of a remarkable era.

Today, Kutná Hora remains one of Bohemia's most popular day-trip destinations thanks in large part to its charming historical center, which joined UNESCO's World Cultural Heritage List in 1995. Further sites of interest are the chilling Sedlec Ossuary, the Czech Silver Museum and Medieval Mine, and the town's most spectacular achievement, St. Barbara's Cathedral.

SIGHTS
Chrám sv. Barbory (St. Barbara's Cathedral)

Named after the patron saint of miners, **St. Barbara's Cathedral** (Barborská St., tel. 775

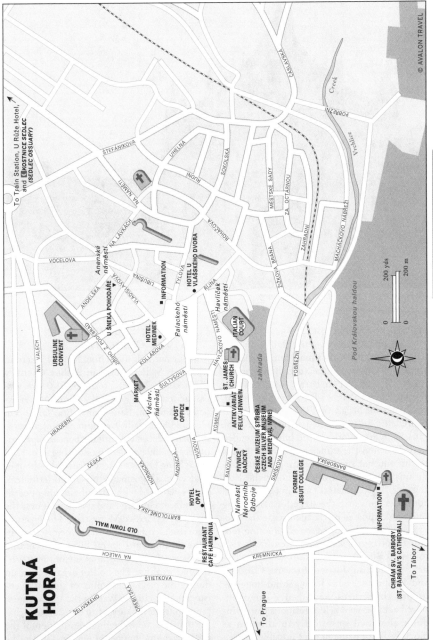

KUTNÁ HORA

© AVALON TRAVEL

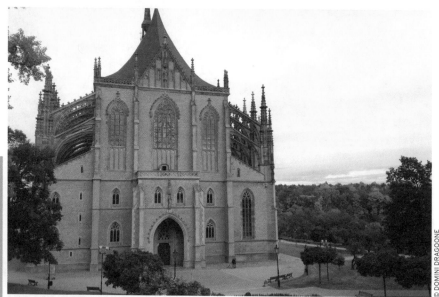

© DOMINI DRAGOONE

St. Barbara's Cathedral in Kutná Hora

363 938, www.khfarnost.cz, Nov.-Mar. daily 10am-4pm, Apr.-Oct. daily 9am-6pm, 60 Kč) is one of the world's most remarkable examples of Gothic architecture. Based on the initial designs of Petr Parléř (who was also responsible for Prague's St. Vitus Cathedral), construction began in 1388 but was interrupted for an extended period due to the Hussite Wars. Work on the building ended in 1558 when the mines and money began to run out, but sporadic renovations and additions continued until the end of the 19th century. The cathedral's soaring arches and countless spires set the stage for a stunning interior dominated by the main altar and decorated with gorgeous frescoes depicting religious motifs and scenes inspired by its rich mining past. Overhead, four wooden statues symbolizing Justice, Bravery, Caution, and Temperance hang from a mind-boggling height, but perhaps the cathedral's most inspired achievement is its enormous glass windows, designed specifically to allow in as much brilliant white light as possible.

◖ Kostnice Sedlec (Sedlec Ossuary)

Roughly one mile south from Kutná Hora train station is Sedlec, home to **Sedlec Ossuary** (Zámecká 127, Sedlec, tel. 326 551 049, www. ossuary.eu, Nov.-Feb. daily 9am-4pm, Apr.-Sept. Mon.-Sat. 8am-6pm, Sun. 9am-6pm, Oct. and Mar. daily 9am-5pm, 90 Kč), a macabre chapel decorated with the bones of approximately 40,000 people. The story began in 1278 when King Otakar II sent Henry, the abbot of Sedlec, on a diplomatic mission to Jerusalem. Henry returned with a small amount of earth taken from Golgotha and sprinkled it over the cemetery of Sedlec Monastery. The grounds were declared holy and the cemetery grew in fame throughout Central Europe, becoming the most sought-after burial site of the powerful and wealthy. The bodies began piling up during the plague epidemics of the 14th century and the Hussite Wars in the 15th century, prompting the building of an underground chapel that was to be the final destination of the ever-increasing number of remains. When the

© JAN LIPOLD

Don't miss the unusual Sedlec Ossuary.

10am-4pm, Tour I 90 Kč, Tour II 140 Kč, combined ticket 160 Kč), offering visitors two tours that detail Kutná Hora's illustrious past. The first tour, "The Town of Silver," outlines the history of Hrádek as well as the town's geological and architectural development. The second tour, "The Way of Silver," however, is what most people opt for. A short explanation of the process of developing silver ore into coins is given before guests are equipped with lamps, helmets, and protective suits and led down into the medieval mines. Reservations are strongly recommended for this tour as it is quite popular.

ENTERTAINMENT AND EVENTS
Kutná Hora International Music Festival
A classical music festival, the **Kutná Hora International Music Festival** (www.mfkh.cz, mid-June) is held in many of the town's most impressive historical landmarks, including the spectacular St. Barbara's Cathedral. Leading Czech musicians are joined by prominent artists from around the world in performing immensely popular compositions from the 13th-20th centuries. Taking in a performance in any one of the town's breathtaking Gothic buildings makes for a truly memorable evening.

Královské stříbření Kutné Hory (Silver Mining Festival)
The **Silver Mining Festival** (late June, tel. 327 512 008, www.stribreni.cz) is a colorful Gothic festival that takes place every year and celebrates Kutná Hora's glory days in the 15th century. The festivities begin with the "arrival" of King Wenceslas IV, which is full of playful pomp and circumstance. Locals join actors by dressing up in costumes of the period and indulge in nonstop concerts, dances, jousts, and competitions that animate the town for an entire weekend.

SHOPPING
Puppets, marionettes, and glass are the biggest-selling souvenirs in Kutná Hora. There

Schwarzenberg family bought the monastery in the late 1800s, they hired local woodcarver František Rint, who hit upon a creative solution to the massive buildup of centuries-old bones. The result is the ossuary as we know it today: a remarkable collection of bones arranged into crosses, columns, chalices, and monstrances as well as giant bells in each of the chapel's corners and an enormous chandelier in the center of the nave containing every bone in the human body. There is even an impressive coat of arms of the Schwarzenberg family. Slightly surreal and bordering on the grotesque, this is one experience you will never forget.

České muzeum stříbra (Czech Silver Museum and Medieval Mine)
Hrádek is a pretty 15th-century castle housing the **Czech Silver Museum and Medieval Mine** (Barborská 28, tel. 327 512 159, www.cms-kh.cz, Apr. and Oct. Tues.-Sun. 9am-5pm, May-June and Sept. Tues.-Sun. 9am-6pm, July-Aug. Tues.-Sun. 10am-6pm, Nov. Tues.-Sun.

BOHEMIA

are numerous shops around town selling them, and your best bet is to do a little comparison-shopping. Typically the shops along the main tourist routes will be slightly more expensive than the ones hidden around corners or down side streets.

Antikvariát Felix Jenewein (Barborská 23, tel. 327 514 304, www.antikvariat-kutnahora.cz, Mon.-Sat. 9am-noon and 1pm-5pm, Sun. 10am-noon and 1pm-4pm) is a used bookstore that has been kicking around since 1991. Filled with old maps, books, paintings, postcards, and antiques, this is a place to check out should you be looking for a piece of Kutná Hora's history to take home with you.

ACCOMMODATIONS

The **(** **Hotel U Vlašského dvora** (28. října 511, tel. 327 514 618, www.vlasskydvur.cz, 1,600 Kč d) is located in the historical center of town, offering guests beautiful views of the area's steeples, churches, and weather-beaten rooftops. Stylish and trendy, the hotel's clean, spacious rooms should satisfy even the finicki-est of travelers, and the friendly staff will be happy to do whatever they can to make your stay a pleasant one.

Hotel Opat (Husova 138, tel. 327 536 900, www.hotelopat.eu, 1,800 Kč d) is a beautiful and affordable hotel located in the eastern end of old town in a peaceful traffic-free area. Its 16 rooms and apartments are comfortable, spa-cious, and well-appointed with phones, satel-lite TV, and high-speed Internet. It's a solid, dependable choice.

The **Hotel Medinek** (Palackého náměstí 316, tel. 327 512 741, www.medinek.cz, 1,600 Kč d) is an affordable option situated opposite the visitor information center in the town's central square. Fifty clean double rooms and apart-ments, helpful staff happy to organize tours and events, a fitness center, a sauna, and an excellent restaurant serving Czech and interna-tional fare should be enough to convince any-one to stay here. If you do, make sure to book a room overlooking the square for the best pos-sible views.

FOOD

(**Pivnice Dačický** (Rakova 8, tel. 327 512 248, www.dacicky.com, daily 11am-11pm, mains 119-399 Kč) is a veritable institution in town and has been operating for over 400 years. Serving up traditional Czech delicacies, international specialties, and extremely inter-esting "alchemical dishes," this is a warm, in-viting, and reputable restaurant that should not be missed.

U Šneka Pohodáře (Vladislavová 333, tel. 327 515 987, www.usneka.cz, Sun.-Thurs. 11am-10pm, Fri.-Sat. 11am-11pm, mains 98-259 Kč) is an excellent pizzeria and a local favorite. The chicken and broccoli pizza is particularly good, though there are plenty of combinations to choose from. The service is very friendly, the decor is warm and inviting, and you get great value for the money. This is an excellent choice should you feel like Italian food during your stay.

Restaurant Cafe Harmonia (Vysokostelská 104, tel. 327 512 275, www.harmonia.wz.cz, daily 10am-11pm, mains 114-329 Kč) is a pop-ular stop that's located to the rear of St. James Church. Excellent soups, salads, and lighter fare are served up to both locals and visitors enjoying the sun on one of the nicer terraces in town.

INFORMATION AND SERVICES

Whatever information you need can be pro-vided to you at the **Information Center** (Sankturinovský dům, Palackého náměstí 377, tel. 327 512 378, www.kutnahora.cz, Apr.-Sept. daily 9am-6pm, Oct.-Mar. Mon.-Fri. 9am-5pm, Sat.-Sun. 10am-4pm). There are plenty of materials here to get you started, and the staff is always on top of all the special events and interesting things to do about town. There are also very useful signs posted everywhere for the benefit of visitors, which make navigating the town a snap.

GETTING THERE
By Bus
Buses for Kutná Hora leave regularly from

Prague's Florenc station and Haje station, with the trip taking roughly 90 minutes. Tickets cost approximately 68 Kč.

By Train

Trains leave for Kutná Hora hourly from Prague's Hlavní nádraží, Holešovice, and Masarykovo nádraží. The journey takes approximately one hour, with the exception of trains leaving from Masarykovo nádraží, which take two hours. The main Kutná Hora station is actually located in Sedlec, requiring transfer onto a local train that will take you to Kutná Hora. Round-trip tickets are about 78 Kč.

By Car

Kutná Hora is 44 miles from Prague. Take Vinohradská Street, which runs east behind the National Theater, all the way to Kutná Hora. Once out of Prague, note that the road turns into Highway 333. The whole trip shouldn't take longer than 50 minutes or so.

There is a main parking lot by St. Barbara's Cathedral. The cost is 50 Kč (flat rate).

Český Krumlov

Legend has it that the name Krumlov comes from the German "Krumme Aue," which, loosely translated, means "crooked meadow." The name is appropriate as the Vltava River snakes its way through town, adding its own layer of unique beauty to what has become one of the Czech Republic's most popular weekend destinations. With its winding cobblestone streets, lazy riverside cafés, and refusal to allow any modern development into its historic town center, Český Krumlov resembles a preserved medieval paradise where time has happily stood still—a feeling that is accentuated by its magnificent castle that overlooks the picturesque countryside and is second only to Prague's in size and stature. Added to UNESCO's World Heritage List in 1992, Český Krumlov is widely considered to be the prettiest town in south Bohemia and the perfect romantic getaway at any time of year.

SIGHTS
Státní hrad a zámek Český Krumlov
(Český Krumlov Castle)

Comprising 40 buildings and palaces as well as five castle courts and a park spread out on 17 acres, **Český Krumlov Castle** (Zámek 59, tel. 380 704 711, www.castle.ckrumlov.cz) dominates the landscape. It was bought in 1602 by Emperor Rudolf II and changed hands a number of times before becoming the property of the Czechoslovak State in 1950. Two major tours are available, taking you through the castle complex's well-preserved interiors that date back to the 16th century. Tours of the Castle Tower and the baroque Castle Theater are also available and are highly recommended.

Tour I (250 Kč) is the most extensive and includes **St. George's Chapel; Renaissance Hall,** with its four lavish rooms decorated with original paintings, panel ceilings, and tapestries from the early 16th century; and the **Schwarzenberg Baroque Suite,** which takes up the entire first floor of the castle and is home to the **Golden Carriage,** a gilded masterpiece built in 1638 in honor of Pope Urban VIII's visit. The highlight of the tour is undoubtedly the **Masquerade Hall,** a masterpiece of the rococo, decorated with wall-to-wall paintings of aristocrats enjoying themselves at a masquerade ball. It served as a sort of waiting room where the town's elite would gather before a performance in the Castle Theater, and its sheer size and meticulous attention to detail is simply breathtaking. It is home to a number of classical concerts in the summer that are hugely popular with visitors and locals alike. Adjacent to it is the equally stunning **Mirror Hall,** which was originally designated a palace and was also the scene of many a social gathering. Its magnificent stonework and gorgeous

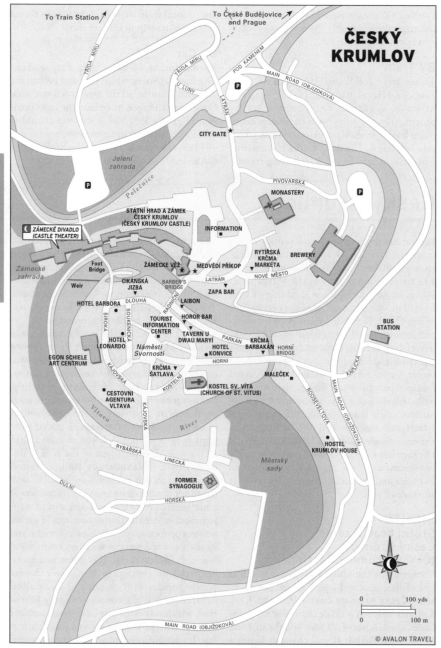

To Train Station

To České Budějovice
and Prague

ČESKÝ KRUMLOV

TŘÍDA MÍRU

TŘÍDA MÍRU

POD KAMENEM

U LUNY

MAIN ROAD (OBJÍZDKOVÁ)

LATRÁN

CITY GATE ★

Jelení
zahrada

Polečnice

PIVOVARSKÁ

MONASTERY

STÁTNÍ HRAD A ZÁMEK
ČESKÝ KRUMLOV
(ČESKÝ KRUMLOV CASTLE)

INFORMATION

ZÁMECKÉ DIVADLO
(CASTLE THEATER)

Zámecké
zahrada

Foot
Bridge

ŽÁMECKE VĚŽ ★

MEDVĚDÍ PŘÍKOP

RYTÍŘSKÁ
KRČMA
MARKÉTA

BREWERY

Weir

CIKÁNSKÁ
JIZBA

BARBER'S
BRIDGE

LATRÁN

NOVÉ MĚSTO

ZAPA BAR

HOTEL BARBORA

DLOUHÁ

RADNIČNÍ

LAIBON

ŠIROKÁ

SOUKENICKÁ

TOURIST
INFORMATION
CENTER

HOROR BAR

TAVERN U
DWAU MARYÍ

PARKÁN

KRČMA
BARBAKÁN

BUS
STATION

HOTEL
LEONARDO

Náměstí
Svornosti

HOTEL
KONVICE

HORNÍ
BRIDGE

KÁJOVSKÁ

EGON SCHIELE
ART CENTRUM

HORNÍ

KRČMA
ŠATLAVA

KOSTELNÍ

MALEČEK

KÁJOVSKÁ

Vltava

CESTOVNÍ
AGENTURA
VLTAVA

KOSTEL SV. VÍTA
(CHURCH OF ST. VITUS)

ROOSEVELTOVA

MAIN ROAD (OBJÍZDKOVÁ)

KAPLICKÁ

River

Městský
sady

HOSTEL
KRUMLOV HOUSE

RYBÁŘSKÁ

LINECKÁ

DŮLNÍ

FORMER
SYNAGOGUE

HORSKÁ

MAIN ROAD (OBJÍZDKOVÁ)

0   100 yds

0   100 m

© AVALON TRAVEL

© JAN HANUS/123RF

Český Krumlov Castle

9am-6pm, Sept.-Oct. Tues.-Sun. 9am-5pm, 50 Kč) is located between the castle's first and second courtyards and surrounded by the residential palace of the Little Castle. It is a rounded six-story Gothic and Renaissance beauty that rises 179 feet in the air and serves as the town's official symbol, immortalized by many a Czech artist, including the renowned Karel Čapek. A tour of the tower is a rewarding experience as visitors are afforded remarkable views of the town and its surroundings from the tower's gallery.

◖ ZÁMECKÉ DIVADLO (CASTLE THEATER)

Dating back to the late 17th century, the **Castle Theater** (May-Oct. Tues.-Sun. 10am-4pm, 250 Kč) is one of the best-preserved baroque theaters in the world. Remarkable as it sounds, the theater's original equipment—machinery, decorations, costumes, and lighting—continues to work, including various acoustic tools that recreate sounds of the elements (wind, rain, and thunder). The castle's archive contains over 2,400 librettos, operas, and ballets as well as nearly 600 authentic costumes from the time. Perhaps the most striking of the theater's features is how it reproduces the effect of candlelight, down to its color and flickering quality, via an electrical system that perfectly creates the illusion of a natural flame. This is an absolute can't-miss for fans of the baroque period.

MEDVĚDÍ PŘÍKOP (BEAR MOAT)

Situated between the castle's first and second courtyards is the very popular **Bear Moat,** which has been delighting children of all ages for years. Bears have been kept in the moat since 1707, and there are four of them being held here today. They are old-timers Kateřina and Vok, along with their son Hubert and his gal, Marie Terezie. The bears are beloved local celebrities, and there is even a Bear Festival held in their honor every Christmas Eve. The castle's official bear keeper starts off the festival day at 6am by placing a number of spruces decorated

paintings bearing a musical motif are worth the price of admission alone.

Tour II (240 Kč) focuses completely on the Schwarzenberg family, who inherited the castle in the first half of the 18th century. The tour includes the **Schwarzenberg Portrait Gallery** and their **19th-century suite,** as well as that of **Duchess Marie Eleonora zu Schwarzenberg,** which includes a reception room, a dining room, a dressing room, and a bedroom, all painstakingly renovated to reflect an authentic look of the period. Although not as varied as the first tour, it nevertheless provides a fascinating look at just how luxuriously the other half lived.

Tours are given April-May and September-October Tuesday-Sunday 9am-5pm, June-August Tuesday-Sunday 9am-6pm.

ZÁMECKÁ VĚŽ (CASTLE TOWER)

Situated on a rocky promontory, the **Castle Tower** (Nov.-Mar. Tues.-Sun. 9am-4pm, Apr.-May daily 9am-5pm, June-Aug. daily

BOHEMIA

with various sweets, biscuits, and fruit in the moat; the public are invited to come in and leave their Christmas offerings. It is the only time of the year where the public is allowed into the moat (while the bears are kept in a separate room). Folks bring numerous gifts, including sweets and honey, all of which are inspected by the bear keeper to ensure nothing harmful is given to the bears. At around 10am the bears are let back into the moat, and the public has a ball as they watch their furry friends go at their gifts with a gusto befitting the holiday season.

Kostel sv. Víta (Church of St. Vitus)

Opposite the castle complex on the other side of the Vltava River is Český Krumlov's second dominant structure, the **Church of St. Vitus** (Horní 156, tel. 380 711 336, www.farnostck. bcb.cz, mass Mon. and Wed.-Sat. 5pm, Tues. 7:30am, Sun. 9:30am, free). Construction of the church began in 1340 but it wasn't until after the Hussite Wars that it was finally completed. It sports three naves with a five-sided

presbytery, along with multiple-story sacristies, the Chapel of Resurrection, and the Chapel of St. John of Nepomuk. Other points of interest are the Statue of Piety from 1350, two organs, and the tombs of the local aristocracy, including Vilem of Rozmberk, a 16th-century diplomat, politician, and one of the highest-ranking noblemen in the Czech Kingdom.

ENTERTAINMENT AND EVENTS
Nightlife

Horor Bar (Másna 129, tel. 775 234 215, Sun.-Thurs. 5pm-4am, Fri.-Sat. 5pm-5am) is located downstairs in a dungeon-type space filled with whips, chains, skeletons, bats, and even a coffin in the back room. Prices are reasonable, the atmosphere is great, and absinthe is served, as is *skoumavky*—little test tubes filled with blood-red liquor. Who knew ghouls had so much fun?

Zapa Bar (Latrán 15, tel. 380 712 559, www.zapabar.cz, daily 6pm-1am) is an excellent choice for those who prefer cocktails to beer. There is a huge whisky selection as well,

The Church of St. Vitus dominates the view of Český Krumlov from the castle.

© TOM DIRLIS

and the Mexican-themed decor is something of a novelty in town. This place is popular with both foreigners and locals, all of whom agree that the mojitos here are some of the best they've ever tasted.

Festivals and Events
The **International Music Festival Český Krumlov** (tel. 380 711 797, www.festivalkrumlov.cz, July-Aug.) has already enjoyed many successful seasons of concert music that explores many musical genres. During the five-week festival, performers from around the world dazzle audiences with their unique brands of homegrown music, including classical, jazz, and rock. Culinary delights are also on offer during various themed nights, which have included French and Irish nights in the past.

SHOPPING
You'll find pretty much the same souvenirs in Český Krumlov as in Prague. There is certainly no shortage of wooden toys, amber, crystal, puppets, ceramics, and gingerbread, so your best bet is to take your time strolling through the center and doing some good old-fashioned comparison shopping. Most of the trinkets offered are tacky or overpriced, but you may find a bargain or two if you're lucky.

One store that stands out, however, is the **Egon Schiele Art Centrum** (Široká 71, tel. 380 704 011, www.schieleartcentrum.cz, daily 10am-6pm), a wonderful museum and shop specializing in prints by Schiele along with other international artists. There are plenty of books available as well as graphics, posters, postcards, and various souvenirs, including coffee mugs and funky T-shirts. If you're stuck for gift ideas, try this place.

SPORTS AND RECREATION
One thing that's really worth your while is to rent a boat and travel along the water, which is where **Maleček** (Rooseveltova 28, tel. 380 712 508, www.malecek.cz) comes in. The outfitter allows you to choose your route and boat and enjoy a trip through town along the river the way past generations used to. Inflatable rafts for 2-6 people are available, as well as 2-person canoes and kayaks. Paddles, life jackets, canoe bags, and maps are provided. Prices vary depending on the routes taken and time spent. This is an excellent way to see the city and its surroundings.

Cestovni agentura Vltava (Hradebni 60, tel. 380 711 988, www.ckvltava.cz) also offers rafting possibilities but does not stop there. Bikes are available for rent, as are Nordic walking tours. If you're the kind of person who likes to stay active and isn't afraid to break a sweat while on holiday, make sure to check this place out.

ACCOMMODATIONS
Located a mere 40 feet off the main square, the **Hotel Leonardo** (Soukenická 33, tel. 380 725 911, www.hotel-leonardo.cz, 2,200 Kč d) is a comfortable historic hotel that has managed to retain a lot of its original Renaissance charm. Rooms are spacious and elegantly furnished and the service is top-notch, as is the buffet breakfast. One potential drawback is the hotel's proximity to all the nighttime action, which occasionally results in guests being within earshot of drunken revelers returning home.

The **Hotel Konvice** (Horní Ulice 144, tel. 380 711 611, www.boehmerwaldhotels.de, 1,500-2,000 Kč d) is known for its friendly owners and excellent views of the old town and castle. Rooms are a bit on the smallish side but nevertheless clean, comfortable, and reasonably priced. The stylish period furniture suits this building, which dates to 1539, and guests feel like they're experiencing the charm of old Europe without roughing it or overpaying.

Located near the central square, **Hotel Barbora** (Široká 89, tel. 380 711 537, www.hotelbarbora.cz, 1,880 Kč d) consists of two buildings built in the 16th century. Small and full of character, some of the 16 comfortable rooms have original wooden ceilings that were handcrafted in the 16th century, while others overlook the river and castle. Its restaurant has been getting raves ever since its reconstruction a few years back, as has its helpful staff, who will go out of their way to make your trip as

BOHEMIA

enjoyable as possible. This is an excellent choice for those who appreciate a personal touch. The ◖ **Hostel Krumlov House** (Rooseveltova 68, tel. 380 711 935, www. krumlovhouse.com, 1,200 Kč d) is a clean, friendly, and completely smoke-free hostel that has earned plenty of positive reviews over the years. The helpful staff is happy to help you find the best bars and restaurants around town as well as organize various activities, including biking, hiking, and horseback riding. If that sounds too strenuous, just chill out in the lounge filled with games, musical instruments, and DVDs, or cook up some comfort food in the clean and well-equipped kitchen. If there's a relaxed and rustic hostel out there that feels a little bit like home, this is it.

FOOD

For excellent food in a medieval environment, try **Krčma Šatlava** (Horní 157, tel. 380 713 344, www.satlava.cz, daily 11am-midnight, mains 190-249 Kč). This cellar restaurant uses candles as its only light source and serves up classic meat dishes cooked on an open fire. Wild boar, baked duck, and mixed grill plates are just some of what's on offer, and the period music, costumes, and sword fighting somehow manage to escape the trappings of kitsch. This is a very popular place, so reserving a table ahead of time is recommended.

The historic **Tavern U dwau Maryí** (Parkán 104, tel. 380 717 228, www.2marie.cz, daily 11am-11pm, mains 130-185 Kč) is located in a medieval house that dates to the mid-16th century. Restored wooden ceilings and intricate ironwork set the scene where diners sink their teeth into traditional Bohemian fare, including chicken, smoked ham, and the immensely popular "Old Time Bohemian Feast," which consists of several meat specialties. This is an excellent and affordable place to enjoy traditional cuisine.

Being vegetarian is not easy in the Czech Republic, but **Laibon** (Parkán 105, tel. 775 676 654, www.laibon.cz, daily 11am-midnight, mains 119-199 Kč) is Český Krumlov's only veggie restaurant. Laid-back, friendly,

and atmospheric, Laibon features a menu filled with delicious vegetarian options like spicy dal, couscous, and curry. There is also a peaceful tearoom and terrace where you can enjoy your meals right along the riverside. It's a welcome choice for those who need a break from the heavy fare found just about everywhere else.

◖ **Cikánská jizba** (Dlouhá 31, tel. 380 717 585, Mon.-Thurs. 11am-2pm and 3pm-11pm, Fri.-Sat. 11am-2pm and 3pm-midnight, mains 99-145 Kč) is an extremely popular Gypsy restaurant that cooks up some of the finest Czech food you'll ever taste. The goulash is astounding, as is the Gypsy pasta with meat and the house specialty of fruit dumplings. Located in a wine cellar that served as the local jail once upon a time, this tiny (seven tables) atmospheric restaurant is a can't-miss choice. If you visit on the weekend, you may get a chance to see live Gypsy music.

A few minutes' walk from the town historic center is **Krčma Barbakán** (Horní 26, tel. 774 663 299, www.krcmabarbakan.cz, Apr. 15-Nov. 1 daily 11am-midnight, Nov. 2-Apr. 14 daily noon-10pm, mains 135-305 Kč). Serving up delicious grilled fish, chicken, and pork dishes with a smile, this highly traditional restaurant will impress you so much you just might come back for seconds of everything.

Rytířská krčma Markéta (Latrán 37, tel. 380 711 453, Apr. 1-Nov. 30 daily 11am-11pm, mains 119-265 Kč) is a very popular medieval-themed restaurant known for its tasty food and huge portions. Mouthwatering dishes like roast chicken or roasted pig cooked over an open fire are sure bets, as is the fantastic time you'll have due to the friendly and energetic vibe. This place is always full, so make sure you reserve a table in advance.

INFORMATION AND SERVICES

Located in the pedestrian zone in the old town center, the **Tourist Information Center** (Náměstí Svornosti 2, tel. 380 704 622, www. ckrumlov.cz/info, Nov.-Mar. daily 9am-5pm, Apr.-May and Sept.-Oct. daily 9am-6pm,

June-Aug. daily 9am-7pm) should be the first stop for anyone new to town. Besides offering the most up-to-date information regarding sights and events, the helpful people here can also help you find accommodations, arrange trips, and exchange money.

GETTING THERE
By Bus
Far more comfortable than the train, the **Student Agency bus** (www.studentagency.cz) for Český Krumlov leaves multiple times every day from Na Knížecí bus station near the Anděl subway station. The trip takes three hours and costs about 200 Kč. Reserving your ticket at least a day before is a good idea, as this is a very popular route. The bus arrives at Český Krumlov bus station, about a five-minute walk from the center of town.

By Train
The train is by far the most inconvenient way to go. Trains leave Prague's Hlavní nádraží a few times a day but require a stop and transfer in České Budějovice. Furthermore, the train station in Český Krumlov is located an inconvenient 20 minutes away from the center of town. The trip can take 3.5-5.5 hours, depending on route taken, and costs approximately 270 Kč.

By Car
Český Krumlov is about 112 miles south of Prague. Take the D1 to Brno. Switch to the E55 heading toward Linz, České Budějovice, and Benešov, taking it all the way to Kamenny Ujezd. Then follow Route 39 into town.

The main parking lot is located below the northern wall of the castle. The cost is 35 Kč an hour.

Karlovy Vary

Approximately 80 miles west of Prague, at the confluence of the Teplá and Ohře Rivers, lies Karlovy Vary—the Czech Republic's largest and most famous spa. Also known by its German name, Karlsbad, the town is surrounded by a romantic hilly countryside, which, when coupled with its pedestrian promenades, early-20th-century art nouveau buildings, and sleepy dreamlike pace, offers visitors an elegance and serenity unrivaled in the entire country. Founded in 1350 by Charles IV, the town's character and curative waters have attracted many illustrious guests over the years, including Beethoven, Mozart, Franz Kafka, Niccolò Paganini, Giacomo Casanova, and Frédéric Chopin to name but a few. Today, the town hosts the highly respected Karlovy Vary International Film Festival and produces a number of popular products like Moser glass, Thun porcelain, Mattoni mineral water, and Becherovka, the nation's beloved herbal liqueur. Aside from the spas and springs, its most renowned landmarks include the Colonnades, the Municipal Theater, and the Russian Orthodox Church of St. Peter and Paul.

SIGHTS
◖ Vřídla
(The Springs)
Karlovy Vary's famous healing springs attract hundreds of thousands of visitors annually from around the world looking to cure various metabolic, digestive, arthritic, and gynecological ailments. The springs share many similarities in their basic compositions, with the main differences being in their temperature and the amount of carbon dioxide they possess, thereby producing varying reported healing effects. Colder springs tend to have a slight detoxifying effect, while warmer waters slow down the formation of bile and gastric stomach juices. The springs range 102-163°F and are all clearly marked with a plaque detailing their mineral content and temperature. The springs themselves are: **Thermal Spring** (Thermal Spring Colonnade, daily 6am-6:30pm), **Charles IV Spring** (Market Colonnade, daily 24 hours), **Lower Castle**

© YULIYA POPOVA/123RF

Karlovy Vary is filled with colorful architecture.

Spring (Castle Colonnade, daily 24 hours), **Upper Castle Spring** (Castle Colonnade, daily 24 hours), **Market Spring** (Market Colonnade, daily 24 hours), **Mill Spring** (Mill Colonnade, daily 24 hours), **Nymph Spring** (Mill Colonnade, daily 24 hours), **Prince Vaclav Spring** (Mill Colonnade, daily 24 hours), **Libuše Spring** (Mill Colonnade, daily 24 hours), **Rock Spring** (near Mill Colonnade, daily 24 hours), **Freedom Spring** (near Spa III, daily 24 hours), **Park Spring** (Military Spa Sanatorium, daily 24 hours), **Snake's Spring** (Park Colonnade, daily 24 hours), and **Štěpánka Spring** (Spa IV, daily 24 hours). The springs are free to the public.

Kolonády
(The Colonnades)
Built during the 19th and 20th centuries, Karlovy Vary's five colonnades are generally busy with people from around the world looking to restore their powers by drinking the town's curative waters. The **Park Colonnade**

(daily 6am-6:30pm) in Dvořák Park was designed by Viennese architects Ferdinand Fellner and Herman Helmer and completed in 1881. It was part of a concert hall and restaurant called the Blanenský Pavilion and originally served as a promenade connecting the concert hall with the Park Spring.

The **Mill Colonnade** (daily 24 hours) is the town's largest, measuring 433 feet long and 43 feet wide. Designed by Josef Zítek between 1871 and 1881, it is easily recognizable thanks to its 124 Corinthian columns supporting a roof that covers five different springs, each labeled with its unique mineral composition and temperature.

Drawing its inspiration from the Swiss architectural style, the wooden **Market Colonnade** (daily 6am-6:30pm) was built in 1883 by Ferdinand Fellner and Herman Helmer and was meant to cover the Market and Charles IV springs for a short while only. Time flew by, apparently, and after nearly 100 years, local authorities thought it would be a shame to tear

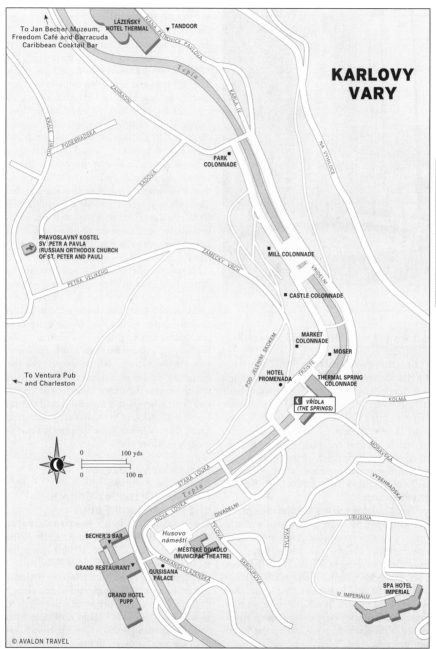

KARLOVY
VARY

To Jan Becher Muzeum,
Freedom Café and Barracuda
Caribbean Cocktail Bar

LÁZEŇSKÝ
HOTEL THERMAL

TANDOOR

NAD JELENIM PAVLOVA

KARLA IV.

NA VÝHLEDCE

ZAHRADNÍ

KRÁLE JIŘÍHO

PODĚBRADSKÁ

SADOVÁ

PARK
COLONNADE

Tepla

PRAVOSLAVNÝ KOSTEL
SV. PETR A PAVLA
(RUSSIAN ORTHODOX CHURCH
OF ST. PETER AND PAUL)

PETRA VELIKÉHO

ZÁMECKÝ VRCH

MILL COLONNADE

VŘIDELNÍ

CASTLE COLONNADE

MARKET
COLONNADE

MOSER

POD JELENÍM SKOKEM

TRŽIŠTĚ

HOTEL
PROMENÁDA

THERMAL SPRING
COLONNADE

To Ventura Pub
and Charleston

VŘIDLA
(THE SPRINGS)

KOLMÁ

0   100 yds
0   100 m

MORAVSKÁ

VYŠEHRADSKÁ

STARÁ LOUKA

Tepla

LIBUŠINA

NOVÁ LOUKA

DIVADELNÍ

TYLOVA

BECHER'S BAR

Husovo
náměstí

MĚSTSKÉ DIVADLO
(MUNICIPAL THEATRE)

SKROUPOVA

GRAND RESTAURANT

MARIÁNSKOLÁZEŇSKÁ

QUISISANA
PALACE

TYLOVA

GRAND HOTEL
PUPP

U IMPERIÁLU

SPA HOTEL
IMPERIAL

© AVALON TRAVEL

BOHEMIA

© MARTINA JOHNSON

Karlovy Vary's Thermal Spring Colonnade

it down and thankfully ordered an overall reconstruction instead.

Located above the Market Colonnade is the **Castle Colonnade** (daily 6am-7pm), which was designed by Friedrich Ohmann and built in 1911-1913. It comprises the Horní pramen (Upper Spring Colonnade) and the Dolní pramen (Lower Spring Colonnade), the latter of which is decorated with a pretty brownstone Spring Spirit relief, added in the 1930s. Closed down for numerous years, it was finally reopened in 2001 following a lengthy reconstruction.

The **Thermal Spring Colonnade** (Mon.-Fri. 9am-5pm, Sat.-Sun. 10am-5pm) was originally a cast-iron work by Ferdinand Fellner and Herman Helmer that was taken down near the beginning of World War II. A temporary wooden colonnade was put in its place, and it stayed until its present glass incarnation was finished in 1974. It is Karlovy Vary's most popular colonnade as it houses the town's main spring, Vřídlo, which shoots water some 50 feet into the air.

Městské divadlo (Municipal Theater)

The first incarnation of the **Municipal Theater** (Divadelní náměstí 21, box office tel. 353 225 537, www.karlovarske-divadlo.cz, daily 2pm-5:30pm and up to one hour before performances) was built in 1717 and stood on a tree-lined avenue behind the Grand Hotel Pupp. Made of wood, it eventually burned down in 1787 and was reconstructed nearly 100 years later (1884-1886), based on the designs of prominent Viennese architects Ferdinand Fellner and Herman Helmer. In 1993 the theater underwent a general reconstruction that lasted six years and cost over 250 million Kč. Its interiors are filled with elegant touches that include rococo lamps on the stairway and a chandelier cast in bronze, but it's the theater's curtain that attracts everyone's attention. Titled *An Apotheosis of Poetic Art,* it was designed by young (and then still relatively unknown) art nouveau artists Franz Matsche, Ernst Klimt, and Gustav Klimt. The theme is theatrical art and its relation to the muses, and it depicts a poet surrounded by three muses who encourage him to gain inspiration from a group of lovers seen on the horizon. Notice as well the two groups in the lower corners. On the right are self-portraits of the artists: Matsche and his violin, Ernst Klimt with a mandolin, and Gustav Klimt with a flute. On the left are Gustav and Ernst Klimt's sisters, who apparently acted as models for three of the muses.

Pravoslavný kostel sv. Petra a Pavla (Russian Orthodox Church of St. Peter and Paul)

The gorgeous five-domed **Russian Orthodox Church of St. Peter and Paul** (Krále Jiřího 1040/2c, tel. 353 223 238, daily 10am-6pm, free) was designed by Gustav Wiedemann and completed in 1898. Reflecting a classic Byzantine style, it was modeled after a church in Ostankino near Moscow and has survived in large part thanks to healthy donations from wealthy Russian guests, whom the church has been serving for over 110 years. Its interior is

The 10 Commandments of Karlovy Vary's Drinking Cure

1. The thermal mineral waters of Karlovy Vary should only be imbibed after having consulted a qualified spa physician.
2. Water should be consumed at the springs in order for the drinker to feel its full medicinal effects.
3. Use only the widely available, traditionally shaped porcelain or glass cups.
4. Do not smoke or drink alcohol. Secondhand smoke is considered to be just as harmful.
5. Combine the drinking cure with light physical exercise such as walking.
6. Try to remain in a relaxed, peaceful state of mind as much as possible.
7. Repeat the drinking cure as recommended by your physician.
8. Do not disturb other patients, regardless of how kind and friendly your motives might be.
9. Do not use the mineral water to water nearby plants, and take special care not to spill it on the floor in the colonnades.
10. Do not touch the spring stand or pipes while taking water from the fountain.

BOHEMIA

decorated with gorgeous paintings and icons (some of which were also gifts) that can keep you occupied for a very long time, and its relief of Russian czar Peter the Great continues to strike pride in the hearts of all Russians who come to visit.

Jan Becher Muzeum (Jan Becher Museum)

Becherovka is one of the nation's most-consumed domestic drinks and one of Karlovy Vary's better-known exports. At the **Jan Becher Museum** (T.G. Masaryka 57, tel. 359 578 142, www.becherovka.cz, daily 9am-5pm, 120 Kč), visitors are taken on a tour of the production plant and learn the basic history, manufacturing, and storage of the liqueur. Aside from the instructional film, exhibitions, and trip through some of the plant's original cellars, guests are also invited to imbibe the country's pride and joy in the museum bar.

ENTERTAINMENT AND EVENTS
Nightlife

Becher's Bar (Mírové náměstí 2, tel. 353 109 483, www.pupp.cz, daily 7pm-3am) is an upscale cocktail bar in the Grand Hotel Pupp and pretty much the only one in town. Fashioned after a typical post-World War I London pub, the bar has a drink menu of over 100 cocktails

that should keep you busy, and there are plenty of gourmet specialties available as well. This is a reasonably priced choice for nighthawks, and the live jazz performed nightly will satisfy any fan of the genre.

Barracuda Caribbean Cocktail Bar (Jaltská 7, tel. 774 708 000, www.barracuda-bar.cz, Mon.-Thurs. 7pm-1am, Fri.-Sat. 7pm-3am) is a warm and fun place decorated in a faux-island bar style that fills up seats and the dance floor with tasty cocktails and catchy hits from the '80s and '90s. It's one of the more popular establishments in town and often attracts local celebrities as well as internationally recognized stars like Daniel Craig.

Festivals and Events

The **Karlovy Vary International Film Festival** (www.kviff.com, first half of July) is the most important of its kind in Central and Eastern Europe and ranks fourth in importance on the continent after Cannes, Berlin, and Venice. The festival ran for the first time in 1946 and suffered under the Communist regime before having life breathed back into it in 1994 by new organizers Jiří Bartoška and Eva Zaoralová. Today, it remains one of the most important cultural events on the country's calendar, attracting thousands of visitors, not to mention actors and directors from all over the world looking to promote their projects. Any fan of the medium will want to visit during the festival's eight-day run and drink up the transformation of this sleepy spa town into one of glamour and excitement. Should you seriously be considering a visit during this time, make sure to book a room well in advance as all accommodations are spoken for months before opening night.

SHOPPING

There are plenty of shopping opportunities in Karlovy Vary, but be forewarned: prices are not what you'd expect them to be outside the capital. Most goods are expensive since the spa resort attracts a certain affluence, but with the right kind of perseverance you'll find what you're looking for and not have to pay an arm and a leg to get it.

Becherovka, the sweet yet spicy domestic drink that can be found in every Czech bar in the country, is produced here and is available in most shops for a decent price. Gold and fur are two of the more common goods here and can be easily found at numerous shops throughout the city. The most popular items bought in Karlovy Vary, however, are crystal and porcelain, both of which can be found at **Moser** (Tržiště 7, tel. 353 235 303, www.moser.cz, Mon.-Fri. 10am-7pm, Sat.-Sun. 10am-6pm), the country's most respected name in glassware.

ACCOMMODATIONS

Hotel Promenáda (Tržiště 31, tel. 353 225 648, www.hotel-promenada.cz, 2,580-3,500 Kč d) is a charming, intimate hotel located in the heart of the city's spa center. The service is warm and welcoming, the rooms are immaculate, and the restaurant is one of the better ones in town. If you're looking for a first-rate, reasonably priced hotel in a city known for being overly expensive, book a room here now.

Housed in a turn-of-the-20th-century building boasting neo-Renaissance, neo-Gothic, and neo-baroque elements is ◖**Quisisana Palace** (Mariánskolázenská 3, tel. 357 079 110, www.quisisana-palace.com, 5,700 Kč d), a superb and luxurious boutique hotel offering 19 gorgeous, comfortable, and well-appointed rooms and suites. There's also a whirlpool, a sauna, steam spa treatments, and air-conditioning—a major plus in these parts. The food on the premises is also quite fantastic, and the staff bends over backward to make sure you have everything you need. It's highly recommended.

Up on a hill overlooking the city is the beautiful and grand **Spa Hotel Imperial** (Libušina 18, tel. 353 203 111, www.spa-hotel-imperial. cz, 3,100 Kč d). Spacious and stylish rooms with marble bathrooms await, as does the Imperial sports center with tennis courts, a

Acquiring a Taste for Becherovka

Becherovka is one of the country's most popular drinks and is available in every bar in the Czech Republic. A product of Karlovy Vary, it is devoid of any chemical preservatives, artificial coloring, or emulsifiers, making it a 100 percent natural alcoholic drink whose recipe hasn't changed in over 200 years. Becherovka's maturation process unfolds in dark oak barrels, some of which date back to the beginning of the 19th century. The sweet herbal liquid spends a few weeks mellowing, its taste turning darker and sharpening before it is filtered and bottled. Although hugely popular among Czechs, it is definitely an acquired taste. Give it a try, but don't be embarrassed if it's not to your liking. Here are a few of the more popular cocktails that use Becherovka as a base:

Beton
1½ ounces Becherovka
⅓ ounce lemon juice
7 ounces tonic water

Red Moon
1½ ounces Becherovka
5 ounces black currant juice
2 ounces soda water

Magic Sunset
1½ ounces Becherovka
5 ounces orange juice
⅓ ounce grenadine

fitness center, and aerobics, not to mention indoor golf with two full-swing simulators of 24 world-famous courses. There is also a beauty salon, an indoor pool, and a concert hall, and the friendly staff will happily help you plan any trips or events you might want should you actually feel like leaving the premises.

FOOD

Freedom Café (Jugoslávská 3, tel. 353 231 621, www.freedomcafe.cz, Mon.-Fri. 8am-8pm, mains 45-93 Kč) is a bright and colorful café with some of the friendliest staff in town. You'll find a decent assortment of breakfasts, sandwiches, salads, and pancakes as well as a large number of coffees, teas, and desserts. It's an excellent place to check out during a lull in the afternoon's sightseeing.

Located near the bus station, **Ventura Pub** (Jízdárenská 1, tel. 353 228 507, www.evropak. cz, Sun.-Thurs. 10:30am-midnight, Fri.-Sat. 10:30am-1am, mains 80-360 Kč) is an excellent Czech restaurant that's a big hit with locals. Traditional meals like roast duck and grilled salmon are prepared to perfection, and the beer on tap is some of the freshest in town. It has excellent service, is very affordable, and the generous mouthwatering portions make this a must for those looking to avoid the tourist traps downtown.

Seeing as it's located in the magnificent Grand Hotel Pupp, it's no surprise that the **Grand Restaurant** (Mírové náměstí 2, Grandhotel Pupp, tel. 353 109 646, www. pupp.cz, daily noon-3pm and 6pm-10pm, mains 279-829 Kč) offers some of the finest dining in town. Luxurious neoclassical surroundings set the stage for the excellent Czech and international fare on the extensive menu. Generous portions are professionally prepared by some of the country's finest chefs and served by friendly and efficient waitstaff. Slightly on the expensive side but well worth the extravagance, the Grand Restaurant is an elegant dining experience you won't soon forget.

Step back in time at **Charleston** (Bulharská 1, tel. 353 230 797, www.charleston-kv.cz, Mon.-Sat. 10am-midnight, Sun.

noon-midnight, mains 169-469 Kč), a warm and inviting restaurant furnished in the old Victorian style. The fish, chicken, and wild game dishes are all excellent, as is the service and live music, which is performed regularly. It's a bit pricy but well worth the extra expense.

While the uninspired no-frills look of **Tandoor** (I.P. Pavlova 25, tel. 608 701 341, www.tandoor-kv.cz, Mon.-Sat. noon-9pm, Sun. noon-6pm, mains 85-190 Kč) may turn some off, those who don't judge books by their covers will be richly rewarded with the finest Indian food in town. Shrimp, lamb, beef, chicken, and vegetarian dishes are prepared to authentic perfection and served by warm and friendly staff. This is a dependable and affordable alternative if you need a break from the local cuisine.

INFORMATION AND SERVICES

The **Infocentrum T.G. Masaryka** (T.G. Masaryka 53, tel. 355 321 171, www.karlovyvary.cz, Mon.-Fri. 8am-6pm, Sat.-Sun. 9am-5pm) is where you want to head to should you have any questions concerning the city's sights or cultural events. The friendly, multilingual staff will be happy to arrange tickets or activities around town for you.

Infocentrum Lázeňská (Lázeňská 14, tel. 773 290 632, Mon.-Fri. 8am-6pm, Sat.-Sun. 9am-5pm) is Karlovy Vary's second official visitor information center and offers the same helpful information and services mentioned above.

GETTING THERE
By Bus

Buses leave regularly from Prague's Florenc station. The trip takes about two hours, and tickets cost approximately 160 Kč. The bus arrives at Dolní nádrazí, about a 10-minute walk from the spas and center. You can also take the local #4 bus; tickets cost 16 Kč, or 20 Kč if you buy them from the driver.

By Train

Trains leave Prague's Hlavní nádraží at least three times a day. Tickets cost 316 Kč, with the journey taking roughly 3.5 hours. Keep in mind that the train takes an indirect route and is 1.5 hours longer than the bus.

By Car

Karlovy Vary is 81 miles from Prague. Take Highway E48 west from Prague all the way to Karlovy Vary. The roads are generally busy, so be sure to exercise caution. The trip shouldn't take more than two hours.

There is plenty of parking all over town. Parking at secure lots (as opposed to on the street) is highly recommended. The cost is 35 Kč an hour.

MORAVIA

Stretching out to the south and east, Moravia is the Czech Republic's famed and beloved wine country—a region characterized not only by its vineyards, lowlands, and wooded hillsides but also by the loose love of life that inevitably comes with the grown grape. Those who venture into Brno and beyond are struck by the less hurried pace, the warm and friendly demeanor

© RICHARD SEMIK/123RF

HIGHLIGHTS

LOOK FOR  TO FIND RECOMMENDED SIGHTS, ACTIVITIES, DINING, AND LODGING.

MORAVIA

(Staré Město (Brno's Old Town): Spend an afternoon taking in the Moravian capital's historic sights, then let your hair down alongside natives who insist (and oftentimes prove) that Brno can be a whole lot more fun than Prague (page 188).

(Kapucínská krypta (Capuchin Crypt): Grotesque, maybe; morbid, sure, but Brno's Capuchin Crypt continues to lure visitors curious to see deceased monks and society big shots in their open coffins and decaying clothes (page 192).

(Náměstí Zachariáše z Hradce (Telč's Town Square): Perfectly preserved

Renaissance and baroque houses, capped off with St. Jacob's Church's 200-foot-tall tower and its inspiring views, make for the perfect romantic morning or afternoon (page 196).

(Státní zámek Telč (Telč Castle): You will be hard-pressed to find more exquisite examples of Renaissance architecture, complete with lavishly decorated interiors guaranteed to make your jaw drop (page 197).

(Pálava Vintage Wine Festival: The most important cultural event in Mikulov is also its most fun, attracting thrill seekers, wine lovers, and anyone else committed to having a great time (page 202).

of the typical Moravian, and the maintenance of the culture's customs. Colorful folk, infectious traditional music, and vibrant village festivals highlight the region's cultural calendar, while its excellent biking and hiking trails afford nature enthusiasts an unforgettably sensuous and serene experience no matter what the time of year. Whereas pubs are Bohemia's natural gathering point, it is the neighborhood *vinárna* (wine bar) that prevails here, attracting locals and those from nearby towns

curious as to what has been growing in the neighboring ground. The strong, sharp taste of *slivovice* (plum brandy) is the liqueur of choice. When it is homemade, it is as much a matter of painstaking preparation as it is pride, and it oftentimes sparks the beginning of a lively and late night. Moravians' food also differs from that of their Bohemian brothers and sisters, involving spicier ingredients more akin to Slovak and Hungarian palates. Whether it's the animated nightlife and historic Old

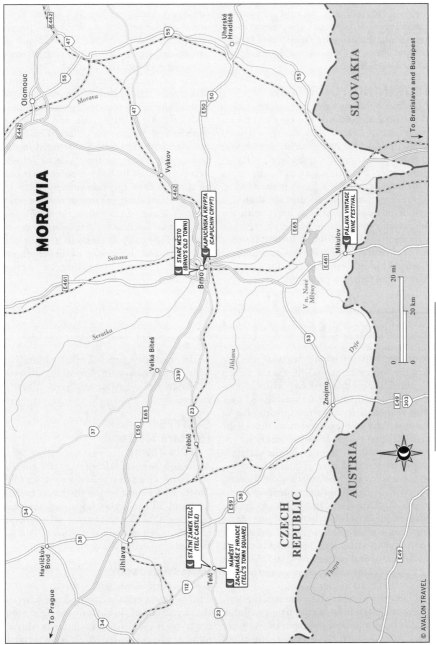

MORAVIA

SLOVAKIA

To Bratislava and Budapest

Olomouc

Uherské
Hradiště

Vyškov

Morava

Brno

STARÉ MĚSTO
(BRNO'S OLD TOWN)

KAPUCÍNSKÁ KRYPTA
(CAPUCHIN CRYPT)

Svitava

Mikulov

PÁLAVA VINTAGE
WINE FESTIVAL

V. n. Nové
Mlýny

Dyje

20 mi

20 km

Velká Bíteš

Svratka

Jihlava

Znojmo

Třebíč

AUSTRIA

CZECH
REPUBLIC

STÁTNÍ ZÁMEK TELČ
(TELČ CASTLE)

NÁMĚSTÍ
ZACHARIÁŠE Z HRADCE
(TELČ'S TOWN SQUARE)

Jihlava

Telč

Havlíčkův
Brod

To Prague

Thaya

MORAVIA

© AVALON TRAVEL

Town of burgeoning Brno or the sleepy timeless beauty of Mikulov and Telč, visitors to the region will undoubtedly experience a lust for life and leisure rarely duplicated in other parts of the Czech Republic.

PLANNING YOUR TIME

Moravia's sights are significantly farther away than those of Bohemia, but they can be experienced in a relatively short time if need be. Three days are enough to do a quick tour through the countryside, grab a bottle of homegrown wine, and beat it back to Prague before your flight leaves. For a deeper understanding of the region, however, 4-5 days are ideal.

The obvious choice is to begin with the Moravian capital, Brno. Spend all the time you want strolling through its historic center or climbing up to Špilberk Castle and the Cathedral of St. Peter and Paul for a taste of history and fantastic panoramic views of the city below. Always bustling with activity, Brno promises an experience you won't soon forget, whether it's an evening at the theater, dinner at a traditional restaurant, or a night out at any of its numerous bars, cafés, or clubs.

From there, it makes sense to visit either Mikulov or Telč, or both of them if you have three or more days at your disposal. Mikulov, with its castle, nature trails, and countless wineries and private wine cellars, is easily an overnight trip for anybody interested in the great outdoors or the finer side of grapes. Leaving Mikulov for last will mean having to go through Brno again on your way back to Prague—something you may or may not want to do. Telč can be enjoyed in a single day, so leaving it for last may make the most sense, as you can fully enjoy its gorgeous town square and castle, and also pick up a number of souvenirs before heading back to Prague in the late afternoon or evening.

Brno

Roughly 140 miles southeast of Prague lies the Moravian capital, Brno, the Czech Republic's second-largest city with its population pushing 400,000. Established over 800 years ago, it prospered quickly due to its proximity to Prague, Vienna, Bratislava, and Budapest—a geographical luxury it continues to profit from today. While certainly not as pretty as Prague, it would be wrong to focus solely on Brno's plethora of concrete functionalist buildings and write it off as just another industrial city. Its historic city center, for example, is full of architectural gems ranging from Gothic to art nouveau, and its two most famous attractions, Špilberk Castle and Cathedral of St. Peter and Paul, rise above the city majestically, adding elegance and historical context to its unique skyline.

Home to a number of universities, theaters, clubs, and cafés, Brno has a dynamic nightlife that is known to rival the capital's. Whether it's a stroll through the streets, a visit to the castle, or an all-nighter full of tasty Moravian wine, Brno's easygoing, fun-loving lifestyle is sure to please anyone who gives it half a chance.

SIGHTS
◖ Staré Město (Old Town)

Although Brno is fairly large and spread out, visitors tend to stay in the compact Old Town, where most of the historical buildings and all the action is. Somewhat oval in shape, Old Town stretches a little over 0.5 mile north to south and about 0.25 mile from east to west.

NÁMĚSTÍ SVOBODY (FREEDOM SQUARE)

This is Brno's main square and the heart of the city. "Square" isn't exactly the right word for it, as it's actually triangular in shape, forming a large reversed "A." It is always busy

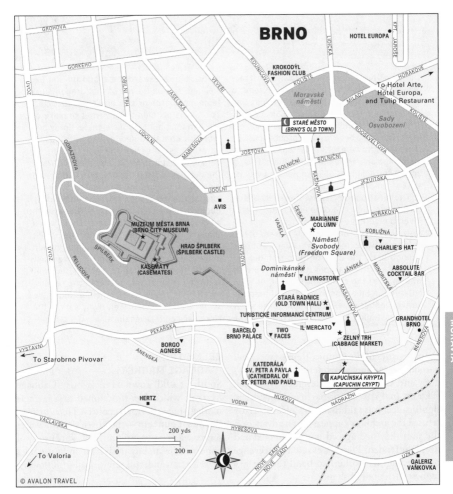

© AVALON TRAVEL

with visitors and locals out for a stroll or simply going about their business, and is also the site of numerous concerts, exhibitions, and various other cultural events throughout the year. At the center of the square is the **Marianne Column,** an attractive and ornate late-17th-century plague column; aside from being a noteworthy piece of sculpture, it also serves as one of the city's more popular meeting points. The southern end of the square leads off to **Masarykova Street.** Lined primarily with shops, it is Brno's busiest and

most commercialized street. Make sure to keep looking up, as many of the buildings have fantastic art nouveau facades that make for plenty of photo ops and a very pleasant stroll.

STARÁ RADNICE (OLD TOWN HALL)

Old Town Hall (Radnická 8) is Brno's oldest secular building, dating all the way back to the 13th century. A quick look will reveal that it has gone through a number of renovations as

The Brno Dragon

The Brno Dragon is one of the town's most recognizable symbols, yet nobody really seems to know what the truth is regarding its origin. One explanation is that it was killed by Sir Albrecht Trut's servants while the town was being established. Some believe it was brought back by crusaders who were returning from one of their many missions, while others maintain it was a gift for the members of Town Hall by a visiting sultan from Turkey.

The most popular story, however, is that the dragon lived in a cave along the Svratka River, devouring everything in sight and terrorizing the local population. A reward of 100 gold coins was offered to whoever was brave enough to rid the town of the beast, but nobody rose to the challenge. One day, a butcher who roamed the continent looking for work entered the Blue Lion Inn and overheard the natives jabbering excitedly about the scaly beast. Listening intently, particularly at the mention of a reward, he stood up and exclaimed, "I shall rid you of that dragon. Just fetch me a large ox pelt and a sack of lime." The townsfolk didn't know what to make of the stranger, but they nevertheless provided him with what he asked for and watched him carefully as he sewed the lime into the ox pelt, loaded it into his wagon, and left. When the butcher located the dragon's lair, he laid his pelt on the ground and waited. It wasn't long before the dragon emerged from hiding, gobbled up the pelt, and washed it down with some of Svratka River's finest. That's when the lime that had been sewn into the ox pelt started to work its magic, beginning to boil and expand until the fearsome monster blew up into tiny little dragon bits. The butcher returned triumphant, pocketed the reward, and left the residents of Brno dancing in the streets. Life has been relatively safe in the Moravian capital ever since.

characteristics of the Gothic, Renaissance, and baroque periods are all evident. The building's door and Gothic portal, designed by Anton Pilgram in 1510, are of particular historical significance. It is said that town officials flatly refused the architect's appeal for an advance on the sum they had agreed upon. Enraged and deeply offended, Pilgram exacted his revenge by ordering his workers to bend the portal's highest turret out of shape.

Suspended in the hall's gateway are two of Brno's most famous attractions. The first is the **Brno Dragon,** which is actually a large alligator whose history is as varied as it is uncertain. The second is the **Wagon Wheel,** which is believed to have come from Jiří Birek, a carpenter from Lednice. The story goes that he bet locals he could cut down a tree, make a wheel out of it, and roll it the 25 miles back to Brno all in a single day. "You're on," said the townspeople, who nearly fainted when he pulled it off. Convinced he was in cahoots with the devil, the people of Brno never did business with him again.

ZELNÝ TRH (CABBAGE MARKET)

South of Old Town Hall is busy Cabbage Market, which has functioned as a farmers market since the 13th century. Here, next to **Parnas Fountain**—the town's main water source when it was built in 1699—are plenty of opportunities to buy fresh fruit and vegetables as well as a wonderful array of colorful flowers.

Hrad Špilberk (Špilberk Castle)

Špilberk Castle has been an inseparable part of Brno's skyline for over seven centuries and is one of its most defining features. Built in the mid-13th century by King Přemysl Otakar II, the castle's looks and relevance changed vastly over the years, beginning as a royal castle and official seat of Moravian margraves, adapting with the times to become a significant baroque fortress, changing into a widely feared prison during the Austro-Hungarian Empire, and finally ending up a barracks. It was declared a

© MARTINA JOHNSON

Brno's bustling Cabbage Market

national heritage monument in 1962 and today houses Brno's leading cultural center, the Brno City Museum. Visitors to Špilberk can also see the castle's casements, a lapidary, a carillon, a baroque pharmacy, and the castle tower, which offers pretty views of the city below.

MUZEUM MĚSTA BRNA (BRNO CITY MUSEUM)

The **Brno City Museum** (Špilberk 1, tel. 542 123 614, www.spilberk.cz, Oct.-Apr. Wed.-Sun. 9am-5pm, May-June Tues.-Sun. 9am-5pm, July-Sept. Tues.-Sun. 10am-6pm, 150 Kč) is one of the city's more important cultural centers. It hosts plenty of concerts and happenings throughout the year and is the place to go to learn everything there is to know about the region's colorful past. There are always new temporary exhibitions being held, while some of the more popular permanent ones include *Špilberk—From Castle to Fortress,* which outlines the castle's development in great detail; *Brno at Špilberk,* which presents some of the most important chapters in Brno's history; and

From Renaissance to Modernism, an exhibition of significant pieces from some of Brno's most distinguished artists from 1570 to 1945.

KASEMATY (CASEMATES)

The castle's **casemates** (Oct.-June Tues.-Sun. 9am-5pm, July-Sept. Tues.-Sun. 10am-6pm, 90 Kč) are one of Brno's most-visited sites despite their grisly history. In 1783, Emperor Joseph II decided to use the dark, windowless rooms as a prison for the land's hardest and most dangerous criminals. The following year, he had wooden cells built, and prisoners serving life sentences were hanged from the walls. Špilberk prison quickly gained the reputation of being the most brutal of all such facilities within the Austrian empire and remained as such until 1855, when Emperor Francis Joseph I put an end to the cruel and unusual punishment.

Katedrála sv. Petra a Pavla (Cathedral of St. Peter and Paul)

Perched atop Petrov Hill overlooking the old

© PAVEL KOHOUT | DREAMSTIME.COM

Špilberk Castle

town is the **Cathedral of St. Peter and Paul** (Petrov 9, tel. 543 235 031, www.katedrala-petrov.cz, church Mon.-Sat. 8:15am-6:30pm, Sun. 7am-6:30pm, tower May-Sept. Mon.-Sat. 10am-6:30pm, Sun. noon-6:30pm, Oct.-Apr. Mon.-Sat. 11am-5pm, Sun. noon-5pm, tower and crypt 35 Kč), one of the city's most recognizable landmarks. Built as a Gothic cathedral on the presumed site of the former Brno Castle, it was converted into the Baroque style in the 18th century and attained its current neo-Gothic form at the turn of the 20th century. Its interior is unspectacular, with a sculpture of the Virgin Mary being of minor interest. There is an original crypt from the 12th century now open to visitors, but it is the cathedral's tower that is worth the effort, as it offers excellent views of the old town and beyond. One thing you might notice while visiting is that the cathedral's bells strike noon at 11am. This can be traced back to a quick-thinking monk who somehow learned during the Thirty Years' War that the Swedes were planning to take the town by noon. If unsuccessful by then, they would

move on. Not wanting to take any chances against the powerful Swedish army, he rang the bells at 11am, prompting the Swedes to pack up and leave and thus saving his beloved Brno.

◖ Kapucínská krypta (Capuchin Crypt)

Below the Cathedral of St. Peter and Paul and adjacent to Zelný trh is the Capuchin Monastery whose biggest attraction is the rather morbid yet intriguing **Capuchin Crypt** (Kapucínské náměstí 5, tel. 511 140 053, www.kapucini.cz, May-Sept. Mon.-Sat. 9am-4:30pm, Sun. 11am-4:30pm, Oct.-Dec. 14 Tues.-Sat. 9am-4:30pm, Sun. 11am-4:30pm, Dec. 15-Feb. 15 Sat. 9am-4:30pm, Sun. 11am-4:30pm, Feb. 15-Apr. Tues.-Sat. 9am-4:30pm, Sun. 11am-4:30pm, 30 Kč). Founded in the middle of the 17th century, it was the final resting spot for many of society's deceased until 1787, when Joseph II prohibited burials within town limits. Today, the remains of various monks and Brno's more distinguished citizens of the day are on display in open coffins, their

Milan Kundera: Brno's Native Son

Born in Brno in 1929, Milan Kundera is one of the 20th century's most notable writers, blending philosophy, essayistic elements, and narrative to create a unique writing style that has produced critically acclaimed novels described as "a feast of many courses." Educated at Charles University and the Film Faculty of the Academy of Music and Dramatic Arts in Prague, Kundera worked as a manual laborer and jazz musician before becoming a professor of literature at the Institute for Advanced Cinematographic Studies. He joined the Communist Party in 1948 and was expelled not once but twice for his unorthodox opinions. At the age of 38, Kundera published his first novel, *The Joke* (1967), a darkly funny, illuminating work revealing how reality under Communist rule takes its revenge on those who play with it. Not surprisingly, Kundera was one of the authors banned from libraries and publication after the Russians invaded Czechoslovakia in 1968, and he was fired from his teaching post less than a year later. In 1975, Kundera moved with his wife, Vera Hrabánková, to France, where he worked as a professor of comparative literature at the University of Rennes. In 1980 he was appointed professor at the École des Hautes Études in Paris. His breakthrough novel, *The Unbearable Lightness of Being*, was published in 1984 and solidified his position as one of Central Europe's, if not the world's, most important and influential writers.

clothing and skin clearly decaying. Although a popular and somewhat fascinating sight, the crypt should be avoided by young children and the faint-hearted.

ENTERTAINMENT AND EVENTS
Nightlife

Charlie's Hat (Kobližná 12, tel. 774 482 229, www.charlies-hat.cz, Sun.-Thurs. 9pm-3am, Fri.-Sat. 9pm-5am) is a fun party place located right in the old town. Head on down to the no-frills, rustic-looking cellar and rub shoulders with students, foreigners, and local party people. Rock and pop music fills the air till the wee hours every night, much to everybody's delight. Be forewarned—its location in a cellar makes it very easy to lose track of time. Don't be surprised if you walk out and the sun has already come up.

Livingstone (Dominikánské náměstí 5, tel. 608 556 055, www.livingstoneclub.cz, Mon.-Sat. 7pm-3am, admission varies) is very popular with students and has been one of the city's go-to clubs for years. Small and intimate, with a main floor for dancing and hobnobbing and an upper floor for chilling with your very affordable cocktail, this place fills to madcap capacity as the night rages on. It's a quintessential example of the local party scene.

Modeled after the industrial clubs of New York, **Two Faces** (Biskupská 1, tel. 775 960 930, www.twofaces.cz, Tues.-Sat. 8pm-5am, admission varies) is a large stylish club that's a big hit with the locals. Four bars, two DJ booths, two dance floors, and a giant video screen are the key ingredients to this late-night success, as are the excellent cocktails and large Roman-type pool that takes center stage during the club's themed summer parties. It's always a fun time.

Festivals and Events

Moravian Autumn (www.mhf-brno.cz, late Oct.) is a highly enjoyable two-week run of classical music concerts performed around the city to the delight of thousands of fans. Symphony orchestras, vocal ensembles, soloists, quartets, and dance troupes all find their way to the stage in some of Brno's finest venues, including the Brno Philharmonic Concert Hall, Janáček Theater, and Brno City Theater. This is a wonderful opportunity to hear superb artists from the Czech Republic and elsewhere

MORAVIA

perform music that still resonates with audiences after all these years.

SHOPPING

Prices are generally cheaper in Brno than in Prague, so odds are you'll find a few deals. For crystal, jewelry, or any number of gift items, check out the pedestrian shopping zone stretching from Náměstí Svobody to the train station. **Galerie Vaňkovka** (Ve Vaňkovce 1, tel. 533 110 110, www.galerie-vankovka.cz, Mon.-Sat. 9am-9pm, Sun. 10am-8pm) is a large shopping center located on the edge of the historical city center between the main train and bus stations. Consisting of 130 shops spread out over two floors, the center offers a wide range of internationally known shops like Levi's and Tommy Hilfiger as well as **Interspar** (daily 7am-10pm), one of the country's more reputable grocery stores.

ACCOMMODATIONS

Winner of the 2013 Hotel of the Year at the Czech Hotel Awards, **Hotel Arte** (Drobného 6, tel. 530 321 281, hotelarte.cz, 2,000 Kč d) is a modern and stylish hotel offering 15 comfortable, affordable, and well-appointed rooms. It is located roughly 10 minutes on foot from the city center in a quiet neighborhood next to an enormous park, which is perfect for a stroll at any time of day. The staff is friendly, speaks excellent English, and is always ready to help solve a problem or plan a day of activities. Top-notch service and comfort make this a hard choice to ignore.

The **Hotel Myslivna** (Nad Pisárkami 1, tel. 547 107 111, www.hotelmyslivna.cz, 1,760 Kč d) is a quiet hotel located in a wooded area overlooking Brno's Exhibition Center, a short 10-minute drive from the center of town. The staff is quite friendly and the rooms are simple, comfortable, and cheerful. There's a sauna, a fitness center, and a billiards table on the premises, and the hotel's restaurant serves fantastic Czech and wild game dishes. This hotel offers excellent value for the money and is perfect for those who prefer some distance between them and the hubbub of the city.

The **Grandhotel Brno** (Benešova 18-20, tel. 542 518 111, www.grandhotelbrno.cz, 2,550 Kč d) is a huge four-star hotel located directly opposite the train station on the edge of the historic old town. Rooms range from small and plain to huge and opulent. Make sure to reserve one facing away from the train station, or else getting to sleep may be more of a challenge than you care for. It's a little on the pricey side, but worth it if money is not an issue.

Barceló Brno Palace (Šilingrovo náměstí 2, tel. 532 156 777, www.barcelo.com, 3,500 Kč d) is located right in the center of town and could very well be the best hotel in Brno. Spacious, elegant, and ultramodern rooms complete with air conditioning, Wi-Fi, and flat-screen TVs await, as does the hotel's staff, who are happy to give directions, arrange a car service, or lead you to the breakfast buffet, which offers a choice of pretty much anything you can think of. This hotel is highly recommended.

Located in a quiet and historic neighborhood a mere 10-minute walk from the center is the **Hotel Europa** (Tř. Kapitána Jaroše 27, tel. 545 421 400, www.hoteleuropa.cz, 1,800 Kč d). The staff is friendly, the rooms are decorated with rich wooden furnishings, and the walls are thick, keeping out all the noise no one wants to deal with while on holiday. It's an excellent and dependable choice for those not interested in staying in the center.

FOOD

Borgo Agnese (Kopečná 43, tel. 515 537 500, www.borgoagnese.cz, Mon.-Sat. noon-midnight, mains 189-479 Kč) is a centrally located and wildly popular restaurant specializing in Mediterranean cuisine that can be enjoyed à la carte or via the degustation menu with paired wines. Dishes range from lamb and duck to fish and pasta, all of which are served by an attentive and professional staff. This is an excellent choice for foodies and those looking to spoil themselves.

Pivovarská Starobrno (Mendlovo náměstí 20, tel. 543 420 130, www.pivovarsk-abrno.cz, daily 10am-midnight, mains 152-459

Kč) offers tasty authentic Czech cuisine like goulash, wild game, and pork and dumplings. The indoor seating area is huge and is decorated like many other traditional Czech restaurants, while the outdoor summer terrace buzzes with activity during the warmer months. If you're really hungry, go for the very filling crispy pork knee and make sure to wash it all down with a freshly tapped light, dark, or mixed Starobrno beer.

Valoria (Bohunická 2, tel. 543 250 462, www.valoria.cz, Mon.-Sat. 11am-11pm, mains 199-489 Kč) is a laid-back yet elegant restaurant with a relaxing outdoor terrace that's a must during the warmer months. A reasonably priced international menu that also features a handful of traditional Czech dishes can be found here, served by friendly and knowledgeable staff who go out of their way to make your experience a memorable one. Reservations are recommended.

The cozy and contemporary **Il Mercato** (Zelný trh 2, tel. 542 212 156, www.ilmercato.cz, Mon.-Fri. 8am-11pm, Sat. 9am-11pm, Sun. 9am-10pm, mains 295-395 Kč) is arguably the city's finest Italian restaurant, with tourist prices to match. The menu isn't extensive, but there are plenty of daily specials focusing on fish, meat, and pasta-based dishes that are expertly prepared and can be enjoyed with a solid selection of French, Italian, and Moravian wines. The open kitchen and steak and fish trays from which you can choose your meal are nice touches, and the multilingual staff is among the finest in town. It's a potential budget-breaker, but well worth the extra expense.

Tulip Restaurant (Třída. Kpt. Jaroše 10, tel. 773 302 021, www.tulip-restaurant.cz, Mon.-Fri. 11am-midnight, Sat. noon-midnight, mains 110-495 Kč) is a bright and friendly establishment with an excellent menu focused on chicken, fish, and steak options that have been getting raves the last couple of years. The prices are fair and the service is professional and attentive, making this an excellent choice for a date, business dinner, or family celebration. Reservations are recommended.

INFORMATION AND SERVICES

Turistické Informacní Centrum (Radnická 8, tel. 542 427 150, www.ticbrno.cz, Mon.-Fri. 8am-6pm, Sat.-Sun. 9am-6pm) provides visitors with pretty much any information they'll need to take full advantage of their time in Brno. From hooking up accommodations to swinging tickets for the hottest shows in town, the fine folks here will be happy to help.

GETTING THERE
By Bus
Buses leave Prague's Florenc station for Brno every hour. The trip takes 2.5-3 hours and tickets cost roughly 220 Kč. Note that tickets should be bought in advance if you're planning on traveling during peak hours or on the weekend. Brno's bus station is a five-minute walk to Old Town.

By Train
Trains leave regularly for Brno from Prague's Hlavní nádraží, with the trip lasting approximately three hours. Tickets cost approximately 210 Kč.

Brno's train station is located in the center of town, a few minutes' walk to Old Town.

By Car
Brno is 139 miles from Prague. Driving to Brno is a straightforward, if at times boring, drive. Simply take the E50 (a.k.a. D1) from Prague all the way to Brno. The trip should take approximately two hours.

Parking in Old Town is not possible, as it's mostly a pedestrian zone. Your best bet is to park at the main train station. The cost is 35 Kč an hour.

GETTING AROUND
There are a number of car rental agencies in Brno, including **Avis** (Brno Turany Airport, tel. 545 521 171, www.avis.com, Mon.-Fri. 8am-7:30pm, Sat.-Sun. 10am-7:30pm, from 1,600 Kč per day), **Budget** (Brno Turany Airport, tel. 545 521 144, www.budget.cz,

MORAVIA

Mon.-Fri. 9am-6pm, from 1,100 Kč per day), and **Hertz** (Millenium Center, Hybesova 42, tel. 225 345 071, www.hertz. cz, Mon.-Fri. 8am-4:30pm, from 1,950 Kč

per day). Booking through the company's website may very well land you a far better deal than renting in person. Check online for more details.

Telč

Anyone interested in peace, quiet, and the picturesque should definitely consider a trip to Telč, widely considered one of the most beautiful holiday spots in this part of Europe. Dating to 1099, this gorgeous little town located on the cusp of Bohemia and Moravia is surrounded by lakes, forests, and countryside dotted with enough castles and ruins to keep any history buff busy. Its pretty Renaissance-influenced castle and square are popular destinations for visitors from around the world and perfect spots to lose yourself in the fairy-tale atmosphere that blankets the entire town. Little wonder that it was added to UNESCO's World Heritage List.

SIGHTS
◖ Náměstí Zachariáše z Hradce (Town Square)

You'll be hard-pressed to find a more enchanting square in the country, lined as it is with arcades and meticulously preserved Renaissance houses complemented by picture-perfect facades. Many of these houses were originally built in the Gothic style during the second half of the 15th century and now boast individually built fronts and gables sporting baroque features. Some of the buildings worthy of attention are **Town Hall** (number 10), whose appearance dates to 1574; the house at **number 48,** which

the pretty Renaissance houses of Telč's town square

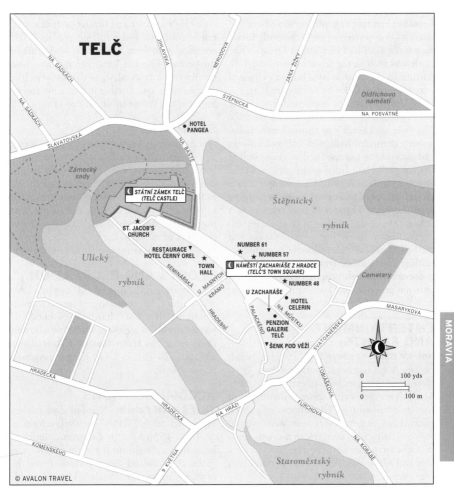

© AVALON TRAVEL

was rebuilt in the baroque style in the 18th century; the Renaissance house with a baroque front at **number 57;** and the sgraffito-covered building at **number 61** with Old Testament motifs. And don't forget 17th-century **St. Jacob's Church** (May and Sept. Sat.-Sun. 1pm-5pm, June-Aug. Mon.-Sat. 10am-noon and 1pm-6pm, Sun. 1pm-6pm, 40 Kč), whose nearly 200-foot-tall tower affords breathtaking views of Telč, its surrounding lakes, and beyond.

Státní zámek Telč (Telč Castle)

Telč Castle (Náměstí Zachariáše z Hradce, tel. 567 243 943, www.zamek-telc.cz, Tour A: Apr. and Oct. daily 10am-4pm, May and Sept. daily 10am-5pm, June daily 9am-5pm, July-Aug. daily 9am-6pm, Tour B: May and Sept. daily 10am-5pm, June daily 9am-5pm, July-Aug. daily 9am-6pm; Tour A 110 Kč, Tour B 90 Kč) is easily one of the most remarkable examples of Renaissance architecture in the Czech

Republic, boasting carefully preserved original interiors that prove the overwhelming influence Italian art had in Central Europe. The castle was built in the second half of the 14th century in the Gothic style but was changed into what we see today by Baldassare Maggi in 1550. Visitors have the opportunity to choose from two tours of these magnificent grounds. The first tour takes you through enormous, lavishly decorated halls with coffered ceilings and astonishing trompe l'oeil works as well as the Knight's Hall, filled with numerous suits of armor, and the African Hall, complete with the stuffed heads of exotic animals hanging from the walls. The second tour takes visitors through the castle's residential quarters, including the library, the dining room, the salon, and the bedroom—all painstakingly recreated according to original designs of the period. While it doesn't overwhelm the senses like the first tour, it is nevertheless a fascinating look at what daily life was like for Moravian nobility.

ENTERTAINMENT AND EVENTS

Hot-Air Balloons above Telč (www.telc.balon. cz, late Aug.) has been operating since 1997, offering contestants the opportunity to compete in two categories: sport ballooning and romantic ballooning. The number of participants seems to grow every year, with over 20 balloons flying high over Telč in previous years. If you're anywhere near the area, stop in for a visit and admire the skies as you've never seen them before.

Take a couple of steps back in time during the colorful and animated **Zacharias's Historic Celebrations** (mid-Aug.), a day dedicated to Telč's most important historical figure. Zachariáš z Hradce (Zacharias of Hradec) was a wealthy nobleman who gained control of the town in the 16th century. Since he was a great admirer of the Italian Renaissance, he invited Italian architects to Telč and they proceeded to transform the town's once Gothic style into the Renaissance paradise it remains today. There are plenty of things to see on Zacharias's day, including

sword fights, dance and theater performances, music concerts, and a full-on medieval fair complete with food, handicrafts, and drink of the period. This is a lot of fun for the whole family and a taste of what things were like many moons ago. Further information can be found at the visitor information office.

SHOPPING

Not particularly known for its shopping scene, Telč is nevertheless a fine place to pick up a bottle of Moravian wine. If you prefer handicrafts or clothing, try walking through the arcades, which offer all sorts of souvenirs, such as postcards, books, ceramic miniatures, and marionettes. Be forewarned that the quality of this kind of merchandise may not be particularly high, so make sure you're not overpaying.

SPORTS AND RECREATION

Cycling around the hills of Telč can be a little trying, but the surrounding beauty is so overwhelming that you'll hardly even notice. If you do decide to see the town by bicycle, rent them from the **train station** (Masarykova 156, tel. 725 754 757, 180 Kč per day) for a reasonable fee.

ACCOMMODATIONS

The **◖ Hotel Celerin** (Náměstí Zachariáše z Hradce 43, tel. 567 243 477, www.hotelcelerin. cz, 1,530-1,750 Kč d) is a romantic, intimate hotel situated right on the main square. The rooms are clean and simply furnished, and the service is warm and attentive. This affordable option is perfect for those fed up with the cold, rather impersonal service that often comes with the bigger chains.

Located in the historic center of town, the **Penzion Galerie Telč** (Na Můstku 37, tel. 774 892 263, www.hoteltelc.cz, 1,600 Kč d) is a wonderful option featuring six spacious and luxurious apartments. The staff is professional yet friendly and willing to go out of their way to make you feel at home, imbuing the premises with a distinct family atmosphere. Many consider this Telč's best value.

The **Hotel Pangea** (Na Baště 450, tel.

Tomáš Baťa: "Our Customer Is Our Master"

Born in Zlín on April 3, 1876, Tomáš Baťa became Czechoslovakia's most innovative and important businessperson after establishing the Bata Shoe Organization in his hometown on August 24, 1894. To offer some perspective on the matter, Bata has so far managed to sell over 14 billion shoes since its inception—over twice the world's current population.

Baťa's operation grew significantly in both size and stature during World War I, when the demand for military shoes skyrocketed. When the dust finally settled, economies had been crippled, currencies were rendered practically useless, and people had barely enough to spend on food, let alone footwear. Baťa's answer was to slash his prices in half, luring customers back into his stores and forcing the industry to follow suit.

As the company prospered, so did neighboring communities. Baťa began building houses, schools, hospitals, and shops near all his factories, creating an environment that allowed everyone to enjoy his success. Possessing a strong sense of social consciousness and responsibility, he was a pioneer of employment welfare and social advancement programs and once stated, "Let's bear in mind that the chances to multiply wealth are unlimited. All people can become rich." It was this sociocapitalist philosophy that got him elected mayor of Zlín in 1923.

A student of Le Corbusier's school of city as machine, Baťa enlisted leading Czech modernist architect František Gahura to design a simple 20- by 20-foot concrete box that could be duplicated quickly and easily. Gahura took the idea and ran with it, adding red brick, glass brick, and steel-framed windows to the mix. The result was that the town's residential buildings now mirrored the factories, stressing Baťa's strong belief of industry being central to one's life.

Baťa continued to modernize the footwear industry by being the first to incorporate factory-style production along with long-distance retailing. He set up factories and companies in a number of countries, including Poland, Yugoslavia, India, Holland, Denmark, the United Kingdom, and the United States. By the time the 1930s rolled around, Baťa and his beloved Czechoslovakia were atop the field of footwear exporters, producing over 80,000 pairs of shoes a day.

Baťa's death came suddenly in 1932—the result of a fatal plane crash. His half-brother Dr. Jan Antonín Baťa took over the operation until the Nazis invaded in 1939, prompting him to flee to Brazil. When the Communists took over, they seized all Bata companies and nationalized them—a sign, no doubt, of their distaste for Baťa's egalitarian capitalism, not to mention the fact that Zlín had already accomplished most of what the Communists were promising, including a level of working conditions unparalleled in Europe at the time.

The company was eventually taken over by Thomas Jan Bata, son of the founder, and its headquarters were moved to Toronto, which is also home to the Bata Shoe Museum. Today, Bata serves roughly one million customers per day, employs over 40,000 people, and is a retail force to be reckoned with in over 50 countries. There is also a Tomáš Baťa University in Zlín, which currently comprises five faculties: Technology, Management and Economics, Multimedia Communications, Applied Informatics, and Humanity Studies.

Tomáš Baťa may not have lived to see his dream of providing shoes to every man, woman, and child on the planet, but he can rest in peace knowing that he and his devoted family have come pretty darn close.

warm and hospitable Hotel Celerin

567 213 122, www.pangea.cz, 1,400 Kč d) is located in a quiet pedestrian zone just two minutes from the town center. The 10 double rooms are clean and comfortable, the desk staff is top-notch, and there is a heated swimming pool on the premises should you need to get your laps in. This is an excellent and affordable three-star hotel that many Czechs opt for when visiting.

FOOD

Situated right on the main square, **U Zachariáše** (Náměstí Zachariáše z Hradce 33, tel. 567 243 672, www.uzachariase.cz, daily 11am-11pm, mains 95-290 Kč) offers diners traditional Moravian fare along with an unbeatable view. Grilled salmon, pepper steak, and roast duck are but a few of the dishes you can dig into while watching the human traffic come and go. The quality of the food and service have come under fire recently, but these complaints tend to be the exception to the rule.

The **Restaurace Hotel Černý Orel** (Náměstí Zachariáše z Hradce 7, tel. 567 243 220, www. cernyorel.cz, daily 7am-10pm, mains 119-239 Kč) serves up traditional Czech fare to what seems like the entire town. Extremely popular due to its reputation for delicious traditional cuisine, this is one place where you may have to elbow your way in for a seat.

Arguably the most charming place to eat in town, **Šenk pod věží** (Palackého 116, tel. 567 243 889, http://senk-pod-vezi.webnode.cz, Apr.-Oct. daily 11am-10pm, Nov.-Mar. Fri.-Sun. 11am-3pm and 6pm-10pm, mains 106-222 Kč) is an excellent choice for tasty Czech fare at reasonable prices. Friendly staff, a good selection of domestic wine, and a great summer terrace are a few more reasons to stop in at any time of day.

INFORMATION AND SERVICES

The **Information Center** (Náměstí Zachariáše z Hradce 10, tel. 567 112 407, www.telc-etc.cz, Apr. Mon. and Wed. 8am-noon and 12:30pm-5pm, Tues. and Thurs.-Fri. 8am-noon and 12:30pm-4pm, Sat.-Sun. 10am-noon and 1pm-4pm, May and Sept. Mon.-Fri. 8am-noon and 12:30pm-5pm, Sat.-Sun. 10am-noon and 1pm-4pm, June-Aug. Mon.-Fri. 8am-6pm, Sat.-Sun. 10am-6pm, Oct. Mon.-Fri. 8am-noon and 12:30pm-5pm, Sat.-Sun. 10am-noon and 1pm-4pm, Nov.-Mar. Mon. and Wed. 7:30am-noon and 12:30pm-5pm, Tues. and Thurs.-Fri. 8am-noon and 12:30pm-4pm) is a handy resource for those who would like to learn more about this beautiful town. The kind staff here can help you with information regarding sights, accommodations, restaurants, trips, public transportation connections, cultural and sport events, and a whole lot more.

GETTING THERE
By Bus

Buses for Telč leave regularly from Prague's Florenc station, but make sure you get on a direct bus, as the others take twice as long to make the trip. Tickets cost approximately 145-189 Kč, with the ride taking roughly 2.5-3 hours. The bus station is 0.5 mile from the center.

By Car

Telč is 103 miles from Prague. Leaving Prague, take the D1 highway east in the direction of Brno and exit at Jihlava. After going through Jihlava, take Highway 38 south, then Highway 23 west. The drive takes roughly two hours. From Brno, take the D1 highway and exit at Jihlava. Pick up Highway 38 after going through town, then take Highway 23 west toward Telč. The drive takes about 1.5-2 hours.

From Mikulov, take the E461/52 north, then the 395 exit toward Pohořelice. At Pohořelice, take the 53 heading for Znojmo/Vienna/Brno, continuing along as the 53 turns into the 412. Take the E59/38 toward Prague/Jihlava-Moravské/Budějovice, then the 23 heading for Jindřichův Hradec-Telč. The drive takes approximately two hours.

Parking is available by the main square. The cost is 30 Kč an hour.

Mikulov

Mikulov, with its enchanting square and 13th-century castle, lies on the Austrian border roughly 155 miles from Prague. The town began to grow economically thanks to its location and climate, which were responsible for the nearly 2,000 acres of vineyards cultivated here by the 16th century. Mikulov also gained a reputation for being a town of religious tolerance, prompting many Jews to relocate here after being exiled from both Viennese and Czech royal towns. It was home to the regional rabbi of Moravia from the mid-16th to mid-19th centuries, and legendary Rabbi Loew, creator of the Golem, lived here as well, founding a yeshiva during his stay.

Mikulov today continues to be one of Moravia's leading wine centers and is home to Víno Mikulov, the largest producer of still wines in the country, with a total production of approximately 15 million bottles a year. It is home to elegant architecture, numerous nature trails, and the fun-filled Pálava Vintage Wine Festival, which attracts wine enthusiasts from all over the Czech Republic and beyond. A short visit will convince even the most finicky of travelers that few towns are filled with so much history and natural arresting beauty as this one.

SIGHTS
Náměstí
(Main Square)

Mikulov's main square is a rather irregularly shaped affair that is nonetheless a Renaissance fan's dream come true, lined as it is with gorgeous well-preserved buildings of the period. One of the square's most prominent features is a **fountain with the statue of Pomona,** the Roman goddess of fruit trees, gardens, and orchards, and who has sat here with her shield since all the way back in 1680. Another attention-grabbing characteristic of the square is its **Plague Column,** which was designed by Josef Prener and built by Ignác Lengelacher in 1724. It depicts three angels, symbolizing faith, hope, and love, as well as the statues of St. Jan Nepomuk, St. Francis Xavier, and St. Karel Boromejský, protector against the black death. The column is ringed with a handful of benches, making it a perfect spot to stop and catch your breath, allowing you to admire the square's remarkable architecture that includes the striking late-16th-century **"U Rytířů"** house, decorated with sgraffiti motifs of knights and war. It is the only house of its kind in town and a perfect example of the late Renaissance style.

Zámek Mikulov
(Mikulov Castle)

Mikulov Castle is a large complex of buildings that was founded by Přemysl Otakar I in 1218. It was acquired by the Liechtensteins in 1249 and went on to change hands and appearances throughout the centuries, being remodeled into late Romanesque, Gothic, Renaissance,

MORAVIA

© MARTINA JOHNSON

Mikulov's main square

and, after fires in 1719, high baroque. It was set ablaze by retreating German forces in 1945, and reconstruction began yet again in 1947. Since 1959, it has been home to the **Regional Museum of Mikulov** (Zámek 1, tel. 519 309 019, www.rmm.cz, Apr. and Oct. daily 9am-4pm, May-June and Sept. daily 9am-5pm, July-Aug. daily 9am-6pm, Nov.-Mar. Tues.-Sun. 9am-4pm, 80-150 Kč), which remains popular due to its interesting exhibition detailing Moravia's long history of wine growing and viticulture. Another object of interest lies in the castle's cellar: Central Europe's second-largest wine barrel, which is 20 feet long, weighs 26 tons, and holds a whopping 26,703 gallons of wine.

Proboštský kostel sv. Václava (Church of St. Wenceslas)

The late Gothic **Church of St. Wenceslas** (Kostelní náměstí 3, daily 10am-noon and 1pm-6pm, free) is located just off the main square and stands on the foundations of a former Romanesque church that burned down sometime around 1426. The relatively modest church sports a five-sided, vaulted presbytery, a triple nave, and lavish stucco interiors. It is also home to one of the country's most valuable church organs, which was the work of renowned organ maker Jan Výmola and dates to 1771.

ENTERTAINMENT AND EVENTS
C Pálava Vintage Wine Festival

The **Pálava Vintage Wine Festival** (tel. 519 510 855, www.palavske-vinobrani.cz, first half of Sept.) is by far the most important cultural event in Mikulov, drawing thousands of merrymakers from all over the country and beyond. For three days straight folks celebrate the actions of one Lord John of Lichtenstein, who, in 1403, set free Czech King Wenceslas IV from a Viennese prison. Upon his return, a large feast was held, and the same thing has been happening here for over half a century. Parades sweep through town, marketplaces spring up, wine is sampled all day and night, and food is consumed with the zeal of hungry nobles. If you

A Quick Guide to Moravia's Wine Regions

The heart and soul of the Czech Republic's wine industry can be found in Moravia's wine region, which stretches from the northernmost tip of Brno to the southernmost tip of Moravia and represents a hefty 96 percent of the country's wine production. The area's average annual temperature of 49°F, 20 inches of rainfall, and relatively warm summers allow for a slower-than-usual ripening of grapes, which results in the retention and concentration of a wide variety of pleasing and popular aromas. The region itself is divided into four subregions: Znojmo, Mikulov, Velké Pavlovice, and Slovácko.

ZNOJMO

Situated in the Bohemia-Moravian Highland, Znojmo's prime wine-growing locations stretch from Kraví Hora to Hnánice in the north, through a series of vineyards in the south that include Šatov, Chvalovice, Vrbovec, Hnízdo, Slup, and Jaroslavice, along with Tasovice and Hodonice in the east. It is primarily a region of white aromatic wines that include Veltlínské zelené, Müller-Thurgau, sauvignon, Ryzling rýnský, and Pálava as well as the pinot varieties of Rulandské bílé, Rulandské šedé, and Rulandské modré.

MIKULOV

Mikulov's wine region is characterized by elevated limestone and sizeable loess drifts located in Pálava, which, when combined with the soils of lower Podyjí and the historical Lednice-Valtice expanse, is responsible for a considerable amount of the wine consumed in the area and in the country at large. The wine communes of Sedlec, Dolní Dunajovice, Pavlov, Perná, Dolní, and Horní Věstonice are responsible for a considerable amount of the wine consumed both in the area and in the rest of the country, which includes Ryzlink vlašský, Rulandské bílé, Veltlínské zelené, and Müller-Thurgau. And don't count out the villages to the north, which include Strachotín, Pouzdřany, and Popice, well known for their Ryzlink rýnský, Tramín červený, and Pálava wines.

VELKÉ PAVLOVICE

Velké Pavlovice represents the heart of Moravia's red wine production thanks to the high content of magnesium found in the soil as well as enviable amounts of limestone loam, marl, sandstone, and conglomerate rock. The center of the region includes the town of Velké Bílovice, which boasts the greatest number of vineyards in the country. In the north, the towns and surrounding areas of Hrušovany and Žabčice produce excellent versions of Veltlínské zelené and Rulandské šedé as well as fragrant and superior varieties of Tramín červený, Pálava, Muškát moravský, and Müller-Thurgau. The region's main axis of vineyards lies along the Brno-Břeclav stretch of highway and includes the historical wine-producing villages of Židlochovice, Velké Němčice, Zaječí, Přítluky, and Rakvice, known for their delicious variations of Veltlínské zelené, Ryzlink vlašský, and Modrý Portugal.

SLOVÁCKO

Slovácko lies in southeast Moravia and is home to heterogeneous natural growing conditions. In the south is the land known as Podluží, whose wine communes are situated in the valley of the Morava River and cooled by northeast winds. The altitude and lightness of the soil dictate the intensity of temperatures during the summer, thereby imbuing white wines such as Ryzlink rýnský, Rulandské bílé, and Rulandské šedé as well as red wines Frankovka and Zweigeltrebe with incomparable vintages. North of Podluží is where you'll find the celebrated wine communes of Hovorany, Čejč, Šardice, and Terezín as well as Ždánice, Archlebov, and Žarošice, known for their unique varieties of Ryzlink rýnský, Rulandské bílé, Muškát moravský, and Müller-Thurgau. The center of the region, however, is Strážnice, whose wine laws date back to Petr of Kravaře in 1417 and whose range of superb vineyard sites produces some of the country's finest Ryzlink rýnský, Rulandské bílé, and Sylvánské zelené.

plan on attending this funfest and staying overnight, keep in mind that you'll have to book a room well in advance.

SHOPPING
Pretty much the only thing worth buying here is the local wine, which flows like mountain water. There is no shortage of wineries and private wine cellars to choose from, most of which offer visitors samples of their latest creations. Your best bet is to simply walk around, soak up the town's wonderful atmosphere, and, having worked up a thirst, experiment at various shops to find the best deals. Many locals may not know much English, but it'll be your taste buds that'll do most of the talking.

SPORTS AND RECREATION
There are plenty of trails to choose from in the region, and a visit to the visitor information center will help you decide which one is best for you. One particularly popular trail, about three miles in length, goes through town, along some natural paths, and then back again. Start at the Château Park and continue on to Goat Hill. After you've enjoyed the beautiful view over town, head north to Turold Hill. You should come across a blue tourist trail. Follow it through the forest as you climb the northeast side of Holy Hill. Reward yourself with another fabulous view of the town before heading down along the Way of the Cross and back into town.

ACCOMMODATIONS
Located just a couple of minutes' walk from the city center, the ◖ **Hotel Galant** (Mlýnská 2, tel. 519 323 353, www.galant.cz, 1,600-2,200 Kč d) is a friendly, professionally run hotel with a warm and helpful staff. It offers 129 modern rooms with Wi-Fi and all the usual amenities, although if you're here in summer, make sure to reserve a room with air-conditioning. The hotel's restaurant serves delicious traditional Czech dishes, and the wine cellar downstairs, seating up to 200 people, is about as fun and Moravian as it gets. This is one of the finer choices in town.

The wonderful **Eliška Hotel** (22. Dubna 1000/28, tel. 519 513 073, www.hoteleliska.cz, 1,120-1,680 Kč d) offers quality accommodations a mere five-minute walk from the main square. The rooms are clean and comfortable and come equipped with satellite TV, Internet, and the usual amenities. Apartments are also available and come with a bath and a terrace. There's an Irish pub on the premises as well, where the Guinness flows freely. It's one of the more stylish and enjoyable hotels in town.

The **Réva Hotel** (Česká 2, tel. 519 512 076, www.hotelreva.cz, 1,000 Kč d) is another excellent and affordable choice. Located right in the historical center, the hotel offers guests tremendous views of Mikulov Castle, Goat Hill, and St. Wenceslas Church. The rooms are clean and bright, with contemporary furnishings, and the hotel staff is exceptionally friendly. There is also a restaurant on the premises with a summer terrace for peaceful romantic dining.

FOOD
The ◖ **Hotel Templ Restaurant** (Husova 50, tel. 519 323 095, www.templ.cz, Sun.-Thurs. 11am-10pm, Fri.-Sat. 11am-midnight, mains 139-279 Kč) will catch your eye for no other reason than it's arguably the brightest building in the entire Jewish quarter. Delicious Czech and international dishes are served by a pleasant staff in elegant surroundings that span five successive rooms. The meals are generously portioned and relatively affordable, but if you're on a tight budget, make sure to check out the daily specials, which are no less impressive.

Serving excellent traditional Czech dishes is the aptly named **Aquarium Restaurant Relax** (Pavlovská 40, tel. 519 324 724, www.aquariumrelax.cz, Sun.-Thurs. 9am-10pm, Fri.-Sat. 9am-11pm, mains 115-324 Kč), which boasts 50 seats and three giant aquariums with fish from all over the world on display. Enjoy tasty duck, beef, and fish options as well as an extensive wine list in a relaxed and smoke-free environment. Attentive waitstaff and more than reasonable prices seal the deal.

INFORMATION AND SERVICES

The **Tourist Information Center** (Náměstí 1, tel. 519 510 855, www.mikulov.cz, Nov.-Mar. Mon.-Fri. 8am-4pm, Apr.-May and Oct. daily 9am-5pm, June and Sept. Mon.-Fri. 8am-6pm, Sat.-Sun. 9am-6pm, July-Aug. Mon.-Fri. 8am-7pm, Sat.-Sun. 9am-7pm) is usually quite busy but very efficient, so you won't be waiting long. This is the place to go if you have any questions regarding sights or cultural events. The kind people here can also arrange concert tickets and accommodations for you as well as an evening in one of the town's many wine cellars. If you feel like exploring on your own, you can find helpful maps and brochures that will get you started.

GETTING THERE
By Bus

Buses leave Prague's Florenc station regularly every day, so routes, times, and prices vary widely. A typical trip takes a little over four hours and costs roughly 269 Kč. The bus station is about 500 feet from the center.

By Car

Mikulov is approximately 155 miles from Prague. Leaving Prague, take the D1 east all the way to Brno, then take Route 52 south to Mikulov. The drive takes roughly 2.5-3 hours.

From Brno, take Highway E65 south to Břeclav, then head east on Route 40 to Mikulov. The drive takes about a half hour.

From Telč, take the 23 out of town, then the E59/38 toward Znojmo. Once past Znojmo, take the 412 toward Brno. Then take the 53 towards Pohořelice until you hit the E461/52 to Mikulov. The drive takes approximately two hours.

Most people park on the street (25 Kč an hour) or at the parking lot just beyond the main square (35 Kč an hour).

MORAVIA

BUDAPEST

The famed Danube River separates Buda's hilly west bank from Pest's bustling streets, thereby offering travelers the best of both worlds—luscious, peaceful surroundings complemented with the infectious energy characterizing a cosmopolitan city. Whether it's a stroll through the Belváros or a night spent enjoying the local wine and cuisine, visitors can't help but be

© TYKHYI/123RF

HIGHLIGHTS

LOOK FOR ◖ TO FIND RECOMMENDED SIGHTS, ACTIVITIES, DINING, AND LODGING.

◖ **Váci utca (Váci Street):** The most famous pedestrian street in the country continues to do big business, luring tourists and residents alike with its memorable mixture of historical landmarks, sidewalk cafés, and trendy boutiques (page 216).

◖ **Dunakorzó (Danube Embankment):** This longtime favorite of both locals and tourists exudes Old World charm, thanks to its pretty outdoor cafés and awe-inspiring views of Buda (page 217).

◖ **Szent István Bazilika (St. Stephen's Basilica):** An awe-inspiring sight, this church boasts a remarkable interior as well as a tower that offers breathtaking panoramic views of the capital (page 222).

◖ **Magyar Állami Operaház (Hungarian State Opera House):** Put on your finest evening wear and head for this neo-Renaissance masterpiece, where the world's finest musicians dazzle sold-out crowds night after refined night (page 229).

◖ **Széchenyi gyógyfürdő (Széchenyi Spa Baths):** This majestic neo-baroque building boasts an enormous swimming pool that can be enjoyed year-round, along with steam rooms, saunas, and Turkish baths (page 237).

◖ **Budavári palota (Royal Palace of Buda):** Dominating Buda's skyline, the Royal Palace is one of the country's most revered architectural achievements and home to the Hungarian National Gallery, Budapest History Museum, National Széchenyi Library, and Ludwig Museum of Contemporary Art (page 243).

◖ **Gellért hegy (Gellért Hill):** A trek up this impressive hill, topped by the battle-scarred but beautiful Citadella, rewards you with some of the most spectacular panoramic views of the city (page 250).

◖ **Aquincum:** A short trip on the HÉV will take you back to the 2nd century, when public baths and sacrificial altars were de rigueur for this former Roman capital (page 253).

◖ **Margit sziget (Margaret Island):** This 1.6-mile stretch of the sublime offers flower gardens, enchanting ruins, and the incomparable Palatinus Strand. Its countless paths and near mystical serenity make this the perfect place to spend a romantic afternoon (page 254).

◖ **The Railroad Circuit:** Drink in the scenery as you ride through the vast Buda Hills on the Cog-Wheel Railroad and the Children's Railroad (page 255).

BUDAPEST

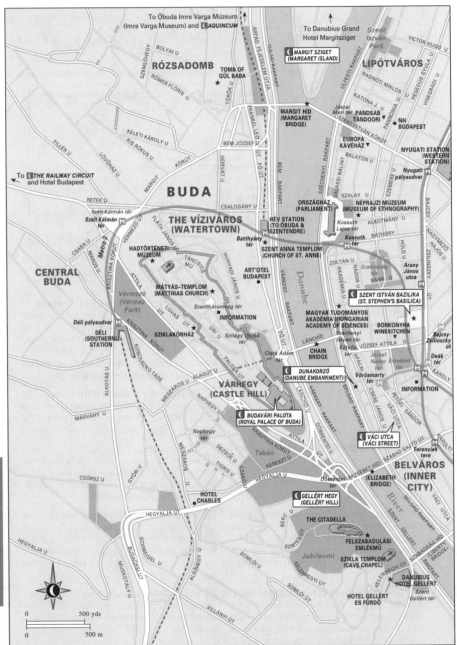

To Óbuda Imre Varga Múzeum
(Imre Varga Museum) and ■ *AQUINCUM*

To Danubius Grand
Hotel Margitsziget

*Szent
István
Park*

VICTOR HUGO U.

SZEMLŐHEGY

BOLYAI U.

RÓMER FLÓRIS U.

RÓZSADOMB

TOMB OF
GÜL BABA
★

TÖRÖK U.

ÁRPÁD FEJEDELEM ÚTJA

ÚJ-AKI RAKPART

ÚJPESTI RAKPART

■ *MARGIT SZIGET
(MARGARET ISLAND)*

LIPÓTVÁROS

RADNÓTI MIKLÓS U.

HEGEDŰS GYULA U.

VISEGRÁDI U.

KELETI KÁROLY U.

KIS RÓKUS U.

FILLER U.

LÓVÖLGY U.

FRANKEL LEÓ ÚT

MARGIT HÍD
(MARGARET
BRIDGE)

Jászai
Mari tér

PANNONIA U.

KATONA J. U.

SZENT ISTVÁN KÖRÚT

PANDSAB
TANDOORI

■ NH
BUDAPEST

EURÓPA
KÁVÉHÁZ ▼

NYUGATI STATION
(WESTERN
STATION)

Nyugati
pályaudvar

BALATON U.

SZEMERE U.

BAJCSY-

NAGYMEZŐ U.

HAJÓS U.

HORVÁT U.

BEM JÓZSEF TÉR

BEM RAKPART

SZALAY U.

BEM
RAKPART

BALASSI BÁLINT U.

BUDA

MARGIT KÖRÚT

RETEK U.

Szell Kálmán tér
*Szell Kálmán
tér*

Metro 2

VÉRMEZŐ ÚT

FLÁTH JÁNOS U.

CSALOGÁNY U.

HÉV STATION
(TO ÓBUDA &
SZENTENDRE)

*Batthyány
tér*

SZÉCHENYI RAKPART

**THE VÍZIVÁROS
(WATERTOWN)**

CSABA U.

MAROS U.

KRISZTINA KÖRÚT

ATTILA ÚT

HADTÖRTÉNETI
MÚZEUM
★

TÁNCSICS
M. U.

HUNYADI JÁNOS ÚT

SZENT ANNA TEMPLOM
(CHURCH OF ST. ANNE)
★

ART'OTEL
BUDAPEST ■

VÁRKERT RAKPART

Danube

ORSZÁGHÁZ
(PARLIAMENT)

*Kossuth
Lajos tér*

NÉPRAJZI MÚZEUM
(MUSEUM OF ETHNOGRAPHY)

ALKOTMÁNY U.

Kossuth

BÁTHORY U.

ZOLTÁN U.

AKADÉMIA U.

*Szabadság
tér*

ARANY
JÁNOS
BANK U.

utca

**CENTRAL
BUDA**

*Vérmező
(Vérmez
Park)*

**MÁTYÁS-TEMPLOM
(MATTHIAS CHURCH)** ★

Szentháromság tér

INFORMATION

*Szilágy Dezső
tér*

VÁRKERT RAKPART

MAGYAR TUDOMÁNYOS
AKADÉMIA (HUNGARIAN
ACADEMY OF SCIENCES)

*Széchenyi
István tér*

■ *SZENT ISTVÁN BAZILIKA
(ST. STEPHEN'S BASILICA)* ★

BORKONYHA
WINEKITCHEN

Déli pályaudvar

**DÉLI
(SOUTHERN)
STATION**

KRISZTINA KÖRÚT

SZIKLAKÓRHÁZ ★

LOVAS ÚT

ÚRI U.

PALOTA ÚT

LÁNCHÍD

CHAIN
BRIDGE

*Eötvös
tér*

APÁCAI U.

*József
Nádor tér*

*Erzsébet
tér*

Bajcsy-
Zsilinszky
út

*Deák
tér*

KOSSUTH LAJOS TÉR

ALKOTÁS U.

MÉSZÁROS U.

ALAGÚT U.

NAPHEGY U.

**VÁRHEGY
(CASTLE HILL)**

*Clark Ádám
tér*

LÁNCHÍD U.

VÁRKERT RAKPART

BELGRÁD RAKPART

■ *DUNAKORZÓ
(DANUBE EMBANKMENT)*

*Vörösmarty
tér*

PETŐFI SÁNDOR U.

KÁROLY KÖRÚT

INFORMATION

MÁRVÁNY U.

*Naphegy
tér*

DEZSŐ U.

KRISZTINA KÖRÚT

ATTILA ÚT

DÖBRENTEI U.

■ *BUDAVÁRI PALOTA
(ROYAL PALACE OF BUDA)*

■ *VÁCI UTCA
(VÁCI STREET)*

VÁCI UTCA

CSÖRSZ U.

GYŐRI U.

MÉSZÁROS U.

TIGRIS U.

CZAKÓ U.

Tabán

KERESZT U.

HEGYALJA ÚT

*Döbrentei
tér*

■ (ELIZABETH
BRIDGE)

ERZSÉBET HÍD

SZABAD SAJTÓ ÚT

*Ferenciek
tere*

**BELVÁROS
(INNER
CITY)**

SZENT GELLÉRT RAKPART

BELGRÁD RAKPART

VÁCI UTCA

HOTEL
CHARLES ■

HEGYALJA ÚT

■ *GELLÉRT HEGY
(GELLÉRT HILL)*

BERC U.

SZIRTES ÚT

River

SZABADSÁG HÍD
(LIBERTY
BRIDGE)

To ■ *THE RAILWAY CIRCUIT*
and Hotel Budapest

BUDAÖRSI ÚT

SCHWEIDEL U.

ALSÓHEGY U.

Jubileumi

THE CITADELLA

FELSZABADULÁSI
EMLÉKMŰ ★

SZIKLA TEMPLOM
(CAVE CHAPEL) ✚

KELEN HEGYI ÚT

HEGYALJA ÚT

MUSKOTÁLY U.

VILLÁNYI ÚT

SOMLÓI ÚT

KELENHEGYI ÚT

DANUBIUS
HOTEL GELLÉRT

*Szent
Gellért tér*

HOTEL GELLÉRT
ES FÜRDŐ

☾

| 0 | | 500 yds |
| 0 | | 500 m |

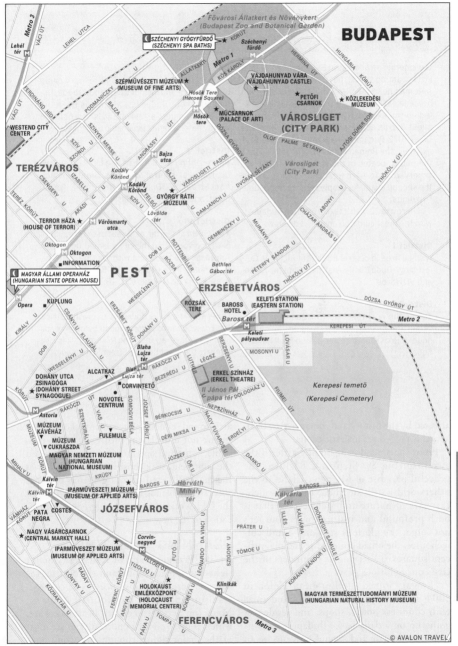

BUDAPEST

Fővárosi Állatkert és Növénykert
(Budapest Zoo and Botanical Garden)

Metro 3

Lehél tér

VÁCI ÚT
LEHEL UTCA
VÁCI ÚT

SZÉCHENYI GYÓGYFÜRDŐ
(SZÉCHENYI SPA BATHS)

Széchenyi fürdő

KÖRÚT
Metro 1
KŐS KÁROLY
HERMINA ÚT
HUNGÁRIA KÖRÚT

ÁLLATKERTI

FERDINÁND HÍDJA

PODMANICZKY
BAJZA U

SZÉPMŰVÉSZETI MÚZEUM ★
(MUSEUM OF FINE ARTS)

Hősök Tere
(Heroes Square)

Hősök tere

VAJDAHUNYAD VÁRA
(VAJDAHUNYAD CASTLE)

★ PETŐFI CSARNOK

★ KÖZLEKEDÉSI MÚZEUM

MŰCSARNOK
(PALACE OF ART)

VÁROSLIGET
(CITY PARK)

WESTEND CITY CENTER

SZINYEI MERSE U

SZÍV U

SZONDI

ANDRÁSSY ÚT

DÓZSA GYÖRGY ÚT

OLÓF PÁLME SÉTÁNY

AJTÓSI DÜRER SOR

TERÉZVÁROS

CSENGERY U

IZABELLA

ARÁDI

Kodály Körönd

Kodály Körönd

Bajza utca

BAJZA

VÁROSLIGETI FASOR

DVŐRÁK SÉTÁNY

Városliget
(City Park)

THŐKŐLY ÚT

TERÉZ KÖRÚT

SZIV U FELSŐ

GYÖRGY RÁTH MÚZEUM ★

DAMJANICH U

CHÁZÁR ANDRÁS U

ABONYI

TERROR HÁZA ★
(HOUSE OF TERROR)

Vörösmarty utca

Lövőlde tér

DEMBINSZKY U

MÚRÁNYI U

ROTTENBILLER U

Oktogon

Oktogon

INFORMATION

PEST

DOB U

RÓZSA U

Bethlen Gábor tér

PÉTERFY SÁNDOR U

THÖKÖLY ÚT

MAGYAR ÁLLAMI OPERAHÁZ
(HUNGARIAN STATE OPERA HOUSE)

ERZSÉBETVÁROS

Opera

KUPLUNG

CSÁNYI U KLAUZÁL U

WESSELÉNYI

ERZSÉBET KÖRÚT DOHÁNY U

RÓZSÁK TERE

BAROSS HOTEL

KELETI STATION
(EASTERN STATION)

DÓZSA GYÖRGY ÚT

KIRÁLY U

DOB U

WESSELÉNYI U

Baross tér

Metro 2

KEREPESI ÚT

Blaha Lujza tér

DOHÁNY UTCA ZSINAGÓGA
(DOHÁNY STREET SYNAGOGUE)

ALCATRAZ

CORVINTETŐ

Blaha Lujza tér

RÁKÓCZI ÚT

LUTHER

LÉGSZ

BEZERÉDJ U

BERZSENYI U

Keleti pályaudvar

MOSONYI U

LÓVÁSÁR U

ERKEL SZÍNHÁZ
(ERKEL THEATRE)

II János Pál pápa tér

DOLOGHÁZ U

FIUMEI ÚT

Kerepesi temetö
(Kerepesi Cemetery)

Astoria

MÚZEUM KÁVÉHÁZ

MÚZEUM ▼ CUKRÁSZDA

NOVOTEL CENTRUM

FULEMULE

RÁKÓCZI ÚT

SZENTKIRÁLYI U

VAS U

JÓZSEF KÖRÚT

SOMOGYI BÉLA

BÉRKOCSIS U

DÉRI MIKSA U

JÓZSEF

ÓRÁ U

NAGY FUVAROS U

ERDÉLYI

NÉPSZÍNHÁZ

DANKŐ U

MAGYAR NEMZETI MÚZEUM
(HUNGARIAN NATIONAL MUSEUM)

MIHÁLY U

KÖRÚT

Kálvin tér

Kálvin tér

IPARMŰVÉSZETI MÚZEUM
(MUSEUM OF APPLIED ARTS)

KRÚDY

BAROSS U

Horváth Mihály tér

BAROSS U

Kálvária tér

DIÓSZEGHY SÁMUEL U

PÁTA NEGRA

COSTES

JÓZSEFVÁROS

ILLES U

KÁLVÁRIA U

KORÁNYI SÁNDOR U

VÁMHÁZ KÖRÚT

NAGY VÁSÁRCSARNOK
(CENTRAL MARKET HALL)

Corvinnegyed

PRÁTER U

FUTÓ U

LEONARDO DA VINCI U

SZIGONY U

TÖMOE U

IPARMŰVÉSZET MÚZEUM
(MUSEUM OF APPLIED ARTS)

ÜLLŐEI ÚT

TIZOLTÓ U

Klinikák

MAGYAR TERMÉSZETTUDOMÁNYI MÚZEUM
(HUNGARIAN NATURAL HISTORY MUSEUM)

RÁDAY U

LÓNYAY U

KÖZRAKTÁR U

FERENC KÖRÚT

ANGYAL U

HOLOKAUST EMLÉKKÖZPONT
(HOLOCAUST MEMORIAL CENTER)

BOKRÉTA U

TOMPA U

PÁVA U

FERENCVÁROS

Metro 3

© AVALON TRAVEL

BUDAPEST

Budapest Addresses and Districts

Deciphering an address in Budapest can seem a little daunting at first, but it's really rather easy. A Roman numeral or four-digit postal code will precede each address. For example, when looking up the excellent Old Man's Music Pub, you might find its address written as: VII. Akácfa u. 13, or 1072 Budapest, Akácfa u. 13. In the first example, the Roman numeral "VII" tells us that the pub is located in the seventh district (Erzsébetváros). To learn what district the pub is in the second example, simply refer to the middle two digits, "07."

There are 22 districts (kerülets) in Budapest, with the most common ones listed below.

District I
A small area in central Buda that includes Gellért hegy, Buda Castle, Matthias Church, Tabán, and Víziváros.

District II
This is the northwest part of Buda, which includes the beautiful and prestigious neighborhood of Rózsadomb as well as hub Széll Kálmán Square.

District III
This district lies on the ancient military camp of Aquincum and includes beautiful Óbuda, the oldest part of Budapest, which has been the site of a commercial revival and is now home to trendy eateries and fashionable up-and-comers.

District V
Representing the Belváros and Lipótváros, this district is as central as it gets. Sights include Váci Street, the Danube Embankment, Parliament, and St. Stephen's Basilica.

District VI
The cultural center of Budapest, Terézváros is where you'll find the city's famed boulevard Andrássy Avenue, along with the Opera House, Nagymező utca (Budapest's Broadway), and lively Franz Liszt Square.

District VII
Otherwise known as Budapest's Jewish district, the Erzsébetváros is surrounded by main roads Károly körút, Király utca, and Rákóczi út. It is also home to the great Dohány Street Synagogue.

---

affected by the history and romance that blankets this ragged yet majestic capital.

From the splendor of Buda Castle to the awe-inspiring St. Stephen's Basilica, the peaceful paradise of Margaret Island to the otherworldly hills of Buda, there is a delicate mix of nature and architecture that is both profound and inspirational. And let's not forget the glorious spas and grand coffeehouses, the broad boulevards and magnificent squares, all serving as reminders of the city's once glorious past.

Hungary joined the European Union in 2004, and its capital continues to modernize with countless hotels, shops, and residences going up on a daily basis. Budapest remains a city on the rise and should prove to be an artistic and economic force to be reckoned with in the not-too-distant future. In the meanwhile, come and sip some of the finest wine on the continent, soak those bones in world-class thermal baths, and enjoy a gorgeous city that successfully blends the comfortable charm of the Old World with the cutting-edge sophistication of the new.

PLANNING YOUR TIME

Unlike Prague, many of Budapest's major sights are spread throughout the city, meaning there are larger distances to be covered, resulting in more time required to do so. Many travelers spend a scant three days here, which allows you the opportunity to see most of the major sights, though you won't have

District VIII
Józsefváros is a sort of Jekyll-and-Hyde neighborhood. Sticking to its main roads will reward you with the wonderful National Museum and busy Kálvin Square. Head for the depths, however, and you'll quickly find yourself in a rather seedy district.

District IX
Ferencváros is a rapidly developing neighborhood that has seen plenty of hip bars, restaurants, and apartment buildings spring up in the last few years. Trendy pedestrian street Ráday utca is an excellent place to have a drink, and the Central Market Hall just up the street is one of the city's most memorable shopping experiences.

District XII
This is home to the beautiful Buda Hills, with winding roads, large houses, and serene hiking trails, not to mention Normafa, which makes for a pleasant summertime getaway or passable ski site in the winter.

District XIII
This is the location of the one and only Margit sziget (Margaret Island).

District XIV
The Városliget is complete with must-see sights such as Heroes Square, the Museum of Fine Arts, Vajdahunyad Castle, and Széchenyi Baths.

TERMS
Hungarian is obviously a complicated language, and its names for various types of roads and streets can cause confusion for the uninitiated. Here are some of the more useful terms that can be learned quickly.

állomás–station
hid–bridge
körút (also abbreviated *krt*)–boulevard
köz–alley or lane
liget–park
pályaudvar (also abbreviated *pu.*)–train station
sziget–island
tér–square
tere–square of
út–road
utca (also abbreviated *u.*)–street
útja–road of

much time to catch your breath and even less time, if any, to enjoy the city's excellent museums and spas. The best way to approach planning a trip to Budapest is to think of it in half days: a half day to visit Margaret Island, a half day to visit the Városliget (City Park), a half day to visit the Buda Hills, and so forth. Again, should you be interested in visiting any museums or spas, both of which are highly recommended, simply add however much time you'd like to allot to either. Four days is enough time to give you a decent sense of what Budapest has to offer, although 5-7 days is ideal.

Budapest's public transportation system rivals Prague's in convenience and overall service, making the entire city easily accessible via bus or subway. It is also a great city to walk around in, and strolls down the Danube Embankment or Andrássy Avenue, or over any of its pretty bridges, are wonderful ways to soak up the atmosphere. While the Belváros is clearly tourist central, the city is so big that huge tour groups are easily avoided in most other districts, thereby allowing you to discover the beauty of Budapest in peace and comfort.

ORIENTATION
Pest
THE BELVÁROS (INNER CITY)
Located in Budapest's fifth district, the Belváros (Inner City) is surrounded by the Kiskörút (Inner Ring), which starts at

BUDAPEST

Szabadság híd (Liberty Bridge) and comprises Károly körút, Múzeum körút, Vámház körút, Bajcsy-Zsilinszky út, and József Attila utca before ending at the Chain Bridge. Its main squares are Deák Ferenc tér, which borders Lipótváros; Vörösmarty tér, which is home to the beginning of popular pedestrian shopping zone Váci utca and neighbors the Danube Embankment; and Ferenciek tere, characterized by the Elizabeth Bridge stretching across to Buda's Gellért Hill.

The major subway stops are Deák Ferenc tér, Vörösmarty tér, and Ferenciek tere.

LIPÓTVÁROS

Lipótváros is located in the northern part of the fifth district next to the Belváros and is bordered by Szent István körút, Bajcsy-Zsilinszky út, Deák Ferenc utca, and the Danube. Its main squares are Széchenyi István tér, located at the foot of the Chain Bridge; Szabadság tér; and Kossuth Lajos tér, home to the mighty Parliament building.

The major subway stops are Arany János utca, Kossuth Lajos tér, and Nyugati pályaudvar.

TERÉZVÁROS

The city's vibrant sixth district is characterized by the grand boulevard Andrássy Avenue, which stretches all the way to Heroes Square and marks the border between Terézváros and Lipótváros. Strolling down the boulevard will bring you to Nagymező utca, otherwise known as Budapest's Broadway, along with vibrant Liszt Ferenc tér and its numerous outdoor cafés and restaurants. Farther up still is the bustling eight-sided square known as the Oktogon, part of the city's Nagykörút (Outer Ring), which begins at Petőfi Bridge and incorporates Ferenc körút, József körút, Erzsébet körút, Teréz körút, and Szent István körút before ending at Margit Bridge.

The major subway stops are Bajcsy-Zsilinszky út, Opera, Oktogon, Vörösmarty utca, Kodály Körönd, and Bajza utca.

ERZSÉBETVÁROS

Situated southeast of Terézváros, Erzsébetváros serves as Budapest's seventh district and is also the location of the capital's colorful Jewish neighborhood. Király utca is a major street full of shops, cafés, and bars, as is Dohány utca, home to the magnificent Dohány Street Synagogue. Klauzál tér, deep in the district, is Erzsébetváros' largest square and historic center.

The major subway stop is Astoria.

THE VÁROSLIGET (CITY PARK)

The end of Andrássy Avenue leads to the Városliget, Budapest's 14th district. The main square is the grandiose Hősök tere (Heroes Square). Its main streets are Dózsa György út, which stretches all the way to Józsefváros, and Állatkerti körút, site of the Circus, Vidám Park, the Zoo, and Széchenyi Spa Baths.

The major subway stops are Hősök tere and Széchenyi fürdő.

JÓZSEFVÁROS

Located southeast of Erzsébetváros, Józsefváros makes up Budapest's eighth district. The Múzeum körút is one of its major routes and is part of the Inner Ring, separating the neighborhood from the Belváros and leading to its main square, Kálvin tér. The other, less-touristy, and far seedier side of the district, the József körút—part of the Outer Ring—remains a haven for prostitution and organized crime.

The major subway stops are Kálvin tér, Blaha Lujza tér, and Keleti pályaudvar.

FERENCVÁROS

The city's ninth district, Ferencváros borders Józsefváros to the south and is separated from the Belváros by the Vámház körút. Major road Üllői út stretches through most of the district, while popular pedestrian street Ráday utca offers color in the form of outdoor cafés and restaurants to what is otherwise a primarily working-class district.

The major subway stops are Corvin-negyed and Klinikák.

Buda
VÁRHEGY, THE VÍZIVÁROS, AND CENTRAL BUDA (CASTLE HILL, WATERTOWN, AND CENTRAL BUDA)

Várhegy (Castle Hill) is designated as Budapest's first district. On the Buda side of the Chain Bridge is Clark Ádám tér, which is the stepping stone to the funicular leading up the hill to the Royal Palace. The Castle District's main square is Szentháromság tér, home to Matthias Church and the Fishermen's Bastion.

Running along the Danube below Castle Hill is the Víziváros, also part of Budapest's first district. Its main street is Fő utca, which leads to central Batthyány tér.

The area loosely known as Central Buda is the assortment of small neighborhoods lying below Castle Hill and characterized by bustling Széll Kálmán tér, located just north of Castle Hill.

The major subway stops are Batthyány tér and Széll Kálmán tér.

GELLÉRT HEGY (GELLÉRT HILL)
South of Castle Hill is Gellért Hill, part of Budapest's 11th district. The hill is reached via the Elizabeth Bridge and stretches out toward Gellért tér and neighboring Liberty Bridge, home of the world-famous Gellért Hotel and Baths.

Gellért Hill is accessed via bus and tram.

ÓBUDA
Located north of Buda along the left bank of the Danube, Óbuda has a lovely and historic main square—Fő tér.

Óbuda is accessed via HÉV train.

THE BUDA HILLS
Beyond central Buda to the east lie the Buda Hills, the majority of which make up the city's 12th district.

The major subway stop is Széll Kálmán tér.

Margit sziget (Margaret Island)
Located in the middle of the Danube and representing Budapest's 13th district, Margaret Island is reached by either the Margaret or Árpád Bridge.

Sights

THE BELVÁROS (INNER CITY)
The Belváros is the historic center of Pest and forms the southern half of its fifth district. Abuzz with shops, restaurants, boutique hotels, and bars, it has caught up to the rest of the Western world in terms of consumerism and commerce, though there is still a sense of the old imperial city lurking around corners and down back streets, beckoning those willing to leave the well-worn tourist routes and delve into an illustrious past.

It is home to some of the city's most important sights, including the famed Danube Embankment, whose enchanting views of Buda have inspired imaginations and romance throughout the centuries. The colorful square Vörösmarty tér is nearby, where street musicians, starving artists, and local peddlers vie for your attention and a few hard-earned forints. And then there's Váci utca—Budapest's bustling pedestrian avenue lined with countless cafés and brightly lit shops selling everything from Prada to paprika.

There is always something to do in the Inner City throughout the year. Whether it's sampling the local cuisine and a wide variety of wines, taking in a jazz show, or nursing a cup of coffee in glorious turn-of-the-20th-century

BUDAPEST

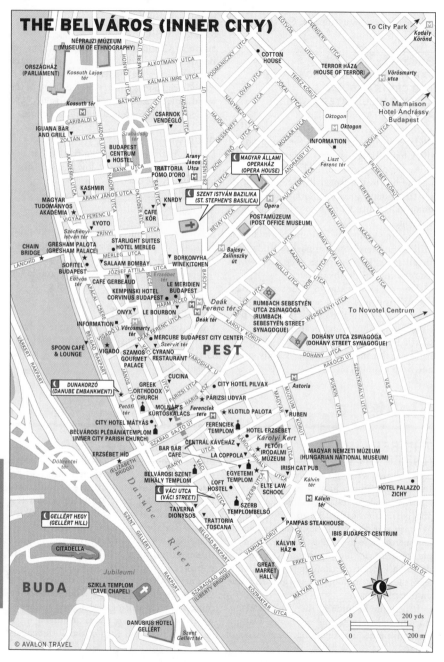

THE BELVÁROS (INNER CITY)

To City Park

Kodály Körönd

NÉPRAJZI MÚZEUM
(MUSEUM OF ETHNOGRAPHY)

COTTON HOUSE

TERROR HÁZA
(HOUSE OF TERROR)

Vörösmarty utca

ORSZÁGHÁZ
(PARLIAMENT)   Kossuth Lajos tér

Kossuth tér

To Mamaison
Hotel Andrássy
Budapest

GARIBALDI U.

Oktogon

Oktogon

IGUANA BAR
AND GRILL

ZOLTÁN UTCA

CSARNOK
VENDÉGLŐ

INFORMATION

Szabadság tér

BUDAPEST
CENTRUM
HOSTEL

BANK UTCA

TRATTORIA
POMO D'ORO

Arany
János
Utca

MAGYAR ÁLLAMI
OPERAHÁZ
(OPERA HOUSE)

Liszt
Ferenc tér

KASHMIR

ARANY JÁNOS UTCA

KNRDY

SZENT ISTVÁN BAZILIKA
(ST. STEPHEN'S BASILICA)

MAGYAR
TUDOMÁNYOS
AKADÉMIA

VIGYÁZÓ FERENC U.

CAFÉ
KÖR

Opera

KYOTO

Széchenyi
István tér

ZRÍNYI

POSTAMÚZEUM
(POST OFFICE MUSEUM)

REVAY UTCA

CHAIN
BRIDGE

GRESHAM PALOTA
(GRESHAM PALACE)

STARLIGHT SUITES
HOTEL MERLEG

MÉRLEG UTCA

Bajcsy-
Zsilinszky
út

LÁNCHID

SOFITEL
BUDAPEST

SALAAM BOMBAY

JÓZSEF ATTILA

BORKONYHA
WINEKITCHEN

Eötvös
tér

CAFÉ GERBEAUD

Erzsébet
tér

LE MERIDIEN
BUDAPEST

APÁCZAI CSERE

KEMPINSKI HOTEL
CORVINUS BUDAPEST

HARM INCĐ

Deák
Ferenc tér

RUMBACH SEBESTYÉN
UTCA ZSINAGÓGA
(RUMBACH
SEBESTYÉN STREET
SYNAGOGUE)

ONYX

LE BOURBON

Deák tér

To Novotel Centrum

INFORMATION

VIGADÓ U.

Vörösmarty
tér

MERCURE BUDAPEST CITY CENTER

Szervit tér

PEST

DOHÁNY UTCA ZSINAGÓGA
(DOHÁNY STREET SYNAGOGUE)

SPOON CAFÉ
& LOUNGE

VIGADÓ

SZAMOS
GOURMET
PALACE

CYRANO
RESTAURANT

VÁROSHÁZ U.

DOHÁNY UTCA

RÁKÓCZI ÚT

CUCINA

DUNAKORZÓ
(DANUBE EMBANKMENT)

GREEK
ORTHODOX
CHURCH

PÁRIZSI UTCA

CITY HOTEL PILVAX

Astoria

PÁRIZSI UDVAR

Petőfi
tér

MOLNÁR'S
KÜRTŐSKALÁCS

HARIS KÖZ

Ferenclek
tere

KLOTILD PALOTA

RUBEN

CITY HOTEL MÁTYÁS

FERENCIEK
TEMPLOM

HOTEL ERZSÉBET

BELVÁROSI PLÉBÁNIATEMPLOM
(INNER CITY PARISH CHURCH)

SZABAD SAJTÓ ÚT

Károlyi Kert

ERZSÉBET HÍD
(ELIZABETH
BRIDGE)

BAR BÁR
CAFE

IRÁNYI

CENTRÁL KÁVÉHÁZ

LA COPPOLA

PETŐFI
IRODALMI
MÚZEUM

MAGYAR NEMZETI MÚZEUM
(HUNGARIAN NATIONAL MUSEUM)

IRISH CAT PUB

BELVÁROSI SZENT
MIHÁLY TEMPLOM

VÁCI UTCA
(VÁCI STREET)

EGYETEMI
TEMPLOM

LOFT
HOSTEL

ELTE LAW
SCHOOL

Kálvin
tér

HOTEL PALAZZO
ZICHY

Kálvin
tér

TAVERNA
DIONYSOS

SZERB
TEMPLOMBELSŐ

TRATTORIA
TOSCANA

PAMPAS STEAKHOUSE

GELLÉRT HEGY
(GELLÉRT HILL)

IBIS BUDAPEST CENTRUM

KÁLVIN
HÁZ

CITADELLA

GREAT
MARKET
HALL

Danube River

Jubileumi

BUDA

SZIKLA TEMPLOM
(CAVE CHAPEL)

ÚLLŐI ÚT

SZABADSÁG HÍD
(LIBERTY BRIDGE)

DANUBIUS HOTEL
GELLÉRT

Szent
Gellért tér

© AVALON TRAVEL

0   200 yds

0   200 m

summer fun at Erzsébet Square

surroundings, you'll find it all available here in the lifeblood of the capital.

Deák Ferenc tér
(Deák Ferenc Square)

Deák Ferenc tér, or simply Deák tér, is easily one of the busiest squares in town as people on their way to work merge with visitors engrossed in their maps. If you have any questions as to where you are or where you're going, fear not, as the very friendly people at **Tourinform** (V. Sütő utca 2, tel. 1/438-8080, www.budapestinfo.hu, daily 8am-8pm) will provide you with answers, maps, and all kinds of informative brochures.

Before moving on to Vörösmarty Square and the Inner City, take a moment to explore lovely **Erzsébet tér (Erzsébet Square)**, whose park across the street merges into Deák Square, forming a sort of border between the Belváros and Lipótváros. In the summertime, the park is constantly full of people young and old chilling out and soaking up the sun. You'll find plenty of beer drinkers, along with guitar players, in-line roller-skaters, and a bevy of Budapesters

cooling their feet in the shallow pool thoughtfully provided in the center of it all. This is a wonderful place to meet locals, read a book, or simply enjoy a beverage and the bustling surroundings.

Vörösmarty tér
(Vörösmarty Square)

Vörösmarty Square is undoubtedly the hub of all social activity in the center. Restaurants, cafés, casinos, airline offices, and a myriad of retail establishments are all close by, serving as a busy backdrop for the scores of artists and musicians vying for their livelihood on any given day. This is also the official beginning of Váci utca, Budapest's—make that Hungary's—most famous promenade.

Nearby is a statue with lions keeping guard over fountains, but it's the **statue of Mihály Vörösmarty,** Hungary's beloved poet and patriot, standing tall in the center of the square that deserves closer scrutiny. Accompanied by a number of eager listeners representing various social classes (a farmer and a peasant girl, a working couple with their son, people in traditional Magyar dress), Vörösmarty recites his patriotic *Szózat* (Appeal), the first verse of which is inscribed in the statue's plinth, which reads, "To your homeland without fail / Be faithful, O Hungarian!" A popular spot for lounging teenagers and visitors in the summer, the statue is wrapped in plastic sheeting every winter in order to protect the Carrara marble from the unforgiving elements.

At the north side of the square is the one and only **Café Gerbeaud** (Vörösmarty tér, 7-8, tel. 1/429-9021, www.gerbeaud.hu, daily noon-10pm), a classic Budapest coffeehouse if there ever was one. Two more nearby sights of historical note are worth mentioning. The first is the pretty art nouveau building at Vörösmarty tér 3, which used to house the **Luxus Department Store**—*the* place back in the day for quality goods before the beginning of the country's political and economic liberalization in the 1980s. The building now sells men's and women's designer wear. The second sight is the **Entrance to the Underground Railroad,** whose original decor was restored in 1996 on its 100th birthday, giving modern commuters a sense of what the public transportation side of things used to be like once upon a time.

Váci utca (Váci Street)

Formed in the 18th century and lined with magnificent architecture from the 19th and early 20th centuries, Váci is easily the city's most popular street. Starting at Vörösmarty Square and leading all the way to Central Market Hall, Váci Street was originally a shopping district that people of all classes and statuses could enjoy. That changed during the first decades of the 20th century, when it became fashionable for Budapest's elite to stroll down the pedestrian-only avenue and freely spend their hard-earned, or in most cases, easily inherited, money. The shops, consequently, became more and more exclusive—and remain so to this day.

Indeed, shoppers today ought to prepare themselves for inflated prices and, while there are many boutiques and popular Western brand outlets to be found, quite a number of shops have adjusted to the healthy jump in tourism and now offer visitors trinkets, T-shirts, and a whole host of kitschy souvenirs. Restaurants, bars, and cafés abound as well, advertising "tourist menus" that typically include meals like goulash, paprika-based meats, and traditional desserts. Some are better than others, and you may want to check out the more mom-and-pop-type establishments located on side streets before making a decision.

A number of colorful characters can be found up and down Váci: musicians young and old busking for a few forints, elderly women hawking traditional hand-woven garments, and visual artists publicly plying their trade to the enjoyment of passersby. There are also a handful of women who like to approach men and lure them into overpriced clubs or offer their company for a fee. All part of a day's work on vivid Váci Street.

Quite a few landmarks dot the pleasant avenue. Starting from Vörösmarty Square, the first left is Kristóf tér, where you'll find the pretty **fishergirl statue** among shoppers and coffee drinkers. Back onto Váci, make sure to pay special attention to the **Pest Theater** (Váci utca 9), whose art nouveau interior is worth a quick look. Still staging popular classic dramas, it was formerly the Inn of Seven Electors, whose claim to fame is allowing a 12-year-old prodigy by the name of Franz Liszt to take the stage back in 1823. Next door is the **Thonite House** (Váci utca 11), characterized by its Zsolnay tiles and now offering Douglas beauty products and Swarovski jewelry. A little farther down, at the corner of Váci utca and Regi posta utca, stands a pretty **fountain of Hermes,** messenger of the Greek gods, who points proudly in the direction of the Danube and not (one presumes) at the McDonald's. The first, or northern, half of Váci utca ends at busy thoroughfare Szabad sajtó út, at the Pest head of the Elizabeth Bridge.

ERZSÉBET HÍD (ELIZABETH BRIDGE)

Originally a decorative chain bridge built between 1897 and 1903, the Elizabeth Bridge was destroyed at the end of World War II by the Nazis retreating into Buda. The clean bright-white version of today was finished in 1964, making it Budapest's second-newest bridge, which also happens to be situated at the narrowest part of the Danube, spanning a paltry 951 feet. On the Pest side, the bridge passes the Inner City Parish Church, while on the Buda side it runs directly into Gellért Hill, consequently requiring a complex set of roads to connect to it. Apparently, this design is the result of a wealthy and rather crafty nobleman, who, owning that stretch of riverbank and being a part of the city council at the time, secured himself a fortune by selling off the land for the purposes of construction.

BELVÁROSI PLÉBÁNIATEMPLOM (INNER CITY PARISH CHURCH)

Located next to Elizabeth Bridge, the **Inner City Parish Church** (V. Március 15 tér 2, tel. 1/318-3108, www.belvarosiplebania.hu, closed for renovation at press time) is the oldest church in Pest, dating all the way back to the 12th century. It is the site of the martyr Saint Gellért's grave as well as numerous historically poignant events, including Hungarian Royal Princess St. Elizabeth's wedding to the son of the Marquis of Thuringia, and the premiere of Liszt's *Missa Choralis* on February 4, 1872, conducted by the composer himself. The church has gone through plenty of transformations over time, operating as a Gothic hall church in the 15th century, a mosque during the Turkish occupation of the 17th century (a remnant of which includes a prayer niche or *mihrab* found on the right side of the church's main altar). After a tremendous fire in 1723, it was rebuilt to reflect the baroque style. As if that weren't enough, it was saved from demolition during the original construction of the Elizabeth Bridge by dint of popular protest and miraculously survived Hitler's bombs in World War II. Something tells me this church will outlive us all, so make sure to pay a visit while *you* still can.

Facing the church, you'll see a small square on the left; this is where the foundation of a Roman military fortress, **Contra Aquincum,** was located. It was an outpost of their settlement at Óbuda at the end of the 3rd century. Notice the smooth sculpture of faceless Roman soldiers forming a tight circle, shields at the ready.

To continue on with the southern half of Váci utca, simply backtrack a little (under the Elizabeth Bridge is quickest) and cross the street.

BELVÁROSI SZENT MIHÁLY TEMPLOM (ST. MICHAEL'S CHURCH IN THE CITY)

St. Michael's Church in the City (Váci utca 47/B, tel. 1/337-8116, www.szentmihalytemplom.hu, Mon.-Sat. 10am-6pm, mass 4pm, Sun. 9am-5pm, mass 10am and 4pm) dates to 1795 and is primarily known for housing one of the city's oldest organs (from 1893). Walking inside is an eerily quiet affair, as most visitors are happy to sit down and get in touch with God or simply collect their thoughts far from the promenade's tourists and pleasure seekers.

SZERB TEMPLOMBELSŐ (SERBIAN ORTHODOX CHURCH OF ST. GEORGE)

Szerb utca is the appropriate home of the splendid **Serbian Orthodox Church of St. George** (V. Szerb utca 2-4, tel. 30/989-6139, daily 10am-3pm, 300 Ft), which was built in the baroque style by the Serbian community in 1698, based on the design of Salzburg architect Andreas Mayerhoffer. It is rather modest in size and far more intimate than you might expect from a church in the center of a capital city. Pews are individual chairs rather than benches, and while its interior has seen better days, it is nevertheless charming in its own way. Make sure to note the two icons on the right side above the pews: one of the Apostle Peter and the other of Paul. They are the only two that survived a devastating flood on March 15, 1838, when the water level in the church reached nearly 10 feet high. Outside the church, embedded in the walls on the left, are the headstones of past Serbian residents.

Dunakorzó (Danube Embankment)

In the late 19th and early 20th centuries, the Danube Embankment was the home of elegant hotels such as the Carlton and the Ritz, along with some of the city's finest restaurants and coffeehouses. It was a colorful, sophisticated scene, one that included members of the upper classes taking the air, world travelers admiring the view, and empty-pocketed Bohemians flirting with women of ill repute. The grand promenade was a place where people could come to experience and observe all of society's walks of life—a luxury that was obliterated by the savage and senseless destruction of World War II.

While paling in comparison to its former glory, the Danube Embankment nevertheless continues to be one of Budapest's favorite locations for locals and visitors alike, all of whom come to enjoy the romantic atmosphere it has somehow managed to retain. The marvelous unobstructed view of Buda can be peacefully admired from a chair or a park bench at any time of day or night, and there are still

BUDAPEST

© TOM DIRLIS

the Danube Embankment

a healthy number of restaurants and cafés in which to relax and watch the flow of human traffic pass by. Also lining the promenade these days are struggling artists, merry musicians, aged vendors selling traditional arts and crafts, and a handful of kiosks offering tours along the Danube. It's a pleasant stroll that stretches from the Elizabeth Bridge to the Chain Bridge, and one that can be savored alone or hand-in-hand with that special someone.

PETŐFI TÉR
(PETŐFI SQUARE)

Petőfi Square is located at the Elizabeth Bridge end of the Danube Embankment. Its center-piece is the **statue of Sándor Petőfi,** Hungary's national poet and author of the historically poi-gnant *Talpra Magyar* (Rise, Hungarian). It was here on October 23, 1956, that hundreds of students came to protest Matyas Rákosi, the Soviet Union's obedient yes-man.

Opposite Petőfi Square stands the **Greek Orthodox Church** (Petőfi tér 2, tel. 1/266-5988, mass Mon.-Sat. 5pm, Sun. 7:30am, 9:15am,

and 10am). Built in 1791-1794 and bankrolled by Greek merchants, it has been a continuous object of dispute between the Patriarchate of Russia, which appropriated it in 1945, and the Orthodox Church of Greece, which maintains rightful ownership. Ecclesiastical disagree-ments aside, visitors are very welcome, and a peek inside is recommended, if only to view its beautiful iconostasis.

VIGADÓ

Located at the Danube Embankment's mid-point is Vigadó tér, home to the majestic **Vigadó** (Vigadó tér 2, tel. 20/429-4124, www. pestivigado.hu), commonly translated as "place for merriment." This is Budapest's second-larg-est and most beloved concert hall, and its 800 seats always sell out any time a concert is an-nounced. Designed by Mihály Pollack, it was destroyed in the 1848 War of Independence and was reconstructed in 1865 based on plans drawn up by Frigyes Feszl. One of the most prominent cultural and entertainment ven-ues at the time and throughout the first half

the Vigadó, Budapest's favorite "place for merriment"

of the 20th century, the Vigadó played host to a number of classical music masters, including Brahms, Saint-Saëns, Debussy, and Franz Liszt, who on one occasion in 1875 shared the stage with Richard Wagner. Badly damaged in World War II, it took a full 36 years before it opened again in 1980 to the delight of an appreciative crowd who kindly chose to overlook the subpar acoustics. The building also houses its very own gallery, considered one of the finest contemporary art exhibition centers in the country; sadly, both it and the concert hall are closed for what appears to be an indefinite period of reconstruction.

A few steps from the Vigadó, sitting on a fence opposite the Restaurant Dunacorso, is the **Little Princess Statue.** Judging by the endless stream of smiling and posing going on, it has to be the most photographed statue in town.

Ferenciek tere (Franciscan Square)

One of the busier junctions in the Inner City, Franciscan Square is a mishmash of bustling activity: Homeless people asking for change, bus lines from Buda passing through or stopping off, shoppers working their way up and down Váci Street, and visitors squinting at maps trying to figure what to see next. Characterized by the Elizabeth Bridge and looming Klotild Palaces, it is also home to the Franciscan Church and gorgeous Párizsi udvar. No matter which way you're headed, odds are you'll end up passing through here at one point or another.

FERENCIEK TEMPLOM (FRANCISCAN CHURCH)

Dating as far back as the 13th century is the rather inconspicuous yet historically rich **Franciscan Church** (V. Ferenciek tere, mass Mon.-Sat. 6am, 8am, 10am, 11am, and 6:30pm, Sun. 6am and every hour until noon, 5pm, 6:30pm, and 8pm). It was built in 1250 in the Gothic style by Béla IV, a member of the third Franciscan order who is widely regarded as Hungary's second founder. Burned to the ground after the Turkish victory at

© CSABA BALASI | DREAMSTIME.COM

the Battle of Mohacs in 1526, it was used as a place of Muslim worship until being returned to the Franciscans in 1690 by Emperor Leopold I. It was rebuilt in its current baroque style during the Counter-Reformation. Life was good for the Franciscan brothers until 1950, when the church was outlawed by the Communist regime. Forty years of imposed exile passed before the church and friary were opened once again on September 1, 1990. The church's frescoes are the work of Károly Lotz and Vilmos Tardos Krenner, and its baroque high altar and magnificent statues are worth close inspection. On the Kossuth Lajos Street side of the church, you'll find a touching relief commemorating Miklos Weselenyi's heroic attempts during the tragic Danube flood of 1838, when the river's raging waters claimed the lives of over 400 people.

KLOTILD PALOTA
(KLOTILD PALACES)
Framing the Pest end of the Elizabeth Bridge are the Klotild Palaces, named after Grand Duchess Klotild Maria Amalia, who, in 1899, purchased the land and assigned Korb Flóris and Giergl Kálmán the task of building two prestigious palaces. The architects overcame the challenges that the two long and rather narrow plots of land presented, creating identical neo-baroque palaces 157 feet in height constructed entirely from stone and topped off with two ducal crowns. The palaces became an immediate symbol of the Austro-Hungarian monarchy's cosmopolitan lifestyle. Renovations to one of palaces were being done at press time, while the other palace is now home to the Buddha Bar Hotel.

PÁRIZSI UDVAR
(PARIS SHOPPING ARCADE)
Another point of interest at Franciscan Square is the **Paris Shopping Arcade** (V. Ferenciek tere 10-11), located on the north side of the square. Although hardly the bustling shopping center it once was, a walk through it is recommended if only to see the amazing night-and-day differences between its two halves.

Entering from the square, one feels transported back to 1913, when it was built according to the designs of Henrik Schmahl. Its intricate ornate features, complete with a stained glass cupola, affect the feeling of being in a quiet church rather than a neglected arcade. When you enter the second half, however, you are greeted with a less-than-inspiring half-forgotten functionalist letdown that's in dire need of renovation.

EGYETEMI KÖNYVTÁR
(UNIVERSITY LIBRARY)
Founded in 1561 by the Archbishop of Esztergom Miklós Oláh, the fabulous **University Library** (V. Ferenciek tere 6, tel. 1/411-6738, www.konyvtar.elte.hu, Mon.-Fri. 10am-8pm, free) originally served as the library of the Jesuit College in Nagyszombat (now Trnava, Slovakia). The eclectic design of the palace was drawn up by Antal Szkalnitzky and construction was done in 1873-1876, making it the first library in Hungary to be open to the public. Currently, it boasts a collection of books and periodicals exceeding 1.6 million volumes, the oldest of which is the manuscript of a Beda fragment dating back to the 8th century. While the entire building is something to be admired, it's the main reading room that's truly remarkable, decorated as it is with delicate frescoes by Károly Lotz and a commanding painting of Franz Joseph by Mór Than. Occasionally, the library holds special exhibitions where some of its most prized prints are taken out of storage and made available to the viewing public.

Egyetem tér
(University Square)
Dominating University Square is the **ELTE Law School** (Egyetem tér 1-3), and across the street, on the corner of Király pál Street and Szerb Street, you'll find a **memorial** embedded in the wall in remembrance of the Danube flood of 1838.

EGYETEMI TEMPLOM
(THE BUDAPEST UNIVERSITY CHURCH)
The **Budapest University Church** (Egyetem tér and Papnövelde utca, daily 10am-6pm,

free), formerly a Pauline monastery, is arguably one of the finest baroque buildings in the city. Built between 1715 and 1744, its architect is widely assumed to be András Mayerhoffer, though nobody seems to be able to verify it. The main facade bears the coat of arms belonging to the order of St. Paul, and between the two bell towers you'll find St. Paul the Hermit on the left and St. Anthony on the right. This church is distinguished from others by its baroque organ, considered by many to be the finest in the country, along with a rare copy of the black Madonna, located above the altar.

PETŐFI IRODALMI MÚZEUM (SÁNDOR PETŐFI LITERATURE MUSEUM)

Named after the country's most important representative of Hungarian letters, the **Sándor Petőfi Literature Museum** (V. Károlyi utca 16, tel. 1/317-3611, www.pim.hu, Tues.-Sun. 10am-6pm, 800 Ft) is a fascinating stroll through the country's literary history. Exhibited here are the manuscripts, home movies, and personal effects of various Hungarian writers you've probably never heard of but who nevertheless made vast contributions to the written word. There's also a captivating sculpture of Ady-Altar's death by Miklós Melocco as well as an ode to ragtime, complete with scratchy, jazzy music streaming through the speakers. The wax figure in blackface, dolls of black musicians, and records on the walls with titles like "Jungle Step" and "My Little Kongo Lady" are offensive by today's standards, but they teach an eye-opening lesson on the evolution of jazz music in Hungary and the rest of Europe.

Behind the Sándor Petőfi Literature Museum is **Károlyi Kert** (Henszlmann Imre utca, daily 8am-dusk), a pretty, well-maintained neighborhood park with swing set and a slide, a mini soccer field, and a fountain with begonias sprouting up around it. A favorite with parents and kids, not to mention the younger set looking to catch up on their reading or gossip, this is a great place to chill out and catch your breath before venturing off elsewhere.

Szervita tér (Servite Square)

Caught between the social hullabaloo of Vörösmarty Square and the endless activity of Franciscan Square, Servite Square is a relatively quiet square punctuated by the Servite Church and a couple of important government buildings.

Just off Váci Street on Servite Square is the 18th-century baroque **St. Anna Church in the Inner City of Budapest** (Szervita tér 6, tel. 1/318-5536, daily 10am-6pm, free), formerly called the Servite Church. Built by János Hölbling and János György Paver, its first stone was laid on September 8, 1725—the day of the Blessed Virgin Mary. The facade and bell tower were rebuilt in 1871, and the relief located above the pediment of the portal portrays the founding saints of the Servite Order: St. Peregrin on the left and St. Juliana on the right. Above the pediment stand Servite legislators St. Augustus and St. Phillip of Beniz. The church remains functional today, with locals escaping the daily grind of the Belváros and spending a few moments of peace on otherworldly matters.

Directly in front of the church stands the **Column of the Virgin Mary.** Facing the church, take the street on the left, named Városház utca (City Hall Street), to find two more buildings of note. The first is—you guessed it—**City Hall,** which pretty much dominates the entire street. Designed by Anton Martinelli, this is Budapest's largest baroque building and was initially used as a hospital in 1711 to care for over 4,000 soldiers injured in the Turkish wars. It became the city's main administration building in 1894.

A little farther down you'll find a lime-green building, **Pest County Hall** (Városház utca 7). Neoclassical in design, this 18th-century building operates as the center of administration for the entire country. Its three inner courtyards are remarkably beautiful and host the occasional classical concert during the summer.

LIPÓTVÁROS

Lipótváros is located in the northern part of the fifth district, next to the Belváros, and is bordered by Szent István körút, Bajcsy-Zsilinszky út, Deák Ferenc Street, and the Danube. Many of the buildings here were built in the 19th century—an imperial past that is balanced out nicely by modern cafés and restaurants as well as plenty of financial and administrative buildings. It is a neighborhood that brims with tourists as well, thanks to some of the capital's most memorable sights, including St. Stephen's Basilica, Gresham Palace, and Parliament.

◖ Szent István Bazilika (St. Stephen's Basilica)

Located in pretty Szent István Square, **St. Stephen's Basilica** (V. Szent István tér, tel. 1/311-0839, www.basilica.hu, daily 9am-7pm, 200 Ft donation) is an awe-inspiring sight to behold. Work on the building began in 1851 based on the designs of Jozsef Hild. Unfortunately, Hild died well before the church's completion, and Miklós Ybl, architect of the Opera House, was called in to finish the job. On close inspection of the structure,

Ybl was shocked to find huge cracks in the building's outer walls. The church's vast dome collapsed less than a week later, forcing the entire project to be declared unsound and paving the way for Ybl's neo-Renaissance design. Overcoming tremendous obstacles and great expense, St. Stephen's Basilica finally opened in 1906.

In the **Szent Jobb Chapel** (daily 9am-7pm) lies Catholic Hungary's most revered and rather bizarre relic: the mummified right hand of St. Stephen, Hungary's first monarch. There are plenty of famous and beautiful works of art decorating the interior, including mosaics designed by Károly Lotz, Alajos Stróbl's statue of St. Stephen on the main altar, and Gyula Benczúr's depiction of St. Stephen offering the Hungarian crown to the Virgin Mary. Those not afraid of heights should definitely make their way up the **tower** (daily 10am-5:30pm, 500 Ft), which offers visitors an amazing 360-degree view of the capital from a height of 213 feet.

The basilica also has a **treasury** (daily

St. Stephen's Basilica

10am-5:30pm, 400 Ft), which features a number of devotional objects from Hungary, Germany, and Austria, as well as a large collection of the garments worn by priests through the centuries.

Széchenyi István tér (Széchenyi István Square)

Positioned at the foot of the Pest side of the Chain Bridge right next to the Danube Embankment, Széchenyi István tér (formerly Roosevelt tér) is too choked with traffic to be considered a square in any pedestrian sense. Nevertheless, it's where you'll find some of the city's more upscale hotels and a couple of noteworthy buildings.

GRESHAM PALOTA (GRESHAM PALACE)

Gresham Palace (V. Széchenyi István tér 6) is situated at the very foot of the Chain Bridge and is rightly considered one of the finest examples of art nouveau architecture in Central Europe. Named after Thomas Gresham, it was commissioned by the Gresham Assurance Company of London in 1904 and completed in 1907 based on designs by Zsigmond Quittner and brothers József and Lászlo Vágó. It operated originally as a luxurious palace for British aristocrats, then became home for Soviet troops during World War II, when it suffered heavy damage, as it did during the 1956 uprising. The palace's woes continued as it fell into disrepair and neglect, serving as a private apartment building during the Communist regime. When Hungary once again established itself as a democracy in 1990, ownership of the palace was transferred to the city's fifth district. Purchased years later by the Four Seasons chain, over $85 million was spent in renovations, resulting in sweeping staircases, mosaics, ironwork, and soaring winter gardens all triumphantly restored, making it one of Budapest's most exclusive luxury hotels.

MAGYAR TUDOMÁNYOS AKADÉMIA (HUNGARIAN ACADEMY OF SCIENCES)

The oldest and most significant building on Széchenyi István Square is the **Hungarian Academy of Sciences** (V. Széchenyi István tér 9). The story goes that on November 3, 1825, county delegates criticized magnates for not bothering to make any sacrifices to create a learned Hungarian society. Not one to be outdone, Count István Széchenyi offered up one year's income from his estate right there and then for just such a purpose. His action was followed by other men of power and wealth who began moving things along, albeit slowly, in a positive direction. The beautiful neo-Renaissance building that was eventually built in 1862-1864 was based on the designs of Friedrich August Stüler, a prominent architect in Berlin. Lecture and session rooms, along with an invaluable scientific library, lie within. The grand gala hall, which stages the occasional concert, was decorated by the ever-present Károly Lotz. A rather inconspicuous monument to the count with deep pockets can be found in the small park in the middle of the busy square.

Szabadság tér (Liberty Square)

Strolling through one of Budapest's most picturesque squares, it is hard to believe that the manicured lawns and comfortable park benches were once the site of a large prison or barracks, the sole function of which was to punish "rebellious Hungarians." Punishment came swiftly and mercilessly, particularly during 1848-1849, when scores of Hungarian freedom fighters were executed at this very location. Torn down just before the turn of the 20th century, the gruesome facility was soon replaced with government offices, banks, and residences. Nowadays, kids play pickup games of soccer, dogs frolic, folks read quietly on their own, and couples seal summer love with a kiss, all with the fresh smell of flowers perfuming the light air.

Two breathtaking testaments to capitalism, both built in 1905 and designed by Count Ignác Alpár, stand on opposite ends of the square. To the west stands the **former Stock Exchange** (Szabadság tér 17), an impressive building influenced by the Secessionist style and full of Greek and Assyrian architectural motifs. It is now home to MTV—not the

BUDAPEST

Sightseeing on the Number 2 Tram

One of the nicest ways to see most of Budapest's major sights is to hop on the fabled number 2 tram and enjoy the ride, all for the price of a regular ticket! The route itself lasts roughly 20 minutes and should be caught at either of its two ends to be enjoyed to the fullest. Make sure you get on the right tram, however, as there's a number 2A out there that doesn't cover the entire route. Highlights include:

Jászai Mari tér
Starting at the Pest end of the Margaret Bridge, you'll see a large conspicuous building between the stop and the river, commonly referred to as "The White House." Formerly serving the Communist Party back in the day, it now houses parliamentary offices.

Szalay utca
To the right is the magnificent Parliament building and to the left the beautiful Museum of Ethnography, formerly the Palace of Justice.

Kossuth Lajos tér
Named after one of the leaders of both the uprising and the 1948-1949 War of Independence, the square is the common destination for visitors to the Parliament building. Here you'll also find a statue of famed freedom fighter Ferenc Rákóczi II.

Széchenyi István tér
The Hungarian Academy of Sciences graces the view on the left, while the gorgeous Chain Bridge leading to Buda sits on the right.

Eötvös tér
A handful of modern and luxurious hotels line the riverbank on the left, as does the historic and still beautiful Dunakorzó (Danube Embankment), Budapest's romantic promenade, perfect for casual strolls and taking in the breathtaking panoramic view of Buda's skyline.

Vigadó tér
Home to the Vigadó, Budapest's glorious concert hall, the way continues with outdoor restaurants and cafés as well as the Elizabeth Bridge, one of the capital's beloved examples of post-World War II architecture.

Március 15. tér
Gellért Hill dominates the skyline here, complete with the statue of Gellért himself and the battle-torn Citadella up top.

Fővám tér
The main sight here is, of course, Central Market Hall, where you'll find a plethora of souvenirs, fruits, and vegetables as well as clothing, traditional food, and much, much more. There's a reason why hundreds of locals and visitors stop here daily.

Közvágóhíd–Millenniumi Kulturális Központ (Millennium Cultural Center)
The Közvágóhíd is on the left, while on the right is the National Theater and Palace of Arts, which comprises a concert hall and theater as well as the Ludwig Museum of Contemporary Art.

© TOM DIRLIS

famed music channel but **Magyar Televizió**, otherwise known as Hungarian Television.

On the opposite side of the square stands the richly decorated **Hungarian National Bank** (Szabadság tér 9, tel. 1/428-2752, www.lk.mnb.hu). Take a moment to enjoy sculptor Károly Sennyei's limestone reliefs, a tribute to commerce in the form of rug merchants, Magyar plowmen, and herders as well as Vikings loading their booty onto a longship. Tours (Mon.-Wed and Fri. 9am-4pm, Thurs. 9am-6pm, free) through the ornate interiors are possible and worth a quick peek should you have some extra time on your hands.

Just up the street is the **U.S. embassy** (Szabadság tér 12), designed by Aladár Kármán and Gyula Ullman and completed in 1900. Originally the home of the Hungarian Hall of Commerce, it has been home to American diplomats since 1935. During World War II, however, it was the Swiss flag that flew out front, and the story is that Jewish refugees hid in the building's lower floors. Currently, the building is heavily guarded, as we've come to expect in today's political climate.

At the very center of the square is the **Soviet War Memorial,** an obelisk with a Soviet star on top—a thorn in the side of many proud Hungarians. Although most of Budapest's other Soviet statues and memorials can now be found at Memento Park, this particular one remains standing in remembrance of the sacrifices Soviet troops made during the city's liberation in 1944-1945. This is the result of an agreement Hungary signed in order to continue paying tribute to the Soviet soldiers buried underneath the monument. It has been the object of nationalistic uproars in the past, as a number of Hungarians feel it should be torn down and replaced with a Hungarian memorial. This feeling got so intense during one past demonstration that nearby cobblestones were uprooted and hurled at police. Now cordoned off by a metal fence, the memorial's perimeter is also regularly patrolled by a couple of police officers to ensure that no more funny business occurs.

Nearby is the interesting **statue of Harry Hill Bandholtz,** a stern-looking U.S. Army general who, in 1919, stopped Romanian troops from looting the Hungarian National Museum using the only thing he had at hand—a whip (presumably the one he's holding behind his back). The statue's inscription says it all: "I simply carried out the instructions of my government as I understood them as an officer and gentleman of the United States Army."

Around Liberty Square

Leaving the square, head behind the Hungarian National Bank onto Hold Street, where you'll find the **former Post Office Savings Bank** (V. Hold utca 4), a magnificent example of Hungarian art nouveau. Built in 1901 and designed by famed architect Ödön Lechner, its facade is full of flower and bee motifs, which were meant to symbolize the bank's fervent activity. Both the cornice and majolica roof ornamentation are, quite simply, astounding.

A little farther down, on the opposite side of the street, **Bejaras Vásárcsarnok** (V. Hold utca 13, Mon. 6:30am-5pm, Tues.-Fri. 6:30am-6pm, Sat. 6:30am-2pm) is a small, local wrought-iron market hall with a handful of vendors selling food, flowers, fruit, and the like. Visiting on a weekday, try to arrive early as many of the stalls close up shop at 4pm.

Continuing on to the junction where Hold Street meets Bathory Street, an **eternal flame** dedicated to Count Lajos Batthyány stands prominently. It's here to commemorate the man who came to office as prime minister after a republic was declared following the 1848 War of Independence, only to be executed at this very spot by the Habsburgs a year later.

Kossuth Lajos tér (Kossuth Lajos Square)

Kossuth Lajos tér, or simply Kossuth tér, is situated on the bank of the Danube and is easily accessible via the M2 (east-west) line of the subway. Named in 1927 after the 19th-century historical figure, the square was previously named the more obvious Országház tér (Parliament Square). Before that, between 1853 and 1898, the square was filled with garbage in an effort to raise the level of its low-lying position next to the river and was dubbed the much less romantic Tömő tér (Landfill Square). Its first recorded name dates back to 1820 and comes to us in German: Stadtischer Auswind Platz, which translates to the rather unimaginative-sounding Unloading Square for Ships.

As you exit Kossuth tér station, cross the number 2 tram tracks and look left to find the melancholy **statue of Attila József.** Looking rather lost and forlorn with his hat in hand and his coat discarded carelessly to his left, Attila sports an eternal hundred-yard stare. One of Hungary's most remarkable poets, his work oftentimes focused on poverty, loneliness, and suffering (themes that plagued him throughout his life), but also expressed his faith in the world's harmony and beauty. He died on December 3, 1937, at the age of 32, when he threw himself under a freight train in Balatonszárszó, an act witnessed by the train's conductor, a sales representative, and, perhaps most poetically, the village lunatic.

Heading straight ahead toward Parliament, the equestrian **statue of Prince Ferenc Rákóczi II** appears on the right. A Transylvanian prince who headed a nearly successful Hungarian uprising against merciless Habsburg rule, he was eventually abandoned by his forces at the Battle of Trenčín (located in present-day Slovakia) on August 3, 1708, when his horse stumbled, throwing him to the ground and knocking him unconscious. Fearing him dead, his forces fled and switched allegiances in the hopes of clemency. It was a slow slide downhill from there; finally abandoned by his remaining allies in 1711, Rákóczi went into self-imposed exile, drifting to Poland and then France and finally settling in Turkey, where he remained until his death in 1735.

Directly in front of the Rákóczi statue is the **1956 Memorial,** a symbolic grave commemorating the several hundred people who were shot down in cold blood on October 25, 1956, during Hungary's tragic uprising against the Soviet Union. The flag waving just behind it with a large hole in the middle is the result of Hungarian revolutionaries who, a couple of days earlier on October 23, tore out the Soviet star that adorned the center of the flag, thereby cementing it as a symbol of Hungarian independence that remains to this day.

Standing tall at the northern end of the square, eyes fixed on and pointing directly at Parliament, is the **statue of Lajos Kossuth,** a revolutionary hero of 1848 whom many Hungarians consider the country's purest patriot and greatest orator. After a brief stint as a lawyer, Kossuth moved on to politics, where his liberal-leaning Parliamentary writings landed him in hot water with the Habsburgs and in prison on the grounds of high treason. A national icon by the time of his release, he took over editing duties at *Pesti Hírlap,* a new Liberal Party newspaper, and became Hungary's de facto dictator when the Habsburgs invaded in 1848. He escaped to Turkey after the Hungarians surrendered in 1849, but continued fighting for the Hungarian cause, giving highly impassioned speeches in both Britain and the United States. He died in Turin in 1894 and is buried in Kerepesi Cemetery. His statue continues to be the scene of highly charged national ceremonies, and you'll be hard-pressed to find a town in Hungary that doesn't have a street, square, or statue dedicated to him.

Walking past the Kossuth statue and around the right side of Parliament will lead you into a charming little park characterized by Imre Varga's striking **statue of Károly Mihályi.** Hungary's first post-World War I president stands alone, with the help of a cane, under two sloping bars forming a makeshift arch high up above him. Behind the statue lies the Danube, with Castle Hill on the left and Margaret Bridge on the right.

If you're feeling nimble and slightly adventurous, take the stairs on the left leading downward and wait for the right moment to cross the busy two-lane road to the **river embankment.** So close now to the Danube you can smell it, the steps that stretch all the way to Margaret Bridge also lead right down to the water so that you can touch the historic river as well. Heading down the embankment, you get a

The Glass Art of Miksa Róth

Miksa Róth is easily Hungary's best-known stained glass and mosaic artist. His colorful work continues to grace numerous sites around the capital, including Gresham Palace, the Music Academy, the Agricultural Museum, St. Stephen's Basilica, and Parliament. Born in 1865, he inherited his father's workshop at the age of 19, back when both he and the craft of glass painting were still in their developmental stages. At 22, Róth was commissioned to decorate the windows of Máriafalva Church (now Mariensdorf, Austria), but his big break came in 1896 when he won a competition that allowed him the privilege of preparing the glass windows for Budapest's Parliament. At Budapest's Museum of Fine Arts Christmas Exhibition in 1898, Róth made waves when he unveiled glass windows prepared using a type of Tiffany glass that had never before been seen in the Austro-Hungarian Empire. As his reputation as an exceptional artist grew, so did the number of awards he received, including the silver medal at the Paris World Exhibition in 1900 and the Grand Prix at the Turin World Exhibition in 1902 as well as at the St. Louis World Exhibition in 1904. Róth continued to represent Hungary's multicolored turn-of-the-20th-century architecture, creating windows in a number of different styles, including secessionist, art nouveau, and Jugendstil, proving that there was little if anything he couldn't do. His work was not limited to Hungary, either. He prepared the windows and mosaics for the Royal Palace in Oslo as well as a magnificent 1,500-square-foot glass cupola for the Teatro Nacional in Mexico City. From the 1920s onward, Róth worked mainly on commissions from the church and state until he decided to close up his workshop once and for all in 1940. He died four years later in 1944.

wonderful view of the back of Parliament and the chance to take a few great photos as well. Be extra careful as you cross the street and head back up the stairs at the end of the embankment. You're now basically back to where you started, at the statue of Hungary's beloved but suicidal poet.

Bridging Kossuth tér and Szabadság tér is tiny **Vértanuk tér (Martyrs' Square).** This is the home of Imre Varga's life-size bronze **statue of Imre Nagy,** the Prime Minister who led the failed uprising in 1956 and was executed two years later. Standing alone on a bridge, hands crossed over one another, he looks pensively toward Parliament, almost as if he knows the end is nigh.

ORSZÁGHÁZ (PARLIAMENT)

Visible from pretty much every riverside point in the city, the **Hungarian Parliament** (V. Kossuth Lajos tér 1-3, tel. 1/441-4904, www.parlament.hu, tickets can be obtained from Gate X daily from 8am or reserved by phone, tours in English daily 10am, noon, 1pm, 1:45pm, and 3pm, 3,500 Ft, 1,750 Ft EU citizens) is without a doubt one of the most remarkable achievements in architectural history. Based on Hungarian architect Imre Steindl's design, this monumental structure was supposed to be ready for the 1896 Millennial Celebrations but wasn't completed until 1902. It is Europe's largest parliament building and ranks third in the world, measuring 880 feet long and 404 feet wide at its center. Other statistics are just as staggering, as its central dome measures 315 feet high (the same height as St. Stephen's Basilica) and its interiors boast 691 rooms and over 12.5 miles of corridors. One thousand people worked to bring this building to fruition using 40 million bricks, 500,000 precious stones, and 88 pounds of gold.

Architecturally speaking, it's an eclectic classic with a Renaissance dome crowning a neo-Gothic facade that stands on a baroque base. Its white neo-Gothic turrets and arches are complemented by a main cupola

BUDAPEST

© TOM DIRLIS

Europe's largest parliament building is in Budapest.

decorated with statues of Hungarian kings—just some of the 90 statues and coats of arms that decorate the building's exterior. Tours are offered daily (entrance at Gate X) and are highly recommended. A few of the things you'll see are the Grand Staircase stretching from the main entrance to the Dome Hall, ceiling frescoes by Károly Lotz, fantastic painted glass windows by Miksa Róth, and the Holy Crown and the Coronation Insignia worn by Hungarian kings since the Middle Ages. There are not enough superlatives in the world to describe Hungary's Parliament building. It simply must be seen to be believed.

NÉPRAJZI MÚZEUM
(MUSEUM OF ETHNOGRAPHY)
With roughly 139,000 Hungarian artifacts, not to mention an additional 53,000 international artifacts, the **Museum of Ethnography** (V. Kossuth Lajos tér 12, tel. 1/473-2400, www.neprajz.hu, Tues.-Sun. 10am-6pm, 1,000 Ft), located directly

opposite Parliament, is one of the largest museums of its kind in Europe. Formerly the Royal Court, this beautiful building combines elements of Renaissance, baroque, and neoclassical architecture with its huge entrance hall, complete with chandeliers and marble staircases, reminiscent of a glorious opera house. The fantastic ceiling fresco by Károly Lotz depicts Justitia, the goddess of justice, a stunning emblem of the building's original purpose. The permanent exhibition is no less than fascinating, beginning with the Kováts family's photographic documentation of large upper-class families, students, and their schooling as well as various aspects of village life. Following that is the Umling family's tradition of fine-painted furniture from the 18th century, which to this day beats the pants off anything IKEA ever made. The exhibitions continue with wonderful folk costumes, farming tools, musical instruments, and the evolution of village life, churches, towns, and feudal estates. There are also temporary exhibitions that come and go but are always affordable (starting from 1,400 Ft) and well worth any history buff's time.

TERÉZVÁROS

Characterized by Andrássy Avenue, Terézváros is easily one of the busiest, most vibrant parts of the city. You'll find the Opera House here, along with the theater quarter and trendy Liszt Ferenc tér (Franz Liszt Square). Shops, museums, cafés, and nightclubs line the streets all the way up to the Oktogon, where the Teréz körút section of the Outer Ring Road cuts through, making it one of the busiest squares in the city and one of the more important intersections for public transportation. Past the Oktogon, the avenue widens, making way for exclusive eateries, neo-Renaissance mansions, and palatial villas, all of which add to the Old World allure of this charming district.

Budapest's finest boulevard, **Andrássy út (Andrássy Avenue)**, is 1.6 miles long, starting from the vicinity of St. Stephen's Basilica and stretching all the way down to Heroes Square

and the Városliget (City Park). The traffic, both human and vehicular, is heavy, with cars and motorcycles dueling for position while shoppers and strollers take full advantage of the boutiques, salons, restaurants, and cafés that abound. Continuing past the Oktogon, shops slowly begin to give way to exquisite palaces and villas as well as to some of the city's most famous and expensive restaurants. Taking in the avenue and its immediate surroundings, it's little wonder that all of it is now a UNESCO-protected World Heritage Site.

Andrássy Avenue from the Basilica to the Oktogon

◖ MAGYAR ÁLLAMI OPERAHÁZ (HUNGARIAN STATE OPERA HOUSE)

The **Hungarian State Opera House** (VI. Andrássy út 22, tel. 1/353-0170, www.opera. hu, guided tours daily 3pm and 4pm, 2,900 Ft) is one of Budapest's most beautiful structures, adding a historical charm to an already-elegant Andrássy Avenue. This neo-Renaissance masterwork was finished in 1884 and has been

© TOM DIRLIS

Budapest's majestic Opera House

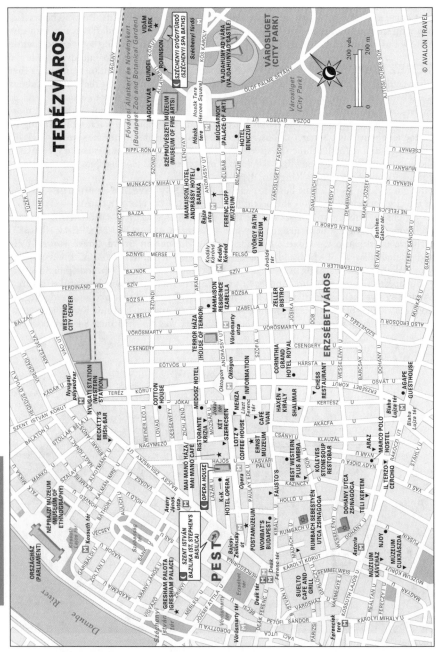

BUDAPEST

TERÉZVÁROS

VÁROSLIGET (CITY PARK)

Városliget (City Park)

© AVALON TRAVEL

200 yds
200 m

VÁGÁNY

VIDÁM PARK

GUNDEL KÖRÚT

BAGOLYVÁR

Állatkerti KÖRÚT

ROBINSON

SZÉCHENYI GYÓGYFÜRDÖ
(SZÉCHENYI SPA BATHS)

Széchenyi fürdő

VAJDAHUNYAD VÁRA
(VAJDAHUNYAD CASTLE)

KÓS KÁROLY

OLOF PALME SÉTÁNY

AUTÓSI DÜBRÉ SÖR

Fővárosi Állatkert és Növénykert
(Budapest Zoo and Botanical Garden)

SZÉPMŰVÉSZETI MÚZEUM
(MUSEUM OF FINE ARTS)

LENDVAY

Hösök tere
(Heroes Square)

MŰCSARNOK
(PALACE OF ART)

DÓZSA GYÖRGY ÚT

RIPPL-RÓNAI U

SZONDI

ANDRÁSSY ÚT

DELIBÁB

HOTEL
BENCZÚR

VÁROSLIGETI FASOR

CSEHÁT U

MUNKÁCSY MIHÁLY U

Hösök tere

MÁNYI U

MAMAISON HOTEL
ANDRÁSSY HOTEL
BARAKA

BAJZA

Bajza
utca

FERENC HOPP
MÚZEUM

BAJZA

BENCZÚR

HERNÁD U

PETERDY U

DAMJANICH U

NÉ FELEJCS U

SZÉKELY BERTALAN U

GYÖRGY RÁTH MÚZEUM

MAREK JÓZSEF U

DEMBINSZKY U

PODMANICZKY U

SZINYEI MERSE U

Kodály
Körönd

FELSÖ

Lövölde
tér

ROTTENBILLER U

Bethlen
Gábor tér

STVÁN U

BETHLEN GÁBOR U

PÉTERFY SÁNDOR U

GARAY U

BAJNOK U

SZIV

SZIV U

SZONDI

ARADI

RÓZSA

ERZSÉBETVÁROS

ALSÓ ERDÖSOR U

MUNKÁS U

FERDINÁND HÍD

RÓZSA

MAMAISON
RESIDENCE
IZABELLA

IZABELLA

ZELLER
BISTRO

JÓSIKA U

DOB U

SZÖVETSÉG U

WESTEND
CITY CENTER

IZA BELLA

SZÓNDI

Vörösmarty
utca

VÖRÖSMARTY U

CSENGERY

HÁRSTA

WESSELÉNYI U

BALZAC

KRESZ GÉZA U

VISEGRÁDI U

VÁCI U

TERROR HÁZA
(HOUSE OF TERROR)

Vörösmarty

CSENGERY

CORINTHIA
GRAND
HOTEL ROYAL

DOHÁNY U

BARCSAY U

VÖRÖSMARTY

SZÓFIA

VÖRÖSMARTY U

EÖTVÖS U

ANDRÁSSY ÚT

Oktogon

Oktogon

ERZSÉBET KÖRÚT

OSVÁT U

Nyugati
pályaudvar

NYUGATI STATION
(WESTERN STATION)

TERÉZ

KÖRÚT

COTTON
HOUSE

JÓKAI

JÓKAI U

MOZSÁR U

MEDOSZ HOTEL

CHESS
RESTAURANT

KERTÉSZ U

AGAPE
GUESTHOUSE

KÁDÁR U

SZENT ISTVÁN KÖRÚT

WEINER LEO U

LOVAG

DÉSSEWFFY

RISTORANTE
KRIZIA

KÉT
SZERECSEN

Liszt
Ferenc
tér

HAXEN
KIRÁLY

SHALIMAR

AKÁCFA

WESSELÉNYI U

Blaha
Lujza tér

MARCO POLO
HOSTEL

Blaha
Lujza tér

BALATON U

STOLLÁR BÉLA U

BIHARI JÁNOS U

NAGYMEZÖ

LOTZ
COFFEE HOUSE

MENZA

CAFÉ
VIAN

CSÁNYI U

KLAUZÁL U

ARAZ

RÁKÓCZI ÚT

BECKETT'S
IRISH BAR

ZICHI JENÖ

Ferenc
tér

ERNST
MÚZEUM

VASVÁRI
PÁL

DÓB

NYÁR U

KÖLEVES
STONESOUP
RESTOBAR

IL TERZO
CERCHIO

NAGY DIÓFA U

NAGY IGNÁC U

SZEMERE U

BAJCSY ZSILINSZKY ÚT

MAI MANÓ HÁZA
MAI MANÓ CAFÉ

HAJÓS

Opera

OPERA HOUSE

LÁZÁR U

PAULAY EDE U

KÁLMÁN IMRE U

MÁRKÓ

VADÁSZ

HOLLÓ U

KAZINCZY

VASVÁRI

K+K
HOTEL OPERA

FAUSTO'S

HOLLÓ U

DOHÁNY UTCA
ZSINAGÓGA

TÉLI KERTEM

VAS U

STÁHLY U

FALK MIKSA U

HONVÉD U

NÉPRAJZI MÚZEUM
(MUSEUM OF
ETHNOGRAPHY)

AULICH U

NAGY IGNÁC U

Arany
János
utca

Arany
János

POSTAMÚZEUM

WOMBAT'S
BUDAPEST

KIRÁLY

RUMBACH
SEBESTYÉN

RUMBACH SEBESTYÉN
UTCA ZSINAGÓGA

PUSKIN

MÚZEUM
CUKRÁSZDA

ORSZÁGHÁZ
(PARLIAMENT)

GARIBALDI U

ZOLTÁN U

BANK U

Kossuth tér

Kossuth
Lajos tér

VÉCSEY

SZÉCHÉNYI

BÁTHORY

SZABADSÁG
tér

SAS U

BÁLINT

SZENT ISTVÁN
BAZILIKA (ST. STEPHEN'S
BASILICA)

Bajcsy
Zsilinszky
út

NÁDOR

Ferenc tér

Deák tér

NÁDOR U

HERCEGPRIMÁS U

PEST

Erzsébet
tér

Deák
Ferenc
tér

BÁRCZY

KÁROLY KÖRÚT

SEMMELWEIS U

GERLÓCZY

VÁROSHÁZ U

Astoria

MÚZEUM
KÁVÉHÁZ

MAGYAR U

MÚZEUM KÖRÚT

AKADÉMIA U

ARANY JÁNOS U

GRESHAM PALOTA
(GRESHAM PALACE)

ZRÍNYI

JÓZSEF ATTILA U

MÉRLEG U

Vörösmarty tér

DOROTTYA U

DEÁK FERENC U

PETÖFI SÁNDOR U

Ferenciek
tere

VÁCI UTCA

KÁROLYI MIHÁLY U

KOSSUTH LAJOS U

REÁLTANODA U

FERENCZY I U

Danube River

Széchenyi
István

VIGADÓ

VÖRÖSMARTY

BÉCSI

PÁRIZSI U

SUELTO
CAFE AND
GRILL

BEST WESTERN
PLUS AMBRA

NJOY

AGAPE

CSEHÁT U

RÖTTENBILLER U

CORINTHIA GRAND HOTEL ROYAL

INFORMATION

PÉTERFY SÁNDOR U

attracting classical music fans ever since with the finest musicians the country has to offer. Couples, families, and friends all don their finest attire for an elegant evening out, and it truly is a sight to behold during intermission, when audience members fill the balcony for a breath of fresh air and wondrous views of the boulevard.

During the afternoon, a walk around the building often rewards visitors with the strains of opera singers warming up for the evening, but if you'd really like an insider's view of this magnificent structure, don't miss out on the informative and entertaining tour.

NAGYMEZŐ UTCA
(NAGYMEZŐ STREET)

Affectionately referred to as Budapest's Broadway, this picturesque street is full of theaters showcasing original works with provocative titles as well as more conventional musicals like *Romeo and Juliet* and *Miss Saigon*. Plenty of intimate cafés and restaurants can be found here, along with a few casinos and a Moulin Rouge dance club. It even sports its very own miniature walk of fame where the footprints of famous thespians have been immortalized in concrete. This is an excellent place to sit back and drink up the charm before heading back out onto Andrássy.

MAI MANÓ HÁZA
(MAI MANÓ HOUSE OF PHOTOGRAPHY)

If you're a photography fan, postpone that return to Andrássy and venture into the **Mai Manó House of Photography** (VI. Nagymező utca 20, tel. 1/473-2666, www.maimano.hu, Mon.-Fri. 2pm-7pm, Sat.-Sun. 11am-7pm, 1,000 Ft). The first floor of the 1894 building served as Mai Manó's residence until the building was bought in 1931 by musical director Sándor Rozsnyai and his wife, Mici Rozsnyai, otherwise known as "Miss Arizona." They built a large three-story club in the building's courtyard (aptly named The Arizona), which became an instant success and remained so until 1944, when the couple was senselessly murdered by the Nazis. Following World War II, the building housed a school and presentation

hall and operated as a branch of the Hungarian Automobile Club for over 30 years. Today, visitors will find some remarkable exhibitions of contemporary photography within its walls as well as historical pieces and those chronicling the careers of some of the medium's most important artists.

ERNST MÚZEUM
(ERNST MUSEUM)

The highly respected **Ernst Museum** (VI. Nagymező utca 8, tel. 1/413-1311, www.ernstmuzeum.hu, Tues.-Sun. 11am-7pm, 990-1,800 Ft) boasts no permanent collection to speak of. It concentrates instead on showcasing a wide variety of constantly evolving modern Hungarian art in interesting new ways. Always one for diversity, the museum also hosts discussions, concerts, and various screenings that continue to grow in popularity.

LISZT FERENC TÉR
(FRANZ LISZT SQUARE)

Home of the diner, drinker, and the very swank, this vibrant square offers opportunities galore to those who want to be seen and heard among others of similar style and fashion. Cafés and restaurants line either side of the strip, offering contemporary cuisine and colorful cocktails in an outdoor environment whose ambience has a distinctly trendy yet friendly pulse. This place is always happening, even in the wintertime, when folks simply carry on with their fun-loving festivities indoors. At the end of the square is the gorgeous Franz Liszt Academy of Music, a superb art nouveau building that doubles as a music university and concert hall.

JÓKAI TÉR
(JÓKAI SQUARE)

If Franz Liszt Square is a beloved princess, then Jókai Square is her awkward, unpopular sister. Featuring a tiny playground with abandoned swings and a sandbox and peppered with a handful of benches more often than not occupied by the local homeless populace, this square, located opposite Franz Liszt Square, is the yin to its neighbor's yang. Pity Mór Jókai,

BUDAPEST

Franz Liszt: From Prodigy to Virtuoso

Known the world over as a child prodigy and the greatest pianist of his, if not all, time, Franz (Ferenc) Liszt (1811-1886) is easily Hungary's most celebrated composer. Born in Raiding on October 22, 1811, Liszt was the son of a steward who was in the service of the powerful Esterházy family. Pushed hard by his father, who immediately noticed little Franz's genius, Liszt performed publicly for the first time at the age of nine. A scant two years later, Antonio Salieri, an old rival of Mozart's, offered the boy free lessons in composition upon hearing a particularly impressive performance at a private home. Liszt studied simultaneously under Carl Czerny, Beethoven's esteemed pupil, and, at the age of 14, wrote his first operetta, *Don Sanche*, which was produced in Paris, where he moved with his family in 1823. Liszt toured extensively and became friends with France's leading artists, including Hector Berlioz and Frédéric Chopin. In 1833 he began seeing Countess Marie d'Agoult, who eventually left her husband and

eloped with Liszt to Switzerland in 1835. They had three children, the youngest of which, Cosima, went on to marry another renowned composer and musician, Richard Wagner. Liszt continued touring, solidifying his reputation as virtuoso, performing recitals and composing symphonic poems that both dazzled audiences and changed the direction of music forever. He separated from his mistress in 1844 and went on to live in Vienna, Rome, and finally Budapest, where he established the Conservatory of Music and served as its first president. In 1886, Liszt embarked on a final tour that saw him perform in Brussels, Paris, Antwerp, and Windsor Castle for Queen Victoria. Liszt decided to visit a Wagner festival that was being hosted by his daughter Cosima, who was grieving the loss of her dearly departed Richard. Suddenly falling gravely ill with pneumonia, Liszt died under the watchful gaze of his loving daughter on July 31, 1886, leaving behind a legacy that is sure to inspire musicians for centuries to come.

whose literary work was far more romantic than the home his statue was given.

The Oktogon

Continuing along Andrássy, past Franz Liszt Square on the way to Heroes Square, you'll come upon the Oktogon, an eight-sided square and intersection that is as busy at it sounds. Full of shops and fast-food eateries, the buzzing never really stops, especially since the Teréz körút part of the Outer Ring Road runs through here as well. This is also the point where Andrássy widens, allowing for a pleasant walk down the middle of the avenue by way of a pedestrian island.

Andrássy Avenue from the Oktogon to Heroes Square
TERROR HÁZA
(HOUSE OF TERROR)

During the years 1944-1956, the building at Andrássy út 60 struck fear into the hearts

of Hungarians. It was here that first the Hungarian Nazis and then the Communist terror organizations ÁVO and ÁVH tortured and killed hundreds of dissidents. Today, it is home to the **House of Terror** (VI. Andrássy út 60, tel. 1/374-2600, www.terrorhaza.hu, Tues.-Sun. 10am-6pm, 2,000 Ft, 1,000 Ft EU citizens), a no-holds-barred memorial dedicated to those who lost their lives on its very premises. There are quite a few exhibits here, starting with a massive mural of the regimes' victims. Video screens portray the Nazi occupation: Hitler's frenzied speeches, people screaming their support, hundreds of soldiers forming a giant pulsing swastika. Other screens show the Soviet occupation, complete with fires, riots, children left for dead, and adults crying openly over the senselessness of it all. And that's just the first room. A walk through the museum is truly a chilling experience that ends in the basement, following an extremely slow elevator ride that features a video explaining in great detail how exactly people were executed. When the elevator finally stops, you find yourself suddenly in the very prison cells that were home to so many unfortunate and innocent people. One cell is so tiny you can barely stand up in it; another is covered in water; and yet another is padded. Those thinking of visiting should know that this is not a typical museum; the faint-hearted or extremely sensitive might want to avoid coming here. Those who do visit, however, will be rewarded with a lasting lesson on a treacherous era as well as one about the dangers of terrorism—no matter what the place or time.

A little farther up the avenue is the **Kodály körönd,** a circular flowerbed. The grandeur of the square has faded over the years as the massive apartments and mansions that surround it can only be described as majestically decrepit. Nevertheless, it still makes for a nice place to sit and rest for a moment and imagine what must have been.

POSTAMÚZEUM
(POST OFFICE MUSEUM)

Recently reopened in the lovely Benczúr House, the quaint **Post Office Museum** (VI. Benczúr utca 27, tel. 1/269-6838, www.postamuzeum. hu, Tues.-Sun. 10am-6pm, 500 Ft) is full of memorabilia from the postal days of yore, including old service desks, wooden telephone booths, and telegram machines. There are also old Communist stamps and swords that postal workers carried (as well as guns later on) to protect themselves from highway robbers in hot pursuit of the booty they were transporting.

GYÖRGY RÁTH MÚZEUM
(GYÖRGY RÁTH MUSEUM)

On Városligeti fasor, one block east of Andrássy and running parallel, is the **György Ráth Museum** (VI. Városligeti fasor 12, tel. 1/342-3916, www.hoppmuzeum.hu, Tues.-Sun. 10am-6pm, admission varies), named after the famous art collector and first-ever director of the Museum of Applied Arts. The villa was built in 1870-1871 and was turned into a museum in 1907. It began to function as an extension of the Ferenc Hopp Museum in 1955

and has showcased colorful Eastern Asiatic arts ever since. Among its permanent exhibitions are a large variety of Chinese ceramics and textiles, Japanese ivory, and an Indian collection that covers several major periods, including the Kushana period of Mathura sculpture and the classical style of the Gupta period. There is also a György Ráth Memorial Room, which involves the restoration of the former owner's original dining room.

FERENC HOPP MÚZEUM
(FERENC HOPP MUSEUM)

Those interested in Asian art will do themselves a great service by visiting the fascinating **Ferenc Hopp Museum** (VI. Andrássy út 103, tel. 1/456-5110, www.hoppmuzeum.hu, Tues.-Sun. 10am-6pm, 400 Ft). Ferenc Hopp visited China during his first trip around the world in 1882-1883, then again during his third and fifth trips in 1903 and 1913-1914. This collection, in the home he bought specifically to house these treasures, is simply phenomenal. The Chinese collection alone consists of over 8,000 items, including furniture, paintings, statues, and ceramics, with its earliest piece dating back to the Zhou period (10th-8th centuries BC). The Japanese collection is no joke either, boasting over 7,000 pieces, a good number of which can be traced back to the Edo period (1603-1867) as well as the Meiji era (1868-1912). The largest part of this particular collection is a stunning group of more than 2,000 works of graphic art.

ERZSÉBETVÁROS

Budapest's seventh district is also the city's Jewish quarter, whose jewel is the remarkable Dohány Street Synagogue. Primarily a blue-collar residential area, the Erzsébetváros oozes character with its crumbling 19th-century buildings, underground bars, and independently run boutiques, minimarkets, and kosher restaurants. It has undergone heavy reconstruction over the last few years, resulting in a slow but steady increase in brightly colored residences, modern hotels, trendy eateries, and hip cafés. A walk through the district will reveal the neighborhood's strong sense of community, where the streets are filled with warm greetings and a promise of things to come.

The magnificent **Dohány utca Zsinagóga (Dohány Street Synagogue)** (VII. Dohány utca 2, tel. 1/343-0420, www.dohanyutcaizsinagoga.hu, Nov.-Feb. Sun.-Fri. 10am-4pm, Mar.-Oct. Sun.-Thurs. 10am-6pm, Fri. 10am-4pm, 2,650 Ft, includes entry to National Jewish Museum) was finished in 1859 and was based on the designs of Ludwig Förster. Built in a neo-Moorish style with additional elements of the Byzantine, Romantic, and Gothic, it is Europe's largest functioning synagogue and the second-largest in the world. It can hold nearly 3,000 people and measures 174 feet long and 87 feet wide, with its two distinct towers reaching over 140 feet in height. In the synagogue's garden is a striking, heart-wrenching Holocaust Memorial designed by Imre Varga that was erected in 1989. It is in the shape of a weeping willow tree and stands on top of the mass graves of Jews who died during the bitter winter of 1944-1945. Each one of the metallic tree's leaves bears the name of a victim of that terrible time.

Next to the synagogue is the **Nemzeti Zsidó Múzeum (National Jewish Museum)** (Dohány utca 2, tel. 1/321-0408, www.zsidomuzeum.hu, Nov.-Feb. Sun.-Thurs. 10am-4pm, Fri. 10am-2pm, Mar.-Oct. Sun.-Thurs. 10am-6pm, Fri. 10am-4pm, 2,650 Ft, includes entry to Dohány Street Synagogue), which stands on the site of the birthplace of Theodor Herzl, the founder of modern Zionism. Inside is a vast collection of various religious relics and ritual objects of the Sabbath and High Holidays as well as a Holocaust Room with powerful photographs and anti-Semitic propaganda of the period.

Down the road a bit from the Dohány Street Synagogue, on Rumbach Sebestyén Street you'll come upon the Moorish-looking **Rumbach Sebestyén utca Zsinagóga (Rumbach Sebestyén Street Synagogue)** (VII. Rumbach Sebestyén utca 11-13, Sun.-Thurs. 10am-3:30pm, Fri. 10am-1:30pm, 500

© SERGII KORSHUN/123RF

the great Dohány Street Synagogue, Europe's largest functioning synagogue

Ft). It's easily recognizable by its yellow-and-red brick facade, and it currently houses art and photo exhibitions of local artists. The building's exterior was restored in recent years, but its neglected interior, complete with stained glass windows, golden columns, and colorful Zsolnay tiles, could do with an overhaul. Nevertheless, the synagogue serves as a unique if somewhat eerie show space.

On adjacent Dob Street you'll find the beautiful but rather indescribable **Carl Lutz Memorial** (Dob 11). It basically features a man lying on his back while another hangs suspended on the wall above him. Lutz was the Swiss vice consul in Budapest in 1942-1945 and worked relentlessly to save Hungarian Jews from Nazi persecution. His efforts resulted in the saving of roughly 62,000 lives. An inscription from the Talmud pays honor to the man and reads: "Whoever saves a life is considered as if he has saved an entire world."

Continuing along Dob Street will bring you to the district's largest square and historic center: **Klauzál tér.** It is a friendly neighborhood park complex with a playground for kids, caged surfaces used for impromptu soccer and basketball games, and a number of benches where visitors can rest their feet, engross themselves in a book, or enjoy a snack bought from the rundown but atmospheric **Vásárcsarnok** (District Market Hall, Klauzál tér 11, Mon.-Sat. 7am-4pm, Sun. 8am-1pm).

THE VÁROSLIGET (CITY PARK)

According to the first available written record circa 1241, the 302-acre-park located behind Heroes Square was originally marshland. The park was formed thanks in large part to tremendous forestation efforts and served as the setting for the all-important Millennial Celebrations that were held in 1896. Nowadays, City Park is a wonderful place to spend the day, be it for a picnic or a stroll around any number of sights, including Vajdahunyad Castle, the Budapest Zoo and Botanical Garden, the Széchenyi Spa Bath Complex, and, of course, Heroes Square.

© TOM DIRLLIS

Heroes Square

Hősök tere
(Heroes Square)

At the northern end of Andrássy Avenue is the giant awe-inspiring Heroes Square, so named because it is home to monuments to the most important figures in Hungarian history. Built in 1896 as part of Hungary's Millennial Celebrations of the Magyar conquest, the striking **Millennial Monument,** dominated by an imposing 118-foot column of the Archangel Gabriel, is the first thing to catch the eye. Gabriel is surrounded by a motley crew on horseback who represent the seven legendary chieftains responsible for the conquest. A stone tablet rests in front of the column. This is the Monument of National Heroes, also referred to as the **Tomb of the Unknown Soldier,** a solemn tribute to Hungary's nameless heroes of war. Behind the monument is a gorgeous semicircular colonnade depicting the most highly regarded men in the country's history, ranging from King Stephen I to Lajos Kossuth. Atop the semicircles are symbols of War and Peace, Work and Welfare, and Knowledge and Glory. This square has been the site of many historical events, including socialist holidays during the Communist era, the ceremonial reburial of Imre Nagy (the Hungarian prime minister during the Hungarian Revolution who was executed in 1956), a visit by Pope John Paul II, and various heated political demonstrations.

MŰCSARNOK
(PALACE OF ART)

On the southern side of Heroes Square is the **Palace of Art** (XIV. Dózsa György út 37, tel. 1/460-7000, www.mucsarnok.hu, Tues.-Wed. and Fri.-Sun. 10am-6pm, Thurs. noon-9pm, 1,800 Ft), also referred to as the Exhibition Hall. Designed by Albert Schikedanz and built in 1896 for the Millennial Celebrations, it was renovated in 1995 and now offers the largest exhibition space for contemporary art in the country. It does not have any permanent exhibitions to call its own, but it offers visitors a peek into the development of local and international art with constantly changing programs that receive critical acclaim.

SZÉPMŰVÉSZETI MÚZEUM
(MUSEUM OF FINE ARTS)

The grandiose neoclassical building on the northern side of Heroes Square is the excellent **Museum of Fine Arts** (XIV. Dózsa György út 41, tel. 1/469-7100, www.szepmuveszeti.hu, Tues.-Sun. 10am-6pm, 1,800 Ft), Hungary's premier gallery of non-Hungarian works of art. The gallery began with a donation by Archbishop Pyrker of Eger, but the most significant portion of the collection (now over 100,000 works strong) was purchased by the state in the 1870s from the Esterházy family. Its permanent exhibitions date back to antiquity, including fascinating Egyptian, Greek, and Roman collections totaling over 1,000 artifacts. The upper floors are a treasure trove of art history, including French works from Édouard Manet, Camille Pissaro, and Paul Gauguin, a comprehensive collection of 13th-to 18th-century Italian paintings, and no less than seven masterpieces by the incomparable El Greco.

Vajdahunyad vára
(Vajdahunyad Castle)

Located behind Heroes Square is the eclectic **Vajdahunyad Castle** (XIV. Városliget, daily 10am-5pm, free admission to castle complex), which is actually an enclave of buildings rather than a proper castle. It was designed by Ignác Alpár for the Millennial Celebrations of 1896 with the intention of displaying the variety of architectural styles found in the Hungarian kingdom. Indeed, a slow walk around the building will reveal a combination of Gothic, Renaissance, baroque, and Romanesque elements. Originally constructed out of cardboard as a temporary exhibit for the 1,000-year anniversary, the castle was such a smash that the city decided to turn it into a permanent structure, which they did starting in 1904, when reconstruction of the castle began using brick and stone.

Inside the castle is the **Museum of Hungarian Agriculture** (Vajdahunyad Castle, tel. 1/363-1117, www.mmgm.hu, Apr.-Oct. Tues.-Sun. 10am-5pm, Nov.-Mar. Tues.-Fri. 10am-4pm,

Sat.-Sun. 10am-5pm, 1,100 Ft), the largest agricultural museum in Europe, also designed by Ignác Alpár. Visitors are treated to a fascinating lesson on the agrarian evolution in Hungary, complete with tools, pottery, excellent recreations of ancient kitchens and migratory dwellings, and informative texts thoughtfully translated into English. Other exhibits include animal skulls and bones, agricultural machines such as steam engines and tractors, and a lighthearted exhibit on the history of wine-making in Hungary that includes colorful period costumes and jewelry.

In the park, opposite the museum, sits a nottoo-friendly-looking hooded figure. Sculpted in 1903 by Miklós Ligeti, this is the famous **Statue of Anonymous,** a monk nobody seems to know much about other than he supposedly lived in the 12th century as the notary to King Béla III. He is also considered to be the author of the *Gesta Hungarorum,* the first-ever book written on the history of the Hungarians. Superstition has it that students who touch his stylus (an old-school writing apparatus) will receive help in their studies.

Fővárosi Állatkert és Növénykert (Budapest Zoo and Botanical Garden)

Located just behind the Museum of Fine Arts is the beautiful **Budapest Zoo and Botanical Garden** (XIV. Állatkerti körút 6-12, tel. 1/273-4900, www.zoobudapest.com, hours vary, 2,500 Ft). Established in 1886, when the collecting of animals was mostly a luxury hobby enjoyed by the rich, it is one of the world's oldest and most respected zoos. The zoo showcases over 2,000 animals, including elephants, tigers, polar bears, kangaroos, and gorillas. You'll find the country's largest tropical garden here as well, boasting roughly 10,000 plant species. Walking past the ornate art nouveau entrance is like entering an oasis in the middle of a bustling city. Animal lovers would be wise to make a stop here if time permits. Make sure to check the website for opening hours, as they vary from month to month.

◖ Széchenyi gyógyfürdő (Széchenyi Spa Baths)

The large yellow neo-baroque building opposite the Circus is none other than the **Széchenyi Spa Baths** (XIV. Állakerti körút 9-11, tel. 1/363-3210, http://budapestgyogyfurdoi.hu/en, daily 6am-10pm, 3,800-4,800 Ft), one of the largest spa complexes in Europe and certainly one of the most popular in town. Its thermal springs were discovered in 1879 and are the city's deepest as well as the hottest, at 165°F. The palatial outdoor swimming pool can be enjoyed year-round, as can the series of steam rooms, saunas, and Turkish baths. Make sure to check out the fantastic whirlpool, and if you're a chess fan, bring your own board and join the seriouslooking but friendly older men in some competitive fun. If you only have time to visit one bath during your stay, make it this one.

Nagy Cirkusz (Hungarian State Circus)

For thrills, chills, and excitement under the big top, try the **Hungarian State Circus** (XIV. Állatkerti körút 12/a, tel. 1/343-8300, www.fnc.hu, box office Wed.-Fri. 10am-6pm, Sat. 10am-7pm, Sun. 10am-6pm, 1,900-3,800 Ft). Putting a smile on children's faces since its inception in 1891, this 1,850-seat venue is open year-round and continues to draw crowds with clowns, trapeze artists, and a wide variety of derring-do. Keep in mind that animals are part of the act, so those particularly sensitive to or active in animal rights issues may want to seek entertainment elsewhere.

Vidám Park

Next to the Circus is family favorite **Vidám Park** (XIV. Állakerti körút 14-16, tel. 1/363-8310, www.vidampark.hu, hours vary, allday pass 4,900 Ft). Offering over 60 different rides, some of which predate World War II, this delightful fairground has a palpable old-fashioned charm now lost at the grand theme-driven amusement parks found elsewhere. Particularly worth your attention is the over 100-year-old merry-go-round that

BUDAPEST

© TOTALPICS/123RF

Széchenyi Spa Baths

comes with authentic Wurlitzer music, the slow-moving (but no less fun) Ferris wheel, and Europe's longest wooden roller coaster. The park has also started to keep its doors open after hours on certain evenings until 1:30am. Make sure to check the website for opening hours as they vary from month to month and tend to change without notice.

Petőfi Csarnok

In the eastern section of the park you'll find **Petőfi Csarnok** (XIV. Zichy Mihály út 14, tel. 61/848-0206, www.petoficsarnok.hu), a leisure center for the city's youth that has enjoyed immense success since opening in 1985. There is a large hall as well as an open-air stage that has hosted countless rock, pop, and classical concerts. The center also organizes various community activities run by the local youth. When not rocking the casbah or doing its best to keep kids out of trouble, it serves as one of Budapest's more popular flea markets.

Közlekedési Múzeum (Transportation Museum)

The **Transportation Museum** (XIV. Városligeti körút 11, tel. 1/273-3840, www.mmkm.hu, Tues.-Fri. 10am-5pm, Sat.-Sun. 10am-6pm, 1,600 Ft) boasts one of the oldest collections in Europe and is full of vintage locomotives, motorcycles, steamboats, and bicycles, not to mention a huge model train set that runs every 15 minutes on the mezzanine level. Well worth a peek if you've bothered to reach this rarely visited section of the park.

JÓZSEFVÁROS

Józsefváros is Budapest's eighth district and is seen as having two distinct parts: the grander Kiskörút side, which attracts tourists thanks to its location near the National Museum and Ervin Szabó Library, and the darker quarters beyond the Nagykörút, historically associated with prostitution and various criminal elements. Most visitors stick to the area around Kálvin Square due to its plethora of shops and restaurants as well as its proximity to Váci Street and the Belváros.

Múzeum körút (Museum Boulevard)

Rivaling Andrássy Avenue in terms of shops and majestic buildings, the Museum Boulevard separates the Belváros from Józsefváros. As you move along on the way to the National Museum, take a short detour down Bródy Sándor Street until you come upon the historically relevant **Magyar Radio Building** (VIII. Bródy Sándor utca 5-7). On October 23, 1956, this street was full of angry students and youth demanding access to the airwaves in order to announce their defiant message: "Withdrawal of the Russian troops! An end to Communist dictatorship!" The ÁVO guards on duty weren't about to let that happen, so they chose instead to open fire, shooting randomly into the crowd of demonstrators. Things got ugly fast, and the masses stormed the building, defending themselves with makeshift weapons they had managed to procure one way or another. The tanks rolled in the following morning and weeks of bloody battle ensued, ending with the revolution's defeat and the start of a 32-year regime of repression.

MAGYAR NEMZETI MÚZEUM (HUNGARIAN NATIONAL MUSEUM)

Built between 1837 and 1847, the **Hungarian National Museum** (VIII. Múzeum körút 14-16, tel. 1/338-2122, www.hnm.hu, Tues.-Sun. 10am-6pm, permanent exhibition 1,600 Ft, admission varies for temporary exhibitions) is easily the largest museum in Hungary. In 1848 it was on the steps of this inspiring neoclassical structure where beloved poet Sándor Petőfi recited his *National Song,* an inflammatory work meant to provoke revolution against the Habsburgs.

There are a number of permanent exhibitions on display, starting with the Lapidarium in the museum's bottom two floors, which house the Medieval and Early Modern Stone Collection as well as the Roman Stone Collection, featuring tombstones from the 1st and 2nd centuries, sarcophagi, and a gorgeous mosaic pavement from the reception hall of a Roman villa. Another exhibit traces the history of the Carpathian Basin from the Paleolithic and Mesolithic Eras all the way to the Avar Period in the 8th and 9th centuries. This fascinating section of the museum is full of amazing relics, including stone tools, golden jewelry, weapons, the first minting of coins, and much more.

The final and largest exhibit extends through 20 galleries and is succinctly called *The History of Hungary from the Foundation of the State to 1900.* The first group of rooms begins with St. Stephen's reign, and in this section you can see a few royal jewels and crowns from the various monarchs who ruled the land. The rise and fall of the Ottoman Empire rounds out the first section and leads into the second, which chronicles Hungarian history through the Revolution, the War of Independence of 1848-1849, and the Millennium anniversary of the country's existence. It is the final leg of the exhibition, however, where things really start heating up; you'll find a whole host of period pieces from World War I, World War II, Nazism, and the 40-year legacy of Communism.

The museum is massive and thorough, which means you should be prepared to spend at least two or three hours in order to get a decent understanding of the region's history. And that's just the permanent exhibitions. There are various temporary exhibitions that come and go regularly, all of which are well worth the time and money spent.

Kálvin tér (Kálvin Square)

Kálvin Square is a rather busy intersection with roads heading toward the airport and westward across the river. Its centerpiece is the neo-Gothic **Inner City Calvinist Church** (Kálvin tér 5), whose main entrance is characterized by a four-columned portico that was designed by well-known Hungarian architect József Hild. Miksa Róth, stained-glass artist extraordinaire, is responsible for the church's impressive windows. The treasury has an excellent collection of liturgical objects dating from the 17th and 18th centuries, but sadly, at press time the church was closed due to nearby construction of the city's much anticipated fourth subway line.

Just off Kálvin Square, down busy Baross utca, stands the **Szabo Library** (VIII. Szabó Ervin tér 1, tel. 1/411-5052, www.fszek. hu, Mon.-Fri. 10am-8pm, Sat. 10am-4pm). Renovated in 1998-2001, this gorgeous neobaroque building was once the home of Count Frigyes Wenckheim. Its main entrance is on Revicky Street, which is also the setting for a short stretch of benches and cafés usually busy with students who have had enough education for the day.

Kerepesi temető (Kerepesi Cemetery)

Although it might seem odd to describe a cemetery as beautiful, it's apt for **Kerepesi Cemetery** (VIII. Fiumei út 16, Nov.-Feb. daily 7:30am-5pm, Mar. daily 7am-5:30pm, Apr. and Aug. daily 7am-7pm, May.-July daily 7am-8pm, Sept. daily 7am-6pm, Oct. daily 7am-5pm). Located just down the street from Keleti Station, it is Budapest's answer to Paris's Père Lachaise, home to everyone who's anyone in Hungarian history. Founded in 1847, its first notable burial was famed poet Mihály Vörösmarty in 1855. Plenty of political leaders, artists, and scientists have followed since then, including Mihály Károlyi, Károly Lotz, Miklós Ybl, Lujza Blaha, and Mór Jókai. There are also three magnificent mausoleums of famous leaders to look for: Lajos Batthyány, Ferenc Deák, and Lajos Kossuth. Along with gorgeous arcades that were built during the years 1908-1911, there is also a striking mausoleum created for the labor movement during the country's 40-year Communist period that's decorated with inspiring images of hard work and all its benefits. Exceptionally well taken care of and a history lesson in itself, the cemetery needs at least two hours of casual strolling to be fully appreciated.

FERENCVÁROS

Development of Budapest's ninth district began in the late 18th century, although it was ravaged by floods in 1799 and again in 1838. It is home to Budapest's most successful soccer team, FTC, as well as the Central Market Hall, whose massive interior is home to countless stalls offering a wide variety of domestic goods that include paprika, sausages, and traditional arts and crafts. Its most fashionable street is the pedestrian-only **Ráday utca,** which is located next to Kálvin Square. Lined on either side with fashionable cafés and restaurants, it is highly popular with people of all ages and walks of life, creating an easygoing, fun-loving atmosphere everybody seems to thrive on. It should be a definite stop during your stay, whether it's for a delicious meal, a cup of coffee, or a good old-fashioned stroll through the neighborhood.

Iparművészeti Múzeum (Museum of Applied Arts)

The **Museum of Applied Arts** (IX. Üllői út 33-37, tel. 1/456-5107, www.imm.hu, Tues.-Sun. 10am-6pm, 900 Ft) was designed by Odön Lechner and completed in 1896, making it the third museum to be built in Europe after its predecessors in London (1857) and Vienna (1864). Its opening had the distinct honor of being the final event of the Millennial Celebrations. This gorgeous art nouveau building, topped with a dome decorated with colorful Zsolnay ceramics, captures the eye from afar and beckons one and all inside. Its collections are extensive, starting with one dedicated to furniture that consists of roughly 4,000 items from the 14th-20th centuries. Its metalwork collection is vast, totaling over 10,000 pieces, including the astounding Esterházy collection, which gives new meaning to the term "treasures." Art nouveau jewelry, astronomical clocks, a wide range of textiles, Christian iconography, and one of the world's largest bookplate collections are but a few of the countless items on display.

Holokauszt Emlékközpont (Holocaust Memorial Center)

The **Holocaust Memorial Center** (IX. Páva utca 39, tel. 1/455-3333, www.hdke.hu, Tues.-Sun. 10am-6pm, 1,400 Ft) is arguably the most architecturally impressive building in the neighborhood, featuring a jagged, asymmetrical exterior and dislocated walls, combining classical elements of form with a variety of modern ones. It's little wonder that architect István Mányi and interior designer István Szenes both won the Ybl Prize for their efforts. The center's main motif is "From Deprivation of Rights to Genocide," tracing the persecution and murder of Hungarian Jews and Roma during that shameful period in history that began in 1938. The museum structures the exhibits to reflect the systematic stages of deprivation. The horror of it all is enhanced by personal accounts that cover the entirety of the exhibition. Opened in 2004, the center continues to grow thanks to private donations of personal relics and effects from survivors.

Magyar Természettudományi Múzeum (Hungarian Natural History Museum)

Although slightly farther away than where most visitors venture, a trip to the **Hungarian Natural History Museum** (IX. Ludovika tér 2-6, tel. 1/210-1085, www.nhmus.hu, Wed.-Mon. 10am-5pm, 1,600 Ft) is nevertheless time well spent, particularly if you have children. Exhibits include over 1.8 million specimens of flora, skeletons of animals from around the world, a gorgeous underwater room full of aquariums, dinosaur eggs, elephant skulls, and a wide array of human bones ranging from the Neolithic period to the Middle Ages.

VÁRHEGY AND CENTRAL BUDA (CASTLE HILL AND CENTRAL BUDA)

Várhegy is rightly considered one of the most beautiful districts in all of Europe. Sitting high above its surrounding neighborhoods overlooking the Danube and Pest, its nearly mile-long plateau is Buda's most striking feature.

Dotted with medieval streets, Gothic arches, and baroque residences, it is where you'll find Buda's majestic palace, the sublime beauty of Matthias Church, and the playful kitsch of Fishermen's Bastion. Filled with tourists in the summer, a shadowy calm falls over the area in the winter, leaving locals in silent contemplation of the palpable history that surrounds them.

Lánchíd (Chain Bridge)

The Chain Bridge is by far Budapest's most famous bridge and a matter of great pride to all Hungarians. Officially opened on November 20, 1849, it was the first bridge to connect Buda and Pest and was responsible for the immediate economic boom that soon followed. As an interesting side note, the tunnel located under the hill just opposite the Buda end of the bridge was constructed in a mere 7.5 months just four years later in 1853. It is 32 feet wide, 32 feet tall, and, at 1,146 feet long, exactly the same length as the Chain Bridge, prompting some Hungarians to joke that they can simply push the bridge into the tunnel when it rains so it won't get wet.

Crossing over the Chain Bridge brings you to **Clark Ádám tér,** the busy roundabout named after the famed Scottish engineer responsible for the Chain Bridge and tunnel. Make sure to look both ways before crossing over to **Budavári Sikló** (funicular, daily 7:30am-10pm, closed every 2nd Mon. for repairs, 900 Ft, 1,800 Ft round-trip), which takes somewhere between 500,000 and one million passengers up the hill every year. Opened in 1870, it was Europe's second funicular and, at the time, the only way to reach the castle grounds. Destroyed in World War II, it was fully restored in 1986 and now uses electricity rather than the steam traction engine that once powered it. The funicular's first carriage offers the least obstructed views, and those who are

BUDAPEST

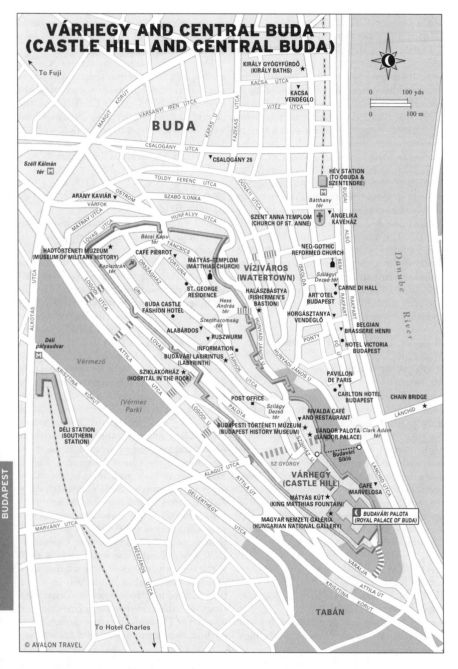

VÁRHEGY AND CENTRAL BUDA (CASTLE HILL AND CENTRAL BUDA)

To Fuji

BUDA

KIRÁLY GYÓGYFÜRDŐ (KIRÁLY BATHS) ★

KACSA VENDÉGLŐ ▼

0   100 yds
0   100 m

Széll Kálmán tér Ⓜ

▼ CSALOGÁNY 26

HÉV STATION (TO ÓBUDA & SZENTENDRE)

Bátthany tér Ⓜ

ARANY KAVIÁR ▼
VÁRFOK

SZENT ANNA TEMPLOM (CHURCH OF ST. ANNE) ✝

ANGELIKA KÁVÉHÁZ ▼

NEO-GOTHIC REFORMED CHURCH ✝

HADTÖRTÉNETI MÚZEUM ★ (MUSEUM OF MILITARY HISTORY)

Kapisztrán tér

CAFÉ PIERROT ▼

Bécsi Kapu tér

MÁTYÁS–TEMPLOM (MATTHIAS CHURCH) ⛪

VÍZIVÁROS (WATERTOWN)

Szilágyi Dezső tér

CARNE DI HALL ▼

Danube River

ST. GEORGE RESIDENCE

Hess András tér

HALÁSZBÁSTYA (FISHERMEN'S BASTION)

ART'OTEL BUDAPEST ▼

BUDA CASTLE FASHION HOTEL

Szentháromság tér

HORGÁSZTANYA VENDÉGLŐ ▼

ALABÁRDOS ▼

RUSZWURM ▼

BELGIAN BRASSERIE HENRI ▼

Déli pályaudvar Ⓜ

Vérmező

INFORMATION ★
BUDAVÁRI LABIRINTUS (LABYRINTH) ★

HOTEL VICTORIA BUDAPEST ▼

SZIKLAKÓRHÁZ (HOSPITAL IN THE ROCK) ★

PAVILLON DE PARIS ▼

(Vérmez Park)

POST OFFICE ■

Szilágy Dezső tér

CARLTON HOTEL BUDAPEST ▼

CHAIN BRIDGE ★

LÁNCHÍD

RIVALDA CAFÉ AND RESTAURANT ▼

DÉLI STATION (SOUTHERN STATION)

BUDAPESTI TÖRTÉNETI MÚZEUM (BUDAPEST HISTORY MUSEUM) ★

SÁNDOR PALOTA (SÁNDOR PALACE) ★

Clark Ádám tér

SZ GYÖRGY

Budavári Sikló

VÁRHEGY (CASTLE HILL)

CAFÉ MARVELOSA ▼

MÁTYÁS KÚT (KING MATTHIAS FOUNTAIN) ★

MAGYAR NEMZETI GALÉRIA (HUNGARIAN NATIONAL GALLERY) ★

BUDAVÁRI PALOTA (ROYAL PALACE OF BUDA)

VÁRALJA

TABÁN

To Hotel Charles

© AVALON TRAVEL

BUDAPEST

The Chain Bridge

Before the construction of the Chain Bridge, people had been ferried over the Danube in boats. Pontoon bridges were used as well but were highly unreliable as they could be swept away during stormy weather. The story is that during a particularly cold December in 1820, Count István Széchenyi had to wait an entire week to cross as he couldn't find a boatman willing to risk maneuvering among the ice flows. Following this trying experience, he declared the donation of an entire year's income toward building a permanent bridge. During a visit to London, he was quite impressed with the work of William Tierney Clark, who had already designed two suspension bridges over the Thames: Hammersmith Bridge and Marlow Bridge. Clark was commissioned immediately, and Scottish engineer Adam Clark (no relation) was hired to oversee construction duties. Blown up by the retreating Nazis in World War II, the bridge was rebuilt quickly and today remains one of the city's dominant symbols.

romantically inclined should definitely take a trip up in the evening in order to enjoy the Pest landscape at its floodlit finest.

Coming off the funicular, you can't help but notice a large statue of an eagle. This is the **Turul,** a mythical winged beast that is the symbol of the Árpád dynasty kings of Hungary. According to legend, the great bird descended from heaven and impregnated Emeshe, who gave birth to wise leader and brave warrior Álmos. He in turn grew up to marry a prominent family's daughter, and through this union a son, Árpád, was born. Marked for greatness, Árpád went on to lead the Magyar conquest of the Carpathian Basin in the 9th century.

Next to the Turul are wrought-iron gates and a set of stairs that lead down to the terrace of the Royal Palace. Here you can enjoy a sweeping view of Pest accentuated by Parliament and St. Stephen's Basilica. A little farther ahead is the **statue of Prince Eugene of Savoy,** considered one of the finer equestrian statues in the city. Prince Eugene was one of the greatest generals to serve the Habsburgs and led successful battles against the Ottoman Turks in the late 17th century. Behind him are the **statues of Csongor and Tünde,** the main characters in Mihály Vörösmarty's time-honored fairy tale *Csongor és Tünde,* which many liken to William Shakespeare's *A Midsummer Night's Dream.*

⟨ Budavári palota (Royal Palace of Buda)

Visible from practically any point in the city, the Royal Palace simply dominates the southern skyline of the Castle District. Dating back to the 13th century, it has a turbulent history, one full of destruction, resurrection, and, above all, survival.

The palace's first incarnation came after the Mongol Invasion of 1241 and is said to have been built by Béla IV. More of a thick-walled fortress than anything else, it was later developed into a proper palace during the reign of King Lajos the Great. In the 14th century, under Sigismund of Luxembourg, it was expanded once again and reflected the Gothic style of the period. It wasn't until the 15th century, however, that the palace hit its stride when it was remodeled yet again, this time by King Matthias. Considered throughout Europe as one of the continent's most extravagant and important works of Renaissance architecture, it attracted nobles, scholars, and artists from far and wide, all of whom wanted to bask in its majesty.

The Turks took Buda in 1541 and ruled for 150 years. While there was some structural damage, it was nothing compared to the complete destruction the palace suffered at the hands of the pan-European Christian army that liberated Buda in 1686. A new

BUDAPEST

© TOM DIRLIS

Buda's Castle Hill

baroque building was built by King Charles III of Habsburg during the years 1714-1723, later extended by his daughter, Empress Maria Theresa. A massive fire in 1810, however, not to mention the War of Independence in 1848-1849, caused further damage, and reconstruction work began once again. Then came World War II. German occupying forces had been using the building as a command post, and during the final months of the war, the Red Army attacked the palace and gutted it completely. Restored once again, the palace now operates as a cultural center, housing the Hungarian National Gallery and Budapest History Museum as well as the National Széchenyi Library and Ludwig Museum of Contemporary Art.

MAGYAR NEMZETI GALÉRIA (HUNGARIAN NATIONAL GALLERY)

Opened in 1957, the **Hungarian National Gallery** (Buda Palace, Bldg. B, C, and D, tel. 1/201-9082, www.mng.hu, Tues.-Sun.

10am-6pm, permanent exhibitions 1,200 Ft) moved to its present location at Buda Palace in 1975. With roughly 100,000 artifacts on display, it is by far the most comprehensive collection of Hungarian painting and sculpture to be found in the entire country. Beginning with a medieval and Renaissance stone exhibition that includes a sculpture of King Béla III's head dating to 1200, the six permanent exhibitions weave their way through Gothic, baroque, and 19th- and 20th-century art and include historical masterpieces like Gyula Benczur's *The Recapture of Buda Castle,* Mihály Munkácsy's *The Convict,* and László Hunyadi's *Farewell.* Some remarkable illustrated altars from the Gothic period are not to be missed, including the 1483 triptych *The Altar of the Virgin Mary from the Church of St. Andrew.* The gallery is enormous and breathtaking in scope, and a good four hours or so should be allotted to it should you want to cover the grounds properly. It's one of the more popular sights in the Castle District, so

ornate gateway to the Royal Palace

getting here early should help you beat the regular crowds.

BUDAPESTI TÖRTÉNETI MÚZEUM
(BUDAPEST HISTORY MUSEUM)

If you've fallen in love with Budapest and want to learn everything there is to know about its history as well as that of the Carpathian Basin, make sure to visit the **Budapest History Museum** (Buda Palace, Bldg. E, tel. 1/487-8800, www.btm.hu, Mar.-Oct. Tues.-Sun. 10am-6pm, Nov.-Feb. Tues.-Sun. 10am-4pm, 1,800 Ft). This fascinating collection includes maps and weapons used during the liberation of Buda from the Turks, outstanding statues from the Roman and medieval eras, and a number of fascinating Gothic sculptures which were serendipitously discovered during an excavation in 1974.

MÁTYÁS KÚT
(KING MATTHIAS FOUNTAIN)

In the Outer Courtyard by the far wall stands the marvelous **King Matthias Fountain,** whose bronze figures relate the tragic tale of Ilonka, a pretty peasant girl who came upon the king while he was out hunting incognito. When humble Ilonka learned the hunter's true identity, the impossibility of them ever getting together came crashing down on her, causing her to die of a broken heart.

SÁNDOR PALOTA
(SÁNDOR PALACE)

Back at the Sikló (funicular) and leading on to the rest of the Castle District is **Sándor Palace** (I. Szent György tér 1-2, not open to the public), whose full restoration was completed in 2000 after suffering near total devastation during World War II. Art historians still argue as to whether its architect was Mihály Pollack or Johann Aman, but they all agree the building was completed in 1806. The palace's first residents were the Count Vince Sándor and his wife, Countess Anna Szapáry, whose son Móric Sándor was a mischievous little fellow known as the Devil's Horseman due to his superb riding skills and habit of entering drawing rooms on horseback. Today, the palace is better known as the official residence of the President of the Republic.

Szentháromság tér
(Szentháromság Square)

Originally a market back in the Middle Ages, Szentháromság Square is not only Castle Hill's highest point, it's also the square all visitors eventually gravitate to, as it's where you'll find two of the area's main attractions: Matthias Church and the Fishermen's Bastion.

Standing smack-dab in the center of Szentháromság Square is the **Holy Trinity Column.** Built by Buda's Council and unveiled in 1706, it was meant to serve as a memorial to those who lost their lives during the punishing plague of 1691. When another epidemic broke out in 1709, a bigger, more ornate memorial was built. The column depicts biblical King David praying for an end to the plague while various saints and cherubs are located under the golden Holy Trinity.

© TOM DIRLIS

the majestic Matthias Church

MÁTYÁS-TEMPLOM
(MATTHIAS CHURCH)

Easily the best-known and most remarkable Catholic Church in Budapest, **Matthias Church** (I. Szentháromság tér 2, tel. 1/355-5657, www.matyas-templom.hu, Mon.-Fri. 9am-5pm, Sat. 9am-1pm, Sun. 1pm-5pm, 1,000 Ft), officially named the Church of Our Lady, was built in the 13th century and has survived countless changes ever since. The church takes its unofficial name from beloved King Matthias, who donated its two towers (his crest is on the south one) and held his two weddings on its premises: the first to Catherine of Podebrad, and, following her death, to Beatrice of Argon.

The church suffered terribly during the 150-year Turkish occupation as most of its invaluable treasures were sent off to Bratislava, and, following the capture of Buda, its role was changed to serve as the city's main mosque. As if that weren't enough, all the magnificent ornate frescoes that graced the church's interiors were whitewashed and its furnishings were completely stripped. When the Turks were overthrown in 1686, a slew of attempts to reconstruct the building according to the fashionable baroque style of the time failed miserably. It wasn't until the end of the 19th century when, thanks to the tremendous work of Frigyes Schulek, the church began to regain its former splendor. A number of early Gothic elements were uncovered during the process, and Schulek added some of his own spectacular touches, including the diamond-patterned roof tiles and various gargoyles.

The church's interior simply overwhelms the senses. Colorful geometric patterns cover the walls and ceiling; dazzling frescoes and stained glass windows by Károly Lotz, Mihály Zichy, and Bertalan Székely blend with gilded altars, stone pulpits, coats of arms, and a whole host of ecclesiastical treasures. There are also a large number of sacred relics such as chalices and vestments on display at the Ecclesiastical Museum, as are replicas of the Hungarian royal crown and other coronation jewels.

the hugely popular Fishermen's Bastion

© TOM DIRLIS

HALÁSZBÁSTYA
(FISHERMEN'S BASTION)

Built in 1905 based on the designs of Frigyes Schulek, the **Fishermen's Bastion** is a pretty piece of fairy-tale kitsch that comes complete with turrets, parapets, and flowing staircases. Incorporating the styles of both neo-Gothic and neo-Romanesque architecture, its seven round towers are meant to represent the seven Magyar tribes that came to Hungary in 896. The view of Pest is simply breathtaking from here, allowing you to see as far away as Margaret Island and view buildings such as Parliament, St. Stephen's Basilica, the Vigadó, and the Inner City Parish Church. As for its name, a local fish market was located behind the church during medieval times, and it was the Fishermen's Guild that defended this part of the castle grounds in the 18th century. Standing in front of the bastion is the impressive bronze equestrian **statue of St. Stephen;** it was unveiled when work on the bastion was completed.

Táncsics Mihály utca
(Táncsics Mihály Street)

Near Szentháromság Square is Táncsics Mihály Street, which was the heart of the Jewish community during medieval times. All of the houses and buildings here are picturesque, to say the least, and a pleasant stroll among them is highly recommended. It's impossible to get lost, as everything reverts back to Matthias Church one way or another, so feel free to "lose" yourself willingly.

The baroque **Erdody Palace** (I. Táncsics Mihály utca 7, tel. 1/214-6770, www.zti.hu, Tues.-Sun. 10am-4pm, 600 Ft) is home to the Musicology Institute of the Hungarian Academy of Sciences, along with the Museum of Music History. Beethoven stayed here in 1800 when the building was a private residence, but today, visitors can learn about the evolution of musical instruments in Hungarian culture and view such unique and interesting examples like the *tárogató, csákány,* and Schunda pedal-cimbalom. Another permanent exhibition, *In Bartók's Workshop,* comprises the great composer's archives and outlines his compositional methods.

A little farther down, at number 26, is the **Medieval Jewish Chapel** (I. Táncsics Mihály utca 26, tel. 1/375-7533, ext. 243, www.btm.hu, May-Oct. Wed.-Sun. 10am-5pm, 800 Ft), now a small Jewish museum complete with frescoes, inscriptions in their original Hebrew, and various artifacts that include maps and prints.

Bécsi Kapu tér
(Bécsi Kapu Square)

At the end of Táncsics Mihály Street is small and unassuming Bécsi Kapu Square. The square's main building is the **National Archives of Hungary** (I. Bécsi Kapu tér 24, not open to the public), a large neo-Romanesque structure with an eye-catching multicolored roof. Around the corner is the **Vienna Gate,** actually a replica of the 16th-century original, but which nevertheless serves as one of the Castle District's entrances. Heading down from here will conveniently lead you to **Széll Kálmán**

BUDAPEST

© TOM DIRLIS

the ruins of Mary Magdalene Tower

tér station (formerly Moszkva tér station). On the opposite corner of the square is the rather basic-looking late-19th-century **Lutheran Church** (I. Táncsics Mihály utca 28, tel. 1/356-9736, http://budavar.lutheran.hu, Mon.-Fri. 9am-1pm, free), which continues to function by holding the occasional concert in the summer.

Kapisztrán tér and Vicinity (Kapisztrán Square)

Just west of Bécsi Kapu Square is Kapisztrán Square, named after Friar John Capistranus, whose statue is easily recognizable; he's the one standing on the back of some poor dead Turk.

Opposite the statue stands the neglected and lonely-looking **Mary Magdalene Tower.** The tower is the only part of this 13th-century Franciscan church that survived World War II, and its stone courtyard, crumbling walls, and busted window now produce a slightly melancholic effect. During the Turkish occupation, this was the only church on the Castle's grounds that Christians were allowed to worship in. Catholics were given the choir while Protestants used the nave.

HADTÖRTÉNETI MÚZEUM (MUSEUM OF MILITARY HISTORY)

The **Museum of Military History** (I. Kapisztrán tér 2-4, tel. 1/325-1600, www.militaria.hu, Oct.-Mar. Tues.-Sun. 10am-4pm, Apr.-Sept. Tues.-Sun. 10am-6pm, 1,100 Ft) houses a rather vast collection of weapons dating from before the Turkish wars all the way to the 20th century, along with uniforms, flags, various military documents, and roughly 28,000 coins. Permanent displays include a commemorative exhibition dedicated to the 150th anniversary of the Hungarian Revolution and War of Independence as well as one commemorating the 90 years following the end of World War I.

The entrance to the museum is found around the corner on **Tóth Árpád sétány**—a pretty promenade with a wonderful view of the Buda Hills. Following it past the museum will bring you to a large patriotic flagpole painted in red, white, and green. Still farther along, on the left side, you'll come to the **symbolic grave of Abdurrahmán,** Buda's last Turkish pasha, who died in 1686. The promenade eventually leads back to Bécsi Kapu Square. Taking it the other way will bring you to Dísz Square and the Royal Palace.

Sziklakórház (Hospital in the Rock)

Located under Buda Castle is the **Hospital in the Rock** (I. Lovas út 4/C, tel. 70/701-0101, www.sziklakorhaz.hu, daily 10am-8pm, guided tours on the hour every hour, 3,600 Ft), a former top-secret nuclear bunker and emergency hospital that went by the code name LOSK 0101/1. Outlining the tragic final days of World War II as well as the beginning of the Cold War, the museum has all kinds of mind-blowing memorabilia on display, including original hospital machinery and beds as well as over 70 wax figures detailing life as it once was. There's also a gift shop offering collectors original bomber jackets, gas masks, hospital stretchers, and a whole lot more. All students and lovers of history will be wise to pay a visit.

THE VÍZIVÁROS AND VICINITY (WATERTOWN)

The narrow strip that runs along the Danube from the Castle District to Margaret Bridge is known as the Víziváros. During the Middle Ages, the area was full of fisherfolk who plied their trade by the river as well as colorful artisans from all walks of life. Residences here are built into the hillside, and many are reached via narrow alleys and stairs, giving the area an aura of centuries past. The neighborhood's main street is **Fő utca,** which runs the length of the Víziváros in a north-south fashion, one block away from the Danube.

The first building worth noticing along Fő Street is the postmodern **French Institute** (I. Fő utca 17, tel. 1/489-4200, www.inst-france. hu, Mon.-Fri. 10am-7pm, Sat. 10am-1pm), designed by George Marois and which has been operating since 1992. The institute stays busy by organizing a large number of classical and jazz concerts, exhibitions, and lectures to a cultured crowd that can't seem to get enough. Aside from a French-language **library** (Tues.-Fri. 10am-7pm, Sat. 10am-1pm), it also houses a bookshop, a theater, and a rather stylish **café** (Mon.-Fri. 9am-11pm, Sat. 11am-11pm).

Farther down at Corvin Square is the **Budai Vigadó** (I. Corvin tér 8, tel. 1/225-6049, www. hagyomanyokhaza.hu, Mon.-Thurs. noon-6pm, Fri. 10am-2pm, box office open Sat.-Sun. 3 hours before concerts, admission varies), Buda's answer to a concert hall and home to the critically acclaimed Hungarian State Folk Ensemble.

Szilágyi Dezsó tér (Szilágyi Dezsó Square)

This small but pretty square has a **neo-Gothic Reformed church** at its center. Its interior is rather simple, but the church possesses excellent acoustics, making it one of the finer places in town to enjoy classical or choral music concerts.

One block over, at the **Bem Rakpart** (Danube bank), is where one of Hungary's darkest moments in history occurred. During the brutal winter of 1944-1945, the fascist Arrow Cross—the Hungarian Nazis—rounded up thousands of Jewish people, bound them in small groups, then tossed them alive into the freezing river.

Batthyány tér (Batthyány Square)

The main square of the Víziváros, Batthyány Square, tends to be busy with shoppers at the **Vásárcsarnok,** a former market hall turned grocery store, or with commuters making use of the subway-HÉV interchange.

SZENT ANNA TEMPLOM (CHURCH OF ST. ANNE)

On the south side of the square is the **Church of St. Anne** (I. Batthyány tér 7, tel. 1/201-3404, daily 6am-6pm for mass), one of Budapest's loveliest baroque buildings. Designed by Kristóf Hamon, construction of the church began in 1740 and was completed by Mátyás Nepauer in 1761. For the next 200 years, the church withstood the ravages of time, including wars, floods, earthquakes, and a plan to have it demolished due to the construction of the city's subway system. Thankfully, cooler heads prevailed and the church underwent reconstruction between 1970 and 1984. Inside, high altar statues of the Virgin Mary and St. Anne leave an impression, as does the striking ceiling fresco by Pál Molnar. Another interesting thing to note is the church's organ, which was consecrated in 1985 and is known today as one of the best of its kind in the country.

KIRÁLY GYÓGYFÜRDŐ (KIRÁLY BATHS)

Dating back to the days of the Ottoman Empire, the **Király Baths** (I. Fő utca 84, tel. 1/202-3688, www.spasbudapest.com, daily 9am-9pm, 2,400 Ft) are truly a step back in time. The steam is so thick you can taste it, and visibility is at a minimum since the only light that manages to stream in comes from the

BUDAPEST

star-shaped openings in the cupola that criss-cross with a handful of lamps.

Margit híd
(Margaret Bridge)

Built in 1872-1876 by a Paris-based firm, the bridge is slightly out of the ordinary due to its V shape. The span twists halfway through to continue along the Nagykörút on one end, while a connecting branch joins the bridge to the southern tip of Margaret Island at the other.

Rózsadomb

Literally meaning "Rose Hill," Rózsadomb was once the neighborhood of choice of past Turkish occupiers but today has the honor of being Budapest's wealthiest and most respectable neighborhood. Many of the city's famous and elite live in the area, and real estate prices are among the highest in the capital. Enjoying easy access to parks, forests, and the hills of Buda, this is a wonderful part of the city to stroll through while admiring both the architectural and natural beauty that surrounds it.

Coming off Margaret Bridge on the Buda side, you'll soon find a street named Mecset (Mosque). A short but rather steep hike up it will lead to a flight of stairs and the **Tomb of Gül Baba** (I. Mecset utca 14, Jan.-Apr. daily 10am-6pm, May-Sept. Tues.-Sun. 10am-6pm, Oct. Tues.-Sun. 10am-5pm, Nov.-Dec. daily 10am-4pm, 400 Ft). It's the final resting place of the Turkish dervish who spread the teachings of Allah with his mighty sword. Ironically, he died during the first Muslim religious ceremony shortly after the Turks took Buda in 1541. The site itself is a small octagonal building surrounded by a splendid colonnaded parapet with a Mediterranean garden featuring roses, tropical fruit trees, Turkish fountains, and excellent views of the city.

◖ GELLÉRT HEGY
(GELLÉRT HILL)

Rising 450 feet above the Danube, Gellért Hill is as vital to Budapest's landscape as either Parliament or Buda Palace. It is easily identified by the **Gellért Statue,** built right into the

hill and surrounded by a colonnade that overlooks a pretty waterfall. Both the hill and statue are named after the Benedictine abbot Gellért, who was an all-important figure during the Magyars' conversion to Christianity under the reign of St. Stephen. Legend has it that shortly following the king's death, Gellért was seized during a pagan rebellion in 1046 and thrown down the hill in a barrel full of nails by those not willing to conform to the Christian faith. A gruesome story to be sure, but not one that should deter you from climbing up and appreciating both the statue and the wonderful view of central Pest below.

To reach the statue and the top of the hill, cross the street upon leaving the Liberty Bridge and follow one of the many footpaths that lead upward; all the paths reach the same point. Even on the hottest of days, the walk up is a pleasant experience as the many trees offer plenty of shade.

The **Szabadság híd (Liberty Bridge)** connects Fővám Square, home of the Great Market Hall, with Gellért Square at the foot of Gellért Hill. Designed by Hungarian János Feketeházy, the bridge was built between 1894 and 1896 and opened officially in the presence of Emperor Franz Joseph, who hammered home the last silver rivet on the Pest abutment. It is 1,095 feet long and 66 feet wide, and its top four masts are decorated with bronze statues of the Turul, the same mythical winged beast that can be found on Castle Hill. There is currently talk of turning the traffic-plagued bridge into a pedestrian-only crossing upon completion of Budapest's long-awaited fourth subway line.

The Citadella

The top of Gellért Hill is dominated by the **Citadella** (XI. Citadella sétány 1, www.citadella.hu, daily 8am-10pm, 300 Ft), built by the Habsburgs between 1850 and 1854 in order to better control the city after their successful suppression of the Hungarian War of Independence. Today, the former barracks operate as budget accommodations, and the structure in its entirety serves the busloads

the Liberation Monument, high atop
Gellért Hill

wartime leader, who lost his son in a plane crash during World War II. The former version of the story is most likely closest to the truth, which is ironic considering that the statue of the Red Army soldier that used to guard the monument was unceremoniously removed shortly after the collapse of Communism.

Hotel Gellért es Fürdő (Gellért Hotel and Baths)

The **Gellért Hotel and Baths** (XI. Kelenhegyi út 4, tel. 1/466-6166, www.spasbudapest. com, daily 6am-8pm, 4,900-5,500 Ft) is one of Budapest's finest thermal bathing complexes. A huge hit with locals and visitors alike, its decadent art nouveau surroundings boast original fittings, mosaics, marble columns, and stained glass windows from 1918, making an afternoon here a most memorable experience. Luckily, one doesn't have to be a guest at the hotel to take advantage of the lavish indoor swimming pool with gorgeous majolica tiles and stone lion heads spouting water, or the separate thermal baths, steam rooms, and saunas. A modest admission fee includes use of the marvelous outdoor swimming pool during the summer months.

In front of the hotel is the **Gellért Fountain,** which stands under a stone dome supported by pillars. A stream of water winds through a complex path that runs in four channels along the ground, representing north, east, south, and west. This is a perfect opportunity to fill up your water bottle either before or after your trip up the hill.

Szikla templom (Cave Chapel)

Located on Gellért Hill opposite the Gellért Hotel and Baths complex is the interesting **Cave Chapel** (XI. Gellért Hill, daily 8am-7pm). Founded by Pauline monks in the 1920s, it was closed down by the Communist police in 1951 and remained sealed until the fall of the regime in 1989. Inside the rather smallish chapel are an intriguing mixture of church elements and natural rock formations that create an extremely calming effect. Services continue to

of tourists that regularly visit. Numerous stalls sell the usual trinkets, tour books, and T-shirts, and there's a restaurant and a couple of makeshift cafés that make for nice spots to rest and fuel up. The view, of course, is stunning and includes just about every sight you can imagine: Castle Hill, Matthias Church, the Chain Bridge, Margaret Island, Parliament, the Danube Embankment, St. Stephen's Basilica, and the rest of Pest stretching out before you. Don't forget your camera or you'll be very sorry.

Felszabadulási emlékmű (Liberation Monument)

Next to the Citadella stands the **Liberation Monument,** depicting a curiously blank-faced woman holding a leaf above her head. Erected in 1947, it was built to commemorate the Soviet soldiers who fought bravely and freed the city from Nazi occupation. Another popular belief, however, is that the statue was originally commissioned by Admiral Horthy, Hungary's

the Gellért Hotel, home of the world-famous Gellért baths

this day and are the only time visitors are not allowed in.

ÓBUDA

As Budapest's oldest district, Óbuda has understandably gone through many significant changes over the centuries. The Roman Empire founded Aquincum here, a settlement dating back to the 1st and 2nd centuries, the remnants of which can still be seen today. In the Middle Ages, Old Buda was called Buda Castle because the royal chancellery made its home here. The Turks dominated the area in the 16th century, and the Zichy counts ruled throughout the 17th century, leading to a massive influx of Germans, who came to outnumber the Hungarians. In the last hundred years or so, Óbuda has grown from a rural settlement to an industrial area that has increased its population exponentially and brought about a consequent rise in stylish offices and villas erected on its hillside.

Óbuda is a wondrous district whose illustrious past crosses over with a promising and vibrant future. It is also extremely conducive to outdoor activities given the number of boathouses along the Danube, the bike paths along the riverside, and the numerous hiking paths in the hills. Time spent here will quickly lead you to understand why the area's most famous writer, Gyula Krúdy, referred to his beloved neighborhood as "the grandfather of all cities."

Fő tér
(Main Square)

Linking old Buda and new is Main Square. The two major roads of ancient Aquincum once crossed here, and the square still remains an important hub of traffic for passengers using the area's trams, buses, and HÉV. The pretty 18th-century houses that surround the square make a picturesque backdrop for the regular concerts, theater performances, and fairs held here, and a walk down its quiet streets will reward you with excellent museums, quaint cafés, and the occasional Roman ruin.

VASARELY MÚZEUM
(VASARELY MUSEUM)

Located by the hub of buses just outside the Árpád híd stop of the HÉV, the **Vasarely Múzeum** (III. Szentlélek tér 6, tel. 1/388-7551, www.vasarely.hu, Tues.-Sun. 10am-5:30pm, permanent exhibitions 800 Ft, admission varies for temporary exhibitions) is dedicated to Hungarian painter Victor Vasarely, who became renowned throughout the world thanks to his eye-opening art that deals primarily with three-dimensional images. The geometrical nature of this extensive collection may indeed induce headaches in those not too interested in modern art, but it will certainly open the eyes and minds of those who are. Along with various ink, tempera, and collage-oriented works, visitors will also be treated to the artist's vision of utopia and his belief that the world can reach harmony through art.

ZICHY KÁSTÉLY
(ZICHY CASTLE)

Zichy Castle (Fő tér 1) can easily be missed if you don't have a look into the courtyard on the right as you enter the main square. Completed in 1757, this beautiful baroque building may be crumbling in places, but it still retains an incontestable elegance. It used to house the Zichy counts who ruled Óbuda 1659-1768. Today, it's home to a couple of interesting museums. The **Óbudai Museum** (III. Fő tér 1, tel. 1/250-1020, www.obudaimuzeum.hu, Tues.-Sun. 10am-6pm, 800 Ft) displays roughly 1,000 historical objects that include pottery, textiles, carvings, and reconstructed living rooms, enlightening visitors on just how differently people lived not that long ago. The **Kassák Museum** (III. Fő tér 1, tel. 1/368-7021, www.kassakmuzeum.hu, Wed.-Sun. 10am-5pm, 600 Ft) is dedicated to respected Hungarian artist Lajos Kassák (1887-1967). Permanent exhibits feature a significant collection of his work, including paintings, sculpture, literature, and typography. Firmly devoted to socialism during his youth, his later works conflicted with postwar communism—so much so that public displays of his work were strictly forbidden.

IMRE VARGA MÚZEUM
(IMRE VARGA MUSEUM)

At the end of Laktanya Street rests a slightly shabby-looking yellow building that houses the **Imre Varga Museum** (III. Laktanya utca 7, tel. 1/250-0274, Tues.-Sun. 10am-6pm, 800 Ft). Quite a few of the famous sculptor's poignant works can be found here, including humorous depictions of military men as well as sculptures of Hungarian heroes Imre Nagy and Béla Bartók. The courtyard also has some touching statues accentuated by serene surroundings.

Just off Fő Square and about 100 feet from the museum is Imre Varga's striking set of sculptures titled *Women with Umbrellas,* which capture both the eye and the imagination.

◖ Aquincum

Although nowhere near any other major sights, a 25-minute trip north on the HÉV to **Aquincum** (Aquincum HÉV station, tel. 1/250-1650, Apr. 15-Oct. Tues.-Sun. 9am-6pm, 1,000-1,600 Ft.) is well worth the time and effort. A key military post of the Roman province of Pannonia Inferior, Aquincum eventually grew to become its capital, reaching a population of 30,000-40,000 inhabitants and covering a major part of today's Óbuda by the end of the 2nd century. When you get off the HÉV at Aquincum station, you can see a **2nd-century amphitheater** right next door. A little farther down on the other side of the street, however, is where all the action is. The ruins that remain are enough to evoke what life must have been like way back then, and if you think they were any less civilized, you're wrong. Helpful texts thoughtfully translated into English reveal the layout of the entire complex, which included residential buildings, public baths, shrines, altars for sacrifices, artisans buildings, and even dwellings that boasted floor heating. A look through a type of viewfinder called a kronoscope magically recreates what some of the buildings (the public bath, the market, and certain houses) must have looked like in their entirety, illustrating just how advanced the Romans were.

If you keep your admission ticket, you can

also visit a tiny but interesting **museum** (tel. 1/250-1650, Apr.-Oct. Tues.-Sun. 10am-6pm, Nov.-Mar. Tues.-Sun. 10am-4pm) on the premises that displays various items from the period, including jugs, glass-bead necklaces, weaponry, and the slightly chilling mummy of a young woman found in a sarcophagus.

◖ MARGIT SZIGET (MARGARET ISLAND)

Margaret Island is a little slice of heaven located between the Margaret Bridge to the south and the Árpád Bridge to the north. It is 1.6 miles long and covers 225 acres. Whether you're traveling alone, with friends, a lover, or the whole family, there is no better place to spend the day relaxing, swimming, sunbathing, picnicking, or simply walking around and appreciating natural beauty.

Originally known as Nyulak szigete (Rabbit Island), it was later renamed after Princess Margaret, daughter of King Béla IV; she entered the island's convent and her burial place is still marked among its ruins. The island was favored by monks who appreciated the island's serenity and by kings for its excellent hunting. Things changed drastically during the Turkish invasion, and the island fell into disuse until the 19th century.

The public opening of a park and entertainment center brought the island back to life, aided by the building of the Margaret Bridge embranchment in 1900, which made it possible for pedestrians to reach the island easily (before that, the island could only be approached by boat). Margaret Island was declared a public park in 1908, right around the time that hot springs were discovered in the area, turning the island into a popular health resort overnight.

Today, the island is a popular destination for visitors and locals in need of escape from the daily rigors of the city. You can spend the entire day strolling up and down the numerous peaceful paths that take you past flower gardens, romantic ruins, a mini zoo, and the Palatinus Strand, Budapest's largest open-air swimming

complex. Joggers will love the 3.3-mile rubber-coated track that encircles the island, and cyclists will appreciate the opportunity to rent bicycles (for one, two, or four people), and there are electric cars available to rent.

Southern Entrance

Starting at the Margaret Bridge entrance and walking past the Margit Sziget Athletic Center, with its tennis courts and well-kept soccer field, you'll quickly find the **Centenary Monument** directly in front of you. Reminiscent of a futuristic pod or cocoon, it was designed by István Kiss and erected in 1972 to commemorate the 100th anniversary of the union of Buda and Pest. Behind it is the delightful **Musical Fountain** that pumps water high into the air accompanied by famous classical tunes. This is a favorite with children, who enjoy running around and spraying each other. Should you care to rent a bicycle, electric car, or take a guided tour by train, here is where you can make those arrangements. If you'd rather walk and see how things go, feel free, as rental opportunities present themselves throughout the island.

A little farther ahead is a pleasant **playground** where children from all over the world make new friends on the slides, swings, and innumerable objects from which to dangle them. Beyond that is the **Hajos Alfred Sportuszoda** (XIII. Margaret Island, tel. 1/450-4214, Mon.-Fri. 6am-4pm, Sat.-Sun. 6am-6pm, 1,800 Ft), a huge swimming pool complex offering a wide range of aquatic possibilities, from high diving to Olympic-size facilities. There are a total of six pools, with three of them dedicated exclusively to beginners. This is an excellent place to have either a relaxed or a more intensive workout. In fact, odds are you'll probably see a handful of Olympic hopefuls here as plenty of serious athletes come to the center to train.

The first ruins you'll encounter are those of the **Franciscan Priory,** which was established near the end of the 13th century and destroyed during Ottoman rule in the 16th century. Not much remains today except for a wall and a few crumbling remnants. The flowerbed in front of it is a nice touch, however.

A pleasant stroll through the middle of the island will reward you further with a small **Japanese Garden,** a large **English-style garden,** an **open-air theater,** an octagonal 187-foot-tall art nouveau **Water Tower** built in 1911, and a **mini zoo** complete with ponies, horses, and baby deer.

Palatinus Strand

Originally opened as a beach along the bank of the Danube in 1919, the **Palatinus Strand** (tel. 1/340-4505, www.spasbudapest.com, Apr. 27-Sept. 1 daily 9am-7pm, 2,600 Ft) was transformed into an open-air complex upon construction of its immense pool in 1921. Fed by the island's thermal springs, the grounds now boast three thermal pools, an artificial wave pool, a water slide, Ping-Pong tables, trampolines, and a whole host of snack bars. Very popular and a tremendous amount of fun, this complex is one reason to bring your swimsuit if you plan on visiting the island, as many have regretted not doing so upon hearing the squeals of laughter and merrymaking that emanate from within the grounds.

Dominican Convent

The ruins of the Dominican Convent, dating back to the 13th century, are arguably the most significant site on the island. Founded by King Béla IV following the Mongol invasion, this became the home of his daughter Princess Margaret, famed for curing lepers and performing other selfless deeds. A marble plaque in the nave of the ruins marks the spot where she was buried and is oftentimes adorned with fresh flowers and lit candles by Hungarians who continue to adore her.

The Promenade of Hungarian Artists begins near the convent—a series of busts featuring some of the nation's finest and most important writers, composers, and the like. Among the famous are Béla Bartok, József Attila, and Franz Liszt.

Nearby is the pretty **St. Michael's Provostship Church of the Premonstratensians,** which can be traced back to the 12th century. Completely destroyed during the Turkish wars in 1541, it wasn't until 1923 when its ruins were excavated. It was reconstructed in 1930-1931 and possesses Hungary's oldest bell, fashioned by Master John Strous in the 15th century.

Northern End

At the far northern end of the island lies a quaint **rock garden** containing twisting little paths and tiny footbridges that wind past pretty ponds, exotic plants, and an artificial waterfall. Turtles and ducklings inhabit the water, something which the kids find entertaining, spending half their time feeding them and the other half frightening them.

THE BUDA HILLS

If you're looking to get away from it all and want to lose yourself in magical natural surroundings, the overwhelmingly beautiful Buda Hills are the perfect place to do so. Densely wooded and dotted with the occasional isolated neighborhood, the hills offer peace of mind and fantastic views that simply cannot be beat. Countless trails lead in and around the area, and while relatively busy during the weekends, it's possible to come here on a weekday and stroll for hours without ever being disturbed. It's easy to forget that you're still within the confines of a city, falling effortlessly into dream states impossible to experience anywhere down below. When you've had your fill of peace and quiet and want to see what sights draw countless visitors in year after year, head for the railroad circuit and let the trains do the climbing.

◖ The Railroad Circuit

One of the most entertaining and breathtaking ways to see the vast Buda Hills is via the railroad circuit, which consists of the Cog-Wheel Railroad and the Children's Railroad. You can spend just a couple of hours if you're in a hurry, or take a more relaxed half day, drinking in the scenery and enjoying the ride more than any particular destination.

Szoborpark (Memento Park)

When Communism finally ended in Hungary, there was much debate as to what to do with all the statues, dedicated to the dreaded political regime, that still decorated the streets. Many wanted to throw them out, eager to quickly forget what had brought so much pain and hardship. Thankfully, cooler heads prevailed, and a collection of 42 statues, memorials, and busts now fill Memento Park—a fascinating outdoor museum that attracts over 40,000 Hungarian and foreign visitors annually, all of whom come to see this remarkable collection reflecting the country's past period of Communist cultural politics. The park includes statues of Lenin, Marx, and Engels as well as memorials dedicated to the Soviet Soldier, Communist Martyrs, and the Republic of Councils, to name just a few. Designed by Akos Eleőd, Memento Park was opened on June 23, 1993, on the second anniversary of the withdrawal of Russian troops from the country. It is both an eyeopener and a history lesson, a living testament to the way things were not that long ago. The park takes approximately 45 minutes to explore, and there's a souvenir shop that sells an informative booklet that includes the history of each exhibit, accompanied by interesting photographs depicting their original locations around town. Predictably, the shop also sells a variety of Communist kitsch, including replicas of Lenin statues, Trabant cars, original Soviet medals, postcards, watches, stamps, and, of course, goofy T-shirts. For those wondering why Stalin isn't represented, the answer is easy: The sole Stalin statue in Budapest was destroyed during the revolution of 1956 when an angry mob brought it down and chopped it up into indiscernible little bits.

FOGASKEREKŰ VASÚT (COG-WHEEL RAILROAD)

Despite being a rather popular tourist attraction, the **Cog-Wheel Railroad** (Városmajor Station, daily 5am-11pm, 300 Ft) is nevertheless an official part of Budapest's tram network. Climbing up 1,066 feet and winding its way through 2.3 miles of track from Városmajor Station (across the street from the Hotel Budapest on Szilágyi Erzsébet fasor in Buda) to Széchenyi Hill, it is a wonderful, picturesque 20-minute trip to the hills that every visitor should experience. It was built in 1874 according to the plans of Swiss engineer Ferenc Salesi Cathry, and its original purpose was to transport residents of Svábhegy (Swabian Hill) to and from their villas. It was only the third steam-traction carriage in Europe at the time, and the line became so popular that it was extended in 1890 to its current terminus. In 1929 it was converted to electric traction out of respect for the environment. One thing that usually comes as a surprise to first-timers is that the route has very few straight stretches; it mainly runs in curves.

GYERMEKVASÚT (CHILDREN'S RAILROAD)

Located a short walk from the Cog-Wheel Railroad's last stop (Széchenyi Hill) is the delightful **Children's Railroad** (www.gyermekvasut.hu, trains run approximately every 45 minutes June-Aug. daily 9am-7pm, Sept.-May Tues.-Sun. 9am-5pm, 1,200 Ft roundtrip). Jokingly referred to as the "greatest toy in the world," this 6.8-mile-long stretch through the Buda Hills was completed in 1951 and originally run by the Communist Youth Organization, who called it the Pioneer Railroad. Today, children ages 10-14 operate switches and signals, print tickets, and keep amused passengers informed of upcoming stops—all in full MÁV (Hungarian State Railroad) uniforms. For those of you wondering, the driver of the train is indeed an adult. A one-way trip takes 45 minutes.

The railroad's first stop is **Normafa.** During the summer, you'll find plenty of locals who have come to escape the daily grind of Budapest. In the winter, the place is packed with ski and snowboard enthusiasts who make the best of what little snow stays on the ground. Another popular stop is **János-hegy.** From here, it's but a few minutes climb up to the top, which, at 1,736 feet, is Budapest's highest point. At the summit you'll find the **Erzsébet Lookout Tower,** named after the much-loved queen during the Austro-Hungarian Empire.

The tower is 77 feet tall and offers remarkable panoramic views of the city and hills. Nearby is the **Libegő** chairlift (Zugligeti út 97, May 15-Sept. 15 daily 9am-7pm, Sept. 16-May 14 daily 10am-3pm, 1,400 Ft roundtrip), which, despite the rather lengthy lines during the summer, offers an enjoyable ride down to **Zugliget,** where you can catch a local bus back to Széll Kálmán Square.

Entertainment and Events

Budapest's nightlife is always vibrant regardless of the time of year. Whether it's trendy Raday Street or Franz Liszt Square, come-as-you-are pubs like Szimpla Kert, or legendary live music venues like Old Man's Music Pub, there is always something happening in the big city to satisfy your inner night owl.

BARS
The Belváros
Taking its name from colorful New York Prohibition agent "Fat Mo" Smith, who, along with his partner Izadore "Izzy" Einstein, made 4,397 arrests and impounded over five million bottles of illegal hooch, **Fat Mo's Music Club** (V. Nyári pál utca 11, Belváros, tel. 1/266-8027, www.fatmo.hu, Sun.-Wed. 5pm-1am, Thurs.-Sat. 5pm-3am) is an excellent choice for fans of blues, soul, or jazz. Friendly English-speaking staff guide you through the extensive menu, which boasts 20 kinds of steak and a cuisine that ranges from Cajun to Mexican fare, not to mention the enviable list of whiskey and wine. This is a fun place any night of the week and easily one of the livelier joints off Váci Street.

If it's tasty pub food you're after, try the ever-popular **Irish Cat Pub** (V. Múzeum körút 41, tel. 1/266-4085, www.irishcat.hu, Sun.-Tues. 5pm-2am, Sat. 3pm-2am, Thurs.-Sat. 3pm-4am), a traditional Irish pub known for its fast, friendly, and attentive service. A happy-go-lucky mixture of Hungarians, expats, and tourists occupy the bar area, while diners dig into delicious Angus steaks under low, rather romantic lighting. The burgers are also delicious and so huge you can barely get your mouth around them. Although slightly pricey by Hungarian standards, it's well within Western traveler budgets and more than fair considering the quality. It's a fine choice for dinner or a couple of drinks when the day's sightseeing is done.

Silenus Étterem & Pub (V. Petőfi Sándor utca 17-19, tel. 20/999-2211, www.silenusetterem.hu, daily 10am-dawn) is a nonstop pub known mostly for its immense global beer selection. Over 100 brews are in stock here as well as a healthy number of ciders, wines, and cocktails. This laid-back watering hole tends to get busy most nights, as does its charming outdoor terrace, although it thins out to a small number of hard-core beer enthusiasts as the night turns into morning. It's well worth a try if you're anywhere near Váci Street, no matter what hour of the day.

Lipótváros
Popular with expats, visitors, and beautiful people of all nationalities, **Café Negro** (V. Szent István tér 11, tel. 1/302-0136, Sun.-Wed. noon-1am, Thurs.-Sat. noon-2am) is a slick cocktail bar-café that has something going on almost every night of the week. During the summer its outdoor patio offers stunning lit-up views of St. Stephen's Basilica, which makes up for the rather pricey drinks.

Advertising itself as Budapest's only authentic Irish pub, **Beckett's Irish Bar**

(V. Bajcsy-Zsilinszky út 72, tel. 1/311-1035, www.becketts.hu, Sun.-Thurs. noon-1am, Fri.-Sat. noon-2am) is a warm, spacious establishment that occupies two vast rooms. Very popular with foreigners, the pub has a huge wraparound bar and outdoor seating during the summer months, which is perfect for people-watching. The prices are a little higher than most in the city, but the English sausages and extensive drinks menu make it well worth it.

Located near Parliament, **Macskafogó Music Pub** (V. Nádor utca 29, tel. 30/921-4666, www.macskafogo.hu, Fri.-Sat. 8pm-4am) is a solid choice if you're looking for something simple yet interesting, dependable yet fun. There's a wide range of drinks on offer as well as a giant TV screen with the latest sports, and a dance floor that fills up as the night flows on. This is the place to go when you can't figure out where to go.

Located inside the art house cinema Toldi, the **Toldi Café** (V. Bajcsy-Zsilinszky út 36-38, tel. 1/472-0397, http://toldimozi.hu, daily

Rom Kocsma (Ruin Pubs)

"Ruin pubs" are drinking holes that spring up unannounced and without any form of advertising in the courtyards and gardens of unused or condemned buildings. They can range from three-level affairs to 10-room party fests, and while some last a mere month or two, others flourish, catching on with the locals and revitalizing what was once a quiet and mostly ignored residential street.

Seeing as they're all unmarked, the only way to identify a ruin pub is by observing two common telltale signs: people drifting in and out of a sketchy building with plastic cups of beer, and a beefy guy incessantly hushing people so as to not disturb the neighborhood's residents.

Crowds tend to be young and cosmopolitan, drinks are on the cheap side, the furniture a ragtag assortment of loose odds and ends, and once inside, you may very well find yourself in the middle of a dance party, an alternative art exhibit, or both.

10am-2am) is a hip, laid-back environment teeming with locals and artsy types catching up with friends or the latest celluloid hero. Likeminded readers should definitely pop their heads in at least once.

Terézváros and Erzsébetváros

Arguably Budapest's biggest bar opening of 2010, the bar **400** (VII. Kazinczy utca 52b, tel. 20/776-0765, www.400bar.hu, Sun.-Wed. 11am-3am, Thurs.-Sat. 11am-5am) has already become a nightlife staple in the Jewish quarter. A large rectangular bar sits in its center, staffed by nearly a dozen busy bar staff serving up reasonably priced drinks in dimly lit, tall-ceilinged surroundings. DJs spin most weekend nights, and a large outdoor terrace accommodates late-night revelers once spring kicks in.

A mixed crowd of travelers and local revelers can be found drinking and dancing the night away at **Alcatraz** (VII. Nyár utca 1, tel. 1/413-1152, www.alcatraz.hu, Thurs.-Sun. 6pm-5am). As its name suggests, the interior is designed to resemble a prison, although there's certainly nothing here that limits anyone's freedom. The friendly, casual staff can be found enjoying themselves as much as anybody else, and the infectious jazz and salsa music will have you pining for an extended sentence.

Bar Ladino (VII. Dob utca 53, tel. 30/874-3733, www.ladino.hu, Sun.-Tues. noon-1am, Wed. noon-3am, Thurs.-Sat. noon-4am), with its high ceiling, wooden tables, spacious surroundings, and local art on the walls is an excellent place to hang out and catch up with friends. It fills up quickly thanks to its affordable drinks and decent pub-type fare, so get here early and soak up the relaxed contemporary atmosphere.

Despite its exposed brick walls and deliberate lack of design, **Kisüzem** (VII. Kis Diófa utca 2, tel. 70/235-4023, Mon.-Wed. noon-2am, Thurs.-Sat. noon-3am, Sun. noon-2am) nevertheless affects an intimate vibe that's typical of the seventh district. You might find a few paintings on the wall now and again showcasing local talent, but simplicity is the name of the game here. An excellent choice

Fat Mo's Music Club

for those interested in conversation over conversation pieces.

Crazy Café (VI. Jókai utca 30, tel. 1/302-4003, www.crazycafe.hu, daily noon-1am) is an incredibly popular bar whose long counter and tables in the back are nearly always full. There's plenty of cheer to go around, as it seems to strike a chord with just about everybody who walks through the door. The vaulted ceiling and walls covered with images of celebrities give this place its own distinct feel, and the reasonable prices, coupled with friendly service, are just the right ingredients to make this a fun, memorable night out.

Cheap beer, street-smart decor, and an overall grungy feel make **Kuplung** (VI. Király utca 46, tel. 30/755-3527, Sun.-Thurs. 5pm-3am, Fri.-Sat. 5pm-5am) a fave with the laid-back, fun-seeking student crowd. Although about as basic as a bar can get, its lack of pretense and emphasis on simply having a good time make this a must-stop for anyone who appreciates a bar's character more than its fancy cocktails or clientele.

Located just around the corner from the Opera House, **Morrison's Music Pub** (VI. Révay utca 25, tel. 1/269-4060, www.morrisons.hu, Mon.-Sat. 7pm-4am) packs them in nightly with catchy tunes, karaoke shows, and nightly drink specials. Popular with the 20-something expat and traveler crowd, this is one of those places where you can easily strike up a conversation with an utter stranger and end up spending the rest of the night becoming friends. It's ridiculously easy to lose track of the time here as well, but nobody ever seems to complain.

Popular with students and night owls alike, **Lámpás** (VII. Dob utca 15, www.alampas.hu, daily 5pm-late) has been everyone's go-to after-hours bar for quite some time now. Exposed walls, haphazard art on the walls, and bookshelves of obscure tomes add to the footloose and fancy-free vibe. Bring a friend and check your ego at the door.

Pótkulcs (VI. Csengery utca 65/B, tel. 1/269-1050, http://potkulcs.hu, Sun.-Wed. 5pm-1:30am, Thurs.-Sat. 5pm-2:30am) is about as typical a bar as you can find in Budapest, from its laid-back outdoor courtyard in the summer to its friendly, beer-drenched indoor venue during the colder seasons. Its popularity rages on with hipsters who don't seem to need much in the way of ostentatious decoration to enjoy themselves and the people around them. This place is perfect for those who want a true taste of the city's bohemian nightlife.

Not far from the Great Synagogue is **Szoda** (VII. Wesselényi utca 18, tel. 1/461-0007, www.szoda.com, Mon.-Thurs. noon-3am, Fri. noon-5am, Sat. 5pm-5am), a comfortable, totally unpretentious, very red bar with old furniture and Japanese anime on the ceiling. It attracts a wide variety of clientele, including students, businesspeople, and those who come for the free Wi-Fi. The prices are cheap, the

A Shot Of *Pálinka*

Almost always served as a shot, *pálinka* is an integral part of Hungarian drinking culture. The word's origin comes from the Slavic word *páliť* (distill). Typically made from plums, apples, pears, apricots, and sometimes cherries, it is a type of brandy that was traditionally an essential part of a villager's diet, which also consisted of items such as bread, lard, and fatty bacon. A shot of *pálinka* would help with digestion and send the imbiber back out to work with a smile. Today, *pálinka* remains an inescapable part of Hungarian culture, finding its way to most tables as the night wears on. Jokingly referred to as "firewater," it typically weighs in at a 40-percent alcohol level, but is no match for the more powerful varieties of the drink commonly referred to as *kerítésszaggató* in Hungarian, which literally means "fence-tearer." These merciless homemade concoctions are not available in stores but are nevertheless common. Simply ask a local Hungarian if they have any and they will take great pride in explaining that their home-brewed *pálinka* is not only better than the commercially available kind but that it will knock your socks off as well. Trust me, they're not kidding.

staff is friendly, and the music is chill. There's also a downstairs, for those who like their parties on the after-hours side of things.

You can trace the roots of **Fészek** (VII. Kertész utca 36, tel. 1/342-6549, www.feszek-muveszklub.hu, daily 8pm-6am) back to the Communist era as it was formerly a Communist artists' club. A huge staircase takes you past large stained glass windows and into a whole lot of fun. There's a beer hall downstairs, a couple of dining areas, a gallery, and a TV room. The large pink courtyard is always full in the summertime, but that shouldn't stop you from heading here and trying to find a seat.

Located opposite the Great Synagogue, **Katapult** (VII. Dohány utca 1, tel. 1/266-7226, daily 10am-2am) is considered one of the better "starter" bars in the area. Loud music and cheap drinks combined with hip bar staff and an irreverent attitude keep Katapult full till the closing bell.

Szimpla Kert (VII. Kazinczy utca 14, tel. 20/261-8669, www.szimpla.hu, daily noon-4am) is a prime example of Budapest's so-called "ruin pubs." Decorated simply (hence the name) with a ragtag mixture of used furniture placed haphazardly throughout its open courtyard, this is one of those places *everybody* in town has been to at least once. It's filled with laid-back locals and open-minded visitors looking for a dose of the authentic. Its utter lack of pretension and casual atmosphere will most likely have you back at least once more during your stay.

Csak Art Bar (VII. Síp utca 4, tel. 30/465-3735, Mon.-Thurs. 4pm-2am, Fri.-Sat. 4pm-4am) is a relative newcomer to the seventh district that's already established itself as a contender for your nighttime attentions. Plenty of eye candy on the walls includes bizarre collages and misshapen mannequins as well as a fantastic array of music being spun that's heavy on hip hop and reggae. It's well worth a visit.

El Rapido (VII. Kazinczy utca 10, tel. 30/279-2861, www.elrapido.hu, Mon.-Thurs. 10:30am-3am, Fri. 10:30am-4am, Sat. noon-4am, Sun. noon-1am) is a mix of café, Mexican pub, flea market, and whatever else you can

© TOM DIRLIS

El Rapido is a café, Mexican pub, flea market…and whatever else you can think of.

think of. It serves delicious burritos, tacos, and quesadillas on the main floor, while all kinds of fun and crazy activity happens downstairs in its ruin pub proper. It's an excellent place to begin or end your bender.

Kék Ló (VII. Kazinczy utca 11, www.tothvirag.com, Mon.-Sat. noon-midnight), or "Blue Horse," is a unique "cloth pub" in that it not only serves up beer and booze to its customers but also fashionable clothing by bar owner and designer Virág Tóth as well. The clothes themselves are on display on run-down shelves and cupboards that lend a decidedly cozy vibe to the place, as do the friendly faces that tend to populate the place.

Józsefváros and Ferencváros

Andersen Dán Étterem és Söröző (VIII. Krúdy Gyula utca 17, tel. 61/781-5551, www.andersenpub.hu, Mon.-Sat. 1pm-2am) offers its own homebrew for the remarkably low price of 1,199 Ft per "meter," meaning ten 0.3-liter glasses. No wonder the place is packed nightly

with fun-loving hopped-up students who keep the place lively till closing time. There are plenty of tables in the labyrinthine cellar, although the bar's manic and flirtatious atmosphere may very well keep you on your feet all night.

Artsy little **Macska** (VIII. Bérkocsis utca 23, tel. 70/372-4725, daily 11am-2am) opened in March 2010 and became an instant hit with the Bohemian set. The space above the bar is used as a gallery, offering light projections and pillows for those who feel like lounging, while the main floor is decked out with comfortable used furniture. Darkly lit, friendly, and what we might commonly call "alternative," Macska is a great place to either chill and chat or start a bar crawl.

Located on trendy Ráday Street, **Jaffa** (IX. Ráday utca 39, tel. 1/219-5285, www.jaffakavehaz.hu, Mon.-Thurs. noon-1am, Fri.-Sat. noon-2am, Sun. 2pm-2pm) is a hip retro-style DJ bar that showcases some of the city's hottest talent on the weekends. The interior is sleek and modern, the atmosphere jovial, and the cocktail list nice and long. This is a perfect place to let your hair down after a day full of traveling or sightseeing.

Housed in two rooms, **Muzikum** (VIII. Múzeum utca 7, tel. 20/221-7767, www.muzikum.hu, Mon.-Wed. 10am-1am, Thurs. 10am-2am, Fri. 10am-3am, Sat. 5am-3am) is both a friendly student-type café and popular music club featuring the finest in jazz, folk, underground, and anything else it feels worthy of showcasing. Tastefully decorated and centrally located, this is an excellent choice for anyone with an eclectic artistic bent.

Buda Castle, Újbuda, and Víziváros

Situated adjacent to Elizabeth Bridge at the foot of Gellért Hill, **Romkert** (I. Döbrentei tér 9, tel. 30/351-5217, www.romkert.eu, Tues.-Sat. noon-3am) is a popular spot for both local students and youthful tourists to meet, which renders this relatively small venue a tad on the overcrowded side on most nights. Nevertheless, it's an excellent place to make new friends while

BUDAPEST

Das ist ein Unikum!

Legend has it that when Kaiser Joseph II of Austria was presented with a strong digestive liqueur by his court physician, Dr. Zwack, the Habsburg monarch exclaimed, *"Das ist ein Unikum!"* (That is special/unique!). Soon after, a relative of the good doctor standardized the recipe and established the Unicum brand. It went on to become one of Hungary's most requested spirits and has maintained its popularity for over 200 years. Made from 40 different herbs and spices, it is best appreciated at room temperature and is reputed to aid digestion. Tar black in color with a syrupy consistency, it tastes somewhat like Jägermeister but is considerably earthier, has a bitter aftertaste, and packs a wallop. It's considered a tad too strong for the average Western palate, although those not brave enough to try the original might be interested in giving Unicum Next a try. Thinner, lighter, and cherry-flavored, it has quickly gained female fans and Western devotees.

blowing off some summer steam. There's no cover charge, but you'll see why when you order a drink, so be forewarned.

Rézmál Café (II. Marczibányi tér 5/a, tel. 70/391-9750, http://rezmal.hu, Mon.-Sat. 2pm-2am, Sun. 2pm-midnight) is a relaxed, simply decorated, straightforward bar-café featuring live music on the weekends. If you're looking for a place on the Buda side conducive to reasonable prices and friendly conversation, you just found it.

Szatyor Bar (XI. Bartók Béla utca 36, tel. 1/279-0290, szatyorbar.blog.hu, Mon.-Fri. noon-1am, Sat.-Sun. 2pm-1am) is a large, colorful, and friendly place sporting a ruin-pub feel that's popular with the younger crowd. Live music and literary readings are a common occurrence, making this an excellent place to party on a Saturday night or chill out on a slow Sunday afternoon.

CLUBS

Those in desperate need of a nightcap ought to seriously consider **Corvintető** (VIII. Blaha Lujza tér 1-2, tel. 20/772-2983, daily 6pm-6am, cover varies). Occupying the top floor and rooftop of the 1970s-style Corvin department store, this after-hours club has been a hot spot with locals and visitors for years. The deep-red dancehall on the top floor throws legendary breakbeat, dubstep, and house parties, while the wide-open patio up top offers gorgeous panoramic views of the city and is an excellent place to wind down and watch the sun come up. It's an excellent bet any day of the week.

A hit with the young, hip, night-is-for-dancing crowd, **Instant** (VI. Nagymező utca 38, tel. 1/311-0704, www.instant.co.hu, daily 1pm-4am, no cover) hosts underground DJs in its cellar, which is crammed with a high-energy crowd shaking their collective moneymaker. The summer months see its massive two-story courtyard open as well as four themed bars equally bursting to capacity. This is definitely the place to come to if you're looking for that loose house-party feel.

Hugely popular with students and 20-somethings, **Living Room** (Kossuth Lajos utca 17, tel. 70/366-3723, www.livingroom.hu, Fri.-Sat. 10pm-5am, cover varies) comprises two basic halls playing different types of music that ranges from Hungarian to top-40 hits. There are no real surprises here, although the club does offer a number of small rooms with curtains that can separate you from the throng should you want to party with your old group of friends or the ones you just met.

Mix (VI. Teréz körút 55-57, tel. 1/301-0528, www.buddha-beach.hu, Fri. noon-5am, Sat. 6pm-5am) is a stylish venue modeled after the trendy clubs of Ibiza and Miami. Top local DJs spin the day's hottest tunes while beautiful young people shake and shimmy on a dance

© TOM DIRLIS

Gödör Klub

floor punctuated with sophisticated lights and lasers. Mojito, anyone?

Piaf (VI. Nagymező utca 25, Terézváros, tel. 1/708-3166, daily 10pm-6am, 1,500 Ft) is not only named after the famous crooner, but it evokes the feel of decadent Paris that is impossible not to love. Plush red furnishings, seductive live jazz, and a downstairs disco that gets pretty wild as the night rages on make this a night out you won't soon forget.

One of the biggest and most popular outdoor summer venues is **Zöld Pardon** (XI. Neumann János utca 2, tel. 1/279-1880, www.zp.hu, Wed.-Sat. noon-5am, cover varies), located in the South-Buda university district by the Rákóczi Bridge. Catering to a predominantly young crowd, its DJ nights are huge hits, as are their live shows featuring all kinds of diverse bands from Hungary and abroad.

LIVE MUSIC

Formerly a Ukrainian stone-carrier whose seafaring days are now well behind it, **A38** (XI. Petőfi Bridge, Buda side, tel. 1/464-3940, www.a38.hu, daily 11am-4am, cover varies) is one of the more unique venues in town to take in a show, permanently moored on the Buda side of Petőfi Bridge, just south of Gellért hegy. Its concert hall is located in the ship's bowels and there is also a restaurant on hand should you get the munchies. During the summer months, the terrace is open and thumps to familiar dance-friendly beats.

In the heart of Erzsébet tér lies the all-purpose übercool **Gödör Klub** (V. Király utca 8-10, Belváros, www.godorklub.hu, Mon.-Wed. 6pm-2am, Thurs.-Sat. 6pm-4am, cover varies), host to a wide range of exhibits, fairs, music concerts, and just about anything else artistic you can think of. This versatile multiple-room space is a favorite during the summer months when hipsters of all shapes and sizes lounge on the steps with a bottle of beer and soak up the sun's rays. This is a great place to people-watch, chill out with friends, and catch some of the local up-and-coming talent.

Szikra Cool Tour House (VI. Teréz körút 62, tel. 1/911-0911, www.szikra.eu, Mon.-Thurs.

BUDAPEST

8am-2am, Fri. 8am-6am, Sat. 10am-6am, Sun. 10am-2am) is a popular, spacious hall offering truly unique cultural experiences thanks to its ever-changing program of the newest, most challenging cinema, theater, and musical concerts around. Anyone interested in what Budapest's alternative arts scene is really about should waste no time getting here.

If you're a fan of live jazz and blues, make a beeline for the **Old Man's Music Pub** (VII. Akácfa utca 13, Erzsébetváros, tel. 1/322-7645, www.oldmans.hu, daily 4:30pm-4am, cover varies). Attracting some of the finest acts in the country, this huge club is packed nightly with a friendly and appreciative crowd. Keep in mind that reservations are a must if you feel like sampling the tasty cuisine.

THE ARTS

A stroll down Nagymező Street, affectionately dubbed "Budapest's Broadway," is enough to assure fans of the arts that the scene is thriving. But it's not just here that one can indulge. Vörösmarty Square and the underpasses of subway stations around town act as ad hoc venues for local buskers entertaining passersby with traditional Hungarian folk music. The magnificent Opera House affords audiences a taste of gifted musicians from around the globe, the Merlin International Theater stages critically acclaimed English-language productions, the Madách Theater plays host to some of the world's most successful musicals, and the Trafó House of Contemporary Arts continues to push the envelope when it comes to modern dance. No matter where your tastes lie, Budapest always has something going on that is sure to both please and inspire even the most demanding of audiences.

Theater

The **Merlin Nemzetközi Színház (Merlin International Theater)** (V. Gerlóczy utca 4, Belváros, tel. 1/317-9338, www.merlinszinhaz.hu, box office Mon.-Fri. 11am-7pm) is a multipurpose arts center, cultural institute, and theater all rolled into one. Nearly half of its repertoire is in English and based on famous international works. Fans of the theater, however, should keep their eyes open for the occasional and usually exceptional Hungarian play translated and performed by local English-speaking talent.

Located one block over on the opposite side of the Opera is the often-overlooked **Új Színház (New Theater)** (VI. Paulay Ede utca 35, Terézváros, tel. 1/269-6021, www.ujszinhaz.hu, box office daily 2pm-7pm). Built in 1907, its art deco facade was designed by Béla Lajta, and its grandiose neo-baroque auditorium comes to us from László Vágó. Formerly the Ballet Institute, this theater has gone through plenty of changes over the years but now offers classic and contemporary Hungarian plays as well as renowned international works. The theater also houses a successful acting school and gallery that offer visual artists the opportunity to introduce their work to a wider audience.

Located in Budapest's vibrant theater district, the **Budapesti Operettszinház (Budapest Operetta Theater)** (VI. Nagymező utca 17, Terézváros, tel. 1/312-4866, www.operettszinhaz.hu, box office Mon.-Fri. 10am-7pm, Sat.-Sun. 1pm-7pm) is a wonderful venue whose past shows have included some of the world's most famous musicals, such as *My Fair Lady, Fiddler on the Roof,* and *West Side Story.* Fully reconstructed at the turn of the millennium, the theater blends the finest in modern stage technology with early-20th-century period furnishings to create a warm, inspiring evening at the theater.

The **Madách Színház (Madách Theater)** (VII. Erzsébet körút 29-33, Erzsébetváros, tel. 1/478-2000, www.madachszinhaz.hu, daily 1pm-6:30pm) was reconstructed in 1999 and possesses three different stages. Its main venue, also known as the Great House, seats just over 800 and regularly plays host to smash musicals like *Cats, Phantom of the Opera,* and *The Producers.* Its second stage is found in the Tolnay Szalon, which typically bases its program on the works of important figures in the world of Hungarian theater. The third stage is found in the Madách Studio, a comfortable

© TOM DIRLIS

Modern technology meets turn-of-the-20th-century furnishings at the Budapest Operetta Theater.

theater seating 180 that hosts professional productions of the medium's most famous playwrights, including William Shakespeare, Anton Chekhov, and Arthur Miller.

Having survived years of political acrimony, revisions, and canceled contracts, the **Nemzeti Színház (National Theater)** (IX. Bajor Gizi Park 1, Ferencváros, tel. 1/476-6868, www.nemzetiszinhaz.hu, Mon.-Fri. 10am-6pm, Sat.-Sun. 2pm-6pm) finally managed to open its doors in 2002. Located along the bank of the Danube, it tends to rely on the classics, including Molière, William Shakespeare, and Anton Chekhov. Despite its spotty and very public history, the theater continues to persevere, believing, as all good theaters do, that the show must go on.

Classical Music and Dance

Designed by Miklós Ybl, Hungary's most important architect of the 19th century, the **Magyar Állami Operaház (Hungarian State Opera House)** (VI. Andrássy út 22, Terézváros, tel. 1/353-0170, www.opera.hu, box office Mon.-Sat. 11am-beginning of performance, Sun. 4pm-beginning of performance) is truly a sight to behold. Completed in 1884, this outstanding example of neo-Renaissance elegance is considered one of Hungary's most important buildings, and it's easy to see why. Its stunning facade is decorated with 16 statues depicting some of history's greatest classical composers, including Mozart, Beethoven, Verdi, and Tchaikovsky. Inside, the massive lobby, grand staircase, and horseshoe-shaped auditorium—in which over 15 pounds of gold were used and whose breathtaking frescoed ceiling was decorated by none other than Károly Lotz—are enough to make you want to return again and again. A tour of the premises (daily at 3pm and 4pm, 2,900 Ft) is highly recommended, as is a show, where you pay a relatively small amount to be automatically transported back to centuries of old. Music fans will definitely not want to miss this.

Located at the end of the square is the **Liszt Ferenc Zeneakadémia (Franz Liszt Academy of Music)** (VI. Liszt Ferenc tér 8, Terézváros, www.zeneakademia.hu), an impressive art nouveau building that is one of the most recognizable in Budapest. It was founded on November 14, 1875, by the pianist and composer himself, although its current incarnation came in 1907 when it was designed by Flóris Korb and Kálmán Giergl at the behest of then-Minister of Culture, Baron Gyula Wlassics. The building's facade includes a statue of Liszt that was sculpted by Alajos Stróbl, and its colorful interior is adorned with frescoes, Zsolnay ceramics, and numerous statues of various significant composers. It now operates as both a concert hall and a music university. You can often hear students practicing, the strains of their soothing, soaring classical music spilling out onto the street.

Informally referred to as the "Peoples' Opera," the **Erkel Színház (Erkel Theater)** (VIII. II. János Pál pápa tér 30, Józsefváros, tel. 1/333-0540, www.opera.hu, box office Tues.-Sat. 11am-beginning of performance,

Sun. 4pm-beginning of performance) impressively seats up to 2,400 people. Built in 1911, it currently serves as the State Opera and Ballet's second home. While some consider it subpar compared to the grand Opera House, it nevertheless fills up nightly with people coming to enjoy the seasonal offerings that include both classic theatrical works and excellent chamber orchestra concerts.

Built in 1909, the **Trafó Kortárs Művészetek Háza (Trafó House of Contemporary Arts)** (IX. Liliom utca 41, Ferencváros, tel. 1/215-1600, www.trafo.hu, box office daily 4pm-8pm) is housed in what used to be the electrical transformer station for south Pest. In the early 1990s a French avant-garde group found the space, which had been left unused for roughly 40 years, and began putting on shows. It was eventually bought by the Budapest City Council, and Trafó opened its doors for the first time during the 1998 Budapest Spring Festival. Focusing on a wide variety of modern dance styles and interpretations, it remains on the cutting edge of all things contemporary, including hugely successful dance programs and two annual music festivals focusing on electronic dance music. The building is also home to the **Trafó Gallery** (Tues.-Sun. 4pm-7pm), which presents eight or nine exhibitions a year in support of young emerging artists, along with the hip **Trafó Bar Tango** (tel. 1/456-2049, daily 6pm-4am), which serves up delicious food and excellent jazz acts in the building's basement. Anyone interested or involved in the arts should definitely make it a point to visit.

Opened in 2005, the **Művészetek Palotája (Palace of Arts)** (IX. Komor Marcell utca 1, Ferencváros, tel. 1/555-3001, www.mupa.hu, daily 10am-6pm) is a remarkable cultural complex that is home to the state-of-the-art National Concert Hall. Awarded the FIABCI Prix d'Excellence in 2006, which is equivalent to winning an Oscar for construction and real-estate development, the concert hall seats 1,699 people and hosts the finest acts in classical, jazz, and world music. Top-notch acoustics, a superb audio-visual system, and a remarkable concert organ make an evening here a truly world-class experience.

At Corvin Square you'll find the **Hungarian Heritage House** (I. Corvin tér 8, Víziváros, tel. 1/225-6049, www.heritagehouse.hu, box office daily 10am-6pm), Buda's answer to a concert hall whose "house band" is the superb Hungarian State Folk Ensemble. The group is the oldest of its kind in Hungary and performs folk dances from all corners of the country. Designed by Arkay Aladár and Kallina Mór, the hall was built between 1898 and 1900 and its art nouveau interior, with wide marble staircase and richly decorated theater hall, make it an excellent venue for fans of traditional music and dance.

Although lacking the distinct charm of older venues around town, the **Budapesti Kogresszusi Központ (Budapest Congress Center)** (XII. Jagelló út 1-3, Gellért hegy, tel. 1/372-5400, www.bcc.hu, box office Mon., Wed., and performance days 3pm-6pm), which also functions as a concert hall, is a surprisingly decent place to enjoy a performance. The acoustics are solid, the seats are plush, and its main room, the Pátria Hall, seats up to 1,800 and is both comfortable and spacious. Shows come and go, so make sure to visit the website for upcoming events.

The **Várszínház (Castle Theater)** (I. Színház utca 1-3, Várhegy, tel. 1/201-4407, www.dancetheatre.hu, box office Mon.-Thurs. 10am-5pm, Fri. 10am-4pm) originally served as a Carmelite Church in the mid-18th century but was rebuilt into a theater on the order of Emperor Joseph II. Its first Hungarian play was *Igaházi*, written by Kristóf Simai and performed on October 5, 1790. One of the theater's most famous guests was Ludwig van Beethoven, who performed here on May 7, 1800. Heavily damaged during World War II, it reopened again in 1978 and is now home to the highly successful National Dance Theater.

Cinemas

Cirko-Gejzir Cinema (V. Balassi Bálint utca 15, Lipotváros, tel. 1/269-1915, www.cirkogejzir.hu) is an excellent art-house theater whose two screening rooms show a wide variety of international, independent, and artistically oriented films. Keep in mind that the program changes daily, so make sure to check the website for showtimes. **Uránia** (VIII. Rákóczi út 21, Józsefváros, tel. 1/486-3400, www.urania-nf.hu) is without a doubt one of Budapest's most beloved and finest theaters. Designed in a Moorish-Venetian style by Henrik Schmahl, its gigantic 700-seat auditorium is more often than not the site of lively and enthusiastic crowds, particularly when the latest Hollywood blockbuster hits town.

The **Művész mozi** (VI. Teréz körút 30, Terézváros, tel. 1/459-5050, www.artmozi.hu) is one of the few alternative cinemas to be found in the city, debuting films from all over the world, including Asia, Europe, and the Americas. There are five screens, which means it shouldn't be too hard to find something interesting, or at least something with subtitles you can understand. There's also a shop in the main hall selling a variety of soundtracks, CDs, and books.

FESTIVALS AND EVENTS

Budapest's events calendar is full of happenings big and small. In spring is the incomparable Budapest Spring Festival, which attracts both musical and visual artists from around the world. During summer the streets and squares are filled with parades, dance festivals, and outdoor concerts on a weekly basis. Two of the season's biggest events are the monumental Sziget Festival and the bone-rattling Hungarian Formula 1 Grand Prix. Wine tasting is the name of the game during fall's Wine Festival, and the Christmas Market and Hungarian Film Week are just two reasons to leave the warmth of your hotel and mingle with winter's merrymakers.

Spring

The **Budapest Spring Festival** (various venues, www.festivalcity.hu, second half of Mar.) is Hungary's largest cultural event and showcases some of the country's finest musicians,

composers, and artists as well as exceptional international talent. Founded in 1981, the festival has grown to roughly 200 events held in 50-60 venues around town and features everything from orchestral and chamber concerts to jazz, contemporary dance, and film screenings. Visitors will do themselves a huge favor by attending at least a handful of the exciting events that keep the city buzzing for two whole weeks.

Summer

The **Sziget Festival** (Óbuda Island, www.sziget.hu, first half of Aug.) is by far the largest musical event to hit Hungary every year and is recognized as one of the world's premier music festivals. Folks from around the globe come to let loose and party hearty on the pretty green island in Óbuda, drinking up the countless shows on multiple stages held in over 60 venues. The island turns into a mini city that week, offering visitors banking services, restaurants, pubs, and shops, not to mention the opportunity to meet like-minded fans. Day passes, week passes, and camping permits are all available, and it's wise to reserve them well in advance as this is one event that is guaranteed to sell out time and again. Every year has a star-studded list of performers, which have included the Chemical Brothers, Nine Inch Nails, Toots and the Maytals, Nick Cave, and Blur.

The **Budapest Summer Festival** (Margaret Island, tel. 1/340-4196, www.szabadter.hu, June-Aug., box office daily 11am-7pm) delights both cultural tourists and fans of the arts alike by putting on highly enjoyable performances at the Margaret Island Open Air Stage, located on the northern tip of the island. There are a wide variety of productions to choose from, including Broadway shows, musicals, children's programs, classical concerts, and pop music performances. Tickets can be bought at the island or at any number of locations throughout the city as well as online from the festival's website.

Built in the mid-1980s, the Hungaroring was meant to invite the Formula 1 World Championship behind the then-iron curtain. Course designers chose Mogyoród, located

11 miles northeast of Budapest, and the **Hungarian Formula 1 Grand Prix** (Mogyoród, www.hungaroinfo.com, end of July-early Aug.) was born. Although one of the slowest tracks on the F1 calendar, race fans flock to the weekend event year after year, making it by far the most popular sporting event of the summer—one that has played host to such greats as Michael Schumacher, Jacques Villeneuve, Ayrton Senna, and Damon Hill. Tickets are typically bought online but can also be purchased at various box offices at the track throughout the three-day affair.

St. Stephen's Day (Aug. 20) is a public holiday that commemorates Hungary's first king. Stephen's biggest contribution to the Hungarian state was converting the nomadic Magyar people to Christianity, and he was canonized for his efforts on August 20, 1083. One of the day's main events is the procession of St. Stephen's holy right hand around the Basilica before returning it to its home inside. Traditional concerts, food and crafts stalls, children's programs, and a street parade all add to the city's festive mood. At night, follow the crowds to Gellért Hill and cap off the fun-filled day by enjoying the massive fireworks display over the Danube that lasts nearly 30 minutes.

Few, if any, events in Hungary are as much fun as the immensely popular **Budapest Parade** (Aug. 26). Seen as the last official event of the summer, the parade attracts hundreds of thousands of people who fill the city's streets and party the day away. Scantily clad youths, world-renowned DJs, and a convoy of over 50 colorful floats are just some of the things that make their way up Andrássy Avenue to the Városliget. The whole spectacle ends with an elaborate fireworks display, and then the real fun begins as most hip bars and clubs hold after-parade parties that rage on till the sun comes up. This is definitely one of those days you want circled on your calendar.

For over 200 years July 14 has symbolized French independence and national unity, and the **Bastille Day Carnival and Market** (I. Fo utca 17, tel. 1/489-4200, www.inst-france. hu, July 14 10am-midnight) is no different.

Sponsored by the nearby French Institute, the Bem quay is closed down for the day and turned into a colorful site that includes enthusiastic dancing and heartfelt singing. Countless booths line the street selling authentic French foods, handicrafts, and sweets, not to mention a large number of delicious wines. This is an excellent opportunity to immerse yourself in a wonderful culture and get caught up in a celebration that oozes joie de vivre.

One of Budapest's most interesting cultural events is the hugely successful **Night of Museums** (various venues, second half of June). Over 45 cities in Hungary open their museums' doors until the wee hours, allowing visitors access to the usual exhibitions as well as those that are generally kept out of the public eye. Budapest alone hosts roughly 400 programs held at over 50 venues; they include guided tours, film screenings, talks, concerts, and dance performances. Over 100,000 people have taken part in recent years, drinking wine and waxing cultural from one end of the city to the other. Entry stickers, which can be bought at participating museums, allow access to all of them as well as free transportation on specially marked buses reserved solely for the night's festivities. This is an incredible way to see all the city has to offer for less than a meal at an average restaurant; it's highly recommended.

With its inception in 1998, the **Jewish Summer Festival** (Erzsébetváros, tel. 1/413-5531, www.jewishfestival.hu, last week in Aug.) has gone on to introduce Jewish culture to an ever-growing number of people. Held the last week of the summer, visitors get a chance to learn more about a culture that stretches back thousands of years through various art forms, including film, theater, photography, readings, and music. Many local and international artists participate in the festival, making it a truly entertaining and informative week.

Fall

The **Budapest International Wine and Champagne Festival** (I. Buda Castle, tel. 1/203-8507, www.winefestival.hu, first half of Sept.) takes place during the first half of

September and is widely considered to be one of the country's most prestigious events. Visitors get the chance to rub elbows with viniculture's finest and learn all aspects of the industry. Food also plays a large role in the festivities, with a grill corner, a fish terrace, and a cauldron farm being just a handful of the gastronomical possibilities available to those not wishing to drink on an empty stomach. The festival's most popular event is the Wine Exhibition and Fair, which takes place at beautiful Buda Castle and allows Hungary's finest winemakers, along with top international merchants, to offer their wares to a very thirsty public. No wine lover should miss this.

The **Contemporary Arts Festival** (various venues, www.festivalcity.hu, early-mid-Oct.) focuses primarily on the contemporary arts in Hungary and attempts to familiarize the public with new artistic forms, trends, and ideas. The program itself is vast and includes dance, jazz, performance art, music, film, theater, and various exhibitions. Reduced from two weeks to 10 days for financial reasons, the festival

nevertheless continues to both educate and entertain art lovers who have been participating annually in ever-increasing numbers.

The **Budapest International Marathon** (throughout the city, tel. 1/273-0939, www.budapestmarathon.com, Oct.) has been "running" since 1984 and has been growing in size ever since. The marathon's starting point is impressive Heroes Square, which also hosts a fair full of show people, concerts, and various booths offering information on sports and lifestyle. Runners head down Andrássy Avenue and then continue past Gresham Palace, the Chain Bridge, Buda Castle, Margaret Island, and the mighty Parliament building. At the end of it all, competitors are given the opportunity to soak in the superb Széchenyi spa baths.

Winter

The **Christmas Market** (Vörösmarty tér, Dec. 1-24) in Budapest is a time-honored tradition loved and anticipated by both Hungarians and foreigners alike. Considered one of the better Christmas fairs in Europe, the market

© BRENDA KEAN/123RF

Budapest's traditional Christmas Market

is an excellent opportunity to buy beautiful handmade folk art and decorations. Roughly 150 programs are scheduled every year, including puppet theaters, folk bands, and dance troupes all joining in the yuletide fun. There's plenty of food available as well, with numerous stalls serving up scrumptious pastries and mulled wine. Two highlights of the market are a visit by the one and only Santa Claus, who listens to countless kids trying to convince him they've been good, and Café Gerbeaud, which becomes a living Advent Calendar as one window is opened daily at 5pm until Christmas Eve.

Established in 1965, the annual **Hungarian Film Week** (various venues, www. hungarianfilmweek.com, first week in Feb.) is the most important film festival in Hungary. All the films in competition are made by Hungarian artists looking to receive critical recognition for their work as well as reach a wider audience. In order to avoid bitter disputes in the past, the festival now has two major awards: Best "Author" Film, which recognizes artistic merit, and Best "Genre" Film, which gives the nod to the film with the most commercial potential. Although nowhere near the stature of the Berlin, Venice, or Cannes film festivals, Hungarian Film Week is nevertheless an excellent opportunity to stay abreast of what's happening in this very exciting and unpredictable medium.

Shopping

When it comes to shopping, the first name on every visitor's lips is Váci Street. This is where locals and tourists with a bit of money to burn come to have a look at what the pricey designer boutiques are offering. You'll find plenty of souvenir and gift shops here as well, peddling everything from traditional costumes to folk art. Many of these shops offer tourist-trap kitsch, but a bit of hunting around should reward you with a treasure or two. The Castle District sees its fair share of shoppers as well, with wine shops and art galleries getting the brunt of the business. Shopping malls abound and include Central Europe's largest, WestEnd City Center, as well as Buda's Mammut, both of which are almost always packed. There's also Andrássy Avenue, which, apart from boasting some of the finer buildings, restaurants, and cafés in town, has plenty of gift shops, boutiques, and bookstores to keep upscale shoppers very happy.

THE BELVÁROS AND LIPÓTVÁROS
Antiques
The state-owned **BÁV** (V. Ferenciek tere 10, tel. 1/318-3733, www.bav.hu, Mon.-Fri.

10am-6pm, Sat. 9am-2pm) has a stronghold on the antiques market in Hungary and has a handful of shops throughout the capital. Its shops specialize in fine art, chandeliers, porcelain, and carpets and tend to have a number of cheap surprises on hand. In case you were wondering, most of BÁV's inventory comprises goods seized by customs.

Located on a street that's home to more than a few antiques shops, **Darius Antiques** (V. Falk Miksa utca 24-26, tel. 1/311-2603, www.dariusantik.hu, Mon.-Sat. 10am-6pm) has had no trouble establishing itself over the years. Trying to distance itself and carve out its own niche in the realm of antiques hunting, it specializes in Biedermeier furniture as well as objets d'art and Viennese antiques.

Nagyházi Galéria (V. Balaton utca 8, tel. 1/475-6000, www.nagyhazi.hu, Mon.-Fri. 10am-6pm, Sat. 10am-1pm) is the largest of its kind in Budapest and mainly stocks furniture, porcelain, and paintings from both Hungarian and international artists. Auctions take place monthly and should be taken advantage of by any serious collector of antiques.

The **Polgár Gallery and Auction House** (V. Petőfi Sándor utca 16, tel. 1/267-4077,

Shopping on Váci Street

Váci Street is Budapest's most famous shopping strip, a mile-long pedestrian area that runs parallel to the Danube and stretches from Vörösmarty Square to Central Market Hall. Disrupted about half way down due to heavily congested Kossuth Lajos Street, its second half can easily be accessed via underpass at Elizabeth Bridge.

The northern part of the street, stretching from Vörösmarty Square to Elizabeth Bridge, is chock-full of well-known fashion outlets and fast food restaurants. Always bustling with locals and tourists bargain-hunting or grabbing a quick snack, it's easily the more congested of the two of Váci's halves, thanks in large part to internationally recognized establishments like Adidas, Mango, Estée Lauder, H&M,

Salamander, McDonald's, Burger King, KFC, and a whole lot more.

The southern part of the street, which runs from the Elizabeth Bridge to the Central Market Hall, is a slightly more subdued affair, focusing mainly on souvenir outlets, ice cream parlors, and family restaurants. You'll find no shortage of opportunities to shell out some of that vacation money on gifts and goulash, however, thanks to the bevy of men and women vying to get you into their restaurant or shop.

Odds are you won't find too many bargains on Váci, but its loose and energetic blend of locals, tourists, shoppers, and street musicians will undoubtedly win you over and have you coming back for one last stroll before you go.

www.polgar-galeria.hu, daily 10am-7pm) specializes in valuable works of art, along with jewelry, antique furniture, and various collectibles. Auctions are held regularly, and art lovers should definitely have a close look at what's on offer as there are many bargains to be had. Overseas visitors should make sure to confirm whether they'll need an export visa for whatever goods they're interested in before entering the bidding.

Art

You'll find some of the city's finest local handiwork at **Magma** (V. Petőfi Sándor utca 11, tel. 1/235-0277, www.magma.hu, Mon.-Fri. 10am-7pm, Sat. 10am-3pm), whose collective of inspired artisans produce exceptional ceramics and woodwork as well as colorful jewelry, embroidered pillows, and stylish handbags.

Rododendron (V. Semmelweis utca 19, tel. 70/419-5329, www.rododendron.hu, Mon.-Fri. 10am-7pm, Sat. 10am-4pm) showcases some of Hungary's finest artists, whose pieces range from cute fridge magnets to arresting artwork to creative clothing and accessories for the

hipster in all of us. Make sure to drop by this unique shop if time permits.

The **Judit Virág Gallery and Auction House** (V. Falk Miksa utca 30, tel. 1/312-2071, http://viragjuditgaleria.hu, Mon.-Fri. 10am-6pm, Sat. 10am-1pm) is a respected seller of quality Hungarian paintings circa the 19th and 20th centuries as well as an excellent variety of colorful Zsolnay ceramics. You'll find a decent collection of their art on display in their exhibition rooms, and even more online. They also hold auctions three times a year, which all serious collectors will want to keep an eye out for.

The **Vándorfény Galéria** (V. Kossuth utca 3, tel. 1/267-5262, www.vandorfeny.hu, Mon.-Fri. 10am-6pm) showcases the works of contemporary Hungarian artists, offering oil paintings, graphics, and enamels to those collectors with a discerning eye. They also have a framing and restoration service to bring your paintings back to life, and will even exhibit their entire collection in your home should you have the interest—and elbow room.

Books and Music

Budapest's first English-language bookshop is

Libri is Budapest's largest chain of foreign-language bookshops.

the very popular **Bestsellers** (V. Október 6 utca 11, tel. 1/312-1295, www.bestsellers.hu, Mon.-Fri. 9am-6:30pm, Sat. 10am-5pm, Sun. 10am-4pm). Opened in 1992, it continues to draw customers from all over the world who are in need of travel books, literary gems, or a good old-fashioned newspaper or magazine. A visit to this bright and well-run shop will satisfy any bookworm.

Központi Antikvárium (V. Múzeum körút 13-15, tel. 1/317-3514, www.kozpontiantikvarium.hu, Mon.-Fri. 10am-6pm, Sat. 10am-2pm) has the distinct honor of being Budapest's oldest, largest, and, some would say, best used bookstore. It's practically a treasure trove of old prints, maps, and photos as well as old and rare books, covering pretty much any topic you can think of. There is also a small English section that has books ranging from literature to philosophy, travel guides, and crime fiction. It's always worth a peek inside.

Libri Foreign Language Bookshop (V. Váci utca 22, tel. 1/318-5680, www.libri.hu, Mon.-Fri. noon-7pm, Sat.-Sun. 10am-3pm)

is Budapest's largest chain of foreign-language bookshops, and this particular location couldn't be more convenient. Two floors of books cover all the major categories, including new titles, classic literature, nature books, language books, guide books, art, history, film—well, you get the picture. Pretty postcards and photo albums can also be bought, and the staff will go out of their way to help you find what you're looking for. English isn't the only language you'll find, as books are also available in German, Russian, French, Italian, and Spanish.

Fashion
Well-respected and immensely popular, **Anda Emilia** (V. Galamb utca 4, tel. 30/933-9746, www.andaemi.com, Mon.-Fri. 11am-6pm, Sat. 11am-2pm) is one of Hungary's finest designers. Her inventive collections focus on soft, restrained, and elegant evening wear while her sleek, understated accessories are a favorite among the capital's modern sophisticated women.

Retrock (V. Ferenczy István utca 28, tel.

30/678-8430, www.retrock.com, Mon.-Fri. 10:30am-7:30pm, Sat. 10:30am-3:30pm) was established by a group of creative young designers who wanted to buck the mainstream. The result is a chic, colorful boutique where retro meets cutting edge, and one-of-a-kind pieces by Hungarian and foreign designers are sold to trendy locals and visitors in the know. Dresses, jackets, skirts, tops, and accessories can all be found here, as can one or two of the designers themselves on occasion.

Located on Budapest's revived Fashion Street, **Byblos** (V. Deák Ferenc utca 17, tel. 30/230-6890, www.roland.hu, Mon.-Sat. 10am-7pm, Sun. 10am-6pm) offers a wide range of clothing and accessories from a number of name-brand designers, including Ralph Lauren, Gianfranco Ferré, and Roberto Cavalli. The prices are a tad high, given the store's fashionable location, but you'll certainly get what you pay for.

Eclectick (V. Irányi utca 20, tel. 1/266-3341, www.eclectick.hu, Mon.-Fri. 10am-7pm, Sat. 11am-6pm) is a local design shop with a great selection of clothes and accessories for trendy young women in the know. Roughly 70-80 percent of their stock belongs to their own brand, while the rest is an excellent variety of hip Hungarian designers like Camou, Red Aster, Kriszta Marosi, and more.

Nanushka (V. Deak Ferenc utca 17, tel. 1/202-1050, www.nanushka.hu, Mon.-Sat. 10am-8pm, Sun. 10am-6pm) is the childhood nickname given to designer Sandra Sandor, whose popular shop hosts a myriad of inspired black, white, and gray women's wear. Comfortable, playful, and subtly sophisticated, her collections have been gaining the respect and credibility of the fashion elite, making her a designer to keep an eye on in the years to come.

Food and Drink

The steady business done by **Szamos Marcipán Cukrászda** (V. Párizsi utca 3, tel. 1/317-3643, www.szamosmarcipan.hu, daily 10am-7pm) is no accident, for it is where some of the finest pastries in the capital are to be had. Cakes, sweets, and ice cream so good it should be illegal keep customers coming back for more. Don't let the location just off Váci Street fool you; this is no tourist trap. In fact, Hungarians make up the majority of the loyal customers.

The chocolates at **Rózsavölgyi Csokoládé** (V. Királyi Pál u. 6, tel. 30/814-8929, www.rozsavolgyi.hu, Mon.-Fri. 10:30am-6:30pm, Sat. noon-6pm) are handmade from 100 percent Dominican cacao beans, which means they all pack quite a punch. The beans are roasted before the chocolates are prepared in the store's workshop and made available to repeat customers with an incurable sweet tooth. Strong fruity and spicy flavors dominate their delicious products, which range from bonbons to truffles.

Gifts

Bomo Art (V. Régiposta utca 14, tel. 1/318-7280, www.bomoart.hu, Mon.-Fri. 10am-6:30pm, Sat. 10am-6pm) specializes in journals, agendas, diaries, postcards, photo albums, and leather-bound books, all of which have been made by hand. If you're looking for a tasteful gift item or simply want to record the memories of your trip in a unique and artistic way, make sure to pay this shop a visit.

Limited-edition pieces are the name of the game at **Eventuell** (V. Nyáry Pál utca 7, tel. 1/318-6926, www.eventuell.hu, Mon.-Fri. 11am-6pm, Sat. 10:30am-2pm). A large number of textile and interior designers offer their wares, which include curtains, cushions, clothing, bedspreads, scarves, jewels, and a whole lot more. The friendly staff is also happy to take orders on any special requests you might have, making this place well worth a look-see.

Budapest Poster Gallery (V. Falk Miksa utca 28, 6th Fl., tel. 1/662-7274, www.budapestposter.com, Mon.-Fri. 2pm-6pm or by appointment) focuses primarily on Hungarian vintage posters from the 20th century depicting a wide range of subjects like films, food, and World War II. Take a step back in time and pick up an affordable one-of-a-kind gift item for the history buff closest to you.

If you don't want to leave Budapest without a souvenir, head straight for **Memories of**

© TOM DIRLIS

Frey Wille makes 24-karat dreams come true.

Hungary (V. Hercegprímás utca 8, tel. 1/780-5844, www.memoriesofhungary.hu, daily 9am-10pm). There are thousands of types of gifts here, ranging from handbags and soccer jerseys to coffee mugs and homemade jams. The prices are decent, the staff is friendly, and the odds that you won't find something to suit your taste are microscopic.

Viola Violetta (V. Veres Pálné utca 10, tel. 1/317-4361, www.violavioletta.hu, Mon.-Fri. 9am-8pm, Sat. 9am-7pm, Sun. 9am-2pm) is arguably the best known and most established florist in Budapest, having served countless weddings and all kinds of social events. Choose from any number of fantastic floral arrangements or relevant gift items, ranging from traditional vases to handmade baskets.

Jewelry
Austrian jewelry makers **Frey Wille** (V. Régiposta utca 19, tel. 1/318-7665, www.freywille.com, Mon.-Fri. 10am-6pm, Sat. 10am-4pm) produce 24-karat gold-plated enamel accessories that have captured the heart and imagination of their devoted customers. Anyone looking for rings, bracelets, or necklaces boasting exceptional design and intricate artisanship will want to check this shop out immediately.

TERÉZVÁROS AND ERZSÉBETVÁROS
Books and Music
Four floors of the newest in literature await you at **Alexandra Könyvesház** (VII. Károly körút 3/C, tel. 1/480-8080, www.alexandra.hu, Mon.-Fri. 9am-9pm, Sat.-Sun. 10am-8pm). There's a decent selection of English books on the second floor, ranging from Penguin classics to Philip Roth and Chuck Palahniuk. A simple yet enticing café sits on this level as well, offering an excellent spot to take a load off and dive into a book before venturing back out onto the streets. If you're interested in Hungarian literature, you'll want to keep an eye out for the various readings held here throughout the year.

Calling itself "a local bookstore with a global conscience," **Treehugger Dan's Bookstore and Cafe** (VI. Lazar utca 16, tel. 61/704-6303, www.treehuggerdans.com, Mon.-Fri. 10am-6pm, Sat. 10am-4pm) is a breath of fresh air (environmental pun intended) in the land of used bookshops. Started in 2006 by environmental activist Dan Swartz, this shop is a favorite meeting spot of locals, travelers, and the green-minded set fully committed to environmental and social justice issues. All lovers of literature and Mother Earth need to check it out at least once during their stay.

Located in the breathtaking Párizs Department store, **Alexandra** (VI. Andrássy út 39, tel. 1/484-8000, www.alexandra.hu, daily Mon.-Fri. 10am-10pm) is one of the finer examples of Hungary's famous bookstore chain, offering newer and classical works in elegant turn-of-the-20th-century environs. There are gifts and wine to choose from as well, not to mention excellent coffee and dessert in the neo-Renaissance-era café located on the top floor.

Fashion
Situated next to the Great Synagogue, **Látomás**

(VII. Dohány utca 16-18, tel. 1/267-2158, www.latomas.hu, Mon.-Fri. 11am-7:30pm, Sat. 11am-6pm) is where you'll find the country's top contemporary designers all under one roof. Unique one-piece creations from over 30 designers include bags, jewelry, clothing, and much, much more. This is where the neighborhood's hipsters come to shop.

Siberia (VII. Wesselényi utca 19, tel. 30/986-5982, daily 11am-9pm) is home to some of the coolest, funkiest shoes you'll find in town. Designed by Anna Zaboeva, who hitchhiked all the way from her native Ukraine for a better life, this incomparable shop showcases a wild and colorful array of formal and informal footwear that will catch the eye of even the most hardened fan of fashion.

Food and Drink

Not far from the Great Synagogue is **In Vino Veritas** (VII. Dohány utca 58-62, tel. 1/413-0002, www.borkereskedes.hu, Mon.-Fri. 9am-8pm, Sat. 10am-6pm), a very friendly store

In Vino Veritas is one of the finer places to buy excellent Hungarian wines.

filled with an impressive range of domestic wines. Ask the knowledgeable staff for help or enjoy browsing for that perfect bottle. High quality at reasonable prices has made this a popular choice among wine lovers for quite some time.

La Petite Française (VII. Király utca 9, tel. 1/321-5711, www.lapetitefrancaise.com, Mon.-Fri. 10am-7pm, Sat. 10am-4pm) is a charming shop specializing in hard-to-find French foods that are both affordable and of the highest quality. A mouthwatering array of wines, chocolates, cheeses, pâtés, and sweets are on display in tasteful arrangements that will make you want to devour everything you see before you. Food buffs will do themselves a huge favor by coming here tout de suite.

Gifts

Dedicated to eco design, print art, and printing techniques, **Printa Akademia** (VII. Rumbach Sebestyén utca 10, tel. 30/292-0329, www.printa.hu, Mon.-Fri. 11am-7pm, Sat. noon-6pm) is a gallery, café, printer, and shop all rolled into one. Recycling is the name of the game here, as evidenced by its earth-conscious art, furniture, and clothing on display. Run by designer Zita Majoros and photographer Claudia Martens, this shop has been gaining repeat customers and street cred since the day it opened its doors.

Lost your iPod? Camera on the fritz? Head on over to **Extreme Digital** (VII. Erzsébet körút 15, tel. 1/450-1452, www.edigital.hu, Mon.-Fri. 10am-6pm, Sat. 10am-2pm) and check out their range of all things high-tech. The prices are fair, the staff is helpful, and there's a repair center on the premises that may come in handy if your pesky gadget stops cooperating at that inopportune time.

Jewelry

Diamonds are the name of the game at **Caprice** (VI. Andrássy út 27, tel. 1/321-2057, www.caprice.co.hu, Mon.-Fri. 10am-7pm, Sat. 10am-4pm), where a dazzling array of jewelry is available, including rings, earrings, and necklaces that have been designed by some of the world's finest artists. Their professionalism and remarkable attention to aesthetic detail are just two reasons this shop does brisk business no matter what the time of year. Run by independent and multitalented designer Judit Wild, **Vadjutka** (VII. Madách Imre út 5, http://vadjutka.hu, Mon.-Thurs. 11am-7pm) is a colorful shop offering a large number of unique and handmade items that will enhance anything you happen to be wearing. It's perfect for those who like they're jewelry light and playful.

Shopping Centers
The **WestEnd City Center** (VI. Váci út 1-3, tel. 1/238-7777, www.westend.hu, Mon.-Sat. 10am-8pm, Sun. 10am-8pm) is located close to Nyugati railroad station and is Central Europe's largest shopping mall. Over 400 stores serve eager shoppers who also have the

WAMP: Showcasing Hungarian Design

Founded in July 2006, WAMP (www.wamp.hu) is a monthly outdoor Hungarian design market that attracts over 4,500 Hungarians, visitors, and expats to its various (and always shifting) locations around town. The market houses over 100 local artists and designers, and visitors are often amazed at the wide array of jewelry, textiles, ceramics, glassware, children's toys, and games on display, all of which make for unique gifts and memorable souvenirs. The market's main objective is to create an established forum where artists of all disciplines can not only find an outlet to sell their work but begin a dialogue with conscientious consumers as well. WAMP has started to organize its monthly endeavor around themes, the most popular of which have been Earth Day, with recycling as its main design, and Street Art, which has included human beat-box performances and urban clothing and merchandise. This is an excellent opportunity both to understand what the country's hottest and most innovative designers are doing as well as to pick up items that far outweigh the usual tourist schlock in both quality and value.

opportunity to relax in the pretty open-air rooftop garden terrace.

JÓZSEFVÁROS AND FERENCVÁROS
Fashion
Leading the pack in alternative clothing for the last 15 years is **Iguana Retro** (VIII. Krúdy Gyula utca 9, tel. 1/317-1627, http://iguanaretro.hu, Mon.-Fri. 10am-6pm, Sat. 10am-2pm), a fantastic shop crammed with all kinds of shirts, dresses, handbags, and a whole lot more, all of them sporting the same unique rebellious rock-and-roll spirit that has established Iguana as a fashionable force to be reckoned with.

Food and Drink
Originally founded in 1993 under the name Budapest Wine Society, **Bortársaság** (IX. Ráday utca 7, tel. 1/219-5647, www.bortarsasag.hu, Mon.-Fri. noon-8pm, Sat. 10am-3pm) has grown to become one of the most important wine traders in the country. You'll find nearly 500 different kinds of Hungarian and foreign wines, along with spirits, sparkling wines, and champagnes. There are a number of locations to choose from, and you can rest assured that if you can't find what you're looking for, odds are it never made it into the country.

The experts at **Magyar Pálinka Háza** (VIII. Rákóczi út 17, tel. 30/421-0487, www.magyarpalinkahaza.hu, Mon.-Sat. 9am-7pm) understand that a proper *pálinka* should warm the body but not burn the throat and are more than happy to help you decide on the variety that's perfect for you. Traditional flavors like plum, pear, and apple are readily available, as are more creative options like walnut, honey, and paprika.

Shopping Centers
Located at the Pest foot of the Liberty Bridge, the **Central Market Hall** (IX. Vámház körút 1-3, tel. 1/366-3300, www.piaconline.hu, Mon. 6am-5pm, Tues.-Fri. 6am-6pm, Sat. 6am-3pm) is Budapest's largest market hall and easily its

Central Market Hall

most popular. Opened in 1896, it then included a network of tunnels that allowed incoming barges to unload their merchandise directly under the market floor. Restored in 1994, its two huge floors are packed with bustling stalls selling a remarkable variety of meats, spices, fruits, vegetables, traditional dolls, clothing, and, of course, local wine and liqueurs. Located on the upper floor are a handful of stalls offering Hungarian staples like goulash and *lángos,* making it a great place to fill up on local food and admire the endless combination of intoxicating colors and smells. If possible, visit on a Saturday morning, when the market is at its busiest and most vibrant.

GELLÉRT HILL TO ÓBUDA
Fashion
Wolford (II. Lövőház út 2-6, tel. 1/318-3733, www.wolford.hu, Mon.-Sat. 10am-9pm, Sun. 10am-6pm) has been one of the more respectable designers of women's fashions for the last 60 years. Specializing in luxury and designer legwear, lingerie, swimwear, and accessories,

this shop is a sure bet for any woman looking to stay modern and classy at the same time.

Food and Drink
Culinaris (III. Perc utca 8, tel. 1/345-0780, www.culinaris.hu, Mon. noon-8pm, Tues.-Sat. 9am-8pm) is a cooking aficionado's dream: fresh fruit and vegetables, olive oils, cheeses, and sparkling wines from around the world, and international foods and ingredients you'd otherwise be hard-pressed to find. If you're feeling like firing up the stove again, check out this place first.

   Chococo (I. Pauler utca 7, tel. 1/787-6997, www.chococo.hu, Mon.-Fri. 8am-10pm, Sat. 8am-6pm, Sun. 9am-6pm) is a chocoholic's dream, offering a large number of chocolaty treats that come in all kinds of shapes, sizes, and mouthwatering flavors. Anyone who has trouble sticking to their diet should stay as far away from here as possible.

Markets
Located next to popular Mamut Shopping

BUDAPEST

Center, **Fény Street Market** (II. Lövőház utca 12, tel. 1/345-4101, www.fenyutcaipiac.hu, Mon.-Fri. 6am-6pm, Sat. 6am-2pm) offers a fine selection of fresh fruit and vegetables as well as ubiquitous food items like sausage and paprika. It's well worth a peek should you be in the vicinity.

Shopping Centers
Not far from the bustling hub of Széll Kálmán Square is **Mammut** (II. Lövöház utca 2-6, tel. 1/345-8020, www.mammut.hu, Mon.-Sat. 10am-9pm, Sun. 10am-6pm), Budapest's busiest shopping mall. There are loads of shops here that include immediately recognizable names like Adidas, Marks & Spencer, and Benetton as well as smaller outlets geared toward the more discerning shopper. Should you need a break, there are plenty of cafés and restaurants on the upper floors and an outdoor fruit and vegetable market next door. Plenty of variety and regular sales keep Mammut at the top of every local's shopping list.

If you've done the rounds and still crave more Mammut, check out **Mammut II** (II. Lövöház utca 2-6, tel. 1/345-8020, www.mammut.hu, Mon.-Sat. 10am-9pm, Sun. 10am-6pm), located directly across the street. Here you'll find more of what you'd expect, with a nice variety of shops that picks up where its counterpart left off.

Opened in late 2009, the four-level, three-acre **Allee** (XI. Október 23. utca 8-10, tel. 1/372-7208, www.allee.hu, Mon.-Sat. 10am-9pm, Sun. 10am-7pm) is the city's youngest shopping center and one of its most vibrant. There are plenty of shops to choose from, representing plenty of internationally recognizable brands like Sony and Levi's, fast-food chains like Burger King and KFC, along with a state-of-the-art cinema and a fitness center.

Sports and Recreation

Hungarians like to stay active, if the number of cyclists and in-line roller-skaters around town are anything to judge by. Traveling around the city by bike is one of the best ways to keep the pounds off as well as discover neighborhood nooks and crannies you might otherwise have missed. For those feeling a little more adventurous, there are caves in the Buda Hills to be explored, while those who simply want to stay fit without getting fancy can head down to Margaret Island and make good use of the rubber track that stretches all around it.

BATHS AND SPAS
Below are descriptions of Budapest's most popular baths. Further information about all of the city's baths, including times, fees, treatments, and which days are same-sex and coed, can be found at www.spasbudapest.com.

At **Széchenyi Spa Baths** (XIV. Állakerti körút 9-11, tel. 1/363-3210, http://budapestgyogyfurdoi.hu/en, daily 6am-10pm, 3,800-4,800 Ft), one of the largest baths in Europe, 15 indoor pools, 3 outdoor pools, and 10 saunas and steam chambers offer everything from aqua-aerobics to Thai massage to carbonic and salt treatments, just to name a few. There's a Wellness Center on the premises, complete with cardiovascular and weight machines as well as a hospital open on weekdays offering a wide array of healing programs, and a buffet and restaurant that will help restore your energy levels after a relaxing and draining day in the water.

The breathtakingly tasteful baths, done in an art nouveau style that's complemented by ceramic tiles, glass roofs, and Roman columns, make the **Gellért Baths** (XI. Kelenhegyi út 4, tel. 1/466-6166, www.spasbudapest.com, daily 6am-8pm, 4,900-5,500 Ft) an experience to remember. It consists of 13 facilities: 3 outdoor pools, 2 effervescent baths, and 8 thermal baths, all of them deriving their medicinal waters from the 118 natural hot springs

Bathing in Luxury

Thermal baths are a distinct part of Hungarian culture, and while a visit to one can be pretty intimidating to a first-timer, it will also be one of the most rewarding experiences on your trip if you forgo your initial shyness and plunge right in.

Your first order of business is to approach the ticket window and choose from the long list of facilities and services available (all in Hungarian). Odds are you'll be looking to use the pool (*uszoda*), thermal pool (*termál*), bath (*fürdo*), steam bath (*gozfürdo*), massage (*masszázs*), or sauna (*szauna*). Once you've purchased your ticket, you'll be given a free locker in the locker room (*öltözo*), or, depending on the establishment, you'll also be able to rent a private cabin (*kabin*) for an additional fee. Whatever you choose, you'll be given a token on a string by the attendant in charge, which allows you to return to your locker or cabin at your leisure.

USEFUL TIPS

- Remember to bring a bathing suit and bathing cap (all long hair must be covered) as well as soap, shampoo, flip-flops, and a towel.
- Treat yourself to the waters for at least two hours in order to fully enjoy their effects.
- Shower thoroughly before entering any of the pools.
- Stay hydrated – keep a water bottle nearby.
- Tip your attendant and masseuse.
- Eat after your time in the baths and take a nap as you'll feel plenty drained. Do not plan on doing any sightseeing immediately afterward.
- Keep in mind that ticket windows close an hour before the baths.

If you feel lost or can't remember anything you just read–just do as the locals do.

bubbling under Gellért Hill. The name of the game here is "massage," as a large number of them are available, ranging from foot massages to aroma massages to underwater jet therapies. There's a also a buffet, dental services, manicure services, a hairdresser, and a currency exchange. And you don't have to be a guest at the hotel to enjoy any of it.

Established in the 12th century, back when monastery baths were being built, **Lukács Thermal Bath** (II. Frankel Leo utca 25-29, tel. 1/326-1659, www.lukacsfurdo.hu, daily 6am-9pm, 3,000-3,100 Ft) first became a spa hotel in the 1880s, added a drinking-cure hall in 1937, a daytime hospital in 1979, and was thoroughly renovated at the end of the 20th century. Boasting eight pools in all, one of which is a mud bath, it offers many of the same services other baths do, including a few unique trademarks such as a drinking cure, physiotherapy treatments, and mud-pack treatments. There is also the possibility of

sunbathing on the roof, a popular activity during the summer months.

The **Rudas Thermal Bath** (I. Döbrentei tér 9, tel. 1/356-1010, www.rudasfurdo.hu, Mon.-Wed. 6am-6pm, Thurs. and Sun. 6am-8pm, Fri.-Sat. 10am-4pm, 3,000-3,300 Ft) is located along the Danube below Gellért Hill and came to be during the Turkish occupation of the 16th century. Deriving its healing waters from three springs—the Atilla, Juventus, and Hungária—its six steam pools and octagonal swimming pool are rich in minerals like calcium, magnesium, sodium and sulfate, among others. Visitors can also enjoy aroma massage, skin-firming massage, body scrubs, drink diets, pedicures, and a whole lot more.

Commissioned by Arslan in 1565, the **Király Baths** (I. Fő utca 84, tel. 1/202-3688, www. spasbudapest.com, daily 9am-9pm, 2,400 Ft) was restored to its former glory following World War II and currently boasts four thermal baths that "borrow" their water from the

BUDAPEST

same springs used by nearby Lukács. Thermal, steam, sauna, and tub baths are available, as are a number of massages, including foot massage and underwater jet massage.

BICYCLING

If you'd like to see Budapest by bike or Segway, **Yellow Zebra Bikes** (VI. Lázár utca 16, Terézváros, tel. 1/269-3843, www.yellowzebrabikes.com, daily 9am-8:30pm) are the ones to contact. A friendly and knowledgeable staff will be more than happy to set you up with a rental or organized tour of all of the capital's major sights. As natives or long-term residents, all of the staff here have an intimate understanding of the city and can let you in on its many secrets and off-the-beaten-path sights. If there's anything you'd like to know about Budapest, this is an excellent place to start.

Just down the street from the Great Synagogue and opposite the hip Szoda bar are the very friendly and helpful folks at **Budapest Bike** (VII. Wesselényi utca 13, Erzsébetváros, tel. 30/944-5533, www.budapestbike.hu, daily 9am-6pm). Started in 2005, they quickly carved out a place for themselves in the market thanks to entertaining and informative tours that continue to grow in popularity. Various trips throughout the city include a general Budapest tour, a Budapest geocache tour, a baths tour, and a chapel tour. There is also a fun-filled pub crawl and wine tour to choose from, both of which are led by natives determined to show visitors a good time.

Bringóhintó (XIII. Margaret Island, Alfréd sétány 1, tel. 1/329-2073, www.bringohinto.hu, daily 8am-dusk, 2,180-4,980 Ft per hour) started in 1991 and has been renting out odd-looking but fun vehicles ever since. Normal mountain and city bikes are available, as are two-seater tandem bicycles and four-person bike-car contraptions. This is a healthy, fun, and relatively easy way to cover all of Margaret Island, especially if you're traveling in a group or with family.

Another fun way to explore Margaret Island is to visit **Sétacikli** (XIII. Margaret Island, Water Tower, tel. 30/966-6453, www.setacikli.

hu, spring-fall daily 10am-6pm, winter Sat.-Sun. 10am-6pm, 1,800-3,000 Ft per hour). Their pedal-operated cars are a big hit with kids, but plenty of adults get into the spirit as well.

CAVING

Pálvölgyi Cave (II. Szépvölgyi út 162, tel. 1/325-9505, www.palvolgyi.atw.hu, Tues.-Sun. 9am-4:15pm, 1,200 Ft) is the prettiest and longest cave in the Buda Hills, stretching a whopping 11 miles under the city. Unfortunately, less than 0.5 mile of it is open to the public, but visitors can still enjoy doing something a little more adventurous than the usual sightseeing while viewing hundreds of remarkable stalactites firsthand. Tours leave every hour and last roughly 50 minutes. The temperature in the caves dips down to about 46°F, so wearing something warm is a good idea. Although there are ladders and stairs to help with your progress, the tour is not recommended for children, the elderly, or those with physical disabilities.

Located not far from Pálvölgyi Cave is the smaller but no less interesting **Szemlőhegyi Cave** (II. Pusztaszeri út 35, tel. 1/325-6001, www.palvolgyi.atw.hu, Tues.-Sun. 10am-4pm, 1,000 Ft), which is covered in unique mineral formations that alternately look like cauliflower or bunches of grapes. Visitors can also enjoy an informative exhibition regarding the caves of Budapest at the entrance hall. Tours run hourly and last approximately 45 minutes. Warm clothing is necessary.

FITNESS CLUBS

Considered by many to be the finest and most comprehensive fitness center in town, the excellent **Danubius Health Spa Resort** (XIII. Margaret Island, tel. 1/889-4914, www.premierfitness.hu, daily 6:30am-9:30pm, day rate 6,900-8,300 Ft) does not disappoint. Yoga, tai chi, aqua aerobics, and Pilates are a few of the more popular activities, and those interested in simple straight-up weight and cardiovascular training will be very satisfied as well. The Danubius has plenty of top-of-the-line equipment available, along with more luxurious options like thermal baths, a whirlpool tub, and indoor and outdoor swimming pools. A full range of massages and medical services are on offer too, making it clear that when it comes time to taking care of both mind and body, the Danubius should be at the top of your list.

Located within the Hotel Marriott is the classy Swedish-owned **World Class Health Academy** (V. Apáczai Csere János út 4-6, Belváros, tel. 1/266-3804, www.worldclass. hu, Mon.-Fri. 6am-10pm, Sat.-Sun. 8am-9pm). This state-of-the-art facility offers everything a health nut could hope for, including top-notch equipment, a friendly, invigorating atmosphere, and a wide variety of programs and services that include a hot tub, a sauna, a steam bath, strength training, cardio training, cycling, Pilates, and yoga. Helpful English-speaking staff make it that much more of a treat to work out here.

ICE-SKATING

City Park Ice Rink (XIV. Olof Pálme sétány 5, Városliget, tel. 1/364-0013, http://mujegpalya. hu, Wed.-Thurs. 9am-1pm, Fri. 9am-1pm and 4pm-8pm, Sat.-Sun. 10am-2pm and 4pm-8pm, 1,200 Ft Mon.-Fri., 1,400 Ft Sat.-Sun.) is Europe's largest and oldest open-air ice-skating rink. Built way back in 1870, the rink has brought plenty of smiles to children's faces and has been the spark of many a romance as well. This is a wonderful place to mingle with locals and stay in shape, all with awe-inspiring Heroes Square right next door. Skate rental is available, and beginners can look to any number of teachers and helpers that are always available.

SKIING

With a panoramic view 1,565 feet above the city, it's little wonder that the gorgeous piece of green known as **Normafa** (XII. Buda Hills, www.normafa.hu) is one of the most popular destinations for Budapesters to escape to during the summer. Located high up in the Buda Hills, it's often overrun by hikers, families, and young lovers enjoying the more-than-idyllic surroundings. In the winter, the area is flooded with skiers, snowboarders, and sledders hoping that the

snow will stay on the ground long enough for them to enjoy it. Those who decide to join in the fun should keep in mind that there is no ski lift or anything resembling it to bring you back up the hill for a second run. Should the time come for you to warm your bones or fill your belly, try a cup of mulled wine or a delicious snack at the pleasant **Normafa Ski House** (XII. Eötvös út 59, tel. 1/395-6508, daily 9am-5pm).

SPECTATOR SPORTS

Soccer is by far the country's most popular sport, and fans will have no shortage of opportunities to root for the home team, be it

American Football in Budapest

When one thinks of Hungary, American football isn't exactly the first thing that springs to mind, but the **Budapest Wolves**, founded in 2004, would like to change all that. Sponsored by Sport 1 television and run by Zsolt Damosy, who is also the promoter of world boxing champion Zsolt Erdei, the Wolves' rough-and-tumble style and never-say-die attitude has done plenty to introduce the sport to Hungarians and win over a few fans in the process.

Currently a force to be reckoned with in the Southeastern European League of American Football (SELAF), the Wolves pull in anywhere from 2,000 to 4,000 fans per game—not bad considering last year's Eurobowl final drew just over 4,000 spectators. The Wolves have high hopes and are constantly on the lookout for ways to improve their organization. Qualified and experienced coaches and players for any of their three teams (Wolves, Wolves 2 Rookies, and under-17 Wolves Juniors) are always a necessity, so if you think you have what it takes, perhaps you can become a star athlete on this side of the pond.

The Wolves play at **Flame Sporttelep** (XIII. Rozsnyai utca 6-8, Újlipótváros-Angyalföld, www.magyarfutball.hu). For more information on the Budapest Wolves and European football in general, have a look at www.wolves.hu and www.eurobowl.info.

league-dominating Ferencvarós Football Club, wildly popular Ujpest FC, or perennial underdogs MTK Budapest. Tickets are very cheap by Western standards, and the enthusiastic crowds are more than infectious. A lazy day at the track is also possible March-November at Kincsem Park.

Soccer

Hungary's most successful soccer club, **Ferencvarós FC** plays at **Ülloi út Stadium** (IX. Üllői út 129, Ferencvarós, tel. 1/215-6025, www.ftc.hu). Known affectionately as either Fradi or FTC, they have won the Hungarian football league 28 times and the cup 20 times. Aside from their successes, the team is also known for having the most vocal and violent fans, many of whom are skinheads or linked to the extreme political right.

Hidegkuti Nándor Stadium (XIII. Salgótarjáni út 12-14, Józsefváros, tel. 1/333-8368, www.mtkhungaria.hu, tickets 500-1,800 Ft) is a relatively small stadium that officially opened in 1912. Home to **MTK Budapest,** its 5,700 seats are rarely filled to capacity, but those who drop by to support the team create more of a family atmosphere than the violent, hooligan-esque environment commonly associated with bigger clubs. If a laid-back day of watching soccer with old fans is your thing, order up your very affordable tickets now.

Szusza Ferenc Stadium (IV. Megyeri út 13, Újpest, tel. 1/231-0088, www.ujpestfc.hu) is home to **Ujpest Football Club,** one of the more popular soccer teams in the country. Originally opened in 1922, the stadium went through extensive renovations in 2000-2001 and now stands as one of the more modern sports facilities in the region. Bathed in purple and white (the team's colors), this has been the setting of many a lively game. Keep in mind that green is the color of bitter rivals Ferencváros, and wearing it will most likely land you in unwanted hot water.

Horse Racing

Originally founded as a gallop track back in 1925, **Kincsem Park** (X. Albertirsai út 2-4, Kőbánya, tel. 1/433-0520, www.kincsempark.com) was then known as one of the more beautiful courses in Europe. Named after a Hungarian wonder horse who won all 54 of her races, the track was redone in 2005 and now allows for trotting races as well. The grandstand was expanded to seat 3,500 visitors and offers a restaurant with a panoramic view of the proceedings on the top floor. Trotting races are held year-round and are usually run on Wednesday and Saturday. Gallop races run March-November every Sunday.

Accommodations

The hotel scene in Budapest is a wide and varied one, ranging from grand historical landmarks like the Hotel Gellért to more unsophisticated functionalist buildings found in the outer districts. You'll find pricey internationally recognized four- and five-star chain hotels in the Belváros and affordable pensions (guesthouses) farther away in the Buda Hills. Budapest's public transportation system is excellent, making it easy to reach the center and all major sights no matter where you choose to stay. In summer, reserving well in advance is strongly recommended, and you'll save a bundle if you do it online. Also, those wanting a double bed should make sure to clearly specify that, as a double room usually means twin beds here.

THE BELVÁROS AND LIPÓTVÁROS
10,000-20,000 Ft

The **Loft Hostel Budapest** (V. Veres Pálné utca 19, tel. 1/328-0916, www.lofthostel.hu, 14,000 Ft d) has been garnering rave reviews since it opened its doors, and it's easy to see why. Spacious and clean dorms, a private room large

Going Local with Budapesting

Budapesting (www.budapesting.com) is a family-run affair that provides apartments and private rooms to travelers looking for a personal touch during their stay in the capital. All accommodations are centrally located and include free bedding, towels, Internet access, parking, coffee, tea, a welcome bottle of wine, and maps to the city. Being picked up from or taken to the airport or train station is also possible for a small fee.

Aside from providing visitors with top-notch accommodations, the fine folks at Budapesting also provide comprehensive tours of the city, along with day-long or overnight trips to nearby towns and Lake Balaton. Highly informative and remarkably hospitable, the main operators, Marton, Peter, and Susie, will go out of their way to make sure you have everything you could possibly need to make your stay a pleasant one and are happy to guide you to the city's best restaurants, bars, shops, or anywhere else your heart desires.

If you're looking for as close to a local experience a foreigner can have, Budapesting is the only service in town that can and will make it happen.

enough to be an apartment, a huge and friendly communal area, and the most helpful staff in town are to blame, as is its close proximity to Váci Street and a myriad of sights, restaurants, and bars. If you're looking for an unforgettable experience without breaking the bank, put this book down and make your reservations now.

Located next to Parliament, **Budapest Centrum Hostel** (V. Nádor utca 26, tel. 30/296-9069, http://budapestcentrumhostel. com, 18,000 Ft d) is not only situated right in the center of the city's action but happens to be one of the friendliest hostels around thanks to the welcoming, hands-on approach of its owner, Alex. Twelve clean and comfortable rooms await, as do free Wi-Fi, towels, tea, coffee, and complimentary breakfast. This is highly recommended to those who want to meet fellow travelers and experience some bona fide Hungarian hospitality.

20,000-30,000 Ft
Originally opened in 1873, the **Hotel Erzsébet** (V. Károlyi utca 11-15, tel. 1/889-3700, www. danubiushotels.com/erzsebet, 21,500 Ft d) took its name from Queen Elizabeth, wife of Emperor Francis Joseph, who ruled the Austro-Hungarian Empire at the time. Located a few minutes' stroll away from Váci Street, the Danube Embankment, and as many shops,

sights, restaurants, and bars as you can handle, guests will most likely never have to see the inside of a bus or subway. Rooms include all the usual amenities like air-conditioning, satellite and pay TV, telephone, Internet access, and soundproof windows. If you're looking for something simple and central that won't break the bank, you just found it.

The **Mercure Budapest City Center** (V. Váci utca 20, tel. 1/485-3100, www.mercure. com, 22,000 Ft d) offers affordable, high-class service. Located on bustling Váci Street near the Café Gerbeaud and Danube Embankment, its 227 rooms and four exclusive suites are a bit on the small size, but tastefully designed and fully equipped. The buffet breakfast is excellent, albeit a tad expensive, but the location simply can't be beat.

The **NH Budapest** (XIII. Vígszínház utca 3, tel. 1/814-0000, www.nh-hotels. com, 28,000 Ft d) is situated behind the Vígszínházis, Budapest's oldest theater. This elegant hotel is home to 160 air-conditioned and soundproof rooms, all of which are equipped with a work space that features free Wi-Fi as well as the usual amenities. The WestEnd City Center, Nyugati train station, and the Danube River are all close by, as are countless means of public transportation, making this a sound choice.

BUDAPEST

30,000-40,000 Ft

Located in bustling downtown Pest, the **City Hotel Mátyás** (V. Március 15 tér 7-8, tel. 1/900-9071, www.ohb.hu/matyas, 35,000 Ft d) is close to all the sights, restaurants, shops, and bars you could hope for. A bar, brasserie, 24-hour reception, and helpful tour desk are available to guests, as are decent service, clean affordable rooms, and the hotel's famous Matthias Cellar Restaurant. This is an excellent choice for those who only have a handful of days in the capital and want to maximize their time without paying an arm and a leg for location.

Sofitel Budapest (V. Széchenyi István tér 2, tel. 1/235-1234, www.sofitel-budapest. com, 35,000 Ft d) went through extensive renovations in 2005 with modern French flair in mind. It boasts 351 rooms, the majority of which offer fantastic views of both the Chain Bridge and Buda Palace. There are also 52 luxury and two presidential suites that radiate the ultimate in contemporary comfort. Facilities include a well-equipped fitness center, a ballroom, 16 state-of-the-art multifunction rooms, and an impressive high-tech boardroom for the plethora of conferences that find their way here. Furthermore, its restaurant, the Paris-Budapest Café, has won raves for its French, Mediterranean, and Hungarian fare.

40,000-50,000 Ft

If it's location you're looking for, you cannot do better than the **City Hotel Pilvax** (V. Pilvax köz 1-3, tel. 1/266-7660, www.cityhotel.hu, 42,500 Ft d). Tucked away on a side street mere minutes from the Danube and busy Váci Street, its accessibility to all the major sights and shops ensures you never have to step foot onto public transportation. The 32 simply furnished rooms are neat and functional and, while they admittedly lack the charm of other hotels, are good enough for those interested more in being in the center of things rather than frills.

In the heart of the city lies the exceptional **Le Meridien Budapest** (V. Erzsébet tér 9-10, tel. 1/429-5500, www.lemeridienbudapest.com, 45,000 Ft d), proud member of the Leading Hotels of the World and accredited with the Five-Star Diamond Award. Its 218 rooms and 26 suites are fully equipped with Wi-Fi, high-speed Internet access, flat-screen TVs, and, of course, top-notch service. There's a health club, a ballroom, and eight boardrooms as well, making this a favorite with businesspeople, diplomats, and high rollers. Its excellent French restaurant, Le Bourbon, has won several awards and remains one of the finer dining experiences in the capital.

◖ Kempinski Hotel Corvinus Budapest (V. Erzsébet tér 7-8, tel. 1/429-3777, www.kempinski-budapest.com, 47,000 Ft d) is quite often the hotel of choice for celebrities and international businesspeople. Overlooking Elizabeth Park, its 335 rooms, 29 suites, and two presidential suites all come with floor heating in the bathroom, built-in safes, and high-tech infotainment systems. Ten meeting rooms as well as a fully equipped business center satisfy every workaholic's needs, while the ballroom is usually the scene of quite a few lavish parties. The Kempinski Spa is also a favorite among guests who take full advantage of the sauna, solarium, steam bath, pool, gym, and massage treatments.

Starlight Suites Hotel Merleg (V. Mérleg utca 6, tel. 1/484-3700, www.starlighthotels.com, 49,000 Ft d) offers comfortable suites that come with a living room, a bedroom, a bath, and living and working areas as well as two TVs, a minibar, and a microwave. In addition, the hotel also has a sauna, a fitness center, and a Turkish bath. Its location mere minutes from Váci Street, the Chain Bridge, a minimarket, and the subway makes this hotel an excellent choice for travelers of all budgets.

TERÉZVÁROS AND ERZSÉBETVÁROS
10,000-20,000 Ft

Marco Polo Hostel (VII. Nyár utca 6, tel. 1/413-2555, www.marcopolohostel.com, 15,000 Ft d) is a popular choice among both individual travelers and larger groups who appreciate the clean rooms and beds as well as there being no curfew or lockout. There are double and quad rooms with telephone and TV, along with 12-bed dormitories with adjoining baths and showers. Its proximity to sights and numerous dining, shopping, and nightlife options make the Marco Polo a no-brainer.

◖**Wombat's Budapest** (VI. Király utca 20, tel. 1/883-5005, www.wombats-hostels.com, 16,000 Ft d) is a large, friendly, and spotlessly clean hostel located within walking distance of every major sight and attraction. Spacious rooms, comfortable beds, and helpful staff are also part of the package here, as is an excellent bar downstairs should you feel like hobnobbing with fellow guests.

Baross Hotel (VII. Baross tér 15, tel. 1/461-3010, www.barosshotel.hu, 18,000 Ft d) is a three-star hotel known for its decent value for the money. With its location near Keleti Station and plenty of public transportation, guests have no problem reaching any and all of Budapest's sights. All 40 rooms and five suites are well maintained and offer air-conditioning, phones, satellite TV, and private safes. A decent buffet is included in the price, and the helpful staff will

do their best to make your stay a memorable one. Simple and unpretentious, this is a good choice for those who like to keep costs down without having to sacrifice basic comforts.

Hotel Benczúr (VI. Benczúr utca 35, tel. 1/479-5665, www.hotelbenczur.hu, 19,000 Ft d) is located in the heart of the city's diplomatic region and a scant two minutes' walk from Heroes Square. Its 153 simple but clean and comfortable rooms are fitted out with all the usual amenities, and the hotel's restaurant and café are fine places to relax and enjoy some contemporary local cuisine. There's also a souvenir shop and a garden for those who like their peace and quiet outdoors.

Located in the heart of Budapest's theater district, the ◖**Medosz Hotel** (VI. Jókai tér 9, tel. 1/374-3000, www.medoszhotel.hu, 20,000 Ft d) is an excellent choice for those looking to remain close to the action without paying an arm and a leg. All the rooms are furnished simply and offer air-conditioning, TVs, and Internet and phone access. Close to the Opera, Franz Liszt Square, and pretty much anything worth seeing, this is an obvious option for the frugal traveler.

20,000-30,000 Ft

Located in busy Blaha Lujza Square, the **Agape Guesthouse** (VII. Akácfa utca 12-14, doorbell 5, tel. 1/317-4833, www.agapeguesthouse.hu, 22,000 Ft d) is a simple subway stop from Keleti Station and a 15-20 minute walk to Váci Street, the Basilica, and Franz Liszt Square. Each of the recently redecorated apartments offers a double bed, a fully equipped kitchen, a bath with a tub, and satellite TV. There is lots of bang for your buck here.

Just off Andrássy Avenue is the **Best Western Plus Ambra** (VII. Kis Diófa utca 13, tel. 1/321-1533, www.hotelambra.hu, 25,000 Ft d), a casual yet professional apartment-hotel. Its 21 rooms are all decked out with striking decor done by local artists as well as the usual amenities (kitchens, satellite TV, minibars, and safes). Close to the Opera House, Basilica, and Franz Liszt Square, this hotel is an excellent choice for those who want to stay close to the action.

© TOM DIRLIS

Wombat's Budapest

BUDAPEST

The **Cotton House** (VI. Jókai utca 26, tel. 1/354-2600, www.cotton-house-hotel-budapest.com, 21,000 Ft d) is a charming hotel with a Jazz Age theme. Each of its 22 rooms is named after a famous celebrity, including Elvis Presley, Humphrey Bogart, and Ernest Hemingway. The hotel is spotlessly clean and presided over by extremely helpful staff. Guests can take advantage of an excellent restaurant in the basement as well as nightly poker tournaments in the Poker Hall. Fun, affordable, and within 10-15 minutes' walk of the main sights, this hotel is a smart choice for those who like a little distance between themselves and the center of town.

30,000-40,000 Ft

Known for its extremely friendly and helpful staff, the centrally-located ❰❰ **Mamaison Residence Izabella** (VI. Izabella utca 61, tel. 1/475-5900, www.mamaison.com, 33,000 Ft d) is a charming, reasonably priced hotel that deserves attention. Thirty-eight suites complete with full-size kitchens, dining areas, and living rooms are what you can expect to find, along with a sauna, a fitness center, complimentary Wi-Fi, and laundry. Clean, comfortable, and quiet, you'll be hard-pressed to find a reason not to stay here.

Mamaison Hotel Andrássy Budapest (VI. Andrássy út 111, tel. 1/462-2100, www.andrassyhotel.com, 33,000 Ft d) is a five-star boutique hotel located within walking distance of the Széchenyi Spa Baths, the Museum of Fine Arts, the Zoo, and Gundel Restaurant, to name but a few. Built in the Bauhaus style in 1937, its 62 guest rooms and seven suites offer the highest quality and comfort, including all the modern amenities you can imagine. As an added bonus, fans of gourmet dining will be pleased to know that the award-winning Baraka restaurant is part of the hotel as well.

K+K Hotel Opera (VI. Révay utca 24, tel. 1/269-0222, www.kkhotels.com, 34,000 Ft d) is one of a distinguished group of privately owned boutique hotels found all over Europe. Its location next to the Opera House is hard to beat, and the hotel's bright, stylish interiors make guests feel immediately at home. Known throughout the continent for its excellent service, the hotel offers 206 tastefully furnished rooms fitted out with state-of-the-art amenities that include air-conditioning, high-speed Internet, and international TV.

Over 50,000 Ft

The ❰❰ **Corinthia Grand Hotel Royal** (VII. Erzsébet körút 43-49, tel. 1/479-4811, www.corinthia.hu, 53,000-75,000 Ft d) is a hard act to beat. Opulently designed and offering guests an unparalleled level of luxury, its 414 rooms plus fully equipped one-, two-, and three-bedroom apartments have been home to politicians, artists, and upper-stratosphere businesspeople. Boasting the country's largest state-of-the art conference and exhibition center as well as the incredibly beautiful Royal Spa, the hotel has firmly established itself as one of Hungary's finest accommodations.

An unparalleled level of luxury awaits at the Corinthia Grand Hotel Royal.

© TOM DIRLIS

JÓZSEFVÁROS AND FERENCVÁROS
10,000-20,000 Ft

⟨ Njoy Budapest (VIII. Rákóczi út 9, 1st Fl. no. 3, doorbell 29, tel. 1/266-1900, www. njoybudapest.hu, 16,000 Ft d) is a bright, cozy, and extremely comfortable hostel located within walking distance of the city center. Complimentary breakfast, coffee, and tea are available, as is a large kitchen, a family room, free Wi-Fi, 24-hour room service, and a whole lot more. It's an excellent and affordable choice for the discerning backpacker.

20,000-30,000 Ft

Right in the thick of hip and happening Ráday Street, **Ibis Budapest Centrum** (IX. Ráday utca 6, tel. 1/456-4100, www.ibishotel.com, 22,000 Ft d) is both a dependable and affordable option in the center of town. Its 126 rooms are comfortable and well maintained, as is the hotel in general, including its bar and garden, which has a terrace. Within walking distance of all the major sights and close to major hubs of public transportation, this is one hotel all visitors to Budapest should consider.

First opened in 1911, the art nouveau building that now houses the **Novotel Centrum** (VIII. Rákóczi út 43-45, tel. 1/477-5300, www. novotel-bud-centrum.hu, 25,000 Ft d) was renovated some years ago in order to make the surroundings more comfortable and pleasant for guests. Spacious, colorful, air-conditioned rooms come with a personal safe, a phone, satellite TV, and Internet access. The helpful staff is more than willing to help you arrange trips and tours around town, and those guests who prefer to stay close to home can enjoy various services, including a sauna, a whirlpool, a fitness room, and massage. This is a four-star hotel that lives up to its rating.

Located on a quiet street close to Kálvin Square, **Kálvin Ház** (IX. Gönczy pál utca 6, tel. 1/216-4365, www.kalvinhouse.hu, 28,000 Ft d) is an exceptionally friendly, warm, and professionally run hotel. Thirty large rooms decorated with tasteful turn-of-the-20th-century furniture are available, all of which are equipped with private baths, phones, and satellite TV. Within easy walking distance of the Liberty Bridge, Váci Street, the National Museum, and Central Market Hall, the Kalvin House is a great affordable choice for travelers seeking service and comfort with a personal touch.

30,000-40,000 Ft

Formerly the residence of Count Nándor Zichy, the **⟨ Hotel Palazzo Zichy** (VIII. Lőrinc pap tér 2, tel. 1/235-4000, www.hotel-palazzo-zichy.hu, 33,000 Ft d) is an excellent four-star boutique hotel located a five-minute walk from the National Museum. Eighty stylish air-conditioned rooms with flat-screen TVs and high-speed Internet access are available, as is a modestly-sized fitness center and an extremely relaxing sauna. Friendly and helpful staff round out what has become one of Budapest's more reliable places to lay your head.

VÁRHEGY AND CENTRAL BUDA
10,000-20,000 Ft

The **Hotel Charles** (I. Hegyalja út 23, tel. 1/212-9169, www.charleshotel.hu, 19,000 Ft d) may not be the prettiest hotel you've ever seen, but it definitely gets the job done by offering fully furnished apartments that can fit 1-4 people. The bus stop directly in front of the hotel allows guests to reach all parts of the city with relative ease, and the 24-hour multilingual reception office can help you plan day trips or simply answer whatever questions you might have. Low on frills but high on service, this hotel is a sensible choice for bargain hunters.

20,000-30,000 Ft

The **Carlton Hotel Budapest** (I. Apor Péter utca 3, tel. 1/224-0999, www.carltonhotel.hu, 29,000 Ft d) is conveniently located at the foot of Fishermen's Bastion and the Castle District, making sightseeing on both the Buda and Pest sides easy as pie. The hotel offers guests 95 rooms complete with air-conditioning, cable

TV, Internet access, a minibar, and a whole bunch more. Helpful staff and spotlessly clean surroundings are two more reasons to enjoy your stay at a hotel that is widely agreed to be great value for the money.

30,000-40,000 Ft

On the Danube Embankment offering magnificent views of Parliament is the trendy and colorful ◖ **Art'otel Budapest** (I. Bem rakpart 16-19, tel. 1/487-9487, www.artotels.com, 34,000 Ft d). Comprising a modern seven-story building and four 18th-century baroque Buda townhouses, guests can choose from being enveloped in modern or turn-of-the-20th-century atmosphere. Its 164 rooms contain state-of-the-art amenities, and renowned American artist Donald Sultan created over 600 works of art for the hotel, which are displayed in all guest rooms as well as common areas. The hotel also boasts an art gallery, an art shop, a sauna, a fitness room, a hair stylist, a beauty parlor, and valet parking. Its balance of art and modernity, along with its proximity to the Castle District and the Chain Bridge leading to Pest, make this a very popular choice.

The **Hotel Victoria Budapest** (I. Bem rakpart 11, tel. 1/457-8080, www.victoria.hu, 35,000 Ft d) is situated on the Buda embankment, allowing all of its 27 air-conditioned rooms to enjoy spectacular panoramic views of the city, including two that have their own balcony. Decked out with the usual amenities such as satellite TV, high-speed Internet, phones, and personal safes, the rooms and the hotel in general are known for being well maintained and spotlessly clean. Buffet-style breakfast, laundry services, a free sauna, and professional service are just a few more reasons to consider a stay in this wonderful hotel.

◖ **St. George Residence** (I. Fortuna utca 4, tel. 1/393-5700, www.stgeorgehotelbudapest. com, 37,000 Ft d) is a fantastic and historic boutique hotel located in the heart of the Castle District. All rooms come with large bedrooms, baths, living rooms, and kitchens, and some of the Gold suites also have whirlpool tubs. Elegant baroque-style furnishings, a romantic courtyard, helpful staff, and some of the finest views of the city are but a handful of reasons to make a reservation right now. It's highly recommended.

Over 50,000 Ft

Well within walking distance of Matthias Church, Fishermen's Bastion, and the Royal Palace, **Buda Castle Fashion Hotel** (I. Úri utca 39, tel. 1/224-7900, www.budacastlehotelbudapest.com, 62,000 Ft d) is a modern, fully-reconstructed four-star hotel perfect for those wanting a dose of luxury during their stay. All of their 25 rooms and suites are modern, spacious, and clean and offer free Wi-Fi, satellite TV, air-conditioning, and plenty of closet space. Pleasant and helpful staff as well as a delicious complimentary breakfast top off this exceptional choice.

GELLÉRT HEGY AND THE TABÁN
10,000-20,000 Ft

The **Hotel Császár** (II. Frankel Leó utca 35, tel. 1/336-2640, www.csaszarhotel.hu, 15,000 Ft d) is a budget bed-and-breakfast in the heart of Buda not far from Margaret Bridge. While the rooms are small, they are nevertheless comfortable, and the staff goes out of its way to make your stay as pleasant as possible. This is a sound choice for the frugal traveler, though bear in mind that trams run in front of the hotel, so reserving a room on the top floor is advised.

Hotel Papillon (II. Rózsahegy utca 3/B, tel. 1/212-4750, www.hotelpapillon.hu, 16,500 Ft d) is located in the lovely and peaceful neighborhood of Rózsadomb, a short 10-minute walk from Buda Castle. Boasting simple yet clean and functional rooms as well as very helpful and friendly staff, this small undiscovered gem is perfect for those preferring a family-style environment to larger, more impersonal hotel chains.

The cylindrical, B-movie-looking **Hotel Budapest** (II. Szilágyi Erzsébet fasor 47, tel. 1/889-4200, www.danubiushotels.com/budapest, 14,000-17,000 Ft d) might be considered by many to be a blight on the landscape, but it also offers travelers an excellent choice in relatively cheap accommodations. All 289 clean no-frills rooms come with a full wall of windows offering great views of either the Danube or the Buda Hills as well as the usual amenities like satellite TV, private baths, and phones. The Restaurant Budapest serves international and Hungarian dishes, while the souvenir shop, newsstand, and business center take care of most travelers' immediate needs. Its proximity to Széll Kálmán Square and the Cog-Wheel Railroad means easy access to Pest and the Buda Hills. This is a smart choice for those needing to keep costs down.

Located on the campus of the Budapest University of Technology and Economics, the **Professor's Guest House** (XI. Stoczek utca 5-7, 7th Fl., tel. 1/463-4103, www.otevszak. hu, 19,500 Ft) is a cheap student dorm-type alternative on the Buda side. Each apartment is equipped with the basics: a phone, a TV, a kitchen, and an Internet connection, making this a viable option for those on a strict budget.

30,000-40,000 Ft
Built just after World War I, the 🌊 **Danubius Hotel Gellért** (XI. Szent Gellért tér 1, tel. 1/889-5500, www.danubiushotels.com, 36,000-52,000 Ft d) remains one of Budapest's best-known and most charming hotels, boasting 234 rooms. The hotel also offers a wide range of health treatments and services, including indoor and outdoor swimming pools, a whirlpool tub, a wave bath, a steam room, manicures, pedicures, and even Thai massage. Then, of course, there are the world-famous Gellért baths, which are free to hotel guests. The service and food remain as good as ever, and the hotel's decaying art nouveau elegance continues to draw guests in.

ÓBUDA AND MARGIT SZIGET
10,000-20,000 Ft
The **Groove Hostel** (XIII. Szent István körút 16, tel. 1/786-8038, www.groovehostel.hu, 16,000 Ft d) has quickly become one of the more popular hostels in town thanks to its

central location near Margaret Island, Nyugati train station, and pretty much any pub, restaurant, or sight you'll care to visit. Big enough so you're not falling over each other though intimate enough to meet fellow travelers, this bright, clean, and friendly establishment is sure to be a hit for years to come.

20,000-30,000 Ft
Danubius Grand Hotel Margitsziget (XIII. Margaret Island, tel. 1/889-4700, www.danubiushotels.com, 25,000 Ft d) sports 154 rooms and 10 executive suites, all located right on breathtakingly beautiful Margaret Island. All rooms are modestly decorated and come with the usual amenities, including satellite TV, Wi-Fi, minibars, and safes. Health nuts will be happy to know that the neighboring Danubius Health Spa Resort is a state-of-the-art facility with indoor/outdoor pools, a whirlpool tub, a thermal bath, and a sauna as well as a large fitness center that hosts 35 exercise stations, two aerobics rooms, a sun terrace, a solarium, and the Hair and Beauty Emporium to boot.

THE BUDA HILLS
10,000-20,000 Ft
High up in the Buda Hills is the **Budai** (XII. Rácz Aladár utca 45, tel. 1/249-0275, www.hotelbudai.hu, 13,800 Ft d). Clean, affordable, and a mere 10- to 15-minute bus ride from the center, this hotel is perfect for those on a tight budget who prefer calm surroundings to bustling city squares. Rooms are basic but well maintained and come with a minibar, satellite TV, and a phone. For the best view of the hills, ask for a room on the top floor, and make sure to enjoy a meal or coffee on the hotel restaurant's terrace.

Helios Hotel & Pension (XII. Lidérc utca 5, tel. 1/246-4658, www.heliospanzio.hu, 20,000 Ft d) is a warm and friendly family-run guesthouse located in the Buda Hills. All rooms are comfortably furnished, and most come with a balcony overlooking the city. A direct bus whisks guests to the city center in 15 minutes, and the 24-hour reception is more than happy to answer questions and arrange any number of sightseeing trips or cultural activities. It's charming, affordable, and the perfect solution to those who like a little peace and quiet with their holiday.

20,000-30,000 Ft

Hotel Molnár (XII. Fodor utca 143, tel. 1/395-1872, www.hotel-molnar.hu, 21,000 Ft d) is a pleasant family-owned and run hotel in the lush greenbelt of Buda. All rooms are spacious and furnished with satellite TV, minibars, and phones and offer attractive views over the city and Buda Hills. Occasional goulash and grill parties are held in the hotel's garden, the aftereffects of which can be burned off in the Scandinavian sauna and fitness room. Its location three miles outside the city center makes this a perfect choice for travelers who appreciate the warm, personal atmosphere of an intimate out-of-the-way hotel, as opposed to the rash of formulaic chain hotels occupying the city center.

Not too far from the Children's Railroad is the **Hotel Normafa** (XII. Eötvös út 52-54, tel. 1/395-6505, www.normafahotel.hu, 27,000 Ft d), which boasts 46 double rooms and 16 suites, all of which are clean, spacious, and stylishly designed. Also of note are their exceptional breakfasts, well-equipped fitness center, heated outdoor swimming pool, and remarkably friendly staff. If you're looking for peace, quiet, and a bit of distance from the incessant bustle of Pest, you just found it.

Food

Hungarians love to eat, which might explain the large and varied number of restaurants found throughout the city. Magyar cuisine continues to dominate the landscape, with establishments ranging from the gourmet to the greasy spoon. Traditional dishes like goulash, fish soup, and wild game should be tried at least once, and snacks like *lángos*—a deep-fried flatbread made from potato-based dough—will keep you going during your long walks about town. International restaurants continue to crop up everywhere, making it easy to find Indian, Greek, Asian, and South American fare regardless of what district you're in. Prices are reasonable by Western standards, and the service, while spotty, continues to improve, with most waitstaff able to speak at least some English, particularly in the downtown core.

THE BELVÁROS
Asian
Not far from the Basilica is **Kyoto** (V. Széchenyi István tér 7-8, tel. 1/801-9862, www.kyotoetterem.hu, daily noon-midnight, mains 2,050-6,100 Ft), whose well-prepared teriyaki, teppanyaki, and Wagyu beef selections keep the place brimming with business. There's also plenty of sushi and sashimi to go around, all of which tends to taste better when enjoyed in the spacious outdoor seating area.

Cafés
At the north side of Vörösmarty Square is the one and only **Café Gerbeaud** (Vörösmarty tér 7-8, tel. 1/429-9000, www.gerbeaud.hu, daily 9am-10pm, 2,450-5,950 Ft), a classic Budapest coffeehouse if ever there was one. Established in 1858, it was bought in 1884 by Swiss confectioner Emil Gerbeaud, whose homemade desserts quickly became the talk of the town and remain unbeatable to this day. Its elegant, ornately designed salons are furnished with chandeliers, marble tables, and gilded ceilings, making it the perfect place to read a newspaper, have a coffee, or simply imagine you're reliving the 19th century. While plenty of outdoor seating is made available during the summer months, it's almost always a challenge to find a vacant table. Do yourself a favor, however, and don't give up, as this is one of those places where you should definitely believe the hype.

Laid-back, filled with ambience, and just plain gorgeous, **Centrál Kávéház** (V. Károlyi Mihály utca 9, tel. 1/266-2110, www.centralka-vehaz.hu, daily 8am-11pm, mains 1,990-5,990 Ft) was founded back when Budapest was still an imperial city, and it shows. A perfect example of a "grand café," it features attentive, bow-tied waiters who serve you with a smile and are very happy to help with the menu. Choice selections include the Wiener schnitzel, mixed grill plate, and the marinated fillet of salmon in cream sauce. Wash it all down with one of the better espressos to be found in the area or with a fine Hungarian wine.

Not far from Váci Street is the warm and colorful **Bar Bar Café** (V. Papnövelde utca 3, tel. 30/867-7987, www.barbarcafe.hu, Mon.-Sat. 1pm-9pm, mains 820-1,120 Ft), owned and operated by an enthusiastic young couple intent on making their coffees, lemonades, and hot chocolates the finest in town. There are plenty of variations to the standard hot and cold beverages, like the sour-cherry *pálinka* coffee, hot chocolate with banana, and mint lemonade served in a jam jar. It's an excellent place to take a load off.

The elegant old-school interior of **Szamos Gourmet Palace** (V. Váci utca 1, tel. 30/570-5973, www.szamosmarcipan.hu, daily 8:30am-9pm, mains 1,880-4,780 Ft) transports you back to the early 20th century, a welcome change from the bustle of modernized Váci Street. The smell of freshly brewing coffee hits you upon entering, as does the tempting sight of cakes, chocolates, and marzipan wrapped in brightly colored paper begging you to indulge. It makes for a perfect midday break.

Molnár's Kürtőskalács (V. Váci utca 31, www.kurtoskalacs.com, daily 9am-10pm, mains 880-1,980 Ft) offers what many believe to be the finest *kürtőskalács* (chimney cake) in the entire country. Originally a festive pastry served at weddings and baptisms, the hot, sticky treat quickly caught on and is traditionally served in eight lip-smacking varieties: vanilla, cinnamon, walnut, almond, chocolate, coconut, cocoa, and poppy seed—all of which can be found here.

© TOM DIRLIS

Molnár's offers the finest *kürtőskalács* (chimney cake) in the country.

Continental

◖ **Onyx** (V. Vörösmarty tér 7-8, tel. 30/508-0622, www.onyxrestaurant.hu, Tues.-Fri. noon-2:30pm, 6:30pm-11pm, Sat. 6:30pm-11pm, mains 9,500-11,500 Ft) is an elegant and luxurious Michelin-star restaurant, representing one of the finest dining experiences to be found in the capital. From its onyx columns and fireplaces to its white-gloved service, you'll spend an unforgettable few hours reveling in their exquisite tasting menus, which come complete with flawless wine pairings. It's not for everyone's budget, but it makes for an unbeatable dinner if you can handle the hefty price tag that comes with it.

French

Located in the Le Meridien Hotel, **Le Bourbon** (V. Erzsebet tér 9-10, tel. 1/429-5500, www.lebourbonrestaurant.com/en, daily noon-10:30pm, mains 2,600-7,900 Ft) boasts a bright colonial-style dining room that plays host to nightly themes dictating the nature of the menu. Themes have included Steak Night Monday, Pasta Night Tuesday, Middle East Wednesday, and Hungarian weekends. The food is always prepared to perfection and served by an attentive and professional waitstaff. There are plans to expand the theme nights, so check the website before visiting to stay informed of developments.

Hungarian

Cyrano Restaurant (V. Kristóf tér 7, tel. 1/266-4747, http://cyrano.hu, daily 8am-midnight, mains 1,790-5,790 Ft) is a slick establishment just off Váci Street that focuses on contemporary Hungarian cuisine. Standards such as goose liver and wild duck breast are expertly prepared, and the wide array of pasta dishes delights diners from all over the world. The cocktails here are fantastic, as is the lively atmosphere and friendly staff. Prices are definitely on the steep side, but well worth it.

If being made to feel like royalty is something you enjoy, head for well-known **Kárpátia** (V. Ferenciek tere 7-8, tel. 1/317-3596, www.

karpatia.hu, Mon.-Sat. 11am-11pm, Sun. 5pm-11pm, mains 3,900-5,900 Ft). Its rich interior reminds diners of the majesty that once enveloped the city, and traditional Hungarian dishes like Lake Balaton pike perch and saddle of venison are perennial winners. All the desserts are homemade, with the strudel in particular standing out. If it's too pricey for your budget, check out the less formal Brasserie, a favorite among locals.

Indian

Kashmir (V. Arany János utca 13, tel. 1/354-1806, www.kashmiretterem.hu, Tues.-Sun. 11am-11pm, mains 1,690-3,590 Ft) is a warm, unpretentious restaurant with an extensive menu of both classic and creative Indian cuisine. Beef, fish, and tandoori dishes make up the majority of the menu, with the tandoori mixed platter being particularly impressive. Vegetarians will be happy to know that there are plenty of tasty options for them, including the mixed vegetable curry and spiced eggplant and potato. For dessert, the *gulab jamun* is a must. Those on a strict budget need not worry as there is a reasonably priced buffet-style business lunch available until 6pm.

Focusing on contemporary Indian cuisine, **Salaam Bombay** (V. Mérleg utca 6, tel. 1/411-1252, www.salaambombay.hu, daily noon-3pm and 6pm-11pm, mains 1,490-3,990 Ft) has established itself firmly in Budapest's restaurant scene. Pretty much any of their chicken, lamb, and vegetarian dishes are excellent, as is the service and atmosphere. Many argue that this is the city's finest Indian restaurant.

International

Don't be intimated by the sleek and upscale interior at **Ruben** (V. Magyar utca 12-14, tel. 1/266-3649, www.rubenrestaurant.hu, daily noon-midnight, mains 1,390-3,990 Ft); it's more affordable than it looks. A decent selection of well-prepared beef, chicken, duck, and vegetarian offerings are available, as is a yummy Hungarian sponge cake that should not be missed. There's plenty of bang for your buck here.

Gimme the Goulash

Popular among herders in the 18th century, Hungary's most famous dish became a staple of Hungarian cuisine in the late 19th century when the country deemed it necessary to establish its national identity and independence from the ruling Habsburgs. For those wondering if the term *gulyás* actually means anything, it does: herdsman.

Every grandmother in the country has her own "authentic" recipe, but *gulyás* is typically a beef dish cooked with onions, paprika, tomatoes, and green pepper. It is neither soup nor stew, but lies somewhere in between. The following is a typical recipe.

HUNGARIAN GOULASH (FOR FOUR PEOPLE)

1.3 lbs. beef sheen or shoulder, or any tender part of beef cut into ¾-inch cubes
2 tbsp. oil or lard
2 medium onions, chopped
2 cloves of garlic
1-2 carrots, diced
1 parsnip, diced
1-2 celery leaves
2 medium tomatoes, peeled and chopped, or 1 tbsp. tomato paste
2 green peppers
2-3 medium potatoes, sliced
1 tbsp. Hungarian paprika powder
1 tsp. ground caraway seed
1 bay leaf
Ground black pepper and salt, according to taste
Water

Heat oil or lard in a pot and stir in chopped onions until they turn golden brown. Sprinkle onions with paprika powder; continue stirring to prevent paprika from burning. Add beef cubes and sauté until they turn white and get a bit of brownish color as well. Let beef cubes simmer. Add garlic, ground caraway seed, salt, ground black pepper, and the bay leaf. Then pour enough water to fill the pot and let it simmer on low heat for a while.

When the meat is half-cooked (approximately 1.5 hours), add the diced carrots, parsnip, potatoes, celery leaves, and more salt if necessary. You'll probably have to add 2-3 cups more water, too. When the vegetables and meat are almost done, add the tomato cubes and sliced green peppers. Cook on low heat for a few more minutes and keep the pot uncovered if you prefer a thicker consistency.

Enjoy!

A three-deck affair, **Spoon Café & Lounge** (V. Vigadó tér 3, tel. 30/655-0200, www.spooncafe.hu, daily noon-midnight, mains 2,990-5,890 Ft) is hard to miss, seeing as it's docked along the Pest embankment by the InterContinental Hotel. The cuisine won't surprise you, as it mostly comprises Hungarian standards, but its location, view, and overall unique experience is hard to beat. It's excellent for an after-dinner drink as well.

Latin American

If you love steak, you most certainly cannot overlook **Pampas Steakhouse** (V. Vámház körút 6, tel. 1/411-1750, www.steak.hu, daily noon-12:30am, mains 2,650-11,850 Ft). At this tastefully designed and reasonably priced Argentinean restaurant, you'll simply devour house specialties like the New Zealand lamb chops and grilled crayfish. There are plenty of Angus steaks to choose from as well, along with various grilled chicken and salmon dishes. Do leave room for the chocolate mousse or you'll be very sorry.

Mediterranean

Trattoria Toscana (V. Belgrád rakpart 13-15, tel. 1/327-0045, www.toscana.hu, daily noon-midnight, mains 2,290-5,450 Ft) is a wonderful Italian restaurant that focuses on Tuscan cuisine. The tomato soup makes a particularly tasty starter, and mains like the

Cucina offers tasty Italian fare in the heart of Váci Street.

linguine with lobster, duck breast, or grilled scampi are popular choices. There are plenty of pastas and pizzas to choose from, and the traditional tiramisu and variety of ice creams are exceptional. If you're a coffee drinker, make sure to try the traditional espresso.

Right in the heart of tourist central is ⟨ **Cucina** (V. Váci utca 20, tel. 1/266-4144, www.lacucina.hu, daily 11:30am-midnight, mains 2,600-5,950 Ft), one of the better Italian restaurants in the downtown core. Inside, you can watch the pizza man do his thing in the middle of the floor or stare in wonder at the huge photo mural of Rome's Piazza Navona. Otherwise, you can sit outside on the terrace and watch the scores of people saunter by. Typical Italian food like pizzas, pastas, fish, and risotto are on offer, all of them delicious and surprisingly affordable given the location.

Serving up the finest Greek food in Pest is ⟨ **Taverna Dionysos** (V. Belgrád rakpart 16, tel. 1/318-1222, www.taverna-dionysos. hu, daily noon-midnight, mains 2,720-6,200 Ft), a warm and friendly restaurant offering fantastic views of the Danube and mouthwatering authentic dishes. All the usual suspects are here: gyros, calamari, and moussaka, not to mention a number of homemade beef, pork, and lamb dishes. The atmosphere is cheery and the service is solid, although there has been some grumbling lately about how long the meals have been taking. It hasn't affected business, however, as reservations are strongly advised.

La Coppola (V. Károlyi Mihály utca 19, tel. 1/235-0425, www.lacoppola.hu, daily 11am-11pm, mains 1,790-5,990 Ft) is a neighborhood favorite, cooking up generous portions of authentically Sicilian pizza, pasta, fish, and meat dishes to a packed split-level crowd night after night. The fish soup, Etna pizza, and homemade tagliatelle with salmon are just a few of the hits here, and those traveling with kids will be happy to know there are toys and distractions for the kiddies on the second floor, should you want to enjoy your meal in delectable peace.

© TOM DIRLIS

Taverna Dionysos serves up the finest Greek food in Pest.

LIPÓTVÁROS
American
KNRDY (V. Október 6. utca 15, tel. 1/788-1685, http://knrdy.com, daily 8am-1am, mains 2,990-11,990 Ft) is Budapest's premier steak house, offering mouthwatering cuts of Wagyu, Argentinian, and USDA prime beef in upscale silver-and-black surroundings that befit the hefty price tag. You can't miss with any of the steak options, and starters like the seared foie gras, Mangalica pork, and tuna tartare top the list in tastiness. Knowledgeable and helpful staff, offering attentive service without being overly intrusive, complement this exceptional dining experience.

Cafés
Located between Nyugati train station and Margaret Bridge, **Európa Kávéház** (V. Szent István körút 7-9, tel. 1/312-2362, www.europa-kavehaz.hu, daily 8:30am-9pm, mains 1,690-3,900 Ft) is usually busy with shoppers and strollers in need of a break. A large selection of

cakes as well as homemade sandwiches await, as does a very pleasant atmosphere and rather friendly service. A simple yet filling breakfast is available as well.

Warm service and excellent value is what you can expect at **Café Jubilee** (V. Szent István körút 13, tel. 1/789-3357, http://cafejubilee.hu, daily 8am-1am, mains 1,750-3,450 Ft), a colorful, cozy café decorated in hip, haphazard way with comfortable couches and armchairs and all kinds of photos and pseudo-clutter adorning its walls and ceiling. The salads are excellent, the goulash hits the spot, and the all-day breakfast is a relief for weary travelers. A solid and affordable find.

Hungarian
Popular with both Hungarians and expats, **Cafe Kör** (V. Sas utca 17, tel. 1/311-0053, www.cafekor.com, Mon.-Sat. 10am-10pm, mains 2,090-4,690 Ft) remains as popular as ever due to the simple fact that it continually serves high-quality food at remarkably reasonable prices. It boasts a rather creative Hungarian menu that is far lighter than at other traditional restaurants. You can't go wrong with the roast chicken or beef tenderloin. Make sure to save room for dessert, as the sponge cake and Gundel pancakes are prepared with the love and attention only a grandmother could give.

Csarnok Vendéglő (V. Hold utca 11, tel. 1/269-4906, www.csarnokvendeglo.hu, daily 10am-10pm, mains 1,280-3,200 Ft) is a cheap local restaurant located near the U.S. embassy that remains mostly unknown to visitors. Steeped in tradition, the menu is heavy on meats and sweets and light on pomp and circumstance. If you want a hearty meal and need to keep costs down, you won't find many places offering more bang for your buck.

Borkonyha WineKitchen (V. Sas utca 3, tel. 1/266-0835, www.borkonyha.hu, Mon.-Sat. noon-midnight, mains 3,350-4,450 Ft) is a cozy and affordable restaurant offering traditional seasonal menus that include duck, seafood, and lamb as well as winning appetizers like Mangalica bacon and crispy duck liver that keep them coming back for more. And there is plenty of wine to choose from: over 200 Hungarian choices, in fact, all of which sit pretty in the enormous fridge behind the bar and all of which are kindly offered by the glass.

Mediterranean

Trattoria Pomo D'oro (V. Arany János utca 9, tel. 1/302-6473, www.pomodorobudapest. com, daily noon-midnight, mains 2,350-6,490 Ft) is a warm, intimate restaurant that offers a wide variety of excellent Italian dishes. The fresh *branzino* is quite good, and the tenderloin with bacon and pepper sauce will satisfy even the most finicky of carnivores. For dessert try the excellent tiramisu or almond chocolate cake, and top the whole thing off with one of the 200 award-winning Italian and Hungarian wines available.

Mexican

For delicious and authentic Mexican-American eats, try **Iguana Bar and Grill** (V. Zóltán utca 16, tel. 1/331-4352, www.iguana.hu, daily 11:30am-1am, mains 1,790-4,690 Ft). Located around the corner from Szabadság Square, this expat staple is colorfully decorated with comical if kitschy retro pictures of old Mexican films, cigarette advertisements, license plates, and mariachi musicians. The menu has everything you'd want in a restaurant like this, offering generous portions of tacos, burritos, quesadillas, fajitas, chilies, and vegetarian options to boot. Jenő's Quesadilla and the aptly named Whoop-Ass Chili are popular choices, but pretty much anything you order is bound to please the palate. It's highly recommended, and advance reservations are advised.

TERÉZVÁROS AND ERZSÉBETVÁROS
American
Suelto Cafe & Grill (VII. Madách Imre tér 1, tel. 1/780-9815, sueltomama.blogspot.hu, Mon.-Thurs. 11:30am-midnight, Fri. 11:30am-2am, Sat. noon-2am, Sun. 1pm-midnight, mains 1,390-2,290 Ft) is a funky little eight-table spot with simple affordably priced fare

like chicken and pasta and burgers served by a lovely and very welcoming staff. It's an excellent choice if you're looking to keep costs down while enjoying a solid meal in intimate surroundings.

Cafés

Mai Manó Café (VI. Nagymező utca 20, tel. 1/269-5642, daily 8am-1am, mains 990-1,750 Ft) is housed in the elegant Mai Manó House on Budapest's Broadway. An excellent and ever-evolving selection of coffees, wines, desserts, salads, and sandwiches, combined with its central location, makes this an excellent choice for unwinding and people-watching. It's perfect for a lazy afternoon.

Café Vian (VI. Liszt Ferenc tér 9, tel. 1/268-1154, www.cafevian.com, daily 10am-1am, mains 1,990-4,990 Ft) is located on trendy Franz Liszt Square and tends to fill up rather quickly in the evenings. There is a lot to choose from here, including a large variety of international breakfasts, salads, pastas, and sandwiches. The grilled honey orange duck breast and Norwegian salmon are superb, as is the decent selection of desserts and coffees. An extensive drinks menu is one more reason to visit and soak up the strip's atmosphere.

Múzeum Cukrászda (VII. Múzeum körút 10, tel. 1/338-4415, daily noon-midnight, mains 990-2,350 Ft) is located between the museum district's university and the National Museum, attracting an eclectic mix of patrons who can oftentimes be found gorging on the scrumptious desserts on offer as well as light salads and sandwiches. An excellent place to start the day or to end the evening.

Cat lovers will not want to miss spending a bit of time at the **Cat Café** (VI. Révay utca 3, tel. 20/617-3301, www.catcafebudapest.hu, daily 10am-10pm, mains 890-1,780 Ft), a clean and friendly place offering a large selection of tea, coffee, sandwiches, and cakes that can be enjoyed in the company of—what else—cats! The resident fur balls walk around freely, happy to play with guests or catch up on a much-needed nap. A cute and playful café that kids can enjoy as well.

You'll find the fabulous Lotz Coffee House on the second floor of the Paris Department Store.

Located in the Paris Department Store on the second floor of the Alexandra bookshop is the magnificent ◖**Lotz Coffee House** (VI. Andrássy út 39, tel. 30/817-0268, Mon.-Fri. 10am-10pm, mains 890-2,780 Ft). Its centerpiece is the breathtaking ceiling, painted in 1910 in bold Renaissance style by the one and only Károly Lotz. It's a masterwork that sets an elegant otherworldly tone to an afternoon filled with delicious coffees and pastries. It's an elegant, relaxing way to spend an hour or two.

Continental

Now located in the Hotel Andrássy, **Baraka** (VI. Andrássy út 111, tel. 1/483-1355, www.barakarestaurant.hu, daily noon-3pm and 6pm-11pm, mains 5,400-6,900 Ft) continues to serve some of the most imaginative and tasty dishes in the city. Enjoy the sophisticated art deco interior while savoring such delicacies as the seared duck breast and roasted red snapper. If there's room for dessert, give the

mouthwatering dark chocolate volcano mojito parfait a try. The menu changes often, so make sure to check the website for current menu recommendations.

Located in the heart of Budapest's Broadway, **Két Szerecsen** (VI. Nagymező utca 14, tel. 1/343-1984, www.ketszerecsen.hu, Mon.-Fri. 8am-midnight, Sat.-Sun. 9am-midnight, 1,690-3,390 Ft) is a popular choice with Hungarian celebrities and savvy locals. A very laid-back, warm, and friendly atmosphere pervades, making it an excellent place to have a drink or grab a bite with a handful of close friends. The caesar salad is excellent, as is the fried monkfish and ravioli filled with spinach and ricotta. This is the kind of place that can easily make a regular out of you.

If you're on the lookout for mouthwatering traditional Hungarian food in addition to Continental cuisine, you cannot overlook **Haxen Király** (VI. Király utca 100, tel. 1/351-6793, www.haxen.hu, Sun.-Thurs. noon-midnight, Fri.-Sat. noon-12:45am, mains 2,290-4,960 Ft). Huge portions served with a smile in a rustic, comfortable setting keep this place busy more often than not, so reservations may not be a bad idea. Devoted carnivores should try the grill platter or venison tenderloin, while those looking for a rich, tasty alternative should opt for the duck casserole. You really can't go wrong here.

A small but diverse menu is what you can expect at ◖ **Chess Restaurant** (VII. Dob utca 63, tel. 1/882-3080, www.chessrestaurant.hu, daily 7am-11pm, mains 2,700-4,900 Ft), a bright, unpretentious establishment with friendly service and very reasonable prices. Dishes change on a seasonal basis but tend to revolve around the pork, beef, seafood, and traditionally Hungarian variety. It's a solid choice known to attract repeat business.

Hungarian

◖ **Zeller Bistro** (VII. Izabella utca 36-38, tel. 30/651-0880, Tues.-Sat. noon-3pm and 6pm-11pm, mains 1,880-4,780 Ft) is a pleasant, laid-back, and affordable restaurant with a warm human touch. Friendly and polite

BUDAPEST

service coupled with homemade dishes cooked with fresh ingredients taken from the owners' farm make a winning combination. Try the duck breast, the beef tartare, or the carrot cake, which has made the place legendary. Try anything you like knowing that it shall not disappoint.

Menza (VI. Liszt Ferenc tér 2, tel. 1/413-1482, www.menzaetterem.hu, daily 10am-midnight, mains 2,190-4,490 Ft) is still the most popular bar-restaurant on Franz Liszt Square, and it's no surprise why. Classic Hungarian dishes like goose liver, pork chops, and beef stew are prepared with care and served either inside in their 1970s cafeteria-inspired surroundings or outside on the square, where you can sunbathe and people-watch to your heart's content. Excellent service and their homemade sour cherry strudel with ice cream are two more reasons to pay a visit.

Indian

Shalimar (VII. Dob utca 50, tel. 1/352-0305, www.shalimar.hu, daily noon-4pm and 6pm-midnight, mains 1,590-4,390 Ft) has placed in the top three as Best Indian Restaurant of the Year in the local papers for a decade now, and the first bite into anything on the menu will quickly show you why. Whether it's the chicken *makhani* or various beef, lamb, and vegetarian dishes, you simply will not be disappointed. The service and ambience can be spotty at times, but it's still well worth a shot should you be in the neighborhood.

International

Téli Kertem (VII. Dohány utca 28, tel. 1/781-6510, daily 4pm-4am, mains 850-1,390 Ft) is a funky, friendly kind of place serving tasty, generously portioned offerings like beef stew with dumplings, honey-ginger chicken with jasmine rice, and a notoriously good Balkan burger. Warm, polite service and excellent value is what keeps this place filled to capacity most nights.

The menu at (**Araz** (VII. Dohány utca 42-44, tel. 1/815-1100, www.araz.hu, daily 7am-11pm, mains 2,550-5,250 Ft) is

primarily focused on French and Hungarian cuisine, offering mouthwatering winners like duck breast, salmon fillet, and shank of lamb in elegant and intimate surroundings. The service is polite and attentive without being intrusive, and the prices have remained more than reasonable despite the restaurant's steady increase in popularity.

Köleves Stonesoup Restobar (VII. Kazinczy utca 41, tel. 1/322-1011, www.koleves.com, daily noon-midnight, mains 1,490-3,190 Ft) is a comfortable laid-back spot in the heart of the Jewish district. The menu reflects Hungarian, Mediterranean, and Jewish (not kosher) delights, with an emphasis on beef, chicken, and lamb. You can also find staples such as duck breast and smoked turkey leg, both of which are scrumptious. There are a handful of options for vegetarians and a small number of desserts, including crepe suzette and sponge cake. This local favorite also has free Wi-Fi and the occasional live music event on the weekends.

Mediterranean

Not far from the Oktogon is **Ristorante Krizia** (VI. Mozsár utca 12, tel. 1/331-8711, www.ristorantekrizia.hu, Mon.-Sat. noon-3pm and 6:30pm-midnight, mains 2,680-5,600 Ft). By mixing the creative and traditional sides of Italian cuisine, owner-chef Graziano Cattaneo has managed to create one of the better Italian restaurants in Budapest. Start off with the excellent porcini soup and follow up with a homemade dish like the salmon filet, veal osso buco, or potato gnocchi with asiago cheese. Definitely leave room for dessert, as you'll want to try the bitter chocolate mousse and caramelized fruit pancake. Reservations are recommended if you're planning on visiting in the evening.

Fans of fine Italian dining will be more than pleased with (**Fausto's** (VI. Székely Mihály utca 2, tel. 1/877-6210, www.fausto.hu, Mon.-Sat. noon-3pm and 7pm-11pm, mains 2,900-6,800 Ft), a consistent favorite on the restaurant scene. Its minimalist setting sets the stage for authentic Italian dishes served with a contemporary twist. Try the spinach gnocchi with calamari and broccoli ragout or sea bass fillet in a lobster and zucchini cream, and top it all off with a sour-cherry and nut cake. Although it's on the pricey side, rest assured this is money well spent. **Il Terzo Cerchio** (VII. Dohány utca 40, tel. 1/354-0788, www.ilterzocerchio.hu, daily 11:30am-11:30pm, mains 1,950-4,850 Ft) is a favorite of Budapest's Italian community, and it's easy to see why. From the brick walls and high arched ceiling to an extensive menu featuring wood-grilled pizzas, steaks, and seafood, this warm and friendly restaurant captures the essentials inherent in an authentic Italian dining experience.

THE VÁROSLIGET
Continental
Close to Heroes Square and located on its own island in City Park Lake, **Robinson** (XIV. Városligeti tó, tel. 1/422-0222, www.robinsonrestaurant.hu, daily noon-4pm and 6pm-11pm, mains 2,700-8,900 Ft) is an ideal restaurant to enjoy a romantic dinner for two. Its summer terrace affords peaceful views of the surrounding landscape, while a fireplace keeps things nice and cozy during the winter. The goulash soup makes for an excellent starter, while main courses like the duck leg with cabbage and free-range chicken continue to be among diners' favorites. The friendly family atmosphere, complemented by wonderful live Latin guitar in the evening, add to a memorable dining experience.

Hungarian
Gundel (XIV. Gundel Károly út 4, tel. 1/468-4040, www.gundel.hu, daily noon-midnight, Sun. brunch 11:30am-3pm, mains 5,900-16,900 Ft) is one of Budapest's best-known restaurants and is equated with the finest in Hungarian cuisine. An impressive art collection covers the walls of its main dining room, giving it an immediate Old World charm sorely lacking in other upscale restaurants. Dishes like their famous foie gras and a gourmet assortment of fish, duck, and meat options are

cooked to perfection and can be washed down with over 100 available wines, including those from Gundel's own wineries. Located next to Gundel, **Bagolyvár** (XIV. Gundel Károly út 4, tel. 1/468-3110, www.bagolyvar.com, daily noon-11pm, mains 1,900-4,900 Ft) is a far less expensive choice that doesn't sacrifice any of the quality. Simple homemade Hungarian dishes are cooked by an all-female kitchen staff and served by waitresses who are consistently warm and friendly. The permanent menu comprises about half a dozen choices, including the tasty but heavy garlic-roasted barbecue pork and veal with egg dumplings. Daily specials are something to keep an eye out for, and desserts like the walnut pancake with chocolate sauce are superb. This is an excellent choice for the budget traveler who'd like to sample well-cooked, authentic Hungarian cuisine.

JÓZSEFVÁROS AND FERENCVÁROS
American
Fun, frolic, and some of the best burgers in town are what you can expect at **Manga Cowboy** (IX. Ráday utca 31, tel. 1/215-8079, www.mangacowboy.hu, Mon.-Fri. 9am-midnight, Sat. 11am-midnight, Sun. 11am-10pm, mains 1,690-3,990 Ft). Colorfully named and perfectly prepared Japanese-American mash-ups like the Kamikaze Burger, Oren Ishii grilled chicken, and Godzilla Combo are served by friendly young waitstaff who dare you to finish all your unbelievably spicy Kill Bill chicken wings.

Black Cab Burger (IX. Mester utca 46, www.blackcabburger.hu, daily 11am-midnight, mains 700-1,400 Ft) has many loyal fans who make the trek to this small, simple, and clean establishment because they maintain it's here where you'll find the city's best burger. Made from scratch with loads of minced meat and a few necessary seasonings, this huge and delicious serving of goodness keeps the limited amount of tables occupied on a consistent basis, so get here early and get in line; it'll be well worth the wait.

BUDAPEST

Paprika Power

If you weren't aware of paprika's popularity before landing in Hungary, you most certainly will be when you get here. Strung up and sold everywhere, Hungarian paprika is the national ingredient, spicing up soups, poultry, and countless meat-based dishes. The following are a few facts that will help you understand Hungary's love of, and association with, the fabled red powder.

FACTS ABOUT PAPRIKA

- Paprika powder is produced by grinding the dried deep red paprika pods of the pepper plant.

- Although it is *the* symbol of Hungarian cuisine, the plant was originally introduced by the Turks during their rule in the 16th and 17th centuries.

- Red paprika isn't the hottest you can find. It's the orange-colored one that will really make you sweat.

- Paprika's heat is caused by capsaicin, a chemical that is extracted from paprika plants and used in pharmaceutical production due to its pain-killing properties.

- Paprika is rich in vitamin C (150 mg per 100 g of paprika), a fact that was discovered by Hungarian scientist Albert Szent-Györgyi, who was consequently awarded the Nobel Prize in 1937.

- Kalocsa and Szeged in the south are the heart and soul of Hungary's paprika production.

TYPES OF HUNGARIAN PAPRIKA

There are eight different brands of paprika generally available in shops, all of which vary in potency and color.

1. Special quality (*különleges*): the mildest of all paprikas; sports the most vibrant red color
2. Delicate (*csípősmentes csemege*): mild paprika full of rich flavor
3. Exquisite delicate (*csemege*): slightly more potent than the Delicate
4. Pungent exquisite delicate (*csípős csemege*): getting warmer
5. Noble sweet (*édesnemes*): the most common type, slightly potent with a bright-red color
6. Half-sweet (*félédes*): a medium-potent paprika
7. Rose (*rózsa*): light red color and mild
8. Hot (*erős*): the papa bear of paprikas; sporting a light brown-orange color, it'll make you blow smoke out your ears

Cafés

The award-winning **Múzeum Kávéház** (VIII. Múzeum körút 12, tel. 1/267-0375, www.muzeumkavehaz.hu, Mon.-Sat. 6pm-midnight, mains 2,800-6,700 Ft) is a time-honored establishment that serves some of Hungary's finest domestic cuisine. Its gorgeous dining rooms are decorated with antique Zsolnay tiles and possess a stunning ceiling fresco by none other than famed artist Károly Lotz. Pretty much anything on the menu is a hit, particularly the catfish in paprika sauce or the unbelievable veal with goose liver and mushrooms. For dessert, try the strudel or traditional cottage cheese dumplings. This is a class act all the way.

Hungarian

Fulemule (IX. Köfaragó utca 5, tel. 1/266-7947, www.fulemule.hu, Mon.-Thurs. noon-10pm, Fri.-Sat. noon-11pm, mains 2,900-5,900 Ft) is an old-school Hungarian restaurant that continues to attract a large number of regulars thanks to its excellent food and generous portions. Enjoy such classic dishes as carp, beef stew, and goose liver, or take a chance on their Jewish menu, which typically includes delicious choices like roast veal and smoked meat brisket. Traditional, affordable, and unpretentious.

Indian

The simple yet dependable **Pandsab Tandoori** (XIII. Pannónia utca 3, tel. 36/270-2974, daily noon-11pm, mains 1,690-2,790 Ft) prepares a number of delicious tandoori specialties from the Punjab region as well as a variety of great breads. Fast, affordable, and authentic, it's an excellent place for lunch or a quick dinner.

International

Considered by many to be Budapest's finest restaurant, **◖ Costes** (IX. Ráday utca 4, tel. 1/219-0696, www.costes.hu, Wed.-Sun. 6:30pm-midnight, mains 4,400-11,500 Ft) offers diners exceptional dishes such as honey-glazed duck breast and crayfish royale, all of which are served up in French-style minimalist surroundings. There are hundreds of wines to choose from as well, not to mention decadent desserts like the milk chocolate mousse. A night here will cost you, but it's money well spent.

Situated behind the Central Market Hall, **◖ Borbíróság** (IX. Csarnok tér 5, tel. 1/219-0902, http://borbirosag.com, Mon.-Sat. noon-11:30pm, mains 2,150-4,450 Ft) is a modern, well lit, and friendly restaurant with tasty fare and an incredible wine list. Try the chicken, butterfish, or duck breast with fresh roasted vegetables, then wash it down with a delicious Hungarian wine that the waitstaff will be more than happy to recommend. It's an excellent and affordable restaurant that's sure to please.

Latin American

Pata Negra (IX. Kálvin tér 8, tel. 1/215-5616, www.patanegra.hu, daily 11am-midnight, mains 1,400-2,200 Ft) is a popular tapas bar right in the thick of the lively Raday strip. Forty different types of tapas are on offer, with the seafood, chorizo, and meatball being the heavy favorites. A large number of vegetarian options as well as tasty lamb, beef, and pork cuts make this affordable option a no-brainer.

VÁRHEGY, THE VÍZIVÁROS, AND CENTRAL BUDA
Asian

Fuji (II. Csatárka utca 54, tel. 1/325-7111, www.fujirestaurant.hu, daily noon-11pm, mains 2,990-14,900 Ft) offers some of the finest sushi in town, though it does come at a price. The sashimi menu offers pretty much any sushi combination you can think of, while delicious offerings like the Fuji Menu include *gyoza* dumplings and beef sukiyaki that you can prepare at your table over a gas flame. This is an excellent dining experience that you won't soon forget, but prepare yourself for a rather hefty bill.

Cafés

Angelika Kávéház (I. Batthyány tér 7, tel. 1/225-1653, www.angelikacafe.hu, Apr.-Oct. daily 9am-midnight, Nov.-Mar. daily 9am-11pm, mains 1,990-4,590 Ft) is a wonderful place to take a break from the day's activities and enjoy a light meal or snack in elegant turn-of-the-20th-century surroundings. If you get there early, you can choose from a number of breakfast options, like three-egg omelets or toasted sandwiches. There are plenty of soups and salads to choose from, and the entrée highlights include grilled salmon and Caribbean chicken wings. The cakes, pastries, and teas are all in a class of their own, and coffee drinkers will be happy to know that there are plenty of iced and piping-hot possibilities.

An institution of sophistication for over 25 years now, **◖ Café Pierrot** (I. Fortuna utca 14, tel. 1/375-6971, www.pierrot.hu, daily 11am-midnight, mains 3,840-6,860 Ft) combines a stylish setting and an unrivaled level of service to create an atmosphere no diner will soon forget. The pike perch with zucchini is excellent, while heartier appetites will appreciate the 21-day-aged beef sirloin. A comprehensive selection of Hungarian wines is ready for the tasting, and the crème brûlée may very well be the best in town. Softly played live piano music in the background completes the effect.

While definitely a tourist standby, **Ruszwurm** (I. Szentháromság utca 7, tel. 1/375-5284, www.ruszwurm.hu, daily 10am-7pm, mains 880-1,780 Ft) is nevertheless well worth seeking out for their unbelievably tasty pastries and desserts. Grab a cake or strudel or homemade lemonade and while away an hour in sugary goodness. Bear in mind that service can be spotty sometimes, most likely due to the large number of occasionally demanding tourists lined up throughout the day.

Continental

Horgásztanya Vendéglő (I. Fő utca 27, tel. 1/212-3780, www.horgasztanyavendeglo.hu, daily 10am-midnight, mains 1,650-4,490 Ft) has been around for as long as anyone can remember and is still considered one of the finest fish restaurants in town. The fish soup is hard to beat, and the trout makes for a memorable main. There are also meat-based Hungarian specialties, but it would be a shame to ignore the variety of fishy delights. If you care for dessert, try the Somloi gnocchi and wash it all down with a light Hungarian wine. Few, if any, leave here disappointed.

János Étterem (I. Hegyalja út 23, tel. 1/202-3414, www.janosetterem.hu, daily noon-midnight, mains 1,650-4,450 Ft) is a dependable restaurant with attentive waitstaff serving up affordable options like smoked ham, veal with paprika, and the ubiquitous goulash soup. The menu changes frequently, but the quality hasn't changed one bit. Consider it five-star dining at two-star prices.

French

Pavillon de Paris (I. Fő utca 20, tel. 1/225-0174, www.pavillondeparis.hu, Tues.-Sat. noon-3pm and 6pm-10pm, mains 3,600-5,900 Ft) is a tastefully decorated French restaurant sporting one of the more romantic courtyards to be found during the summer months. Popular dishes include the duck breast with lavender and honey sauce and rack of lamb in mustard and persillade. There is also a fine selection of French cheeses available, complemented with a top-notch selection of French and Hungarian wines.

Belgian Brasserie Henri (I. Bem rakpart 12, tel. 1/201-5082, www.belgasorozo.com, daily noon-midnight, mains 2,090-5,990 Ft) boasts an extensive beer list and well-prepared French menu that includes excellent choices like the confit pork riblets with shrimp, fried Corsendonk Agnus Dei chicken breast with roquefort cheese, and rosé duck breast with sauce of orange and mango. It's a winner all around, as evidenced by the brisk business it does night and day. Reservations are recommended.

Hungarian

Kacsa Vendéglo (I. Fő utca 75, tel. 1/201-9992, www.kacsavendeglo.hu, daily 6pm-1am, mains 3,300-6,500 Ft) is an elegant, comfortable, upscale restaurant specializing in duck. While various beef and wild game dishes can be had, it's the duck in all its forms that most are drawn to. Try the crispy duck with sour cherry, pineapple, or orange sauce, or the wild duck stuffed with plums—or any other interesting combination that strikes your fancy. With live music in the evening, this is a perfect place to celebrate an anniversary or enjoy a romantic dinner for two.

Carne di Hall (I. Bem rakpart 20, tel. 30/446-9004, www.carnedihall.eu, Mon.-Sat. noon-midnight, mains 2,790-4,690 Ft) is a popular cellar restaurant serving well-prepared Hungarian dishes like goose liver, duck breast, and salmon fillet. Excellent service and a decent range of available wines help keep this cozy restaurant at the top of many locals' lists.

Alabárdos (I. Országház utca 2, tel. 1/356-0851, www.alabardos.hu, Mon.-Fri. 7pm-11pm, Sat. noon-3pm and 7pm-11pm, mains 3,400-6,500 Ft) is a long-standing professionally run restaurant offering classic Hungarian dishes with a contemporary edge. There's a tasting menu available as well as expertly prepared duck, rabbit, pork, and veal selections that are reasonably-priced, albeit a tad smallish in portion.

Café Marvelosa (I. Lánchíd utca 13, tel. 1/201-9221, www.marvelosa.eu, Tues.-Sat. 10am-10pm, Sun. 10am-6pm, mains 2,390-2,870 Ft) is a warm and cozy establishment with vintage artwork on the walls that makes you feel like you're having lunch at your quirky grandmother's house. The menu is basic but well prepared, and the service is prompt and friendly. The real gem is the dessert menu boasting a cottage cheese dumpling that will change your entire world view. It's perfect for a lazy afternoon.

International

Rivalda Café and Restaurant (I. Színház utca 5-9, tel. 1/489-0236, www.rivalda.net, daily 11:30am-11:30pm, mains 2,600-5,700 Ft) is a classy yet comfortable restaurant with exceptional outdoor seating and a number of well-prepared international meals on its menu. The sautéed foie gras, Mediterranean chicken, and Argentine steak are all winners, as are the handful of classic Hungarian dishes like the breast of pheasant and wild boar ragout. Prompt service and a fine wine selection are two more reasons to make the trek to Buda.

Csalogány 26 (I. Csalogány utca 26, tel. 1/201-7892, www.csalogany26.hu, Tues.-Sat. noon-3pm and 7pm-10pm, mains 2,400-5,500 Ft) is a simple bistro with a winning, unpretentious atmosphere allowing diners to enjoy the short yet fantastic menu in comfort. Brought to you by friendly and knowledgeable staff are such delights as Norwegian salmon, roast pork, and scallops in butter squash, all of which can be washed down with a number of fantastic domestic wines. It's always a reliable choice.

Trófea Grill Étterem (II. Margit körút 2, tel. 1/438-9090, www.trofeagrill.eu, daily noon-midnight, mains 3,899 Ft Mon.-Fri., 5,499 Ft Sat.-Sun.) offers an all-you-can-eat Hungarian buffet of exceptional quality that ranges from venison to duck to catfish and a whole lot more in between. There are also a number of tasty soups to open with and a large salad bar for those inclined toward healthier options. Excellent service and excellent value make this a solid choice for lunch or dinner.

Russian

Arany Kaviár (I. Ostrom utca 19, tel. 1/201-6737, www.aranykaviar.hu, daily noon-3pm and 6pm-midnight, mains 3,500-9,900 Ft) is an upscale Buda restaurant with an elegant finely lit interior: the perfect place to have a romantic dinner with that special someone. The French-influenced Russian menu is carefully selected every month and offers delicious

choices such as the classic chicken Kiev and lamb with vegetable ragout. If undecided, consider the Gourmet Menu option, which comprises the finest assortment of food available at the restaurant, selected from the most popular courses on offer.

ÓBUDA AND MARGIT SZIGET

Hungarian

One of the more popular choices on the Buda side is **Kisbuda Gyöngye** (III. Kenyeres utca 34, tel. 1/368-6402, www.remiz.hu, Tues.-Sat. noon-11pm, mains 2,780-4,990 Ft). Its antique furniture and frescoed ceiling provide a very intimate environment for savoring international gourmet dishes as well as Hungarian favorites. The Serbian catfish fillet and venison steak with cranberries come highly recommended, as does the rum and chocolate pancake, a delicious, decadent dessert.

Kéhli Restaurant (III. Mókus utca 22, tel. 1/368-0613, www.kehli.hu, daily noon-11:30pm, mains 1,990-3,990 Ft) is a traditional restaurant with slightly rustic decor and hearty Hungarian dishes like fried pike perch, stuffed cabbage, beef goulash, baked lamb, and a whole lot more. The service is friendly, the live music unintrusive, and the prices more than reasonable. This is always a dependable choice.

Zöld Kapu (III. Szőlő utca 42, tel. 1/387-7028, www.zoldkapuvendeglo.hu, daily 10am-10pm, mains 1,990-3,990 Ft) is an excellent Hungarian restaurant offering tasty affordable meals in portions generous enough to keep most people from being able to finish a three course meal. Whether it's beef or poultry or lamb or veal, you'll find a wide variety to choose from and a lovely garden area you can enjoy it all in during the warmer months. There's great value for your money here.

International

Symbol (III. Bécsi utca 56, tel. 1/333-5656, www.symbolbudapest.hu, daily 11:30am-midnight, mains 1,800-4,680 Ft) is an elegant and appealing restaurant that serves up creative fusion dishes with an Italian and Hungarian bent. Pizzas, pastas, and an eclectic choice of meat, fish, and poultry dishes is what you can expect as well as a decent selection of wines and desserts. It's a solid choice should you happen to be in the neighborhood.

Mediterranean

Gyradiko (III. corner of Királyok útja and Pünkösdfürdő utca, tel. 1/243-4986, http:gyradiko.hu, Mon. 1pm-11pm, Tues.-Wed.

11am-11pm, Thurs.-Sat. 11am-1am, Sun. 11am-11pm, mains 760-2,800 Ft) offers what many insist is the finest Greek food in town, particularly the gyros platter, which is the most popular dish by far. Leaning toward a fast-food vibe, the warm and friendly staff work overtime trying to quell the long, seemingly endless line of hungry customers dying for another bite of Hellenic heavenliness. Highly recommended.

Information and Services

VISITOR INFORMATION OFFICES

There is no shortage of visitor information possibilities in Budapest, but the main company that handles most visitors is **Tourinform** (main office, V. Sütő u. 2, tel. 1/438-8080, www.budapestinfo.hu, daily 8am-8pm). Helpful, efficient, and English-speaking staff are more than happy to provide you with information regarding sights, tours, day trips outside the capital, and much more. You can also pick up plenty of free leaflets, booklets, and maps that are quite comprehensive and invaluable to the first-time visitor.

Another centrally located office can be found at Franz Liszt Square (VI. Andrássy út 47, tel. 1/322-4098, www.budapestinfo.hu, daily noon-8pm), which provides the same useful information and is just a few minutes away from St. Stephen's Basilica and the Opera. Those flying to Budapest should make sure to check out the **Tourinform Ferihegy** (Terminal 1, tel. 1/438-8080, www.budapestinfo.hu, daily 8am-10pm) branch for all pertinent information before heading into the heart of the city. If you think you might need instant information at any given hour of the day, be sure to contact the visitor information 24-hour hotline (tel. 1/438-8080).

EMERGENCY SERVICES

The **Budapest Police Command** (V. Vigadó utca 4, daily 24 hours) is always available to visitors at its Deák Square location. If your passport is lost or stolen, report it immediately to the Budapest and Pest County Directorate of the **Office for Immigration and Citizenship** (XI. Budafoki út 60, tel. 1/463-9165, daily 24 hours) or your country's embassy.

Should an emergency occur, contact the appropriate number:

• Ambulance: 104

• Police: 107

• Fire: 105

• General emergency: 112

MEDICAL SERVICES

There are many hospitals in Budapest, including **MÁV Kórház** (VI. Rippl-Rónai utca 37, emergency room entrance, tel. 1/269-5656) and **Országos Traumatológiai Intézet** (VIII. Fiumeti út 17, tel. 1/333-7599), which serve both adults and children. For adults only, there is the **BM Kórház** (VII. Városligeti fasor 9-11, tel. 1/322-7620), while the **Heim Pál Gyermekkórház** (VIII. Ülloi út 86, tel. 1/210-0720) deals exclusively with children.

FirstMed Centers (I. Hattyú utca 14, 5th Fl., tel. 1/224-9090, www.firstmedcenters.com, daily 24 hours) is an English-speaking clinic that offers emergency care around the clock. **Medicover Health Centre** (VI. Teréz körút 55-57, tel. 1/465-3100, www.medicover.com/hu, Mon.-Fri. 7am-8pm) is the leading private health care provider in the region that charges either a flat fee or a fee for specific services. For immediate 24-hour dental care, try **SOS Dental Service** (VI. Király utca 14, tel. 1/333-8888, www.smilistic.com, daily 24 hours) or **Profident** (VII. Karoly körút 1, tel. 1/342-2546, www.profident.com, daily 24 hours). The word for pharmacy in Hungarian is *gyógyszertár*. All pharmacies will be able to provide you with the proper medicine you need to control or cure most common ailments. Should you need a pharmacy after regular business hours, the location of the nearest 24-hour one is displayed on all pharmacy doors. Don't panic if the pharmacy looks closed when you get there. Ring the bell and wait patiently. A small fee is added for nighttime service. Some all-night pharmacies around town are **ALMA Pharmacy** (VIII. Baross tér 9, www.almapatika.com), **Déli Pharmacy** (XII. Alkotás út 1/b, tel. 1/355-4691), **Óbuda Pharmacy** (III. Vörösvári út 86, tel. 1/368-6430), **Örs Vezér Pharmacy** (XIV. Örs vezér tere, tel. 1/211-3861), **Szent Margit Pharmacy** (II. Frankel Leó út 22, tel. 1/212-4311), and **Teréz Pharmacy** (VI. Teréz körút 41, tel. 1/311-4439).

BANKS AND CURRENCY EXCHANGE

Banks tend to offer the best exchange rates in Budapest but keep relatively short hours. They are generally open Monday-Thursday 8am-4pm and Friday 8am-3pm. The most reputable banks around town are **CIB Bank** (II. Medve utca 4-14, tel. 1/212-1420, www.cib.hu), **Erste Bank** (V. Párisi utca 3, www.erstebank.hu, Mon. 8am-6pm, Tues.-Thurs. 8am-4pm, Fri. 8am-3pm), and **OTP Bank** (V. Nádor utca 6, tel. 1/483-2300, www.otpbank.hu, Mon. and Wed. 8:45am-6pm, Tues. and Thurs. 8:45am-5pm, Fri. 8:45am-4pm).

Currency exchange offices are all over the city. Should you want to forgo the banks or you need to change money after they've closed, hunt around for the best deal, as rates vary widely.

POSTAL SERVICES

Budapest has plenty of postal outlets throughout the city, so there really is no excuse for not sending that postcard to Mom. All post offices are open Monday-Friday 8am-6pm, with the exception of the two head post offices near the city's main railroad stations. The first is near **Nyugati Railroad Station** (VI. Teréz körút 51, Mon.-Sat. 7am-9pm) and the second by **Keleti Station** (VIII. Baross tér 11, Mon.-Sat. 7am-9pm, Sun. 8am-8pm). Most post offices offer both the sending and receiving of faxes as well as cash possibilities for VISA, VISA Electron, Eurocard/Mastercard, Maestro cards, Eurocheques, and American Express traveler's checks.

INTERNET

There are countless Internet cafés throughout the city. Prices vary wildly depending on their proximity to the city center. A few of the better ones are **FOUGOU** (VII. Wesselenyi utca 57, tel. 1/787-4888, fougou.uw.hu, daily 7am-2am, 31 terminals, 200 Ft per hour), **NET 7 Cafe** (VIII. József körút 14, tel. 1/798-4991, Mon.-Fri. 7am-midnight, Sat.-Sun. 10am-11pm, 20 terminals, 300 Ft per hour), and **Vista NetCafe Internet Center** (XIII. Váci út 6, tel. 70/585-3924, daily 24 hours, 40 terminals, 500 Ft per hour). Those traveling with a laptop will be happy to know that many cafés, bars, and restaurants offer free Wi-Fi to their patrons. These establishments advertise this service on their doors or windows, making it easy for you to choose whichever one strikes your fancy.

LAUNDRY

There are very few coin-op launderettes to be found in Budapest as most Hungarians have their own washing machine, however the self-explanatory **Self-Service Laundry** (VII. Dohány utca 37, tel. 1/781-0098, www.laundrybudapest.hu, daily 9am-midnight) is a fine option with helpful staff and reasonable prices. The **Liliom Textilcare Salon** (IX. Liliom utca 7-9, tel. 1/215-6782, www.liliomszalon.hu, Mon.-Fri. 7am-7:30pm, Sat. 8am-2pm), is another solid choice thanks to its modern facilities and English-speaking staff. For full-service washing and dry-cleaning, try the highly rated **Tiszta Kék** (VI. Teréz körút 62, tel. 1/374-0767, www. tisztakek.hu, Mon.-Fri. 7am-7pm, Sat. 8am-2pm) or **Horváth** (VIII. Népszínház utca 53, tel. 1/313-4508, www.kelmefesto.hu, Mon.-Thurs. 7am-5pm, Fri. 7am-4pm).

Getting There

BY AIR

Budapest Ferenc Liszt International Airport (tel. 1/296-7000, www.bud.hu) is located in southeast Pest, approximately 15 miles from the center of town. The airport has two main terminals.

Taking a cab from the airport to downtown can cost anywhere from 5,000 to 6,000 Ft, and while it's the most convenient option, there is a cheaper alternative. The airport's regularly running **minibus service** (tel. 1/296-8555, www.airportshuttle.hu, daily 24 hours) offers trips to the center for 3,200 Ft pp, with each vehicle seating anywhere from 8 to 11 passengers. Tickets can be purchased online or from the company's service desks located in both the airport's terminals. While certainly cheaper, it does, however, have one slight disadvantage: Depending on the number of people in the vehicle as well as the distances between destinations, it might be a while before you finally make it to your hotel.

BY TRAIN

A large number of trains from across Europe roll into **Keleti Station** (VIII. Kerepesi út 2-4, tel. 1/313-6835), which is located in Pest's somewhat sketchy Baross Square. The station is conveniently located on the red subway line, making it easy to reach and a snap to get to any part of the city.

Other major railroad stations include Nyugati Station and Déli Station. The occasional international train arrives at **Nyugati Station** (VI. Teréz krt. 55, tel. 1/349-0115), but it mainly serves the Danube Bend and Great Plain. It is located on the Outer Ring and borders the 5th, 6th, and 13th districts. It can be reached via the M3 Budapest subway line (Nyugati pályaudvar). **Déli Station** (I. Krisztina körút 37/A, tel. 1/355-8657) is located in central Buda at the terminus of the M2 Budapest subway line. Few international trains arrive here, and most routes serve Lake Balaton and Transdanubia.

Trains from Budapest to Prague leave regularly, roughly 5-6 times a day, and the trip takes 7-9 hours. The national train website, www.mav-start.hu, is very useful, offering complete up-to-date information regarding Hungary's railroad system and schedules.

BY BUS

Just about all international buses from the UK and continental Europe make **Népliget Station** (Népliget autóbusz-állomás, Ferencváros, IX. Üllői út 131, tel. 1/219-8086) their final destination.

Volánbusz (www.volanbusz.hu) is the country's main international bus line and runs daily buses from Prague. The trip generally takes 7.5-8 hours and fares start at 5,000 Kč. Passengers are asked to check in one hour beforehand (or 15 minutes prior to leaving at the very latest). Fares and schedules change often, so make sure to check the Volánbusz website for the most up-to-date information.

BY CAR

An International Driving Permit is no longer necessary in order to drive legally in Hungary, but a valid UK, U.S., or Canadian license most certainly is. A handful of highways connect Hungary to the rest of Europe, the most important being the E60 (or M1) which connects Budapest with Vienna and the west, and the E65, which connects Budapest with Prague and points north. The roads are generally hassle-free, as are the Austrian and Slovak borders, though you may be required to present your driver's license and registration.

In regard to distances to Budapest, Prague is 347 miles, Vienna is 154 miles, Warsaw is 339 miles, and Berlin is 428 miles.

Driving from Prague to Budapest takes 5-6 hours and is quite simple. Take the D1/E65 out of Prague toward Brno. As you approach Brno, take the D2/E65 toward Bratislava. Entering Slovakia, continue along the E65/E75/M15 toward Hungary. Entering Hungary, continue along the M15, which turns into the M1. Take the M1 all the way to Budapest.

Getting Around

Budapest is a rather large city, which means you'll most likely have to jump on a bus, tram, or subway at some point during your stay. The system is efficient and rather simple to get the hang of, so don't worry and just jump right in. If you need of a taxi, use caution and stick to the companies recommended here. If you're traveling around by car, know that Hungarians are rather aggressive drivers and don't always follow the common rules of the road. Keep your eyes open at all times.

PUBLIC TRANSPORTATION

Budapest's highly efficient network of public transportation services includes roughly 200 bus lines, 34 tram lines, three subway lines, and four above-ground suburban train lines (HÉV). The majority of services run daily 4:30am-11:30pm, although night buses serve the major routes during the wee hours. All three subway lines connect at Deák tér station, with trains running every two minutes during peak times and up to every 15 minutes late in the evening. The HÉV's lines run to and from various points on the city's outskirts, but only the one running to Szentendre in the north (located at Buda's Batthyány tér station) is of any real concern to visitors.

BKV (Budapest Transportation Company, www.bkv.hu) runs Budapest's public transportation system, including all buses, trams, subways, suburban railroads, and trolleys as well as the Cog-Wheel Railroad and the funicular leading to Buda Palace. For more information regarding all things public transportation, have a look at their website.

Tickets

Tickets are available at subway kiosks, newsstands, and machines located at bus and tram stops throughout the city. Typical tickets are good for one entire journey of any length without transfer. This includes the Cog-Wheel Railroad but not the HÉV stops that lie outside the city's boundaries. (Special tickets can be bought to allow for a change of route and travel beyond Budapest.) A single ticket costs 350 Ft or 450 Ft if bought from the driver.

There is a large range of books of tickets, and daily, weekly, and monthly passes are available as well. A one-day pass costs 1,650 Ft, a three-day pass 4,150 Ft, and a seven-day pass 4,950 Ft. It's a good idea to buy a book of 10 tickets at a discounted price of 3,000 Ft, but this depends on how much you plan on using the public transportation system.

Tickets must be validated at the start of each trip by inserting them into the orange boxes found near the doors of all buses, trolleybuses, trams, and HÉV trains, and in front of the escalators at subway stations. Make sure to validate your ticket, as there are plenty of inspectors patrolling the routes. Some wear uniforms while others travel undercover, but all sport a blue armband and carry badges with a photo ID. The old "I'm a foreigner, how could I be so stupid?" routine has worn thin, and inspectors no longer allow their lack of English language skills to get in the way of their job. If you haven't validated your ticket, you will be penalized.

BY TAXI

There are two kinds of taxis in Budapest: the ones that belong to large organized fleets and the ones that are run privately. Whatever you do, avoid the latter, as they are legally allowed to determine their own rates and are oftentimes on the hunt for tourists who just don't know any better. Hailing a cab on the street or choosing one from a taxi stand guarantees that the base rate you will be charged before getting in will be significantly higher than if you had called ahead. The most reputable taxi company to contact when in need of a driver is **City Taxi** (tel. 1/211-1111, www.citytaxi.hu). Other dependable companies include **Fő Taxi** (tel. 1/222-2222, www.fotaxi.hu) and **Buda Taxi** (tel. 1/555-5555, www.budataxi.hu).

There is a basic charge of roughly 300 Ft during the day and 420 Ft at night on entering the taxi. Rates are then calculated by kilometers traveled with a maximum of 240 Ft per kilometer being charged during the day and a maximum of 336 Ft at night. Larger, better-known taxi companies occasionally offer lower rates, depending on the time of day and the distance traveled. If you are happy with the driver and service, rounding the bill up or tipping 10 percent is common practice.

BY CAR

Driving in and around Budapest is not an enviable task as traffic is a common problem thanks to pedestrian zones and never-ending construction. Reckless drivers who change lanes at the last possible second or speed up suddenly in order to beat out a red light add to the maddening equation, making Budapest's excellent public transportation system a logical and less stressful alternative.

Despite the capital's unpredictable roads, Hungary has an excellent highway system that makes it easy to get around the country as well as to connect to neighboring ones. There are three main types of roads. The first is motorways (preceded by an M), which link Budapest with Lake Balaton and Vienna via Győr and run to Miskolc via Debrecen and Szegred via Kecsemét. The second type is national highways, characterized by a single number; they spread out from the capital. The third type is the secondary or tertiary roads, which are identified by two or three digits. Traveling the open road is not free, and your car must have an appropriate highway sticker that can be bought at gas stations and some kiosks. For further information regarding prices, routes, and maps, check out www.motorway.hu.

Parking

Parking is very difficult to find in the center of both Pest and Buda, but relatively easy elsewhere. Tickets can be purchased from machines located on the street and must be left on the dashboard, clearly visible through the windshield. Fees change often and vary depending on location.

Car Rental

Renting a car can be an expensive affair, but a bit of hunting ought to reward you with a decent deal. Make sure to have your passport and credit card handy, and if reserving a car before arriving in Hungary, double-check to ensure you've got the reservation confirmation with you.

Hertz (V. Apáczai Csere János utca 4, tel. 30/337-4456, www.hertz.hu, Mon.-Fri. 8am-5pm, Sat. 8am-1pm, from 13,500 Ft per day) is a reliable option with offices at the airport as well. **Fox Autorent** (VII. Hársfa utca 53-55, tel. 1/382-9000, www.fox-autorent.com, from 14,500 Ft per day) has gained plenty of repeat business and is highly recommended. **Avis** (V. Arany János utca 26-28, tel. 1/318-4240, www.avis.com, Mon.-Fri. 7am-6pm, Sat.-Sun. 8am-2pm, from 15,500 Ft per day) is another solid option that also has offices at the airport.

BEYOND BUDAPEST

Flowing 1,775 miles through nine different countries, the Danube is Europe's second-longest river after the Volga. As the Danube enters the Carpathian Basin, it is forced by surrounding hills and mountains through a narrow, twisting valley before continuing on its merry way to the capital. The shape of the river at this point is commonly referred to as the Dunakanyar,

© JÁNOS MISETA/123RF

HIGHLIGHTS

LOOK FOR ◖ TO FIND RECOMMENDED SIGHTS, ACTIVITIES, DINING, AND LODGING.

◖ **Szabadtéri Néprajzi Múzeum (Skanzen Open-Air Ethnographical Museum):** This ambitious museum has recreated villages from the 18th and 19th centuries. Spend the afternoon immersing yourself in Hungary's colorful past (page 316).

◖ **Bazilika (The Basilica):** Esztergom's main attraction is the largest church in the country. Check out the world's biggest oil painting and the creepy crypt before heading up to the cupola for stunning panoramic views of St. Stephen's birthplace (page 317).

◖ **Siófoki Nagystrand (Siófok Beach):** Suntan central by day, hedonist haven by night, Hungary's most visited beach has it all (page 323).

◖ **Tihanyi Apátság (Tihany Benedictine Abbey):** This gorgeous abbey contains the world's oldest existing document in Hungarian; the adjoining Tihany Museum will teach you everything you ever wanted to know about the region's turbulent past (page 332).

◖ **Balaton Festival:** Keszthely's biggest cultural event officially kicks off the summer season with a multitude of street performers, outdoor concerts, and theater productions culminating in the highly anticipated Balaton Ballroom Dance Competition (page 340).

© AVALON TRAVEL

or Danube Bend. It is a remarkably scenic part of the country, with green valleys and forested hills rising up from the river. There are also a handful of pretty little towns along the bend that are easily reached from Budapest and make for delightful day trips.

The most popular town in the region is undoubtedly the charming artist colony Szentendre. Characterized by a romantic embankment, lively cafés, and winding cobblestone streets, it is a picturesque part of Hungarian history that simply cannot be missed. Esztergom is also well worth a trip out of the big city as it is the birthplace of the one and only St. Stephen as well as the site of the great Basilica, Hungary's largest church. And who can overlook lovely Lake Balaton? Central Europe's largest lake fills up quickly and not so quietly over the summer months as visitors from around the world come to satisfy their Dionysian desires in Siófok, sip from the springs of Balatonfüred, imbibe the mouthwatering wines of Badacsony, and bask in the beauty of Keszthely.

While life might be a little slower outside the capital, it's certainly no less exciting. The wine flows as freely as the waters of the Danube, colorful festivals run throughout the summer

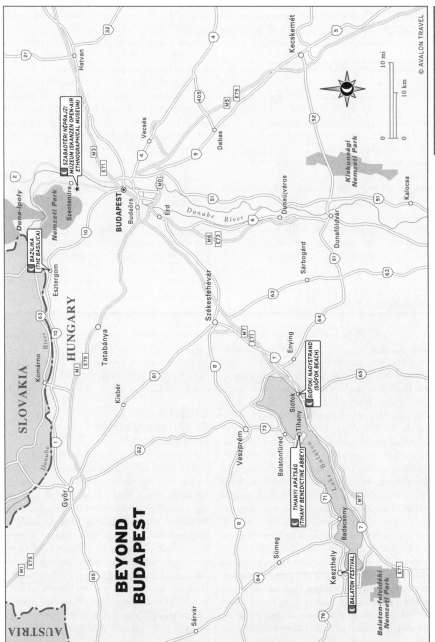

© AVALON TRAVEL

BEYOND BUDAPEST

AUSTRIA

SLOVAKIA

HUNGARY

Danube River

Danube

Komárno

Győr

Esztergom

Duna-Ipoly Nemzeti Park

BAZILIKA (THE BASILICA)

Tatabánya

Kisbér

SZABADTÉRI NÉPRAJZI MÚZEUM (SKANZEN OPEN-AIR ETHNOGRAPHICAL MUSEUM)

Szentendre

BUDAPEST

Budaörs

Érd

Vecsés

Hatvan

Dabas

Kecskemét

Kalocsa

Kiskunsági Nemzeti Park

Dunaújváros

Dunaföldvár

Sárbogárd

Székesfehérvár

Enying

Siófok

SIÓFOKI NAGYSTRAND (SIÓFOK BEACH)

Tihany

Balatonfüred

TIHANY APÁTSÁG (TIHANY BENEDICTINE ABBEY)

Veszprém

Lake Balaton

Badacsony

Keszthely

BALATON FESTIVAL

Balaton-felvidéki Nemzeti Park

Sümeg

Sárvár

10 mi

10 km

months, and locals mix with foreigners to create an international air of fun and adventure that is as uplifting as it is memorable.

PLANNING YOUR TIME

How much time you spend beyond Budapest really depends on what you're hoping to get from your trip. To be sure, the traditional way of seeing Szentendre and Esztergom is to leave the capital in the morning and return in time for dinner and a nightcap. This is definitely the best way to appreciate each town, and unless you fall particularly in love with either destination, an overnight stay will not be necessary.

Lake Balaton, on the other hand, is a whole other kettle of goulash. Though most places are easily accessible, there really is no point in heading there unless you plan on spending at least two or three days. Keep in mind, however,

that this is the absolute minimum you should schedule, and it will most likely restrict your trip to a quick tour of the nearest towns. If you plan on touring a substantial part of the lake and want to soak up its endless beauty, 4-5 days will give you a good start; a week will feel like you've died and gone to Hungarian heaven. Siófok, Balatonfüred, and Keszthely are all well worth an overnight stay, if not more, while Tihany and Badacsony can be enjoyed in half a day apiece if time is short.

Travel outside of Budapest is easier than you think. The HÉV from Batthyány tér in Buda serves those headed for Szentendre, and numerous buses, trains and boats leave for Esztergom daily. Lake Balaton is also easily reached by bus, train, or boat, and travel in and around the Balaton region is likewise easily managed via the same modes of transportation.

Szentendre

Despite being choked with tourists during the summer months, Szentendre nevertheless remains an atmospheric, picturesque town whose location a mere 13 miles north of Budapest makes it an easy and logical choice for either a half-day or full-day trip. Serbian settlers established themselves here in the Middle Ages, which accounts for the handful of Serbian Orthodox churches located around town as well as the palpable Mediterranean feel of Szentendre's very own Dunakorzó—a romantic river embankment lined with lively outdoor cafés and restaurants. The town's inherent beauty inspired an artists colony to develop here in the early 20th century and continues to serve as home and muse to roughly 100 artists. Most visitors stick close to the main square and its environs, preferring the shopping opportunities to almost anything else, but if you're feeling slightly adventurous, try losing yourself down one of the town's many winding cobblestone streets. Odds are you'll end up

losing the masses and come upon a more residential area of town, which you'll be happily surprised to note is just as pretty and romantic as Szentendre's well-worn main drag.

SIGHTS
Fő tér and Vicinity (Main Square)

Szentendre's main square is chock-full of pretty baroque and rococo architecture as well as tons of tourists who fill the surrounding cafés, shops, and restaurants all day and night throughout the summer months. Busy **Bogdányi utca (Bogdányi Street),** with its long strip of shopping opportunities, begins here, while the remaining streets twist and turn in different directions, leading to various churches, museums, and quieter locales. Here on the square, there are two immediate buildings that add to the illustrious history and romantic atmosphere: Blagovestenska Church and Ferenczy Museum.

BLAGOVESZTENSZKA SZERB ORTODOX TEMPLOM (BLAGOVESTENSKA CHURCH)

Blagovestenska Church (Fő tér 4, tel. 26/314-457, May-Sept. Tues.-Sun. 10am-6pm, 300 Ft) is one of the finer examples of baroque architecture found on the main square. It is a Serbian Orthodox church that was built in 1752 based on the designs of Andreas Mayerhoffer. The main entrance windows and bell tower sport rococo flourishes, as does the iconostasis found inside. Many of the furnishings located under the vaulted nave are authentic pieces dating to the 18th century. For those wondering, "Blagovestenska" means the feast of the Annunciation of the Blessed Virgin Mary, to whom the church is dedicated.

FERENCZY MÚZEUM (FERENCZY MUSEUM)

Named for Károly Ferenczy, the **Ferenczy Museum** (Kossuth Lajos utca 5, tel.

strolling through Szentendre

© PETER VIRAG

26/310-244, www.femuz.hu, Tues.-Sun. 10am-6pm, 1,000 Ft) pays homage to one of the country's finest Impressionist painters; he made Szentendre his home between 1889 and 1892. There are nearly 8,000 works on display chronicling the work of local artists from the 19th century to the present day. Included is the work of Ferenczy's children, twins Noémi (a tapestry artist) and Béni (a sculptor).

KOVÁCS MARGIT MÚZEUM (MARGIT KOVÁCS MUSEUM)

Dedicated to Hungary's most famous ceramics artist, the **Margit Kovács Museum** (Vastagh György utca 1, tel. 26/310-244, daily 10am-6pm, 1,000 Ft) was for years the country's most visited collection of art. Visitors will be amazed by the range and imagination of this remarkable artist, whose works here include an extensive selection of friezes, folk art, and heartbreakingly realistic statuettes.

ENTERTAINMENT AND EVENTS

Szentendre's cultural calendar is full throughout the year. A good idea is to check listings while in Budapest and then make the short trip into town should something strike your fancy.

The **Szentendre Summer Festival and Theater** (tel. 26/301-701, www.szentendre.hu, late June-late Aug.) is a highly anticipated event that involves a wide range of theater, concerts, exhibitions, and children's programs that take place all over town. Very entertaining children's shows are performed every Sunday morning, and popular jazz and folk evenings are held in the Barcsay Museum garden every Saturday night.

The **Spring Days of Szentendre** (second half of Mar.) coincides with Budapest's Spring Festival, whose tremendous popularity has inspired a chain of similarly spirited events throughout the country. The aim of the festival is to promote the outstanding work of local artists and musicians. Chamber orchestras, choirs, folk dance ensembles, and amateur theater are a few of the things visitors can expect to find at this fun and animated festival.

SHOPPING

There is no shortage of shopping opportunities in Szentendre. Indeed, it can feel sometimes like the whole town is one big marketplace. Fő tér, the main square, has a number of shops selling various handicrafts and souvenirs. Just off the square is Bogdányi Street, filled with shops selling crystal, folk costumes, antiques, fabrics, shirts, and, of course, local artwork by resident painters. There is also a collection of kiosks by the Danube Embankment selling more of the same.

ACCOMMODATIONS

There are plenty of options for those who would like to stay in Szentendre overnight. Most come in the form of *panziós* (guesthouses), which vary greatly in price. To properly enjoy everything the island has to offer, try staying somewhere that isn't directly in the thick of all the tourist action. This will ensure peaceful surroundings and a better understanding of what the people here are really like.

The completely renovated **Bükkös Hotel** (Bükkös part 16, tel. 26/501-360, www.bukkoshotel.hu, 20,500 Ft d) offers wellness services that include biosauna, Finnish sauna, massages, a steam room, and a jetted tub. There are 22 clean, simply furnished rooms as well as an excellent restaurant that allows you to grill authentic Hungarian and wild game specialties at your own table.

◖ The Rosinante (Szigetmonostor 2015 hrsz 057/2, tel. 26/722-000, www.rosinante.hu, 16,500 Ft) is a romantic country inn located in a lovely and peaceful conservation area on the island. Twenty fully equipped rooms are available, along with an outdoor swimming pool, a whirlpool, and a sauna. There is also an excellent Hungarian restaurant on the premises, and the bright and friendly staff is always available to arrange tours and activities for all its guests.

The three-star **Hotel Róz** (Pannónia utca 6/b, tel. 26/311-737, www.hotelrozszentendre.hu, 14,000 Ft d) offers guests 10 clean and comfortable air-conditioned rooms that are furnished simply and boast pretty views of the Danube. Its fine restaurant serves up filling breakfasts and old-fashioned Hungarian dishes, which can be enjoyed in the elegant dining room or on the lovely outdoor terrace.

FOOD

Restaurants operating in well-established tourist destinations are bound to be pricier than the norm, and Szentendre is no different, particularly the dining establishments located at the main square. There are, however, renowned restaurants serving authentic Hungarian fare at reasonable prices, a few of which are listed here.

Housed in a former 18th-century smithery, **Rab Ráby** (Kucsera Ferenc utca 1/a, tel. 26/310-819, www.rabraby.hu, daily noon-10pm, 1,450-2,690 Ft) is a very popular restaurant that serves delicious traditional Hungarian fare. Its lovely summer patio makes for pleasant, relaxed dining, and its rather chaotic interior, filled with handcuffs, chains, full suits of armor, and a wide array of metallic doohickeys, make this a memorable time for both the visual and tactile senses.

Almost always busy with both Hungarians and the tourist trade, **◖ Aranysárkány Vendéglő** (Alkotmány utca 1/a, tel. 26/301-479, www.aranysarkany.hu, daily noon-10pm, mains 2,550-4,790 Ft) is an excellent traditional Hungarian eatery that offers up tasty meat dishes like lamb and steak as well as standard Eastern European fare that includes stuffed cabbage and dumplings. The long wooden tables and friendly service provide a warm, hospitable atmosphere that has become legendary in these parts.

Bar Centro (Péter Pál utca 2/B, tel. 70/383-0383, www.barcentro.hu, Wed.-Fri. 8am-11pm, Sat.-Sun. 9am-11pm, mains 1,200-2,350 Ft) is a warm and intimate restaurant that serves simple yet tasty fare that includes sandwiches, salads, meat and cheese platters, and a handful of Hungarian standards. The service is attentive and the atmosphere relaxed, making it a perfect pit stop for those needing an hour or two off from the Szentendre strip.

INFORMATION AND SERVICES

Tourinform Szentendre (Dumtsa Jenő utca 22, tel. 26/317-965, www.tourinform.hu, Mon.-Thurs. 10am-5:30pm, Fri.-Sun. 10am-6pm) is staffed with very helpful people who can provide you with maps of the area as well as help with concert and exhibition schedules, accommodations, and common side trips outside town.

GETTING THERE
By HÉV

Take the HÉV from Batthyány tér in Buda. Trains leave roughly every 20 minutes 4:30am-11:30pm. The trip takes approximately 45 minutes and costs 1,280 Ft round-trip. The HÉV station is a 10-minute walk from the main square.

By Car

Szentendre is 13 miles from Budapest. Take Lajos utca across from Margaret Island north until it becomes Szentendrei út in north Budapest. This then becomes Rákóczi utca, Batthyány utca, and finally Dózsa György út, which will lead you directly to Szentendre.

Parking is available throughout the town and along the river. It costs anywhere from 100 to 200 Ft an hour.

By Boat

You can catch a boat from Vigadó tér on the Danube Embankment each morning at 10am. It returns from Szentendre at 6pm. The trip takes roughly 1.5 hours and costs 2,500 Ft. Various kiosks line the embankment representing companies who may offer different departure and arrival times. Boats tend to run from May until the end of September or middle of October.

VICINITY OF SZENTENDRE

If you're looking for something outside of town that's both educational and fascinating, try the Skanzen Open-Air Ethnographical Museum, located two miles southwest of Szentendre. A bus leaving from Szentendre's bus station (located adjacent to the HÉV) will get you there quickly and easily. If driving, follow Route 10 north and turn left on Sztaravodai út.

🄲 Szabadtéri Néprajzi Múzeum (Skanzen Open-Air Ethnographical Museum)

Founded in 1967, the **Skanzen Open-Air Ethnographical Museum** (Sztaravodai út, tel. 26/502-500, www.skanzen.hu, Tues.-Sun. 9am-5pm, 1,700 Ft) is an ambitious collection of over 300 buildings representing the past architecture, life, and traditions of Hungary's different regions. Situated in Duna-Ipoly National Park, the museum comprises several recreated villages from the 18th and 19th centuries that include buildings such as a fire station, a tavern, and a shepherd's hut. Arguably the most fascinating part of the immense collection is the furniture, textiles, and household equipment that give visitors a clear and fascinating picture of what life was really like back then. Shops selling traditional foods, crafts, and souvenirs are also on the premises.

Esztergom

Located approximately 31 miles northeast of Budapest, a mere stone's throw from the Slovak border, Esztergom served as both the capital of Hungary from the 10th to mid-13th centuries and as the Royal Seat up to the end of King Béla IV's reign. Esztergom is also famous for being the birthplace of Vajk, otherwise known as St. Stephen, Hungary's beloved king who was crowned here in the year 1000. The town went on to flourish, particularly during the 14th and 15th centuries, when it rivaled Buda in cultural significance. Its importance and stature disappeared altogether, however, during the unforgiving 150-year Turkish rule of the 16th and 17th centuries. Today, Esztergom's winding streets, church towers, narrow stairs, and alleys continue to evoke an atmosphere of historical importance and artistic beauty, particularly when it comes to the magnificent Basilica, Hungary's largest and grandest church.

SIGHTS

◖ Bazilika
(The Basilica)

The mighty masterpiece known simply as the **Basilica** (Szent István tér 1, tel. 36/402-354, www.bazilika-esztergom.hu, Mar. 27-Oct. 27 daily 8am-6pm, Oct. 28-Mar. 26 daily 8am-4pm) is the largest church in the country, measuring an impressive 328 feet tall and 351 feet long. From 1543 to 1683, the Basilica suffered both negligence and damage under Ottoman rule, except for the beautiful **Bakócz Chapel,** which somehow survived relatively intact. Built by Tamás Bakócz (archbishop 1497-1521), it is one of Hungary's finest examples of Renaissance architecture and boasts elaborately

© PETER VIRAG

Esztergom's mighty Basilica

carved red marble. Following the expulsion of the Turks, the Hungarian Catholic Church reestablished itself in Esztergom in 1819, and a few years later, in 1822, Primate-Archbishop Sándor Rudnay laid the foundation stone of a new cathedral. Two architects, Pál Kühnel and later, following Kühnel's death, János Packh, were responsible for the masterpiece we enjoy today, which had its ceremonial consecration on August 31, 1856. Franz Liszt composed his *Esztergom Mass* for the occasion and conducted its first performance from the organ loft.

The centerpiece of the great Basilica's interior is the vast altarpiece depicting the Assumption of the Blessed Virgin Mary. Painted by Michelangelo Grigoletti, it measures 44 feet by 21.7 feet, making it the world's largest oil painting done on a single piece of canvas. Upstairs, an interesting collection of liturgical objects in the **treasury** (Mar. 1-Oct. 31 daily 9am-5pm, Nov. 1-Jan. 12 Tues.-Sun. 10am-4pm, 800 Ft) includes some very pretty chalices, jewels, and vestments from the baroque period as well as the coronation cross dating all the way back to the Árpád era—the same one Hungarian kings swore on. A creepy **crypt** (Mar. 1-Oct. 31 daily 9am-5pm, Nov. 1-Feb. 28 daily 10am-4pm, 200 Ft) where the remains of archbishops, assistant bishops, canons, and exiled anti-Communist Cardinal Mindszenty rest is also open to visitors, as is a **cupola** (Apr. 1-Oct. 31 daily 9:30am-5pm, 600 Ft), whose steep climb pays off with a wonderful view of the entire town.

Keresztény Muzeum (Christian Museum)

The **Christian Museum** (Mindszenty tér 2, tel. 33/413-880, www.christianmuseum.hu, Mar.-Nov. daily 10am-5pm, 900 Ft) is located on the second floor of the Primate's Palace and boasts the country's largest collection of ecclesiastical artwork, ranking just behind the National Gallery and Museum of Fine Arts in scope and significance. The museum was founded in 1875 by Archbishop János Simor and contains remarkable Hungarian work from the late Gothic period, along with Austrian, German,

Italian, and Flemish paintings from the 13th to 18th centuries. There are also a large number of tapestries and icons on display, rounding out a fascinating set of exhibitions outlining religion's vital role in Hungarian history.

ENTERTAINMENT AND EVENTS

Esztergom isn't exactly known for its nightlife, and many restaurants pull double duty, offering diners tasty grub and well-made drinks. One or two trendy or all-night bars do crop up now again; simply asking the locals will put you in the right direction. The cultural calendar is filled with various art exhibitions and classical music concerts, though the two biggest events are clearly the St. Stephen's celebrations and summer theater performances at the Basilica.

Nightlife

Termál Sörkert (Kis-Duna sétány Belváros, daily 9am-10pm) is an affordable, bare-bones outdoor bar that is packed more often than not by a predominantly young crowd enjoying the warm summer night. It's a fun and laid-back option without the frills.

Gambrinus Music Pub (Vörösmarty utca 3, Mon.-Thurs. 11am-2am, Fri. 11am-3am, Sat. 3pm-3am, Sun. 3pm-2am) is a popular pub-type bar that attracts both locals and visitors looking to let their hair down and enjoy the evening with a glass of Hungarian wine or beer, or a tall cool pint of one of the finest Czech brews, as the name of the establishment implies.

Festivals and Events

The Basilica offers up a gorgeous backdrop during the **Esztergom Castle Theater Festival** (June-Aug.) as a wide variety of plays ranging from historical epics, operas, comedies, and musicals are performed during warm summer nights. Performances are in Hungarian but with such fantastic scenery are nonetheless enchanting.

August 20 is St. Stephen's Day in Hungary, one of the biggest holidays of the year as the entire country celebrates the king and founding of

Fascinating Facts

- Susan Polgar, daughter of internationally renowned chess coach Polgar Laszlo, made chess history by breaking the game's gender barrier when she became the first woman ever to qualify for the men's World Chess Championship and earn a Grandmaster title.

- Those old enough to remember television in the 1980s will undoubtedly recall the acerbic yet lovable primetime alien, ALF. Sporting a huge snout and orange fur, he was played by three-foot-tall Hungarian actor Michu Meszaros, who got into the hairy suit every time full body shots were required.

- On June 9, 2007, a whopping 6,637 Hungarian couples entered *Guinness World Records* for the largest gathering of simultaneous kissing. The record was previously held by the Philippines, which only got to enjoy its place at the top for a handful of months before the Hungarians smooched their way to history.

- World-famous philanthropist George Soros was born in Hungary and grew up during the Holocaust. He left to study at the London School of Economics and has had a hand in shaking up the world's finances ever since.

- Ex-Lax, the chocolate-flavored laxative that has provided relief the world over, is the brainchild of Hungarian inventor Max Kiss. Tired of the unpleasant bitter taste that was synonymous with laxatives at the turn of the 20th century, Kiss sweetened the taste of the active ingredient, phenolphthalein, to produce the second-best-selling laxative in the world.

- Edward Teller, father of the hydrogen bomb, was born in Budapest in 1908. He moved to the United States in the 1930s, where he eventually became a member of the Manhattan Project. Teller was also an important figure in the development of thermonuclear energy.

- Beloved film actor Tony Curtis was the child of Hungarian natives who left for the United States in search of a better life. Although he was born in the Bronx, New York, Curtis never forgot his roots and returned to Hungary in 2003 to shoot two 30-second spots for Hungarian tourism.

- During the Middle Ages, the Carpathian Basin was home to Europe's most developed mining system and was responsible for the production of 80 percent of the continent's gold.

the Hungarian state. Imagine, then, the popularity of **St. Stephen's Days** (Aug. 18-20) in Esztergom, which is where he was crowned on Christmas Day in 1000. The party starts early and ends late with a whole host of outdoor concerts, theater, food, fun, and frolicking in between. This is one of the more highly anticipated events on the town's cultural calendar and is not to be missed.

SHOPPING

While certainly not a shopping mecca by any stretch of the imagination, Rákóczi Square does offer supermarkets, banks, and bustle. There is also a daily outdoor market on Simor János Street, with stalls selling fruits and vegetables as well as clothes, souvenirs, wine, and a whole bunch of reasonably priced bric-a-brac.

ACCOMMODATIONS

Most people come to Esztergom for the day and leave well before the need for sleep and shelter arises. Should you get smitten with the place, however, and want to stay overnight, you'll find no shortage of guesthouses and small hotels in and around the city center.

Alabárdos Panzió (Bajcsy Zsilinszky utca 49, tel. 33/312-640, www.alabardospanzio.hu, 9,900 Ft d) is a charming little bed-and-breakfast with 21 rooms with en suite baths and four apartments located right in the heart of Esztergom. Its cheerful atmosphere is infectious, and while their rooms are a little on the small side, they are nevertheless clean, comfortable, and quiet. **Ria Panzió** (Batthany utca 11-13, tel. 33/313-115, www.riapanzio.com, from 14,000 Ft d) is a quiet and charming guesthouse located within a short walk of both the Basilica and the Danube. Rooms are a little on the small side, though clean and comfortable, and blend in nicely with the overall friendly family-run atmosphere. Breakfast is generous and tasty, and the excellent Csülök Csárda restaurant is located right next door as well.

The **Gran Camping Pension and Dormitory** (Nagy-Duna sétány 3, tel. 33/411-953, www.grancamping-fortanex.hu, from 10,000 Ft d) is a great choice for budget travelers and those who would like to meet like-minded wanderers. Situated on Prímás Island, it offers guests spacious, brightly lit bungalows, simple but clean guest rooms, and a well-maintained hostel with 160 beds. Recreational possibilities are endless, with tennis courts, a soccer field, a playground, and a swimming pool on the premises, along with a restaurant and a shop. The town center is an easy 10-minute walk from the grounds, and Slovakia is a hop, skip, and a jump from neighboring Maria-Valeria Bridge.

FOOD

Esztergom has plenty of restaurants, with most offering traditional Hungarian dishes at relatively reasonable prices. The following are some of the better dining experiences to be had around town.

Located underneath the Basilica is the very well-known **◖ Prímás Pince** (Szent István tér 4, tel. 33/313-495, www.primaspince.hu, Mon.-Sat. 11am-11pm, Sun. noon-10pm, mains 2,200-3,900 Ft). Enjoy traditional Hungarian dishes like goulash, wild game soup, and pike perch in its cavernous cellars, which ooze a modern intimate atmosphere that makes the already excellent food even better.

Not just another cellar restaurant, **Csülök Csárda** (Batthyány utca 9, tel. 33/412-420, www.csulokcsarda.hu, daily noon-10pm, mains 1,790-3,980 Ft) offers plenty of *csülök*

(trotter) specialties as well as a delicious paprika chicken and wide array of pork, turkey, and steak dishes. Generous portions, friendly service, and a rustic environment make this an excellent choice for either lunch or dinner any day of the week.

Anonim Vendéglő (Berényi utca 4, tel. 33/631-707, daily noon-10pm, mains 1,800-3,150 Ft) is located inside a historic town house decorated in traditional Hungarian style and offering some of the most mouthwatering dishes in town. The menu changes regularly but always offers excellent pork, beef, chicken, and fish specialties that can be washed down with one of the many Hungarian and international wines on offer.

INFORMATION AND SERVICES

Centrally located **Gran Tours** (Széchenyi tér 25, tel. 33/502-001, www.grantours.hu, Mon.-Fri. 8am-4pm) is where you should head to if you need any information about Esztergom. Apart from providing visitors with city maps, brochures, and general information, the staff are also happy to help you exchange money, book accommodations, reserve concert tickets, and arrange for a guided tour of the area.

GETTING THERE
By Bus
Numerous buses depart frequently from Árpád híd bus terminal, which is located at the Árpád híd subway station in Budapest's 13th district. The faster ride (via Dorog) takes roughly 75 minutes but can vary depending on traffic. Tickets cost approximately 850 Ft. The bus station is in the center, about five minutes from the main square and 15 minutes from the Basilica.

By Train
Trains to Esztergom leave Budapest's Nyugati station every 30 minutes or so. Tickets cost 1,680 Ft and the trip lasts roughly 1.5 hours. Note that the Esztergom train station is about a 20-minute walk from the center and all major sights.

By Car

Leave Budapest by taking Highway 11 north (Szentendre-Visegrad-Esztergom, 40 miles) or Highway 10 (Budapest-Dorog-Esztergom, 28 miles).

Parking is available everywhere. It costs anywhere from 100 to 200 Ft an hour.

By Boat

Traveling to Esztergom by boat can be a very pleasurable experience. The popular river tour provider **MAHART** (V. Belgrád rakpart, tel. 1/484-4010, www.mahartpassnave.hu) has a boat leaving Budapest every morning at 9:30am from Vigadó Square on the Danube Embankment. The trip takes 1.5 hours and costs 7,500 Ft round-trip.

Lake Balaton

Affectionately nicknamed the "Hungarian Sea," Lake Balaton is both Central Europe's largest lake and Hungary's premier holiday destination. Its 124 miles of shoreline offer visitors a multitude of activities, from enjoying a swim in silky waters to sailing, windsurfing, fishing, and a whole lot more. The rolling hills and historic vineyards of the north will please hikers and wine enthusiasts alike, while the lively southern shore will prove to be more than enough fun for even the most energetic of partiers. Waterfront towns, spa resorts, natural wonders, and picture-perfect historical landmarks all come with the territory, making Lake Balaton an excellent choice for families, couples, and lone travelers looking for fun, relaxation, adventure, and the quintessential Hungarian summer experience.

The lake's **south shore** is easily reached from Budapest, which is one reason why it attracts thousands of tourists year after year. Another is its famed nightlife that knows no end and has few, if any, limits. Filled to near capacity with countless resorts, high-rises, shops,

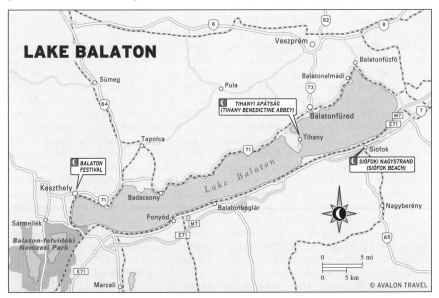

© AVALON TRAVEL

© TOM DIRLIS

Lake Balaton

bars, restaurants, and discos, it is *the* place in Hungary to spend long days at the beach and even longer nights out on the town. Siófok, the south shore's largest and busiest resort, remains the lake's HQ of hedonism, luring hordes of fun-loving students and 20-somethings looking to work on their tans before drinking and dancing till they drop. If it's a nonstop party you're after, you'll most definitely find it here.

Lake Balaton's **north shore** is the yin to the south shore's yang—a destination for travelers more interested in a journey through the country's history and culture, where teeming resorts and drunken revelers are replaced with picturesque towns and centuries-old vineyards. At the far west of the shore is Keszthely, one of the region's largest towns and home to the gorgeous Festetics Palace. Nearby are the fine wines and basalt hills of Badacsony, whose natural environs are some of the finest in the entire region. There is also the beautiful 18th-century baroque Benedictine Abbey of Tihany as well as the popular Balatonfüred, Hungary's oldest spa resort. No matter where you go in the

north, you'll find peaceful surroundings, Old World hospitality, and a relaxation of spirit that is as rare as it is invigorating.

SIÓFOK

Located on the southeastern end of the lake, Siófok began to come into its own during the 1860s when it was first connected to Budapest by rail. Easily accessible from the capital, it quickly grew into the largest resort town on the lake and continues to be the country's prime location for hedonists. Lined with bars, restaurants, hotels, and clubs, Siófok attracts a young student crowd that comes to soak up rays during the day and get their freak on at night. Despite the countless hotels, burger joints, strip bars, and nightclubs, however, the town has somehow managed to preserve some of its Old World charm. Tree-lined promenades take visitors past majestic villas, while both the Aranypart (Gold Coast) to the east and the Ezüstpart (Silver Coast) beckon bathers into their soothing shallow waters. Buildings such as the Water Tower in central Szabadság Square

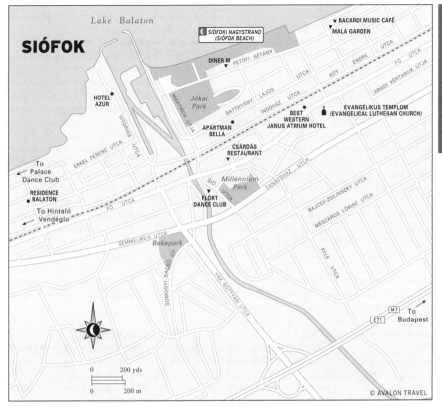

as well as the Evangelical Lutheran Church are worth noting, as is peaceful Millennium Park. For the most part, however, people come to Siófok to eat, drink, and be merry, though not necessarily in that order.

Sights
◖ SIÓFOKI NAGYSTRAND (SIÓFOK BEACH)

The most visited beach in the country, let alone on the lake, **Siófok Beach** covers an area of over 20 acres and holds roughly 13,000 people. During the day, sun-lovers young and old take a dip, catch some rays, or engage in one of the many water sports on offer. By night, the beach turns into a hedonist's heaven with numerous bars, discos, concerts, and casinos. The beach

is also the site of the world famous **Coke Club,** which attracts thousands of tourists every year thanks to its nonstop nightlife and excellent outdoor concerts.

MILLENNIUM PARK

Built in 1994, **Millennium Park** is a peaceful oasis in the center of town spanning over four acres. Well-manicured lawns are home to gorgeous flowers and statues as well as a picturesque musical pavilion and water fountain. At night, the small lake is a wonderfully romantic spot for lovers bathed in the park's lights. Always open, it is the perfect place for those who need to get away from the frantic activity that tends to envelop the rest of the town during the summer months.

EVANGÉLIKUS TEMPLOM (EVANGELICAL LUTHERAN CHURCH)

Siófok's **Evangelical Lutheran Church** (Fő utca 220, tel. 84/310-549, www.siofok-lutheran.eu, June-Aug. Mon.-Sat. 10am-noon and 4pm-6pm) was designed by Ybl Prize-winning architect Imre Makovecz and stands as one of the town's most original and architecturally thought-provoking buildings. Combining traditional elements with modern touches, the church is 80 percent wood and was mainly financed by Siófok's Finnish sister town, Oulu, which is also the name of the park the church resides in. Massive angel wings stretch above either side of the main entrance protecting all those who enter. Inside, the church seats 150 people and is home to László Péterffy's noteworthy *Statue of the Resurrected*, located above the eastern altar.

Entertainment and Events

Siófok is without a doubt the nightlife capital of Lake Balaton, and finding somewhere to quench your thirst or put your dancing shoes to good use will not be a problem. There are countless bars, clubs, cafés, and the like vying for your attention, time, and money, and they are all full of like-minded fun lovers and thrill seekers. Most people come here to party, and you can join them in doing so well into the night.

NIGHTLIFE

Twenty years later, the **Palace Dance Club** (Vécsey Károly utca 20, tel. 84/350-698, www.palace.hu, daily 10pm-5am, cover varies by theme/party) is still Siófok's best-known club, attracting over 300,000 visitors a year. Inside are two stories full of house, techno, and trance fans partying on the dance floor and tables as well as in the massive outdoor garden, which is perfect during warm summer nights. Plenty of weekend programs and theme nights are scheduled, including the very popular Foam and Free Beer Parties. Free Palace buses leave from the water tower in the center of town every hour starting at 9pm, and if you see one cruising around town, simply wave and the kind bus

driver will stop and let you on. This place is a must for any serious clubber.

Bacardi Music Café (Petofi sétány 5, tel. 20/599-6397, www.bacardi-music-cafe.hu, daily 4pm-5am, cover varies by theme/party) is another institution in Siófok that packs in both students and tourists on a regular basis. Inside you'll find a spacious seating area done up in comfortable bamboo as well as a dance floor that heats up as the hours fly by. There is also an outdoor patio where people can chill from the block rockin' beats and catch up with friends or attempt to make new ones.

Flört Dance Club (Sió utca 4, tel. 20/333-3303, www.flort.hu, daily 9pm-5am, cover varies by theme/party) was established in 1989 and has not looked back since, seeing as this twin-level club is almost always packed with the lake's most beautiful men and women. Trance, house, and techno are spun by international DJs on a nightly basis, and the club's various theme nights and parties are almost always sellouts.

FESTIVALS AND EVENTS

During the **Golden Shell Folklore Festival** (first week of July), Siófok changes from a hedonistic party town into a slightly more cultured, international folklore center. Dance troupes from all over the world perform traditional dances to adoring audiences that are invited to take part in the demonstrations and learn a few moves themselves. There are plenty of parades, performances, and concerts throughout the week, offering a nice break from the usual club fare that typically overruns the town.

An annual three-day event, the **Balaton International Egg Festival** (mid-Oct.) honors and attempts to further promote the consumption of eggs. Plenty of outdoor concerts take place during the festival as well as a number of egg-based contests, including a children's egg-drawing event and an adult egg-based recipe contest. One of the most entertaining events is the Egg Ball, which offers dancers the opportunity to party until the sun comes up. Although an egg festival may sound a little strange to some travelers, the event brings in thousands of visitors every year.

Shopping

Sometimes it feels like Siófok is one big souvenir stand, pulsating with tourists in dire need of souvenirs and beach accessories. The center of town, particularly **Kálmán Promenade,** is jam-packed with shops and stalls managed by smiling shopkeepers eager to make a sale. Postcards, beach towels, leather goods, embroidery, and a whole host of arts and crafts are available, all of which make for a memorable gift item or souvenir. Prices can be rather inflated at times, so don't be embarrassed to haggle should you feel it necessary.

Accommodations

There are plenty of accommodations options for visitors to choose from, ranging from upscale wellness centers to guesthouses. Many affordable guest rooms are available in private homes with remarkably low prices and a family atmosphere to boot. A trip to the Tourinform office will arm you with plenty of phone numbers and addresses, but bear in mind that Siófok is a ridiculously popular tourist destination and that you take your chances by not reserving a room ahead of time.

The **Hotel Azúr** (Erkel Ferenc utca 2/C, tel. 84/501-400, www.hotelazur.hu, 49,500 Ft d) is situated directly on the shore and has the distinction of being the largest four-star hotel in Balaton. Its brightly colored and tasteful Mediterranean decor provides a warm, welcoming environment that is home to 222 clean, comfortable, and spacious rooms and luxury suites. The rooms are all fashioned with balconies and equipped with movie channels, Wi-Fi, safes, minibars, and air-conditioning. The hotel also boasts its own beach as well as a number of saunas and steam rooms, a thermal bath, and one of the finest indoor pools you'll ever see. As far as the region goes, this is about as good as it gets.

Residence Balaton (Erkel Ferenc utca 49, tel. 84/506-840, http://hotel-residence.hu, 41,000 Ft d) is a popular hotel offering 57 modern, spacious, and well-appointed rooms. There are a number of wellness treatments available here, including massages, aromatherapies, and facials, along with a private beach just a few minutes' walk from the hotel. Friendly, affordable, and professionally run, it's little wonder this is one of the more successful hotels in the area.

Located just a few minutes' walk from the train station, the **Best Western Janus Atrium Hotel** (Fö utca 93-95, tel. 84/312-546, www.janushotel.hu, 31,000 Ft d) is a friendly and professional family-run boutique hotel offering modern and comfortable rooms designed to reflect different periods and cultures—the Paris room, the Audrey Hepburn room, the India room, and so on. While the rooms may be a tad too small for some peoples' tastes, their proximity to shops, restaurants, the beach, and downtown core more than make up for it.

Apartman Bella (Batthyány Lajos utca 14/A, tel. 84/510-078, www.siofokbella.hu, 16,000 Ft d) is a reasonably priced and popular option. The 12 apartments vary in size, with 1-3 bedrooms holding 2-6 people. All apartments have their own terraces as well as kitchens or kitchenettes, fridges, satellite TV, and minibars. Located a couple of minutes' walk from the beach, port, and center, it is an excellent choice for travelers of all tastes and budgets.

Food

Most of the food in town is of the traditional Hungarian variety, but there are plenty of kiosks and smallish eateries serving up a variety of snacks and foods such as hamburgers and pizza. Prices vary greatly, so have a look around before settling on a place that suits both your tastes and budget.

Csárdás Restaurant (Fő utca 105, tel. 84/310-642, www.csardasetterem.hu, daily noon-9pm, mains 1,290-3,200 Ft) is a highly reputable establishment located in the center of town that serves up tasty Hungarian fish and meat dishes. Its three halls are decorated with light traditional touches, and its outdoor seating is nearly always full during the holiday season. Also on offer are over 20 kinds of Hungarian wine, which go down splendidly during the live gypsy music concerts in the summer.

Near the railroad is **Hintaló Vendéglő** (Vécsey útca 6, tel. 84/350-494, http://hintalo-etterem-siofok.hu, May 15-Sept. 20 daily noon-midnight, mains 1,320-2,820 Ft), an excellent traditional Hungarian restaurant that should not be missed. It's decorated in a charming rustic style, and the friendly staff deliver mouthwatering meat, fish, and wild game delights that are sure to please all palates. Dinnertime is the right time here as dishes are prepared in a *bogrács* (cauldron) as well as grilled on an open fire outdoors.

Diner M (Petofi stny. 3, tel. 84/510-074, www.dinerm.hu, late May-June and Sept. daily 10am-2am, July-Aug. daily 24 hours, mains 890-3,790 Ft) is not only a step back in time but an American one at that. Playing off the classic diners of the 1950s, Diner M incorporates booths, stools, jukeboxes, and muscle cars to recreate a piece of Americana known and loved the world over. Diners can choose from club sandwiches and chili dogs, burgers, and milk shakes while listening to old Elvis and rockabilly records. Some say it's tacky; others say it doesn't belong. Whatever it is, it certainly distances itself from the usual fare found around town.

Located in the small hotel of the same name, **◖ Mala Garden** (Petőfi sétány 15/a, tel. 84/506-688, www.malagarden.hu, daily 11am-midnight, mains 1,890-3,790 Ft) offers diners an excellent variety of Thai, Indian, and Mediterranean cuisines as well as traditional homemade chicken, pork, and duck dishes. Pull up a chair in the modern yet comfy dining room or head for the patio, which offers a soothing and inspiring view of the lake. Reservations aren't necessary but are a good idea as word of this relative newcomer to the scene has built a solid reputation in a very short time.

Information and Services

Tourinform Siófok (Water Tower, tel.

The 1950s are alive and well at Diner M in Siófok.

© TOM DIRLIS

84/310-117, www.tourinform.hu, Mon.-Sat. 8am-8pm, Sun. 9am-1pm) is located right under the town's massive water tower and provides visitors with maps and information regarding Siófok, its sights, and Lake Balaton in general. Help is available if you need to find accommodations, and tickets for various events can be arranged here as well.

Getting There
BY TRAIN
Trains leave regularly from Budapest's Keleti and Déli train stations. The journey typically lasts 1.5-2.5 hours depending on route taken and costs 2,200-2,800 Ft. The train station is located near Millennium Park, in the center of town.

BY CAR
Siófok is 70 miles from Budapest. Driving from Budapest to Siófok couldn't be easier. Simply take Highway M7 south all the way to town, then follow the "Siófok Centrum" sign into the center of town.

Plenty of parking is available both in the center and by the lake. It costs anywhere from 100 to 200 Ft an hour.

BALATONFÜRED
Located at the northeastern end of the lake, Balatonfüred is a picturesque town surrounded by gently sloping hills that grew in popularity as a result of its curative springs and warm, invigorating climate. First mentioned in the estate registration of Tihany Abbey in 1211, it was home to spa houses as early as the 18th century and quickly became a favorite destination of liberal-minded politicians and artists. A lively and sophisticated social and cultural scene followed, which inevitably led to a development boom in the 19th century. Today, it is home to beautiful villas, residential districts, and churches as well as a number of hotels that manage to strike a balance between the old world and the new. Among the town's highlights are Vaszary-Villa and the Lajos Kossuth Spring, not to mention a romantic stroll along the pier.

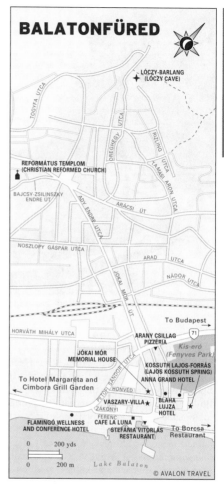

Sights
VASZARY-VILLA
Formerly the summer resort of Archbishop Kolos Vaszary, **Vaszary-Villa** (Honvéd utca 2-4, tel. 21/200-2454, www.furedkult.hu, Wed.-Sun. 10am-6pm, 1,500 Ft) was renovated in 2010 and now serves as Balatonfüred's cultural center. Art exhibits, literary readings, and musical performances are the norm here, as are highly reputable classes for kids who have an interest in the visual arts.

© TOM DIRLIS

chilling by the lake in Balatonfüred

KOSSUTH LAJOS-FORRÁS (LAJOS KOSSUTH SPRING)

Situated opposite the State Hospital for Heart Disease in Gyógy Square is the **Lajos Kossuth Spring,** also referred to as the "Drinking Hall." Built in 1800 in a neoclassical style, it was originally named after Emperor Joseph Francis I, who visited Balatonfüred in 1852, but was renamed to honor Hungary's beloved radical following the end of World War II. Originally used to treat stomach and kidney conditions, its spring is now used primarily to relieve various cardiovascular ailments.

JÓKAI MÓR MEMORIAL HOUSE

Built in 1870, the **Jókai Mór Memorial House** (Honvéd utca 1, tel. 21/200-2453, www. furedkult.hu, Wed.-Sun. 10am-6pm, 900 Ft) allows visitors to see how the famous 19th-century writer lived, including the desk where he penned a number of well-known short stories about his beloved Balaton as well as his most famous novel, *The Golden Man.*

LÓCZY-BARLANG (LÓCZY CAVE)

Though not particularly impressive in size, **Lóczy Cave** (Öreghegyi utca, tel. 87/555-291, May-Sept. daily 10am-6pm, 500 Ft), with its 394-foot-long, 63-foot-deep subterranean setting is an excellent experience for cave enthusiasts. Discovered in 1882, its pretty calcium carbonate formations, coupled with layers of limestone dating back millions of years, leave an indelible impression, as do the bubbling hot waters below. The site is named after the famed Lajos Lóczy, who spearheaded countless forays into Hungary's caves. The 20-minute guided tour offered is an excellent lesson in the region's evolution over the centuries.

REFORMÁTUS TEMPLOM (CHRISTIAN REFORMED CHURCH)

Commonly referred to as the "white church," the **Christian Reformed Church** (Óvoda utca 1, tel. 87/342-795, mass Sun. 9:30am) is a single-towered classicist beauty whose foundation stone was laid in 1828. Inside, the whitewashed walls and alluring plainness of its huge hall provoke silent fascination, while its large choir on the northern side is reminiscent of the grandeur of Tihany Abbey. Behind the church is a relatively new multistory rectory that is home to offices and a congregation hall, adding to what is already one of the town's most valuable and recognizable landmarks.

Entertainment and Events

Balatonfüred's nightlife has slowed down a bit over the years but still heats up during the summer with Hungarians and tourists from all over the world shedding their bathing suits and suiting up in their sexiest outfits. Bars tend to open early and close whenever the party winds down, offering you plenty of opportunities for a bit of hedonistic fun.

NIGHTLIFE

Café La Luna (Zákonyi Ferenc espl. 4, tel. 70/935-7488, Sun.-Thurs. 8am-midnight, Fri.-Sat. 7am-2am) is a friendly and affordable

© TOM DIRLIS

Vaszary-Villa is Balatonfüred's cultural center.

café-bar with plenty of outdoor seating right by the shore. Whether it's a delicious cocktail or a glass of Hungarian wine you're looking for, look no farther.

The **Waikiki Cocktail Bar** (Tagore espl. 1, tel. 70/636-6713, daily 9am-2am) serves up everything from ice cream to cocktails on a lovely terrace offering gorgeous panoramic views of the lake. It has a Mediterranean-type of vibe, complemented by fair prices and friendly service.

FESTIVALS AND EVENTS

Hungary entered *Guinness World Records* in 2007 by holding a 192-hour megaconcert during the **International Guitar Festival** (tel. 30/289-1239, www.balatongitar.hu, end of June). The event is an annual huge success. When not breaking records, the festival hosts leading guitarists from all over the world whose styles range from classical to rock to flamenco. This is one festival that no lover of the six-string should miss.

The **Blue Ribbon Regatta** (tel. 1/460-6925, beginning of July) was first held on Lake Balaton in 1934 and has been going strong ever since. The route runs from Balatonfüred to Balatonkenese, Siófok, Keszthely, and back to Balatonfüred, and at 124 miles is Europe's longest round-the-lake race. Held every odd-numbered year, this is arguably the Hungarian sailing season's most popular race.

Held annually since 1825, the **Anna Ball** (end of July) is undoubtedly Balatonfüred's most eagerly anticipated social event of the year and is celebrated on whatever weekend falls closest to July 26—the day the name Anna is celebrated. The highlight of the event is the choosing of the Belle of the Ball, who, along with her runners-up, rides across town in carriages before taking a trip around the lake on *Nemere II*, one of the town's most impressive sailing boats. Other events during this fun and romantic weekend are dance performances, brass band concerts, and theater productions.

The neoclassical Lajos Kossuth Spring was built in 1800.

Shopping

While there are no shops that particularly stand out per se, numerous stalls and holes-in-the-wall offer all kinds of souvenirs ranging from wine to traditional foods and toys. Prices are affordable and relatively standard, though a bit of comparison shopping may result in a surprise deal or two.

Accommodations

The four-star **(Anna Grand Hotel** (Gyógy tér 1, tel. 87/581-200, www.annagrand.hu, 56,000 Ft d) is Balatonfüred's crown jewel in accommodations as well as the setting for the annual Anna Ball. Located in the middle of the historical district, a mere 300 feet from the promenade, it offers 100 rooms with all the amenities as well as three suites fit for royalty. A world-class restaurant and spa center are two more reasons to start saving your forints now.

The **Flamingó Wellness and Conference Hotel** (Széchenyi utca 16, tel. 87/581-060, www.flamingohotel.hu, 21,000 Ft d) is a modern four-star hotel situated right on the shores of Lake Balaton. Its 181 rooms, apartments, and family suites are both spacious and spotlessly clean, offering gorgeous views of Tihany and its abbey. There are plenty of shops and restaurants nearby, and the hotel's wellness and spa services include an indoor pool, a whirlpool tub, a steam bath, a sauna, massages, a beauty salon, and a solarium. Those looking for a bit of pampering while on holiday will definitely want to consider the Flamingó.

The very affordable three-star **Blaha Lujza Hotel** (Blaha Lujza utca 4, tel. 87/581-210, www.hotelblaha.hu, 17,500-19,000 Ft d) is a pretty period-piece hotel that used to serve as home to the famous Hungarian singer of the same name. Its 22 rooms are simply furnished yet comfortable, but there is no air-conditioning available. Nevertheless, its traditional decor, friendly staff, and proximity to the lake all add up to a sensible choice for those who appreciate intimate surroundings without paying exorbitant rates.

The **Hotel Margaréta** (Széchenyi utca 53, tel. 87/343-824, www.hotelmargareta.hu, 13,000 Ft d), is a simple centrally located hotel that does what it's meant to do—take care of its guests without any frills or fanfare. Boasting 50 spacious double rooms complete with balconies, showers, TVs, and fridges as well as a helpful staff happy to make your stay in town a pleasant one, the Margaréta is an excellent choice for travelers looking for little more than a comfortable place to lay their head after a long day.

Food

The **Cimbora Grill Garden** (Széchenyi utca 23, tel. 87/482-512, www.cimboragrillkert.hu, daily noon-11pm, mains 1,900-3,200 Ft) is an outdoor affair that seats up to 150 people who have come with an appetite. A wide variety of grilled meat dishes, including ribs, pork chops, chicken, goose, and turkey, is available, along with a salad bar offering 10 types of salad. Be prepared to eat plenty and get your hands a little dirty in the process.

Located next to the pier, **Stefánia Vitorlás Restaurant** (Tagore Promenade 1, tel. 30/546-0940, www.vitorlasetterem.hu, daily 10am-midnight, mains 1,700-3,950 Ft) is home to a huge sunny terrace that seats up to 600 people. Diners will be impressed with the quality of the food, which includes delicious Hungarian specialties like veal in smoked cheese and Balaton fish soup, along with the professional service. There are also over 40 desserts to tempt you, including a mouthwatering strawberry yogurt cake. Aside from the tasty fare, guests can't discount the remarkable view, which allows you to dine and daydream at the same time.

Situated right by Tagore Promenade, **Borcsa Restaurant** (Tagore sétány, tel. 87/580-070, www.borcsaetterem.hu, Mon.-Thurs. 11am-9pm, Fri.-Sun. 11am-11pm, mains 1,790-4,790 Ft) offers diners delicious grilled meat, fish, and poultry dishes as well as a covered terrace allowing for beautiful views of the lake. Hugely popular with locals and tourists, it's well worth at least one visit.

Arany Csillag Pizzéria (Zsigmond utca 1, tel. 87/482-116, www.aranycsillagpizzeria.hu, daily noon-11pm, mains 1,580-2,680 Ft) is one of the better pizzerias in town and a solid choice for those looking for an alternative to Hungarian cuisine. Grab a seat in its rustic interior setting or outside on its patio and dig into any number of pizza, pasta, fish, or vegetarian dishes. The service is friendly, the food consistently mouthwatering, and the prices more than affordable. Little wonder the place is almost always packed. Reservations are recommended.

Information and Services

The accommodating folks at **Tourinform** (Blaha utca 5, tel. 87/580-480, www.tourinform.hu, Dec.-Feb. Tues.-Fri. 9am-4pm, Sat. 9am-3pm, Apr. 2-June 15 Mon.-Fri. 9am-5pm, Sat. 9am-3pm, June 16-Aug. 31 Mon.-Sat. 9am-7pm, Sun. 10am-4pm, Sept.-Oct. Mon.-Fri. 9am-5pm) are happy to arm visitors with a number of brochures and publications regarding the region and the country in general. Information about cultural events, restaurants, hotels, and sights is readily available, as are plenty of books, maps, postcards, and CDs.

Getting There

BY TRAIN

Trains leave Budapest regularly from Déli station. The trip takes 2-3 hours depending on the route taken and costs 2,520-3,120 Ft. The train station is a 15-minute walk from the lake.

BY CAR

Balatonfüred is located roughly 87 miles from Budapest along main road 71. If coming via Veszprém, take main road 73 and change to 71 in Csopak.

Parking is available all over town and by the lake. It costs anywhere from 100 to 200 Ft an hour.

BY BOAT

The town's port is very active during the summer season and can be reached from a number of spots, including Tihany and Siófok.

TIHANY

The Tihany Peninsula became Hungary's first nationally protected area in 1952 and has managed to maintain its charming traditional fishing village quality despite the surge of development elsewhere in Balaton. Its unique landscape is characterized by the Inner and Outer Lake (both formed in volcanic craters) as well as Csúcs, Nyereg, and Apáti Hills, which were once the setting for very active volcanoes. Due to the peninsula's thermal activity, approximately 50 geyser cones cover the area, not to mention the Geyser Field, which formed over three million years ago. Tihany village, the area's main historical attraction, dates back to 1055, when it was founded by King Andrew I. Its beautiful 18th-century baroque Benedictine Abbey is undoubtedly its best-known and most impressive monument.

Sights

◖ TIHANYI APÁTSÁG (TIHANY BENEDICTINE ABBEY)

Established by King Andrew I in 1055, **Tihany Benedictine Abbey** (András tér 1, tel. 87/538-200, http://tihany.osb.hu, daily 9am-6pm, 1,000 Ft includes museum) was erected in honor of St. Anianus. It is home to its founder's sarcophagus as well as a copy of the abbey's deed, which is the oldest existing document containing the Hungarian language. During the Turkish occupation of the 16th and 17th centuries, the medieval monastery was transformed into a fortress and eventually destroyed. Reconstruction began in 1716 and was finished in 1752, giving the two-steeple church its present baroque form. Its interior is filled with remarkable wood carvings as well as banisters decorated with angels and arguably the most beautiful carved baroque pulpit in the country, all of which were created by gifted artist Sebestyen Stuhlhof. Next door is the **Tihany Museum** (tel. 87/448-650, http://tihany.osb.hu, daily 9am-6pm, 1,000 Ft includes abbey), likewise housed in a pretty baroque building and features a wealth of information about the region's tumultuous past and enduring culture.

VISSZHANG HEGY (ECHO HILL)

A path on the left side of the church leads up to Echo Hill, which affords splendid views of the lake. Words shouted from the top of the hill are meant to reverberate back from the walls of the church and produce an echo, though sadly, the effect has begun to wane due to increased noise and development.

Entertainment and Events

The **Lavender Festival** (tel. 87/538-022, late June-early July) in Tihany is a unique opportunity to visit an enormous lavender plantation and take part in the lavender harvest. Visitors are taken on organized trips by professionals who are happy to inform them of the flora and fauna in the area as well as help them pick the fragrant flowers.

Every year, Tihany's **Summer Theater Festival** (tel. 87/448-804, early July-late Aug.) hosts a wide array of popular cultural programs in an open-air theater. Locals and visitors from all over the world have enjoyed spectacular performances that have included productions of both Hungarian and internationally known plays as well as concerts, dance performances, and children's theater. Tickets can be obtained at the Tourinform office in town.

Shopping

Part of the fun in Tihany is to stroll around and have a look at all the wares being sold along the cobblestone streets. There is certainly no shortage of local handicrafts, embroidery, wine, and earthenware pots to choose from, along with a wide variety of wooden trinkets ranging from bracelets to chess sets.

Levendula (Batthyány utca 18, May.-Dec. daily 10am-6pm) is a charming little shop offering a number of handmade products made from lavender. Gift-seekers can choose from lavender-based bags, dolls, candles, cups, painted tiles, soap, and lots more. A refreshing change from the usual fare one finds on the main shopping strip, Levendula is an excellent opportunity to procure a memorable and aromatic souvenir.

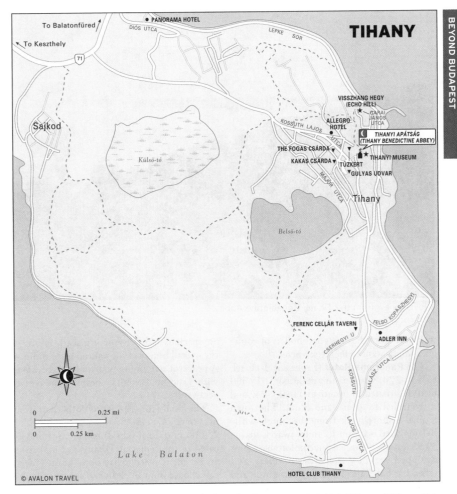

Paprikaház (Kossuth Lajos utca 16, daily 10am-6pm) is quite the sight to behold, what with the entire front and sides of the building covered with the country's beloved paprika. Peppers aren't the only thing you'll find here, however, as a large number of typical Hungarian foods and spices are available, making this an excellent stop for armchair and professional cooks alike.

Accommodations

Located at the top of the Tihany Peninsula is the four-star **Hotel Club Tihany** (Tihany-Rév utca 3, tel. 87/538-564, www.clubtihany.hu, 38,000 Ft d), whose 330 rooms and bungalows are always filled to capacity in the summer. The rooms themselves are brightly decorated and come with TV and Internet access, although the odds are you won't be using them much. A swimming pool and the Cure Center, offering everything from physiotherapy to total health packages, are also available. Those traveling with children will be hard-pressed to find better accommodations, but those who'd rather

© TOM DIRLIS

a lovely view from the Tihany Benedictine Abbey

stay away from the hoots and hollers of young ones might want to look elsewhere.

The **Panorama Hotel** (Lepke sor 9-11, tel. 87/538-220, www.panoramaht.com, 25,500 Ft d) is situated in beautiful Tihany Bay and surrounded by peace and quiet. The town is just a short walk from the hotel, while Balatonfüred is a scant 1.2 miles away. Offering 39 adequately furnished but comfortable rooms equipped with TVs, phones, minibars, and safes, the hotel also has a popular sauna and solarium available for guests. This is an excellent choice for those who like to be relatively near the action but look forward to going home to a peaceful night's sleep when the fun is over. Reservations in advance are strongly recommended, as is asking for a room with a view of the bay.

The **Adler Inn** (Felsőkopaszhegyi utca 1a, tel. 87/538-000, www.adler-tihany.hu, 19,500 Ft d) is an elegant hotel situated among Tihany's vineyards less than a mile from the center. Open from the middle of March to the end of October, its 11 rooms and apartments are spacious and stylishly furnished, adding to the overall beauty of the natural surroundings. A peaceful swimming pool and terrace, along with a top-notch sauna, complete the perfect getaway.

The family-run **Allegro Hotel** (Batthyány utca 6, tel. 87/448-456, www.allegrohotel.hu, 23,000 Ft d-26,500 Ft d) is the only hotel located in the center of Tihany and makes for an excellent place to lay one's head. Guests can choose from 14 clean and spacious double rooms with en suite baths as well as a family suite, most of which offer superb views of the lake. There's also a swimming pool and two sun decks that are ideal for chilled-out mornings or afternoons. If time allows, make sure to have the staff arrange a horse and carriage ride up to the hotel's own vineyard and wine cellar, where you can imbibe some of the region's finest wines.

Food

The Fogas Csárda (Kossuth Lajos 9, tel. 87/448-658, www.fogascsarda.hu, Mar.-Nov.

15 daily 11am-11pm, Nov. 16-Feb. Fri.-Sun. 11am-11pm, mains 1,800-3,900 Ft) is the oldest traditional restaurant in Tihany and very well known to both tourists and Hungarians. Located near the abbey, it offers fish, wild game, and traditional dishes in a rustic setting decorated with handcrafted furniture and local art and crafts. This is an excellent choice for those wanting a taste of the authentic, though it can get overrun by tour groups now and again.

Among the vineyards on Mount Cser you'll find the exemplary **Ferenc Cellar Tavern** (Cserhegy 9, tel. 87/448-575, www.ferencpince.hu, Apr.-Nov. daily noon-11pm, mains 1,950-3,650 Ft), which serves up delicious Hungarian fare like red-hot goulash, garlic pork chops, and fresh pike perch and zander. Diners enjoy both the grub and the extraordinary view, washing it all down with any number of locally produced wines.

Originally a farmhouse, **Kakas Csárda** (Batthyány utca 1, tel. 87/448-541, www.kakascsarda.hu, daily 9am-7pm, mains 1,350-2,950 Ft) has been impressing diners with a wide range of Hungarian specialties since 1983. Fish, game, chicken, pork, beef, and lamb are all offered, along with delicious homemade bread and local Balaton wines. Whether dining in their rustic interior or on their lovely garden terrace, you're sure to enjoy this authentic and delicious experience.

Located a few minutes' walk from Tihany Abbey, **Tűzkert** (Batthyány utca 15, tel. 70/519-8513, www.tuzkert.hu, Apr.-Oct. daily 10am-10pm, mains 1,900-3,400 Ft) has been feeding grateful guests its special brand of Hungarian specialties since 2002. All of its traditional meals, which include goose, chicken, and wild boar, are prepared in their wood oven without the aid of any artificial flavors or preservatives. Excellent service and comfortable seating on the garden terrace are more reasons this place remains busy throughout the season.

Gulyas Udvar (Mádl Ferenc tér 2, tel. 87/438-051, www.gulyasudvar.hu, daily 11am-11pm, mains 1,450-2,990 Ft) is a pleasant restaurant located in the heart of Tihany. Offering both international and Hungarian fare ranging from chicken fillet to grilled trout as well as a comfortable terrace and nightly barbecues, this is a safe bet for even the pickiest of palates.

Information and Services

Brochures, books, and a whole range of information can be found at the **Tourinform Office** (Kossuth Lajos utca 20, tel. 87/448-804, www.tourinform.hu, Mon.-Fri. 9am-7pm, Sat.-Sun. 10am-6pm). The friendly staff are happy to answer your questions and also sells postcards, stamps, maps, and various books offering more detailed information about the region.

Getting There

BY BUS

A local bus to Tihany can be taken from Aszófő, a mere three miles away. Balatonfüred also has a bus serving Tihany, which can be caught just outside the Balatonfüred railroad station. Buses run hourly; the trip lasts about 30 minutes and costs 160 Ft. One of the stops the bus makes is in front of the abbey steps.

BY CAR

Tihany is roughly 89 miles from Budapest. From Budapest, take Highway M7 south, then main road 71 from Balatonaliga.

There are small lots all around the village. Parking costs anywhere from 100 to 200 Ft an hour.

BY BOAT

You can opt to travel via ferry (590 Ft) from Szántód. The trip lasts 10 minutes, with ferries leaving every 40 minutes.

BADACSONY

Hungary's finest poets and painters have described Badacsony and its surroundings, located at the western end of the lake, as the most beautiful landscape in the country. It is characterized by enormous basalt hills, the most famous of which are the Badacsony (1,227 feet), the Gulács (1,289 feet), the Csobánc (1,234 feet), and Szent György-hegy (1,362 feet). A winding 500-foot-long path makes its way up Badacsony Hill and is lined with charming old

© TOM DIRLIS

docked in Badacsony

wine cellars selling the local produce, which just happens to be some of the country's most famous and delicious wines. Calm, quiet, and surrounded by awe-inspiring natural beauty, Badacsony makes for a wonderful day away from the rigors of reality.

Sights

BASALT HILLS

These wondrous geological relics resemble coffins from a distance, adding another poetic layer of beauty and mystique to the area. The various formations of solidified basalt are legendary, with some of the more popular examples being the Stone Gate of Badacsony and the "organs" of Szent György. The hills' numerous shapes and geological souvenirs of the past outline the development of volcanic activity in the area, and it is interesting to note that one reason given for the region's superior wine is the volcanic ash found in the soil. Badacsony's famous vineyards, meanwhile, are located on the southern slopes between Badacsony Hill and the lake.

Entertainment and Events

What else can one expect from a town revered far and wide for its tasty wine than a festival honoring the godly grape? All of the region's traditions come to life during the carefree days of the **Badacsony Wine Festival** (late July-early Aug.), which includes demonstrations on winemaking then and now as well as a number of outdoor concerts and theatrical performances guaranteed to keep one and all entertained.

Shopping

Pretty much the only thing worth buying in Badacsony is some of its delicious wine. The **Sipos Wine House** (Szőlő utca 13, tel. 87/471-153, www.siposborhaz.hu, May-Sept. daily 10am-6pm) is an excellent place to start. The vineyard is located at the foot of Badacsony Mountain, ensuring this decades-old family business the finest of harvests season after season. Apart from offering excellent vintages at remarkably affordable prices, they are also happy to arrange wine tastings at similarly reasonable fees (800-1,800 Ft pp).

Accommodations

【 **Hotel Bonvino Wine and Spa** (Park utca 22, tel. 87/532-210, www.hotelbonvino.hu, 44,000 Ft d) is a luxurious hotel with all the trimmings located near the shores of Lake Balaton. Each of the rooms is air-conditioned and comes with a flat-screen TV and a minibar. There's also an indoor pool on the premises as well as a jetted tub, a Finnish sauna, a steam cabin, spa treatments, and both indoor and outdoor playgrounds for the kids. It's a tad on the pricey side, but well worth the extra dough.

Obester Panzió (Római út 203, tel. 30/213-0225, www.obesterpanzio.hu, 14,800 Ft-16,800 Ft d) is a charming guest house offering eight comfortable double rooms as well as two apartments perfectly suited for 3-4 people. Enjoy hearty grilled Hungarian dishes on their delightful terrace, which offers fantastic views of the lake, and wash it all down in the wine cellar with any number of delicious homegrown wines.

Food

The **Szent Orban Wine-House and Restaurant** (Kisfaludy Sandor utca 5, tel. 87/431-382, www.szeremley.com, Fri.-Sun. noon-9pm, mains 1,900-3,950 Ft) is a gourmet restaurant that adds an element of traditional elegance to Badacsony's limited dining options. Serving regional dishes that include pike perch and wild game, it is also an excellent place to imbibe some of the country's finest wines while absorbed in the lovely panoramic view from the summer terrace.

Hungarian and international cuisine is the name of the game at **Kisfaludy-House Restaurant** (Kisfaludy Sándor utca 28, tel. 87/431-016, www.kisfaludyhaz.hu, May-Oct. daily 11am-11pm, mains 1,900-5,100 Ft), where the 200-seat terrace teems to capacity during the high season. Grilled meat, seafood, and an ever-changing list of chef's specials are what keeps bringing people in, along with the lively Romany musicians who play Hungarian standards throughout the night.

Located high in the hills, 【 **Borbarátok** (Római utca 88, tel. 87/471-000, www.borbaratok.hu, daily noon-midnight, mains 1,450-4,350 Ft) offers mouthwatering traditional Hungarian dishes as well as a breathtaking view of the lake. Fish, chicken, and meat offerings are all prepared with loving care and served with a smile. Locally grown wines and a true sense of Hungarian authenticity are a few more reasons to make the trek up the hill. It's highly recommended.

Information and Services

Maps, guides, and a whole host of information on the region can be acquired at **Tourinform Iroda** (Park utca 14, tel. 87/531-013, www.badacsony.com, Oct.-Apr. Mon.-Fri. 9am-3pm, May-June and Sept. Mon.-Fri. 9am-5pm, Sat.-Sun. 9am-3pm, July-Aug. daily 9am-7pm). Guided tours can be arranged here, and various souvenirs, postcards, and the like are on sale as well.

Those who spend at least one night in Badacsony qualify for the Badacsony Card, which can be obtained from local lodgings. The card allows holders to use all beaches for free and entitles them to 10 percent off at participating restaurants and wine cellars.

Getting There

BY TRAIN

The easiest way to get to Badacsony is by train. Coming from Budapest, trains leave frequently from Déli station. Trips take 3.5-4.5 hours and cost 3,130-4,275 Ft. From anywhere else in the region, simply get off the train at the Badacsony stop. The train station is a couple of blocks from the town center.

KESZTHELY

Situated at the far western tip of the lake, Keszthely is not only one of the region's largest towns but one of its most beautiful as well, attracting thousands of tourists during the warm summer months. The town began to develop rapidly in the 14th century, when crossing trade routes brought unprecedented wealth and commerce. Destroyed during the Turkish Wars, it was brought back to life in

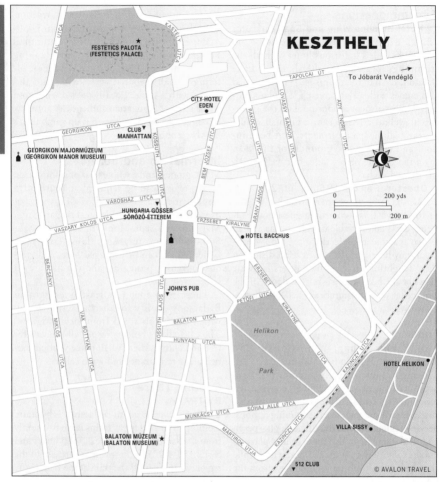

KESZTHELY

To Jóbarát Vendéglő

FESTETICS PALOTA
(FESTETICS PALACE)

CITY HOTEL
EDEN

CLUB
MANHATTAN

GEORGIKON MAJORMÚZEUM
(GEORGIKON MANOR MUSEUM)

HUNGARIA GÖSSER
SÖRÖZŐ-ÉTTEREM

HOTEL BACCHUS

JOHN'S PUB

Helikon

Park

HOTEL HELIKON

VILLA SISSY

BALATONI MÚZEUM
(BALATON MUSEUM)

512 CLUB

© AVALON TRAVEL

TAPOLCAI ÚT

0   200 yds
0   200 m

the 18th century by the powerful Festetics family, who became the area's sole landowner and was responsible for building a city hospital, a grammar school, and Europe's first agricultural college, the Georgikon. By the end of the 19th century, Keszthely had firmly established itself as a premier bathing resort that boasted soothing waters and an architecturally eclectic town center. Today, much of the era's architecture remains, and the town's numerous museums, monuments, and landmarks, particularly the elegant Festetics

Palace, help make it one of the lake's finest holiday destinations.

Sights
FESTETICS PALOTA
(FESTETICS PALACE)

Festetics Palace (Kastély utca 1, tel. 83/312-190, www.helikonkastely.hu, daily 9am-6pm, free) is the fourth-largest palace in Hungary, boasting 101 rooms, a protected park, and a museum tracing the history of the town's most influential family. Commissioned by Kristóf

Festetics, construction of the U-shaped two-story baroque palace began in 1745 and was extended and altered over the years by his sons Pál and György. Visitors to the palace will be treated to an amazing collection of exhibitions found in the **Helikon Palace Museum** (Kastély utca 1, tel. 83/312-190, Sept.-June daily 10am-5pm, July-Aug. daily 9am-6pm, 2,500 Ft). Highlights include the outstanding Helikon Library, whose floor-to-ceiling oak bookcases were built by a local carpenter and have managed to remain intact over the years, along with various trophies, weapons, and residential rooms furnished with invaluable pieces from the period. To the west of the palace are the immaculately kept Festetics Palace Grounds, which are decorated with pretty statues and fountains, reminding visitors of an elegance and style of a long-ago era.

BALATONI MÚZEUM (BALATON MUSEUM)

Founded in 1898, **Balaton Museum** (Múzeum utca 2, tel. 83/312-351, www.balatonimuzeum. hu, May and Sept.-Oct. Tues.-Sun. 10am-6pm, June-Aug. daily 10am-6pm, Nov.-Apr. Tues.-Sat. 9am-5pm, 800 Ft) has the distinct honor of being the oldest museum in the country. Inside, visitors will find numerous educational exhibits covering everything there is to know about the region. An impressive diorama outlines the lake's enormous variety of flora and fauna, while other rooms detail the region's local dress, jewelry, and pottery as well as its rich history of fishing, boating, and bathing. This is an excellent choice for those interested in familiarizing themselves intimately with the area's rich archaeological, geological, and natural evolution.

GEORGIKON MAJORMÚZEUM (GEORGIKON MANOR MUSEUM)

Detailing the area's agricultural history, the **Georgikon Manor Museum** (Bercsényi Miklós utca 67, tel. 83/311-563, May-Oct. Tues.-Sat. 10am-5pm, Sun. 10am-6pm, 600 Ft) is located on the site of Europe's first-ever agricultural college. A wide variety of exhibitions

concerning the college's history, the traditions of viticulture and viniculture, and the hard life of farmers and servants help visitors understand the unforgiving challenges of agriculture through the centuries. Tools, carts, coaches, and farming machinery complete the effect.

Entertainment and Events

Many of the bars and clubs are of the neon-lit or strip variety, but there are a number of loose and friendly establishments that are second homes to students and night owls alike. A stroll through town will quickly enlighten you as to which ones are up your alley.

NIGHTLIFE

John's Pub (Kossuth Lajos útca 46, tel. 30/237-9025, www.johnspubkeszthely.hu, Mon.-Thurs. noon-midnight, Fri.-Sat. noon-4am) is a pretty straightforward type of place with plenty of wood furnishings and tons of drink-happy youngsters. This place gets pretty busy on weekends and even busier during

Keszthely's Balaton Museum, the oldest museum in the country

theme nights and special parties. It's loads of fun if you can keep up.

For a walk on the wild side, try **512 Club** (Csík Ferenc Sétány 2, tel. 70/250-2950, www.512club.hu, Mon.-Thurs. noon-3am, Fri. noon-5am, Sat. 6pm-5am, no cover), a long, dark alternative bar that can get pretty rowdy, especially when it hosts live concerts. Music ranges from ska and punk to rock, providing a refreshing change from the countless techno beats that typically fill the night air.

【 BALATON FESTIVAL

The **Balaton Festival** (mid-late May) is easily Keszthely's biggest and most important cultural event. It is held to symbolically usher in the lake's summer season and is an eclectic mix of what some might call "high" and "low" art. It traditionally opens with a classical concert at Balaton Theater, which paves the way for a variety of similar concerts held at various upscale venues. The streets, on the other hand, are filled with jugglers, clowns, and various other street performers, all getting in on the act and entertaining the swelling crowds. Outdoor pop and rock shows fill the night air, and there are plenty of other dance and theater productions to enjoy as well. The festival closes with the hugely popular Balaton Ballroom Dance Competition, capping off two weeks of not-to-be-missed fun.

Shopping

There are plenty of shops and street vendors catering to the tourist trade by selling handmade arts and crafts, embroidery, wine, and various gift items. The best shopping in town, however, is located just down the hill from the main square. There you'll find Keszthely's **open-air market,** which buzzes with activity daily from dawn to mid-afternoon. Plenty of good buys are to be found, with vendors selling fruit and vegetables, spices, trinkets, clothing, and lots more. One word of advice: If you feel the price is a little high, it probably is. Don't be afraid to haggle!

Accommodations

There are plenty of places to choose from in Keszthely, ranging from huge hotels to pretty pensions. As always, the best deals are to be found at guesthouses and private rooms, the addresses and contacts of which can be made readily available to you with a simple visit to the town's Tourinform office.

Open seasonally, the 【 **Hotel Helikon** (Balatonpart 5, tel. 83/889-600, www.hotel-helikon.hu, early spring-late fall, 30,000 Ft d) is a pricey three-star affair situated right on the shore. Its 232 rooms and suites are comfortable, well kept, and equipped with satellite TV, minibars, and balconies that offer nice views of the lake. A wide variety of sports facilities and health services are available, including indoor and outdoor tennis courts, a swimming pool, a sauna, a solarium, bowling, a hairdresser, manicures, and pedicures. This is a reliable option for those who prefer big hotels and a certain level of luxury.

Located in the center of town, **City Hotel Eden** (Kisfaludy utca 11, tel. 83/312-213, www.hoteleden.hu, 23,500 Ft d) offers large clean rooms with satellite TV, Wi-Fi, and soundproof windows as well as a peaceful garden with its own swimming pool. The friendly staff are always happy to answer your questions, help arrange tours, and do whatever they can to make your stay a pleasant one. This is an excellent and affordable choice.

The **Hotel Bacchus** (Erzsébet királyné st 18, tel. 83/314-096, www.bacchushotel.hu, 19,000 Ft d) is hard to beat when it comes to location, situated as it is right in the heart of town. The friendly staff do their best to make your stay a pleasant one, and the simply furnished though relatively comfortable rooms should be suitable for most easygoing travelers. The on-site restaurant serves excellent Hungarian fare including fish and wild game specialties, and the hotel's wine cellar-museum allows guests both to learn about and to purchase some of the country's finest wines. Overall, this is a solid choice, but a few have observed that the value for money is somewhat on the lower end of the scale.

The **Villa Sissy** (Erzsébet királyné utca 70, tel. 83/315-394, www.villasissy.hu, 7,000-12,000 Ft d) is a quiet romantic getaway

© TOM DIRLIS

the quiet and romantic Villa Sissy

located a mere two-minute walk from the lake-front. Clean, spacious, tastefully decorated rooms and apartments accommodate a maximum of 13 people, which helps maintain an intimate family-type atmosphere. This is a great and affordable option for budget travelers who will be staying a night or two and want to stay close to the action.

Food
Friendly service and authentic Hungarian meals are what you can expect from **(Jóbarát Vendéglő** (Martinovics utca 1, tel. 83/311-422, http://jobarat.blogspot.cz, daily 11am-10pm, mains 1,850-4,150 Ft). The menu changes on a weekly basis but you can expect tasty and generous portions of meat, chicken, pork, and fish, all of which can and should be enjoyed with their fine selection of domestic wines.

Hungaria Gösser Söröző-Étterem (Kossuth Lajos utca 35, tel. 83/312-265, daily 9am-11pm, mains 1,800-3,100 Ft) is a spacious traditionally decorated Hungarian restaurant with outdoor seating that is always packed in the summertime. Mouthwatering meat dishes and spicy soups are the most popular choices, and there's an excellent selection of local wines to choose from as well. Music and entertainment are provided in the evening, which tends to get the guests excited and, not surprisingly, a lot more thirsty.

Despite being a relative newcomer to the scene, **Club Manhattan** (Georgikon útca 2, tel. 20/912-5251, www.clubmanhattan.hu, daily 11am-10pm, mains 850-2,490 Ft) has already established itself as one of the finer dining establishments around. Exposed brick and checkered tablecloths lend the place a homey Old World vibe, while the menu of Hungarian classics as well as oversize comfort foods like burgers and sandwiches leaves nothing to be desired. Friendly service and a fun, carefree vibe make this a hit with all who pass through its doors.

Information and Services
Tourinform Keszthely (Kossuth Lajos utca 30, tel. 83/314-144, www.tourinform.hu, Mon.-Fri. 9am-5pm, Sat. 9am-12:30pm) will be able to address any questions or concerns you may have. They provide plenty of information about the town and its surroundings as well as help finding accommodations, dining tips, and tickets for any cultural event that may tickle your fancy.

Getting There
BY TRAIN
Trains leave Budapest's Déli station more or less hourly on a daily basis. The trip takes approximately 3-4.5 hours and costs 3,410-4,005 Ft. The train station is on the lakeshore, about a 15-minute walk to the center.

BY CAR
Keszthely is 117 miles from Budapest. If coming from Budapest, take the M7 motorway south toward Balaton. When you get to Balatonszentgyörgy, keep your eyes open for Highway 76, which will take you to Keszthely.

Parking is available on the street. It costs anywhere from 100 to 200 Ft an hour.

BACKGROUND

The Land

GEOGRAPHY
The Czech Republic

Covering an area of approximately 30,450 square miles, the Czech Republic is geographically considered a midsize European country, on par with Austria or Ireland, representing a scant 2 percent of the European Union and sporting a relatively low population that hovers somewhere around 10.3 million.

Located smack-dab in the heart of Europe, it shares borders with Germany to the west, Poland to the north, Austria to the south, and former family member Slovakia to the east. The country comprises Bohemia and Moravia as well as the tiny southern tip of Silesia. These three lands are further broken down into 14 regions, the largest being Central Bohemia, home to the nation's capital.

The Czech Republic lies between two mountain ranges, characterized by the Czech Highlands, along with the Šumava, Český les, Krušné hory, Krkonoše, Orlické hory, and Jeseníky Mountains, which form the hilly central and western parts of Bohemia, and the West Carpathian Mountains (Beskydy), located in Moravia along the Slovak border. Krkonoše, which creates a natural border with neighboring Poland, is the country's highest

mountain range and is also home to Sněžka, the Czech Republic's tallest mountain, which stretches to a height of 5,256 feet.

Being a landlocked country, the Czech Republic does not have access to the sea. The nation's famed river, the Vltava, runs 269 miles and is navigable from Prague to Mělník, where it empties into the Elbe. The Elbe, meanwhile, runs southwest across Bohemia, receiving the Vltava, Jizera, and Ohře Rivers before continuing on its way to Germany. The Morava River flows south toward the Danube River, draining most of Moravia in the east, while the Oder River rises in the northeastern part of the country, flowing north toward Poland.

Hungary

Hungary is approximately 35,919 square miles in size, roughly the size of Indiana. Measuring about 155 miles from north to south and 326 miles from east to west, it shares borders with Slovakia to the north, Ukraine to the northeast, Romania to the east, Serbia and Croatia to the south, Slovenia to the southwest, and Austria to the west.

Hungary comprises three regions: the Great Plain, the Transdanube, and the Northern Hills. The Great Plain is situated east of the Danube River and makes up over half of the country's overall territory. Surrounded by mountains, it is characterized by its wastelands, swamps, sandy areas, and fertile soil. The Transdanube, meanwhile, lies in the west, bounded by the Danube and Drava Rivers, and consists for the most part of rolling hills leading to the Austrian Alps. It is home as well to the Bakony Mountains, which feature dolomite and limestone plateaus and reach heights of 1,300-2,300 feet. Finally, the Northern Hills lie north of Budapest, running in a northeastern direction toward the border with Slovakia. Forested ridges, rich coal and iron deposits, and the production of world-famous Tokaj wine personify the region.

When it comes to bodies of water, the mighty Danube leads the way, with a third of it located in Hungary. The rest flows through Germany, Austria, the former Yugoslavia, and Romania. The Drava River runs along the border with Serbia and Croatia, while the Rába, Azamos, Sio, and Ipoly Rivers make their way along the Slovak border. Lake Balaton is, of course, the country's largest and best-known lake. It outsizes Lake Velence, located southeast of Budapest, and Lake Ferto, on the Austrian border.

CLIMATE

Prague

Prague's **winter** temperatures range 22-37°F, with the season literally being the night to summer's day, averaging a mere 2-3 hours of sunshine daily. Long, cold, and gray winters in the capital are best battled with a piping hot cup of *svařák* (hot mulled wine) and a firm belief that the sun will indeed rise again one day. On the upside, there are fewer tourists choking the streets, so a walk down the cobblestones is a far more pleasant experience, and Christmastime is a colorful, enchanting affair with carp peddlers and brightly lit outdoor markets filling the center's squares. Occasionally, virgin white snow blankets the city for a magical day or two, adding a wintry layer of almost unbearable beauty to all of Prague's marvelous monuments.

Temperatures naturally start to rise come **spring,** averaging 30-65°F. The city slowly starts to awaken from its deep slumber, smiles begin to appear on people's faces, and gardens and castles once again open their doors to the public.

Things are in full swing by the time **summer** rolls around, with tourists descending on the capital in full force. The streets are crowded, the bars, beer gardens, and cafés are packed, and business booms all around. Temperatures hover at a reasonable 75-80°F, and the sun doesn't set till 9:30pm or so, making up, it would seem, for all its time off in the winter.

The most colorful time of year and arguably the prettiest is the **fall** season, which sees temperatures begin to dip steadily from the comfortable mid-60s in September to low 30s in November. Days begin to perceptibly shorten, with the sun starting to set around

© FESUS ROBERT/123RF

Hungarian landscape near Tihany

dinner time, letting us all know that the party's over and winter's darkness is just around the corner.

Budapest

January and February are **winter**'s coldest months in Budapest, with temperatures around 30-35°F, although they can and do quickly fall well below that. Damp, snowy, and devoid of tourists, the city is best experienced with friends and loved ones over a glass of wine at your favorite restaurant or bar.

Things start to pick up in the **spring,** its warmer temperatures (38-62°F) and promises of sunshine adding a discernible bounce to everybody's step. It can get rather wet, however, particularly during May, when showers seem to appear out of nowhere.

Summer temperatures in Budapest average 68-72°F, but often reach Mediterranean proportions of more than 80°F. Tourist season reaches its zenith, Hungarians head for Lake Balaton, and a wide range of outdoor concerts and festivals pop up on a regular basis. Easily

the busiest time in the capital, it is also the liveliest and most exciting.

The **fall** brings with it milder temperatures that make September and October the best, most comfortable months for sightseeing. Starting at around the mid-60s in September, the mercury starts dropping to the low 40s by the time November rolls around.

FLORA AND FAUNA
The Czech Republic

Despite the fact that large areas of original Czech forests have been cleared due to expanding development and the need for timber, woodlands remain a distinct and beloved characteristic of the country's landscape. The average forest comprises a healthy mix of oaks, fir, and spruce, but the country's symbolic tree is the linden. The most historic tree, a cultural symbol for almost 1,000 years, is called the Klokočovská linden and can be found in the Železné Mountains. Various regions in the country have established nature reserves to protect what have been designated particularly important landscapes, the most notable of which are the Šumava Forest, the Moravian karst, and the Jizera Mountains. Considering its small size, the Czech Republic has relatively diverse wildlife. In its forests and wetlands, the most common types of species you are bound to come across include hares, otters, martens, minks, and marmots. The woods and fields are home to pheasants and partridges as well as plenty of wild boars, ducks, red deer, and geese. You might catch a lucky break and get to see an eagle, a vulture, or a heron, and if you happen to find yourself in the northeastern part of Moravia, you may even see a wolf or a brown bear. The country's rarer species, including storks, ospreys, bustards, and eagle owls, are protected by various organizations sponsored by the state.

Hungary

Just over 12 percent of Hungary's land is covered by meadows and pastures, while roughly a further 19 percent is made up of mainly deciduous forests. The forests are full of oak, lime, and beech, with oak by far the predominant type of tree.

There are some 2,200 species of plants to be found in the country, most of which are indigenous to Central Europe. Quite a few rare and endangered flowers are protected, the most important of which are the fragrant hellebore (*Helleborus odorus*) in the Mecsek Mountains, the wild peony (*Paeonia officinalis* var. *banatica*), the pheasant's eye (*Adonis vernalis* L.), sage (*Salvia nutans*) on the Great Plain, and the meadow anemone (*Pulsatilla pratensis* subsp. *hungarica*) in the Nyírség.

Somewhere in the neighborhood of 45,000 animal species live in Hungary. The forests abound with roe deer, wild boars, and foxes, while lower-lying regions and cultivated areas are home to rabbits, partridge, quail, and pheasant.

The country's rivers and lakes are full of a wide variety of fish, including carp, catfish, pike, eel, trout, and Lake Balaton's world-famous (and delicious) pike perch.

The Great Plain is a huge migration center for a large range of birds, the most common of which are storks and swallows as well as laughing geese, wild geese, and herons. During the spring and autumn, huge flocks of migratory birds make their way from north to south and then back again, while some head to Africa for the winter.

Hungary's bird reserves protect many endangered species, including peregrine falcons, striped-headed reed warblers, spoonbills, ibis, egrets, bitterns, and red herons, while protected waterbirds include bustards and avocets.

History

THE CZECH REPUBLIC
Early Settlers

The oldest settlers of Czech lands are believed to be a Celtic tribe called the Boii, who inhabited the area somewhere around the 4th century BC. They gave Bohemia its name and defended the region successfully for nearly 1,000 years before being ousted by Germanic tribes who were in turn destroyed by Attila the Hun in 451 AD.

The Great Moravian Empire

It wasn't until the 6th century AD that Slavs entered the picture and began to settle the territory. Slavic leader Mojmir established the Great Moravian Empire along the Morava River in 830; it grew to encompass modern-day Bohemia, Slovakia, southern Poland, and western Hungary. The empire found itself between the powerful Frankish Kingdom to the west and the Byzantium to the east. Not wanting to be overcome by the influence of the Frankish Kingdom, Mojmir's successor, Prince Rostislav, sent word to the Byzantine Empire to send aid in the form of priests. Two missionaries named Cyril and Methodius arrived and began spreading Eastern Christianity. Most famously, they created a Slavonic script, known better as the Cyrillic alphabet, which continues to be used to this day in countries such as Russia and Bulgaria.

The Přemyslid Dynasty

The short-lived empire was replaced by the 400-year-long rule of the Přemyslid Dynasty. The first Přemyslid prince, Bořivoj, founded Prague Castle in 880. His grandson, "Good King" Wenceslas, went on to become one of the most famous rulers in the Přemyslid line and is today the patron saint of the Czech people. He was murdered by his jealous younger brother Boleslav, who vied for political power of his own and got it—only to lose it to Saxon King Otto I, who conquered Bohemia in 950 and made it a part of the Holy Roman Empire. Prague became a bishopric in 976, a Slav alliance was formed with Přemysl princes ruling the land on the German's behalf, and Bohemia began to boom. Prague grew rapidly

statue of Charles IV, at the foot of Charles Bridge in Prague

© LUCIE ERICKSEN

as a result of its advantageous geographic position at the crossroads of several trade routes. Construction of the Judith Bridge (now the Charles Bridge) began in 1172, Old Town was founded in 1234, Lesser Town in 1257, and Přemysl Otakar II saw his Czech kingdom expand all the way to the Mediterranean Sea. Nothing lasts forever, however, and things quickly started to go downhill when Otakar II was killed in 1278 at the Battle of Moravske Pole by the invading Roman King Rudolf Habsburg. The final nail in the coffin came in 1306 when the last Přemysl, Wenceslas III, was assassinated in Olomouc.

John of Luxembourg and Charles IV

John of Luxembourg ascended to the Czech throne in 1310 and stayed there until his death in 1346. During this time, both Prague and the Czech territory continued to grow, seeing the foundation of the Hradčany district in 1320 as well as Old Town Hall in 1338. In 1346, despite being blind, John of Luxembourg entered the Battle of Crécy and was killed. His son fought, too, but managed to survive and go on to bring Bohemia into a golden age, establishing Prague as a cultural capital and turning it into one of the most prosperous cities in the region. His name was Charles IV.

In 1344, Charles IV elevated the Prague bishopric to an archbishopric. On April 7, 1348, he established what is now Charles University, the oldest university in Central Europe. Charles IV didn't stop there, however. He began construction of New Town and Charles Bridge as well as the reconstruction of St. Vitus Cathedral and the building of Karlštejn, the Czech Republic's most famous and popular castle. All of his historic accomplishments led to him being crowned Holy Roman Emperor in 1355—one more reason why he is still lovingly referred to today as the father of the Czech nation.

The Hussite Era

Charles IV's son, Wenceslas IV, was having a heck of a time. Private wars, highwaymen, plague—not to mention the fact that the church had started focusing far more on wealth and power than the good word of God. Critics began to demand that the church renounce its power and property, something that wasn't going to happen any time soon. Consequently, a reform movement began. It was led by Jan Hus, who, in 1403, started preaching and fighting against the outright corruption of the church. The number of his enemies within the church grew, and he was eventually arrested and burned at the stake on July 6, 1415.

The murder of Hus sparked a massive protest by his followers, the Hussites. In 1419, the first Defenestration of Prague occurred, which culminated in seven councilors being thrown out the window of Prague's New Town Hall. Religious battles swept the country in 1420-1434, and in 1436 an agreement was finally reached. The Catholic Church, for the first time in its history, would allow more than one religion to be practiced on the territory it controlled. This foreshadowed the European Reformation, which proved to be a huge step forward for religious freedom. In 1458, George of Poděbrady, a moderate Hussite, became the country's new king and based his rule on peace, tolerance, and diplomacy despite being largely ignored by many European rulers and the pope.

The Habsburg Dynasty to Joseph II

In 1526, Ferdinand I of Habsburg took over the Czech throne and immediately moved the seat of power to Vienna, reducing Prague Castle to little more than a Habsburg vacation home. He was succeeded by Rudolf II, who was crowned in 1576 and moved the court back to Prague in 1583. Obsessed with art and science, it was under his reign that the nickname "Magic Prague" came to be, attracting the likes of Tycho Brahe and Johannes Kepler and creating an environment where legends like the Golem were born.

Rudolf II's brother, Matthias, took over and took little time in stripping Protestants of the rights they had been granted in the

past. This, of course, sparked Prague's Second Defenestration, and in 1618, out the window (of Prague Castle this time) went more oppressive councilors, starting what was to become the hugely destructive Thirty Years' War. The Protestants were routed in 1620 at the Battle of White Mountain, and less than a year later, 27 Protestant leaders were rounded up and executed in Old Town Square. What followed was the banning of all religions save Roman Catholicism, the suppression of the Czech language, the overtaking of Protestant properties, and the killing of anyone who dared get in the way. Little wonder this period is often referred to as the Dark Age.

Things finally began to improve under Marie Therese's rule of the Austrian Empire 1740-1780. She and her son (and successor) Joseph II mercifully reduced the power of the Catholic Church, kicked the pushy Jesuits out in 1773, and issued the Edict of Tolerance in 1781, which allowed for religious minorities to have political and religious rights.

The National Revival

As the 18th century came to an end, a National Revival, attempting to resurrect the Czech language, culture, and identity, began. Josef Dobrovský and Josef Jungmann were two figures who successfully introduced the study of the Czech language in schools, while historian František Palacký authored a much-needed *History of the Czech People*. Czech literature saw the light of day again with novelist Božena Němcová and poet Karel Hynek Mácha, the first Czech dictionary was published between 1834 and 1839, and Czech cultural institutions began to appear in the form of the National Theater and the National Museum.

Fighting for more and more political rights, a group called the Young Czechs attacked the establishment and older, passive Czechs who remained unsuccessful in their negotiations with the Habsburgs. Their efforts were finally rewarded in 1891 when they swept the elections to the Diet with the help and support of Realist Party leader Tomáš Garrigue Masaryk.

The 19th century was also characterized by

the Industrial Revolution, which saw the introduction of factories, the building of a railroad between Prague and Vienna, and a massive influx of people moving to the city from the countryside in search of new and exciting work. A nation was slowly being formed.

The First Republic and World War II

An independent Czechoslovakia was born on October 28, 1918, following the collapse of the Austro-Hungarian Empire. Two years later, a Czechoslovak Constitution was drafted, and the nation's first elected president, Tomáš Garrigue Masaryk, set up shop at Prague Castle.

Czechoslovakia enjoyed a parliamentary democracy, absorbed 70 percent of the industry from the former Austro-Hungarian Empire, and ranked among the strongest of the world's economies. In the mid-1930s, however, German inhabitants of the border areas began calling for autonomy. When diplomacy between the Czech and German governments failed, the Czechoslovak armed forces seized the disputed areas. In 1938, Britain and France, no friends of the Germans but admittedly unprepared for war, signed the Munich Pact along with Germany and Italy, allowing Adolf Hitler the right to invade and claim Czechoslovakia's border areas. The utter selling out of the land and its people still stings some of the older Czechs, who recall a bitter phrase repeated over and over again at the time: *O nás, bez nás* ("About us, without us").

The Germans invaded Czechoslovakia on March 15, 1939, and occupied the country until the end of World War II in 1945. May 5, 1945, marks the day of the Prague Uprising, when citizens took matters into their own hands. Their cause was helped by the Soviet Red Army on May 9, which helped ensure the liberation of Prague. In the western part of the country, meanwhile, it was the U.S. Army that liberated town after town (like Plzeň, which still commemorates the day with a parade) under the leadership of General Patton.

The Communist Era

Following the end of World War II, the Communist Party won the national election in 1946, with further elections to come in the following two years. Interested in gaining complete power, however, the party staged a coup on February 25, 1948, marking the beginning of a totalitarian regime that would last the next 40 years. Approximately 95 percent of all privately owned companies became properties of the state, and political trials and executions were handed down to anyone who opposed the new law of the land.

In the 1960s, a wave of political and cultural freedom was briefly enjoyed when Alexander Dubček, secretary of the Communist Party, attempted to create a brand of "socialism with a human face," guaranteeing people's basic rights and decreasing the number of political persecutions that had plagued the country for so long. The famed "Prague Spring," an outward and effusive display of the people's growing freedoms and happiness, began to disturb the Soviet Union, which saw these changes as potential threats to the system. So, on August 21, 1968, five Warsaw Pact member countries invaded Czechoslovakia, and the nation's representatives, including Dubček, were dragged to Mother Russia for a "chat." It was there that they were coerced into signing the Moscow Protocol, which allowed Soviet forces to "temporarily" stay on in Czechoslovakia, just to make sure everything ran smoothly.

The period that followed, 1968 through the mid-1980s, is known as the "normalization" period, when the party tried to right the wrongs of the last couple of years and bring things back to the way they were before the attempted reforms. This sparked the Charter 77 movement, whose members spoke out as proponents of freedom and human rights. One of those members was a young Václav Havel, who grew more and more vocal against the Communists' blatant lack of respect for the people and the truth.

Things finally began to move forward in 1985 when Mikhail Gorbachev found his way to the top of the Soviet Union and, realizing that the entire Soviet bloc was starting to crumble under the weight of severe economic problems, introduced a slow yet definite course of change.

The Velvet Revolution and Beyond

Gorbachev's perestroika and the fall of the Berlin Wall in the autumn of 1989 were signs that fundamental changes were on their way. On November 17, 1989, police in Prague violently broke up a demonstration commemorating the 50th anniversary of the closing down of Czech universities under Nazi rule. The papers circulated the story widely, and three days later, the streets were filled with roughly 200,000 people demanding the government's immediate resignation.

Things moved quickly, and in January 1990, former dissident and political prisoner Václav Havel was elected to power following the country's first democratic elections in over 40 years.

Unable to find a mutually beneficial bilateral model for the coexistence of the Czech and Slovak nations, Czechoslovakia split in two on January 1, 1993, becoming the Czech Republic and Slovakia.

The Czech Republic has gone on to blossom into one of the more successful post-Communist countries since then, joining NATO in 1999 and the European Union on May 1, 2004. With a robust tourism industry and the Communist hangover just about cured, the future looks bright indeed.

HUNGARY
The History of the Carpathian Basin

Celts settled Gellért Hill in the mid-1st century BC and were eventually conquered by the Romans, who extended their rule to the region lying west of the Danube. Their settlement of Aquincum grew into the capital of Pannonia province, which was inhabited by an impressive 30,000 people. During four centuries of rule, the Romans created a sophisticated civilization that was responsible for the founding of many of western Hungary's present-day towns.

Mass migrations brought the Visigoths,

Ostrogoths, and Lombards as well as the Huns and Avars, whose empires eventually collapsed, leaving western and southern Slavs to settle the Basin.

King Stephen

In 896 the Carpathian Basin was conquered by Magyar tribes, who made the mighty Danube the heart of their homeland. They made the flatlands their first home, including what is today's downtown Pest, which was then a large island. On Christmas Day, 1000, King Stephen was crowned with the blessing of the pope and became Hungary's first king. Believing firmly in the importance of bringing Christianity to the pagan practices of the Magyars, King Stephen invited Bishop Gellért to come help. Gellért, however, was rewarded by being thrown into a barrel and pitched off the hill by pagans who had little interest in being converted. King Stephen nevertheless succeeded, introducing measure after measure until he eventually Christianized the land.

statue of King Stephen, in front of the Fishermen's Bastion in Budapest

The Mongol Invasion

The Mongols invaded and destroyed Pest in 1241, besieging the Magyar army and effectively ending Hungary after a mere 300 years of existence. All looked lost, but internal conflicts within the Mongol Empire resulted in them leaving the country the following summer. King Béla IV began reconstruction of the country, building castles and fortifying towns, and inviting German and Italian settlers, whom he encouraged to participate in the urban development of the land. Known as "the second founder of the state," Béla IV went on to plan the construction of Buda Castle, raise Buda and Pest to the rank of towns (after which they began to flourish), and founded the Dominican convent on Margaret Island.

King Matthias

The rule of King Matthias (1458-1490) is widely considered to be the golden age of medieval Hungary. He built a centralized monarchy through sheer will and political savvy, created a highly respected mercenary army, and laid down the foundations for the development of commerce and industry.

The first printing press was established in 1473, the study of science flourished, and, by the time of his unexpected death in 1490, Matthias left behind a rapidly growing economy that ranked alongside those of the most developed European countries.

The Turkish Occupation

Buda was occupied by the Turks in 1541, kicking off 150 years of rule that saw the entire Great Plain become part of the Ottoman Empire, which already stretched across three continents. The laws of Islam prevailed over Christianity, and the Ottoman tax system hit Hungarian serfs hard. The law restricted their freedom of movement, stone houses were not allowed to be built, and damaged houses could not be repaired without permission. Battles broke out intermittently, but the Turks beat the insurgents back again and again, destroying and plundering the country along the way.

The Habsburgs

Hungary began undergoing reconstruction under Habsburg rule in the 18th century, including Buda Palace, which had been gutted and abandoned. The country joined the rest of Europe in widespread revolution, however, culminating on March 15, 1848, with Sándor Petőfi's passionate reading of his *National Song* from the steps of Pest's National Museum. The revolution was quelled the following year, but a corner had been turned, and Hungarians began to have more of a say concerning matters that directly affected them. The result was the Compromise of 1867, which brought with it both stability and prosperity. It also reorganized the Habsburg Empire on a dualist basis where both the Austrian Empire and Hungarian Kingdom became independent states with separate legislative bodies and governments.

Budapest developed at an astonishing speed, and Buda and Pest were joined with Óbuda in 1873, creating a new and thriving capital. New bridges were built, as were streetlights, the first underground railroad in continental Europe, and Andrássy Avenue. The compromise's high point came in 1896 when massive Magyar Millennium celebrations took place to commemorate 1,000 years of the Magyars settling the land. A new Parliament building was constructed, as was monumental Heroes Square. By the time the turn of the century rolled around, Budapest rivaled Vienna as a capital of culture and had truly come into its own as a political, administrative, and commercial force.

The World Wars

The assassination of heir to the Austro-Hungarian throne Archduke Ferdinand in Sarajevo on June 28, 1914, aligned Hungary with the Central Powers. This alliance forced the country into World War I, resulting in the loss of one million Hungarian lives. By the summer of 1918, a Hungarian National Council had come into existence. Headed by Count Mihály Károlyi, it demanded a separate peace and Hungarian independence.

Bending under immense pressure, Archduke Joseph appointed Károlyi prime minister, and Hungary was proclaimed a republic on November 16, 1918.

The Treaty of Trianon was signed following the end of the World War I, the provisions of which were remarkably severe. Hungary's territory was reduced to one-third of its former size, resulting in the sudden estrangement of roughly three million Hungarians. Then there was the enormous indemnity it was forced to pay, immediately destroying an economic region that had thrived for centuries.

In the hopes of recovering at least some of the land lost due to the treaty, Hungary slowly began to align itself with the Axis Powers, who brought about the Vienna Verdicts in 1938 and 1940, returning some of the land previously annexed to Slovakia and Romania. Hungary's alliance with the Axis Powers, however, meant participating in what was shaping up to be another world war, and in 1941, Hungary found itself entering World War II. Casualties that numbered in the hundreds of thousands, plus damages to towns inflicted by the Allies, inspired countrywide resistance to the war. Sensing this and not wanting to lose support, Hitler occupied Hungary in March 1944, setting up a puppet government that was more than happy to follow orders. More troops were sent to the front, and Hungarian Jews were sent to German death camps. By the time the Soviet army drove out the last of the Germans in April 1945, roughly 500,000 Hungarian lives had been lost and over 40 percent of the country's national resources destroyed. The Treaty of Trianon raised its ugly head once again and Hungary was for a second time made to pay crippling reparations.

1956

A much-needed period of reconstruction took place after the war, while democratic elections brought about the formation of a coalition government. This did not go down well with the Hungarian Communist Party, however, who, with the support of the occupying Soviet army, began a series of unlawful arrests and deportations to dreaded Siberia, managing in a short time to assume power and introduce the country to a relentless reign of terror.

Resistance began to grow over time, and on October 23, 1956, a revolution erupted in the streets, toppling Mátyás Rákosi's regime and introducing the government of Imre Nagy, who announced the beginning of a new Hungary and the country's withdrawal from the Warsaw Pact. As Soviet troops withdrew, the people celebrated and began to feel that things would finally return to normal. On November 4, however, Soviet tanks rolled in and crushed the uprising within days, arresting, deporting, or simply executing anyone who stood in their way. Imre Nagy was deported to Romania, only to be brought back to Hungary for a circus of a trial that ended with his execution in 1958.

Goulash Communism

The 1960s saw the introduction of what was commonly referred to as "goulash communism." By improving the overall living standard (albeit slightly) and allowing a modicum of flexibility in regard to travel to the West, the regime of János Kádár tried to appease a wary public. He also incorporated the slogan "Who is not against us is with us" into the daily vocabulary in the hopes of building solidarity.

The economy began to suffer under this system of "socialist planning," however, and massive debts began to amass. This led to inflation, a lower standard of living, and an overall feeling of hopelessness that was now felt by those within the Communist Party as well. In the end, János Kádár was forced to resign, and Miklós Németh's reform-Communist government took over.

1989 and the New Millennium

In the summer of 1989, representatives of the government met with budding opposition parties to discuss the possibilities and potential of a multiparty democracy. Simultaneously, Hungary opened its borders to citizens of Soviet-occupied East Germany who were looking to flee westward. The result was the beginning of a domino effect that led to the eventual fall of Communism and a democratically elected government that took power in May 1990.

A new and revitalized economy led to a flurry of construction and renovation that saw the restoration of such architectural gems as Gresham Palace and the conversion of Váci Street into a pedestrian zone. The political, economic, and cultural changes continued to evolve, and in 2004, Hungary joined the European Union, solidifying its opportunity to once again become a key player in Central Europe.

Government and Economy

THE CZECH REPUBLIC
Government
A new constitution was adopted on December 16, 1992, establishing the Czech Republic as a parliamentary democracy. Having adopted many of the Western world's liberal governmental principles, the constitution calls for a bicameral parliament comprising the Chamber of Deputies, elected every four years, and the Senate, elected on a district basis every six years. Both the president and prime minister share executive power. The former selects the latter, who runs the government and keeps the president abreast of all appointments to it.

There are a number of political parties representing the country's various interests, including the Civic Democratic Party, the Civic Democratic Alliance, the Freedom Union, the Christian and Democratic Union-Czech People's Party, the Czech Social Democratic Party, and the Communist Party. Interesting to note is the Green Party, which entered parliament for the first time at the beginning of the millennium. A relative newcomer on the scene, it has enjoyed modest success with its youth-oriented campaigns, making it a party to keep an eye on in the future.

Economy
When Communism fell in 1989, the Czech government introduced a new economic program that included price liberalization, the opening of markets to foreign trade and investment, internal convertibility of the country's currency, privatization of state-owned enterprises, and tax reform. Led by President Havel and Prime Minister Klaus, the country's well-educated and skilled labor force, proximity to Western Europe, and low level of foreign debt resulted in it becoming one of the great post-Communist success stories of the East. The tourism and service industries began to flourish, too, as reports of the capital's astonishing beauty and liberal atmosphere surfaced. The fairy-tale ended within a few years, however, as it became painfully clear that the government was not restructuring key sectors of the economy, nor was it creating transparent financial market regulations. In 1996, out and out corruption in the banking sector resulted in the collapse of eight state-controlled banks. Necessarily severe economic measures followed, leading to a major depreciation of the Czech currency and a recession in the late 1990s. The economy rebounded at the turn of the century and grew quickly once again when the Czech Republic entered the European Union in 2004. Today, Czechs—particularly those who live in Prague, where business continues to grow steadily and the unemployment rate is a microscopic 1 percent—enjoy a higher standard of living than most former Communist states.

HUNGARY
Government
Throughout the 19th and 20th centuries, Hungary's political system was mostly autocratic in nature, though the period between 1867 and 1948 did see a functioning parliament, a multiparty system, and an independent judiciary. Then came the Communist

© CRAIG ERICKSEN

the Hungarian Parliament building

takeover in 1948, and a Soviet-style system was incorporated wherein all legislative and executive branches of the government fell under the control of the Communist Party. Opposing political parties were abolished, and the Hungarian Social Democratic Party was forcefully merged with the Communist Party to form the Hungarian Workers Party.

Dramatic political reforms began to take place after the fall of Communism in 1989, beginning with an all-encompassing revision of the 1949 constitution, which included approximately 100 changes and reintroduced a multiparty parliamentary system of democracy that included free elections. The legislative and executive branches were once again separated and an independent judicial system was established, as was a constitutional court elected by parliament.

Today, the National Assembly holds ultimate legislative power, electing the president of the republic, the Council of Ministers, the president of the Supreme Court, and the chief prosecutor. The Council of Ministers is led by the prime minister and is responsible for the administration of the state. The president, meanwhile, commands the armed forces but otherwise has limited authority.

Economy

Hungary was primarily an agrarian country up to World War II, but the Soviet Union introduced an industrialization policy in 1948 as well as a centrally planned economy that created millions of new jobs. As time passed, the number of those employed in the agricultural sector began to decline significantly, representing a mere eighth of the population by the end of the 1980s. Meanwhile, the industrial workforce grew to roughly one-third of the employed population, with iron, steel, and engineering given the highest priority. New technologies and high-tech industries were ignored, however, and by 1989 Hungary's new market and parliamentary system inherited an economy plagued with debt and underdeveloped export sectors. The sudden opening of the country and abolition of state subsidies led to the eventual collapse of its iron, steel, and engineering industries as well as a GDP that decreased by 25 percent, leading to a 14 percent unemployment rate in the early 1990s. Things started to look up by the new millennium, however, thanks in large part to Hungary's very welcoming foreign investment policies, along with the modernization of telecommunications and establishment of new industries like automobile manufacturing. Today, roughly one million small and medium-size businesses operate in the country, state ownership of businesses has fallen to approximately 20 percent, and an increasingly profitable tourism industry indicate that Hungary has finally begun to right itself.

People and Culture

THE CZECH REPUBLIC

The Czech Republic's population weighs in at just over 10 million people, with roughly 1.2 million living in Prague. The capital remains rather homogenous, as the vast majority of people are of Czech origin. Slovak and Roma minorities are the second and third largest ethnic groups, just ahead of the significantly large expatriate community, which numbers in the tens of thousands and mostly comprises Americans, Brits, Germans, and the French. Minority groups from South Asia as well as Africa and Russia have continued to grow in size, adding a cosmopolitan flavor and appeal to Prague that was clearly lacking before Communism fell and the floodgates opened.

Culture

While just as friendly, considerate, and warm as anybody else, Czech people can seem rather distant and at times downright rude to first-time visitors, particularly when it comes to the service industry. This is in large part due to a still lingering Communist hangover in which

Easter Traditions

While the Czech Republic is easily one of the most secular countries in the world, Czechs are nevertheless eager to observe centuries-old traditions when it comes to celebrating Easter. Most traditions have faded over the years, but two have withstood the test of time: the popular coloring and decorating of eggs as well as the more controversial "whipping" of women and young girls.

Pagan Slavs believed that whipping brought wealth, luck, and a healthy harvest for an entire year, the logic being that the vitality of the young twigs braided together to form a whip or *pomlázka* would be transferred to those being whipped. The lucky women who find themselves on the receiving end of such unique attention (usually concentrated on the backs of their legs) reward the men with painted eggs as well as a brightly colored ribbon that is tied to the whip before the male in question moves on to the next house. In some villages, however, whipping the women of the house isn't enough, as another tradition dictates that women are to be thrown in a bath of cold water so that they experience an "Easter dousing," which, of course, is known to chase away both illness and evil spirits.

Luckily, no one takes these traditions all that seriously anymore, although sales of whips come Easter time continue to shoot through the roof. And you might be relieved to know that the whipping itself has been replaced by light, good-natured whacks on a female loved one's bottom for old time's sake. The smart ones still keep a safe distance between themselves and the bathtub.

many don't feel the necessity to overexert themselves at their jobs or are simply tired of the nonstop flow of foreigners that come and go. Nevertheless, Czechs will open up quickly if you attempt a word or two of their language or somehow demonstrate that you're a respectful visitor and not just one of the masses who have come for the booze and bordellos. Typically mild-mannered, understated, and sporting a dark sense of humor, Czechs are also often very tolerant people, sexually open-minded, proud of their absurdly delicious beer, and fiercely loyal to their national soccer and hockey teams. Many Czechs love the outdoors and often leave the rigors of the city on the weekend, heading to their cottages for rest, relaxation, and outdoor recreation.

Religion

If there's a heaven for atheists, the Czech Republic is most certainly it. Thanks to 40 years of Communist rule that taught atheism as part of the curriculum and systematically stripped the church of all its power, Czechs are the most atheistic people in Europe and admit as much with a certain sense of pride. Catholicism is the country's traditional religion, but only 30 percent of people claim to loosely believe in "something," while less than 10 percent of the population claims to attend church services more than once a month. When asked about their distaste and disinterest in all things ecclesiastical, most Czechs will tell you they have a hard time distinguishing between Communism and religion; after all, both limit one's freedom and demand that people comply with their ideals. Not very Bohemian, now, is it?

Language

As you might expect, the Czech language is the predominant tongue spoken in the Czech Republic, though some of the older Czechs can speak German and Russian, which was mandatory in schools before the Velvet Revolution. Prague is no different, of course, but many do speak at least a bit of English, primarily in the shops, restaurants, and bars located in the downtown core. As you leave the center, however, your chances of finding someone to communicate with in English begin to diminish.

Food and Drink

Typical Czech meals focus primarily on bread, meat, and potatoes, with fresh fruit and vegetables being an afterthought at best. A standard breakfast usually involves a bread roll smothered in jam and butter, a touch of yogurt, or eggs and sausage. Bakeries serving croissants and pastries are also popular stops for those on their way to work. Lunch is the average Czech's main meal of the day and is generally had between noon and 2pm. This is when the nation's most common meal—dumplings, sauerkraut, and roast pork—is typically enjoyed. Dinner, served anywhere from 5pm to 7pm, is oftentimes a much smaller and simpler affair, consisting of rye bread and an assortment of sausage and deli meats. Vegetarians will most likely be limited to soups and salads when patronizing a Czech establishment, while restaurants specializing in various foreign cuisines

Czech beer

© LUCIE ERICKSEN

Superstitions

Hungarians, it turns out, are just as superstitious as everyone else. While they believe that a black cat, spilled salt, broken mirrors, and the number 13 are all harbingers of terrible luck, there are nevertheless a few other superstitions that are unique to the culture and still believed to this day.

For example:

- If a framed picture falls from your wall, a family member will become ill.
- If a black dog crosses your path, you will have a fight with someone.
- If your left palm itches, money is on the way. If your right palm itches, you'll spend carelessly.
- If your left ear starts to ring, good news is around the corner. If your right ear starts to ring, bad news is on the way.
- If the first person you speak to New Year's Day is a man, you'll have good luck throughout the year. If you happen to speak to a woman first, bad luck will abound.
- The weather on each day between the 13th and 24th of December will forecast the weather for each coming calendar month, respectively.
- If you are suddenly seized by a fit of hiccups, it's a surefire sign that someone is talking behind your back.
- If any animals appear in your dreams, someone in your family is about to die.

(Asian and Indian, for example) may offer more variety. Beer is the standard alcoholic drink throughout the country, followed by wine and any number of spirits. Coffee and a wide assortment of teas top the nonalcoholic category.

HUNGARY

Historically speaking, Hungary was a multicultural country since its beginnings in the 10th century, but the geographical changes that came after the end of World War I left it with a predominantly homogeneous population of ethnic Hungarians—a fact that remains to this day. Over 90 percent, in fact, of Budapest's two million people are Hungarian, with the Roma being the largest of the ethnic minority groups, followed by the Slovaks. Plenty more minority groups make Hungary their home, however, including Germans, Russians, Greeks, and Poles. There is also a small expatriate community comprising mostly North Americans and Brits who have either opened up small businesses or work for any number of multinationals.

Culture

Hungarians are a hospitable people who generally will go out of their way to make a guest feel welcome. They are typically very friendly to foreigners and will do what they can to help if able to communicate in English. Lively, active, and fun-loving, Hungarians also often enjoy having dinner and drinks with friends, following the latest soccer game, and unwinding at any one of the country's many baths. They are fiercely proud of their culture and will talk to you at length about their glorious history as well as their admittedly uncertain future.

Religion

Despite having been exposed to a wide variety of religions as a result of being ruled by everyone from the Austrian Habsburgs to the Ottomans, Hungary nevertheless remains a relatively secular country, with roughly one-third of the population claiming no religious affiliation whatsoever. About 50 percent of Hungarians are Roman Catholic, most of whom live in the northern and western sections of the country. Protestants account for just over 20 percent of the populace, while the Jewish community, with centuries-long roots in the country, was estimated to be around 400,000 before 1939. Today, following the decimation of World War II, that number is closer to 80,000.

Language

Hungarian is the main language spoken widely throughout the country, posing quite a few difficulties for visitors who find it nigh impossible to make heads or tails of the bizarre sounding Finn-Ugric language. Most Hungarians who can't speak English will throw in a German word or two in hopes of making themselves clearer, rarely realizing that this doesn't help most visitors. English is generally spoken by most under the age of 30, though, particularly in the service industry and at most museums and city sights. The odds of finding someone who speaks English do start to work against you, however, the farther you stray from the capital.

Food and Drink

Typical Hungarian meals are generally known to be meat-heavy and generously spiced with paprika, though there are plenty of other options, such as goose liver, wild game, and pike perch. Breakfast can be a typical eggs-and-sausage affair or a lighter meal consisting of yogurt, fresh fruit, pastry, or fruit-filled pancake. Lunch is mainly served at noon and is the day's most important meal. It usually begins with a seasonal or fish soup and is followed by a meat dish like paprika chicken or traditional favorite *gulyás* (goulash). Dinner is typically served between 6pm and 7pm and can range from an assortment of fantastic Hungarian salamis to a fish or meat dish. If you're looking for something other than meat, you'll usually have a handful of fish-based meals to choose from as well as the occasional salad, but that's about it. There are countless dessert options, as the country abounds in mouthwatering pastries, ice creams, and cakes, all of which are guaranteed to satisfy your sweet tooth. Wine is by far the alcoholic drink of choice as Hungarians have no shortage of domestic product to choose from. On the nonalcoholic side of things, coffee tops the list, with tiny cups of espresso being the most popular.

The Arts

THE CZECH REPUBLIC
Cinema

For such a small country, it really is amazing just how many quality films are made in the Czech Republic. While only 15 or so films are produced each year, a handful have managed over the years to win the prestigious Academy Award for Best Foreign Picture: *Obchod na korze* (*The Shop on Main Street,* by Jan Kadar and Elmar Klos), *Ostře sledované vlaky* (*Closely Observed Trains,* directed by Jiří Menzel), and *Kolja* (by Jan Svěrák). Recent nominations for the coveted prize include 2000's *Musíme si pomáhat* (*Divided We Fall,* by Jan Hřebejk) as well as 2003's offering, *Želary* (directed by Ondřej Trojan). The country's most successful filmmaker, however, is undoubtedly the incomparable Miloš Forman, responsible for such classics as *One Flew over the Cuckoo's Nest, Amadeus,* and *Man on the Moon.*

Czech films are typically offbeat in nature, wielding a dark sense of humor and unconventional narratives that make for unique cinematic experiences. Lately, however, it seems that the originality of the films that the Czechs are known for has begun to suffer thanks in large part to having to compete with international (primarily American) releases. The result is a tendency to rely on formulaic storytelling or an endlessly nostalgic revisiting of the nation's past, usually in the form of World War II mini epics or Communist-era dramedies.

Aside from its domestic endeavors, Prague also hosts a large number of foreign productions that come here to capitalize on professional crews and exceptional locations at relatively low costs. Past productions include *Mission Impossible, The Brothers Grimm, Hart's War, From Hell,* and *Oliver Twist.*

Literature

With a roster of literary giants that includes Bohumil Hrabal, Milan Kundera, Franz Kafka, and Nobel Prize winner Jaroslav Seifert, the Czech Republic is clearly well represented in the field of belles lettres. Dating back to the 12th century in the form of folk poetry and liturgical texts, Czech literature hit its stride during the national revival of the mid-19th century with the outlandish and oftentimes nightmarish works of Karel Jaromír Erben (*Kytice*), Božena Němcová (*Babicka*), and the country's greatest Romantic poet, Karel Hynek Mácha, known primarily for his exceptional lyrical work *Maj.*

The start of the 20th century, particularly the years 1918-1939, represents a high point in Czech literature, with an incredible body of work coming from masters of the narrative form like Franz Kafka (*The Metamorphosis*), Karel Čapek (*RUR*), and Jaroslav Hašek (*The Good Soldier Svejk*).

It wasn't until the 1960s that things started to look up again, as writers such as Vaclav Havel (*The Garden Party*), Josef Škvorecký (*Cowards*), Milan Kundera *(The Unbearable Lightness of Being*), Bohumil Hrabal (*Closely Observed Trains*), and Ivan Klíma (*A Ship Named Hope*) came into form, fighting the Communists on home turf or producing some of their finest work while in exile abroad. This rebellious streak continued on into the 1970s when samizdat, the practice of reproducing banned works on personal typewriters and distributing copies secretly both inside and outside the country, took off, lending much needed exposure to the powerfully subversive material.

The fall of Communism has seen a sharp decline in the number of celebrated Czech writers, with the possible exception being Jachym Topol, whose down-and-dirty vision of post-Communist Prague made for excellent reading when it first came out in 1994, but now seems terribly out of date due to Prague's rapidly changing nature.

Music

The Czech Republic has a rich and diverse musical history that notably starts in the 18th century with influential composer Johann Stamitz, who founded the Mannheim school of symphonists and had a significant effect on the great Mozart. Also influential was Josef Mysliveček, who wrote operas and symphonies that were highly respected in Italy, where he came to be known as "il divino Boemo"—the divine Bohemian.

Classical music began to blossom during the 19th century with renowned composers such as Bedrich Smetana, who was the first to incorporate Czech nationalism into his work, as in his famed opera *Prodaná nevesta* (The Bartered Bride) and his powerful cycle of symphonic poems *Má Vlast* (My Country). Then, of course, there was Antonín Dvořák as well as Leoš Janáček and Bohuslav Martinů, each of whom left their mark on international stages and who continue to be immortalized today with orchestral concerts performed regularly around the world.

Today, the Czech Republic's most famous (and oldest) recording artist is still Karel Gott—dubbed "the Czech Elvis" by his fans, who remain loyal to the cheesy pop singer who started soon after the King himself. On the alternative, indie side of things, there is no shortage of bands gracing Prague's stages. Monkey Business is a hugely successful funk band led by the vocal stylings of American Tonya Graves; Charlie Straight, Anna K., and Tatabojs continue to churn out light radio-friendly rock and pop tunes; Kabat reigns supreme in the heavy metal department (still a popular genre here); and old-timers Cechomor blends traditional folk and rock to create a rootsy and unique Czech sound.

HUNGARY
Cinema

The provisional Soviet-led government

Etyekwood and Korda Studios

Located roughly 15 miles from Budapest, Etyek is home to a nearly 5,000-acre wine-growing region known for producing dry, acidic, light wines. More recently, however, Etyek has become synonymous with production of a much different sort—movies. Nicknamed "Etyekwood" by the press, the tiny town is now home to Korda Studios, which came to be thanks to Hungarian-born American producer Andrew G. Vajna and businessman Sándor Demján, who is responsible for the very successful WestEnd City Center. This major film production studio boasts a state-of-the-art postproduction suite, a 65,000-square-foot soundstage, and the largest indoor water tank in Europe. There are big plans for the studio, with both founders banking on American productions being lured to Hungary in an effort to save costs as well as domestic filmmakers looking to capitalize on the government's pledge to reimburse 20 percent of production costs for each film made at Korda. The hope is that Hungary will once again be thrust into the limelight of international film production, and judging by the growing number of films that have been bypassing Prague due to its absurdly unfair tax laws, it looks like this is one dream that might come true.

established the Hungarian Film Industry in 1948, which was to promote the land and its people through a nationalistic context, in essence a sophisticated propaganda machine. After the 1956 uprising, young filmmakers coming up in the system began to make films filled with symbolic and allegorical inside jokes that bit the hand greasing the machine. A Hungarian New Wave was born, and by the early 1970s Hungarian cinema was widely considered to be one of the most exciting, daring, and original in Eastern Europe. Ironically, it was the collapse of Communism that led to the particularly troubling state domestic cinema finds itself in today. Now that the gates to the world are open, audience members are far more inclined to spend their money watching a genre film rather than one dealing with intricate social conflict. In other words, Hungarian art films have taken a backseat to American blockbusters, reaching maybe a few thousand viewers, and are unable, therefore, to make much of their money back, let alone earn a profit.

There have been a few success stories, however, particularly with famed director Istvan Szabo's Oscar for Best Foreign Film for his hugely popular *Mephisto*. Hungarian expatriates have made quite a name for themselves abroad as well, starting with Michael Curtis (*Casablanca*), the Korda brothers, and Adolph Zukor (the founder of Paramount Studios) in the 1920s-1940s. Hungarians who fled after the 1956 uprising have continued the tradition in the form of producer Andrew Vajna (*Nixon, Lethal Weapon*), Peter Medak (*The Ruling Class, Let Him Have It*) and screenwriter Joe Eszterhas (*Flashdance, Basic Instinct*).

Literature

The earliest and most significant examples of the written Hungarian language can be found in the *Halotti Beszéd és Könyörgés* (Death Speech and Prayer) as well as *Ómagyar Máriasiralom* (Old-Hungarian Mary-Lamentation), the first Hungarian poem, which dates all the way back to 1300.

The 16th century saw the rise of Gáspár Heltai and his moralistic fairy tales; Sebestyén Tinódi Lantos, whose verse recounted famous battles against the dreaded Turks; and the religious, heroic, and romantic elements of Bálint Balassi, widely agreed to be one of the country's finest poets.

The next major movement came in the 19th century, when some of the country's most revered writers began expressing themselves in the Romantic style. There was Ferenc Kölcsey, who composed the Hungarian national anthem; Mihály Vörösmarty, who became poet laureate after penning his epic poem *Zalán futása* (*Zalan's Run*); Sándor Petőfi, who stirred the country's heart with his patriotic and revolutionary poems; and János Arany, credited with single-handedly introducing Hungary to the ballad form.

Attila József reworked popular poetry and took it in the direction of the avant-garde during the first half of the 20th century, while the second half saw Dezső Tandori and Ottó Orbán delve deeply into postmodernist narrative. Péter Esterházy's *Termelési regény* (*Production Novel*), Péter Nádas' *Emlékiratok könyve* (*Book of Memoirs*), and György Konrád's *A cinkos* (*The Accomplice*) all enjoyed significant success in the 1980s, while Imre Kertész received the Nobel Prize for Literature in the new millennium (2002) for his heartbreakingly beautiful novel *Sorstalanság* (*Fateless*), which deals with the Holocaust as seen through the eyes of a young boy.

Music

Hungary has enjoyed a rich musical culture for centuries, mixing classical elements with folk music and gypsy rhythms to create a sound unique to its land and people. *Verbunkos,* a traditional Hungarian dance music coupled with Western harmonies and forms, was made popular by Ferenc Erkel (1810-1893), who was also the first to use the Hungarian language in opera with *László Hunyadi* and *Bánk bán.* Representing a high point in Hungarian classical music was, of course, the incomparable Franz Liszt (1811-1886), whose blend of European romanticism and Hungarian traditions catapulted him to the top of the classical music scene in

the second half of the 19th century. Operettas enjoyed a respectable degree of success at the turn of the 20th century with composers Ferenc Lehár (1870-1948), Imre Kálmán (1882-1953), and Jenő Huszka (1875-1960) representing their country on the international stage. Then came Béla Bartók (1881-1945), another seminal Hungarian composer of international repute who turned to the traditions of Hungarian folk music and made them into his own unique works, including the opera *Bluebeard's Castle,* ballets *Wooden Prince* and *Miraculous Mandarin,* and numerous string quartets and piano concertos. During the oppressive 1960s, rock music was the rebellious melody of choice with bands like Illés, Omega, and Lokomotiv GT, along with singers Klári Katona, Zsuzsa Koncz, and Kati Kovács expressing their distaste and disillusionment in the form of political protest. Things loosened up and by the mid-1980s all sorts of musical genres were coming into their own, including, of all things, the rock opera, whose popularity can be attributed to its national and religious themes more so than the music itself. Hits of the time included *István the King* and *The Excommunicated.*

Today, Hungary's contemporary music scene continues on in vibrant style, spanning any number of genres. Electronic dance music started gaining popularity after the changes in 1989 and continues on today, with Anima Sound System, Yonderboi, and Neo being some of the more popular acts. Ganxsta Zolee pioneered gangsta rap in Hungary, while Dopeman and LL Junior provide mainstream hip-hop to the masses. Ektomorf sits atop the heavy metal scene, and bands like Aurora, PICSA, and Prosectura continue to prove that punk is not dead.

Architecture

Both Prague and Budapest boast some of the most breathtaking architecture to be found in the world, let alone Europe. From palaces to churches, museums to hotels, visitors are treated to a wide range of styles that span centuries and inspire awe in all who lay eyes on them.

Perhaps the biggest difference between the two cities is the fact that a number of Budapest's buildings and monuments were destroyed over and over again throughout the years due to bloody wars, whereas Prague's were for the most part (and rather miraculously) spared from any significant damage. As a result, some of Budapest's finest architecture is actually an amalgamation of styles. For example, take its magnificent Parliament building, which incorporates Renaissance, neo-Gothic, and Baroque elements, or the Royal Palace of Buda, which was originally designed in the Gothic style, later rebuilt to gel with the Renaissance tastes of the time, and finally reconstructed as a baroque building.

Painstaking care is taken in both countries to restore historical landmarks to their original designs. Even the most casual passerby will be amazed at the overwhelming aesthetic beauty found in both cities. The following is a small sampling of some of the architectural gems to be found.

GOTHIC

The Gothic style of architecture flourished in this part of the world from the 13th to the 16th centuries and was particularly embraced in Prague. Its main features are pointed arches, ribbed vaults, and flying buttresses, with an emphasis on verticality meant to signify a sort of "reaching up to God." There are plenty of well-preserved examples of Gothic architecture in Prague today, with the Church of Our Lady Before Týn in Old Town Square and the mind-blowing Charles Bridge being its most famous examples. Other notable sights are the Powder Tower, Old-New Synagogue in Josefov, and the eastern side of St. Vitus Cathedral.

RENAISSANCE AND NEO-RENAISSANCE

The Renaissance movement began in the 16th century, and its style emphasized symmetry, proportion, and an overall influence by the architecture of classical antiquity. In Prague, the Royal Summer Palace (otherwise referred to as "The Belvedere") and Schwarzenberg Palace are two shining examples. St. Stephen's Basilica, the Hungarian Academy of Sciences, and Budapest's majestic Opera House are the Hungarian capital's most significant contributions to the neo-Renaissance movement.

BAROQUE AND NEO-BAROQUE

The baroque movement swept through Europe during the 17th and 18th centuries, focusing primarily on broader forms, adding colonnades, domes, and large ceiling frescoes to works as well as creating dramatic contrasts in the usage of light and shade. Neither Prague nor Budapest lack for wonderful demonstrations of the style. Prague's most exquisite example is undoubtedly the magnificent St. Nicholas Church in Malá Strana, which never ceases to wow visitors. Not to be outdone, the Church of St. Nicholas in Staré Město, the Clementinum, Wallenstein Palace, and the Loreto serve as fine examples of the period. In Budapest, the enormous City Hall, Franciscan Church, and Church of St. Anne are just a handful of buildings displaying an undeniable mastery of the form, while the Klotild Palaces and Széchenyi Spa Baths are must-sees for those interested in neo-baroque.

© TOM DIRLIS

the Museum of Czech Cubism in Prague

ART NOUVEAU

The highly stylized and dynamic curvilinear designs that characterize art nouveau began cropping up at the end of the 19th century and peaked in popularity at the turn of the 20th century. Oftentimes incorporating floral motifs and basking in opulence, the buildings are a symphony for the eyes. In Prague, the best-known examples of the flamboyant style are the gorgeous Municipal House and the well-preserved exterior of the Grand Hotel Evropa. In Budapest, the art nouveau movement was influenced by Middle Eastern design and incorporated more traditional Hungarian elements as well, creating a unique synthesis of styles that is noticeable in the Museum of Applied Arts, Gresham Palace, and the lavish Gellért Hotel and Baths.

CUBIST

Prague was a hotbed of cubist activity in Central Europe, primarily during the years 1910-1920. The style is easily recognizable thanks to its emphasis on striking triangular and pyramidal forms as well as its focus on diagonal lines instead of horizontal or vertical ones. The most celebrated architectural examples of the movement are undoubtedly Adria Palace and the House of the Black Madonna, which is also home to the interesting and informative Museum of Czech Cubism.

Cubism, despite its influence and popularity in Prague, failed to impact the architecture of Budapest.

MODERNIST

The modernist movement began shortly after the establishment of an independent Czechoslovakia in 1918 and flourished during the years leading up to World War II. Linking design with function (hence the term "functionalism") as well as uncommon beauty with purpose, its use of brick, stone, prefab materials, and glass swept the city and left behind many exemplary uses of the form, including the Church of the Most Sacred Heart of Our Lord, Veletržní palác (Trade Fair Palace, home to the National Gallery Collection of 19th-, 20th-, and 21st-Century Art), Mánes Gallery, and the residential Baba Settlement.

In Budapest, the influence of Modernism can be found primarily in residential architecture.

ESSENTIALS

Getting There

BY AIR
Prague

Václav Havel Airport (tel. 220 111 888, www.prg.aero) is located in Dejvice, roughly 12.5 miles northwest of the downtown core. The **Czech Airline CSA** (tel. 239 007 007, www.csa.cz) provides direct flights to some U.S. cities. Other major airlines regularly stopping in Prague are **Lufthansa** (tel. 234 008 234, www.lufthansa.com), **Air France** (tel. 233 090 933, www.airfrance.cz), **Austrian Airlines** (tel. 227 231 231, www.aua.com), and **British Airways** (tel. 239 000 299, www.britishairways.com).

Budapest

Budapest Ferenc Liszt International Airport (tel. 1/296-7000, www.bud.hu) is located in southeast Pest, approximately 15 miles from the center of town. The airport has two main terminals. Terminal 1 generally handles airlines offering budget travel like **EasyJet** (tel. 1/296-8368, www.easyjet.com), **Germanwings** (tel. 1/296-8369, www.germanwings.com), and **Norwegian Air Shuttle** (tel. 70/332-4009, www.norwegian.com). Terminal 2, meanwhile, is home to leading international carriers **British Airways** (tel. 1/777-4747, www.britishairways.com), **Air France** (tel. 1/483-8800,

www.airfrance.com), **KLM** (tel. 1/296-5747, www.klm.com), and **Lufthansa** (tel. 1/411-9900, www.lufthansa.com).

BY TRAIN

A multitude of regional and continental rail passes are available, and they're a very good idea for anyone who would like to travel extensively throughout the continent. If you're coming from North America, you'll want to book ahead online. The two most important sites are **Euro Railways** (www.eurorailways. com) and **RailEurope** (www.raileurope.com), both of which offer scores of deals depending on age, length of stay, and distances traveled.

Prague

All international trains make their final stop at either **Nádraží Holešovice** (Holešovice Station, Vrbenského 1, Holešovice, tel. 296 191 817) or **Hlavní nádraží** (Main Station, Wilsonova 2, Nové Město, tel. 224 214 886). Trains from Budapest to Prague leave 5-6 times a day, and the trip takes 7-9 hours. Visit www.idos.cz for schedules and fares of all trains, buses, and planes, both leaving and crisscrossing the country.

Budapest

A large number of trains from across Europe roll into **Keleti Station** (VIII. Kerepesi út 2/6, tel. 1/313-6835), which is located in Baross Square. Trains from Prague to Budapest leave around the clock and number up to 10 a day, with the trip taking 7-9 hours. The national train website, www.elvira.hu, is very useful, offering complete up-to-date information regarding Hungary's railroad system and schedules.

BY BUS
Prague

Florenc bus station (Křižíkova 6, Žižkov, tel. 900 144 444, florenc.cz) is where all domestic and international coaches come and go. On the premises is a **Eurolines office** (Křižíkova 2b, tel. 245 005 245, www.elines.cz, Sun.-Fri. 6:30am-10:30pm, Sat. 6:30am-9pm), which can help you reserve a seat on any one of their numerous buses connecting Prague with the rest of the continent. Buses leave Budapest for Prague three times a week. The trip takes 7.5-8 hours, and a round-trip ticket costs roughly 12,000 Ft. Visit www.idos.cz for schedules and fares of all trains, buses, and planes, both leaving and crisscrossing the country.

Budapest

Just about all international buses from the United Kingdom and the rest of Europe make **Népliget Station** (Népliget autóbusz-állomás, Ferencváros, IX. Üllői út 131, tel. 1/219-8000) their final destination. **Volánbusz** (www.volanbusz.hu) is the country's main international bus line and runs the routes coming from Prague. The trip generally lasts 7.5-8 hours, and fares start at 990 Kč. Passengers are asked to check in one hour beforehand (or 15 minutes prior to leaving at the very latest). Fares and schedules change often, so make sure to check the Volánbusz website for the most up-to-date information.

BY CAR
Prague

A valid UK, U.S., or Canadian driver's license is required for you to lawfully drive in the Czech Republic. The country's highways are continually being upgraded, which means traffic jams and various delays are not out of the ordinary. For travel on the highways, a sticker must be bought at a border crossing, gas station, or post office and affixed to your windshield. The validity of coupons is as follows: "R" is valid for one year, "M" for one month, and "D" for one week.

If you're approaching Prague from the east, you'll cross through Zilina, Slovakia; those from the south will pass through Linz, Austria. If coming from the west, Waldhaus-Rozvadov will serve as your border crossing, and Reitzenhain-Pohranicí will greet those coming from the northwest.

While Prague boasts highway connections from five major directions, the country's highway network leaves plenty to be desired, as it is incomplete and suffers from poor upkeep.

Nevertheless, two major highways lead to the Czech border: the D5 (or international E50) stretches southwest past Plzeň and on to Germany, while the D1 (or international E65) heads to Brno and continues on to Slovakia. With regard to distances to Prague, Budapest is 347 miles, Vienna is 194 miles, Warsaw is 320 miles, and Berlin is 220 miles.

Driving from Budapest to Prague takes 5-6 hours and is quite simple. Take the M1 out of Budapest toward Bratislava. Take the Bratislava exit, continuing along the D2/E65 into Slovakia. Follow the D2/E65 through Slovakia, into the Czech Republic, toward Brno. As you approach Brno, take the D1/E65 toward Prague. Continue along the D1/E65 until you reach Prague.

RULES OF THE ROAD

People drive on the right side of the road in the Czech Republic. Wearing your seatbelt is mandatory, and child seats for young children are required on all roads. There is absolutely zero tolerance when it comes to drinking and driving. That means you cannot have had anything alcoholic to drink before getting behind the wheel, no matter how tiny or insignificant the amount. Use of a cell phone while driving is against the law (although a hands-free device is OK). Headlights must be on no matter what time of day you're driving. Always stop behind trams when passengers are getting on and off at a stop where there is no pedestrian island, and avoid driving on tram tracks unless there is no other choice. Speed traps are common in the Czech Republic, so it's always best to observe the speed limits: 130 km/h (81 mph) on the highways, 90 km/h (56 mph) on roads, and 50 km/h (31 mph) in towns and villages.

Budapest

An International Driving Permit is no longer necessary in order to drive legally in Hungary, but a valid UK, U.S., or Canadian driver's license most certainly is. A handful of highways connect Hungary to the rest of Europe, the most important of which are the E60 (or M1), which connects Budapest with Vienna and the west, and the E65, which connects Budapest with Prague and points north. The roads are generally hassle-free, as are the Austrian and Slovak border crossings, thanks to the European Union's Schengen Agreement. In regard to distances to Budapest, Prague is 347 miles, Vienna is 154 miles, Warsaw is 339 miles, and Berlin is 428 miles.

Driving from Prague to Budapest takes 5-6 hours and is quite simple. Take the D1/E65 out of Prague toward Brno. As you approach Brno, take the D2/E65 toward Bratislava. Entering Slovakia, continue along the E65/E75/M15 toward Hungary. Entering Hungary, continue along the M15 which turns into the M1. Take the M1 all the way to Budapest.

RULES OF THE ROAD

People drive on the right side of the road in Hungary. Those sitting in the front seat are required to wear seat belts at all times. Children under the age of six cannot sit up front and must always have their seat belts on. There is a zero tolerance rule in effect regarding alcohol consumption before getting behind the wheel. Headlights must be on at all times. All cars in Hungary must be equipped with a first-aid kit, reflective warning triangle, and spare bulbs (any officer who stops you and finds you without one or more of these items will most likely write you up). The car should also have a clearly visible sticker indicating the country it has been registered in. The speed limits are 130 km/h (81 mph) on the highways, 90 km/h (56 mph) on roads, and 50 km/h (31 mph) in towns and villages.

Visas and Officialdom

PRAGUE
Visa Requirements
Those wishing to visit the Czech Republic will be wise to consult their local Czech embassy or consulate before traveling, as requirements change often. Currently, citizens of the European Union, United States, and Canada do not need a visa for visits under 90 days. Keep in mind that visas cannot be obtained at the border; they must be applied for in advance at a Czech embassy outside of the Czech Republic (but not necessarily the one in your country). The entire process can be quite frustrating and time consuming, so it's best to start this process well in advance. For further information, check out the Ministry of Foreign Affair's website (www.mzv.cz).

Customs
EU nationals visiting the Czech Republic are not required to make a formal customs declaration, provided the quantities of such personal products as alcohol and tobacco fall within the limits set. Visitors bringing in goods purchased in other EU countries where tax and duty has already been paid will not be required to pay tax and duty in the Czech Republic. Non-EU citizens who have bought products in the EU and have already paid tax and duty on them will be required to produce a receipt in order not to pay a second time. Personal effects including laptops, cameras, clothing, and gifts totaling no more than 7,600 Kč are not subject to duties. Prohibited goods include narcotics, pornographic or offensive material, firearms, ammunition, and animal and plant products. Customs allowances for non-EU nationals include: 200 cigarettes, 100 cigarillos, 50 cigars, or 250 grams of tobacco; one liter of spirits over 22 percent alcohol by volume or two liters of fortified wine, sparkling wine, or other liqueurs, and two liters of still table wine. For goods bought in the EU, the allowances are considerably more generous: 800 cigarettes, 400 cigarillos, 200 cigars or 1,000 grams of smoking tobacco; 110 liters of beer, 20 liters of fortified wine, 90 liters of wine, and 10 liters of spirits. For more information, visit the official website of the Czech Customs Administration (www.cs.mfcr.cz).

Embassies and Consulates
Most major embassies and consulates can be found in the center of Prague. The **U.S. Embassy** (Tržiště 15, tel. 257 022 000, http://prague.usembassy.gov) is located in Malá Strana, not far from the square. The **British Embassy** (Thunovská 14, tel. 257 402 111, http://ukinczechrepublic.fco.gov.uk/en) is also in Malá Strana, along with the **French Embassy** (Velkopřevorské náměstí 2, tel. 251 171 711, www.france.cz), which is situated opposite the John Lennon Wall. The **Canadian Embassy** (Muchová 6, tel. 272 101 800, www.canada.cz), meanwhile, is located in Prague 6.

BUDAPEST
Visa Requirements
Visitors to Hungary will need a valid passport to gain entry, except for citizens of Austria, Belgium, Croatia, France, Germany, Italy, Liechtenstein, Luxembourg, Slovenia, Spain, and Switzerland, who need only produce a national identity card. Citizens of the European Union, United States, Canada, Australia, and New Zealand do not need a visa. U.S. and Canadian citizens are allowed to stay in Hungary for a maximum of 90 days. Those citizens who enter the country with the intention of becoming employed or staying longer than 90 days, however, do need a travel visa. Hungarian visa requirements tend to change often, so it's best to consult with your local Hungarian embassy or consulate before traveling.

Customs
EU nationals visiting Hungary are not required

to make a formal customs declaration provided the quantities of such personal products as alcohol and tobacco fall within the limits set. Visitors bringing in goods purchased in other EU countries where tax and duty has already been paid will not be required to pay tax and duty in Hungary. Non-EU citizens who have bought products in the EU and have already paid tax and duty on them will be required to produce a receipt in order not to pay a second time. Personal effects including laptops, cameras, clothing, and gifts totaling no more than 92,000 Ft are not subject to duties. Prohibited goods include narcotics, pornographic or offensive material, firearms, ammunition, and animal and plant products. Customs allowances for non-EU nationals include 200 cigarettes, 100 cigarillos, 50 cigars, or 250 grams of tobacco; one liter of spirits over 22 percent alcohol by volume or two liters of fortified wine, sparkling wine, or other liqueurs, and two liters of still table wine. For goods bought in the European Union, the allowances are considerably more generous: 800 cigarettes, 400 cigarillos, 200 cigars, or 1,000 grams of smoking tobacco; 110 liters of beer, 20 liters of fortified wine, 90 liters of wine, and 10 liters of spirits. For more information, visit the official website of the National Tax and Customs Administration of Hungary (NTCA) at http://nav.gov.hu.

Embassies and Consulates

Every major country has an embassy or consulate in Budapest. The heavily fortified **U.S. Embassy** (V. Szabadság tér 12, tel. 1/475-4400, www.usembassy.hu) is located close to Parliament in pretty Szabadság Square. The **Canadian Embassy** (II. Ganz utca 12-14, tel. 1/392-3360, www.canadainternational.gc.ca/hungary-hongrie) is located on the Buda side. The **British Embassy** (V. Harmincad utca 6, tel. 1/266-2888, www.britishembassy.hu) is located very near the main pedestrian shopping street Váci utca, and the **French Embassy** (VI. Lendvay utca 27, tel. 1/374-1100, www.ambafrance-hu.org) is just a short walk from Heroes Square.

Tips for Travelers

TRAVELERS WITH DISABILITIES

Odds are that travelers with disabilities will encounter a bit of difficulty in Prague, as quite a number of buildings (not to mention subway stations, hotels, and the like) do not provide proper wheelchair access. The **Prague Wheelchair Association** (Benediktská 6, tel. 223 325 831) publishes a free brochure outlining barrier-free sightseeing routes, galleries, restaurants, and shops; it can be picked up at its office. You can also contact **Accessible Prague** (Moravanu 51, tel. 608 531 753, www.accessibleprague.com), whose services include helping to arrange transportation, accommodations, and personal assistance.

Budapest is another European capital that sorely lacks in wheelchair access. While an increasing number of hotels are slowly starting to catch on, there are still plenty of barriers around town. An excellent resource, however, is **MEOSZ** (III. San Marco utca 76, tel. 1/388-5529, www.meosz.hu), which is the National Association of People with Mobility Impairments. Scroll down a little on their website until you find the icon of the British flag on the left. It will lead you to a list of sights, restaurants, hotels, museums, and the like that offer comfort and accessibility to all their visitors.

GAY AND LESBIAN TRAVELERS

While definitely not as loud and proud as in other major cities, the gay community in Prague is nevertheless a thriving one. There are a small number of bars and clubs that cater specifically to gay men and lesbians, many of which are friendlier than their straight counterparts. For up-to-date listings regarding the scene, check out the very helpful and informative **GayGuide** (http://prague.gayguide.net).

The gay community in Budapest is a healthy, albeit low-key, one. Plenty of bars and clubs spring up only to close moments later, leaving everyone to wonder what comes next. In order to find out and stay on top of an ever-changing scene, make sure to visit **Budapest Gay City** (www.budapestgaycity.net) or **GayGuide** (http://budapest.gayguide.net).

FEMALE TRAVELERS

Some women may initially be surprised or put off by the blatant sexuality found on billboards and reflected in the rather provocative styles of dress in both countries, but they are simply reflections of a liberal attitude toward sex. Both cities abound in strip clubs and "gentlemen's clubs" (meaning brothels), and Czech and Hungarian women, while strong-willed and independent, have little, if any, motivation not to flaunt what they've got. Despite the overt exhibitions of flesh and open displays of interest and affection, women here are generally far safer than in most large American cities, with assaults being very low in number. Of course, caution and common sense are always a good thing to practice, which means that dark alleys, train stations, parks, underpasses, and the outer districts should generally be avoided if traveling alone at night.

CONDUCT AND CUSTOMS
Prague
GENERAL ETIQUETTE

It's rare to hear Czech people raise their voices in public, with the exception of the occasional drinker barking at the moon after the bars let out. North Americans and southwestern Europeans tend to be a whole lot louder when entering shops or having a conversation over coffee or dinner—a habit that Czechs and those having lived here long enough oftentimes find hard to take. Try to keep your voice at whatever level the establishment is operating at. Of course, all this goes right out the window when entering a bar or club. Other shining examples of good behavior are helping mothers with baby carriages up and down stairs or getting on and off trams. Always offer your seat to an elder when on public transportation and try to remember to say "Dobrý den" (good day) when entering a shop. Finally, if invited to a Czech home, make sure to take your shoes off, as most people wear slippers indoors. Some of the more thoughtful hosts provide guests with slippers of their own.

TERMS OF ADDRESS

Although generally polite and pleasant, Czechs as a whole tend to be rather reserved when meeting new people, much more so than North Americans and Western Europeans, who think nothing of hugging, kissing, and exchanging jokes from the get go. A smile and firm handshake will suffice during initial introductions. Always address elders and those you are meeting for the first time in the plural form, which is a clear sign of social courtesy and respect. Typically, both you and the person being addressed will switch to more informal speech before you know it. Although Czech is a very complex and difficult language, learning a few pleasantries will go a long way in ingratiating yourself, as all Czechs appreciate foreigners who make an effort to speak their language.

Budapest
GENERAL ETIQUETTE

Having a good time is paramount to Hungarians, so as long as your behavior is on par with everybody else's, you'll be OK. If invited to a Hungarian's home for dinner, be on time (or at least no more than five minutes late) and always bring a gift. Preferred items are chocolates, flowers, or Western liquor. Do not bring wine, as Hungarians pride themselves on their own ability to choose something suitably tasty. On the streets, helping the elderly and mothers with children is commonplace and expected.

TERMS OF ADDRESS

While close friends kiss each other on both cheeks, a friendly handshake is just fine when being introduced for the first time. If a man is greeting a woman, he should wait for the woman to extend her hand first. When addressing elders or people in a business context, use titles, surnames, and the plural (more polite) form. Hungarian tradition dictates that all names appear surname first, followed by the person's given name.

HEALTH AND SAFETY
Common Afflictions

The most common complaints from travelers to these destinations are minor in nature and usually revolve around sunburn and insect bites. In Prague, however, you may want to steer clear of traditional mayonnaise-heavy sandwiches and salads sold in supermarkets as they often sit out for hours and have been the cause of quite a few cases of salmonella. Tap water in both Prague and Budapest is perfectly safe.

Medical Services

Medical care is decent in both countries, and payment by cash will automatically get you the quick and proper attention most locals on insurance only dream of. Rates rival those in Western countries, so you'll be wise to double-check your health plan and see what kind of coverage (if any) it provides in Central and Eastern Europe. If you're on any medication, make sure to bring enough to last you the entire trip; bringing copies of your prescriptions is also a good idea.

Insurance

It's a good idea to confirm beforehand whether your insurance policy covers treatment in the Czech Republic and Hungary. If it does, verify whether any incurred costs will be covered by the policy up front or whether you will be reimbursed on your return home. Should your particular policy not provide coverage in this part of the world, find a travel medical insurance company that does, either online or through a trusted travel agent.

Safety

Prague is remarkably safe during the day and at night. The biggest problem continues to be petty theft, be it a scarf or a pair of gloves that goes missing at a bar or restaurant, the occasional shortchange at a kiosk or by a particularly clever waiter, or pickpocketing, which usually occurs wherever there are large groups of tourists or on the trams heading for Prague Castle. Your best bet is to keep your valuables in your hotel safe and just enough money on you to get through the day.

Budapest is a relatively safe city with little violent crime, but a number of pickpockets work the public transportation system. Always keep your valuables in the hotel safe and your money in an inside or front pocket. Watch for the numerous underpasses used to cross some of the major streets. If it's late at night and you're having second thoughts, feel free to bend the law and jaywalk.

Information and Services

MONEY
Prague
CURRENCY

The currency used in the Czech Republic is the crown (*koruna*). The crown's two most common abbreviations are Kč and CZK. Bills come in denominations of 100, 200, 500, 1,000, 2,000, and 5,000 Kč. Most shops will happily provide change for up to 1,000 Kč, but if you have a 2,000 or 5,000 Kč bill, you're best off using it at a bar, restaurant, or supermarket. Coins come in denominations of 1, 2, 5, 10, 20, and 50. At the time of writing, the crown was roughly 19 Kč to both the U.S. and Canadian dollar, 29 Kč to the British pound, and 25 Kč to the euro. For the most up-to-date rates, be sure to check out www.xe.com.

CHANGING MONEY

Exchange rates vary slightly across town, and it's a good idea to do a bit of comparison shopping before making a transaction. Banks generally charge less commission, but you are confined to their business hours (Mon.-Fri. 8am-5pm). Be wary of those offering "No Commission," as their rates are usually the worst and oftentimes result in creative calculations. Exchanging money on the street is strongly discouraged, no matter what rates you are offered. It's a common enough occurrence for visitors to walk away from a transaction thinking they've made the deal of a lifetime only to realize soon afterward that the money they received in return for theirs was not Czech currency (usually it's Bulgarian).

CREDIT CARDS AND ATMS

Although not as commonplace as in North America or Western Europe, credit cards are becoming more and more common as an alternative method of payment. Most restaurants and shops in the city center will accept the world's better-known plastic as well as euros, but it never hurts to ask if you're not

sure. Plenty of ATMs are to be found around town, with most paying out on major credit and charge networks like Visa, MasterCard, Cirrus, and Delta. Just be certain that the symbol on your card matches one of those advertised on a given machine.

TAXES

A 19 percent value added tax (VAT) is added beforehand to all goods, so there is no pesky arithmetic for visitors to get bogged down in. In other words, the price you see is the one you pay. Nonresidents are eligible for VAT reimbursement if they purchase products at shops advertising "Tax Free Shopping" and obtain the appropriate VAT Refund Form from staff. Refunds can be obtained at the border or from Václav Havel Airport at the customs desk in the Departure hall. You must be prepared to present your sales receipt, passport, and refund form. Eligible purchases are those totaling over 1,000 Kč that are taken out of the country within 30 days of sale.

COSTS

The cost of living in Prague is nowhere near as low and alluring as it once was, but it is still relatively affordable for Western visitors. Meals in the city center generally run 150-250 Kč a plate, but can easily reach 800-1,000 Kč at some of the fancier places. A glass of domestic wine should cost roughly 35-50 Kč, while a beer hovers somewhere around 30-50 Kč. These, of course, are average prices and can grow exponentially depending on the location and establishment.

TIPPING

Czechs aren't necessarily the best tippers, which may account for some of the surly service you're bound to encounter. Foreigners are expected to tip the standard 10-15 percent, but feel free to tip nothing if the service was particularly unprofessional. One common form of payment is for the waiter to come to your table and tell you the total cost of your meal. The diner then hands over the money and tells the waiter how much tip to keep. For example, if your bill comes out to 225 Kč and you'd like to leave a 25 Kč tip, simply hand over your money and say "250." The waiter will then give you back the appropriate change. When taking a cab, keep your eye on the meter. If you feel like your driver was honest, then an appropriate tip would be to round up to the next 10 or 20 Kč.

Budapest
CURRENCY
Hungary's unit of currency is the forint, typically abbreviated as Ft or HUF. Bills come in denominations of 200, 500, 1,000, 5,000, 10,000, and 20,000, while coins come in denominations of 1, 2, 5, 10, 20, 50, and 100 Ft. Should you get either a 10,000 or 20,000 Ft bill from the ATM, save it for purchases totaling over 1,000 or 2,000 Ft, as it's generally too large an amount to use when buying something small like a cup of coffee. At the time of writing, the forint was roughly 229 Ft to the Canadian dollar, 234 Ft to the U.S. dollar, 350

Ft to the British pound, and 306 Ft to the euro. For current rates, head to www.xe.com.

CHANGING MONEY
Although you'll have no problem finding plenty of independent currency exchange booths throughout the city center, it is widely understood that they generally charge higher rates than most, despite their large signs advertising 0 percent commission. Changing money on the street, no matter how sweet the offer may sound, is even worse, not to mention illegal. Individual banks and travel agencies are far more reliable and recommended. Keep in mind that they are free to set their own rates, so a bit of comparison shopping won't hurt. You will also see signs throughout the downtown core, as well as at train stations and the airport, that read "Bureau de Change." They typically have the fairest rates, so make sure to have a look at what they're offering as well.

CREDIT CARDS AND ATMS
Withdrawing forints shouldn't be a problem as plenty of banks have 24-hour ATMs that accept most, if not all, popular credit, debit, and charge cards, including AMEX, Diners Club, Cirrus, EnRoute, Euro/Mastercard, JCB, and VISA. These cards can also be used in hotels, restaurants, and shops. Many establishments have signs at the front entrance advertising which cards they accept.

TAXES
A 20 percent value-added tax (VAT), called ÁFA, is included in the sales price of goods in Hungary. Foreigners are entitled to a refund if items bought in stores advertising "Tax Free Shopping" total a minimum of 50,000 Ft, less than 90 days pass between the time of purchase and time of export, and items leaving the country remain in new condition (cannot have been used in Hungary). Make sure to ask the sales staff for a Fiscal Receipt and VAT Reclaim Form (your export and tax refund documents), as well as a Tax Free envelope. Put the credit card receipt into the envelope, or, if paying by cash, include the sales receipt and your receipts

---

Prague Card

The Prague Card (www.praguecitycard.com) is a two, three, or four-day pass to more than 50 museums and monuments around town, including Prague Castle, the Powder Tower, Old Town Hall, and the National Museum. It can be purchased at visitor information centers all over town as well as at travel agencies, hotels, and the airport. The cost is 950 Kč for two days, 1,050 Kč for three days, and 1,300 Kč for four days. Though somewhat pricey, the Prague Card is nevertheless practical if you're planning on soaking up as much culture as possible. If you're only interested in visiting a handful of museums and sights, however, individual tickets to the respective places are definitely the way to go.

Budapest Card

Those planning on packing in as much sightseeing as possible during their stay might want to opt for the Budapest Card. Available at visitor information offices, hotels, travel agencies, subway ticket offices, and the airport, it offers a number of discounts around town, including unlimited travel on public transportation, free or discounted entry to 60 museums, and discounts on selected restaurants such as Gerbeaud, spas such as Széchenyi and Palatinus Strand, and services such as Budget Rent-A-Car. Valid for 24, 48, or 72 hours, the card's rather hefty price tag comes in at 4,500, 7,500 and 8,900 Ft, respectively. While certainly offering a wide array of potential savings, keep in mind that many of the major museums offer free admission, so check out the card's specifics at www.budapest-card.com, or if you're already in town, simply ask a tourist information assistant whether the card is suitable for your particular trip.

from changing money into forints. You can be refunded in cash at the airport IBUSZ office or be reimbursed via bank check or transfer by mailing all original documents (VAT invoice, VAT refund form, exchange or credit card receipt) in the Tax Free envelope within six months of the date of purchase. Make sure you have all the relevant documents stamped by Hungary Customs before leaving or else a refund will not be possible.

COSTS

Hungary remains a very affordable place for travelers, who have the luxury of choosing from a wide variety of hotels, restaurants, and shops. An average meal will cost 1,300-2,200 Ft, while a glass of beer goes for roughly 400-800 Ft, depending on the brand. Clearly, prices in general are slightly more expensive in the downtown core, but still a bargain when compared to Hungary's Western neighbors. One big advantage is that Budapest has stocked its collective commercial shelves with many of the same products found elsewhere, but at a noticeably lower price.

TIPPING

Tipping is a big deal in Hungary, with everyone from the hairdresser, waiter, taxi driver, or thermal spa attendant getting a piece of the action. This is not to suggest, however, that tipping is mandatory. If the service was particularly bad, feel free to tip nothing as an expression of your dissatisfaction. When in restaurants, always ask if a service charge has been added to your bill, as it's a relatively commonplace procedure. If it has been added, a tip is not necessary. If it hasn't, then 10-15 percent is standard. Do not leave your tip on the table. If your bill was brought in a booklet, leave the tip inside. If not, give the tip to the waiter.

BUSINESS HOURS
Prague

Most shops in Prague open at 8:30am or 9am on weekdays and close at either 5pm or 6pm. Saturday openings are at the same time but end earlier, usually around 1pm or 2pm. Specialty shops, department stores, and supermarkets, particularly those close to the city center, may stay open as late as 9pm or 10pm. Banks, on the other hand, tend to share the same operating hours: Monday-Friday 8am or 9am to 4:30pm or 5pm.

Budapest

The majority of shops are open Monday-Friday 10am-6pm and Saturday 10am-1pm or 2pm. Most shops close on Sunday, although those in central shopping areas usually stay open and follow Saturday's hours. Food shops tend to open earlier, at either 6am or 7am, and close at 6pm or 7pm on weekdays, while weekends have them opening at 7am or 8am and closing at 1pm or 2pm. Certain food shops (designated as "nonstops") operate daily 24 hours. Most banks, meanwhile, are open Monday-Thursday 8am-3pm and Friday 8am-2pm.

MAPS AND VISITOR INFORMATION
Prague

The **Prague Information Service** (tel. 221 714 444, www.praguewelcome.com, daily 9am-7pm) is the first and foremost tourist authority on all things Praha. Whether it's basic information regarding the country, culture, transportation, accommodations, cultural events, day trips, or organized tours, you'll find everything you need right here. Plenty of maps and brochures can be picked up at their four

Balaton Card

The Balaton Card is an exceptional offer that will go a long way in saving you money should you plan on staying in the Lake Balaton area for a while. The price is currently 3,810 Ft and provides the following discounts throughout the region:

- 20 percent off lines and cruise ships crossing the lake (not valid for ferries)
- 10-15 percent off accommodations
- 10-15 percent off restaurants
- 20-30 percent off the entry fee at Lóczy-cave in Balatonfüred
- 10-20 percent off renting sports equipment, sailing, go-karting, and tandem skydiving
- 10 percent off quality wines offered by a number of wine cellars
- 10 percent discount at various beauty salons
- 10 percent discount on towing costs in case of a breakdown
- 10-100 percent off private beaches

Make sure to visit www.balatoncard.hu for further information and a full, up-to-date list of the discounts offered.

branches: Rytířská 31 (Mon.-Sat. 10am-7pm), Staroměstské náměstí 1 (Mon.-Sat. 9am-8pm, Sun. 10am-7pm), Prague Airport (daily 8am-8:30pm), and Lesser Town Bridge Tower, Malá Strana (Apr.-Oct. daily 10am-6pm).

For general information about the country, three websites will help you get the ball rolling. The first is the Czech Republic's official tourism site run by the **Czech Tourist Authority** (www.czechtourism.com). The second is overseen by the Czech Republic's **Ministry of Foreign Affairs** (www.czech.cz). Last, but not least, there's **CZeCOT** (www.czecot.com), a highly informative Czech tourism server.

Maps of Prague can be bought at pretty much any bookshop, newsstand, or hotel, and can be had for free at various visitor information offices. Most consider the series of maps called *Plán města Prahy,* published by Kartographie Praha, to be the best. They vary in terms of size and detail, so you should be able to find the one that's perfect for your particular trip.

Budapest

There is no shortage of visitor information possibilities in Budapest, but the main company that handles most visitors is **Tourinform** (Main office, VI. Liszt Ferenc tér 9-11, tel. 1/322-4098, www.budapestinfo.hu, daily noon-8pm). Helpful, efficient, and English-speaking staff are more than happy to provide you with information regarding sights, tours, day trips outside the capital, and much more. You can also pick up plenty of free leaflets, booklets, and maps that are quite comprehensive and invaluable to the first-time visitor.

Another centrally located office is **Tourinform Deák** (V. Sötö utca 2, tel. 1/438-8080, www.budapestinfo.hu, daily 8am-8pm), which provides the same useful information and is mere minutes away from many of the more popular sights, including Váci Street, Vörösmarty Square, and the Danube Embankment. Those flying to Budapest should make sure to check out the **Tourinform Ferihegy** (Terminal 1, tel. 1/438-8080, www. budapestinfo.hu, daily 8am-10pm) airport branch for all pertinent information before heading into the heart of the city. If you think you might need instant information at any given hour of the day, be sure to note the visitor information 24-hour hotline (tel. 1/438-8080).

For general information regarding the entire country, contact the **Hungarian National Tourist Office** (350 5th Ave., Suite 7107, New York, NY 10118, 212/695-1221, www.gotohungary.com). Other informative sights include **HungaryZIN** (www.hungaryzin.com) and **Budapest.com** (www.budapest.com).

Free maps can be obtained from all visitors centers and can also be found at the back of local publication *Budapest Funzine*. Mr. Gordonsky's colorful **City Spy maps** (www.cityspy.info) are also quite useful, but if you want a bona fide detailed map outlining the entire city and its environs, a trip to any bookstore in the center will offer a number of them to choose from.

COMMUNICATIONS
Prague
POSTAL SERVICES
When sending mail, be patient, as odds are there will be a lengthy line to wait in. Make sure whatever it is you're sending is properly and clearly addressed, and in the case of packages, wrapped in plain paper where all pertinent information can be easily found and read. Postcards and letters can be dropped into any of the orange mailboxes located outside all post offices and around the city.

Both postcards and letters weighing up to 20 grams cost 18 Kč sent within Europe. Sending them outside Europe costs 24 Kč.

TELEPHONE
Prague's telephone lines underwent a major digital overhaul over a decade ago, and now all numbers have nine digits, with regional and mobile prefixes integrated into the nine-digit number. The Czech Republic's international dialing code is 420. If you'd like to make a long distance call from here to your loved ones abroad, simply dial 00 followed by the country and city codes. The prefix for Canada and the United States is 1, and the United Kingdom's is 44.

There are a handful of public pay phones that still take coins, but they are few and far between, not to mention perpetually broken. Most nowadays take prepaid calling cards, which can be bought at kiosks and newsstands. They come in varying denominations and can be used at pay phones to make local and long-distance calls. You can also buy prepaid SIM cards from the major phone companies serving the area, which include Vodaphone, T-Mobile, and O2, all of whom have branches in every shopping mall. Rates are highest 7am-7pm on weekdays and lowest after hours and on weekends and public holidays.

NEWSPAPERS AND MAGAZINES
There are plenty of international newspapers and magazines available in Prague, including *The Guardian, International Herald Tribune,* and *Atlantic Monthly.* Most can be found at kiosks or English-language bookshops, along with plenty of locally produced news and coverage. The most established English newspaper in town is the weekly **Prague Post** (www.praguepost.com), which has as many critics as it does readers. Nevertheless, it delivers the country's news and has an excellent arts and entertainment section detailing all of the city's most important cultural happenings. For financial news, the **Prague Tribune** (www.prague-tribune.cz) covers markets, trends, and all things moving and shaking in a region that continues to develop rapidly. Independently produced local mags dealing with life in the expat lane, as well as literary zines showcasing some of the local talent, come and go overnight and are hard to pin down. Whatever is being printed at the time of your visit, however, will surely be available at all English-language bookshops.

RADIO AND TV
Czech television centers around four main stations. ČT1 and ČT2 are both state-funded channels and offer viewers anything from domestically produced dramas to the latest episode of *Mad Men.* ČT2 does have some

programs of interest, including a weekly film club that often plays English movies as well as jazz and classical concerts. The country's two private stations, Prima and Nova, serve up the usual sitcom and dramatic fare imported from the United States, Canada, Germany, and France. Keep in mind that everything is dubbed here, so even if you do manage to find something you like, odds are you won't understand it. Most residents opt for a cable package of some kind that usually includes channels like CNN or Sky.

Radio stations in Prague tend to play the same old pop and top-40 formats we're all accustomed to. There is, however, the excellent Radio 1 (91.9 FM), which spins everything from hip-hop to indigenous music. This, of course, is both its strength and its weakness, as it's very eclectic but rather unpredictable as well. To stay abreast of what's happening in the world, tune in to the BBC World Service at 101.1 FM.

Budapest
POSTAL SERVICES
When sending mail, be patient, as odds are there will be a lengthy line to wait in. Make sure whatever it is you're sending is properly and clearly addressed and, in the case of packages, wrapped in plain paper where all pertinent information can be easily found and read. Postcards and letters can be dropped into any of the red boxes found outside all post offices and on numerous streets around the city.

Stamps for postcards sent within Europe cost 220 Ft, while those for letters weighing up to 20 grams cost 280 Ft. Sending mail to North America is slightly pricier, with stamps costing 250 Ft for postcards and 315 Ft for letters up to 20 grams. For a full list of rates, check out www.posta.hu.

TELEPHONE
Phone numbers in Budapest have seven digits, plus the area code 1. Phone numbers outside Budapest have six digits, plus a two-digit area code. If you want to reach somebody staying in another part of the country, dial 06, wait

for the tone, then dial the area code and phone number. Mobile phones begin with 06-20, 06-30, 06-31, or 06-70 and are then followed by seven digits. You must dial all the numbers (06 prefix included) if you are calling from a landline or pay phone, as well as if you are calling from another mobile phone provider. If calling someone who uses the same provider, dialing the first four numbers (e.g., 06-30) is not necessary. Hungary's international access code is 36, while the outgoing code is 00 plus the relevant country and city codes.

Public pay phones operate on 20, 50, and 100 Ft coins or prepaid phone cards, which can be bought at post offices, newsstands, and most kiosks. As in most places, international calls are cheapest when made after standard business hours or on weekends and public holidays.

NEWSPAPERS AND MAGAZINES
Aside from the plethora of foreign newspapers available at most English-language bookshops, there are a handful of domestically produced English publications that have significant circulations. The first is the fluffy, tabloid-leaning *Budapest Sun* (www.budapestsun.com), which reports the country's news on a daily basis. Many buy the paper simply for its entertainment and events listings. Those interested in matters political or business-oriented will want to grab a copy of the more respectable *Budapest Business Journal* (www.bbj.hu), which keeps readers informed of the massive changes the country and the region are currently going through. People who would like to know what's going on around town should definitely pick up *Budapest Funzine* (www.funzine.hu). This is a free publication geared toward both tourists and expats with plenty of tips and inside information on shopping, restaurants, nightlife, and a whole lot more. It's very informative and not too shabby a read either.

RADIO AND TV
Hungarian television is led by national channel MTV, a barren landscape of dreary variety shows, game shows, and soap operas. Commercial channels such as Duna TV, TV2,

and RTL Klub are not much better. Many residents spring for a satellite package of some sort, but most of the channels end up being in German, with the occasional Russian, Polish, or Italian one thrown in to spice things up. If you're staying at one of the pricier hotels, you may get CNN, which may not sound like much but will make you appreciate the boob tube all the more when you finally return home.

On the radio, you can catch the excellent BBC on 92.1 FM, which is more or less the only thing in English on a regular basis. Some stations have the occasional hour or two of an English-speaking DJ or interview, but those are few and far in between.

WEIGHTS AND MEASURES
Electricity in the Czech Republic and Hungary is 220 V and 50 Hz. Most outlets have the typical European two-pin socket (also referred to as "Europlugs"), while some also have a protruding third (safety ground) pin. If you're planning on using any North American appliances or electronic equipment, make sure to bring an adapter, as they are not easy to find and are overpriced when available.

Both the Czech Republic and Hungary are on Central European Time and Central European Summer Time (CET). This puts the time in Prague and Budapest one hour later than London, six hours later than New York, and nine hours later than Los Angeles. The 24-hour clock is used officially and oftentimes in conversation as well.

Czechs and Hungarians use the metric system. Road signs display distances and speeds in kilometers, and you fill up your car with liters of gas. A large glass of beer is half a liter, while smaller items are measured using decagrams (*deka;* 10 gram units) and deciliters or (*deci;* 10 centiliter units). For example, enough lunchmeat for a couple of sandwiches would be 10 *deka* (100 grams) and a typical glass of wine would be 2 *deci*.

RESOURCES

Glossary

CZECH

antikvariát: second-hand bookshop
cukrárna: sweet shop
divadlo: theater
dům: house or building
hospoda: pub
hrad: castle
jízdenka: ticket for public transport
kavárna: café or coffee shop
Kč: Czech crown (also abbreviated CZK)
kino: cinema
knihkupectví: bookshop
kostel: church
lékárna: pharmacy
město: town
most: bridge
nádraží: train station
náměstí: town/public square
obchod: shop
ostrov: island
pěší zóna: pedestrian zone
pivo: beer
potraviny: food shop or mini-market
sleva: discount
trh: market
ulice: street
vinárna: wine bar
vlak: train
zahrada: garden, park
zastávka: bus, tram, or train stop

HUNGARIAN

antikvárium: second-hand bookshop
bolt: shop
borozó: wine bar
édességbolt: sweet shop
egyház: church
élelmiszerbolt: grocery shop or mini-market
Ft: Hungarian forint (also abbreviated HUF)
gyógyszertár: pharmacy
ház: house or building
híd: bridge
jegy: ticket
kávéház: café or coffee shop
könyvesbolt: bookshop
leszámítolás: discount
megálló: bus, tram, or train stop
mozi: cinema
pályaudvar: train station
park: garden, park
piac: market
sétálóutca: pedestrian zone
sör: beer
söröző: pub
sziget: island
színház: theater
tér: town/public square
utca: street
vár: castle
város: town
vonat: train

Czech Phrasebook

PRONUNCIATION GUIDE

Czech is a relatively difficult language to learn. Just ask the multitude of foreigners who have lived here for years and still trip over their tongues. Nevertheless, it's the effort that counts, and many Czechs will be both pleased and flattered that you tried. When reading signs, menus, etc., keep in mind that the language is written phonetically, so there are no tricky silent letters. Also helpful to know is that most words are stressed on the first syllable.

a as in "lap"
á as in "father"
c "ts" as in "gets"
č "ch" as in "choose"
ch like an "h" but throatier
e as in "bet"
é as in "fair"
i as in "knit"
í as in "knee"
j like "y" in "yellow"
ň like "ny" as in "canyon"
o as in "cot"
ó as in "boring"
ř no English equivalent; a combination of a rolled "r" and soft "g"
š "sh" as in "shore"
u as in "look"
ú as in "doom"
ů as in "doom"
y as in "knit"
ý as in "knee"
ž like "s" in "measure"

BASIC AND COURTEOUS EXPRESSIONS

Hello/Good day Dobrý den
Hi Ahoj
Good morning Dobré ráno
Good evening Dobrý večer
Good night Dobrou noc
How are you? Jak se máte?
I'm fine Mám se dobře
Please/You're welcome Prosím

Thank you Děkuji
Yes Ano
No Ne
and/or a/nebo
Excuse me Promiňte
Sorry Pardon
Goodbye Nashledanou
Cheers Na zdraví
Bon appetit Dobrou chuť
I don't speak Czech Nemluvím Česky
Do you speak English? Mluvíte Anglicky?
My name is... Jmenuji se...
I understand Rozumím
I don't understand Nerozumím
I don't know Nevím

TERMS OF ADDRESS

I já
you vy (formal), ty (informal)
he on
she ona
we my
they oni
Mr./Sir pan
Mrs./Madam paní
Miss slečna
friend přítel

TRANSPORTATION AND DIRECTIONS

Where is...? Kde je...?
from/to od/do
here tady
far daleko
near blízko
map plán
downtown centrum
highway silnice
straight rovně
go right doprava
go left doleva
address adresa
north sever
south jih

east *východ*
west *západ*

ACCOMMODATIONS
hotel *hotel*
guesthouse/family hotel *penzion*
key *klíč*
bathroom *toaleta*
shower *sprcha*
bath *koupel*
manager *ředitel*
towel *ručník*
soap *mýdlo*
toilet paper *toaletní papír*

FOOD
breakfast *snídaně*
lunch *oběd*
dinner *večeře*
menu *jídelní lístek*
water *voda*
juice *džus*
coffee *káva*
tea *čaj*
milk *mléko*
eggs *vejce*
fruit *ovoce*
vegetables *zelenina*
bread *chléb*
meat *maso*
chicken *kuře*
beef *hovězí*
pork *vepřové*
fish *ryba*
soup *polévka*
french fries *hranolky*
salt *sůl*
pepper *pepř*
the bill *účet*

SHOPPING
I need... *Potřebuji...*
I want... *Já chci...*
I would like... *Rád bych (teď)...*
How much does it cost? *Kolik to stojí?*
money *peníze*

SIGNS
Out of Service *Mimo Provoz*
Open *Otevřeno*
Closed *Zavřeno*
Toilets *Toalety*
Men *Páni/Muži*
Women *Dámy/Ženy*
Entrance *Vchod*
Exit *Východ*

NUMBERS
0 *nula*
1 *jeden*
2 *dva*
3 *tři*
4 *čtyři*
5 *pět*
6 *šest*
7 *sedm*
8 *osm*
9 *devět*
10 *deset*
11 *jedenáct*
12 *dvanáct*
13 *třináct*
14 *čtrnáct*
15 *patnáct*
16 *šestnáct*
17 *sedmnáct*
18 *osmnáct*
19 *devatenáct*
20 *dvacet*
21 *dvacet jedna*
22 *dvacet dva*
23 *dvacet tři*
30 *třicet*
40 *čtyřicet*
50 *padesát*
60 *šedesát*
70 *sedmdesát*
80 *osmdesát*
90 *devadesát*
100 *sto*
1,000 *tisíc*

TIME AND DATES
What time is it? *Kolik je hodin?*

today *dnes*
tomorrow *zítra*
yesterday *včera*
now *ted'*
next week *příští týden*
day *den*
week *týden*
month *měsíc*
year *rok*
century *století*

Days
Monday *pondělí*
Tuesday *úterý*
Wednesday *středa*
Thursday *čtvrtek*
Friday *pátek*
Saturday *sobota*
Sunday *neděle*

Months
January *leden*
February *únor*
March *březen*
April *duben*
May *květen*
June *červen*
July *červenec*
August *srpen*
September *září*
October *říjen*
November *listopad*
December *prosinec*

Seasons
spring *jaro*
summer *léto*
fall *podzim*
winter *zima*

Hungarian Phrasebook

PRONUNCIATION GUIDE

The Hungarian language is hands down one of the most difficult and complex languages on the continent, so learning even the basics will take some work. Understanding pronunciation is key, as is practicing. Like anywhere else, an honest attempt at using the language will put you in the good graces of any native speaker. Like the Czech language, stress almost always falls on the first syllable. Long vowels have either a single or double acute accent, while short vowels have no accent or the two-dot umlaut. In most cases, the sound of long vowels is slightly elongated.

a "o" as in "not"
á as in "father"
c "ts" as in "lets"
cs "ch" as in "church"
e as in "let"
é as in "say"
gy like "di" in "medium"
i like "ee" in "feet" (short)
í like "ee" in "feet" (long)
j like "y" in "yes"
ly like "y" in "yes"
ny like "ny" in "canyon"
o like "a" in "fall"
ó as in "law"
ö like "u" in "fur" (short)
ő like "u" in "fur" (long)
r rolled "r"
s "sh" as in "shop"
sz "s" as in "sofa"
u as in "full"
ú as in "root"
ü as in German *über* (short)
ű as in German *über* (long)
w "v" as in "very"
zs like the "s" in "pleasure"

BASIC AND COURTEOUS EXPRESSIONS

Hello/Good day *Jó napot*
Hi *Szia!*
Good morning *Jó reggelt*
Good evening *Jó estét*
Good night *Jó éjszakát*
How are you? *Hogy van?*

I'm fine Jól
Please Kérek/Kérem
Thank you Köszönöm
Yes Igen
No Nem
and/or és/vagy
Excuse me Elnézést
Sorry Bocsánat
Goodbye Viszlát!/Viszontlátásra!
Cheers Egészégedre
Bon appetit Jó étvágyat
I can't speak Hungarian Nem beszélek magyarul
Do you speak English? Beszél angolul?
My name is... A nevem...
I understand Értem
I don't understand Nem értem
I don't know Nem tudom

TERMS OF ADDRESS
I én
you ön (formal), te (informal)
he/she ő
we mi
they ők
Mr./Sir úr
Mrs./Madam hölgy
friend barát

TRANSPORTATION AND DIRECTIONS
Where is...? Hol van...?
from/to honnan/hova
here itt
far messze
near közel
map térkép
downtown belváros
highway autópálya
straight egyenesen
right jobb
left bal
address cím
north észak
south dél
east kelet
west nyugat

ACCOMMODATIONS
hotel szálloda
bathroom fürdőszoba
shower zuhany
bath kád
towel törülköző
toilet paper vécépapír

FOOD
breakfast reggeli
lunch ebéd
dinner vacsora
menu étlap
water víz
juice gyümölcslé
coffee kávé
tea tea
milk tej
eggs tojás
fruit gyümölcs
vegetable zöldség
bread kenyér
meat hús
chicken csirke
beef marhahús
pork sertéshús
fish hal
soup leves
french fries hasábburgonya
salt só
pepper bors
the bill fizetek

SHOPPING
I need... ...van szükségem
I want... Kérek...
I would like... Szeretnék...
How much does it cost? Mennyibe kerül?
money pénz

SIGNS
Out of Service Nem működik/Üzemen kívül
Open Nyitva
Closed Zárva
Toilets Toalettek
Men Férfi
Women Női

Entrance *Bejárat*
Exit *Kijárat*

NUMBERS
0 *nulla*
1 *egy*
2 *kettő (két)*
3 *három*
4 *négy*
5 *öt*
6 *hat*
7 *hét*
8 *nyolc*
9 *kilenc*
10 *tíz*
11 *tizenegy*
12 *tizenkettó*
13 *tizenhárom*
14 *tizennégy*
15 *tizenöt*
16 *tizenhat*
17 *tizenhét*
18 *tizennyolc*
19 *tizenkilenc*
20 *húsz*
21 *huszonegy*
22 *huszonkettó*
23 *huszonhárom*
30 *harminc*
40 *negyven*
50 *ötven*
60 *hatvan*
70 *hetven*
80 *nyolcvan*
90 *kilencven*
100 *száz*
1,000 *ezer*

TIME AND DATES
What time is it? *Mennyi az idő?*
today *ma*
tomorrow *holnap*
yesterday *tegnap*
now *most*
day *nap*
week *hét*
month *hónap*
year *év*
century *évszázad*

Days
Monday *hétfő*
Tuesday *kedd*
Wednesday *szerda*
Thursday *csütörtök*
Friday *péntek*
Saturday *szombat*
Sunday *vasárnap*

Months
January *január*
February *február*
March *március*
April *április*
May *május*
June *június*
July *július*
August *augusztus*
September *szeptember*
October *október*
November *november*
December *december*

Seasons
spring *tavasz*
summer *nyár*
fall *ösz*
winter *tél*

Suggested Reading

All of the books listed here can be found online at most of the Web's major book sites, as well as at the local English-language bookshops listed in the *Shopping* sections of Prague and Budapest.

PRAGUE
Literature

Hašek, Jaroslav. *The Good Soldier Švejk*. Czech literary icon Jaroslav Hašek's most famous and celebrated work. This subversive satire illustrates the futility of war through the eyes of a solider far more interested in drinking and card playing than the bureaucratic machine he's caught up in.

Havel, Václav. *To the Castle and Back*. Fascinating memoir from the Czech Republic's former president, outlining his years in office and the transition from Communism to democracy. Offers firsthand accounts and revealing insights on the challenges of creating a new government, as well as his thoughts on the war in Iraq, the role of the United States in a global context, and the future of the European Union.

Hrabal, Bohumil. *I Served the King of England*. The story of Ditie, an ambitious waiter focused on accumulating $1 million and as many sensuous experiences as he can. Depicting the absurdities of the nation's history during the middle of the 20th century, it is a work full of memorable characters and situations ranging from the hilarious to the downright tragic.

Kafka, Franz. *The Castle, The Metamorphosis,* and *The Trial*. The masterworks from Prague's most famous writer blend perfectly with the city's cobblestone streets and Gothic atmosphere. Perfect reading during the dark and mysterious winter months.

Klíma, Ivan. *Love and Garbage*. Poetic novel focusing on a banned Czech writer who now cleans Prague's streets alongside a motley crew that is likewise outcast from society. A moving meditation on love, freedom, and death from one of the country's premier writers.

Kundera, Milan. *The Joke, The Book of Laughter and Forgetting,* and *The Unbearable Lightness of Being*. The Czech Republic's most successful literary export is a must-read for anyone interested in familiarizing themselves with the absurdity and romance of the land and its people.

Meyrink, Gustav. *The Golem*. This is the classic telling of Rabbi Loew's fabled monster. Phantasmagorical, surreal, and wonderfully weird, Meyrink paints a picture of Prague that is much different from Kafka's, or anyone else's for that matter.

Neruda, Jan. *Prague Tales*. Famous collection of bittersweet vignettes depicting life back in 19th-century Malá Strana. Half the fun is reading the stories, while the other half is walking down the streets immortalized in them.

History, Politics, and Culture

Banville, John. *Prague Pictures: A Portrait of the City*. A wonderfully written collection of anecdotes dealing with Banville's pre- and post-Communist visits to Prague mixed in with interesting and enlightening tidbits of historical fact.

Farley, David and Sholl, Jesse. *Travelers' Tales Prague and the Czech Republic: True Stories*. Politics, history, and sociology all find their way into this excellent mix of entertaining personal experiences and memorable adventures. From well-known Czechs to foreigners who live and love in the country, these stories range from the poetically poignant to the laugh-out-loud funny.

Havel, Václav. *Disturbing the Peace, Living in Truth,* and *Letters to Olga.* These works offer remarkable insight to one of the country's most important and influential leaders. In these three volumes we find his thoughts, letters written to his wife while imprisoned, and his most significant contributions to political writing.

Ripellino, Angelo Maria. *Magic Prague.* A wild and wonderful blend of art, literature, history, and fantasy that celebrates the magical capital's haunted heart.

Sayer, Derek. *The Coasts of Bohemia: A Czech History.* A thoroughly researched book detailing the Czech peoples centuries-long search for their national identity, offering a treasure trove of information regarding Czech art, theater, architecture, language, music, and literature.

BUDAPEST
Literature
Esterházy, Péter. *Celestial Harmonies.* This ambitious literary work attempts to outline the lives of the writer's aristocratic family who played no small role in Hungarian history. Split into two parts—the first, an exercise in post-modern vignettes, and the second a more traditional form of narrative—the book takes some effort to get through, but nevertheless rewards readers with a deeper understanding of the land, its politics, and its people.

Fischer, Tibor. *Under the Frog.* This satirical novel follows the exploits of two basketball players representing the Hungarian national team from the end of World War II to the Hungarian uprising in 1956. Although a remarkably funny read, the book also manages to intelligently examine the repression leading up to the uprising, as well as the brutality of its bloody end.

Kertész, Imre. *Fateless.* This haunting novel by Nobel prize winner Imre Kertész is an absolute must for visitors to the country, as well as literature fans in general. Written from the perspective of a 14-year-old Hungarian Jew imprisoned in Auschwitz and Buchenwald, it is guaranteed to stay with readers long after they've finished.

Kosztolányi, Dezső. *Skylark.* Widely regarded as a masterpiece of 20th-century Hungarian literature, Kosztolányi's beautiful book portrays provincial life during the Austro-Hungarian monarchy. Centering around an elderly Hungarian couple and their unattractive spinster daughter (Skylark), the author turns family sentiment upside down in this short, enjoyable read.

Nádas, Péter. *A Book of Memories.* Jumping back and forth between the Stalinist era and post-Communist Eastern Europe, this exceptional though demanding work portrays a society full of secrets, tension, and fear, where the personal and political often become the same thing.

History, Politics, and Culture
Frigyesi, Judit. *Béla Bartók and Turn-of-the-Century Budapest.* An interesting perspective on one of Hungary's most acclaimed composers. Frigyesi delves deep into the country's intellectual society at the time—a remarkably talented and diverse group of individuals who collectively attempted to find wholeness and identity in a rapidly developing world.

Kontler, Laszlo. *A History of Hungary.* This comprehensive review of Hungarian history begins with the pre-historic age and takes the reader all the way to the present day.

Kontler examines the country's economics, revolutions, geographical setting, and social structure in an attempt to understand the country's current challenges in a new Europe.

Lessing, Erich. *Revolution in Hungary: The 1956 Budapest Uprising.* Lessing was one of the first photographers to document the uprising and its aftermath. The remarkable photos he took during the period are found in this eye-opening volume. Interspersed with easy-to-read essays highlighting this painful, bloody chapter in Hungarian history, the book relies heavily on the photographs to tell the time's stories, which range from hope and jubilation to the bitterness of broken dreams.

Schopflin, George. *Politics in Eastern Europe, 1945-1992.* An impressive analysis of Communism and its aspirations, as well as how it was able to stabilize its grip on the people and the reasons that led to its collapse.

Internet Resources

PRAGUE
Travel
www.praguewelcome.com
One of Prague's official tourist information portals, this site offers plenty of help regarding historical sites, accommodations, and city events. You can also learn more about reserving tickets for various cultural events going on around town, as well as arrange day or overnight trips out of the city.

www.discoverczech.com
Another informative site that has all kinds of pages dedicated to the Czech Republic including detailed information regarding apartments, hotels, car rental agencies, and a whole lot more.

www.myczechrepublic.com
This is an excellent resource for learning all kinds of interesting things regarding Czech culture, history, cuisine, and language. The site also features a blog, chat function, and message boards that offer plenty of opportunities to interact with past visitors and current residents.

Culture
www.expats.cz
www.prague.tv
Both of these sites are treasure troves of invaluable information, providing visitors and residents of Prague with a remarkable amount of up-to-date travel, cultural, and relocation material, as well as classifieds, message boards, job opportunities, and lots more to keep you occupied for hours. If you want to keep your finger on the pulse of Prague, bookmark both sites immediately.

www.praguebeergarden.com
A concise and informative site regarding many of the better pubs, breweries, and beer gardens around town. A great place to start planning your next crawl.

News and Information
www.praguemonitor.com
Those wanting to stay abreast of politics and culture will do themselves a favor by visiting this highly informative and typically well-written site.

www.radio.cz
Radio Praha's site serves up-to-the-minute articles covering every major news event in the country and region. Visitors to the site also have the option of listening on demand or connecting to live broadcasts.

www.livingprague.com
A detailed site and labor of love from a friendly expat who informs visitors of the latest in travel tours, accommodations, concerts, and a whole lot more.

BUDAPEST
Travel
www.budapestinfo.hu
Sponsored by the Budapest Tourist Office, this is a highly informative site that also assists in booking hotels and securing tickets for a wide range of events.

www.gotohungary.com
The Hungarian National Tourist Office in New York has an exceptional site that includes historical information, as well as a cultural calendar, suggested itineraries, tour packages, and a whole lot more.

www.visit-hungary.com
If you're still looking for more information after visiting the above two sites, try the new and improved www.visit-hungary.com.

www.bestofbudapest.com
Excellent site detailing all kinds of cultural happenings, as well as up-to-date information on travel, dining out, and accommodation.

Culture
www.pestiside.hu
For a light-hearted and typically zany look at life in Hungary, make sure to visit this highly entertaining and informative site.

www.caboodle.hu
At www.pestiside.hu, you'll find a link to this site, an excellent and fun portal that is loaded with information regarding all the important happenings around town.

www.happyhunwine.com
For wine enthusiasts, a visit to this site will get you started on better understanding the country's history of wine, as well as its relevant wineries and regions.

News and Information
www.budapest.hu
Very informative and up-to-date site outlining the day's and week's news from around the city, country, and EU proper.

www.met.hu
Up-to-the-minute weather reports from around the country.

Index

List of Maps

MAP SYMBOLS

══════	Expressway	🄲	Highlight	✈	Airport	⚲	Golf Course
─────	Primary Road	○	City/Town	✗	Airfield	🅿	Parking Area
─────	Secondary Road	◉	State Capital	▲	Mountain	▲	Archaeological Site
═ ═ ═ ═	Unpaved Road	❋	National Capital	✦	Unique Natural Feature	⛪	Church
─ ─ ─ ─	Trail	★	Point of Interest			⛽	Gas Station
··········	Ferry	•	Accommodation	☌	Waterfall	⬱	Dive Site
─•─•─•─	Railroad	▼	Restaurant/Bar	▲	Park		Mangrove
══════	Pedestrian Walkway	■	Other Location	⬤	Trailhead		Reef
ㅍㅍㅍ	Stairs	⛺	Campground	⚡	Lighthouse		Swamp

CONVERSION TABLES

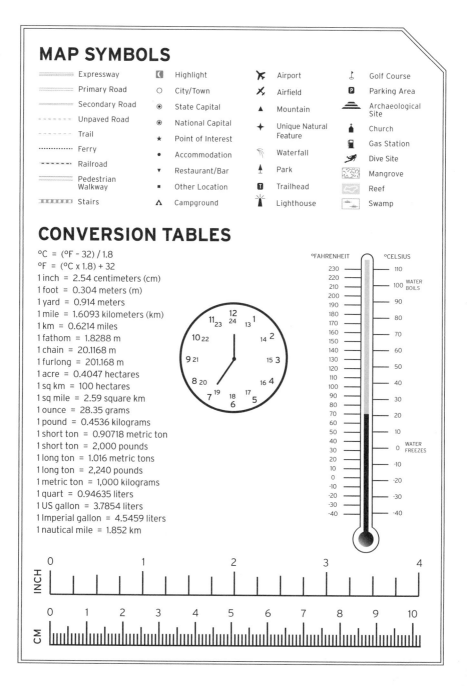

°C = (°F - 32) / 1.8
°F = (°C x 1.8) + 32
1 inch = 2.54 centimeters (cm)
1 foot = 0.304 meters (m)
1 yard = 0.914 meters
1 mile = 1.6093 kilometers (km)
1 km = 0.6214 miles
1 fathom = 1.8288 m
1 chain = 20.1168 m
1 furlong = 201.168 m
1 acre = 0.4047 hectares
1 sq km = 100 hectares
1 sq mile = 2.59 square km
1 ounce = 28.35 grams
1 pound = 0.4536 kilograms
1 short ton = 0.90718 metric ton
1 short ton = 2,000 pounds
1 long ton = 1.016 metric tons
1 long ton = 2,240 pounds
1 metric ton = 1,000 kilograms
1 quart = 0.94635 liters
1 US gallon = 3.7854 liters
1 Imperial gallon = 4.5459 liters
1 nautical mile = 1.852 km

MOON PRAGUE & BUDAPEST

Avalon Travel
a member of the Perseus Books Group
1700 Fourth Street
Berkeley, CA 94710, USA
www.moon.com

Editor and Series Manager: Kathryn Ettinger
Copy Editor: Christopher Church
Graphics and Production Coordinator: Lucie Ericksen
Cover Design: Faceout Studios, Charles Brock
Moon Logo: Tim McGrath
Map Editor: Kat Bennett
Cartographers: Stephanie Poulain, Kat Bennett
Indexer: Rachel Kuhn

ISBN-13: 978-1-61238-760-4
ISSN: 1941-4773

Printing History
1st Edition – 2008
3rd Edition – July 2014
5 4 3 2 1

Front cover photo: building detail, Old Town, Prague
© Doug Pearson/Getty Images
Title page photo: Chain Bridge, Budapest © rudi1976/
123RF
Front matter photos: pages 6, 8 top-right and bottom,
9 bottom-left, 10-bottom, 14, 16, 20, 21: © Lucie
Ericksen; page 7: © Anke Leifeld/123RF; page 8
top-left: © Renata Sedmakova/123RF; pages 9 top,
10 top-left and 11 bottom-left: © Domini Dragoone;
page 9 bottom-right: © Vladyslav Siaber/123RF;
page 10 top-right: © anasztazia/123RF; page 11 top:
© Martin Dimitrov/123RF; page 11 bottom-right:
© piccaya/123RF; page 15: © marcovarro/123RF;
page 17: © sborisov/123RF; page 18 left: ©
Artur Bogacki/123RF; page 18 right: © Sergii
Figurnyi/123RF; page 22: © zechal/123RF; page
23: © Petr Podrouzek/123RF; page 24: © Vacclav/
Dreamstime.com; page 27: © Pablo Debat/
Dreamstime.com
Back cover photo: aerial view of Old Town Square,
Prague © Jennifer Barrow/123RF

Printed in Canada by Friesens

KEEPING CURRENT

If you have a favorite gem you'd like to see included in the next edition, or see anything
that needs updating, clarification, or correction, please drop us a line. Send your com-
ments via email to feedback@moon.com, or use the address above.